Only as I write this dedication do I truly realize the enormous extent to which my family provided me with support while I was writing this book.

To Ozzie, my one-of-a-kind husband, thank you for your unconditional love, immense tolerance, and unselfish assistance during this writing process. To Alex, my beloved son, thank you for understanding "Mommy has to write." You bring me so much joy, and I am very proud of you. You both are the greatest gifts God has given to me, and I love you infinity.

To my family, Dad, Mal, Les, Jude, Pete, Ryan, Danielle, Mom Diaz, Jason, Mylissa, and Mike, thank you for always asking me, "How is the book coming?" providing encouragement, and believing in me.

And to Mom, thank you for your everlasting guidance and prayers from Heaven. I love and miss you always.

Survey of
Athletic Injuries

for Exercise Science

Linda Gazzillo Diaz, EdD, ATC, LMT

William Paterson University
Department of Kinesiology
Wayne, New Jersey

JONES & BARTLETT
LEARNING

World Headquarters
Jones & Bartlett Learning
5 Wall Street
Burlington, MA 01803
978-443-5000
info@jblearning.com
www.jblearning.com

Jones & Bartlett Learning books and products are available through most bookstores and online booksellers. To contact Jones & Bartlett Learning directly, call 800-832-0034, fax 978-443-8000, or visit our website, www.jblearning.com.

Substantial discounts on bulk quantities of Jones & Bartlett Learning publications are available to corporations, professional associations, and other qualified organizations. For details and specific discount information, contact the special sales department at Jones & Bartlett Learning via the above contact information or send an email to specialsales@jblearning.com.

Production Credits

Executive Publisher: William Brottmiller
Acquisitions Editor: Megan R. Turner
Editorial Assistant: Agnes Burt
Editorial Assistant: Kayla Dos Santos
Production Editor: Joanna Lundeen
VP, Manufacturing and Inventory Control:
  Therese Connell

Composition: Cenveo Publisher Services
Cover Design: Kristin E. Parker
Rights and Photo Research Coordinator:
  Amy Rathburn
Cover Image: © Jim Cummins/age fotostock
Printing and Binding: Edwards Brothers Malloy
Cover Printing: Edwards Brothers Malloy

Library of Congress Cataloging-in-Publication Data

Diaz, Linda Gazzillo.
    Survey of athletic injuries for exercise science / by Linda Gazzillo Diaz. — 1st ed.
        p. ; cm.
    Includes bibliographical references and index.
    ISBN 978-1-4496-4843-5 — ISBN 1-4496-4843-6
    I. Title.
    [DNLM: 1. Athletic Injuries—Case Reports.   QT 261]
    RD97
    617.1'027—dc23
                                    2013009734
6048
Printed in the United States of America
17 16 15 14 13   10 9 8 7 6 5 4 3 2 1

Brief Contents

Contents

Preface

Survey of Athletic Injuries for Exercise Science provides necessary knowledge to health and exercise science professionals, physical educators, coaches, massage therapists, nurses, students, and other individuals who work with physically active populations. Each chapter features **Case Studies** that expand your knowledge by providing real-world applications for the topics discussed in the chapter.

Part 1 provides students with the background information necessary to develop an overall understanding of the concepts related to injuries and illnesses.

Chapter 1: Legal Issues covers pertinent information that will equip students with an understanding of various legal concepts related to exercise science. Negligence and how to avoid litigation by utilizing particular defenses against negligence are thoroughly discussed. Comparable and contributory fault, foreseeability, liability, assumption of risk, and Good Samaritan laws are explained.

Chapter 2: Classification of Injuries and Illnesses addresses types of sports-related injuries and illnesses, how they occur, and their signs and symptoms. The chapter includes a description of injury categories including fractures, dislocations, sprains, and strains. Pathogens that cause illnesses, including bacteria, viruses, and fungi, are examined. The body's healing process is explained in detail.

Chapter 3: Bloodborne Pathogens identifies the prominent bloodborne pathogens that can infect athletes, including human immunodeficiency virus, hepatitis B virus, and hepatitis C virus. The chapter explains the Occupational Safety and Health Administration (OSHA) standards with regard to avoiding pathogen transmission, along with workplace universal precautions.

Chapter 4: Wound Care and Bandaging categorizes the wounds that an athlete can sustain, including lacerations, incisions, abrasions, and puncture wounds. The differences between open and closed wounds are discussed. Wound treatment, including cleaning, dressing, and bandaging the wound, is described.

Chapter 5: Emergency Care focuses on life-threatening injuries and illnesses and the care you give to assist individuals in these dire situations. This chapter explains how to conduct a primary survey in order to identify life-threatening illnesses and conditions. These life-threatening illnesses and conditions include angina, heart attack, cardiac arrest, stroke, seizure, diabetic conditions, and environmental illnesses.

Chapter 6: Basic Injury Examination and Care distinguishes the differences between a primary and secondary survey. It includes directions on how to perform a basic examination on an injured athlete, along with how to treat injuries with rest, ice, compression, and elevation (RICE).

Chapter 7: Wellness, Exercise, and Fitness explains the concepts of wellness, physical activity, exercise activity, and fitness. Various types of exercise, including cardiorespiratory and strength training, as well as the principles of conditioning, are explained. Athlete assessment and testing protocols are also described in this chapter.

Chapter 8: Nutrition and Supplementation explains the differences between macronutrients and micronutrients. The chapter discusses considerations for devising an athlete's weight management program.

The chapters in **Part 2** focus on athlete injuries and illnesses associated with particular body parts, and identify the characteristics, mechanism or cause, signs and symptoms, immediate treatment, and prevention of each injury and illness.

Chapter 9: The Head and Face covers life-threatening injuries to the head, including mild traumatic brain injury and intercerebral, epidural, and subdural bleeding. Facial injuries to the eyes, ears, nose, and mouth are explained.

Chapter 10: The Upper Extremity includes injuries to the neck, shoulder, elbow, forearm, wrist, hand, and fingers. Upper extremity, acute, and chronic injuries are described.

Chapter 11: The Core Body identifies injuries to the spine, thorax, and abdomen, as well as illnesses that occur to the thoracic and abdominal organs. Posture evaluation is also discussed.

Chapter 12: The Lower Extremity introduces injuries to the hip, thigh, knee, patella, lower leg, ankle, foot, and toes. The chapter also depicts some conditions that occur specifically in younger populations.

Part 3 examines various infections and health conditions that affect athletes' participation in physical activity and sports.

Chapter 13: Systemic and Local Infections depicts various common and life-threatening infections that an athlete can sustain. The chapter identifies the signs, symptoms, and treatment for infections.

Chapter 14: Special Populations discusses cardiovascular, immunological, metabolic, neuromuscular, orthopedic, respiratory, and other conditions that affect an individual's participation in physical activity and exercise. The chapter identifies the conditions' characteristics and limitations, which are important to consider when assisting the athlete in devising an exercise program.

FEATURES OF *SURVEY OF ATHLETIC INJURIES FOR EXERCISE SCIENCE*

- Each chapter begins with **Chapter Objectives**, which highlight the critical points to be discussed in each chapter.
- **Tips from the Field** boxes provide recommendations for common practices and skills that can be utilized with athletes.

- Bolded **Key Terms** are defined in the margins throughout the chapters and compiled into a **Glossary** at the end of the book.
- **Discussion Questions**, located at the end of the each chapter, challenge student comprehension of the material covered in the chapter. Many questions present students with realistic scenarios, and require students to think critically about potential courses of action in response to the situations.

THE ATHLETE, THE EXERCISE SCIENTIST, AND THE REFERRAL PROCESS

In the text, the term *athlete* is used frequently; it describes all individuals who participate in some form of physical activity or exercise. Likewise, throughout the text the term *exercise scientist* or *exercise science professional* is employed. For the purpose of this text, any individual who works with athletes is considered an exercise scientist or exercise science professional.

For many injuries and illnesses noted within the text, athlete referral to emergency medical services (EMS), advanced medical personnel, a physician, or the like is necessary for the athlete to obtain appropriate care. Whom you refer the athlete to depends on various factors including your employer's policies, employment position, professional credentials, and qualifications to provide immediate athlete care. However, regardless of these factors, in any circumstance in which the athlete is in a life-threatening, limb-threatening, or serious situation, call 911 immediately.

THE HEALTHCARE TEAM

While at your facility, you will assist your injured or ill athletes. However, many other individuals make up the healthcare team and assist you in providing athlete care. Some of these individuals include primary care and orthopaedic physicians, optometrists, dentists, nurses, athletic trainers, physical therapists, nutritionists, registered dieticians, massage therapists, psychologists, emergency medical technicians (EMTs), paramedics, exercise physiologists, exercise scientists, strength and conditioning coaches, personal trainers, coaches, and parents. Each individual plays a critical, specific role in affording your athlete the utmost care before, during, and after injury and illness.

NOTE TO THE STUDENT: YOUR ROLES AND RESPONSIBILITIES

Your chosen profession as an exercise scientist requires you to work with athletes on a regular basis. Consequently, you will have many roles and responsibilities. The focus of this text is to explain your role when dealing with your athletes' injuries and illnesses. Injury and illness knowledge, as well as proper first aid training, are necessary in order to treat the athlete when she or he becomes injured or ill. Likewise, all exercise science professionals should maintain current cardiopulmonary resuscitation (CPR) and automated external defibrillator (AED) certification.

Before your athlete participates in physical activity and exercise, he or she needs to be screened. Your role in this task includes identifying any risk factors that the athlete may have and determining if the athlete is ready for participation.

Another role and responsibility is to be a teacher. You continually instruct athletes on how to perform proper physical activity and exercise skills, monitor their nutrition and exercise programs, choose healthy foods, identify signs and symptoms of injury or illness, and help maintain their mental and physical health and wellness.

You also have a role as a motivator. Motivation is the key for any athlete to be compliant with and adhere to his or her physical activity, exercise, wellness, and nutritional programs. You are a guiding force in assisting your athletes to reach their goals.

The athlete will come to you for advice regarding his or her program, and perhaps personal, physical, and mental aspects that affect his or her quality of life. Consequently, for your role as advisor and counselor, you must be well prepared to assist your athlete as necessary.

As your athlete's supervisor, you are directly responsible for her or his safety while at your facility. You must adhere to facility safety policies in order to prevent injuries and illnesses.

At all times, ethical behavior and honest communication are important. Exercise science professionals must exhibit the utmost respect for their athletes' lives at all times. All activities performed must not jeopardize the athletes' health and well-being.

Throughout your career, your athletes will unfortunately sustain injuries and illnesses. They will rely on you to reach their wellness, exercise, and fitness goals. By appropriately utilizing the information in *Survey of Athletic Injuries for Exercise Science*, you can assist your athletes in obtaining and maintaining a good quality of life.

About the Author

Linda Gazzillo Diaz, EdD, ATC, LMT is a Professor and Athletic Training Education Program Director at William Paterson University of New Jersey. She earned a Bachelor of Science in Health Education/Athletic Training from Penn State University in 1991, a Master in Exercise and Sport Sciences/ Athletic Training with a specialization in Sport Business Management from the University of Florida in 1993, and a Doctorate of Education in Educational Administration/Higher Education from Rutgers University in 1999. Dr. Gazzillo Diaz has been a certified athletic trainer since 1991 and a licensed massage therapist since 1992. Presently, she teaches athletic training, exercise science, and kinesiology core classes within the William Paterson University Department of Kinesiology, where she has been a faculty member since 1995. Dr. Gazzillo Diaz was a volunteer athletic trainer with the U.S. Olympic Committee at the Olympic Training Center in Lake Placid, New York, in 2002; the Winter World University Games in Forni Alvoltri, Italy, in 2003; and the Summer Paralympic Games in Athens, Greece, in 2004. Currently, she is a Special Olympics New Jersey Medical Team Volunteer and has been active with the organization since 1996.

Acknowledgments

During the course of writing this text, many people assisted me in countless ways. I would like to acknowledge the Jones & Bartlett Health Professions Team, because they are the most significant contributors in regard to making this text a reality. Thank you Shoshanna Goldberg, who was Executive Editor at the time; Megan Turner, Acquisitions Editor; Agnes Burt, Editorial Assistant; Kayla Dos Santos, Editorial Assistant; Amy Rathburn, Rights and Photo Research Coordinator; Joanna Lundeen, Production Editor; Toni Ackley, Copyeditor; Troy Liston, Artist; and Maureen Johnson, Proofreader. Without your guidance and incessant work on this project, I would have never fulfilled my goal of writing this text.

I graciously thank the models who unselfishly spent hours with me to take photos for this text, including William Paterson University Athletic Training Education Program students Jackie Applegate, Carlye Bianco, Kimberly Conover, Dana Ewen, Peter Fusco, Kristin Grazevich, Nick Hodgman, Lauren Kravitz, Irene Manthi, Shawn McNally, and Rayna Yacoub; William Paterson University Exercise Science student Jonathan Padron; William Paterson University Exercise Science Faculty members Dr. Michael Figueroa and Dr. James Manning; my husband Ozzie Diaz; and my son, Alex Diaz. Thank you to Dr. Racine Emmons for brainstorming with me. And finally, a special thank you to Dr. Rich Blonna, who offered me words of wisdom at the beginning of this endeavor.

You all have played an integral role in producing this text, and I thank you from the bottom of my heart.

© Jim Cummins/age fotostock

Reviewers

The author would like to thank the following Jones & Bartlett Learning reviewers for their many suggestions that improved the textbook:

Dave Hammons, AT
Boise State University
Boise, ID

Kristi R. Hinnerichs, PhD, ATC, CSCS*D
Wayne State College
Wayne, NE

Jessica Mutchler, MSEd, ATC
Old Dominion University
Norfolk, VA

Adam Raikes, LAT, ATC
Utah State University
Logan, UT

Part I

© Photodisc

Chapter 1

Legal Issues

CHAPTER OBJECTIVES

After you have read this chapter, you will be able to understand:

- Negligence and its four elements
- The differences between omission and commission
- The concept of foreseeability, and examples of how harmful acts may and may not be foreseeable
- How comparable and contributory fault affects a plaintiff's compensation in a negligence claim
- The use and importance of assumption of risk documents
- Good Samaritan laws and how they protect a first aider
- How to defend yourself against negligence

In the present day, the potentiality of litigation in the workplace is real. As an exercise scientist, you are responsible for your athletes' well-being. However, exercise scientists who supervise, instruct, and care for athletes are especially at risk for being sued. As a professional, you must continually be cognizant that providing improper first aid injury and illness care for an athlete may have legal ramifications. These statements are not an attempt to discourage you from assisting an injured or ill athlete; on the contrary, caring for your injured and ill athletes is imperative (**Figure 1-1**). However, it is prudent to obtain proper first aid and cardiopulmonary resuscitation (CPR) training and understand the legalities that govern your actions prior to working with and providing care to athletes. Knowledge of legal issues affecting you as an exercise scientist is crucial. With this knowledge, you can guide your actions to

Figure 1-1 It is important for exercise scientists to properly instruct athletes on how to perform activities correctly and safely.

provide injured and ill athletes proper care, while protecting yourself as best as possible from litigation.

NEGLIGENCE

The term **negligence** is utilized quite frequently in a variety of contexts. A student could be negligent in completing an assignment. A physician could be negligent

> **Negligence** When a person did not act as a reasonable, prudent person would, and damages occurred to another person or his or her property.

3

when diagnosing a child's illness. Regardless of how negligence is utilized, the term means that a person did not act as a reasonable, sensible, or prudent person would. Negligence is a part of tort law. A **tort** is not a criminal act against someone, but a civil wrong that occurs to a person's body or property, caused by another person. In tort law, negligence is unintentional harm (Cotten & Wolohan, 2010; Osborne, 2001). For exercise science professionals who care for athletes, negligence can cause injury or illness. A caregiver must act in a reasonable manner when tending to athletes. If the caregiver does not act responsibly, then the athlete could become ill or injured.

> **Tort** A civil wrong that occurs to a person's body or property; not a criminal act.

For a caregiver (defendant) to be found negligent in a court of law, the injured athlete (plaintiff) has the burden of proving that the defendant did not provide care to the plaintiff as any other reasonable person would. In order for the plaintiff to be awarded damages, usually in the form of money, the plaintiff has to prove that the defendant took part in the four components of negligence: (1) a duty existed by the defendant to the plaintiff, (2) the defendant failed to perform the duty, (3) the defendant failing to perform the duty was the actual cause of the plaintiff's injury or illness, and (4) injury or illness (i.e., damages) occurred to the athlete (Wong, 2010). In court, the plaintiff does not have the burden to prove the four elements of negligence by a reasonable doubt as in criminal cases; however, every element must be proven in order for the plaintiff to win the case (Avery, 2009).

DUTY

An athlete (plaintiff) can claim that negligence caused his or her injury or illness; however, for this claim to go forward in court, the defendant (caregiver) had to have a **duty** to the athlete. In other words, the defendant was liable and responsible for the athlete's well-being, and had a special relationship with the athlete at the time of injury. Many professionals, including exercise scientists, have an inherent duty to athletes due to the nature of their employment. Coaches have a duty to their athletes. Personal trainers have a duty to their clients. Physical education teachers have a duty to their students. These three professionals have a responsibility and duty to the people they serve due to their education, qualifications, and certifications (Wong, 2010). If the plaintiff cannot prove that the defendant

> **Duty** When a person is liable and responsible for the athlete's well-being, due to the special relationship with the athlete at the time of injury.

had a duty to them, negligence cannot be proven and the case will be dismissed.

STANDARD OF CARE

When a defendant has been charged with negligence, the plaintiff must show that the defendant not only had a duty to care for the plaintiff at the time of injury or illness, but also did not meet the expected standard of care. The standard of care is the manner in which the defendant acted as compared to other defendants with similar qualifications (Cotten & Wolohan, 2010; Pozgar, 2010).

Consider the following scenario: A first aid-certified physical education teacher conducts an indoor wiffle ball tournament in physical education class. A student participant is injured when a wiffle ball is hit into his eye, causing immediate vision problems. The physical education teacher summons the school nurse and simultaneously dials 911 to obtain emergency care for the student. Until emergency medical services (EMS) arrives, the physical education teacher provides first aid to the student.

In this scenario, the court first determines if the physical education teacher had a duty to the student participant. In this case the court will most likely find that the physical education teacher did have a duty to the student due to the nature of the teacher–student relationship. The court then determines if the physical education teacher's standard of care prior to and after the incident was appropriate for the student and the situation at hand. The court compares the actions of this physical education teacher to other physical education teachers with the same training, qualifications, and certifications. The court's findings determine whether the defendant appropriately met the standard of care.

FAILURE TO ACT

The second step in proving that a caregiver–defendant is negligent is for the athlete–plaintiff to show the defendant failed to act and perform a duty for the plaintiff. This failure to act exists if the defendant participated in an act of omission, misfeasance, or commission. Omission, also called nonfeasance, is when a person does not perform an act that he or she is qualified to do (Pozgar, 2010; Prentice, 2010).

Consider the following scenario: Many football coaches are required by their institutions and organizations to maintain first aid certification. During practice, a football player incurs a deep, large, bleeding, open wound. The coach chooses to continue practice and does not provide first aid care for his athlete. Days later, the athlete sustains a systemic, secondary illness and infection. The athlete's condition apparently resulted from the coach's lack of first aid care for the wound. In this scenario, the football coach has taken part in an act of omission.

Misfeasance occurs when a person is legally able to perform an act that he or she is qualified to do, but performs the act improperly. In regards to the previous scenario, let's say the football coach instead tended to the athlete's wound by cleaning it with soap and water, without applying antibiotic ointment or a bandage, and then allowed the athlete to return to play with an uncovered open wound. Consequently, the athlete's wound became infected. The football coach has then participated in an act of misfeasance. He was qualified and knowledgeable on how to provide proper first aid care for an open wound but he did not apply all of the appropriate care as he should have.

Commission, also called malfeasance, occurs when a person performs an act that he or she is not qualified to perform on another person (Prentice, 2010). To change the scenario again, the football coach cared for his athlete's deep, large, bleeding, open wound, but decided to stitch the wound himself instead of referring the athlete to a physician or calling 911 for emergency services. The football coach is not qualified to suture wounds. Days later, the athlete's wound is infected and he has a systemic illness due to the coach's care. In this scenario, the football coach participated in an act of commission.

In any of these scenarios, by the nature of the coach–athlete relationship, the coach has a duty to perform proper first aid on his players as any other reasonable coach would. However, the coach failed to act in a proper manner and could be found negligent.

FAILURE TO ACT AS THE PRIMARY CAUSE OF INJURY

In order to prove negligence, the plaintiff has the burden of showing that the defendant's failure to act in a reasonable manner is the primary cause for the plaintiff's injury or illness. The plaintiff has the opportunity to make various claims. A plaintiff can claim that physical bodily injury or illness resulted from the defendant's failure to act in a reasonable manner. Likewise, he or she can claim to have suffered negative emotional, psychological, or social damages due to the defendant's failure to act. The plaintiff can also claim that he or she has lost employment and earnings due to the defendant's failure to act (American Academy of Orthopaedic Surgeons [AAOS], 2012). In the previous scenarios, the football coach took part in acts of omission and commission. However, if these acts did not directly cause the illness, then the plaintiff's negligence claim is dismissed. Despite the fact that the plaintiff has experienced injury or illness, often it is very difficult for the plaintiff to prove that the defendant's actions were the proximate cause.

ACTUAL HARM OR DAMAGES OCCURRED

A coach may have had a duty to his or her athlete, and breached the duty to provide a reasonable standard of care that caused the athlete's injury or illness, but the athlete must prove that actual harm resulted. Let's return to the wiffle ball tournament scenario, but this time the physical education teacher breached her duty to the student, which caused an immediate vision problem. The student sued the physical education teacher for negligence that caused vision loss. The student did not sue the physical education teacher for any other damages; however, if the student's vision returned to normal, then no actual damages occurred. Consequently, the negligence claim would be dismissed. Even though damages did not occur, the student may attempt to prove that a potential for harm to his eye or vision existed. Negligence claims of what could have occurred, or the potentiality of harm, will not hold up in court (Osborne, 2001). Therefore, this negligence claim of what could have happened to the student's eye would be dismissed.

FORESEEABILITY

Even though a special relationship exists between people, such as a personal trainer and his or her client, a duty or obligation from one person to another may not exist. When a court of law finds insufficient foreseeability for the personal trainer to safeguard the client's health and welfare, then the personal trainer does not have a duty to the client. Foreseeability is the ability of a person to anticipate danger and resultant harm that could occur to others sharing in the special relationship. Even when a person conducts him- or herself in a reasonable manner, an unforeseeable act can cause harm to another person (Cotten & Wolohan, 2010). When an act is not foreseeable, then the person who performed the act cannot be found negligent.

Reflect upon the following scenario: A Little League baseball team is playing a game during a partly cloudy day. As usual, throughout the day and immediately prior to the game, both teams' coaching staff and the umpires view the weather forecast. Not one meteorologist predicted rain or stormy weather for this day. The home team coach also utilized a lightning detector, which did not detect lightning. The visiting team is in the field. Unexpectedly, out of nowhere, lightning strikes an outfielder. The home team coach calls 911 immediately. Despite the coaches' efforts to provide CPR, the player is pronounced dead by EMS. In this scenario, the coaching staffs and the umpires were unable to foresee that lightning, coming from 30 miles away, would strike a player. The coaching staffs and the umpires had been particularly cognizant of the weather report throughout the course of the day and immediately prior to the game. No meteorologists predicted lightning storms on this day, and the working lightning detector did not reveal any threat. This unfortunate event was not foreseeable. A jury ultimately determines foreseeability in any negligence case. In this particular scenario it is evident that the coaches and umpires could not foresee the lightening strike so it is unlikely that they would be found negligent (Cotten & Wolohan, 2010).

COMPARABLE FAULT

> **Comparable fault**   When the court assigns some fault to both the defendant and the plaintiff.

When a defendant is found negligent, the court will determine if **comparable fault**, also called comparable negligence, exists. Although the defendant is deemed negligent, in some cases the plaintiff contributed to the damages that he or she incurred. Comparable fault in a negligence case is when the court assigns some fault to both the defendant and the plaintiff (Fitzgerald, 2005; Hekmat, 2002). In comparable fault cases, after hearing the case the court typically assigns blame to both the defendant and plaintiff as a percentage of total faults. The court determines how much the plaintiff contributed to the negligence. Judgment, in the form of monetary compensation, is then awarded to the plaintiff. Because the plaintiff is to some extent at fault, the compensation will not meet the plaintiff's original demands. Instead, the compensation is a percentage of the demanded award, which is usually derived from the defendant's percentage of fault from the total demanded compensation.

Most states have adopted this principle of comparable fault; however, in the past, most states utilized the principle of

> **Contributory negligence**   When a plaintiff is deemed to be responsible to some extent for her or his injury.

contributory negligence. As with comparable fault, contributory negligence is found when a plaintiff is deemed to be responsible to some extent for the injury. The major difference between contributory negligence and comparative fault is in how the compensation is awarded. Unlike comparable fault, if contributory negligence is found, with the plaintiff contributing to the injury to any extent, then no compensation whatsoever is awarded to the plaintiff. Because the contributory negligence principle seems very unyielding, many states changed their statutes to utilize comparable fault instead. Only four states, Alabama, Maryland, North Carolina, and Virginia, and the District of Columbia currently utilize the contributory negligence principle in court (Cotten & Wolohan, 2010).

Consider the following scenario regarding comparable fault: A personal trainer works at We R Fit Gym. He and his client have been working together to increase the client's muscle mass and strength for approximately 1 year. The personal trainer repetitively explains and demonstrates to his client how to utilize the equipment properly and safely. The client understands how to utilize the equipment and does so as taught by his personal trainer. One day, the client comes into the gym for a training session with the personal trainer. The client is angry, and in an unsettled mood. The personal trainer recommends to the client that he not train today due to his disposition. However, the client willingly and voluntarily participates in the day's training session. In a hesitant but usual manner, the personal trainer instructs his client to perform the daily training session activities, which are written on the client's chart. The client begins the training session and the personal trainer assists another client. Without the personal trainer's direction, the client decides not to follow the charted activities. The client proceeds to increases his resistance on the lumbar spine extension machine. Immediately upon beginning the exercise, the client feels a tearing sensation in his lower back and experiences excruciating pain. The client reports the event to the personal trainer. The personal trainer immediately calls for an ambulance to transport his client to the emergency room (ER), and then cares for the injury. As per the ER physician's prescription, the client must lie in bed to rest his back for a minimum of 1 week. Consequently, the doctor's orders result in the client being unable to work during this time. Due to the nature of his employment, the client does not get paid when he is not working, nor does he get worker's compensation.

The client decides to sue the personal trainer for negligence. The client demands monetary compensation in the sum of $100,000 for pain and suffering and loss of wages. In this case, the court considers comparable fault. The client voluntarily participated in the training session against the personal trainer's professional judgment. The personal trainer previously taught the client how to properly and safely utilize the equipment. The client had always utilized the equipment as instructed for previous training sessions. The personal trainer set up the daily activities as usual, which the client disregarded. Consequently, the client is injured due to lack of judgment and failure to follow the personal trainer's directions. The personal trainer may be found negligent to some extent, however. The personal trainer did not prevent the client from training on that day due to his angry and unsettled mood. Also, the defendant may be found negligent because he left the client temporarily, to assist another client, which caused a temporary lack of supervision. However, the court will use the comparative fault principle and find the client contributed to his injury. In this scenario, the court judges what percentages the defendant and plaintiff were at fault and awards a percentage of monetary compensation according to the percentage the defendant was at fault. If the court states that the defendant was 25% at fault and the plaintiff was 75% at fault, then the court would award $25,000 of the $100,000 original demands to the plaintiff.

VICARIOUS LIABILITY

In the previous scenario, the personal trainer's employer, We R Fit Gym, would also be liable for the client's injury, and consequently named in the lawsuit. We R Fit Gym is liable due to vicarious liability. Vicarious liability, also called *respondeat superior*, is when an employer is responsible for its employ-

> **Doctrine** A rule or principle of law.

ees' negligent acts. This **doctrine** is imposed only if the employee was working in his or her employment capacity under the employer's direction. If the employee is not working under his or her employer's direction at the time the negligent injury occurred, then the employer is not held liable by vicarious liability (Wong, 2010).

Consider this example: The personal trainer, who works for We R Fit Gym, decides to train his client at his own home. He is training his client on his personal time. The personal trainer has the client pay him in cash for services after each training session. The personal trainer is an independent agent in this instance, and is not working for We R Fit Gym. If the client is injured as in the previous scenario, then We R Fit Gym is not held responsible for the personal trainer's negligence. Whenever an employer has a "master–servant" (Pozgar, 2010, p. 241) relationship with its employees, then vicarious liability exists. Other common master–servant relationships include a school district and a physical education teacher, a school district and a school nurse, an athletic director and coaching staff, a strength and conditioning coach and athletic team members, and coaching staff and their athletes (Wong, 2010).

ASSUMPTION OF RISK

> **Assumption of risk** When an athlete knowingly recognizes the inherent risk of injury, and voluntarily participates in the activity.

In many athletic activities, due to the inherent nature of the activity, the risk of injury is possible. **Assumption of risk** is when a person knowingly recognizes the inherent risk of injury by participating in an activity, and then voluntarily participates in the activity anyway. This inherent risk is evident in sports such as football, ice hockey, and rugby. For other activities such as running, weight lifting, and golf, the risk of injury is not as significant. Regardless, most athletes understand that by the activity's nature injury can result.

In order to participate in activities, the athletes voluntarily accept the risk of injury. Assumption of risk is categorized as either implied or express. Implied assumption of risk is when an athlete assumes the inherent danger associated with an activity. Express assumption of risk is when the participant recognizes the potential for harm and signs a waiver relieving the organization from any liability for incurred injury (Fitzgerald, 2005; Pozgar, 2010). In most traditional athletic activities, implied assumption of risk is prevalent. Depending on the events that occur, implied assumption of risk varies in regard to the court's judgment and award. The judgment varies depending on whether the danger is inherent in the athletic activity and the plaintiff willingly participated, or whether the defendant was negligent and the plaintiff had knowledge of this negligence and participated in the athletic activity regardless.

Consider the following two scenarios. In one scenario, a high school senior football player and his parents knowingly assume the inherent risks of football. The athlete voluntarily participates and his parents voluntarily allow him to do so. During a game, the athlete is hit by an opposing player and suffers a season-ending knee injury. The player's parents attempt to sue the coach and school district for damages, because the player will no longer be recruited by universities to play football as a scholarship athlete. The coach and university are not found negligent, because no duty to the athlete existed. The injury was a direct result of football, a collision sport, and its inherent dangers. Consequently, no compensation is awarded to the plaintiff.

In the second scenario, a head coach and assistant baseball coach have batting practice using an L screen. The assistant coach notices that the screen has a tear in it. He informs the head coach. The head coach does not fix the tear or have the assistant coach use another L screen. The head coach mandates that the assistant coach use the screen during batting practice despite the defect. Standing behind the screen, the assistant coach pitches the ball to an athlete. The athlete hits the ball, which penetrates the L screen at the tear. The assistant coach gets hit in the face with the batted ball and suffers a fractured cheekbone. The assistant coach sues the head coach and the school district for negligence. In this case, the assistant coach knowingly participated in the act of having batting practice using a defective screen. The head coach is negligent because he has a duty to the assistant coach as his supervisor. He also has a duty to remove the screen from use and utilize a functional screen that is not defective. Although the head coach's negligence caused the assistant coach's injury, the assistant coach contributed to his own injury by utilizing the screen despite knowing the danger. Consequently, the damages awarded are treated as in a comparative fault case. The assistant coach is awarded only a percentage of the demanded monetary compensation because he contributed to his own injury.

Express assumption of risk occurs when an athlete knowingly and voluntarily participates in activities with inherent danger, but prior to participation he or she signs a **waiver** or release of liability (**Box 1-1**). A waiver is a type of contract presented to an athlete by an organizing body with which the athlete participates. Once the athlete signs the waiver, the organization (e.g., We R Fit Gym, the school district) is released from liability if the athlete is injured. If the organization wishes to utilize waivers, the director or administrator must consider various issues when developing and instituting these documents. The waivers must be written clearly without fine print to make the athlete aware of the inherent risks of injury by participating in the activity. They must utilize words that the athlete fully understands; this means common language, not legal jargon, must be utilized. The waiver must be written in the athlete's first language (e.g., English, Spanish, French). The organization also should have an attorney who has legal knowledge regarding athletic participation waivers review the document before use.

> **Waiver**   A type of contract that releases an organization under which the athlete participates from liability.

When presenting the waiver to an athlete, make sure he or she recognizes and acknowledges the activity's inherent risks. Be certain the athlete understands injury may occur as a result of participation. He or she must voluntarily agree to participate in the activity and willingly sign the waiver. These steps in signing the waiver must take place for the waiver to be upheld in court (Cotten & Wolohan, 2010; Pozgar, 2010). However, as in all legal cases, the court makes the ultimate decision as to whether to uphold the waiver. The court considers whether the athlete understood the waiver and its contents clearly enough before voluntary participation. If the athlete did not clearly understand what he or she was signing, then the waiver is not enforced and the organization is held liable for the athlete's injury. The court also determines whether the athlete was coerced or forced to sign the waiver by an organization's employee. If the athlete was coerced or forced to sign the waiver, then the waiver is not enforceable. Even if an athlete clearly understands the waiver's terms, willingly signs it, and voluntarily participates in the activity, but an employee or participant inflicts careless or deliberate harm on the athlete, then the waiver is enforced and the organization is held liable for the athlete's injury.

Consider another scenario at We R Fit Gym: It is winter in the northeast United States. A client joins We R Fit Gym and signs a waiver. This waiver releases the gym from any liability if the client is injured while participating in weight training and conditioning activities at the gym. One snowy day, the client enters the gym and begins his weight training session. At the end of the session, the client exits the gym through a commonly used exit door. Unknown to the client, the exit has a great amount of ice located immediately outside of the door on the sidewalk, which is on We R Fit Gym's property. The client exits the gym, slips on the ice, falls hard on the ground, and breaks his fibula. This injury ultimately prevents the client from performing his employment duties. Consequently, he is unable to work for weeks, and is not paid by his employer. Also due to the nature of the injury, complications, and multiple surgeries, the client incurs major medical bills that are not entirely covered by his employer's medical insurance. The client sues We R Fit Gym for negligence. In the suit, the client claims the assumption of risk waiver should not be upheld, and demands monetary compensation for salary lost, medical bills, and pain and suffering. In this case, We R Fit Gym's waiver that the client voluntarily signed most likely will not be upheld. We R Fit Gym has the responsibility to keep the gym and the grounds safe for its patrons. Ice had accumulated at the doorway on the We R Fit Gym's property where the patrons exit. The We R Fit Gym staff was careless and did not remove

---

Box 1-1	An Example of a Basic Waiver

I, _____ (name), attest that I am voluntarily participating in the activities that We R Fit Gym provides. I entirely understand that there is an inherent risk of injury, including the possibility of disabling injuries and even death, while participating in these activities, and I knowingly and willingly assume this risk. I also attest that I have voluntarily signed this waiver, and was not coerced to do so.

_____   _____
Participant Signature   Date

_____   _____
Witness Signature   Date

the ice prior to opening the facility. Therefore, due to the gym's duty and lack of action to secure the safety and welfare of its clients, We R Fit Gym is negligent. The waiver did not state that We R Fit Gym is released from liability for any risk—only the risk inherent in participating in the weight training and conditioning activities. Therefore, in this scenario the waiver the client signed that releases We R Fit Gym from any liability is upheld and judgment is in the client's favor.

In most assumption of risk cases when adults have signed waivers, and the requirements necessary to uphold the waiver are in place, the court upholds the waiver. Again, the court determines whether to uphold the waiver on a case-by-case basis. However, it becomes increasingly difficult for the courts to uphold waivers when parents sign waivers on behalf of their minor children. This difficulty occurs because some minor children do not or cannot truly understand the inherent risks of athletic activity. Also, the courts have to discern whether it is reasonable for the parents to sign a waiver on behalf of their minor children. Parents who sign on behalf of their minor children essentially relinquish their children's rights (Wong, 2010). Ultimately, waivers may or may not be upheld in court. Regardless, organizations that utilize waivers have instituted one means to defend themselves and their employees against litigation.

GOOD SAMARITAN LAWS

All 50 states and the District of Columbia have some type of **Good Samaritan laws**. Good Samaritan laws are statutes that protect someone from legal liability when they are assisting an injured or ill person. The person being helped is typically a stranger, and requires some sort of first aid care. Often these laws are considered first aid immunity. The Good Samaritan laws are different among the states, but in general they provide some protection for people providing necessary first aid care to others in emergency and life-threatening situations. HeartSafe America's website (http://www.heartsafeam .com/pages/faq_good_samaritan) provides each state's Good Samaritan laws. The laws apply if you provide first aid to an injured or ill person in certain circumstances. In all cases, you are protected if you provide first aid in an emergency situation, at the immediate emergency location, with good intentions, in a prudent manner, and without any monetary or other compensation (Cotten & Wolohan, 2010).

Even though Good Samaritan laws exist, in certain situations the person providing first aid (the first aider) is required

> **Good Samaritan laws**
> Statutes that protect people from legal liability when assisting injured or ill people in an emergency situation.

to obtain consent from the injured person before performing first aid skills. If the victim is a conscious adult, the first aider obtains consent to assist the victim. If the victim is a child and the guardian is present, the first aider obtains consent from the guardian in order to assist the child. In an emergency situation, if the victim is a minor without a guardian present, or is an unconscious adult, then consent is implied and the first aider can begin assisting the victim immediately (AAOS, 2012).

How the Good Samaritan laws are written and the laws' content in each state's statutes determine which first aid actions are considered covered under the laws. A scenario where Good Samaritan laws often apply, again depending on the state, is as follows: You are a coach for a recreational junior high soccer team. Your team is playing a game on your home field. Parents, family members, and spectators fill the bleachers. During halftime, one parent in the stands screams. Her husband is apparently unconscious on the bleachers. You and your assistant coach run to the victim to see what is wrong. The woman says that her husband was clutching his chest, and then suddenly passed out. You tell your assistant coach to call for an ambulance immediately. You have had CPR training in the past. You find that he is not breathing and begin CPR immediately. You do not remember the accurate number of breaths and compressions, but you assist the man anyway. Unfortunately, the man does not survive. The woman attempts to sue you in court for your actions, under the pretense that you were not currently certified in CPR and did not remember the exact proper CPR skill set when you provided care for her husband. In this instance, in most states, Good Samaritan laws prevail and you would not be held responsible for the man's death. Likewise, the court would rule that you are not responsible for any compensation to his wife.

Although it is rare for first aiders to be sued in court, the Good Samaritan laws do not apply in all cases. In some states, the first aider is protected when she or he participates in ordinary acts of omission; however, in many states, the first aider cannot act in a willful, reckless manner that causes additional injury (AAOS, 2012). Consider the previous scenario where you are a coach for a recreational junior high soccer team. In this case, a parent in the stands screams because her toddler son is having trouble breathing. You and your assistant coach run to the boy, who is wheezing. The mother tells you that he has not previously been diagnosed with asthma. Against your will, your assistant coach, who has asthma, decides to give two puffs of her rescue inhaler to the toddler. The toddler reacts adversely to the medication and his situation becomes worse. He stops breathing and goes unconscious. You call for an ambulance. The ambulance arrives minutes later. The EMTs perform CPR and revive the boy. Unfortunately, he has minor brain damage. In this case, the courts find that the Good Samaritan laws do not prevail for the assistant coach because her first aid conduct for the boy was reckless and caused further harm. The assistant coach is under your and the employer's supervision. Even though your assistant coach gave the boy her medication against your will, vicarious liability prevails. You and your employer are named in the lawsuit along with the assistant coach.

If you choose to provide first aid to an injured person, you have the duty to stay with that person until EMTs or another equally or more qualified person assists the victim (AAOS, 2012). However, one issue to consider when deciding to provide first aid care for bystanders is that most states do not have laws that mandate a person has a duty to provide first aid assistance to an injured or ill person in the first place (Cotten & Wolohan, 2010; Pfeiffer & Mangus, 2012). Although no duty may exist, your personal ethics and morals come into play when you witness an emergency situation in which a person is seriously injured or ill.

It is extremely important to know the Good Samaritan laws in your state. Good Samaritan laws provide you, as a first aider, some protection against lawsuits in emergency situations, so hopefully you and other bystanders will be willing to assist the injured and ill victims in these unfortunate situations.

STATUTE OF LIMITATIONS

When an injured person decides to file a negligence claim against another person, he or she does not have an unlimited amount of time to file a lawsuit. The **statute of limitations** is a finite number of years in which a person can file a negligence claim. The statute of limitations is determined by and varies from state to state. In most states, the statute of limitations is from 1 to 4 years. An exception to this rule is when the damages occurred to a minor. In this case, the statute of limitations begins when the child turns 18 years old (Cotten & Wolohan, 2010). Also, in some states the statute of limitations begins when the person has been given notice or has knowledge that the negligent act created the injury or illness. The statute of limitations also begins when a person "should have discovered the injury" (Pozgar, 2010, p. 207). Often, even with each state's designated statute of limitations, the courts have difficulty determining when the statutory period began.

The court must determine whether the plaintiff knew or should have known that the negligent act caused the injury, and the date when this knowledge occurred. Consider the

> **Statute of limitations**   A finite number of years that a person has to file a negligence claim in court. The statutes of limitations are determined by each state and vary from state to state.

previous case in which the assistant coach provided first aid assistance to the toddler boy at the soccer game. Instead of being permanently injured immediately, consider that the boy has no apparent injury or illness after the incident. Years later, when the boy is a 20-year-old adult and attends college, he begins to have migraines, memory loss, a cognitive deficit, and vision problems. His mother tells him what occurred at the soccer game many years before. He decides to file a lawsuit against the assistant coach for damages that occurred when he was a toddler. The plaintiff sues and demands monetary compensation for medical bills and pain and suffering.

The courts consider a variety of factors in this case. First, as previously determined, the court finds that the Good Samaritan laws do not prevail in this case. Also, the court considers the state's statute of limitations in regard to the plaintiff's age. The injury occurred when the plaintiff was a minor. In most states the statutory time period begins when the child turns 18 years old. If the statute of limitations is greater than 2 years, then the man can file the lawsuit. If the statute of limitations is less than 2 years, then the man cannot file the lawsuit. The court recognizes that this incident was a probable cause of the injury and illnesses he incurred. However, in this case the court determines that the man should have known of the incident because his parents should have informed him.

Depending on the situation, the statute of limitations can complicate an injured person's ability to sue another person in court. Although each state has its own rules governing the statute of limitations for negligence cases, all states do have one aspect in common: If a person attempts to file a lawsuit after the statute of limitations, then the lawsuit will not ensue.

DEFENSES AGAINST NEGLIGENCE

You can take action and attempt to defend yourself against negligence claims. What you do to protect yourself can mean the difference between being found negligent in court and liable for damages, or not. Because you instruct and supervise athletes on a continual, daily basis, you are responsible for their lives. You have the duty to protect your athletes from harm; however, you have to protect yourself in case one of your athletes chooses to sue you for negligence. To best prepare yourself for legal action, take the steps shown in **Table 1-1** to make sure you have the best protection against these tortuous claims.

As previously discussed, important defenses from negligence are waivers, release of liability, or assumption of risk agreements. Utilize these documents whenever you are responsible for athletes' safety and well-being, and regardless of whether you are self-employed or work for an organization or institution. Similar to these documents are contracts, which can also include assumption of risk elements. If you

Table 1-1	A Checklist for Defending Against Negligence

You should complete the following actions as part of your "to do" checklist in order to actively prepare yourself for a defense against a negligence claim:

☐ Utilize waivers, releases of liability, and assumption of risk agreements with your athletes.

☐ Utilize contracts that specify the terms of use for the athlete at your facility.

☐ Have all athletes complete a medical history questionnaire prior to participation.

☐ Have every athlete complete a preparticipation examination (PPE), performed by a physician (MD or DO).

☐ Mandate that all athletes who have preexisting or questionable injuries and/or illnesses must be cleared for participation by a physician (MD or DO).

☐ Create, maintain, and practice emergency action plans (EAPs) at your facility.

☐ Warn the athletes of the inherent dangers of the activities.

☐ Provide proper training and instruction to the athletes within your qualifications.

☐ Supervise the athletes appropriately.

☐ Provide proper, well-fitted, and safe equipment for the athletes' use.

☐ Hire qualified employees to work with the athletes.

☐ Obtain quality professional certifications.

☐ Participate in continuing education activities.

☐ Purchase liability and malpractice insurance for yourself and your employees.

are the owner of We R Fit Gym, you can have each client sign a contract that provides not only information such as the gym's terms of use and fees required from the client, but also assumption of risk elements.

Tips from the Field

Tip 1   All important documents such as the athlete's assumption of risk, PPE, and medical history questionnaire paperwork must be duplicated and stored in two separate locations. One copy of the documents should be electronic and password protected, on a computer hard drive. The other copy should be on paper, which is filed by the athlete's name in a locked filing cabinet. A third location could be on a password-protected flash drive. The paper copies can be scanned into the computer and saved as electronic PDF files. Computer software programs also exist to record your athlete's information. Access to these confidential documents should be limited to the personnel who would need them and have the legal right to view them.

Other documents utilized to avoid negligence claims include a preparticipation exam (PPE), a medical questionnaire, a medical participation notice, an emergency medical treatment consent form, and daily treatment and injury report documentation. A PPE along with a medical questionnaire help you to identify an athlete's predisposing medical conditions, both physical and psychological, which could cause injury or illness during participation at your facility. The PPE should be performed by and the medical questionnaire verified by a licensed physician. This physician verification is particularly important if you are self-employed. The physician signs and dates the forms and states whether the athlete is allowed to fully participate in your organization's activities. Whether the forms are scanned and downloaded into a computer or kept in a hard copy, these documents must be kept in a protected, confidential file. Confidentiality is important in regard to all athletes' files. Your athletes' personal health information is protected by the Health Insurance Portability and Accountability Act of 1996 (HIPAA), which prevents athlete health information sharing between various entities without his or her permission. This information includes all medical information. Unless the athlete signs a waiver giving you permission to disclose his or her personal health information to others, you are not allowed to share that athlete's information with anyone. Likewise, you do not have access to your athlete's health information from his or her physician or other healthcare providers. If the athlete needs or wants you to have his or her health information, he or she must sign a waiver at the physician or healthcare provider's offices allowing you to obtain that health information.

Tips from the Field

Tip 2   If the athlete has any questionable or previous injuries, illnesses, or conditions, as identified to you by the athlete's medical history questionnaire, do not let the athlete participate in any activity at your facility. Require the athlete to have a PPE and obtain a physician's (MD or DO) clearance for the athlete to participate in the activity prior to participation. The physician writes the clearance, or lack thereof, on prescription paper or letterhead. This paperwork is kept in the athlete's files.

At least once per year, review the athlete's participation forms with her or him. This regular review is important to determine whether the athlete's medical status has changed. By having these forms completed by the athlete (and reviewed and co-signed by the athlete's parents or guardians if the athlete is a minor), and the athlete's medical clearance verified by a licensed physician, you have taken additional steps to protect yourself against a negligence claim.

Tips from the Field

Tip 3 When you are working with a minor athlete (under the age of 18), regularly communicate with his or her parents or guardians regarding the child's progress, changes in his or her training program or activity, and any concerns regarding their child. When you communicate with the parents regarding their child, give them the opportunity to respond to your comments, questions, and concerns. Allow them to ask questions. By communicating with the parents regarding their child, you give them proper notification, warning, and knowledge of the activity and situation at hand.

Another defense against negligence is to always have emergency action plans (EAPs) at your facility. EAPs are written documents that prepare you, the staff, and your athletes for various emergencies. By having EAPs, you show your organization's preparedness for protecting your clients' safety and welfare at your facility if an emergency occurs. EAPs specify the course of action to be followed by the facility's staff in case of emergencies, such as when an athlete is injured or comes down with an illness, a fire breaks out, or an environmental emergency occurs. EAP components include the location of emergency phones and emergency numbers. Staff members have particular roles, such as who is responsible for calling 911, who remains with the injured athlete, and who meets the ambulance. The EAP addresses facility access, including how emergency personnel enter and exit. The EAP also depicts the emergency exit routes for each facility area. It delineates who has access to all rooms, fields, gates, and the like while the facility is in use. The emergency and first aid supplies location is also noted in the EAP, as is the location of all athlete emergency and health information, and who has access to the confidential information. An employee is assigned to keep the crowd, including other athletes and employees using the facility, under control. The personnel involved in instituting the EAPs must understand each EAP's purpose and their role in the EAP. Likewise, each EAP is practiced by the employees in a simulated manner on a regular, continual basis to be certain that the emergency plans run smoothly and appropriately.

Tips from the Field

Tip 4 If an injury does occur to your athlete at your facility, make sure you document the incident immediately. Write in detail the day, time, pertinent athlete information, events that occurred, and care given. Write legibly and clearly in ink. Do not use white-out or other erasable devices or ink. Sign and date the injury report and keep it somewhere safe. If you are summoned to court by the injured athlete you can utilize this documentation to recall events and perhaps present it in court.

Other than utilizing various forms of documentation, you should perform certain actions to prevent yourself from being sued. If you are a coach, physical education teacher, exercise scientist, or someone who works with, instructs, and supervises athletes, you have a duty to do the following:

- Warn the athletes of the activity's inherent dangers
- Provide proper training and instruction
- Supervise the athletes appropriately
- Provide proper equipment for their use
- Hire qualified employees

Informing the athlete of the activity's inherent risks includes not only having him or her read and voluntarily sign waivers, but also thoroughly explaining the risks involved and answering any questions the athlete has in regard to the risks. If you are in charge of hiring qualified personnel, consider your state laws and the policies of your organization and its governing bodies. The New Jersey State Interscholastic Athletic Association (NJSIAA), for example, is a governing body for interscholastic athletics in New Jersey (http://www.njsiaa.org). The NJSIAA requires all interscholastic secondary school coaches to complete a fundamentals of coaching course designated by the NJSIAA. Also, coaches must complete Sports First Aid, CPR and AED certification, and Concussion Awareness courses in order to coach. Depending on your organization, facility, institution, or the like, you may want to consider hiring appropriate healthcare personnel, or you may be required to do so. Laws in each state vary, as do the policies within organizations' governing bodies, in regard to the availability of healthcare personnel on site. To protect your organization from negligence lawsuits, you can hire physicians, athletic trainers, physical therapists, psychologists, EMTs, or other healthcare personnel to assist in caring for your athletes. Always cover your bases to make sure your athletes are safe and well cared for. At the same time, you will protect yourself from litigation by hiring appropriate personnel.

Once the athlete understands the activity's inherent risks and voluntarily signs the waiver, you need to provide her or him with proper training and instruction. If an athlete is attempting a new activity, show her or him how to properly and safely perform the activity. If a client at We R Fit Gym is going to utilize the leg press machine for the first time, demonstrate and clearly explain the purpose of the exercise, how to utilize the machine properly and safely, and what to do if she has difficulty or pain when completing the exercise. After you have instructed her to use the equipment properly, continually supervise the athlete to make sure she is utilizing the proper techniques and performing the activity safely, as you instructed her. When the athlete is working with equipment, or has equipment to wear, it is your responsibility to make sure the equipment is safe, in good working order, properly fitted for her, and frequently checked and reconditioned according to safety standards. Utilize all equipment as intended by the manufacturer. Any unapproved alterations and/or equipment modifications render the product unsafe to use by manufacturers' standards. If the athlete uses this altered product and is injured as a result, the manufacturer is released of liability. The individual who altered the equipment could be held liable for damages. If you are the employer or the person in charge of hiring staff, hire competent, certified, knowledgeable employees. Thoroughly interview each prospective employee, review the applicants' qualifications, and acquire character references and employment recommendations. If you perform all of these actions, you demonstrate your desire to ensure the health, safety, and welfare of your athletes. These actions are extremely important if an athlete claims that you are negligent.

Various actions that you take to protect yourself from a negligence claim can enhance your personal and professional development as an exercise scientist. Obtain professional certifications in your field. By obtaining high-level, national, professional certifications, you demonstrate that you are knowledgeable and skilled in your field. Some organizations claim to offer respected certification programs, but in reality the certifications are not highly regarded and are very simple for a candidate to obtain. Investigate and seek out the reputable organizations in your field of work and obtain the corresponding certifications. One well-respected organization is the National Strength and Conditioning Association (NSCA), which offers a Certified Strength and Conditioning Specialist (CSCS) certification that is nationally recognized and challenging to obtain. Candidates must have at minimum a bachelor's degree and pass a rigorous certification exam. The NSCA also offers an NSCA-Certified Personal Trainer (NSCA-CPT) certification. Because the NSCA is a highly respected organization in the personal training and fitness field, the certifications that a personal trainer or certified strength and conditioning specialist hold from the NSCA show that the professional has met the stringent education, knowledge, and testing requirements. (Please note that this organization is only one example of the highly regarded national organizations that provide additional certifications and credentialing for professionals in your field of expertise.) If a personal trainer holds additional respectable certifications and credentials, an athlete can be reasonably assured that he or she is under the supervision of a highly knowledgeable professional.

Finally, by participating in continuing education activities, you further protect yourself from being found negligent. In professional fields, such as exercise science, information and practices are continually changing based on new research activities and conclusions. Professionals must be up to date with the latest information, technology, and best practices. Because you are working with, supervising, and teaching other people who depend on your expertise, it is imperative to continue your education for as long as you are employed and practicing in your field. If you are well-versed, knowledgeable, and utilize current, research-based best practices with your athletes, you have another defense against a negligence claim. Some professional organizations demand that credential holders complete continuing education and report these activities to the professional organization. For example, once you have earned credentials through the NSCA, you are required to participate in continuing education activities based on the NSCA's continuing education policies (see http://www.nsca.com for these policies). This organization's continuing education policies ensure that its credentialed professionals stay abreast of new, evolving information and best practices in the strength and conditioning realm. The continuing education requirements for other professions depend on the profession's and/or professional's affiliation with a national, regional, or state organization as well as individual state rules and regulations. Some of the continuing education activities required include attendance at seminars, workshops, laboratories, and webinars. Continuing education participation can assist you if you are brought to court for a negligence claim. You can demonstrate to the court that you are up-to-date with the most current information and best practices in your field. You can also explain how you used the knowledge and best practices with your athlete. With this continuing education and its application, you have another defense in court against a negligence claim.

Even if you take all of the aforementioned actions to prevent and defend yourself against the potential for negligence litigation, unfortunately you may still be named as a defendant in a negligence claim. What will happen if you are brought to court for a negligence claim? Fortunately, professional liability and malpractice insurance exists that can assist you as a defendant in a negligence lawsuit. If you are employed by an organization, often your employer provides this insurance at no cost to you. Determine whether your employer provides this insurance, obtain a copy of the insurance policy, and investigate the coverage terms. While working under the direction of the employer, this liability and malpractice insurance should minimally provide you legal defense and fees. The insurance policies only provide you with certain monetary limits per lawsuit per year. However, your employer's insurance may not provide you adequate coverage while on the job, and in most instances does not provide you any coverage when working outside your duties for your employer.

Consider this scenario: You are working for We R Fit Gym. The gym provides liability and malpractice insurance for all employees. Each personal trainer has $1 million of insurance coverage per claim (i.e., lawsuit) per year, with a maximum of $3 million total per year. You decide to begin your own personal training business in your home, separate from We R Fit Gym. One of your clients sustains an injury at your home while performing training techniques that you instructed. She files a negligence claim against you. You do not have any professional liability and malpractice insurance other than the insurance provided by We R Fit Gym. Because you were training your client under your personal business and not as an employee of We R Fit Gym, your We R Fit Gym liability and malpractice insurance is not applicable to cover you for this claim. You have to pay all legal defense fees, among other expenses, which most likely will prove to be extremely costly. As a professional, purchase liability and malpractice insurance for as long as you work with athletes. Even if your employer provides this insurance for you, it is always prudent to purchase your own personal liability and malpractice insurance as a supplement to your employer's insurance. By having this professional liability and malpractice insurance, you can rest easy knowing that if you find yourself as a defendant in a negligence claim you have adequate protection and representation.

SUMMARY

As an exercise scientist, you must be aware of and knowledgeable about legal issues that can affect you. You work with athletes and are responsible for their lives, so you have a standard to uphold not only in your athletes' eyes, but also in the eyes of the courts. If you actively recognize these legal issues, and take action to be a prudent, responsible professional when working with your athletes, you will be on the right track to avoid the courtroom.

DISCUSSION QUESTIONS

1. In regard to the four components of negligence, which component(s) do you feel would be the most difficult for a plaintiff to prove in a negligence claim? Why do you feel this way?

2. Describe an example of a foreseeable event in the exercise science field that could cause harm or damages to another person.

3. Would vicarious liability exist at your place of employment with a negligence claim? Why or why not?

4. If you came across an injured person who desperately needed first aid, what could you do to protect yourself from being named in a negligence lawsuit?

5. What specific actions can you take during your daily activities and employment to protect yourself from being a defendant in a negligence claim?

CASE STUDY

One Seemingly Harmless Decision Creates Huge Legal Ramifications

Mike is a new performance enhancement trainer at the Garden State Performance Training Center. He is meeting today with Meredith, who is a new client. Meredith is a 6-foot-tall, 130-pound, 18-year-old collegiate volleyball player who is very athletic and fit. She wants to continue increasing her speed and power, especially when she jumps to spike a ball. Mike plans to help her attain her goals. Today she meets Mike at the center to complete the necessary paperwork, including a medical history, insurance, and assumption of risk forms. Mike aspires to begin her first training session after the paperwork has been completed. As per the Garden State Performance Training Center policies, if a new client does not have medical conditions that would preventing her from participating on the same day that she completes the medical questionnaire, then she can begin her first training session immediately. Meredith indicates on her medical questionnaire that she has "heart problems." When Mike questions what the "heart problems" entail, Meredith says, "I think my doctor said I have something minor like a heart murmur, but I am not sure." Mike knows that athletes with heart murmurs have participated in his strenuous training activities before without any problems. He tells Meredith that he needs a clearance note from her doctor before she participates. Meredith says she just saw her doctor last week when she returned from college, and her doctor said she can participate in all athletic activities. Meredith is anxious to begin her training session today, and knowing that she may not be able to do so is getting her visibly upset. After briefly thinking about the situation, Mike decides to allow Meredith to participate in one session before obtaining the medical clearance. After all, Meredith said her doctor allowed her to participate in all athletic activities last week when she saw him.

Mike begins the hour training session with Meredith. She is performing high intensity vertical jumping and sprinting activities. She seems to be doing very well with the activities, but is breathing very fast and shallow. With approximately 10 minutes remaining in the session, Meredith begins to complain of chest pain and dizziness. Mike immediately stops her session, and asks her what is wrong. Meredith says that she "feels lightheaded and out of breath." She continues to say that her "heart is pounding hard and hurts." Mike notices Meredith's face is pale and she is unsteady when standing. Mike helps her sit comfortably in a chair, and leaves her briefly to go to the sign-in desk to call 911. When Mike returns to Meredith she is unconscious and not breathing. Mike begins CPR without any protective barriers. Within a few minutes, the EMTs arrive and take over. They apply an automated external defibrillator (AED) and are able to restart her heart, but Meredith is still unconscious. Mike's supervisor, Pamela, arrives at the scene and asks Mike what happened. The EMTs take Meredith to the hospital via ambulance. Now that the scene is cleared, Pamela orders Mike to come to her office to discuss what happened.

1. How should Mike have handled this situation differently from the beginning, so as to avoid any potential litigation?

2. What legal issues does Mike have to consider in this scenario?
3. Will Mike be liable for any damages resulting from this event?
4. Will the Garden State Performance Training Center be liable for any damages?

REFERENCES

American Academy of Orthopaedic Surgeons (AAOS). (2012). *First aid, CPR, and AED advanced* (6th ed.). Sudbury, MA: Jones and Bartlett.

Avery, G. (2009). Negligence: A prescribing dilemma. *Practice Nurse*, 38(10), 36–39. Retrieved April 1, 2011, from http://search.ebscohost.com

Cotten, D. J., & Wolohan, J. T. (2010). *Law for recreation and sport managers* (5th ed.). Dubuque, IA: Kendall Hunt.

Fitzgerald, T. B. (2005). The "inherent risk" doctrine, amateur coaching negligence, and the goal of loss avoidance. *Northwestern University Law Review*, 99(2), 889–929. Retrieved April 1, 2011, from http://search.ebscohost.com

Hekmat, R. R. (2002). Malpractice during practice: Should NCAA coaches be liable for negligence? *Loyola of Los Angeles Entertainment Law Review*, 22(3), 613–642. Retrieved April 1, 2011, from http://elr.lls.edu/issues/v22-issue3/index.html

Osborne, B. (2001). Principles of liability for athletic trainers: Managing sport-related concussion. *Journal of Athletic Training*, 36(3), 316–321. Retrieved April 1, 2011, from http://www.ncbi.nlm.nih.gov/pmc/articles/PMC155425/

Pfeiffer, R. P., & Mangus, B. C. (2012). *Concepts of athletic training* (6th ed.). Sudbury, MA: Jones and Bartlett.

Pozgar, G. D. (2010). *Legal and ethical issues for health professionals* (2nd ed.). Sudbury, MA: Jones and Bartlett.

Prentice, W. E. (2010). *Essentials of athletic injury management* (8th ed.). New York: McGraw-Hill.

Wong, G. M. (2010). *Essentials of sports law* (4th ed.). Santa Barbara, CA: Praeger/ABC-CLIO.

Chapter 2

Classification of Injuries and Illnesses

CHAPTER OBJECTIVES

After you have read this chapter, you will be able to understand:

- Various mechanisms of tissue injury
- The healing process, including the three phases of healing
- The signs and symptoms of injury and illness
- The differences between acute and chronic injuries
- The classifications of injuries and illnesses
- The microorganisms that cause illnesses

Numerous types of injuries and illnesses exist. An athlete can experience an injury or be overcome by an illness that can be minor or severely disabling. Whether an injured athlete has a broken bone, a muscular injury, or a skin infection, the body must heal in order to return to its original state. The healing process is a systematic means for tissue to respond to the injury and allow the body to resume normal function. This chapter explains the tissue response to injury and introduces you to the general classifications of injuries and illnesses. By understanding these general classifications, you will be able to identify various types of injuries and illnesses.

MECHANISM OF INJURY

Various mechanisms of injury exist. A mechanism of injury is the cause of the injury or the manner in which the injury occurs. Compression, separation (tensile), and shear forces are three very common mechanisms of injury for both soft tissue and bony injuries (**Figure 2-1**).

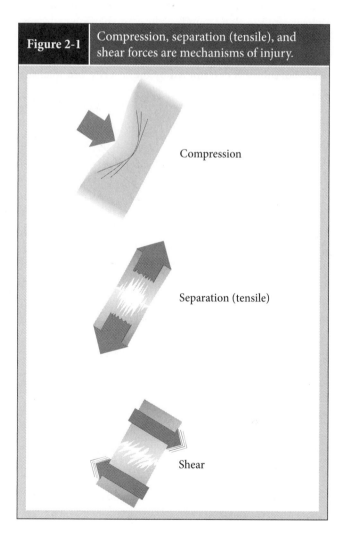

Figure 2-1 Compression, separation (tensile), and shear forces are mechanisms of injury.

Compression

Separation (tensile)

Shear

Compression forces occur when the tissue is crushed between two or more objects. During a workout, a weightlifter drops a weight on her foot. Her foot is compressed between the weight and the floor. Consequently, she sustains a metatarsal fracture due to the compressive mechanism of injury.

Tissue separation, or tension, occurs when a structure is pulled apart from either one or both ends. The tissue is stretched beyond the anatomical limit, which is the maximal length the tissue can withstand, and as a result the tissue tears (Eaves, 2010). For example, an athlete twists his ankle in a manner that stretches a ligament. The ligament cannot withstand the force and the athlete sustains an ankle ligament tear, or sprain. The mechanism of injury in this example is a separation force placed on the tissue.

A shear force is applied to the body when one or more forces move across the tissues. If more than one shear force crosses the tissues, the forces typically move in opposite directions. If a soccer player's thigh is kicked by an opponent wearing cleats, the cleats move across and shear the skin. Consequently, a skin wound, such as an abrasion or laceration, can occur.

Regardless of the mechanism of injury, the extent or degree of injury is determined by the severity and intensity with which the force is applied. The size of the area affected also determines the severity of injury. The injury most likely will be more severe if a great amount of force or stress is applied over a small area versus a larger area. In a previous example, a weightlifter dropped a weight on her foot. If the weightlifter dropped the same amount of weight on her thigh, the force applied to the tissue would be less than the force applied to the foot, because the thigh is a larger area than the foot (Anderson, Hall, & Martin, 2000). Also, the speed of the force can cause varying severity of injury. If a baseball player is hit by a 95 mile per hour (mph) pitch versus a 40 mph pitch at the same bodily area thrown from the same distance, the severity of injury caused by the 95 mph pitch will be greater. As you can see, many factors come into play to determine the severity of injury.

Tips from the Field

Tip 1   Remember that each athlete has a different tolerance to and perception of pain. When you ask an athlete how much pain they are experiencing, ask them to rate their pain on a scale of 1 to 10, with 1 being the least pain they have ever experienced and 10 being the most pain they have ever experienced. After they have given you their rating, ask them to describe the circumstance or scenario in which they felt that level of pain before. This information can give you an idea of the severity of injury.

THE HEALING PROCESS

After an injury occurs to an athlete, the healing process begins. The healing process is imperative for an injured or ill athlete. This process is a means to repair the tissues, return the body back to its uninjured state, and restore the body's equilibrium. The three phases of the healing process are the inflammatory phase, the fibroblastic repair phase, and the maturation-remodeling phase (Bahr & Maehlum, 2004; Booher & Thibodeau, 2000; Pfeiffer & Mangus, 2012). These phases occur in a continuum, which means they overlap each other (**Figure 2-2**). The three phases do not have a rigid time frame when one phase ends and the subsequent phase begins. However, completion of each phase is imperative for the tissue to heal properly. When the healing process is complete, an athlete should be able to obtain normal, pre-injury function.

The Inflammatory Phase

The inflammatory phase is the first phase in the healing process for **acute injuries**. This phase can arguably be considered the most important phase. If the inflammatory phase does not properly follow an intended course of events, then the damaged tissue will not move on to the fibroblastic phase. This lack of progression can cause further injury, in particular **chronic injury**, which is discussed later in this chapter.

> **Acute injury**   Occurs when the body is suddenly afflicted by trauma or damage to its tissues, which consequently initiates inflammation.
>
> **Chronic injury**   Occurs when an injury is no longer acute, yet remains in the later inflammatory phase or early fibroblastic repair phase of the healing process.

The inflammatory phase begins at the time of injury. Immediately when tissue is damaged vasoconstriction occurs. Vasoconstriction is defined by the blood vessels' lumen, or opening, becoming narrowed and smaller in diameter. Vasoconstriction often takes place for an extremely short amount of time, typically 5 to 10 minutes (Prentice, 2011). During this time, blood flow is slowed to the injured area. After vasoconstriction occurs, vasodilation begins.

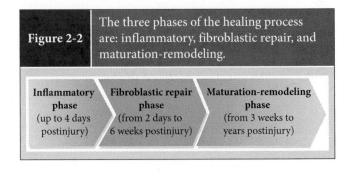

Figure 2-2   The three phases of the healing process are: inflammatory, fibroblastic repair, and maturation-remodeling.

Inflammatory phase (up to 4 days postinjury)	Fibroblastic repair phase (from 2 days to 6 weeks postinjury)	Maturation-remodeling phase (from 3 weeks to years postinjury)

Vasodilation is when the blood vessels' openings become larger in diameter. The vasodilation occurs during the beginning stages of the inflammation phase. The damaged tissue; cells, such as white blood cells or mast cells; and enzymes release chemical mediators that cause the vasodilation (Prentice, 2011). Two chemical mediators that are seemingly detrimental to the athlete, yet important to the healing process, are histamine and bradykinin. Histamine causes vasodilation, which increases blood flow to the injured area. It also causes redness, an increased temperature at the injured site, and blood vessel permeability. Like histamine, bradykinin creates blood vessel permeability, and also causes pain at the injured site and surrounding areas (Pfeiffer & Mangus, 2012).

When the blood vessels are vasodilated and their walls are permeable, the damaged red and white blood cells and the plasma fluid in the blood exit the blood vessels. This plasma fluid and cells are called **exudate**. How much exudate is formed depends on factors such as the extent of injury, chemical mediators released, and blood vessel permeability (Prentice, 2010). Exudate accumulates in the space outside the blood vessels. The exudate becomes viscous and remains stagnant along the soft and bony tissues. Due to its viscosity, the exudate creates the appearance of swelling and **ecchymosis** (**Figure 2-3**). As the exudate increases, the pressure increases at the injury site. The pressure causes cellular death due to lack of oxygenated blood flow to the area (Eaves, 2010), and pressure on nerve endings causes pain at the injury site. The exudate also prevents the veins from functioning properly. Usually the venous system brings waste, including carbon dioxide, damaged cells, and extracellular fluid, through the circulatory system to clean up the injured area after the trauma. However, the restoration cannot occur until other chemical mediators are released.

Chemical mediators that assist in returning the area to its pre-injury state are heparin, serotonin, leukotrienes, and prostaglandins (Prentice, 2011). Heparin is an anticoagulant, which helps make the exudate less viscous, making venous return possible. Serotonin helps the blood vessels to vasoconstrict and become less permeable. Consequently, the amount of fluid and cells exiting the blood vessels is minimized. Leukotrienes and prostaglandins both impede inflammation and decrease swelling.

At the end of the inflammatory response phase and in response to other chemical mediators, phagocytes go to the

> **Exudate** Formed by plasma fluid and cells; it is located in the space outside of the blood vessels.

> **Ecchymosis** A black and blue, bruise-like color of the skin that can occur with internal bleeding.

Figure 2-3 The black and blue color seen at the inner thigh in this picture is called ecchymosis.

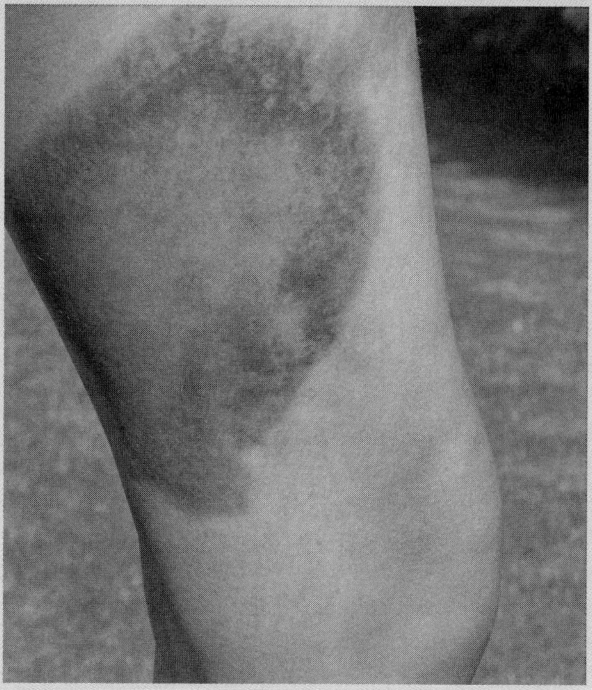

© sgm/ShutterStock, Inc.

injury site to debride the area. Phagocytes include cells such as leukocytes, neutrophils, and macrophages. They consume the waste materials, damaged cells, and foreign matter around the tissues (Pfeiffer & Mangus, 2012). Assisting the phagocytes are platelets, which are sticky substances that attach to the exposed collagen fibers on the blood vessels' walls. These platelets create a plug that helps limit the size of the inflamed area.

At this time, thromboplastin is released from the damaged cells. Thromboplastin initiates a series of events that causes the clot to be formed. The existence of thromboplastin makes prothrombin change to thrombin, which is the sticky substance comprising the clot (Prentice, 2011). A clot begins to form, which, like the platelet plug, limits the size of the inflamed area. The clot also prevents further blood flow to the injured area. As the clot forms, phagocytes continue to debride the area.

This phase of healing is characterized by specific signs and symptoms of inflammation. Signs of inflammation are characteristics that are physically observable. Symptoms of inflammation are characteristics that are not physically observable, but are subjective and reported by the athlete. Signs of inflammation include redness, swelling, increase in tissue temperature, and loss of function (**Figure 2-4**). The predominant and most common symptom of inflammation that the athlete experiences is pain. As the inflammatory phase subsides and the second phase of healing begins, these signs and symptoms of inflammation notably subside. The inflammatory phase can take up to 4 days to complete before the fibroblastic repair phase commences (Bahr & Maehlum, 2004).

The Fibroblastic Repair Phase

Usually around the second day postinjury marks the end of the inflammatory phase. At this time, the inflammatory phase overlaps with the beginning of the fibroblastic repair phase. The fibroblastic repair phase has a longer duration than the inflammatory phase, and can take up to 6 weeks to complete. This phase of healing is characterized by a decrease in signs and symptoms of inflammation, continuation of phagocytic activity, fibroblastic activity, and formation of collagen tissue and a fragile scar.

By the time the fibroblastic repair phase begins, the signs and symptoms of inflammation have decreased. New capillaries form at the injury site, which brings oxygenated blood to the area, while phagocytes continue to rid the injured site of debris (Bahr & Maehlum, 2004). Consequently, pressure decreases, which in turn decreases pain and swelling at the site. With

decreased pain and swelling, the athlete is able and willing to move the area. This voluntary movement increases range of motion, or amount of available motion, at the injured area.

Fibroblasts are cells that have the ability to form **collagen** fibers. They are located in connective tissue and migrate to the injured area. The fibroblasts begin

> **Collagen** A strong protein that comprises bone, soft tissue including skin, cartilage, and other connective tissues.

to create a loose meshwork of unorganized collagen at the injury site. The collagen creates a fragile scar at the site of the previously formed clot. This scar formation process is called fibroplasia (Booher & Thibodeau, 2000). Over weeks, the collagen begins to re-form and strengthen as the fibroblasts decrease in number, and thus ends the fibroblastic repair phase.

Tips from the Field

Tip 2   Athletes who have injuries in the fibroblastic repair phase of healing are able to participate in limited activities (with a physician's clearance note, of course). However, if they have any signs or symptoms of inflammation, or even soreness, before, during, or after activity, then their activity must be modified or reduced further. In some cases you may need to stop activity that entails that area (i.e., if it is a lower body injury, you can have your athlete perform upper body activities until the signs and symptoms subside).

The Maturation-Remodeling Phase

During the fibroblastic repair phase, collagen is laid down in a disorganized fashion, which creates a fragile scar. However, as stress is applied to the area, the collagen lines up parallel to how the stress is applied (Booher & Thibodeau, 2000). This organization of the collagen scar tissue fibers occurs in the beginning of the maturation-remodeling phase, which is the final phase of healing. It usually begins around 3 weeks postinjury, and overlaps the end of the fibroblastic repair phase. This final phase of healing is significantly longer than the fibroblastic repair phase and can take years to complete.

As the phase progresses, scar formation continues. Stress on the scar aligns the scar tissue fibers parallel to each other and the lines of stress. This stress creates more organized scar tissue. However, this stress must be applied in a manner that does not disrupt the scar. If too much stress exists, then scar disruption occurs and the healing process takes much longer than originally planned. Over time, the collagen fibers become more organized, and the scar continues to strengthen and decrease in size (Booher & Thibodeau, 2000).

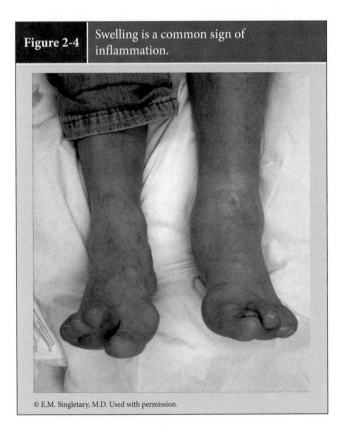

Figure 2-4 | Swelling is a common sign of inflammation.

© E.M. Singletary, M.D. Used with permission.

BONE HEALING VERSUS SOFT TISSUE HEALING

Bone healing is similar to soft tissue healing in regard to the events that occur in the inflammatory phase; however, once the fibroblastic repair phase begins, bone healing is different than soft tissue healing. During the fibroblastic repair phase, osteoblasts from the surrounding bone move to the break, or fracture, in the bone. These osteoblasts, which are a type of fibroblast, form a callus at the injured site (**Figure 2-5**). The callus is a combination of collagen and cartilage, which fills in the break in the bone. Over time, as with soft tissue healing in the maturation-remodeling phase, this bony callus becomes hard and strong (Pfeiffer & Mangus, 2012). Stress is applied to assist the callus to properly form into bone. However, usually some immobilization of the fracture is necessary to promote proper healing. A physician determines whether the fractured bone should be immobilized for days, weeks, months, or not at all. The physician makes this determination depending on various factors including the severity of the fracture, secondary injuries and complications, bone(s) injured, and the athlete's age and health. With proper treatment of the fracture, the injured site will heal and become continuous with the surrounding bone.

SIGNS VERSUS SYMPTOMS

Every injury has its typical signs and symptoms. Signs of injury are physically observable characteristics of injury. Signs are also objective, which means that you are able to see a sign as another person would. The injured athlete's perception cannot change the signs of the injury that you see. Unlike signs

Figure 2-5	A bony callus forming at the site of a metatarsal fracture.

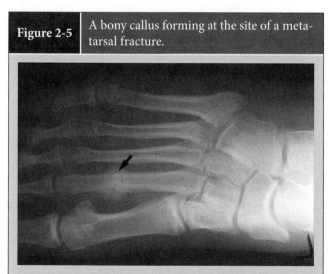

Reproduced with permission from Johnson TR, Steinbach LS (eds). Essentials of Musculoskeletal Imaging. Rosemont, IL: American Academy of Orthopaedic Surgeons; 2004:623.

Figure 2-6	Deformity is a sign of a dislocation.

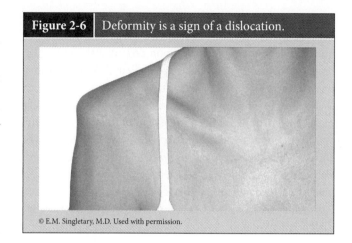

© E.M. Singletary, M.D. Used with permission.

of injury, symptoms are characteristics of injury that are not physically observable. Instead, symptoms are subjective to the injured person. You cannot see the symptoms that an injured athlete experiences. Because you cannot see symptoms, you can only take the injured athlete's word that the symptom exists. Both signs and symptoms are equally important to determine what type of injury an athlete has sustained, and to consequently render the proper treatment.

Numerous common signs and symptoms of injury exist. Some typical signs include differences in tissue temperature, asymmetry, and malalignment as compared to the opposite, uninjured, or **contralateral** side; ecchymosis; swelling; deformity (**Figure 2-6**); redness; hives; **crepitus**; and loss of function. Some common symptoms include pain, soreness, fever, nausea, **tinnitus**, headache, and numbness. Signs and symptoms of injury are often the same for a multitude of injuries, which makes determining the athlete's injury or illness difficult.

> **Contralateral**   The opposite side of the body symmetrical to the injured side. If the injury is at the right knee, then the contralateral side is the left knee.
>
> **Crepitus**   A crackling or grating sensation that you and an athlete may feel during movement or palpation when a structure is injured.
>
> **Tinnitus**   Ringing in the ears.

ACUTE VERSUS CHRONIC INJURIES

An acute injury occurs when the body is suddenly afflicted by trauma or damage to its tissues. Consequently, acute injury initiates inflammation and promotes all inflammatory process events. Acute injuries have a specific, sudden mechanism of injury. An athlete can typically describe and pinpoint the exact time the injury occurred. For example, an athlete at We R Fit Gym who drops a weight on his foot can describe the exact moment that he fractured his foot. His injury is acute because he had a specific, sudden mechanism or cause of injury. Likewise, immediately upon dropping the weight on his foot, the healing process, in particular the inflammatory phase, begins.

Chronic injuries are unlike acute injuries because with many chronic injuries the athlete cannot identify a specific, sudden mechanism of injury. Also, the signs and symptoms of chronic injuries develop more slowly than with acute injuries. For example, an athlete at We R Fit Gym complains of diffuse pain at both shoulders that has been increasing for 3 weeks. She cannot recall any specific time of injury when she immediately felt symptoms or noticed signs of inflammation. This scenario is very typical when an athlete has a chronic injury.

Another common reason why an injury is deemed chronic is due to the athlete having an acute injury and not receiving proper treatment for the injury. If acute injuries are not treated appropriately, they do not heal properly. The injury does not move through the healing process continuum as it should. Consequently, the injury becomes chronic. This process often occurs with mild to moderate injuries. For example, athletes with acute mild to moderate sprains and strains commonly learn to adapt to or ignore the associated discomfort and other inflammatory signs and symptoms. The athlete continues to participate in activities instead of obtaining proper treatment for the acute injury. In most cases this continued participation hinders the healing process and prolongs the signs and symptoms.

Consider the following scenario: During a Friday night championship game, a basketball player goes up for a lay-up and on her way down she lands with her foot on another player's foot. She inadvertently twists her ankle into inversion, which creates a mild sprain of her anterior talofibular ligament on the lateral side of her ankle. She experiences immediate pain and disability. Almost as quickly as the pain appears, it subsides and she is able to run down the court to play defense. Her team wins the game. She is so excited that she does not pay attention to her acutely injured ankle. The weekend arrives and she has mild ankle pain, swelling, and no loss of motion. She continues to perform her activities of daily living, which include Saturday morning basketball practice. The athlete decides not to see a physician for evaluation, nor does she provide any first aid treatment to her ankle. This scenario is typical for how an athlete's acute injury, due to no or improper treatment, can easily predispose an acute injury to become a chronic injury.

Another reason why an injury becomes chronic is due to an athlete's inability to recognize his or her injury when experiencing a subacute or overuse injury. A subacute injury exhibits very minimal signs and symptoms as compared to an acute injury, and is usually caused by microtraumas to a body structure. Overuse injuries occur from repetitive motions, and over time the structure is damaged. Overuse injuries can begin as subacute injuries and become chronic injuries. Because chronic injuries do not have a specific, identifiable, sudden mechanism of injury, it is often difficult for an athlete to recognize his or her injury. Chronic injuries are noted as having a mechanism of injury that begins as subacute and occurs over time from repetitive use of the structure involved.

Consider another scenario: A baseball pitcher constantly throws overhead. This constant throwing puts a significant amount of stress on his shoulder musculature and tendons. After every practice and game he believes his shoulder soreness is due to high intensity throwing. He does not consider that his shoulder is injured. Therefore, he does not mention the soreness to his coach. Three weeks later, he goes to his coach and explains that on some days, during and after throwing, his shoulder "feels fine" and on other days his shoulder is "extremely painful." The athlete now complains of loss of motion and strength. The fibroblastic repair phase of healing occurs after the inflammation phase and 3 weeks into the healing process. However, the athlete is still experiencing symptoms of injury that are consistent with the inflammatory phase. He may not have experienced a sudden acute mechanism of injury, but instead he sustained small, subacute injuries that occurred over time. Unfortunately, now the baseball player has sustained a chronic shoulder injury.

Most chronic injuries fluctuate between the inflammatory and fibroblastic repair phases. These injuries have a difficult time progressing through the fibroblastic repair phase and reaching the maturation-remodeling phase. Often, for the chronic injury to heal properly a physician or qualified allied healthcare professional elicits minor trauma, such as friction massage, to the chronic injury site. This microtrauma precipitates an inflammatory response, and reverts the injury to the beginning of the inflammatory response phase. A chronic injury may take many months or even years to heal.

In many instances, chronic injuries can be avoided if athletes closely listen to their bodies and heed acute injury signs and symptoms. Educate your athletes to report any acute inflammatory signs and symptoms of injury to their physician immediately upon recognizing them. Even if the athlete experiences mild signs and symptoms, he or she must receive care to promote the healing process and attempt to avoid chronic injury.

CLASSIFICATION OF INJURIES

The body is composed of numerous commonly injured anatomical structures. Likewise, various forces are placed on and created by these structures. Consequently, your athletes are predisposed to injury at some point in their lives. After reading this chapter, you will be able to classify what type of injury your athlete has experienced. Along with acute and chronic injuries, experts have classified injuries into two additional categories based on the tissue type involved. These categories are soft tissue injuries and bone injuries. Soft tissue and bone injuries are acute and chronic and further broken down into numerous classifications. Common soft tissue injuries include sprains, strains, tendinopathies, muscle spasms, contusions, bursitis, and skin wounds. A fracture is a common bone injury, while common joint injuries include dislocations and subluxations.

Soft Tissue Injuries

Sprain

A sprain is an injury to a ligament in which the ligamentous fibers are stretched or torn. A sprain typically is caused by a sudden, acute mechanism of injury such as a twisting (shear) or pulling apart (tension) of a joint. A joint is the articulation between two or more bones, which are held in close proximity to each other by ligaments. A ligament can be stretched or completely torn (ruptured); however, not all fibers in a single ligament are always ruptured. A single injured ligament may have intact, stretched, and torn fibers at the same time. As with other acute injuries, when a sprain occurs the healing process begins. The signs and symptoms of inflammation develop immediately after injury. During the healing process, scar tissue fills the space where the ligament tear occurred. The ligament and the scar tissue have plastic qualities. Plasticity means that the tissue does not have elasticity. Elasticity means that the tissue can be deformed or stretched and return to its original length. Because a ligament has plastic qualities, when it is stretched the ligament remains at that length. This fact is the same for scar tissue laid down when a ligament heals. After injury, the damaged ligament and resultant scar tissue are not strong enough to withstand significant stress. Consequently, it is very common for an athlete to have subsequent injuries occur to the same ligament.

A sprain is classified by using terminology describing its degree of severity. In 1964, the American Medical Association (AMA) charged a Subcommittee on Classification of Sports Injuries with creating standardized athletic injury nomenclature. The Subcommittee finalized the content in 1966, and *Standard Nomenclature of Athletic Injuries* was published by the AMA soon thereafter (AMA, 1966). Since that time, the medical field has utilized this nomenclature as a standard for explaining the severity of injuries. Three degrees of severity for sprains exist—first-, second-, and third-degree. The severity of injury increases from first-degree being the least severe to third-degree being the most severe. With first-degree sprains, the ligaments are stretched, but ligamentous fibers are not necessarily torn. First-degree sprains are often referred to as Grade 1 sprains. These sprains exhibit mild signs and symptoms of inflammation, which include a slight increase in tissue temperature, minimal skin redness at the injured site, mild loss of motion, mild swelling, discomfort to mild pain, and mild stiffness due to edema. Second-degree sprains are often referred to as Grade 2 sprains. These sprains occur when many of the ligament's fibers are completely torn, yet some remain intact. Grade 2 sprains exhibit moderate signs and symptoms of inflammation. An athlete with a second-degree sprain experiences a definitive increase in tissue temperature, skin redness at the injured site, moderate loss of motion, moderate swelling, significant pain, and joint instability. Third-degree, or Grade 3, sprains are the most severe sprains. The ligament is completely ruptured and the tissue is entirely torn. Consequently, the signs and symptoms of third-degree sprains are severe. Third-degree sprains exhibit a greater localized increase in temperature than do second-degree sprains, notable redness, and significant loss of motion, swelling, pain, and joint instability.

Regardless of the degree of injury, when an athlete suffers a sprain she or he will be adversely affected to some extent. Your role is to provide immediate, proper care and medical referral for an athlete with a sprain.

Strain

A strain is an injury to a muscle, tendon, or most commonly the musculotendinous junction (MTJ) where the muscle and tendon meet (Pfeiffer & Mangus, 2012). The muscle and tendon fibers may be stretched or torn. Not all fibers in one muscle or tendon are necessarily affected. Unlike ligaments, which are plastic, muscles are elastic. Of course, if muscle or tendon fibers cannot withstand the stress applied and are stretched beyond their anatomic limit they rupture. The common mechanisms of injury for a strain include a sudden muscle stretch while at rest, or a quick, forceful muscle contraction. Strains are similar to sprains in that strains are classified into the three degrees previously described. First-, second-, and third-degree strains all have similar signs and symptoms to sprains in regard to pain, redness, swelling, and loss of function. However, with all strains, muscle spasm occurs to some extent and pain is most pronounced during muscle function.

To preliminarily determine whether the injury is a sprain or a strain before you refer your athlete to a physician or summon emergency services, you can keep one rule of thumb regarding ligaments in mind. Ligaments are not contractile tissues as muscles are. Therefore, if an athlete has sprained a ligament, the pain most likely is more pronounced when the joint is passively moved versus actively moved. With passive motion, no muscle contraction occurs. The joint is separated and the bony joint surfaces are moved apart. This passive motion and joint surface distraction consequently stretch the ligament, causing pain. When a muscle or tendon is injured, pain is more pronounced with active movement. Active movement occurs when muscles contract to move the joints through a range of motion. The concentric (shortening) or eccentric (lengthening) contraction of the muscle causes pain. This rule of thumb is not always foolproof, because at times, sprains and strains can occur simultaneously.

Tendinopathy

Tendinopathy is a term describing injury to the tendons. The injuries include tendinitis, tenosynovitis, and tendinosis. Tendinitis is an inflammatory condition of the tendon, whereas tenosynovitis is an inflammatory condition of the synovial sheath that surrounds the tendon. Tendinosis is tendon degeneration. Signs and symptoms of tendinopathies include pain during activity that decreases after activity, crepitus, loss of motion, swelling, and **point tenderness**. The mechanism of injury for tendinitis and tenosynovitis can be acute or chronic. An acute mechanism of injury includes a sudden contraction or stretch of the tendon, which is similar to a strain's mechanism of injury. More commonly, the mechanism of injury for tendinitis and tenosynovitis is microtrauma that occurs to the structure due to repetitive

> **Point tenderness**
> Discomfort or pain when an injured area is touched.

overuse. Microtraumas are small injuries to the fibers that collectively, over time, create a chronic injury. The repetitive overuse does not necessarily originate from improper mechanics or function. On the contrary, tendinitis and tenosynovitis often occur with proper function. However, the intensity, quantity, duration, and repetition of tendon function all play a part in the tendinopathy. Tendinosis occurs if tendinitis continues to be a chronic condition and proper treatment is not given. As a result, the tendon does not heal and degenerates.

During activity, athletes create continuous, repetitive joint movements by muscular contractions. Some athletes have more repetition during activities than others. For example, by nature of their sport, swimmers and baseball players have repetitive shoulder motion. The athletes perform at a high level of intensity in order to gain optimal performance. If the athletes do not rest adequately between activities and modify their activity in regard to intensity, duration, and function, then the shoulder can become inflamed due to microtraumas. Soreness is a common symptom of microtrauma. Unfortunately, athletes do not often heed this symptom, and additional microtraumas occur during each subsequent activity. Without rest or treatment for this soreness, the microtraumas eventually summate and cause a major inflammatory process. This inflammation can be extremely disabling to an athlete and will hinder their function to some extent (**Figure 2-7**).

| **Figure 2-7** | An inflamed Achilles' tendon. |

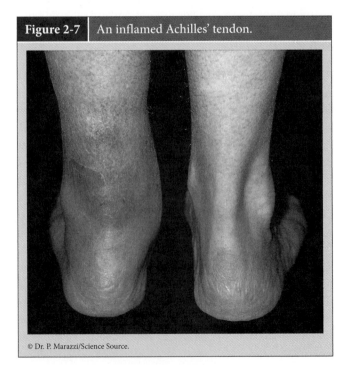

© Dr. P. Marazzi/Science Source.

Muscle Spasm

Muscle spasms, or muscle cramps, are involuntary contractions of the muscles (Binkley et al., 2002). The muscles become stiff and hard, which results in pain and loss of motion. Various mechanisms of injury for muscle spasms exist. When a joint, muscle, or bone is injured, the surrounding muscle involuntarily contracts in order to protect the injured area from further harm. A direct blow to a muscle; a sudden, forceful movement, in particular an unexpected stretch; or overuse of a muscle, especially when the muscle is fatigued, can also cause the muscle spasm. If an athlete stretches her hamstrings to the extent that the muscle group cannot tolerate the stretch, the muscles spasm to protect against further injury. If a boxer is punched by another boxer in the abdomen, which injures an internal organ, the abdominal muscles contract and become hardened (guarding) in order to protect the internal organs from further injury. Muscle spasms also occur if a body part remains in a still position over time. Muscle spasms often occur in the neck due to sleeping in the same, and potentially awkward, position for hours. Muscle spasms can also occur from dehydration and lack of electrolytes in the body (Binkley et al., 2002). If an athlete does not hydrate enough or ingest adequate electrolytes before exercise, the athlete may succumb to muscle cramping, which is a heat-related illness. Muscle cramping particularly occurs when exercising in a hot and humid environment due to the amount of water and electrolytes lost when an athlete sweats. If you educate your athletes on proper hydration before, during, and after activity, you can prevent this heat-related muscle cramping from occurring.

Contusions

A bruise is another name for a contusion. The mechanism of injury for a contusion is a compression force. Typically this force originates from an object compressing a muscle against the underlying bone (Prentice, 2011). The direct blow from the object crushes the muscle fibers, causing injury to the muscle fibers, capillaries, and underlying structures. The object causing injury can be stationary, such as a weight rack that your athlete walks into, or it can be moving, such as a batted baseball. The contusion's severity depends on a multitude of factors, including the size and speed of the object striking the muscle as well as the size, thickness, and strength of the muscle. In regard to object speed, an object traveling at high speed and striking the body would cause a more severe contusion than the same object traveling at a lower speed. For example, consider the speed of a baseball when a batter hits a line drive and strikes the pitcher in the quadriceps. Then consider the catcher tossing the ball slowly with a high arc at the pitcher, who fails to catch it and gets hit on his quadriceps. The athlete undoubtedly will have a more significant contusion as a result of the high-speed batted ball. Also, if an athlete has strong, large, hypertrophied muscles, then these muscles can withstand greater compression forces as compared to muscles that are weak, small, and atrophied.

Once a muscle is contused, inflammation begins. Signs and symptoms of a contusion are the same as for sprains and strains—pain, redness, increase in tissue temperature, swelling, and loss of function are typical immediately after injury. Hematomas—blood from damaged, bleeding tissues and capillaries—can accumulate around the muscle and under the skin. The hematomas can sometimes be visible if they form at the skin surface. These hematomas cause ecchymosis. Whenever a severe contusion with significant signs and symptoms occurs to one of your athletes, suspect that the underlying bone, internal organs, or structures other than the muscle are also injured. Consequently, you should refer your athlete to a physician for evaluation.

Bursitis

Bursae are fluid-filled sacs located throughout the body. They assist in shock absorption and decrease friction between various anatomical structures in the body, such as ligaments, tendons, bones, and skin. Commonly injured bursae include the prepatellar bursa, which is located at the knee between the skin and the patella; the olecranon bursa, which is located between the skin and the olecranon of the elbow; and the trochanteric bursa, which is located at the hip between the greater trochanter and the gluteal muscles. Bursae can be injured in either an acute or a chronic manner. Acute bursitis is caused by a direct, forceful blow to the body. A common mechanism of injury for acute olecranon bursitis, for example, is a direct blow to the elbow while in maximal flexion against a nonyielding object such as a wall. The injured bursa immediately fills with fluid and appears very swollen. The athlete experiences pain and loss of function at the area. Interestingly enough, the athlete may not have point tenderness when touching the swollen bursa, but most likely has pain when touching the bone under and around the bursa. The bursa may feel like a ball of encapsulated jelly, which can be moved back and forth without eliciting pain. The athlete may not be willing to move the joint due to pain, or may even be unable to move the joint. This inability to move the area is due to the significantly larger bursa taking up space and stretching the skin, thereby preventing movement.

Consider the following scenario: An ice hockey player is competing in a game. He goes after the puck at full speed with his stick in hand. His opponent checks him into the boards.

At that moment, his elbow is flexed and his elbow pad slides just enough for his olecranon to strike the board. The athlete feels immediate pain and disability. A few minutes later, when he returns to the bench, his pain has decreased; however, he is unable to flex his elbow. The olecranon bursa is approximately the size of a golf ball. The athlete touches the bursa and moves it around without much pain. When the athlete touches the underlying olecranon, however, he has significant point tenderness. This point tenderness suggests that the direct blow against the boards may have caused a fracture to the underlying bone. Consequently, the athlete was referred to see a physician for x-rays (**Figure 2-8**).

Bursae can also be injured by a chronic mechanism of injury. This mechanism of injury includes overusing a muscle or tendon, and repetitive friction over a bursa. In these cases, the signs and symptoms of injury are similar to those of acute bursitis; however, they appear slowly, perhaps over hours or days. Also, typically the immediate swelling after an acute bursa injury is more pronounced and appears localized. With chronic bursa injuries, the swelling is more generalized. With knee bursitis, an athlete could have chronic inflammation due to repetitive activities such as deep knee

Figure 2-8 | Acute elbow bursitis.

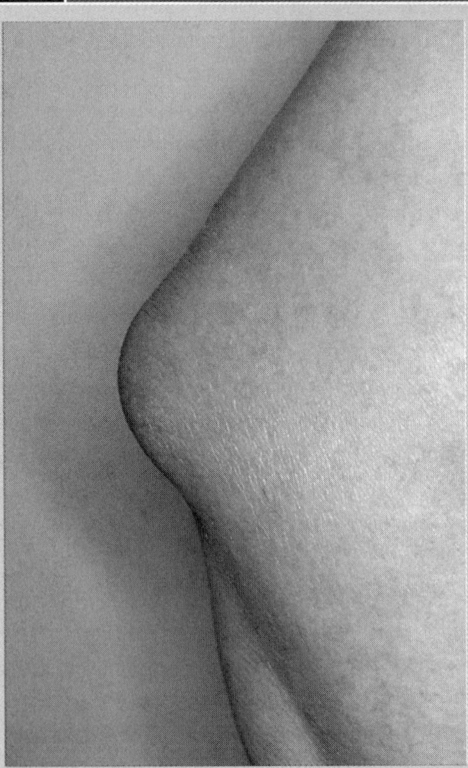

© SPL/Science Source.

flexion activities or continual kneeling. For example, an athlete at We R Fit Gym begins an intense squat program with heavy resistance. Her body, in particular her knees, are not accustomed to this exercise. Over a period of days, the athlete begins to feel discomfort and point tenderness. She notices generalized puffiness around the front of the knee. These signs and symptoms continue to increase as the days and activities progress. The athlete's knee function deteriorates. Finally, she decides to see a physician who diagnoses her with chronic knee bursitis. The athlete is allowed to continue training, but with limited knee flexion activities until the signs and symptoms of injury subside.

The injuries discussed in this section are the most common soft tissue injuries that your athletes will experience. The injury severity varies immensely from athlete to athlete and injury to injury. The injury may be so mild that the athlete is able to continue activity participation. On the other hand, the injury may be so severe that the athlete is not capable of or allowed to participate for a period of time. No two soft tissue injuries are the same, and your athletes may experience more than one soft tissue injury simultaneously. Regardless of how many soft tissue injuries your athletes may experience, your role in educating and providing immediate care and referral is imperative to the athletes' well-being and return to full pre-injury function.

Bone Injuries

Fractures

Most likely at some point during your career, one of your athletes will sustain a fracture. Fractures are disabling to an athlete for a variety of reasons. When an athlete breaks a bone, the bone is immobilized with a splint or cast for a period of weeks to allow proper healing. Sometimes it is necessary to perform surgery to assist in realigning the broken bones into their proper position. Fractures typically do not occur as a single injury. Often another injury exists along with the fracture, such as a ligament rupture, muscle contusion or strain, and nerve and blood vessel injury. Mechanisms of injury for fractures include compression, tension, and shear forces. The signs and symptoms of fractures include the typical signs and symptoms of inflammation, which are pain, swelling, loss of function, redness, and increase in temperature. Other signs and symptoms include crepitus, deformity, joint locking due to bony fragments lodged in the joint space, and loss of sensation due to nerve injury.

Fractures are classified as closed or open, displaced or nondisplaced, and complete or incomplete. Most fractures are closed fractures, which occur when the broken bones do not protrude through the skin. When the broken bones protrude through the skin, the bones create an open wound, and the fracture therefore is classified as an open or compound fracture. These fractures are more troublesome than closed fractures because the open wound is susceptible to infection, which could become **systemic** and potentially fatal. Likewise, significant external bleeding may occur, which can also be fatal (**Figure 2-9**). Fractures also are classified as displaced or nondisplaced. If the ends of the fractured bones are not in proper alignment with each other, then the fracture is displaced. If the ends of the bones remain in alignment, then the fracture is nondisplaced. Displaced fractures are often more severe and have the potential to cause additional trauma due to bone movement. When the fractured bones have been pushed out of alignment, more opportunity exists for injury to other structures, including nerves and blood vessels. When fractures are open they are also displaced. Closed fractures can be displaced or nondisplaced. Fractures can occur through the entire bone, creating two or more separate pieces, which is called a complete fracture. An incomplete fracture is when the fracture line does not pass through the entire bone, which leaves part of the bone intact.

> **Systemic**   Throughout the entire body.

Specific terminology is used to describe the type of fracture line. Some of the more common fractures are classified as transverse, oblique, greenstick, comminuted, compression (impacted), spiral, avulsion, stress, or epiphyseal fractures (**Figure 2-10**).

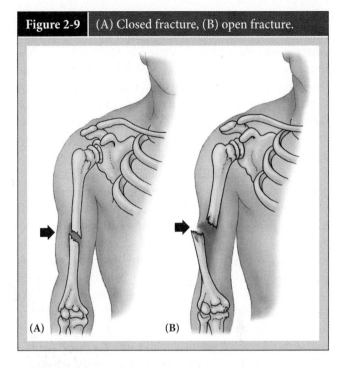

Figure 2-9   (A) Closed fracture, (B) open fracture.

(A)   (B)

A transverse fracture is a complete fracture with a fracture line that is perpendicular to the long axis of the bone (Starkey, Brown, & Ryan, 2010). An oblique fracture line is similar to the transverse fracture line, except it runs on a diagonal to the

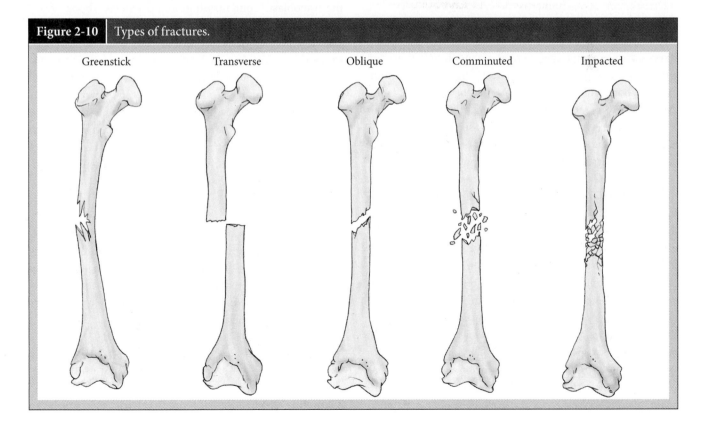

Figure 2-10   Types of fractures.

Greenstick   Transverse   Oblique   Comminuted   Impacted bone's long axis. A greenstick fracture typically occurs in young children whose bones are not completely finished growing and have not entirely hardened. These fractures are incomplete fractures. The side opposite the force is broken, but the side where the stress was applied is intact. A comminuted fracture is a complete fracture with numerous tiny pieces. These bone fragments are floating around in the space between the ends of the bones. They also can dislodge from the space and move around among the tissues, causing further damage.

Compression or impacted fractures occur when stress is applied to the ends of the long bones. This type of fracture can occur if an athlete jumps or falls from a great height, such as a tall ladder or the roof of a house. The compressive forces from the ground and the athlete's body on the femur or tibia can cause the compressive fracture. Likewise, this same mechanism of injury can cause a compression fracture of the spinal vertebrae.

Spiral fractures occur as a result of torsion and compression forces. These forces are directed along the long axis of the bone, and create a spiral fracture line appearance. Consider how a spiral fracture can occur to a football player during a game. The athlete is running with the ball and is tackled. The force causes his hand to be planted on the ground. The hand creates a compressive force up the radius and ulna to the humerus. During the tackle, his body, including his shoulder joint, rotates, which creates torsion. Consequently, a spiral fracture occurs to the humerus.

Avulsion fractures occur when a piece of bone is pulled off the main bone by a ligament or tendon. When a torsion stress occurs to a joint, the ligament or tendon sometimes can withstand the force. Consequently, the ligament or tendon pulls the bone from its attachment, creating a fracture. Often avulsion fractures are difficult to distinguish from a sprain or a strain at the ligament's or tendon's insertion, respectively. Ultimately when an avulsion fracture is suspected, refer the athlete for x-rays to obtain a correct diagnosis.

A fracture that occurs from repetitive or atypical stress over a period of time is referred to as a stress fracture. Stress fractures typically occur in weight-bearing bones due to the force continually placed on them by the athlete contacting the ground or another surface in a repetitive manner. Therefore, these fractures are not considered to have an acute, traumatic mechanism of injury. Most stress fractures occur to the lower extremities due to the constant pounding during running or jumping activities. The muscles and bone cannot readily dissipate the constant, repetitive force. Over time, which could be many weeks, the bone begins to break down. A particular stress fracture symptom is pain that occurs before and after weight-bearing activity. Sometimes the athlete has a dull aching pain at night that wakes them. They often are able to function, but pain causes their function to decline. The athlete will have point tenderness at the site of the stress fracture. If you suspect your athlete has a stress fracture, stop the athlete's training activities and refer them to a physician for evaluation. The physician will most likely order x-rays for the athlete. When viewing an x-ray, you cannot see a stress fracture unless it has already healed. On an x-ray, the healed stress fracture appears as a stark white line on the bone.

> **Tips from the Field**
>
> **Tip 4** If you are unsure whether your athlete has sustained a stress fracture, immediately have your athlete stop any sign- and symptom-provoking activities, and refer them to a physician for evaluation. Do not forget to get a clearance note from the athlete's physician prior to allowing your athlete to return to activity.

Epiphyseal fractures can be dangerous if they occur to young children. The epiphysis is at the end of the bone where new bone is formed. This bone formation occurs during the growing years. Once an adult has stopped growing, the epiphyseal plates, or growth plates, close and solidify. Epiphyseal fractures occur at these growth plates. When a growing athlete sustains a fracture at this site, the fracture can be extremely detrimental to their limb growth. The fracture may disrupt the osteoblast (bone forming) and osteoclast (bone breakdown) activity. Consequently, the bone may stop growing and close prematurely, creating a shortened limb as compared to the other side. Any mechanisms of injury previously discussed can cause an epiphyseal fracture, and the signs and symptoms are similar to other fractures. Epiphyseal fractures may occur as stress fractures or as acute, traumatic fractures. All acute fractures are medical emergencies. Therefore, to ensure proper athlete care, your primary role in treatment of the athlete's acute fracture is summoning emergency personnel immediately.

Joint Injuries

Injuries to the joints are common. Not only can the ligaments and tendons that cross over joints become injured, but the bony articulation at the joint also can be damaged. Stresses placed on the joint from bodily movements and outside forces can cause dislocations and subluxations, which are two very common joint injuries.

Dislocations

Dislocations, or luxations, are acute joint injuries that occur when one end of a bone is forced out of its normal position relative to the other bone (**Figure 2-11**). The mechanisms of

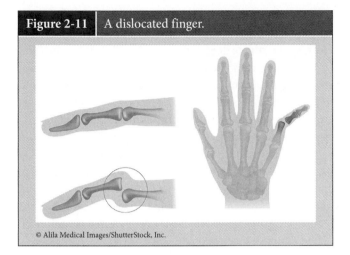

Figure 2-11 | A dislocated finger.

© Alila Medical Images/ShutterStock, Inc.

injury for a dislocation are a direct blow to the joint by an outside force or a force created by the athlete's body along with the bones moving in a manner in which they are unaccustomed. Some joints are more easily dislocated than others. The glenohumeral (shoulder), patellofemoral (kneecap), and phalangeal joints (fingers) are typically the most frequently dislocated joints. These joints are most commonly dislocated due to their shallow bony articulations. Signs and symptoms of dislocations are readily apparent. Obvious deformity is a very prevalent sign exhibited when a dislocation occurs. The bone protrudes from its normal position, creating disfigurement. Swelling may or may not be present. The athlete cannot move the joint because the bones are out of place. The athlete has significant pain, and possibly some sensation loss. Picture a quarterback preparing to throw the football with his arm in a cocked position. Suddenly the opposing lineman goes for the ball and tackles the quarterback. The opponent's force pushes the quarterback's arm in a posterior, or backwards, position, which results in a shoulder dislocation. In another scenario, a basketball player attempts to catch a ball that forcefully hits the tip of her finger. The ball forces her finger to move out of alignment. The distal phalange dislocates and moves on top of the middle phalange.

Unfortunately, once an athlete dislocates a joint, the chance of the same joint dislocating again increases. Additional dislocations are possible due to the joint structures, including the capsule, ligaments, tendons, and muscle, becoming significantly stretched and injured with the first dislocation. Consequently, the bones that comprise the joint are not held as tightly in place as they were prior to injury. The force necessary to dislocate the same joint a second time does not have to be as great as with the initial injury. Keep in mind that the force needed to cause a dislocation can also cause a concurrent fracture, along with nerve and blood vessel damage at the injury site (Anderson et al., 2000). Because secondary injuries are possible with dislocations, they must be treated as medical emergencies. Only physicians are qualified to relocate the bones. Never put the bones back into normal alignment, because you can do further harm to your athlete. Instead, call your local emergency number immediately.

Subluxations

Subluxations occur when a bone within a joint moves out of normal alignment and then spontaneously moves back into normal position. The movement out of normal joint alignment occurs due to an outside force, such as a direct blow from an object, or an internal force, such as a forceful muscle contraction. Unlike dislocations, subluxations can be acute or chronic (Starkey et al., 2010). The mechanism of injury for an acute subluxation is the same as for a dislocation. An example of an acute subluxation is when a humeral head rapidly moves out of normal joint position and then immediately back into normal joint position on its own. This injury is classified as acute due to the traumatic mechanism of injury. Similar to a dislocation, the possibility for future subluxations exists. After an athlete sustains his or her first acute subluxation, he or she may have repetitive subluxations of the same joint. These recurrent subluxations are classified as chronic. Along with the glenohumeral joint, chronic subluxations often occur at the patellofemoral joint.

The signs and symptoms of subluxations include pain, point tenderness, loss of function, swelling, and possible loss of sensation. Unlike dislocations, because a subluxed joint is in normal alignment, you do not see deformity. However, because the joint was out of normal alignment temporarily, consider that secondary injury may have occurred. Therefore, in order for your athlete to obtain proper care, refer her or him for immediate physician evaluation.

THE BODY'S RESPONSE TO ILLNESS

Athletes are prone to illnesses like any other person. The healthier the athlete is psychologically and physically, the less chance she or he will acquire an illness; however, athletes cannot entirely prevent illnesses. A variety of common causes of illness exist, including nutritional deficiencies, lack of exercise, impaired immunity, mental stress, heredity, toxins, and microorganism infection (Neighbors & Tannehille-Jones, 2000). Over time, lack of exercise, or even a lack of minimal physical activity, decreases bodily function, causing weakened muscle and bones, and immune system deterioration. Consequently, the athlete's immune system cannot fight infection properly and illness results. Mental stress can increase to the point where the body can no longer tolerate the stress.

Again, the immune system weakens and illness can invade the body. Hereditary illness is due to abnormalities in an athlete's chromosomes in utero. These chromosomal abnormalities may not cause illness until later in life, or perhaps not at all (Neighbors & Tannehille-Jones, 2000).

Toxins are poisonous substances produced by a living cell that enters an athlete's body and causes illness. A bee creates a toxin as a defense mechanism, which is released when the bee stings a person or an animal. For some athletes, this sting may be deadly, because the venom released causes an athlete to go into anaphylactic shock. Anaphylactic shock occurs when a person is severely allergic to a toxin, such as bee venom. The toxin causes swelling in and constriction of the air passages, which makes the person unable to breathe. Consequently, anaphylactic shock is a serious medical emergency.

Microorganisms entering the body can cause illness and infection. The three microorganisms that commonly cause illness are bacteria, viruses, and fungi. These microorganisms are the predominant causes for athletes' everyday illnesses.

Bacteria are cells that reproduce in the body and produce systemic illnesses and localized infections. When an illness affects the entire body it is a systemic illness; a localized illness or infection is when the bacteria affect only a particular area. Many types of bacteria exist. Some bacteria are very strong and difficult to eliminate from the body, such as methicillin-resistant *Staphylococcus aureus* (MRSA), whereas others are more easily destroyed, such as *Campylobacter*, which causes food poisoning (Crowley, 2010). Fortunately for athletes, antibiotics can be used to break down the microorganisms and return the athlete's body to a normal state. Bacteria also cause common illnesses and infections such as acne, sinus infections, strep throat, meningitis, gastroenteritis, and Lyme disease (Pommerville, 2012).

Viruses are smaller microorganisms than bacteria; however, unlike bacteria, viruses must attach to a host cell in the athlete's body in order to live and replicate (Neighbors & Tannehille-Jones, 2000). Viruses can replicate and mutate. This mutation makes it extremely difficult to destroy the virus with any medicinal agent. Antibiotics or other drugs are not able to destroy the virus as they effectively destroy bacteria. Consequently, over-the-counter (OTC) and prescription drugs are utilized to alleviate the athlete's signs and symptoms. The viral illness must run its course. The athlete's immune system attempts to fight the virus, break it down, and eliminate it from the body. Common viral illnesses include herpes simplex 1 virus (cold sores), conjunctivitis (pink eye), rhinoviruses (head colds), and verruca virus (warts) (Pommerville, 2012). Fortunately, vaccines exist that can help prevent an athlete from obtaining certain viruses. Common immunizations include those for hepatitis B virus (HBV), influenza (flu), and measles, mumps, and rubella (MMR). In response to these immunizations, the body creates antibodies that fight the virus, so the athlete does not acquire the illness or infection.

Fungi are plantlike organisms that thrive in dark, moist environments. Many fungal infections occur on the skin and remain localized, such as tinea corporis (ringworm), tinea cruris (jock itch), tinea pedis (athlete's foot), and *Candida albicans* (yeast infection). Although rare, fungal infections can become significant systemic illnesses. Usually, normal bodily bacteria prevent fungi from causing a systemic illness, such as a pulmonary fungal infection. However, if bacteria are not functioning properly, acute systemic fungal illness can occur (Crowley, 2010). Fungal infections can be treated by antifungal oral and topical medications.

Regardless of the microorganism, bacteria, viruses, and fungi can be contagious, meaning they can be spread from athlete to athlete, either by direct contact, such as touching the infected area, or by indirect contact, such as the transference through water molecules in saliva or a sneeze. An ill athlete is considered contagious for a specific period of time, but this duration varies depending on the microorganism. Common contagious illnesses and infections include the flu, pink eye, ringworm, and herpes.

Tips from the Field

Tip 5   If your athlete has any skin lesions that appear as pustules, rashes, hives, or any unusual, unfamiliar markings, immediately have your athlete see a doctor. Your athlete must not be permitted to participate in activities with your organization or in your facility until they have received written clearance from their physician and provided it to you. The skin lesion may be infectious and contagious. Immediately disinfect any object and area that your athlete has contacted, because the microorganism causing the potential infection could be transferred to your other athletes.

SUMMARY

Now that you have learned about the healing process and classification of injuries and illnesses, various classifications, mechanisms, and signs and symptoms of injury are familiar. This information will assist you in providing athlete care.

DISCUSSION QUESTIONS

1. What are the key events that occur in the three phases of healing?
2. What is the difference between a sign and a symptom of injury and illness?

3. What are differences between sprains and strains? What can you do to preliminarily determine if an athlete has a sprain or a strain?

4. How can an injury go from being acute to chronic? What classifies an injury as being chronic?

5. Why are compound fractures medical emergencies? Why could an athlete's life be threatened if she has a compound fracture?

6. Why is it important that exercise scientists do not reduce a dislocated joint? What could happen to the athlete if an untrained person relocates the bones?

7. What is bursitis, and how can it affect an athlete's performance?

8. What microorganisms cause illnesses, and how do they differ? What general treatments can be utilized to rid the organisms from the body and decrease signs and symptoms of illness?

CASE STUDY

Listen to Your Body

Megan is a 15-year-old, slender cross-country runner at Ocean Crest High School. She has just won the county championship meet. As a result, Megan has an automatic entry into the state championship meet, which takes place in 1 month. The state championship meet distance is twice as long as any other meet she has ever participated in. Likewise, it takes place on unfamiliar terrain for Megan, which includes rugged, steep hills. To prepare for this meet, Megan's coach instructs her to train 5 days per week. He says that he will run with her each day, because he wants to motivate and push her to her training limit.

Megan's training intensity is significantly increased as compared to her previous training for the county championship. She runs farther each day on various surfaces including dirt, blacktop, and all-weather track. Megan begins training up and down hills, which she is not accustomed to doing. After a few days of intense training, as a gift her mother purchases Megan new running sneakers, which she wears the next day to train. Megan sees that she is progressing after just a few days of vigorous training. She thinks to herself that if she also runs on weekends, she will improve faster and become better. Consequently, Megan decides to train on her 2 days off, making her training schedule 7 days per week. She does not schedule any rest days.

After about 2 weeks of training, Megan begins to experience some discomfort in the bottom of her right foot at the end of her workouts. She believes that the discomfort will go away on its own. Also, Megan is afraid to tell her mother or coach about the discomfort because she is fearful that she would not be allowed to continue her 7 days per week training. Megan tries to ignore the discomfort and work through it. A few days after her discomfort began, the discomfort turns into dull, aching, constant pain after the workouts. The pain not only is considerably worse after workouts, but Megan also starts to feel the pain during the workout. Then she begins to experience aching on the bottom of her right foot even when her foot is at rest while she is sitting or lying down.

One day during a workout, the pain is so bad that it begins to affect her gait and she starts to limp. She is not able to put her right foot flat on the ground and instead walks on her right foot's toes. At this point, she still tries to complete the workout, but due to the pain the workout suffers considerably to the point where she cannot run at all and complete the workout. Megan cannot tolerate the pain and finally realizes that her foot is not getting any better. She immediately tells her coach and mother about what has occurred over the last 3 weeks. The next day, her mother takes her to the doctor, who says that Megan cannot run for a month or more, which prevents her from competing in the state championship meet.

1. What types of injuries could Megan have?
2. What factors led to Megan's injury?
3. What could Megan have done when she first began to train for the state championship meet in an attempt to prevent this injury?

REFERENCES

American Medical Association. (1966). Annual reports. *Journal of the American Medical Association*, 198(4), 403. Retrieved May 31, 2011, from http://jama.ama-assn.org/content/198/4/397.full.pdf+html

Anderson, M. K., Hall, S. J., & Martin, M. (2000). *Sports injury management* (2nd ed.). Philadelphia: Lippincott, Williams & Wilkins.

Bahr, R., & Maehlum, S. (Eds.). (2004). *Clinical guide to sports injuries: An illustrated guide to the management of injuries in physical activity*. Champaign, IL: Human Kinetics.

Binkley, H. M., Beckett, J., Casa, D. J., Kleiner, D. M., & Plummer, P. E. (2002). National Athletic Trainers' Association position statement: Exertional heat illnesses. *Journal of Athletic Training*, 37(3), 329–343. Retrieved June 3, 2011, from http://www.nata.org/sites/default/files/ExternalHeatIllnesses.pdf

Booher, J. M., & Thibodeau, G. A. (2000). *Athletic injury assessment* (4th ed.). New York: McGraw-Hill.

Crowley, L. V. (2010). *An introduction to human disease: Pathology and pathophysiology correlations* (8th ed.). Sudbury, MA: Jones and Bartlett.

Eaves, T. (2010). *The practical guide to athletic training.* Sudbury, MA: Jones and Bartlett Learning.

Neighbors, M., & Tannehille-Jones, R. (2000). *Human diseases.* Albany, NY: Delmar Thompson Learning.

Pfeiffer, R. P., & Mangus, B. C. (2012). *Concepts of athletic training* (6th ed.). Sudbury, MA: Jones and Bartlett Learning.

Pommerville, J. C. (2012). *Guide to infectious diseases by body system* (2nd ed.). Sudbury, MA: Jones and Bartlett Learning.

Prentice, W. E. (2011). *Principles of athletic training: A competency-based approach* (14th ed.). New York: McGraw-Hill.

Prentice, W. E. (2010). *Essentials of athletic injury management* (8th ed.). New York: McGraw-Hill.

Starkey, C., Brown, S. D., & Ryan, J. (2010). *Examination of orthopedic and athletic injuries* (3rd ed.). Philadelphia: F.A. Davis.

Chapter 3

Bloodborne Pathogens

CHAPTER OBJECTIVES

After you have read this chapter, you will be able to understand:

- The similarities and differences among the bloodborne pathogens hepatitis B virus (HBV), hepatitis C virus (HCV), and human immunodeficiency virus (HIV)
- The signs and symptoms of bloodborne pathogen infection
- How an athlete develops acquired immune deficiency syndrome (AIDS)
- How bloodborne pathogens are transmitted from athlete to athlete
- The components of the Occupational Safety and Health Administration (OSHA) bloodborne standard
- How to protect yourself and your athletes from contracting bloodborne pathogens

In the exercise science field, we work closely with athletes during our daily professional activities. Because we frequently work in close proximity to our athletes' bodies, the potential for exposure to athletes' bloodborne pathogens exists.

> **Direct contact** When a person's infected blood has physically touched another person's body.

One means to acquire bloodborne pathogens is through **direct contact** with an athlete's infected blood or bodily fluids. Exercise science professionals do not commonly come in contact with athletes' blood or bodily fluids; however, one unfortunate incident can result in infection. Consequently, we must make every attempt to prevent transmission of

bloodborne pathogens. This chapter gives an overview of bloodborne pathogens, including how to protect yourself from being exposed.

THREE COMMON BLOODBORNE PATHOGENS

According to the U.S. Department of Labor's Occupational Safety and Health Administration (OSHA) (1991), bloodborne pathogens are microorganisms in the blood that cause disease. These pathogens are also found in some bodily fluids such as vaginal secretions, semen, cerebrospinal fluid, and synovial fluid. Research has shown that hepatitis B virus (HBV) and human immunodeficiency virus (HIV) are also found in saliva, although in very small quantities as compared to blood; therefore, theoretically saliva is a viable mode of transmission (Neighbors & Tannehille-Jones, 2000; Van der Eijk et al., 2004). Sweat does not contain bloodborne pathogens.

As exercise scientists, we must take an active role in preventing transmission of bloodborne pathogens in the workplace. At some point during your professional career, one of your athletes will have an open, bleeding wound. If your athlete sustains this type of injury under your supervision, you are responsible for providing first aid. Always consider that your athletes may have acquired bloodborne pathogens. Treat them appropriately while protecting yourself from infection.

One means to protect yourself from bloodborne pathogen infection is to assume that all athletes are passive carriers, meaning that an athlete can transmit a bloodborne pathogen to other people and infect them, even though the athlete does not exhibit any signs or symptoms of illness at the time of transmission. By assuming that all athletes are passive carriers, you can appropriately utilize personal protective equipment (PPE) at all times when providing first aid. PPE includes items such as disposable latex gloves, protective eyewear, and disposable facemasks and gowns.

Tips from the Field

Tip 1 Before purchasing latex gloves for your first aid kit, determine if you are allergic to latex. A latex allergy creates mild to severe signs and symptoms. If you notice that your hands are red, itchy, painful, or have the appearance of hives or a rash after wearing latex gloves, then you are mildly allergic to latex. More severe allergic reactions include difficulty breathing, chest tightness, and other signs of anaphylactic shock. If you are allergic to latex, utilize nitrile or vinyl disposable gloves. Likewise, some athletes are allergic to latex, so it is prudent to have nitrile or vinyl gloves in your first aid kit.

Three prevalent bloodborne pathogens are HBV, hepatitis C (HCV), and HIV. Athletes can be passive carriers of any of these bloodborne pathogens. Consequently, be aware that these bloodborne pathogens may be prevalent during your activities as an exercise science professional.

Hepatitis B Virus

Hepatitis B virus (HBV) is a bloodborne pathogen that originally was thought to be found only in blood, and transferred only via open wounds, contaminated needles, and blood transfusions. However, HBV is also found in other bodily fluids such as semen, vaginal fluid, synovial fluid, and cerebrospinal fluid. As exercise scientists, our primary concern regarding HBV in our daily employment activities is coming in contact with our athlete's blood, or saliva in large quantities. Also, HBV exists in dried blood for approximately 1 week (American Academy of Orthopaedic Surgeons [AAOS], 2008; Prentice, 2010). Therefore, dried blood found on towels in your facility's locker room dirty laundry bin, or on the bathroom sink after an athlete has shaved, may contain HBV for up to 1 week. Another cause for concern is that athletes can be HBV passive carriers for years. You will not know that your athlete has acquired HBV unless he or she discloses this condition to you.

> **Antigen** A substance that, when introduced into the body, stimulates the immune system to produce antibodies. Antibodies help the body to destroy foreign substances such as bacteria.

When an athlete is infected with HBV, the virus travels to the liver where it multiplies over approximately 6 weeks to 4 months. During this time, some of the virus coating is released into the blood. A blood test confirms if the **antigen** and

some infectious viral components are in the blood (Crowley, 2010). Signs and symptoms of HBV infection include continual fatigue, weakness, loss of appetite, and nausea. The athlete may complain of a constant headache and abdominal pain, and also may have a fever and exhibit **jaundice**, dark-colored urine, and light-colored stools (Abramowitz, 1999). An athlete with these signs and symptoms may not rec-

> **Jaundice** A yellowing of the skin and whites of the eyes that can occur with liver inflammation, infection, or disease.

ognize that they have been infected with HBV because many of these signs and symptoms mimic those of the flu. If an athlete approaches you with questions regarding their symptoms, or you notice they are exhibiting signs of illness, immediately refer them to a physician. The athlete may just have a cold or flu; however, they should be evaluated by a physician to obtain a proper diagnosis and treatment. Fortunately for many athletes who are infected with HBV, the body eliminates the virus and the athlete undergoes no further illness (AAOS, 2008). For some athletes, however, the HBV turns into a chronic infection without signs and symptoms for years. Over time, the chronic HBV infection destroys the liver, causing liver **cirrhosis** or cancer, and then death (Abramowitz, 1999).

> **Cirrhosis** An irreversible liver disease that occurs over time. The liver tissue is replaced with scar tissue, and eventually liver function terminates.

The incidence of HBV infection has declined over recent years, mainly due to first aiders and healthcare providers being cognizant of the methods of transmission and means to prevent transmission. The decrease in HBV infection also has been attributed to the healthcare community's attempt to publicize the benefits of HBV immunization, and making the vaccine more available to the public. For example, since 1990 babies born in hospitals are given the first dose of the HBV vaccine before they leave the hospital (Centers for Disease Control and Prevention [CDC], 2009a). Many exercise scientists are being proactive and have their primary care physician inoculate them. The vaccine consists of three medicinal doses within 6 months. The vaccine is approximately 95% effective against acquiring the virus. Likewise, many employers are requiring exercise scientists to be vaccinated for HBV as a prerequisite for employment. If you work in a facility where your role is to provide first aid or medical care to athletes, or you handle blood or other potentially infectious materials (OPIM), then OSHA regulations require your employer to offer you the series of HBV vaccinations at no cost to you (AAOS, 2008; OSHA, 1991). Your employer must pay the cost for your three medicinal doses. A month or so after you have received the last dose, a blood test is necessary to determine whether an adequate number of antibodies have been created. If HBV does enter your body, the antibodies fight against the virus and destroy it. Consequently, if your blood contains enough antibodies then you are immune to HBV.

Hepatitis C Virus

According to the AAOS (2008), hepatitis C virus (HCV) is "the most common chronic bloodborne infection in the United States" (p. 19). HCV is found in the blood and passed from person to person via openings in the skin, such as open wounds or mucous membranes. HCV is most commonly passed by sharing contaminated needles during illicit injectable drug use. Since 1992, blood screening technology and procedures for donated blood transfusions have been significantly improved (Mayo Clinic, 2011). All donated blood is thoroughly tested for pathogens such as HCV; therefore, the incidence of transmission through transfusions is rare. The primary concern for exercise scientists in the workplace is HCV transmission via open bleeding wounds. Also, according to the Centers for Disease Control and Prevention (2009b), HCV can live outside the body for between 16 hours and 4 days. Many of the signs and symptoms for HCV infections are the same as for HBV infection. HCV infection first produces flu-like symptoms such as loss of appetite, vomiting, nausea, fever, and fatigue. Additional signs and symptoms include jaundice, joint pain, dark urine, and clay-colored stools (CDC, 2009b). However, in approximately three-quarters of HCV cases, the person is asymptomatic (AAOS, 2008). Similarly to HBV, most athletes do not recognize that they have been infected with HCV. They assume they have the flu and ignore the possibility of HCV infection.

An HCV-positive athlete must be continually under a physician's care, and have his or her blood tested regularly to determine whether the HCV is adversely affecting the liver. An athlete can be infected with HCV and sustain only minimal liver damage; however, in many cases, an athlete develops serious liver disease such as cirrhosis or liver cancer. It may take up to 20 or 30 years after infection for the liver to develop these serious diseases (Mayo Clinic, 2011). If liver damage is significant, then the athlete needs a liver transplant.

Unlike HBV, no vaccine for HCV exists. Antiviral HCV medications are utilized to decrease symptoms, but the medication does not destroy or eliminate the virus from the athlete's body.

Human Immunodeficiency Virus

Human immunodeficiency virus (HIV) causes acquired immune deficiency syndrome (AIDS). HIV is found in blood and bodily fluids such as semen and vaginal and cerebrospinal fluids. HIV has been shown to exist in sweat, saliva, and tears; however, no evidence exists that these bodily fluids cause HIV transmission because the minute amounts of the virus in the bodily fluid are not enough to cause infection. Therefore, exercise scientists, in particular personal trainers and strength and conditioning specialists who work with sweaty athletes daily, do not need to worry about HIV transmission when coming in contact with athletes' sweat.

Similar to HBV and HCV, HIV enters the body via an open wound or mucous membrane by direct contact with HIV-infected blood. Therefore, always use PPE when an athlete is bleeding. After entering the body, HIV invades healthy cells and lives in these cells in order to replicate. The virus destroys CD4+ (helper) T **lymphocytes**, more commonly known as T cells, which are blood cells that fight off infection (CDC, 2010a). Consequently, after the T cells are destroyed by HIV, the body cannot protect itself against illness and disease. Over time, the immune system is destroyed (**Table 3-1**). Unlike HBV, HIV cannot live outside the body for more than a few hours. Therefore, HIV does not thrive in dried blood as HBV can.

> **Lymphocytes** White blood cells in the body that help the immune system fight illness and disease.

Similar to an athlete whose blood tests have confirmed HBV or HCV infection (referred to as being HBV or HCV "positive"), an HIV-positive athlete can be a passive carrier and transmit the virus to uninfected athletes. The HIV-positive athlete can be infected for up to 10 years before she or he exhibits signs and symptoms of illness (Prentice, 2010). About 25% of HIV-positive athletes are asymptomatic and do not know that they are infected (AAOS, 2008). In many

Table 3-1	The Sequence of Events in HIV Infections and Their Significance	
Event	**Significance**
HIV invades CD4+ (helper) T lymphocytes cells and becomes part of cell DNA	Individual is infected for life
Virus proliferates in infected cells and sheds virus particles	Virus present in blood and body fluids
Body forms anti-HIV antibody	Antibody is a marker of infection but is not protective
Progressive destruction of helper T cells	Compromised cell-mediated immunity
Immune defenses collapse	Opportunistic infections Neoplasms

cases, the athlete exhibits signs and symptoms of HIV infection that mimic the flu for about a week or two. The athlete experiences fatigue, fever, night sweats, joint pain, headaches, nausea, weight loss, and small infections. If your athlete complains of these signs and symptoms, or you identify that they are ill while at your facility, discontinue the athlete's activity and refer them to a physician for evaluation.

To determine whether an athlete is infected with HIV, a blood test is performed to test for HIV antibodies. When a virus enters the body, the body needs time to create antibodies. A large enough quantity of antibodies may not be created immediately after HIV transmission, and the blood test will be negative. According to the CDC (2010a), the body produces enough antibodies to be detected by a blood test approximately 25 days after exposure and transmission. For about 97% of people, enough detectable antibodies in the blood are apparent by 3 months. The first blood test performed to detect the antibodies is either a Single Use Diagnostic System for HIV-1 (SUDS), otherwise known as a rapid HIV test, or an ELISA or EIA (enzyme-linked immunosorbent assay) test. If these preliminary tests find that no HIV antibodies exist, then the athlete is HIV negative. No other tests need to be performed. If either the rapid HIV or ELISA test detects antibodies, then another, different, confirmatory HIV test must be performed. One common confirmatory test is the Western Blot test. If the Western Blot test also detects antibodies, then the athlete is deemed HIV positive.

Tips from the Field

Tip 2   Never ask an athlete or a coworker if they are HIV positive. If you know an athlete or a coworker is HIV positive, never disclose the information. HIV-positive people are protected under the Americans with Disabilities Act (ADA), and their status must be kept confidential. The ADA protects HIV-positive people from discrimination in the workplace. If you know an athlete or a coworker has HIV, do not discriminate against them in any way. HBV- and HCV-positive people also qualify for protection under the ADA if they experience a physical or mental impairment that disables them in the workplace.

Acquired Immune Deficiency Syndrome

HIV weakens the athlete's immune system, and eventually the virus causes acquired immune deficiency syndrome (AIDS). The length of time for an HIV-infected athlete to develop AIDS varies from athlete to athlete, but it can be up to 8–10 years (AAOS, 2008). Prior to being diagnosed with

AIDS, the athlete experiences three stages of illness: primary HIV infection, the asymptomatic stage, and the symptomatic stage (Pommerville, 2012). During primary HIV infection, the athlete exhibits many of the flu-like signs and symptoms previously mentioned. In the asymptomatic stage the athlete is symptom-free; however, a blood test will confirm a decrease in the number of T cells. In both the primary HIV infection stage and asymptomatic stage, the athlete most often does not experience significant symptoms. At this time, the HIV-positive athlete is a passive carrier and can unknowingly transmit the virus to others. The third stage is the symptomatic stage. In this stage, a blood test reveals a severe decrease in T cells. The athlete exhibits significant weight loss and signs and symptoms of **opportunistic infections**. This third and final phase progresses to AIDS, which is diagnosed when HIV has significantly destroyed the athlete's T cells, as determined by a blood test. The athlete has signs and symptoms of the disease including severe weight loss, fatigue, nausea, vomiting, weakness, and diarrhea. The athlete may develop disorders such as stomach ulcers, pancreatitis, esophagitis, and skin infections.

> **Opportunistic infections**   Illnesses or diseases that invade the body of an athlete who has AIDS.

Once the athlete has been diagnosed with AIDS, his or her body will not be able to fight any opportunistic infections due to the significant immune system damage. Usually, when a bacterium, virus, fungus, parasite, or other pathogen enters a healthy athlete's body, the body's immune system fights off the pathogen, destroys it, and eliminates it from the body. When an athlete has AIDS, however, the immune system cannot fight even the most common pathogens. Opportunistic infections thrive in the athlete's body and take over the systems and functions. Consequently, the pathogen creates deadly illness and disease. Common opportunistic infections include Kaposi's sarcoma and other cancerous tumors, pneumonia, and tuberculosis. Kaposi's sarcoma, which is caused by a herpes virus, is the most common type of cancer that affects an athlete with AIDS. This cancer forms under the skin and in the mouth, throat, nose, and organs, causing lesions with a reddish-purple appearance, which may be painful (National Institutes of Health, 2011). From initial AIDS diagnosis, an athlete's life expectancy is approximately 3 to 5 years (Neighbors & Tannehille-Jones, 2000). Life expectancy can be increased by taking antiviral medication such as zidovudine (AZT), which assists in slowing the viral replication. However, to date, AIDS is ultimately fatal. No vaccine exists for HIV, and no cure exists for AIDS.

EXPOSURE TO AND TRANSMISSION OF BLOODBORNE PATHOGENS

> **Exposure**   Contact with blood or other potentially infectious bodily fluids via mucous membranes, eyes, nose, mouth, broken skin, or injection into skin or mucous membranes.

High-risk activities create **exposure** incidents to bloodborne pathogens. Two high-risk activities are unprotected sexual intercourse and sharing contaminated needles. Semen, vaginal fluids, and blood all carry a high concentration of bloodborne pathogens. In sexual intercourse, the bloodborne pathogens are exposed to and transmitted through the mucous membranes. If athletes share contaminated needles when injecting illicit drugs, they are exposed to bloodborne pathogens that are transmitted directly into the bloodstream. The needle most likely contains minute amounts of infected blood from an infected user. When an uninfected user uses the same needle to inject the drug, the bloodborne pathogens have a significant opportunity to be transmitted. These high-risk activities do not occur in everyday employment, but keep in mind that you do not know what high-risk activities your athletes take part in on their personal time.

In the exercise science field, unless you are handling blood on a daily basis, the potential for exposure to bloodborne pathogens is minimal. Typically, an exposure incident occurs if an infected athlete's blood is transferred to your skin, eyes, nose, mouth, or mucous membranes. The following scenarios depict exposure incidents: You are coaching a wrestler who sustains a significant nosebleed during practice. As you assist the athlete by providing first aid, he sneezes in front of your face. The nasal discharge and blood sprays onto your face, and into your eyes and nasal passageways. Although you do not know if your athlete is infected with a bloodborne pathogen, you have experienced an exposure incident. In another instance, you are training an athlete at We R Fit Gym. After her spinning class, she decides to eat a bagel at the snack bar. She slices her finger on the knife and has a deep, bleeding, open wound. She panics and runs to you screaming for help. She grabs your hands with her badly bleeding hand, right on your healing open wound. This scenario depicts another exposure incident. Finally, you are working with an athlete in your kickboxing studio. She comes to you claiming she was accidentally kicked in the stomach by a training partner. She says she is nauseous. As you are consoling her, she vomits. You notice the vomit is laced with blood, which was transferred to your ungloved hands. These three exposure incidents, although uncommon

and seemingly unusual, can realistically occur while you are on the job or during personal activities. Any time you come in direct contact with an athlete's blood, whether or not you know the athlete's blood is infected with bloodborne pathogens, it is considered an exposure incident. You must take the appropriate course of reporting the incident, and testing must occur after an exposure. These processes are discussed later in this chapter.

Just because you or an athlete is exposed to a bloodborne pathogen does not mean that transmission will occur. The infected blood must actually enter an uninfected person's body via openings in the skin, eyes, nose, mouth, or mucous membranes. The pathogens must then enter the bloodstream, and the virus must attack and take over a healthy, host cell to begin replicating. This sequence of events is considered actual bloodborne pathogen transmission. Although you must be extremely cautious, HIV is difficult to transmit from person to person. It is easily destroyed by changes in temperature (Neighbors & Tannehille-Jones, 2000). HIV cannot live outside the body, but HBV can live in dried blood for up to a week, and HCV can live outside the body for up to 4 days. Consequently, HBV and HCV transmission can still occur during this time, so always be careful and use PPE when touching any objects at your facility that have dried blood on them.

OSHA BLOODBORNE PATHOGEN STANDARD

In 1991, the Occupational Safety and Health Administration (OSHA) Bloodborne Pathogens Standard 29 CFR 1910.1030 (OSHA, 1991) was published (**Figure 3-1**). The standard was instituted to protect any employee, including exercise scientists, who have the potential to be exposed to bloodborne pathogens or OPIM while on the job (AAOS, 2008). The regulations were set forth to recommend specific procedures regarding bloodborne pathogen exposure prevention in the workplace. Also, the standard defines what to do if an exposure incident occurs, as well as your employer's role in reporting and following up with the exposure. The OSHA standards regulate your employers' actions regarding bloodborne pathogen training for employees, **work practice controls**, employee medical history,

> **Work practice controls**   Policies and procedures that your employer creates to assist you in reducing the chances of bloodborne pathogen exposure in the workplace.

and status reviews. If you are an employer, you must abide by the OSHA standards, and implement them appropriately and effectively for your employees' and athletes' safety.

Figure 3-1 | OSHA Bloodborne Pathogen Standard.

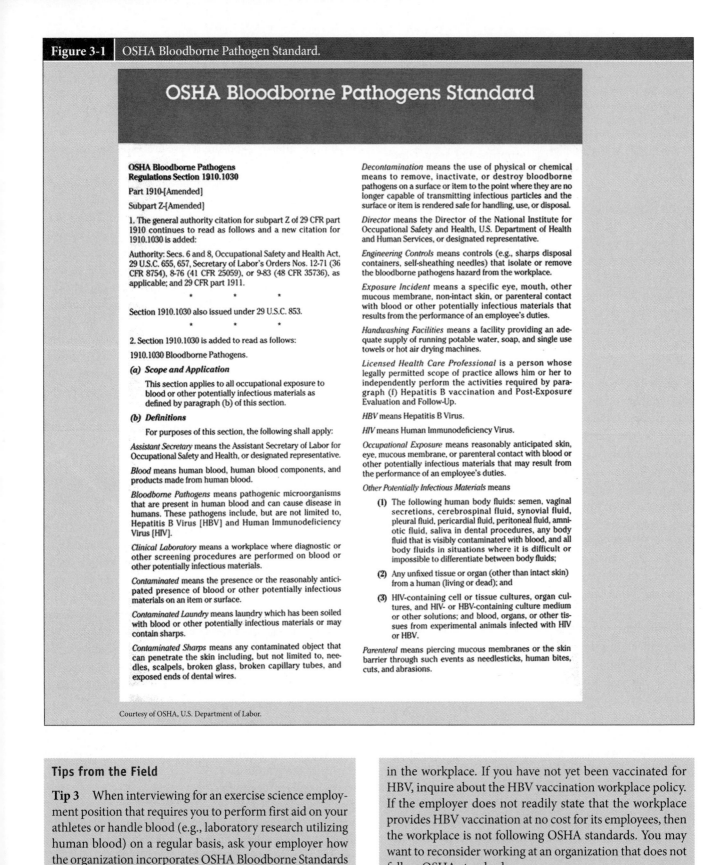

OSHA Bloodborne Pathogens Standard

OSHA Bloodborne Pathogens Regulations Section 1910.1030

Part 1910-[Amended]

Subpart Z-[Amended]

1. The general authority citation for subpart Z of 29 CFR part 1910 continues to read as follows and a new citation for 1910.1030 is added:

Authority: Secs. 6 and 8, Occupational Safety and Health Act, 29 U.S.C. 655, 657, Secretary of Labor's Orders Nos. 12-71 (36 CFR 8754), 8-76 (41 CFR 25059), or 9-83 (48 CFR 35736), as applicable; and 29 CFR part 1911.

* * *

Section 1910.1030 also issued under 29 U.S.C. 853.

* * *

2. Section 1910.1030 is added to read as follows:

1910.1030 Bloodborne Pathogens.

(a) Scope and Application

This section applies to all occupational exposure to blood or other potentially infectious materials as defined by paragraph (b) of this section.

(b) Definitions

For purposes of this section, the following shall apply:

Assistant Secretary means the Assistant Secretary of Labor for Occupational Safety and Health, or designated representative.

Blood means human blood, human blood components, and products made from human blood.

Bloodborne Pathogens means pathogenic microorganisms that are present in human blood and can cause disease in humans. These pathogens include, but are not limited to, Hepatitis B Virus [HBV] and Human Immunodeficiency Virus [HIV].

Clinical Laboratory means a workplace where diagnostic or other screening procedures are performed on blood or other potentially infectious materials.

Contaminated means the presence or the reasonably anticipated presence of blood or other potentially infectious materials on an item or surface.

Contaminated Laundry means laundry which has been soiled with blood or other potentially infectious materials or may contain sharps.

Contaminated Sharps means any contaminated object that can penetrate the skin including, but not limited to, needles, scalpels, broken glass, broken capillary tubes, and exposed ends of dental wires.

Decontamination means the use of physical or chemical means to remove, inactivate, or destroy bloodborne pathogens on a surface or item to the point where they are no longer capable of transmitting infectious particles and the surface or item is rendered safe for handling, use, or disposal.

Director means the Director of the National Institute for Occupational Safety and Health, U.S. Department of Health and Human Services, or designated representative.

Engineering Controls means controls (e.g., sharps disposal containers, self-sheathing needles) that isolate or remove the bloodborne pathogens hazard from the workplace.

Exposure Incident means a specific eye, mouth, other mucous membrane, non-intact skin, or parenteral contact with blood or other potentially infectious materials that results from the performance of an employee's duties.

Handwashing Facilities means a facility providing an adequate supply of running potable water, soap, and single use towels or hot air drying machines.

Licensed Health Care Professional is a person whose legally permitted scope of practice allows him or her to independently perform the activities required by paragraph (f) Hepatitis B vaccination and Post-Exposure Evaluation and Follow-Up.

HBV means Hepatitis B Virus.

HIV means Human Immunodeficiency Virus.

Occupational Exposure means reasonably anticipated skin, eye, mucous membrane, or parenteral contact with blood or other potentially infectious materials that may result from the performance of an employee's duties

Other Potentially Infectious Materials means

(1) The following human body fluids: semen, vaginal secretions, cerebrospinal fluid, synovial fluid, pleural fluid, pericardial fluid, peritoneal fluid, amniotic fluid, saliva in dental procedures, any body fluid that is visibly contaminated with blood, and all body fluids in situations where it is difficult or impossible to differentiate between body fluids;

(2) Any unfixed tissue or organ (other than intact skin) from a human (living or dead); and

(3) HIV-containing cell or tissue cultures, organ cultures, and HIV- or HBV-containing culture medium or other solutions; and blood, organs, or other tissues from experimental animals infected with HIV or HBV.

Parenteral means piercing mucous membranes or the skin barrier through such events as needlesticks, human bites, cuts, and abrasions.

Courtesy of OSHA, U.S. Department of Labor.

Tips from the Field

Tip 3 When interviewing for an exercise science employment position that requires you to perform first aid on your athletes or handle blood (e.g., laboratory research utilizing human blood) on a regular basis, ask your employer how the organization incorporates OSHA Bloodborne Standards in the workplace. If you have not yet been vaccinated for HBV, inquire about the HBV vaccination workplace policy. If the employer does not readily state that the workplace provides HBV vaccination at no cost for its employees, then the workplace is not following OSHA standards. You may want to reconsider working at an organization that does not follow OSHA standards.

All employees who could potentially come in contact with bloodborne pathogens must go through annual bloodborne pathogen training. According to the OSHA standards, the employer provides the training during work hours at no cost to the employee. The training includes information on bloodborne pathogens, exposure, transmission, and prevention. Work practice controls include procedures that employees practice to prevent bloodborne pathogen exposure and transmission. Work practice controls include washing your hands after removing gloves (**Figure 3-2**) and using an eyewash station and sharps containers. In any area where a possibility for bloodborne pathogens or OPIMs exists, eating, drinking, smoking, applying cosmetics, and handling contact lenses are prohibited (AAOS, 2008). Employees need to make every attempt to prevent spraying or splattering of blood. On a minimum annual basis, employers reevaluate the work practice controls. The organization must ascertain that it is taking all precautions to prevent bloodborne pathogen and OPIM exposures. Also, at least once per year, the employer evaluates the employees' medical history and status to determine the employees' health. Your role in reevaluating your employees' medical history and status is not to determine whether they have been infected with a bloodborne pathogen; rather, it is to make sure they are healthy and able to perform their jobs.

Universal Precautions

To prevent bloodborne pathogen transmission, exercise scientists must follow universal precautions. Universal precautions are standardized, sequenced actions utilized by a caretaker when assisting a bleeding athlete or when OPIMs exist. Universal precautions are not necessary when dealing

Figure 3-2 Hand washing is a primary means of preventing exposure to and transmission of bloodborne pathogens.

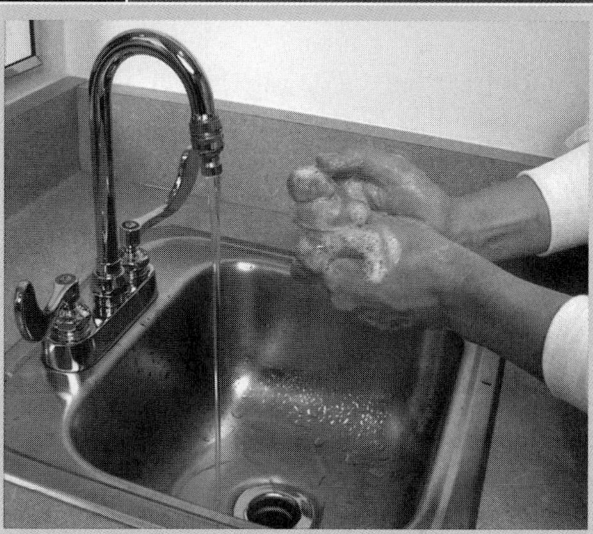

Courtesy of Kimberly Smith and Christine Ford/CDC.

with sweat, tears, vomit, or spit, unless blood appears in these bodily fluids. Universal precautions include the utilization of PPE. PPE must be included in your facility's first aid kit, which must be readily accessible to all employees. Necessary first aid kit materials include disposable gloves, a face mask, a gown, protective eyewear, sterile roller gauze and pads, breathing barriers for administering cardiopulmonary resuscitation (CPR), and hand sanitizer. **Table 3-2** gives an example of items to include in a workplace first aid kit.

Table 3-2	Sample Workplace First Aid Kit	
Items		**Minimum Quantity**
Adhesive strip bandages (1" × 3")*		20
Triangular bandages* (muslin, 36"–40" × 36"–40" × 52"–56")		4
Sterile eye pads (2" × 2")		2
Sterile gauze pads (4" × 4")		6
Sterile gauze pads (3" × 3")*		6
Sterile gauze pads (2" × 2")*		6
Sterile nonstick pads (3" × 4")*		6
Sterile trauma pads (5" × 9")*		2
Sterile trauma pads (8" × 10")		1
Sterile conforming roller gauze (2" width)		3 rolls
Sterile conforming roller gauze (4.5" width)		3 rolls

(continues)

Table 3-2	Sample Workplace First Aid Kit (*Continued*)	
Items		**Minimum Quantity**
Waterproof tape (1" × 5 yards)		1 roll
Porous adhesive tape (2" × 5 yd)*		1 roll
Elastic roller bandages (4" and 6")		1 of each
Antiseptic skin wipes, individually wrapped*		10 packets
Antibiotic ointment, individual packets*		6 packets
Disposable (medical exam) gloves (various sizes)*		2 pairs per size
Mouth-to-barrier device (either a face mask with a one-way valve or a disposable face shield)		1
Disposable instant cold packs		2
Sealable plastic bags (quart size)		2
Padded malleable splint (SAM Splint, 4" × 36")		1
Emergency blanket		1
Scissors		1
Tweezers		1
Hand sanitizer (61% ethyl alcohol)		1 bottle
Biohazard waste bag (3.5 gallon capacity)		2
Mini flashlight and batteries		1
List of local emergency telephone numbers		1
First aid guide*		1

*Item meets the ANSI/ISEA Z308.1-2009 minimum standard for the workplace first aid kit. Optional items and sizes may be added based on the potential hazards.

Tips from the Field

Tip 4   Keep a small Ziploc® bag in your car that contains the following: at least three pairs of disposable latex or nitrile gloves, a few packages of 4" × 4" sterile gauze, a large gauze roll, and a CPR pocket mask. If you have to provide first aid to control bleeding or administer CPR and have access to your car, the basic, appropriate PPE items are available for use. These PPE items are crucial to assist you in preventing bloodborne pathogen transmission. Check the gloves and pocket masks periodically. Changes in temperature detrimentally affect the materials over time. For example, hot temperatures and direct sunlight cause nitrile glove disintegration. Over time, latex gloves stick together and become weak, which causes rips and holes. The pocket mask material also slowly breaks down.

Figure 3-3	Always wear gloves when dealing with an athlete's blood or bodily fluids.

© Joe Belanger/ShutterStock, Inc.

Before touching a bleeding athlete, put on latex, nitrile, or similar protective gloves (**Figure 3-3**). In situations where a large quantity of blood or the potential for blood to spurt, spray, or splatter exists, such as if an athlete is severely cut, vomiting blood, or has an open fracture, wear face and body protection, including items such as a disposable face mask and gown. When you are finished providing first aid to the athlete, dispose of the bloody materials properly. If the materials,

| Figure 3-4 | Properly dispose of saturated PPE in biohazard containers. |

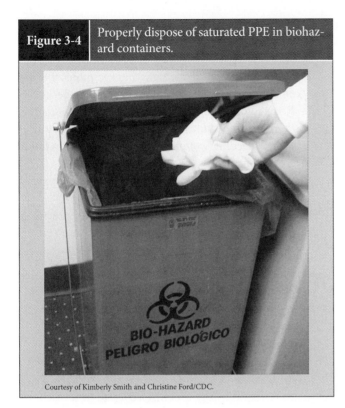

Courtesy of Kimberly Smith and Christine Ford/CDC.

Saturated When materials, such as gauze, bandages, or a towel have soaked up the maximum amount of blood or bodily fluid they can hold.

such as gauze or bandages, are **saturated**, place them in a properly labeled biohazard container or bag (**Figure 3-4**). You can store biohazard bags in your first aid kit. If the materials are not saturated, then place them in regular garbage. Never reach into a biohazard container or bag to remove any materials. Once you are finished with the first aid care, then carefully and properly remove your gloves (**Figure 3-5**). When you remove your gloves, do not touch your skin with a bloody glove. Make every attempt to remove the gloves inside out with a clean portion of the glove. Immediately after removing the gloves and placing them in the proper receptacle, wash your hands with soap and water. If soap and water are not available, use a hand sanitizer or other commercially prepared sanitizing lotion, gel, or towelette. As soon as you can, wash your hands with soap and water.

Tips from the Field

Tip 5 When caring for an athlete's open wound, always utilize PPE regardless of whether you know an athlete is a bloodborne pathogen carrier. While caring for a bleeding athlete, if he proclaims, "I don't have HIV, so you don't have to use gloves," a simple, direct, and ethical response could be, "I treat all of my athletes the same and wear gloves when I provide first aid." Regardless of whether an athlete discloses his or her infectious status to you, always wear gloves!

Universal precautions also include cleaning surfaces that have been exposed to blood and OPIM. Always clean the surface area where the blood was located, along with any contaminated items, equipment, floors, and the like, while wearing gloves. Many commercial liquid disinfectant cleaning solutions are available that destroy HIV, HBV, HCV, other viruses, and bacteria. These cleaning solutions must be used as directed. Some solutions require you to leave the solution on the contaminated area for a period of time before wiping the area, in order to destroy the pathogens. Many of these commercial cleaning agents are utilized effectively for daily equipment cleaning. According to the CDC (2010b), a bleach and water solution with a ratio of 9 parts water to 1 part bleach is also effective. Because the bleach and water solution loses its effectiveness in 24 hours, the solution must be prepared daily. A bleach and

| Figure 3-5 | How to properly remove gloves. |

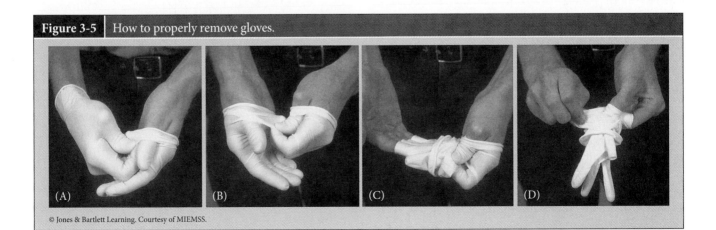

(A) (B) (C) (D)

© Jones & Bartlett Learning. Courtesy of MIEMSS.

water solution is not always the cleaning solution of choice, however, because it breaks down and discolors materials.

Universal precautions require use of breathing barriers in order to prevent transmission of bloodborne pathogens. If you perform CPR, utilize a breathing mask as a barrier, whether or not the athlete has open bleeding facial wounds. Do not clean the barrier with the aforementioned cleaning solutions in order to reuse it. Breathing barriers must be utilized only one time on one athlete. Dispose of the barrier appropriately in a biohazard container.

Reporting exposure incidents and follow-up care are part of universal precautions. If you experience an exposure incident, report the incident immediately to your employer or supervisor. Once you report the exposure incident, your employer should provide you with an immediate medical evaluation, provided you give your employer consent to do so. The employer bears the cost of antibody blood testing, counseling, and follow-up care. Your employer also investigates the exposure incident, including how and why it occurred. It is your employer's responsibility to determine whether any workplace controls must be modified. The employer also investigates what steps can be taken at the facility to prevent a future exposure.

SUMMARY

The bloodborne pathogens HBV, HCV, and HIV are three serious viruses that cause significant disease and, especially in the case of HIV, death. These viral infections, associated illnesses, and diseases are entirely preventable. Exercise scientists must take an active role in preventing bloodborne pathogen exposure and transmission. Throughout your career, very few instances will arise requiring you to provide first aid to a bleeding athlete. However, you most likely will assist a bleeding family member, friend, or acquaintance at some point. Continue to utilize universal precautions and PPE in these situations. If we all utilize universal precautions when dealing with bloodborne pathogens, we can promote a decline of HBV, HCV, and HIV transmissions in the future.

DISCUSSION QUESTIONS

1. What are the three bloodborne pathogens discussed in this chapter? Which of them is preventable via immunization?
2. What are the different ways an athlete can contract bloodborne pathogens?
3. Which bodily fluids carry bloodborne pathogens? What are the different ways that an exercise scientist can contract a bloodborne pathogen in the workplace?
4. What are the three stages of HIV infection that eventually lead to AIDS? Describe who is considered a passive carrier. In which stages can the athlete be a passive carrier?
5. HBV, HCV, and HIV have many similar signs and symptoms. Describe the signs and symptoms that are *different* among the three bloodborne pathogens.
6. Name some of the OSHA universal precautions that an exercise scientist must follow when treating an athlete with a bleeding wound or when other bodily fluids are present.
7. What are your employer's responsibilities if you experience an exposure incident in the workplace?
8. What are some PPE that you must use when providing first aid care to a bleeding athlete?

CASE STUDY

What a Bloody Mess!

Ms. Anderson is a physical education teacher at Welcoming High School. She has just completed a week of teaching her freshmen students a volleyball unit, including skills, etiquette, and modified rules, in preparation for a class volleyball tournament. Today the boys and girls begin the tournament in class. Ms. Anderson stresses to the students that as a safety precaution they must adhere to the modified rules she has previously taught and explained to them. In particular, she emphasizes that students are not allowed to spike the ball in her physical education class. Ms. Anderson instituted this rule in an attempt to prevent any unnecessary harm to students who do not possess the skills, strength, and experience to properly defend a spiked volleyball.

To begin the tournament, Ms. Anderson divides the class into four, equally skilled teams. All four teams play at once on two courts. The first day of the tournament went smoothly and the students appeared to have a great time. However, on the second day of the tournament a student named George becomes agitated due to his team's poor performance. He feels that he is doing all of the work to score points for his team. George also believes his teammates are not contributing as much as he has been. He expects much more of his teammates, and he becomes incredibly mad. At this point, he cannot control his anger. It is George's turn to rotate into the attack line. George's teammate sets the ball close to the net right by George. George spikes it with extreme force into the opposing court. The ball hits his opponent, Monica, squarely in the face. She immediately begins to bleed profusely from both nostrils. George immediately helps Monica and gets blood all over his hands.

Monica's teammates yell for Ms. Anderson, who is settling a scoring issue on the adjoining court. Ms. Anderson goes over to see what all of the commotion is about. When she arrives, Monica is sitting on the gymnasium floor with both hands covering her nose and mouth. There is a small pool of blood beneath her, and blood all over her hands. George is crouching next to Monica and is helping her. He has Monica's blood all over his hands. Ms. Anderson asks Monica and George what happened, and if there is anything else wrong other than her bloody nose. Monica states that she is very dizzy and her vision is a bit blurry. Ms. Anderson asks a student, John, to run to get the school nurse. In the meantime, Ms. Anderson begins to panic because she knows that she needs to stop Monica's bleeding. The only items Ms. Anderson has in her pocket are tissues.

1. What should Ms. Anderson do first?
2. Should Ms. Anderson consider Monica a bloodborne pathogen passive carrier? Why or why not?
3. What universal precautions should Ms. Anderson take to protect her, George, and Monica from bloodborne pathogen transmission?
4. What should be done about the pool of blood on the gymnasium floor?
5. How should Ms. Anderson have been more prepared for this bleeding incident?
6. What PPE should Ms. Anderson have on-site in the gym?
7. George has Monica's blood on his hands. Is Ms. Anderson required to report this exposure incident?

REFERENCES

Abramowitz, M. (1999). How to avoid hepatitis B & C. *Current Health*, 25(6). Retrieved June 24, 2011 from Academic Search Complete, http://search.ebscohost.com

American Academy of Orthopaedic Surgeons (AAOS). (2008). *Bloodborne pathogens* (5th ed.). Sudbury, MA: Jones and Bartlett.

Centers for Disease Control and Prevention (CDC). (2009a). Hepatitis B FAQs for the public. Retrieved June 24, 2011, from http://www.cdc.gov/hepatitis/B/bFAQ.htm

Centers for Disease Control and Prevention (CDC). (2009b). Hepatitis C FAQs for the public. Retrieved June 24, 2011, from http://www.cdc.gov/hepatitis/C/cFAQ.htm

Centers for Disease Control and Prevention (CDC). (2010a). Basic information about HIV and AIDS. Retrieved June 27, 2011, from http://www.cdc.gov/hiv/topics/basic/index.htm

Centers for Disease Control and Prevention (CDC). (2010b). Cleaning up body fluid spills on pool surfaces. Retrieved March 3, 2013, from http://www.cdc.gov/healthywater/swimming/pools/cleaning-body-fluid-spills.html

Crowley, L. V. (2010). *An introduction to human disease: Pathology and pathophysiology correlations* (8th ed.). Sudbury, MA: Jones and Bartlett .

Mayo Clinic. (2011). Hepatitis C. Retrieved June 30, 2011, from http://www.mayoclinic.com/health/hepatitis-c/DS00097/DSECTION=causes

National Institutes of Health (NIH). (2011). Kaposi's sarcoma. Retrieved June 28, 2011, from http://www.nlm.nih.gov/medlineplus/kaposissarcoma.html

Neighbors, M., & Tannehille-Jones, R. (2000). *Human diseases*. Albany, NY: Delmar Thompson Learning.

Occupational Safety and Health Administration (OSHA). (1991). Standard 29 CFR 1910.1030. Retrieved June 22, 2011, from http://www.osha.gov/pls/oshaweb/owadisp.show_document?p_table=STANDARDS&p_id=10051

Pommerville, J. C. (2012). *Guide to infectious diseases by body system* (2nd ed.). Sudbury, MA: Jones and Bartlett Learning.

Prentice, W. E. (2010). *Essentials of athletic injury management* (8th ed.). New York: McGraw-Hill.

Van der Eijk, A. A., Niesters, H. G. M., Götz, H. M., Janssen, H. L. A., Schalm, S. W., Albert, D. M. E., et al. (2004). Paired measurements of quantitative hepatitis B virus DNA in saliva and serum of chronic hepatitis B patients: Implications for saliva as infectious agent. *Journal of Clinical Virology*, 29(2), 92–94. doi: 10.1016/S1386-6532(03)00092.

Chapter 4

Wound Care and Bandaging

© Jim Cummins/age fotostock

CHAPTER OBJECTIVES

After you have read this chapter, you will be able to understand:

- The various types of wounds that an athlete can incur
- The signs and symptoms of, and differences between external and internal bleeding
- How to provide first aid care for open and closed wounds
- How to apply dressings and bandages
- When to refer an athlete with an open wound or internal bleeding to a physician or the emergency room (ER)

Wounds are extremely common soft tissue injuries that frequently occur to athletes. Undoubtedly, a time will come when you must provide first aid care for an athlete who has sustained a wound at your facility. You will have to determine the wound type and severity. Many wounds are minor and can be adequately treated without advanced medical care; however, you will have to determine if referral to a physician or emergency medical services is warranted. Determining whether a wound is life threatening is imperative for an athlete's survival. It is crucial that you recognize the types of wounds, mechanisms of injury, and signs and symptoms. You must know how to provide adequate first aid care for wounds, which often includes applying dressings and bandages. Also, when treating or in close proximity to an athlete's open bleeding wound, you must always use universal precautions. This chapter offers you useful information regarding wounds that will certainly assist you in your practice and activities of daily living.

BLEEDING

Capillaries, veins, and arteries are the three types of blood vessels in the body. Although capillary, venous, and arterial bleeding are all similar in that blood exits the damaged blood vessel, other signs of bleeding for each vessel are dissimilar. Capillaries are the smallest and most numerous of the three types; arteries are the largest. Capillary bleeding is the most common type of bleeding that your athletes will experience (American Academy of Orthopaedic Surgeons [AAOS], 2012). Capillary blood seeps from a wound very slowly, and usually in smaller amounts in comparison to venous and arterial bleeding. The blood appears red. A scenario when capillary bleeding occurs is the following: Your athlete is running on the road for her workout. She slips on some gravel and loses her balance. She falls and slides across the pavement, scraping her leg on the blacktop. The wound immediately but slowly begins to bleed. In most cases, capillary bleeding is not difficult to control with first aid skills.

Unlike capillary bleeding, venous and arterial bleeding are rare and occur only with severe, traumatic mechanisms of injury. Although venous and arterial bleeding are both notably serious, arterial bleeding typically leads to fatalities or neurological dysfunction (Yasa et al., 2008). Venous blood flows out of the body comparable to how water flows out of a garden hose. It exits the blood vessel in a steady manner and commonly in large quantities. These factors make venous bleeding difficult to control. Due to the carbon dioxide in venous blood, the blood is darker red than capillary blood. On the other hand, the high oxygen content in arterial blood cause this blood to look much brighter red than capillary blood. Arterial blood does not seep out like capillary blood, nor does it continuously and steadily pour out like venous blood. Instead, arterial blood shoots out of the blood vessel with each heartbeat. Each time the heart beats, a large quantity of blood exits the artery with significant force. The blood exiting the wound is plentiful and difficult to stop with common first aid skills. Immediate surgery is necessary to treat a severed artery (Yasa et al., 2008). Whenever you recognize venous or arterial bleeding, summon advanced medical care at once by calling 911, and treat the athlete for **shock**. Venous and arterial bleeding are life-threatening for the athlete. Therefore, act immediately and quickly to help save your athlete's life (**Figure 4-1**).

> **Shock**   A life-threatening condition that occurs when oxygenated blood in the body is not getting to the vital organs, including those in the chest, abdomen, and brain.

Often venous and arterial bleeding occur simultaneously due to the close proximity of the veins and arteries. If one vessel is damaged, it is highly probable that the other vessel is damaged. Consider how arterial and venous bleeding occurs simultaneously in the following scenario. Two collegiate ice hockey players are racing for the puck. Both players check each other and lose their balance. One player's skate strikes the front of the other player's neck and lacerates the skin and underlying tissues. As the injured player stands up and exits the ice to sit down on the bench, the coach looks at the ice. The injured player is leaving a trail of blood and, by looking at its appearance on the ice, the coach immediately knows his athlete has a life-threatening injury. On the ice are two trails of blood. One trail appears as a dark red, steady line from where the athlete was injured and continues all the way to the bench. The other trail appears in spurts or sprays over the ice. A spray of bright red blood follows a void area, and alternates blood and void the entire distance to the bench. It is evident that the athlete has both his jugular vein and carotid artery injured by the skate. These two blood vessels are located in the neck in close proximity to each other. The vein expels dark red blood in a continuous stream, while the artery expels blood with each heartbeat, which created the bright red blood spray followed by a void, then another blood spray, and so on. This scenario demonstrates how veins and arteries can be simultaneously injured. This venous and arterial external bleeding is a life-threatening, medical emergency. EMS must be summoned immediately to transport the injured athlete to the emergency room. While waiting for the ambulance, the coach must provide appropriate first aid to the athlete. Appropriate first aid is discussed later in this chapter.

You can easily determine what type of bleeding an athlete is experiencing by remembering the characteristics of capillary, venous, and arterial bleeding. By knowing the manner in which the blood is exiting the wound, the quantity of blood produced, and its color, you can decide if the bleeding is capillary, venous, or arterial. Make this determination immediately, so you can provide appropriate first aid skills and know whether to summon EMS.

External and Internal Bleeding

Regardless of whether a capillary, vein, or artery is bleeding, the blood exits the body, remains in the body, or possibly both simultaneously. When blood exits the body, either from the skin via an **open wound** or another opening in the body, such as the nose, mouth, or ears, then

> **Open wound**   A cut in the skin through which external bleeding occurs.

the bleeding is considered external bleeding. An example of external bleeding is when your athlete is playing basketball at your gym and is hit in the nose by the ball. As a result, capillaries are damaged in his nasal passageway, his nose begins to bleed, and the blood exits through his nostrils. You can easily determine if a person is bleeding externally due to the visible blood. However, internal bleeding is very different.

Internal bleeding occurs when a blood vessel is damaged and releases blood inside the body. The blood does not exit through any wound or opening in the body and remains within the skin. Internal bleeding occurs with various injuries and illnesses. Injuries caused by a direct blow often bleed internally. Often you cannot see signs of internal bleeding. Ecchymosis, or a black and blue skin color caused by internal bleeding, may be present. Usually the area that is injured and bleeding

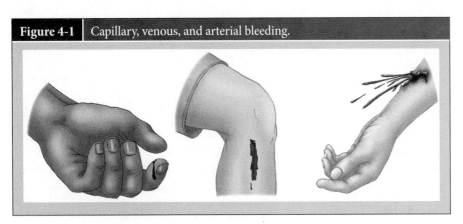

Figure 4-1   Capillary, venous, and arterial bleeding.

Figure 4-2	Ecchymosis is a sign of internal bleeding.

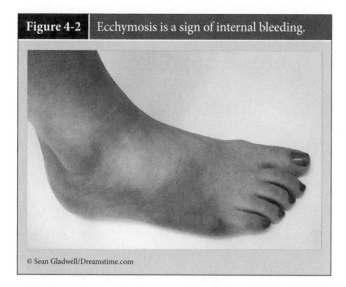

© Sean Gladwell/Dreamstime.com

Figure 4-3	An abrasion.

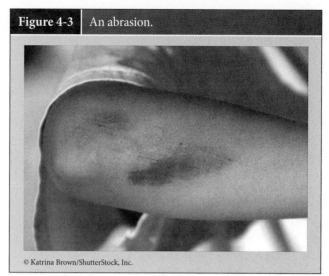

© Katrina Brown/ShutterStock, Inc.

is painful, tender to the touch (point tender), and rigid. An example when internal bleeding could occur is when your athlete drops a free weight on her foot and hours later ecchymosis appears (**Figure 4-2**). Another example of internal bleeding is when, in physical education soccer class, your student is kicked in the thigh by another student, injuring the underlying muscle and blood vessels. Because the bleeding in this **closed wound** occurs within the underlying tissues and an open wound does not exist, signs of bleeding, such as ecchymosis, may not be apparent. Consequently, it may be difficult to determine if your athlete is significantly injured when she has a closed wound and internal bleeding.

> **Closed wound**   An injury to the tissues underlying the skin. Unlike open wounds, bleeding occurs but does not exit the body.

OPEN WOUNDS

Open wounds are common in our everyday life. Minor open wounds occur frequently when we sustain a paper cut, a pinprick, or a blacktop skin abrasion. We can experience more severe open wounds from objects such as glass breaking the skin, a steering wheel during a car accident, or a knife while cutting food. Whether these open wounds are simple, complex, or life threatening, they are classified to help you determine the first aid necessary and whether referral to advanced medical care is warranted. The six classifications of open wounds are abrasions, incisions, lacerations, punctures, avulsions, and amputations.

Abrasions

Abrasions occur when the skin comes in contact with a surface or an object that rubs against the skin (**Figure 4-3**). The rubbing removes minute portions of the skin, leaving an open wound. The surfaces that rub against the skin and cause abrasions are most often rough surfaces, such as blacktop, concrete, and sand. Picture a softball player wearing her standard uniform, which includes shorts and high socks. When her teammate hits the ball, she runs and slides into second base. An abrasion occurs as a result of the rubbing of the grainy sand on the **lateral** side of her unprotected knee. Smooth surfaces such as a tiled or gymnasium room floor also can cause abrasions. Think about a middle school physical education class having scooter races. A student is lying on her stomach on the scooter and is pushing it with her hands and feet. Suddenly, while going fast down the floor, she falls off her scooter. Her forearm forcefully rubs against a portion of the floor and she consequently sustains an abrasion on her forearm.

> **Lateral**   A structure's location furthest away from the midline when the body is bisected into right and left halves through the umbilicus.

Abrasions are typically painful. The athlete usually feels a stinging or burning sensation. These wounds are also prone to infection due to dirt-carrying bacteria that becomes imbedded in the wound, coupled with lack of bleeding (Jones, 2007). To an extent, blood coming out of a wound actually helps eliminate some dirt, bacteria, and other small foreign debris from a wound. Generally speaking, because abrasions do not bleed a lot, they have a greater potential for infection than do other wounds that tend to bleed more readily.

Incisions

Incisions are open wounds that appear to have smooth edges (**Figure 4-4**). Sharp objects, such as smooth blade knives

Figure 4-4	An incision.

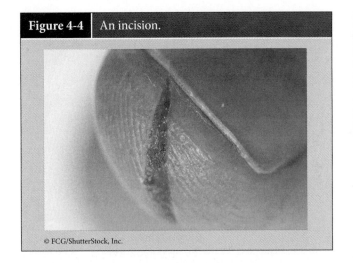

© FCG/ShutterStock, Inc.

Figure 4-5	A laceration.

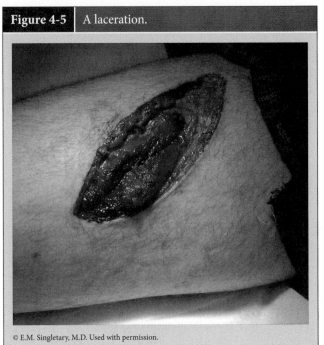

© E.M. Singletary, M.D. Used with permission.

and glass, can cause incisions. These objects may cause incisions that appear to be superficial, but in reality are very deep (Jones, 2007). Paper cuts are incisions that are superficial; a smooth blade knife can cause a very deep incision. Often the object causing the incision may be so sharp that the athlete does not even feel the object strike the skin. Consider the following scenario: Your athlete has just completed a workout and is standing next to you in We R Fit Gym. He is drinking orange juice in a glass from the snack bar. He suddenly drops the glass on the tile floor, which shatters next to you. You immediately close off the area and clean up the glass so other athletes do not get injured. Due to the hectic scene, you did not notice that your lateral lower leg is bleeding from an incision caused by the shattered glass. Superficial incisions can cause minimal to no pain. Deep wounds usually cause sharp and throbbing pain. Incisions tend to bleed significantly, depending on their length, depth, and location. The skin may not **approximate**. The cut edges may seem to pull away from each other. The quantity of blood can be minimal to immense. Incisions to the scalp tend to bleed enormously due to the vast quantity of capillaries in the tissue.

> **Approximate** When the damaged, cut portions of the skin of an open wound fall back in line and are in close proximity.

Lacerations

Lacerations are very similar to incisions because they may be superficial or deep, with minimal or immense bleeding (**Figure 4-5**). These wounds can be caused by sharp objects striking the skin, or by an object crushing, pulling, or grinding against the skin. Consider the following scenario: After a training session with your athlete, she decides to run on her own. She goes to the local high school and runs around the track. As part of her workout she runs up and down the metal stadium bleachers. While running up the bleachers, she does not plant her foot well, slips, and falls. She hits her shin as she falls down. The metal stadium bleacher causes a crushing, grinding force against her skin that pulls the skin apart, creating a laceration. The appearance of lacerations differs from incisions. Whereas an incision's skin has straight, clean edges, lacerated skin appears jagged and uneven. Consequently, like an incision, the edges may not approximate. Due to the skin's jagged edges, skin may also appear missing. As with incisions, the pain varies depending on the laceration's size and depth. Other than the wound appearance, lacerations and incisions have similar characteristics.

Punctures

Punctures occur when an object penetrates the skin (**Figure 4-6**). An object can be small like a splinter, or large like a knife. When an object punctures the skin it may fall out of or remain in the wound. Some objects protrude from the wound. Most puncture wounds are not life-threatening, but secondary complications, such as infection, can occur (McDevitt & Gillespie, 2008). In general, puncture wounds do not bleed much in comparison to incisions and lacerations. However, as with other wounds, punctures cause pain. The pain may be dull, aching, or sharp. The amount of pain produced often indicates the extent and depth of the injury (McDevitt & Gillespie, 2008). The object's size determines

Figure 4-6 | A puncture.

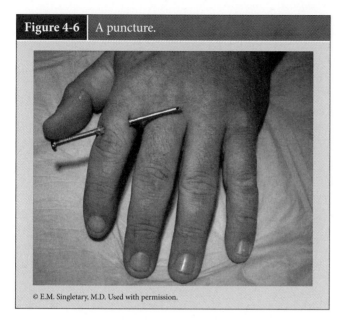

© E.M. Singletary, M.D. Used with permission.

Figure 4-7 | An avulsion.

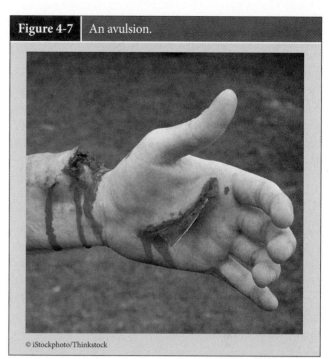

© iStockphoto/Thinkstock

not only the depth of injury, but also the extent of injury. A large puncturing object, such as a knife, undoubtedly causes greater trauma, bleeding, and pain than a smaller object, such as a pin. Swelling and ecchymosis may also arise around the wound. Many puncture wounds occur to the foot because we bear weight and put pressure on our feet when we stand, walk, and run. Common objects that cause punctures to the feet include glass, nails, and shells on the beach. Puncture wounds also commonly occur to the fingers and hands because we use implements, equipment, and objects during the course of the day. Typical objects that puncture hands and fingers include pins, needles, wood (splinters), nails, and fishhooks.

Avulsions

Avulsions are wounds where the skin is torn and some tissue is actually ripped off (**Figure 4-7**). The mechanism of injury is a traumatic event. For example, athletes should not wear jewelry, in particular earrings and rings, during activity. Before someone works out with weights, does yard work, works in construction, or uses equipment they must always take their rings off. These activities can cause someone to catch their ring on an object while the ring is on their finger, and forcefully pull the ring off. When the ring pulls off, it tends to get caught on the knuckle and pulls the skin and underlying tissues off of the bone. This type of avulsion injury causes significant pain and bleeding.

Amputations

Similar to avulsions, amputations occur when a significant traumatic force entirely cuts off a part of the body (**Figure 4-8**).

Amputations occur as a result of a traumatic force. Usually these wounds occur to smaller body parts, such as fingers, toes, and earlobes. However, in some major traumatic events, such as automobile accidents, loss of a limb is very possible. Objects causing amputations include knives, saws, mechanical power equipment, and glass. To prevent amputations, misuse of these objects and utilizing defective equipment must be avoided. As an example, never allow your athletes to work out at your gym wearing any jewelry including earrings, other body piercings, and rings. If your organization neglects to have and enforce a no jewelry policy, you may be found negligible if an amputation due to jewelry occurs to an athlete.

Figure 4-8 | An amputation.

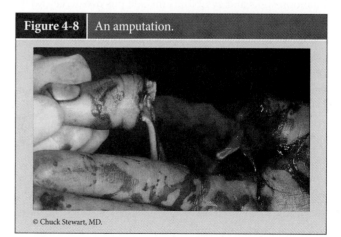

© Chuck Stewart, MD.

Signs and symptoms of amputations include minor to major bleeding, which depends on the size and location of the body part that has been amputated; significant pain; shock; and the body part severed from the body (MedlinePlus, 2011). In the case of amputations, shock occurs due to the significant external bleeding. Because blood is exiting the body at the open wound, oxygen is not distributed as needed to the brain and vital organs. If the athlete is in shock for a period of time, death can result.

In some cases, amputated body parts can be reattached by surgeons. In other cases, as determined by physicians, the body part may not be able to be reattached. Also, the physician may determine that for adequate healing and to obtain better functional capabilities, the athlete is better off with a **prosthesis** rather than reattachment of the amputated body part.

> **Prosthesis**   A synthetic body part that is custom made to replace an amputated body part.

INFECTION

With any open wound, a possibility of infection exists (**Figure 4-9**). Infection results from improper initial treatment and inappropriate continuous care of a wound. Also, debris, bacteria, or other pathogens that were initially in or remain in the wound can cause infection. Regardless of the type of open wound, the penetrating object may have debris, bacteria, or other pathogens on it. Therefore, any open wound can become infected. Punctures are particularly prone to infection. Debris or a pathogen on the puncturing object can be pushed far down into the puncture hole. Because small punctures, in particular, bleed minimally, the pathogen remains in the puncture. If the puncture is not cleaned properly, the pathogen remains in the wound. Over time, the pathogen creates infection. Wound infection signs and symptoms vary. Common signs and symptoms include pus discharge, swelling, and redness in and around the wound (Cutting & White, 2004). An athlete with an infection may also complain of pain at the wound, general body fatigue, and fever. Usually an infected wound does not appear to progress through the healing process. If your athlete's wound is infected, refer her or him to a doctor.

One notable type of bacteria that causes infection, and even creates a life-threatening illness for your athletes, is the bacterium that causes tetanus. It is a fallacy that only puncture wounds can be stricken by the tetanus bacteria. Likewise, it is not true that only rusty metal objects carry the bacteria. On the contrary, the bacteria causing tetanus can enter the body

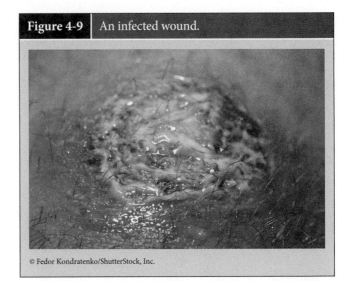

Figure 4-9   An infected wound.

© Fedor Kondratenko/ShutterStock, Inc.

via any open wound and any object. Typically, dirty objects tend to have the tetanus bacteria on them. Within 1–3 weeks from when the tetanus bacteria enter the body, a first sign of infection is "lockjaw," a serious facial muscle spasm. Along with lockjaw, other immediate signs of infection include fever, sweating, and irritability. Soon thereafter the spasms occur to other muscles. These spasms can cause muscle ruptures, fractures, and breathing difficulty (PubMed Health, 2011). The potential for significant, life-threatening illness from tetanus is why getting an initial vaccination for tetanus, as well as a **booster vaccination** every 10 years, is imperative.

> **Booster vaccination**   A dose of the antigen administered to the body, after the original vaccination was given, in order for the body to create additional antibodies to fight against infection.

FIRST AID FOR EXTERNAL WOUNDS

External, open wounds require appropriate first aid care. If proper first aid is not rendered, then proper wound healing does not occur. Likewise, to complicate matters, without proper first aid and wound healing, wound infection can occur. Many exercise scientists have formal basic or advanced first aid training and know how to provide proper first aid for wounds. If you do not have formal first aid training, you can and should heed general guidelines to provide your athletes with adequate, appropriate care.

When providing first aid care for open, bleeding wounds, the first step you take is to stop the bleeding. In order to stop the bleeding, with gloved hands apply direct pressure to the

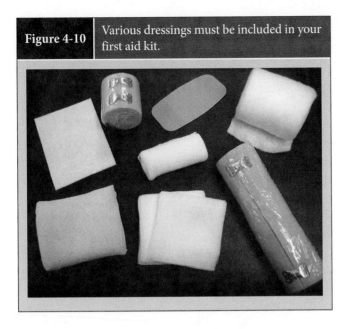

Figure 4-10 Various dressings must be included in your first aid kit.

wound with a clean, preferably sterile, dressing. These dressings, such as gauze sponges or squares, must be in your organization's first aid kit (**Figure 4-10**). The dressings will become saturated with blood if there is venous, arterial, or severe capillary bleeding. Keep the wet dressings on the wound and add additional dressings on top. Do not remove any dressings; otherwise, bleeding most likely will resume. Continue to provide direct pressure over the wound. Have someone call 911, and comfort your athlete by talking to him or her. If a wound exhibits only minor capillary bleeding, the dressings most often do not become saturated. Slowly and carefully remove the dressings, dispose of them properly, and continue with your first aid skills. At any time, if the dressings stick to the wound, do not attempt to remove them. However, if you must remove the dressings to bandage the area, wet the dressings with small amounts of water or saline until they come loose from the wound. If you are not able to remove the water-soaked dressings easily, continue with your first aid skills and refer the athlete to a physician. Remember, when applying dressings; do not put direct pressure on an impaled object, a wounded eye, or a fracture (AAOS, 2012). Also, especially with a potential underlying fractured bone, minimize movement of the area and stabilize it; otherwise, further injury can result. Fortunately, the majority of minor open wounds stop bleeding within about 5 minutes. Shock typically does not result from minor bleeding; however, keep in mind that some athletes are not able to tolerate the sight of blood, and will go into shock.

Tips from the Field

Tip 1   When providing first aid care for an open wound, take all necessary first aid supplies out of the first aid kit before providing care. One mistake that a caregiver could make is to have gloves on, touch the bleeding wound, and then with the bloody gloves put their hands back into the first aid kit. The caregiver would thus contaminate the entire first aid kit with blood, and possibly bloodborne pathogens. If you care for an open wound and forget to take an item out of the first aid kit, properly take off the gloves, dispose of them appropriately, retrieve the materials you need from the first aid kit, apply new gloves, and then care for the bleeding wound. Try to avoid this delay in care by removing all necessary first aid items before touching the bleeding athlete. Taking time to think about which materials you require will assist you in providing efficient and timely first aid care. Often you will have a coworker or bystander who can assist you in retrieving materials from the first aid kit and hand them to you for application. For example, taking off the wax-lined tabs on adhesive bandages is difficult because it often sticks to the gloves. Your coworker, who is not wearing gloves, could easily prepare these bandages and materials for you. Be careful not to get blood on your coworker when obtaining the materials from him or her. Have your coworker put the items down for you to take, to prevent exposing your coworker to the blood.

Tips from the Field

Tip 2   You can "double glove" when providing first aid care. *Double glove* means to apply two gloves on each hand before touching the bleeding athlete. If you need to take off your gloves to go back into your first aid kit because you forgot to take out an item (as described in Tip 1), or if you need additional items, you can take off the outer layer gloves and have the second layer underneath.

After the bleeding has stopped, continue to provide care to your athlete by cleaning the wound. For major wound bleeding, cleaning the wound is not a priority. With major bleeding, your athlete needs immediate advanced medical care before she or he goes into shock from loss of blood. In contrast, for minor wound bleeding, clean the wound immediately to remove bacteria, pathogens, and debris, as well as promote proper healing. Once the bleeding has stopped, carefully remove the dressings and gently wash the wound with antibacterial or ordinary soap and clean water. In place of soap and water, you can also use a commercially prepared cleaning agent. Over the years, various companies have created wound

> **Antiseptics** Substances that assist in cleansing a wound and destroying pathogenic bacteria that may have entered the wound.

antiseptics in various forms including liquids, gels, ointments, and aerosols. Some research has shown that utilizing these commercially prepared wound cleaning agents produces better wound healing and decreases healing time as compared to using soap and water (Cutting, 2010). One benefit of having these agents in a first aid kit is that they are readily available for immediate wound cleaning, especially when soap and water are not accessible. While cleaning the wound, carefully observe the wound to see if any debris is in the wound. If debris is embedded in the wound, do not remove it. Continue to clean the wound and flush it with water, then dress and bandage the wound, and call for medical assistance.

Many different dressings have been created and are useful for providing wound care. Some dressings are formulated not

> **Antimicrobial** A substance that attempts to kill pathogens such as bacteria, viruses, and fungi.

to stick to the wound, while others have **antimicrobial** agents incorporated into them to help prevent infection. Specialized dressings exist and are often used by medical personnel. One specialized dressing is an occlusive dressing, which is a nonabsorbent dressing that creates a film over the wound. Occlusive dressings are built to seal out debris, air, moisture, bacteria, and other pathogens. Hydrocolloid dressings contain particles that combine with the blood from the wound and form a gel that creates a moist environment and promotes healing. Butterfly bandages or Steri-Strip skin closures hold the wound edges together. Some of these specialized dressings are very expensive and some are not. Some wounds require these specialized dressings, and others require only basic gauze and nonadherent dressings.

When using sterile gauze or a nonadherent dressing, choose the appropriate dressing size to completely cover the wound. For very minor wounds, a typical commercial adhesive bandage, which contains a nonadherent dressing, most often will suffice. Prior to applying the adhesive bandage, apply an antibacterial ointment to the wound, as per the directions on the product package. This ointment helps prevent any debris or pathogens from getting into the wound. Once you have placed the ointment on the wound with a cotton-tipped applicator and applied the dressing, you may or may not need to apply a roller gauze bandage. Typically, if the athlete is continuing activity or if the wound is minor yet large, then placing a roller gauze bandage on the wound is appropriate (**Figure 4-11**).

The roller gauze bandage holds the dressing in place during activity. To apply the roller gauze to an extremity, begin at

Figure 4-11 | Apply a roller gauze to secure dressings.

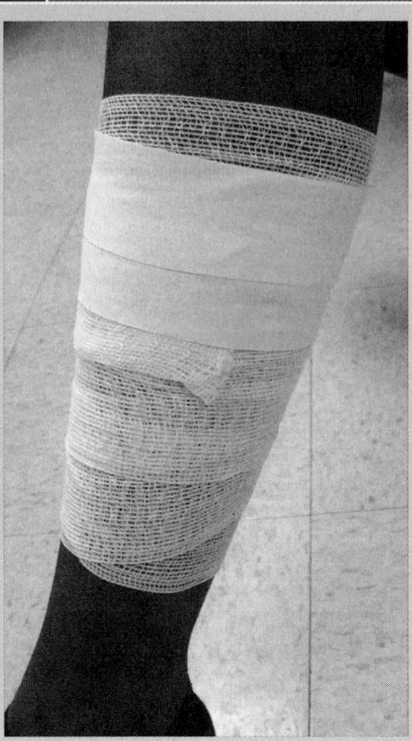

the end of the wound closest to either the hand or foot. Unroll the roller gauze upwards toward the head. As you unroll the roller gauze bandage, place it so it overlaps by about half the width of the previously applied roller gauze bandage. As you unroll the roller gauze, do not wrap the wound and extremity too tightly, which will cut off circulation, or too loosely, so the roller gauze will fall off. Completely cover the wound. When you are finished, you may have excess roller gauze. Cut the excess roller gauze with safety, blunt-tipped scissors. Place elastic or paper tape on the unsecured end of the roller bandage. Apply enough tape to secure the roller gauze bandage and keep it from falling off. Once the roller gauze bandage has been applied, ask your athlete if it feels comfortable, is not too tight or loose, and does not restrict movement.

While you are applying the roller gauze bandage, and once you have finished, check the athlete's circulation to make sure it is normal. Do so by comparing the color of your athlete's hands and feet, depending on where the roller gauze bandage has been applied. The color should be pink and the temperature should be the same on the contralateral extremities. Also check the athlete's capillary refill. With two of your fingers, press the fingernail or toenail bed on the extremity with the open wound. The nail bed color should be pink without pressure, and change to white with pressure. Upon releasing your pressure, the nail bed should immediately turn back to pink. This refill of blood into the nail bed demonstrates adequate circulation through the extremity to the fingers and toes. If the athlete is responding well to your first aid treatment, consider whether you need to refer him or her to the ER for stitches.

Tips from the Field

Tip 3   Have the athlete assist you as much as possible when providing first aid for his or her bleeding wound. When an athlete approaches you for help, hand him or her something clean, such as a towel, T-shirt, or sweatshirt, to hold over the wound and apply direct pressure to it. If you have sterile gauze readily available, you can give him or her the gauze to hold over the wound. Do not hand the item or dressing directly to the bleeding athlete. He or she may grab the item or dressing with a bloody hand, which may touch you. Instead, put the item down on the athlete's lap if he or she is sitting, or on a table or hard, nonfabric chair, which can be easily cleaned. By putting the item down and having the athlete pick it up to use, you will not have contact with the athlete's blood. In the meantime, while the athlete is applying his or her own direct pressure with a dressing, access your first aid kit, put on gloves, and get the first aid materials prepared.

To Stitch or Not to Stitch?

Before you dress and bandage an open wound, inspect it carefully and ask yourself, "Does this wound need stitches?" You can utilize a few criteria to determine whether to refer your athlete to a physician for stitches. Whenever an athlete has a laceration or incision on the face, hands, or head, you must refer them to their physician or the ER immediately for stitches. Even if the wound is minor in these areas, stitches are necessary to help minimize scarring. Also, if the wound is very severe or greater than an inch long, the damaged ends do not approximate, it does not stop bleeding in a short amount of time, or you can see the underlying tissues in the wound, then the athlete must be referred to the ER for stitches right away (Prentice, 2011). The stitches help slow the bleeding significantly, assist with proper healing, and minimize skin scarring (**Figure 4-12**). Whenever there is a question as to whether your athlete needs stitches, refer your athlete to a physician.

Additional Considerations with Open Wounds

Certain open wounds call for special first aid care. When dealing with a puncture wound, do not remove any large object

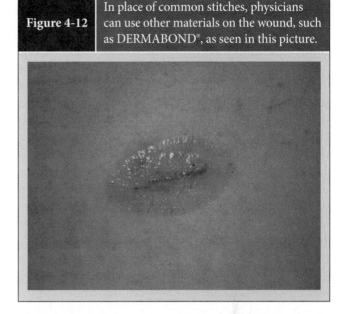

Figure 4-12   In place of common stitches, physicians can use other materials on the wound, such as DERMABOND®, as seen in this picture.

that is protruding from or is inside the wound. Objects such as nails, knives, and glass are examples of protruding objects. The protruding object may have severed an artery or a vein. Leaving the object in place may prevent significant bleeding by blocking off a major blood vessel. If the object is removed, further tissue damage may occur. Any object protruding from the eye should not be removed. For a small puncture object, such as a common splinter or a bee stinger, carefully help your athlete to remove the object if you feel comfortable doing so, with tweezers or the side of a credit card, respectively. For larger objects that must not be removed, take special care not to move the object and keep the athlete as still as possible. Call 911 immediately for help. In the meantime, place bulky dressings and bandages around the object to stabilize it and minimize bleeding. For an eye puncture, use dressings and bandages around the object to keep it still. Both eyes move together. Therefore, to minimize movement of the injured eye and the protruding object, bandage both eyes. Stay with your athlete to comfort him or her, to treat him or her for shock, to give cardiopulmonary resuscitation (CPR) if necessary, and to afford the emergency medical technicians (EMTs) details of the injury when they arrive.

When dealing with an avulsion, provide first aid care as discussed, but also consider how washing the wound in running water and soap would affect your athlete. Consider the following scenario: You are working in We R Fit Gym and overseeing the weight training floor from your office. One of your athletes is performing upper body weight lifting with free weights. Suddenly, you hear a deafening scream. You run onto the floor and see Kyle holding his severely bleeding hand. You approach Kyle and ask him what happened. He said that he finished his set and was attempting to put the free weight back onto the rack. He was not paying attention and put the weight down on his third and fourth fingers. Kyle's fingers became caught between the free weight and the metal rack. The weight was so heavy that it crushed his two fingers. When he pulled his fingers from under the weight, he noticed they were cut severely, and skin was avulsed from them. Kyle looked at his fingers and immediately went into shock. In this scenario, would you wash the wound? In this case, washing his fingers under running water would probably complicate the injury and make it worse. The force of the water could very well turn his avulsed fingers into amputated fingers. To provide Kyle with immediate care, call 911. Then control bleeding, bandage the wounds, and treat Kyle for shock.

Hopefully your athletes will never have an amputation. However, if they do you must think about what you should do with the amputated body part. Call 911, then dress and bandage the wound while treating for shock. If possible, retrieve the amputated body part and place it in a plastic bag. Place this bag in another plastic bag containing ice. Inform the EMTs that you have the body part, and make sure it accompanies the athlete to the hospital. The physicians might be able to reattach the amputated body part.

Tips from the Field

Tip 4   If your athlete has a nosebleed, you can utilize many effective, commercially prepared nosebleed materials. These materials come in a variety of forms including powder and granules. However, many of these nosebleed preparations are expensive. An inexpensive and very effective means to stop the bleeding is to utilize a small piece of a cut, regular-sized tampon and insert it into the bleeding nostril. A tampon's size, absorbency, and ability to assist in clotting are perfect for bleeding nostrils. After you take the tampon out of the packaging, estimate the size of the tampon needed in order to fit only part-way up the athlete's nostril. Cut the tampon across its width before you place it in the athlete's nostril. When you cut the tampon, make sure it is long enough so some of the tampon sticks out of the nostril, because you do not want the tampon to be difficult to remove. When you insert the tampon, make sure it is far enough in so it will not fall out. Do not insert the tampon too far up the nostril because it could get lodged in the cavity and cause further injury. If both nostrils are bleeding, put a piece of cut tampon in each nostril. You may want to put a regular-sized tampon or two, along with blunt-tipped medical scissors, in your workplace first aid kit in case you must assist an athlete with a nosebleed.

CLOSED WOUNDS

Unlike open wounds, which bleed externally, closed wounds bleed internally. Internal bleeding does not necessarily mean that the bleeding occurs deep down in the tissues; rather, the bleeding can occur at the skin and upper tissue layers. Also, internal bleeding can occur with solid and hollow internal organs in the thorax and abdomen. With internal bleeding, the blood does not break through the skin. Similarly to open wounds, closed wounds exist on a continuum from minor bleeding to life-threatening bleeding.

Typical minor internal bleeding would be from ruptured capillaries. A simple contusion is an example of a closed wound with minor internal bleeding. Contusions are caused by a direct blow of an object to your athlete's body. The object can be propelled at your athlete, your athlete can run into an object, or both the object and your athlete can be moving and collide together. Internal bleeding can occur in your gym as per the following scenario: Your athlete is walking to the locker room while talking to a workout partner. She is not paying attention and bumps her forearm into the stationary bicycle handlebar. She feels immediate pain, which quickly subsides. The next day, she notices minor ecchymosis in the area. She has sustained a contusion with minor internal bleeding.

An example of a major closed wound in which internal bleeding occurs is with an abdominal organ injury. Usually these closed wounds occur due to a significant blunt force trauma to the abdomen. The force causes a contusion or even laceration of the organ. Significant abdominal internal bleeding typically causes abdominal muscle **rigidity** and **guarding**. Consider the following scenario: You are coaching high school baseball. Your centerfielder sees the batted ball approaching him high in the air. He runs to the ball. At the last second, he realizes he is too short and will not catch the ball. Your athlete dives for the ball. When he dives, his gloved arm buckles underneath him. His elbow is bent and forcefully moves backward into his abdomen. Within minutes your athlete exhibits signs of shock. He has a lacerated spleen, which bleeds profusely. This spleen injury and associated internal bleeding are life-threatening.

> **Rigidity**   Occurs as a result of an abdominal organ injury. The abdominal muscles become stiff upon palpation.

> **Guarding**   Occurs when an abdominal organ is injured. The abdominal muscles spasm and become tense in order to protect the injured abdominal organs from further injury.

First Aid for Closed Wounds

When your athlete sustains a closed wound at your facility, provide immediate first aid care. First, ask your athlete what happened to cause the wound, which helps you determine the mechanism of injury. Attempt to identify the symptoms of injury. Ask them how they are feeling, to describe the pain, and to note any abnormal sensations. Determine the signs of injury by looking at the wound and the athlete in general. Is there ecchymosis or deformity at the impact site? Are they holding the area to support or protect it? Do they move the injured area freely? Does their face look pale or blue? Do they have difficulty breathing or are they breathing more rapidly than usual? The mechanism of injury, along with the signs and symptoms of injury, assist you in determining whether the wound is minor or life-threatening. If blunt force trauma was applied to the thorax or abdomen, check for signs of shock, including rapid breathing and pulse, and treat as necessary. As with any life-threatening injury, be prepared to call 911 and provide CPR. Likewise, if you cannot determine the severity of the closed thoracic or abdominal wound, always call 911 immediately, treat for shock if signs and symptoms exist, monitor the athlete's airway, breathing, and pulse, and use RICE if the circumstances allow. If you have determined that the closed wound is minor, such as a mild contusion, use RICE, which stands for rest, ice, compression, and elevation. Refer your athlete to their physician for further evaluation. Do not forget to obtain a physician's medical clearance from your athlete before allowing them to resume participation at your facility.

Tips from the Field

Tip 5 If an athlete complains of pain in an area such as the abdomen, chest, or musculature, it is imperative to find out the specific details of the mechanism of injury. If your athlete says she or he was kicked, hit, punched, or had some other kind of blunt force trauma to the area, then assume she or he has internal bleeding. The bleeding may be minor or severe. Regardless, when you suspect internal bleeding, refer your athlete for a medical evaluation or phone 911 in emergent situations.

Applying Bandages for Closed Wounds

When your athlete sustains a minor closed wound at your facility that causes mild to moderate pain or disability, wrap the area with an elastic bandage to provide support and compression to the area (**Figure 4-13**). This elastic bandage, also called an elastic wrap, relieves some pain until his or her

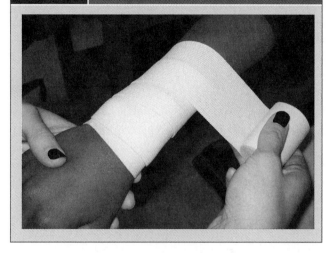

| Figure 4-13 | Elastic bandages can help minimize pain and provide support to an injured area until the athlete can see a physician. |

physician examines the athlete. Elastic wraps are not necessary for significant, major closed wounds because you must call 911 and treat the athlete as previously discussed. Elastic wraps typically are a brownish color and come in various widths, including 2 inches, 4 inches, and 6 inches, and lengths of 5 yards or 10 yards. You can always cut the wrap with blunt-tipped scissors to obtain the appropriate length, if you need to do so. Keep a variety of elastic bandages in your organization's first aid kit or supply cabinet. Before beginning to wrap the injured body part, choose the appropriate size bandage. Typically 2-inch width and 5-yard length wraps work well for wrist injuries. For athletes with large thighs, 6-inch width and 10-yard length wraps are best.

When beginning to wrap the closed wound, start distally, or furthest away from the head. Therefore, if you are wrapping the upper arm, start by the elbow and wrap upward toward the shoulder. If you are wrapping the calf, start by the ankle and move toward the knee. Wrap the elastic bandage in the same manner as you wrap a roller gauze bandage. Overlap the bandage by half of the width of the previously applied layer of wrap. Avoid leaving the skin exposed, which occurs when the wrap is not applied properly. Holes or "windows" in the applied wrap will not provide the appropriate compression for the athlete and can more easily slide off. As you apply the wrap, smooth it out with your available hand to prevent any bumps in the wrap, which prevent proper compression. Pull the wrap so it has tension, but not so tight that it cuts off circulation to the extremity. When you have covered the injured area once, any leftover wrap can continue to be applied, or you can cut off the remainder with blunt-tipped scissors. Secure the elastic bandage with the clips provided with the wrap, or athletic tape secured around the wrap's loose end. While you are applying the wrap, ask the athlete if it is comfortable, and watch for signs of decreased circulation. After you finish applying the wrap, check for proper circulation as when applying a roller gauze bandage.

SUMMARY

Open and closed wounds will most likely be common injuries occurring to your athletes while participating in activities at your facility. Fortunately, these wounds are not often severe, and require only minimal first aid care until your athlete can see his or her physician. Frequently, your athlete will not need to see a physician and can continue participation safely. However, sometimes an athlete will be severely injured at your facility and require advanced medical care. Your role in these instances is to recognize that a significant injury exists, call 911, and provide immediate first aid care to your athlete until EMTs arrive. Always remember when dealing with open wounds to follow universal precautions and Occupational Safety and Health Administration (OSHA) standards. When in doubt about an athlete's need for advanced medical care, call 911.

DISCUSSION QUESTIONS

1. What are the three primary types of blood vessels in the body? What are the differences in how they bleed externally when injured?
2. Name six signs and symptoms of an infected open wound.
3. Describe how you provide first aid for your athlete with a minor open bleeding wound.
4. Why is it important to leave large impaled objects in the wound?
5. Describe different methods to check for circulation after applying a bandage.
6. Under what circumstances must you refer an athlete to a physician or the ER for stitches?
7. What are some ways a bystander can assist you when providing first aid care for your injured athlete's open wound?
8. Describe the mechanism of injury for closed wounds. When can a closed wound be life-threatening?

CASE STUDY

To Play or Not to Play?

It is Friday night at North Hudson High School. The school is wrestling their rivals, South Hudson High School, for the conference championship. North Hudson is down by 2 points with only the 152-pound weight class left to wrestle. Diego is North Hudson's senior star wrestler and the reigning county champion at 152 pounds. The match is running smoothly and Diego is beating his opponent by 6 points with one period remaining. As long as he continues to wrestle smart he should win and take home the conference championship for his school.

The wrestlers start the period in neutral position. The referee blows his whistle and the wrestlers aggressively approach each other and begin to wrestle. Within the first 10 seconds, the wrestlers simultaneously go for a shot and butt heads. There is a loud thud, and both wrestlers fall to their knees. Immediately, blood starts to pour down from Diego's forehead onto his face. His blood drips all over the wrestling mat. He is in significant pain. He places his hands on the wound as a reaction to the pain and in order to control the bleeding. Diego stands up steadily, and begins to turn toward his coach. Diego's coach, Coach Cornell, immediately runs out onto the mat with the team's medical kit to help Diego.

Unfortunately, no other medical personnel are at the wrestling meet, so Coach Cornell must provide first aid to Diego. He hands Diego a towel from the bench to place over his cut, and begins to put on a pair of latex gloves. Afterwards, Coach Cornell slowly removes the towel from Diego's wound to examine the injury. The coach sees a deep 1-inch horizontal laceration just above the outer edge of Diego's left eyebrow. The two cut skin edges are not approximating and seem to have been torn away from each other. Coach Cornell also recognizes that the bleeding has stopped. Coach Cornell asks Diego, "How are you feeling?" Diego says, "I feel okay." Coach Cornell asks, "Do you have any head, neck, or back pain or vision difficulty?" Diego responds, "No, but some blood ran into my eye." He adamantly tells Coach Cornell that he wants to stay on the mat and finish the match to win the county championship for his team. Diego says, "Coach, just bandage me up and put me back in!"

1. Should Coach Cornell allow Diego to continue wrestling? Why or why not?

2. What should Coach Cornell do to control the bleeding?

3. What types of dressings and bandages should he apply to attempt to protect against infection and to keep the wound closed?

4. Should Coach Cornell advise Diego's parents to transport him to the hospital? Why or why not?

REFERENCES

American Academy of Orthopaedic Surgeons (AAOS). (2012). *First aid, CPR, and AED standard* (6th ed.). Sudbury, MA: Jones and Bartlett.

Cutting, K. F. (2010). Addressing the challenge of wound cleansing in the modern era. *British Journal of Nursing*, 19(11), S24–S29. Retrieved August 21, 2011, from http://search.ebscohost.com

Cutting, K. F., & White, R. (2004). Defined and refined: Criteria for identifying wound infection revisited. *British Journal of Community Nursing*, 9(3), S6–S15. Retrieved August 21, 2011, from http://search.ebscohost.com

Jones, M. (2007). Repair of minor wounds. *Practice Nurse*, 33(12), 31–34. Retrieved August 21, 2011, from http://search.ebscohost.com

McDevitt, J., & Gillespie, M. (2008). Managing acute plantar puncture wounds. *Emergency Nurse*, 16(5), 30–36. Retrieved August 21, 2011, from http://search.ebscohost.com

MedlinePlus. (2011). Amputation—traumatic. Retrieved August 26, 2011, from http://www.nlm.nih.gov/medlineplus/ency/article/000006.htm

Prentice, W. E. (2011). *Principles of athletic training: A competency-based approach* (14th ed.). New York: McGraw-Hill.

PubMed Health. (2011). Tetanus. Retrieved August 21, 2011, from http://www.ncbi.nlm.nih.gov/pubmedhealth/PMH0001640/

Yasa, H., Ozelci, A., Yetkin, U., Gunes, T., Gokalp, O., Yilik, L., et al. (2008). Our experiences in the management of carotid artery injuries. *Internet Journal of Thoracic and Cardiovascular Surgery*, 11(2), 13. Retrieved August 21, 2011, from http://search.ebscohost.com

Chapter 5

Emergency Care

CHAPTER OBJECTIVES

After you have read this chapter, you will be able to understand:

- The components of an emergency action plan
- The steps involved in taking a primary survey
- The differences among cardiac arrest, heart attack, and angina
- The signs, symptoms, and management of a stroke
- How to assist an athlete who is having a seizure
- The different types of shock and how they affect the body
- The differences among hypoglycemia, hyperglycemia, and diabetic ketoacidosis
- The signs and symptoms of different types of heat- and cold-related illnesses
- How to deliver proper treatment to athletes

No matter where you work or what activities you and your athletes participate in, emergency situations will arise. Emergency situations that occur to athletes at the workplace can include life-threatening or **limb-threatening** injuries and illnesses. Although you will rarely experience these emergency situations while supervising athletes, when they arise you are obligated to provide emergency care. Therefore, adequate knowledge is crucial to recognize signs and symptoms of life-threatening or limb-threatening injuries and illnesses, as well as provide proper emergency care for your athletes.

Limb-threatening When an athlete sustains a significant injury resulting in loss of motor function and/or sensation of the arm(s) or leg(s).

EMERGENCY ACTION PLAN

An important part of providing appropriate care for athletes is creating and implementing an emergency action plan (EAP) for your facility. An EAP is a crucial component of any organization's policies and procedures. The EAP includes written procedures that designate actions to help you and other employees respond to an emergency situation, allowing you to provide immediate, appropriate athlete care. The EAP is communicated to all personnel on a regular basis, perhaps as part of an annual employee orientation. EAP components include first responder and other personnel roles, activation of the emergency medical services (EMS) system, availability of emergency equipment, and athlete care.

The EAP designates that the first person on the scene of an emergency is considered the "first responder" who activates the EAP. The first responder provides immediate care to the injured athlete. The first responder also commands the scene and gives direction to other employees who can help. Other personnel at the scene assist the first responder in a variety of activities. These personnel have duties that include assisting the first responder with providing athlete care, activating the EMS system by calling 911, obtaining emergency equipment, controlling bystanders, unlocking any entrances for EMS access to the facility, and meeting the ambulance at a designated area. The specific employee roles depend on factors such as the organization type, athlete population, and venue demographics.

Activation of the EMS system begins when the first responder instructs another employee or bystander to call 911. The EAP designates the imperative information that the caller gives to the dispatcher. This information includes the type of emergency, the number of injured athletes, the extent of injuries, and the care being provided. The caller should also tell the dispatcher the best way to enter the venue and access the injured athlete, while also informing the dispatcher that someone will be waiting at that entry point for EMS.

Tips from the Field

Tip 1 Make sure you know the proper procedures for summoning EMS in your town. In some instances, 911 may not be the direct number that you use to summon EMS. For example, some higher education institutions require on-campus emergency situations to be reported to the campus police, and not directly to EMS. The campus police may have a direct phone number, which may not be 911, that must be utilized in order to summon help. Therefore, keep all emergency personnel phone numbers (i.e., campus police, first aid squad, fire company) on your cell phone, in the first aid kit, and visible on the walls at your place of employment. Make sure your staff knows the policies regarding summoning EMS.

Emergency equipment utilized to care for injured athletes should always be on site and easily accessible. Emergency equipment at your facility may include an automated external defibrillator (AED); wheelchairs; crutches; vacuum, air, and other splinting materials; and fire extinguishers. Instruct all employees on how to utilize the equipment properly, and immediately train all employees on any newly purchased equipment. Have the equipment calibrated and checked for safety annually or as required by the manufacturer.

Athlete care is the last component of the EAP. The care provided assists in stabilizing the athlete until EMS arrives. Your goal is to provide the athlete with the best possible care and chance for survival. Typically the first responder provides and commands athlete care; however, if another person present is more experienced or holds higher credentials to provide care (e.g., a physician, an EMT), then that person should be the primary care provider. The first responder can, however, continue to activate the EAP. When the EAP is in place, and regularly communicated to and practiced by the employees, the employees can appropriately handle an emergency.

SAFETY FIRST

Even though you have an obligation to provide care for your injured athletes in an emergency situation, always put your safety first. If your athlete is in an environment that is unsafe for you to enter, then you do not enter the area. For example, if your athlete is lying on the ground and appears unconscious, and you enter the room and smell an unusual odor, you must not enter the room. The odor may be a poisonous substance that can cause you to become another victim. Instead, call 911 or your local emergency number immediately. In exercise science professions, unsafe environments in your place of employment could include a building fire, a poisonous gas or substance leak, or an armed assailant. In these or any other dangerous environments, you will desperately want to help your athletes; however, do not be foolhardy and take the chance of entering the scene, or you may become another victim. Your role in these situations is to call 911 immediately. Meet the emergency personnel when they arrive at the scene and describe in detail what has occurred.

THE PRIMARY SURVEY

Before providing emergency care to an athlete, always complete an initial evaluation, known as a primary survey. A primary survey is performed to determine if your athlete is experiencing a life-threatening injury or illness that warrants emergency care. Some injuries and illnesses that can be considered emergency situations are unconsciousness, traumatic spine injuries, stroke, cardiac arrest, heart attack, shock, choking, asthma attacks, seizures, and diabetic emergencies.

An Unconscious Athlete

To begin the primary survey, first determine if the athlete is unconscious, meaning he or she is in a state of not being aware of his or her surroundings, and is not responsive to verbal or tactile (touch) stimuli. Unconsciousness can be caused by a variety of illnesses and injuries, including head injuries, shock, cardiac arrest, and heat stroke. As an example of how your athlete can become unconscious, think about an athlete playing a competitive racquetball game in your gym. During a long rally, he runs to return the ball, and does not realize where his body is relative to the wall. As he strikes the ball, his body's momentum is so great that he cannot stop. He strikes his head hard onto the wall. This blunt force trauma to the head causes him to be knocked out, or rendered unconscious. Immediately upon becoming unconscious, he falls to the ground, lies motionless, and is unaware of his surroundings. He is not able to respond to your verbal or tactile stimuli for a period of time.

Two stimuli that can be used to arouse your athlete from an unconscious state are voice and touch. When an athlete is lying motionless, determine if she is unconscious by approaching her while shouting her name and "Are you okay?" At the same time, gently tap her shoulder to see if she responds. By no means shake the athlete because she may have a spine injury. If you shake or move an unconscious athlete with a spine injury, you can do further harm to the athlete. Make sure the athlete stays as still as possible.

You may say to yourself, "How do I know if an athlete has a spinal injury?" Well, you may not always know. However, suspect the athlete has sustained a spinal injury if he or she falls from a significant height such as a ladder that is taller than he or she is, if he or she has a traumatic accident such as a car accident, or if he or she sustains a direct blow to the head by an object or another person. Also, if you did not see the athlete go unconscious, but he or she is motionless and lying on the floor, always suspect that the athlete has a spinal injury. Consequently, stabilize the athlete's head, neck, and spine in the position that you find them until advanced medical care arrives.

Regardless of whether the athlete has a spinal injury, once you determine that the athlete is unconscious, immediately send someone to phone 911 or your local emergency number. If no one is around to call for you, position the athlete in the modified HAINES position, call 911, then return to the athlete and continue care (**Figure 5-1**). HAINES stands for high arm in endangered spine. The purpose of the modified HAINES position is to attempt to maintain an open airway while you phone 911. This position is also better than any other recovery position for keeping the spine in a neutral position as much as possible when you must leave the unconscious athlete to summon advanced medical care (Blake et al., 2002). If the athlete vomits while in the modified HAINES position, the vomit will drain from the mouth instead of blocking the airway.

To put your athlete in this position, lie them on their side with their head resting on an outstretched arm, spine straight, and knees flexed. In this position, monitor the athlete's breathing. If their breathing stops, carefully roll them on their back, maintaining in-line stabilization, and administer

cardiopulmonary resuscitation (CPR) until EMS arrives and takes over.

Checking for Breathing

After you have determined the athlete is unconscious, check to see if the athlete is breathing. If the athlete is lying face down, tilt your head to the side and put your face by their nose and mouth to see if you can hear or feel their breaths. If possible, check to see if their chest is rising and falling, which would indicate that they are breathing. Put your hand gently on their back to see if you can feel the thorax expanding with each respiration. If the athlete is breathing, stay close to their face and monitor their breathing until advanced medical personnel arrives. If you cannot tell whether they are breathing, then you must log roll the athlete onto their back.

To log roll the athlete, it would be beneficial to have additional coworkers or athletes assist you (**Figure 5-2**). When you log roll an athlete, it is important to keep the head, neck, and spine in a straight orientation. This procedure is called in-line stabilization, which means you are keeping the head, neck, and spine in line with each other as if the person were standing or lying flat on his or her back.

When log rolling the athlete, the athlete's head and neck must move as a unit with the spine at all times. If you are the first person to approach the athlete, take the lead at the athlete's head and stabilize the athlete's head and neck. To do so, place your hands on either side of the athlete's head, keeping in mind that your arms will shift position as you roll the athlete. Sometimes it is easier to cross your arms and then place your hands on either side of the athlete's head. Make sure you cross your arms in a manner so when you have rolled the athlete on his or her back, your arms end up straight and in a comfortable position to continue to maintain in-line stabilization.

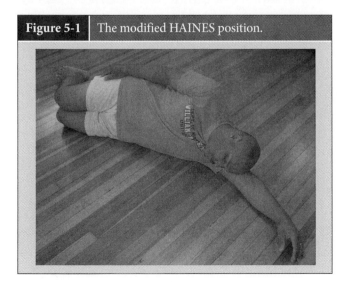

Figure 5-1 | The modified HAINES position.

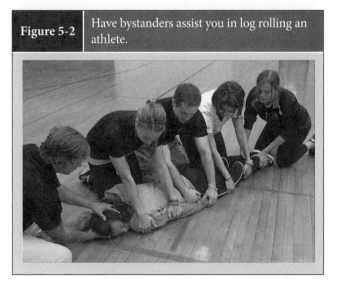

Figure 5-2 | Have bystanders assist you in log rolling an athlete.

Your assistants are all positioned on one side of the athlete, at the arms, hips, and thighs. One assistant is at the feet. Direct your assistants in regard to which direction to roll the athlete. Roll the athlete opposite the resting direction of his or her face. Choose a command such as "ready, set, roll" or "on three: one, two, three," and tell your assistants before you roll the athlete what the command is. Direct your assistants to keep the athlete's body in line at all times. This log roll technique is not easy. All employees must work together efficiently. Consequently, your organization should make in-line stabilization and log rolling an athlete a regular part of employee training.

Once the athlete is on his or her back, check for breathing again (**Figure 5-3**). If you are stabilizing the head and neck, then it is better for one of your coworkers to check to see if the athlete is breathing. You do not want to remove your hands from the unconscious athlete's head and neck because movement can occur (**Figure 5-4**).

If you are the only person around to assist your athlete, and you cannot tell whether he or she is breathing while lying on his or her stomach, log roll the athlete yourself while maintaining in-line stabilization (**Figure 5-5**). Get on the side of the athlete opposite his or her face. Kneel as close to the athlete as possible by placing your knees so they touch the athlete's side, and sit on your heels. Place the hand closest to his or her head on the back of his or her neck, and grasp the neck firmly. Place your other hand at the hip that is farthest away

Figure 5-4 Maintaining in-line stabilization is imperative for an athlete who may have sustained a spinal injury.

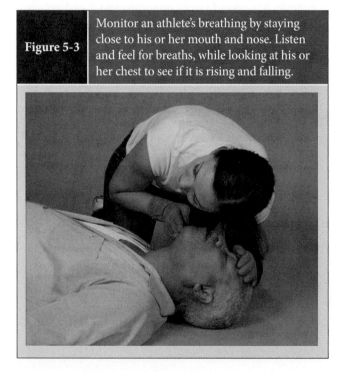

Figure 5-3 Monitor an athlete's breathing by staying close to his or her mouth and nose. Listen and feel for breaths, while looking at his or her chest to see if it is rising and falling.

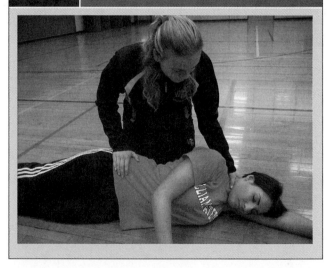

Figure 5-5 If you are by yourself with an unconscious athlete, log roll her while maintaining in-line stabilization.

from you. Maintaining in-line stabilization, roll the athlete toward you, onto your thighs, and then carefully and slowly move backward on your knees to allow the athlete to rest on the ground. At this point, with the athlete face up, you must continue your primary survey.

Checking for Severe Bleeding

Severe bleeding can be the cause of the athlete's unconsciousness. Severe bleeding can also make an unconscious athlete's situation worsen rapidly due to the lack of oxygenated blood getting to the brain and internal organs. As you determine whether the athlete is unconscious by seeing if he or she is unresponsive, you must also examine the athlete from head to toe to see if he or she is bleeding severely (**Figure 5-6**). While you are checking the athlete's breathing, look to see if there is blood around his or her body, on his or her clothes, or on the surrounding ground, all of which indicate external bleeding. External bleeding often accompanies internal bleeding, which is indicated by bruising of the skin. If you see that the athlete is bleeding severely, and you have someone available to assist you, have your assistant use personal protective equipment (PPE), or clean clothing, blankets, or towels, to put pressure

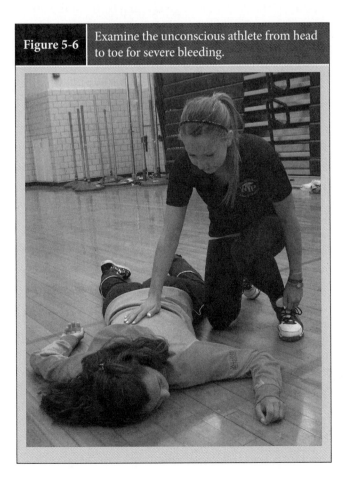

Figure 5-6 Examine the unconscious athlete from head to toe for severe bleeding.

on the bleeding site in an attempt to stop or slow down the loss of blood. If you are alone, then your priority is to check for breathing and determine whether your athlete needs CPR.

Cardiopulmonary Resuscitation

The layperson's adult CPR does not incorporate a circulation check, so once you have determined that the athlete is not breathing, begin CPR immediately. CPR can potentially save the life of an athlete who is experiencing **cardiac arrest**. By utilizing CPR skills on an athlete in cardiac arrest, you will manually force the heart to pump oxygenated blood to the brain and vital organs. If oxygenated blood is reaching the brain and vital organs, then the athlete's tissues can be sustained for a short period of time. In the past, only one type of CPR existed. This CPR technique included mouth-to-mouth or rescue breathing, which entails placing your mouth over the athlete's mouth and breathing oxygenated air into his or her lungs. Utilizing a breathing barrier, such as a disposable pocket mask (**Figures 5-7** and **5-8**), is imperative during rescue breathing to prevent disease transmission and to promote adequate oxygen entering the athlete's respiratory tract. After two rescue breaths, you compress the chest 30 times at a rate of 100 compressions per minute at the mid-sternum in order to compress the heart between the sternum and the vertebrae (**Figure 5-9**). The series of compressions and breaths results in oxygenated blood moving through the adult athlete's body. If another person can assist you in delivering CPR to an adult

> **Cardiac arrest** When an athlete's heart is significantly damaged, it will no longer function properly and stops beating.

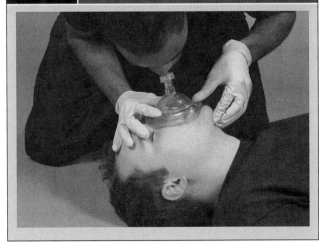

Figure 5-7 Breathing barriers protect against disease transmission and promote administration of air into the respiratory tract.

| Figure 5-8 | Some breathing barriers are small enough to store in your pocket while working with athletes. |

athlete, then deliver the two rescue breaths while your assistant delivers 30 chest compressions. When your assistant becomes tired, he or she should call for a position switch, which is done after you complete two breaths. This type of CPR is defined as full CPR by the American Red Cross (2013).

The latest development in CPR is hands-only CPR. This type of CPR is usually utilized if you witness an athlete collapse with no warning (American Red Cross, 2012). Unlike full

| Figure 5-9 | Application of CPR. |

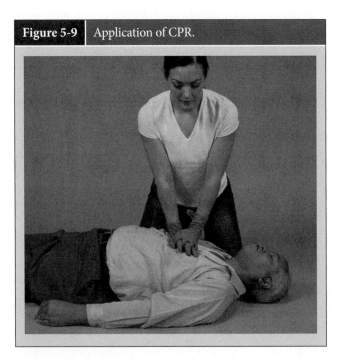

CPR, with hands-only CPR you use your hands to administer chest compressions and do not make any mouth-to-mouth contact; no rescue breaths are given. You push hard and fast on the chest. Similar to full CPR, with hands-only CPR you force the heart to mechanically pump blood throughout the body; however, because you are not performing rescue breaths, no additional oxygen is being introduced into the athlete's blood. Only the oxygen that was in the blood when the athlete ceased breathing remains in the body. Even though no additional oxygen is entering the athlete's blood, performing hands-only CPR will mechanically circulate the blood throughout the body, which can increase the athlete's chance of survival compared to not performing CPR at all.

Regardless of whether you utilize full or hands-only CPR, continue administering CPR until the athlete begins to breathe, you are too tired to continue, advanced medical personnel arrive, an automated external defibrillator (AED) is brought to the scene, another trained person takes over for you, or the scene becomes unsafe for you to continue (American Academy of Orthopaedic Surgeons [AAOS], 2012; American Red Cross, 2012).

Because you work regularly with athletes in exercise science or a related profession, becoming certified in CPR is imperative. Some employers will require you to initially obtain and then maintain CPR certification. You are legally bound to assist your athletes at your facility and perform CPR if needed. However, outside of your facility, even if you are not certified in CPR and you witness an athlete suddenly collapse, you can assist the athlete. You can give compressions by "pushing hard and fast" (American Red Cross, 2012), or at the very least call 911. If you perform full or hands-only CPR even if you have not obtained CPR certification, you will be protected by your state's Good Samaritan laws.

Automated External Defibrillators

Even though you can utilize CPR as a lifesaving technique to manually force an athlete's heart to pump oxygenated blood to the brain and vital organs, in most circumstances, for adults, CPR alone cannot restart the heart and make it beat on its own. The use of an AED (**Figure 5-10**) is absolutely necessary to restart the heart, make it beat in a normal fashion, and distribute blood throughout the body. Often when adults fall unconscious due to the heart stopping, the heart is actually not beating normally and cannot sustain a normal rhythm from its electrical conductivity. The heart is often in ventricular tachycardia or ventricular fibrillation, and therefore does not pump blood throughout the body. Ventricular tachycardia is when the heart beats very fast, at approximately 100 beats per minute or more. Also, the heart will have a few irregular beats

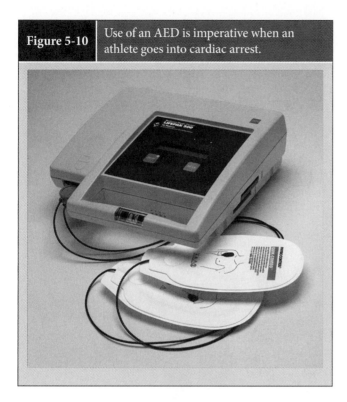

Figure 5-10 | Use of an AED is imperative when an athlete goes into cardiac arrest.

in a row (MedlinePlus, 2010). Ventricular fibrillation can also occur, especially after a person has a heart attack (Mayo Clinic, 2011). Ventricular fibrillation is when the heart beats with an unusual, irregular rhythm, or fibrillates. In this instance, adequate blood and oxygen cannot get to the brain and vital organs.

A heart attack is different than cardiac arrest in that the athlete is experiencing part of the heart dying, but he or she is still breathing. In adult athletes, a heart attack can result in cardiac arrest, which typically involves ventricular tachycardia or ventricular fibrillation. The only means to correct ventricular tachycardia or ventricular fibrillation is to utilize an AED. An AED is a machine that delivers electrical shocks to an athlete who has experienced cardiac arrest involving ventricular tachycardia or ventricular fibrillation. The AED's purpose is to briefly stop the heart in order for it to reset itself, and then beat normally. You probably have seen AEDs mounted on the wall in places such as hospitals, airports, restaurants, schools, shopping malls, and movie theaters. Without an AED, the chance of survival for the athlete is very small. For every minute that defibrillation by an AED is delayed after the athlete sustains cardiac arrest, the chance of survival decreases by 7–10% (Rho & Page, 2007). The chance of survival for an athlete in cardiac arrest increases significantly when CPR and AED use is initiated immediately after the athlete succumbs to cardiac arrest.

Utilizing an AED is very easy for a layperson. Once you press the AED's on button, the AED verbalizes instructions for you to follow. The AED begins by directing you to place the adhesive conduction pads in the correct areas on the athlete. Each adhesive pad is attached to a wire and an adapter, which is plugged into the AED. To make it easy for you to place the pads, the adhesive pads have pictures depicting where the pads must be placed on the athlete. Then the AED directs you to plug in the adapter. The AED verbalizes when it is analyzing the heart's rhythm. It also states whether to deliver a shock by pressing the shock button, or whether you should simply continue to administer CPR. It is extremely important that no one, not even yourself, is in contact with the athlete while a shock is being delivered. If someone is touching the athlete while he or she is being shocked, the shock may not be effective for the injured athlete. Also, the person touching the athlete will also be shocked, and possibly sustain a significant injury.

As part of gaining CPR certification, you should gain AED certification also. CPR and AED certification courses are offered by a variety of national organizations. Two of the most renowned national organizations that provide these courses are the American Heart Association and the American Red Cross. Exercise science and other professionals who work with athletes should become certified in CPR and AED even if their employers do not require the certifications. As with CPR, Good Samaritan laws will protect the layperson to an extent when he or she has utilized an AED on an injured athlete. In 2000, the Cardiac Arrest Survival Act (CASA) became federal law; it provides some immunity for laypersons using an AED on a cardiac arrest victim (Rho & Page, 2007). Therefore, do not be afraid to utilize an available AED on a cardiac arrest victim.

THE PRIMARY SURVEY AND ATHLETIC EQUIPMENT

At times, you will have to perform a primary survey on an athlete who is wearing equipment. Football, hockey, and lacrosse players wear helmets and shoulder pads, which can be a hindrance to you when completing a primary survey. Nevertheless, in life-threatening situations, a primary survey must be performed regardless of the equipment worn. If the athlete is wearing shoulder pads with a jersey and you find that the athlete is not breathing, cut the shoulder pad laces or remove the Velcro attachments at the chest and open the pads enough to access the chest. In most cases the shoulder pads do not need to be removed entirely, but the chest must be exposed so you can appropriately place your hands on the sternum to perform CPR and for the AED pads to be placed appropriately on the athlete's body. Helmets should not be removed; a football helmet, for example, assists in maintaining the cervical spine in a stabilized position, especially when the athlete is secured to a spine board. The face mask, however, must be removed immediately or lifted upward by its hinges to allow for rescue breathing. Depending on the helmet, specialized tools such as pruners, cordless screwdrivers, and other devices that can cut through or remove the clips holding the face mask on the helmet are necessary. Be cognizant of the helmets your athletes wear and the tools required for emergency face mask removal. Practice removing the face mask in a simulated situation. Your goal is to remove the face mask quickly and safely, while minimizing any movement of the head or cervical spine. At all times while you are caring for an athlete wearing a helmet, another person should be stabilizing the athlete's head and spine. When faced with an injured athlete wearing equipment, your first reaction may be to immediately remove the equipment. However, keep in mind that you can provide appropriate care to your athlete while keeping his or her equipment on.

LIFE-THREATENING SITUATIONS

Unfortunately, because you work with athletes daily, you will undoubtedly be presented with emergency life-threatening situations. Hopefully, you will have CPR and AED training and knowledge, as well as immediate access to an AED, to assist you in proper lifesaving efforts for your athlete. Often, by simply and properly recognizing these emergency situations, calling for an ambulance, and keeping the athlete comfortable and stable, you will give him or her a chance to survive. Even though these actions may seem trivial and you want to do more to help the athlete, these actions can save his or her life. Some emergency life-threatening situations include heart attack, stroke, seizures, choking, shock, asthma exacerbations, diabetic emergencies, and environmental emergencies.

Heart Attack

A heart attack is caused by the same heart condition as cardiac arrest, but as noted previously, an athlete who has a heart attack does not necessarily succumb to cardiac arrest. Similar to cardiac arrest, a heart attack occurs when, over time, portions of the heart muscle die due to coronary artery damage. Coronary arteries deliver oxygenated blood to the heart (**Figure 5-11**). Damage to an artery causes insufficient oxygenated blood flow to the portion of the heart muscle tissue affected by the damaged coronary arteries. Consequently, that portion of the heart tissue dies due to lack of adequate oxygen.

The athlete experiences the heart attack signs and symptoms as a portion of the heart muscle dies. Heart attack signs and symptoms include chest pain, shoulder pain, jaw pain, the

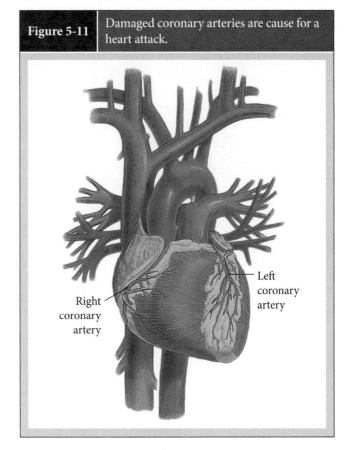

Figure 5-11   Damaged coronary arteries are cause for a heart attack.

Right coronary artery

Left coronary artery

feeling of indigestion, nausea, sweating, shortness of breath, and dizziness (**Table 5-1**). Some of these signs and symptoms are very noticeable and others are mild. For example, a man who experienced a heart attack described the pain by stating that it felt like "an elephant was sitting on his chest." He said the pain was excruciating and his chest felt like it was being squeezed. Another man said that his heart attack only "felt like constant indigestion." Women often have more subtle signs of heart attack, including nausea, lightheadedness, fatigue, shortness of breath, and sweating. Consequently, they tend not to recognize that they are having a heart attack. They often do not have chest pain, which is the primary heart attack sign for men. If an athlete exhibits any of these signs and symptoms, or complains about them without having undue cause for the occurrence (e.g., shoulder pain when a shoulder injury has occurred), suspect that your athlete is having a heart attack.

When you are with an athlete who is experiencing heart attack signs or symptoms, have him sit down and relax in whatever position is comfortable, and make sure he is breathing normally. Ask the athlete whether he has a heart condition

Table 5-1	Emergency Care for a Heart Attack	
Condition	**What to Look For**	**What to Do**
Heart attack	• Chest pressure, squeezing, or pain • Pain spreading to shoulders, neck, jaw, or arms • Dizziness, sweating, nausea • Shortness of breath	1. Help victim take his or her prescribed medication. 2. Call 9-1-1. 3. Help victim into a comfortable position. 4. If the victim is alert and not allergic to aspirin, give four chewable aspirin or one regular aspirin. 5. Assist with any prescribed heart medication. 6. Monitor breathing.

> **Angina** Occurs when a part of the heart does not get enough oxygenated blood. The athlete feels pain similar to an athlete who is experiencing a heart attack, but most often not as severe.

and if he takes medication to make the symptoms subside. Some athletes with heart conditions such as **angina** will take low dose or baby aspirin each day to help prevent a heart attack. Some athletes with angina also take medication such as nitroglycerine when an angina episode occurs. If an athlete knowingly has angina and an episode occurs, assist him in taking the appropriate medication. If after approximately 5 to 10 minutes the medication did not work to relieve the symptoms, the athlete did not have his medication available, or the symptoms are increasing rapidly, then call for EMS immediately. If the athlete does not knowingly have angina, but is experiencing heart attack signs and symptoms, call 911 immediately.

When an athlete is experiencing a heart attack, have him take one regular dose adult aspirin. The aspirin can assist in alleviating the symptoms by preventing blood from clotting in the coronary arteries, consequently promoting blood flow to the heart (AAOS, 2012). Also, some athletes with heart conditions will have prescription drugs that must be utilized during a heart attack. These drugs spontaneously destroy blood clots

in the coronary arteries, which allows oxygenated blood to reach the heart normally. Even if you are unsure whether your athlete is having a heart attack, it is prudent to be cautious when providing care. Any delay in help can be fatal. Calling for advanced medical care is crucial for the athlete's survival. Also keep in mind that until EMS arrives you must always be prepared to administer CPR and utilize an AED if your athlete suddenly goes into cardiac arrest.

Stroke

Decreased arterial blood flow to the heart can cause an emergency situation for the athlete; similarly lack of arterial blood flow to the brain can have the same result. When arterial blood flow to the brain is insufficient or blocked, or the brain is bleeding internally, then the athlete may suffer a cerebrovascular accident (CVA), which is most commonly known as a stroke. Stroke signs and symptoms include weakness, **paralysis**, numbness, or tingling on one side

> **Paralysis** The inability to move a body part, with or without an inability to feel sensation.

of the body; vision problems; slurred speech; sudden headache; dizziness; confusion; and chest pain (Das et al., 2011) (**Table 5-2**).

Table 5-2	Emergency Care for a Stroke	
Condition	**What to Look For**	**What to Do**
Stroke	• Sudden weakness or numbness of the face, an arm, or a leg on one side of the body • Blurred or decreased vision • Problems speaking • Dizziness or loss of balance • Sudden, severe headache	1. Call 9-1-1. 2. Have the victim rest in a comfortable position. 3. If vomiting, roll the victim to his or her side.

An athlete can suffer a stroke with no warning, and some stroke signs and symptoms can mimic other conditions. Therefore, attempt to detect signs and symptoms of a stroke quickly in order to obtain advanced medical care for your athlete in a timely manner. First, ask the athlete if she has lost any feeling or has any weakness in her face, arms, or legs. Have the athlete make facial expressions, such as smiling and frowning, and see whether her face droops or she is unable to perform the expressions. Then have the athlete close her eyes while you lightly touch her arms, fingers, and legs, and ask whether she can feel your touch. If the athlete says that she can feel your touch, ask her to describe where you are touching her. This test will determine if she has sensation in those areas. Next, determine if the athlete can perform various motions. Instruct her to raise her arms up over her head. While sitting in a chair, have her flex and extend her knees. If the athlete is not able to perform these upper and lower body movements, ask her what she believes is preventing her from moving these areas (e.g., pain, weakness, muscle tightness). Throughout this entire process, evaluate the athlete's speech, to determine if it is slurred, and her memory. If your athlete exhibits these signs or symptoms, then suspect that your athlete has experienced a stroke. You must act quickly and call 911 without delay. Have the athlete rest in a comfortable position and monitor her breathing until advanced medical help arrives.

Seizures

Another emergency situation occurs when an athlete experiences a seizure. Seizures are caused by unexpected, abnormal electrical discharges from the brain and spinal cord. When an athlete is seizing, a change in behavior or abnormal, uncontrollable motor function results. Sometimes the athlete experiences an **aura**, which indicates a seizure is forthcoming. According to Miller & Berry (2011), seven types of seizures exist, which are classified according to the severity of the signs and symptoms.

> **Aura** An abnormal feeling of the mind and body that may come directly before an athlete experiences a seizure.

The most severe seizure is a **tonic-clonic** seizure, which is also called a grand mal seizure. It is pretty easy to recognize the signs and symptoms of an athlete who is having a tonic-clonic seizure. The athlete will have significant muscular contractions, making the body appear very stiff while it is convulsing. Although the athlete's

> **Tonic** A state in which the muscles are in constant contractions.
>
> **Clonic** A state in which the muscles rapidly and forcefully contract and then reflexively relax.

eyes may be open, he will be unconscious and not aware of his surroundings. The athlete will not be able to respond to your verbal or **tactile** commands. The athlete's eyes may appear to roll into the back of his head with his teeth clenched. He will be breathing very rapidly. You will have to wait for the seizure to run its course.

> **Tactile** The sense of touch.

During a tonic-clonic seizure, the athlete's muscles, including facial muscles, are maximally and continuously contracted throughout the seizure. The athlete will also be convulsing. He may fall to the ground with stiff limbs, and his body will shake. The athlete might bite his tongue, causing it to bleed, and lose bladder or bowel control during the seizure. The seizure may continue for a few minutes. When the seizure is over, the athlete will very slowly regain consciousness. He will be dazed, confused, and unaware of what happened. He may also be embarrassed, anxious, irritable, and sullen.

You play an important role in assisting an athlete having a grand mal seizure. Recognizing the signs and symptoms of a seizure is important in order to prepare for what will follow. Protect the athlete and bystanders from harm as best you can. Have bystanders move away from the seizing athlete. Also have them clear the area of objects such as tables, chairs, equipment, or anything that could harm the seizing athlete should the athlete fall or move into them. Immediately designate someone to call 911. Allow the seizure to run its course. Do not restrain the athlete, shake him, or put anything in his mouth. Restraining the athlete can cause further harm to the athlete, yourself, or bystanders. If the athlete bites his tongue or is bleeding elsewhere, immediately put on gloves to protect yourself from bloodborne pathogens. Loosen any of the athlete's tight clothing, if possible. If the athlete is seizing on the ground, place something soft, such as a sweatshirt, pillow, or rolled towel, under his head so he does not forcefully hit his head on the floor, causing a head injury. Stay with the athlete during the course of the seizure, noting how long the seizure lasts. The length of the seizure is important as part of the information to give the EMS personnel when they arrive on the scene. When the athlete's seizure is over, be mindful that the athlete may or may not be conscious. Monitor his breathing at all times. Often the athlete's breathing after a tonic-clonic seizure may be very faint, so make sure his airway is open and he is breathing normally. If the athlete is conscious, he may be embarrassed, confused, or disoriented. Talk to the athlete, comforting and reassuring him that you are there to help and that EMS is on the way. Stay with the athlete until EMS arrives. Whether he is unconscious or conscious and breathing after the seizure is over, the best position to place the athlete in is the modified HAINES position (Blake et al., 2002).

The mildest seizures are absence or petit mal seizures. Unlike tonic-clonic seizures that exhibit various signs and symptoms, absence seizures have subtle signs and symptoms. Consequently, it is not as easy to determine if an athlete is experiencing an absence seizure. Children are more likely to have petit mal seizures than adults are. During this time, the child appears to be staring at an object and daydreaming with a dazed look on his face. For a short amount of time he will be unable to respond to your voice, because he is oblivious to his surroundings. Usually as the child gets older, the absence seizures will stop.

As with tonic-clonic seizures, allow the absence seizure to run its course. The seizure usually resolves in less than 20 seconds, typically with no injury. Attempt to arouse the athlete by talking to him, calling his name, and saying, "Are you okay?" Do not shake the athlete. Stay with the athlete until the seizure is over, and comfort him once he becomes aware of his surroundings. EMS is rarely necessary to treat an athlete who has sustained an absence seizure, because emergency situations do not typically result. However, refer the athlete to his physician for a thorough examination.

Choking

When a conscious athlete has food, drink, or any other object in her mouth, the possibility of choking is real. Choking occurs when the object goes into the trachea and blocks air flow when an athlete is conscious or unconscious. Most often choking athletes are conscious. For example, an athlete can choke when she is eating and talking at the same time. When an athlete is conscious and coughing or talking due to an object entering her airway, then she is getting sufficient oxygen to supply her brain. Encourage her to continue coughing. By having the athlete cough, the object may dislodge from the airway and be expelled. However, if she cannot cough, speak, or breathe, or has a high-pitched wheeze or squeal sound coming from her, then her airway is sufficiently blocked. At this point you must give the athlete abdominal thrusts, which some people refer to as the Heimlich maneuver (**Figure 5-12**). Ask the athlete, "Are you choking?" If she nods, then ask her if you can assist her. If she nods, then she has given you consent to help her. Both of you must stand; position yourself behind the athlete. Support the athlete and deliver five back blows between the shoulder blades with the heel of your hand. Then wrap your arms around the athlete's waist, and put your thumb into your right hand and make a fist. Find the athlete's navel with your left hand's middle finger, with your index finger lying next to your middle finger. Then place the thumb side of your right fist above your index finger above the navel. Place your left hand over your right hand and deliver five slow, controlled, strong thrusts to the abdomen. Deliver these thrusts in and upward to the abdomen in

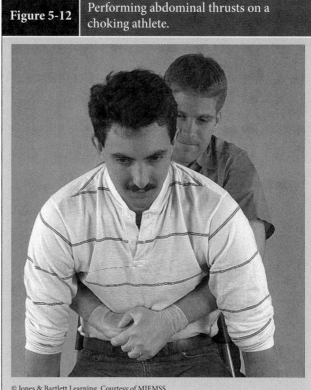

Figure 5-12 Performing abdominal thrusts on a choking athlete.

© Jones & Bartlett Learning. Courtesy of MIEMSS.

single attempts. Continue the five back blows and five abdominal thrusts until the object is expelled and the athlete is able to breathe or until your athlete goes unconscious. If the object is expelled and the athlete is able to breathe, monitor her breathing. If she is having any difficulties breathing or has any pain resulting from the choking incident, then call 911. If a previously conscious and choking athlete becomes unconscious have someone call 911 and apply your CPR skills until EMS arrives.

If the food or object does not dislodge after a short period of time, the athlete will not have enough oxygen to the brain. Consequently, she will become unconscious and still be choking. To assist an unconscious choking adult athlete, begin to perform your CPR skills. Compress the chest 30 times at a rate of 100 compressions per minute, and then look in the mouth to see if the object has been dislodged. If the object is in the mouth, remove it with a finger and attempt to deliver two rescue breaths utilizing your pocket mask. If you do not see an object in the athlete's mouth, deliver two rescue breaths, and then continue with 30 compressions. This cycle of 30 compressions, object check, and two rescue breaths continues until the athlete begins to breathe, air goes into the athlete but the athlete is still not breathing (which will require you to begin full CPR), another qualified person or EMS arrives to take over for you, or you are too exhausted to continue.

Shock

Whenever an injury or illness occurs, a life-threatening condition called shock can result. Shock is the body's reaction to the loss of or diminished blood flow to the body. Blood is shunted away from the body's core. Consequently, the hemoglobin in the red blood cells is unable to supply the brain and vital organs with oxygen. If shock is not treated immediately, then the athlete can die.

Various types of shock can occur to an athlete. A common type of shock that occurs as a result of injury is hemorrhagic shock. For example, hemorrhagic shock occurs when a vein or artery is severed and the athlete is bleeding externally or internally. The shock causes a decreased quantity of blood in the circulatory system. Therefore, adequate blood and oxygen are not delivered throughout the body to sustain proper function.

Hypovolemic shock occurs with a loss of body fluids. If an athlete has an illness that involves severe diarrhea and vomiting, dehydration may occur. If the athlete is not taking in adequate fluids to replenish the fluids he or she has lost, hypovolemic shock may occur due to the dehydration.

During and after a heart attack, an athlete can experience cardiogenic shock. When a heart attack occurs, a diminished quantity of blood flows through the body. Consequently, lack of oxygen is delivered to the body tissues and leads to shock.

Psychogenic shock is brought on by witnessing or hearing about a drastic event. The athlete then experiences various emotions such as fear or grief. These emotions can cause the athlete to go into shock. For example, an athlete is lifting weights at We R Fit Gym. He decides to perform cleans as part of his workout, and increases the weight from his last session. As he lifts the bar, he cannot handle the increased weight, and his right shoulder dislocates. The athlete looks at his shoulder, which is severely deformed, and due to the pain he is overcome with fear. He immediately goes into psychogenic shock. In this case, the athlete's blood vessels quickly become dilated, resulting in blood moving away from the brain and vital organs, which diminishes the organs' oxygen supply.

Neurogenic shock typically occurs when an athlete experiences severe spinal cord trauma. This trauma results in spontaneous **autonomic nervous system (ANS)** dysfunction. Signs of neurogenic shock include hypotension, or low blood pressure; bradycardia; and neurological disruption. The hypotension causes blood to move toward the

> **Autonomic nervous system**   Controls automatic bodily functions such as the abdominal organs, pupils, heart rate, breathing, digestion, and other unconscious or involuntary functions of the body.

extremities and away from the brain and core body. For example, a wide receiver is running a pattern across the middle of the field. He jumps up for a high pass. While he is airborne, the defender hits his legs, causing him to spin and flip over in the air. When the receiver lands, he hits the turf head first, sustaining a cervical spinal cord injury. Due to the nature of the injury, and that ANS signals to the blood vessels are disrupted, he immediately goes into neurogenic shock.

Other types of shock include septic shock and anaphylactic shock. Septic shock occurs when an athlete has a significant bacterial or fungal infection. The common bacteria *Streptococcus pneumonia*, which causes ear infections, meningitis, and pneumonia, is often the cause of septic shock (Centers for Disease Control and Prevention [CDC], 2008). The infection precipitates a series of events that result in lack of blood flow, which causes a lack of oxygen to the tissues. As with other types of shock, the heart has to work much harder in order to increase the blood flow and oxygen to the tissues. These events cause tissue death and possibly the athlete's death.

Anaphylactic shock also is a serious condition that can result in death. Anaphylactic shock is caused when an **allergen** enters the athlete's body. Common allergens include various nuts, especially peanuts; bee stings; shellfish; medications; latex; and dairy products. The effects of anaphylactic shock range from mild to life-threatening. A mild reaction includes hives or a rash appearing on the skin. However, in severe cases, the blood vessels dilate, become permeable, and release blood and fluid into the body. Swelling, most often around the face and neck, occurs as a result. Also, the respiratory passageways become swollen, which results in breathing difficulty. Consequently, within minutes the athlete cannot breathe and, if the condition is not treated quickly, the athlete will quickly become unconscious and die.

> **Allergen**   A substance or object that causes sensitivity or an allergy.

Most types of shock have similar signs and symptoms. The most common include a glassy-eyed stare; disorientation; agitation; irritability; confusion; nausea; thirst; pale, moist, and cool skin; sunken eyes; a rapid, weak pulse; decreased blood pressure; increased respiration rate; and dilated pupils. Certain types of shock also have very specific signs and symptoms. A sign of an athlete experiencing cardiogenic shock is neck vein protrusion. Septic shock will also result in fever and red skin. Anaphylactic shock has signs and symptoms of hives, breathing difficulty, fainting, and unconsciousness.

After you have recognized that your athlete is experiencing shock, immediately provide care. Signs and symptoms of shock can be reversed if proper and immediate treatment is given. However, if an athlete has been in shock for some time and immediate care is not provided, then death can occur. When you identify that an athlete is in hemorrhagic, hypovolemic, neurogenic, or psychogenic shock, help the athlete lay down comfortably on her back with her feet raised approximately 8 to 12 inches, in an attempt to redistribute blood to the core body. If the athlete has a significant lower body injury, such as a dislocation or fracture, or has sustained a spinal injury, do not raise the feet because you may cause further harm. Because the blood has been shunted away from the core of the athlete's body, she may shiver and feel cold. Keep the athlete warm by putting a blanket, a jacket, or any soft material over her (**Figure 5-13**). If she has lost blood and fluid, she may feel thirsty. Do not give her anything to drink by mouth because she most likely will not be entirely coherent, and you would not want her to choke. While you are providing care, talk to and comfort her. Reassure her that she will be okay, and talk to her about other interests to take her mind off of the injury, illness, or situation at hand. If your athlete does not quickly return to a normal state within a few minutes, call 911 immediately.

If you suspect an athlete is in cardiogenic, septic, or anaphylactic shock, call 911 immediately. For an athlete in cardiogenic shock, be prepared to administer CPR if she goes into cardiac arrest. For anaphylactic shock, ask the athlete if she has an epinephrine auto-injector (one common brand is the Epi-pen); if so, assist her in obtaining it so she can administer it to herself immediately (**Figure 5-14**). Regardless of what type of shock the athlete is experiencing; the athlete's life is on the line. You must react immediately, care for the athlete, and summon advanced medical care.

Figure 5-13 Treating an athlete in shock includes talking to the victim; keeping her warm; raising her legs if she does not have a head, spine, or lower extremity injury; and calling 911.

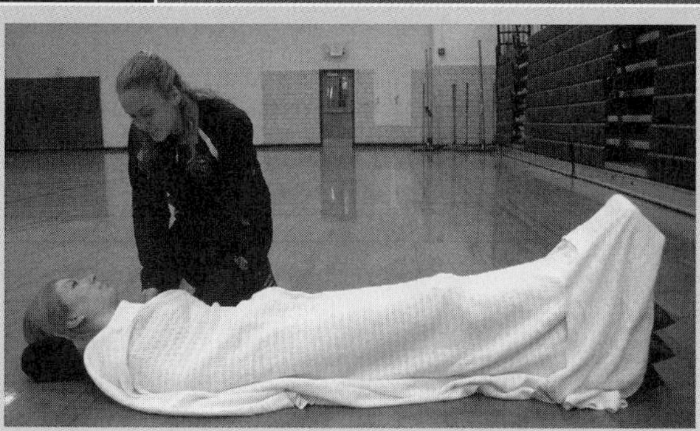

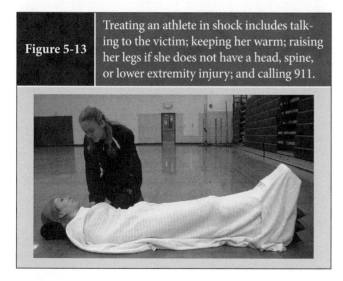

Figure 5-14 An Epinephrine auto-injector, such as an Epi-pen®, can reduce the signs and symptoms of anaphylactic shock, and assist in saving the athlete's life.

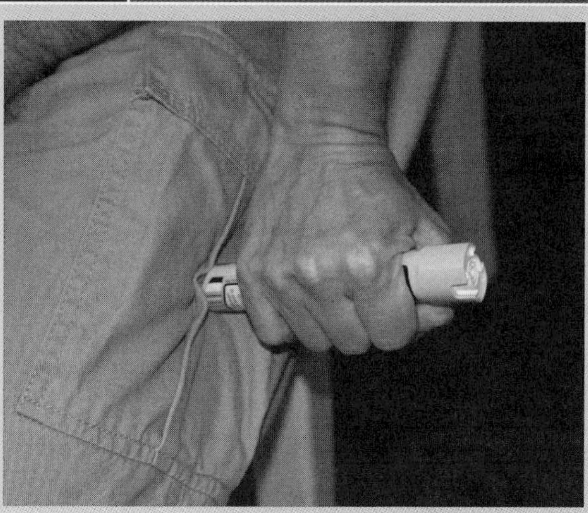

© Jones & Bartlett Learning. Courtesy of MIEMSS.

Asthma Exacerbations

Many athletes have a respiratory tract condition called asthma. Asthma is a chronic condition that occurs when the respiratory tract becomes inflamed and the bronchi become constricted. Typically, asthma exacerbations, formerly called "asthma attacks," occur due to an allergen or another substance detrimentally affecting the athlete's respiratory tract. Allergens and other substances that trigger asthma exacerbations include air pollution, smoke, aerosols, perfume and other strong-smelling substances, dust, medication, pet dander and fur, and food. Also, exercise and various emotions can cause asthma exacerbations.

Physiologically, asthma can occur due to inflammation, bronchospasm, or both. An allergen enters the respiratory tract, and over a period of time an inflammatory response is triggered. The inflammatory response onset occurs within minutes to weeks after allergen exposure. Airway inflammation of the bronchi and bronchioles occurs. The inflammation triggers the creation of mucous in these passageways, which causes decreased airflow. Acute exacerbations have a rapid onset and cause the bronchi and bronchioles to spasm. The smooth muscle lining of these passageways becomes constricted due to the muscles' contraction, which also decreases airflow (Gorse, Blanc, Feld, & Radelet, 2010) (**Figure 5-15**). Because the air entering the respiratory tract is decreased,

| Figure 5-15 | The effects of asthma on the smooth lining of the respiratory tract. |

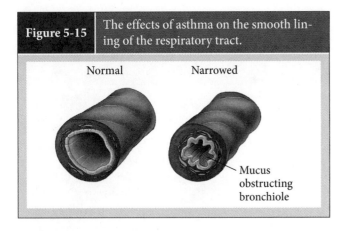

Normal   Narrowed

Mucus obstructing bronchiole

oxygen exchange in the lungs is also decreased. Consequently, asthma exacerbations are life-threatening.

Because asthma exacerbations are life-threatening, it is crucial to recognize the signs and symptoms of asthma exacerbation immediately. Common signs and symptoms include wheezing, shortness of breath, increased respiratory rate, coughing, chest tightness, headache, and nausea (Gorse et al., 2010; Mangus & Miller, 2005). Because the athlete is experiencing the effects of reduced airflow into her respiratory tract, she most likely will be anxious, nervous, and unsettled.

Proper immediate care for an athlete having an asthma exacerbation is essential. First, ask the athlete if she is asthmatic. If she says that she is, then ask her if she has medication. Most medications that help treat acute asthma exacerbations are called rescue inhalers. These rescue inhalers are metered dose inhalers (MDIs) that expel a specific dose of prescription medication (**Figure 5-16**). When taken properly, the MDIs typically alleviate acute asthma exacerbation signs and symptoms. In most instances these MDIs work very quickly to normalize the athlete's respiratory rate and quality. If your athlete says she has an MDI, help her obtain the medication and have her administer it as prescribed. If the medication does not relieve the symptoms shortly after administration, call 911. If she does not have her MDI with her, attempt to calm her down, put her in the most comfortable position to facilitate her breathing, and have her take slow, regulated, deep breaths. If the exacerbation does not subside within a couple of minutes, then call EMS. Also, if at any time her lips, face, nails, or skin turn **cyanotic**, then you need to call 911. If

| **Cyanotic**   A blue color of the skin that occurs when lack of oxygen and increased carbon dioxide are present in the tissues. |

the athlete is unaware that she is asthmatic and has an exacerbation, then treat her in the same manner as an asthmatic athlete who does not have an MDI.

Tips from the Field

Tip 2   If you have an asthmatic athlete who utilizes a rescue inhaler, ask if he or she can get an extra inhaler from his or her doctor to keep at the facility, depending on your facility's policies. For example, many public schools allow a student to have a spare inhaler stored in the nurse's office in a locked medicine cabinet. The spare inhaler must be labeled with the athlete's full prescription including the athlete's name, medication, dosage, and prescribing doctor. If your facility does not allow employees to store spare inhalers for its athletes, then suggest to your athlete to keep a spare inhaler with him or her at all times with his or her personal belongings. Your athlete will then always have the medication on hand in case of an asthma exacerbation. By always having a spare inhaler accessible to your athlete, you can assist your athlete in avoiding a major asthma exacerbation emergency.

Asthma can be life-threatening due to insufficient oxygen to the brain and vital organs. Consequently, when your athlete experiences an exacerbation, take a brief, thorough history and treat the athlete without delay.

Diabetic Emergencies

Diabetes mellitus is a condition characterized by high blood glucose (sugar) levels due to the pancreas being unable to properly produce the hormone insulin. Diabetes can also be caused by the body being unable to utilize the insulin that the pancreas has produced and secreted into the body. The body

| Figure 5-16 | Metered dose inhalers are used to decrease the signs and symptoms of an asthma exacerbation. |

Asthma medication for an attack.

Keep victim sitting up.

uses insulin to break down food, notably simple sugars and complex carbohydrates, so it can use these nutrients for energy.

Two types of diabetes exist. Type 1 was formerly known as juvenile-onset diabetes, and Type 2 was formerly known as adult-onset diabetes. In Type 1 diabetes the athlete's body does not produce insulin. Consequently, the athlete cannot break down sugar and carbohydrates. This type of diabetes typically is diagnosed in children and young adults. In order for an athlete with Type 1 diabetes to properly process food and for his body to function properly, the athlete must self-administer insulin and monitor his blood glucose daily. Consequently, Type 1 diabetes is sometimes referred to as *insulin-dependent diabetes*. Unlike those with Type 1 diabetes, athletes with Type 2 diabetes can produce insulin, but the body is not able to produce sufficient amounts or the body's cells are unable to utilize the insulin properly. Most often, athletes who are affected by Type 2 diabetes are those who are sedentary, overweight, and have improper dietary habits. Typically, athletes with Type 2 diabetes will be prescribed a nutritious, balanced, low-calorie diet in conjunction with a daily exercise program.

As with individuals with Type 1 diabetes, individuals with Type 2 diabetes must monitor their blood sugar levels daily. However, individuals with Type 2 diabetes may not need supplemental insulin in order to manage or treat their condition. Over time, a proper diet and adequate exercise may be sufficient to control the athlete's blood sugar levels at a normal range. If this treatment is not working to normalize the athlete's blood sugar levels, then insulin may be prescribed by his physician. Without adequate treatment for both Type 1 and Type 2 diabetes, various secondary illnesses, including, but not limited to, eye conditions, including retinopathy, glaucoma, cataracts, and blindness; foot conditions, including decreased circulation and nerve damage; ulcers; hearing loss; kidney disease; stroke; and skin disorders can result.

Signs and symptoms of diabetes mellitus include unusual, significant fatigue; hunger; weight loss; and thirst. Athletes with Type 2 diabetes also may feel tingling in their feet or hands, suffer from recurring infections, have skin wounds that do not heal quickly, and have blurred vision (American Diabetes Association, 2012). Whether an athlete has Type 1 or Type 2 diabetes, detrimental conditions can result. Hypoglycemia, hyperglycemia, and diabetic ketoacidosis are three potentially life-threatening conditions that can occur to a diabetic athlete (**Table 5-3**).

A diabetic athlete can experience hypoglycemia or low blood sugar. An athlete who exercises and does not eat nutritious snacks before exercise will break down sugar in the body and utilize it during activity. If the athlete does not eat carbohydrate snacks before, during, and after exercise, then sugar in the body is not replaced. Consequently, the body's sugar level will be very low. Another cause of hypoglycemia is high insulin and low sugar in the body. For example, a Type 1 diabetic athlete administers her daily insulin, but does not eat an appropriate quantity of food during the day. Her insulin level will be high and blood sugar level will be low. Signs and symptoms of hypoglycemia include dizziness, confusion, weakness, fatigue, and headaches. In severe cases hypoglycemia can lead to insulin shock. The athlete may lose consciousness, have a seizure, or fall into a coma (Miller & Berry, 2011).

Hyperglycemia or high blood sugar occurs when excess sugar is in the blood, insulin levels are too low, or insulin is not being used properly. For example, if a Type 1 diabetic athlete forgets to take his insulin, his blood glucose levels will become elevated throughout the course of the day as he eats. Signs and symptoms of hyperglycemia include glucose in the urine, as measured by chemstrips (**Figure 5-17**); glucose in the blood, as measured by self-monitoring blood glucose equipment; and increased appetite, thirst, and urination (Miller & Berry, 2011).

Hyperglycemia can lead to a life-threatening condition called diabetic coma, also known as diabetic ketoacidosis. Diabetic ketoacidosis occurs when the athlete's blood glucose levels remain high and the athlete's body is unable to effectively utilize the glucose for energy. Consequently, the body uses fat as an energy source instead of glucose. The athlete will

Table 5-3	Signs and Symptoms of Hypoglycemia, Hyperglycemia, and Diabetic Ketoacidosis	
Hypoglycemia	**Hyperglycemia**	**Diabetic Ketoacidosis**
Dizziness	Glucose in the urine as measured by chemstrips	Signs and symptoms of hyperglycemia as well as:
Confusion	Increased appetite	Fruity-smelling breath
Weakness	Increased thirst	Fatigue
Fatigue	Increased urination	Nausea
Headache		Breathing difficulty
Seizure		Muscle aches
Loss of consciousness		Blurred vision
Coma		

Figure 5-17	Chemstrips dipped into urine can detect levels of blood glucose.

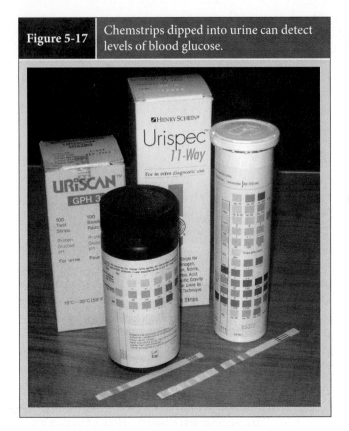

Figure 5-18	If an athlete is experiencing hypoglycemia, give them a small amount of glucose.

Tips from the Field

Tip 3   In order to prepare for an athlete who is experiencing hypoglycemia, keep a small tube of flavored cake icing (noting the expiration date) or sugar packets in your first aid kit. If one of your diabetic athletes has low blood sugar signs and symptoms, have them ingest one of these simple sugars to immediately raise their blood glucose. The flavored icing works well because it is palatable and can be squirted easily into the athlete's mouth.

exhibit and experience signs and symptoms of hyperglycemia, along with a fruity-smelling breath due to the production of ketones. Ketones are chemicals created by the body when fat is broken down and utilized by the body as an energy source. Other signs and symptoms of diabetic ketoacidosis include fatigue, nausea, breathing difficulty, muscle aches, and blurred vision (Mangus & Miller, 2005).

Whenever you recognize that an athlete is exhibiting signs and symptoms of diabetes mellitus, take your athlete's history and ask her if she is diabetic. If she says that she does not know if she is diabetic or has not had her blood glucose levels tested recently, then recommend that she promptly see her physician to be examined. An athlete's treatment varies depending on whether she exhibits signs and symptoms of hypoglycemia, hyperglycemia, or diabetic ketoacidosis. To treat an athlete with hypoglycemia, have her ingest a small amount of simple sugars. Give her a small spoonful of granulated sugar, a few sips of orange juice, or glucose tablets or gel, provided she is completely coherent (**Figure 5-18**). Once the sugar is in her body, the signs and symptoms of hypoglycemia should decrease rapidly, and the athlete should return to a normal state very quickly. If the athlete does not progressively return to a normal state within a few minutes, then immediately refer the athlete to her physician or EMS.

If the athlete is experiencing hyperglycemia, ask her if she has taken her insulin that day. If she has not taken her insulin and has it with her, then have her administer it immediately. If the athlete does not have her insulin with her or does not take insulin, then refer her to a physician or summon EMS immediately. Athletes who continuously have bouts of hyperglycemia must be put on a strict exercise and diet regimen. For Type 2 diabetics, insulin may be prescribed to control the high blood sugar.

If at any time you smell an athlete's breath and it is fruity-smelling, or you see signs of diabetic ketoacidosis, give her water to drink and have her administer her insulin immediately. Call her physician to see if she can be examined immediately. If the athlete's physician is not available, dial 911 to summon EMS. Diabetic ketoacidosis can result in coma or death if not treated immediately.

Environmental Emergencies

Our athletes frequently exercise indoors, in places such as gyms or clinics. To keep our athletes motivated and interested in exercise, we can vary their specific exercises and change the exercise environment. When working with an athlete outdoors, educate him or her in regard to heat- and cold-related illnesses, along with the danger of lightning.

Heat Illnesses

Heat illnesses typically occur outdoors when the environmental temperature and **relative humidity** are high. When the relative humidity is high, the air carries a large quantity of water molecules. When we exercise, our muscles and core body create heat. As the environment increases

> **Relative humidity** The number of water molecules in the air, which is designated by the percent of air saturation.

in temperature, our body temperature also increases. In order to eliminate heat, the body sweats. The sweat is dissipated into the air by evaporation of the water molecules that comprise the sweat. The air can readily accept these water molecules provided that the air is not saturated with water molecules. Less evaporation will occur as the relative humidity increases. Consequently, the athlete's body will not sufficiently eliminate heat, and will be in danger of succumbing to heat illness. The hot, humid environment predisposes an athlete exercising outdoors to various heat illnesses including heat syncope, heat cramps, heat exhaustion, and heat stroke.

Heat syncope occurs when an athlete is exercising in the hot, humid environment and becomes dizzy and lightheaded. As a result he suddenly faints (Binkley, Beckett, Casa, Kleiner, & Plummer, 2002). Fainting typically occurs due to blood vessel vasodilation, blood pooling at the extremities, and dehydration (CDC, 2011). When an athlete faints and falls to the ground, the blood is then redistributed to the vital organs and brain. After fainting, the athlete typically returns to full consciousness within a short amount of time.

After noticing the athlete has fainted, approach him immediately and perform a primary survey. Make sure that he has no life-threatening conditions; if he does, then call 911 and care for him immediately. Remove the athlete from the environment and bring him to a cool environment such as a room with fans or air conditioning. Have the athlete sit comfortably while drinking plenty of cool water or low carbohydrate drinks to rehydrate. The athlete should revert back to his normal state shortly with rest, external cooling of the body, and rehydration.

Heat cramps are involuntary, painful muscle spasms that typically occur at the gastrocnemius or abdominal muscles while exercising in a hot, humid environment (Binkley et al., 2002). As with heat syncope, heat cramps can be a result of dehydration and a lack of electrolytes in the body. The athlete will be sweating and fatigued. Due to the muscle pain and cramping, the athlete will stop his activity. At this point, care

for the athlete by having him rest in a cool environment. Give him water or electrolyte drinks in order to rehydrate. Assist him in massaging and gently performing static stretches for the involved muscles. You can also apply ice or perform ice massage on the painful muscles. Once the athlete is rehydrated and the pain and cramps are alleviated, the athlete can return to activity with caution. However, it is prudent to recommend to the athlete to continue his exercise session indoors where the temperature is controlled and heat illness is unlikely.

Heat exhaustion is notably more serious than heat syncope or heat cramps. After exercising in the hot, humid environment for a period of time, the athlete loses a significant amount of water and electrolytes. If the athlete does not continuously replace the fluids, then he most likely will succumb to heat exhaustion. Signs and symptoms of heat exhaustion are profuse sweating; pale skin; rapid, weak pulse; increased respirations; lightheadedness; and dizziness. The athlete's core body temperature will be elevated toward 104°F, and he will have clammy, moist skin (Binkley et al., 2002; CDC, 2011).

To care for a person experiencing heat exhaustion, immediately move him to a cool area, preferably one with air conditioning and/or fans. Remove all sweaty clothes, except for undergarments in order to be discreet, so the surrounding air can cool the skin and sweat evaporation can occur (Binkley et al., 2002). Apply ice packs or ice towels to the athlete's body, especially at the neck, armpits, and groin. Have the athlete rehydrate by drinking water or electrolyte drinks. Although some researchers state that in order to effectively monitor an athlete's core body temperature, you must utilize a rectal thermometer (Binkley et al., 2002), the use of this device is beyond the scope of your training and you should not utilize this temperature monitoring method. Instead, utilize a temporal or oral thermometer to consistently monitor the athlete's core body temperature, and determine if your efforts to decrease the temperature are working. Once the athlete has returned to a normal state, he should rest for the remainder of the day. Refer the athlete to a physician if your athlete has more than one bout of heat exhaustion. Call EMS if your athlete does not show a progressive decrease in heat exhaustion signs and symptoms as you are providing care.

Heat exhaustion can progress to a more serious, life-threatening condition called heat stroke. Heat stroke occurs when the athlete's body is unable to regulate the core temperature. The athlete is severely dehydrated, his pulse is rapid and strong, and his respirations are increased. The athlete's core body temperature may go up to 106°F. His skin appears hot, red, and dry. However, an athlete who has just been sweating will still have sweat on his body when in heat stroke, so his skin will not be dry. The athlete is extremely disoriented, and does not respond to your questions or commands. The athlete can become unconscious and slip into a coma at any time. Therefore, heat stroke is a medical emergency and the athlete must be transported to a hospital via EMS immediately. After calling 911, provide quick, immediate care to the athlete. Similarly to heat exhaustion, move him to a cool environment, preferably with air conditioning. Other than his undergarments, remove his hot, sweaty clothes. Place him in a cold immersion tub up to his neck (Binkley et al., 2002), making sure that he does not slip under water. Monitor his core body temperature continually. When the core body temperature decreases to 102°F, you can remove him from the tub to prevent further cooling and harm to the athlete (Binkley et al., 2002). Do not give him any fluids by mouth. He will not be able to control his intake because he will not be entirely conscious, or conscious at all, and could aspirate the fluid. Heat stroke can cause death, so you must provide this emergency care to your athlete quickly.

Tips from the Field

Tip 4   If you do not have access to a cold immersion tub to cool an athlete who is experiencing heat stroke, an effective means to bring down the body temperature is by saturating towels in an ice water bucket, and then spreading them out on the athlete, avoiding the athlete's eyes, nose and mouth. Pour ice all over the towels. With the wet towels on the athlete, the ice will more readily adhere to the towels and consequently cool the athlete. If you apply loose ice to the athlete's skin, it will slide off his or her body and not effectively decrease core body temperature.

Educate your athlete on preventative measures so he will not be afflicted with a heat illness. Your athlete should be certain that he is hydrated before, during, and after exercise. He should drink approximately 8 ounces of water or electrolyte fluid every 15 minutes. Advise him to wear light-colored and -textured clothing, which wicks sweat and heat away from the body. Monitor the environment by utilizing a heat index chart to determine if the athlete can safely exercise outdoors (**Figure 5-19**). A heat index chart utilizes relative humidity (%) and temperature (°F) to predict the chance of the athlete succumbing to heat illness if he participates in prolonged physical activity outdoors. A high heat index is high relative humidity along with high temperature, which creates a scenario of extreme danger for athletes participating in prolonged activity outside. If the heat index indicates that your athlete is in danger of heat illness, have him exercise inside if possible. Also, even if the heat index indicates less likelihood of the athlete succumbing to heat illness, have him exercise during the morning

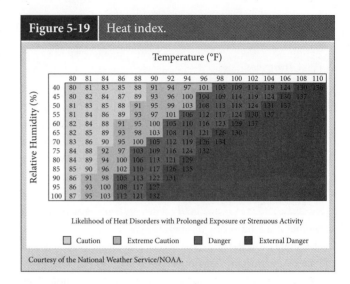

Figure 5-19 | Heat index.

Likelihood of Heat Disorders with Prolonged Exposure or Strenuous Activity

☐ Caution   ☐ Extreme Caution   ☐ Danger   ☐ External Danger

Courtesy of the National Weather Service/NOAA.

or evening when the environment is less hot and humid. If the athlete wishes to exercise outdoors, he must acclimatize his body and spend short amounts of time exercising each day in the hot, humid environment. In time, his body will become accustomed to working in this environment, which assists in preventing heat illness. Overall, in order to prevent heat illness, the athlete must be cautious and adjust his behaviors if he wants to successfully exercise outdoors in a hot, humid environment.

Cold Illnesses

As with heat illnesses, athletes can sustain cold illnesses when exercising outdoors. Cold illnesses include frostnip, frostbite, and hypothermia. Although low environmental temperatures can cause cold illnesses, if the environmental conditions are also wet (i.e., rain or snow) and windy, then the chances of an athlete sustaining a cold illness is higher than with cold air alone. Consequently, athletes should take precautions in exercising in the cold as they would in the heat.

Normal body temperature is approximately 98.6°F. In order for the body to create heat in cold temperatures, it shivers. When body temperature drops even slightly from the athlete's norm, shivering occurs. Along with shivering, the body attempts to protect itself by shunting blood away from the extremities toward the trunk, vital organs, and brain in an attempt to provide adequate oxygen to these areas. Because the blood is moving away from the extremities, areas such as the fingers and toes, as well as unprotected areas such as the nose and ears, are susceptible to frostnip and frostbite. When the body temperature decreases further, to about 95°F, then the body becomes hypothermic.

Frostnip is the least severe of the three cold illnesses. Frostnip occurs when the athlete is in the cold for a period of time and his or her body temperature decreases. The fingers, toes, ears, cheeks, and nose are typically affected. Ice crystals form within these tissues. The tissues feel very cold and begin to lose color and feeling. Fortunately, as soon as the tissues are warmed up the ice crystals dissipate. Warm the tissues by putting them in proximity to warm air (blowing on them) or a warm object (by a heating element), or by putting them in the armpits (an area of core body warmth). The athlete should not rub the area. The athlete will not suffer permanent tissue damage with frostnip.

Most athletes utilize the term *frostbite* for what is truly frostnip. Frostbite is more severe than frostnip and can affect the superficial or deep tissues. Typically, frostbite affects the same areas as frostnip, such as the ears, nose, fingers, toes, and cheeks. Superficial frostbite begins when ice crystals form in the tissues, which become frozen. The athlete's skin appears waxy and without typical color due to the lack of oxygen. The athlete complains of numbness and loss of function due to tissue stiffness. Over time, if the athlete does not get out of the cold environment, then his or her condition can turn into deep frostbite. With deep frostbite, the tissues are so numb that the affected areas are no longer painful. The tissues are extremely hard and cannot be moved either actively or passively. Blisters typically begin to form on the skin (**Figure 5-20**). As with frostnip, the athlete must get out of the cold environment and rewarm the area immediately. Help him or her remove any wet and cold clothing, put on dry clothing, and cover him- or herself with warm blankets. Place the frostbitten body part in warm, but not hot, water. The athlete can also use warm water bottles to assist in warming the area. If blisters are present,

dress the blisters with nonadherent gauze pads and dressings, in order to prevent infection and the tissues from sticking to each other. While you are treating the athlete for frostbite, call 911 to have him or her transported to an emergency room for immediate treatment.

Hypothermia is the most severe of the three cold-related illnesses. This life-threatening illness occurs with prolonged exposure to the cold environment. The body temperature decreases to 95°F or lower. The body conserves heat and oxygen in the blood by moving it to the brain and vital organs. The blood vessels also become constricted. The athlete begins to have major nervous system and brain dysfunction. He or she becomes confused, disoriented, and lethargic. The athlete's speech is slurred, vision is impaired, and gait and body movement are uncoordinated. The body tissues are hard and stiff. The athlete experiences intense shivering until the body temperature falls to 86°F, when shivering stops. Eventually, if the athlete does not get out of the cold environment and get advanced medical care immediately, the athlete's heart rhythm will become dangerously irregular, and his or her breathing rate and quality will be significantly decreased. Ultimately, without emergency care, the hypothermic athlete will become unconscious, enter into a coma, and die. Therefore, your first priority is to make sure he or she is out of the cold and call 911. Lay the athlete down and attempt to rewarm him or her by removing cold, wet clothing and replacing it with many layers of warm blankets over the entire head and body. In order to allow adequate breathing, do not cover the nose and mouth. Stay with the athlete and be prepared to give CPR if necessary.

To prevent cold-related illnesses, an athlete must take precautions when exercising in the cold, wet, windy weather. If at all possible, suggest to your athletes to avoid exercising in extremely cold, wet, windy weather. A wind chill chart will assist you in determining how readily your athletes can sustain cold-related illnesses (**Figure 5-21**).

If your athlete insists on exercising in cold, wet, and windy conditions, educate him or her to wear appropriate clothing that insulates his or her body. Many exercise clothing companies have formulated fabrics that help keep the body warm in the cold. Layered clothing maintains an insulated state, and keeps body heat around the body. If the athlete gets too warm while exercising, he or she can remove clothing to regulate his or her body temperature. All extremities, as well as the head, must be adequately covered. Have the athlete continually hydrate when exercising in cold environments, just as he or she would in hot, humid environments. He or she should drink plenty of water and electrolyte drinks. Being hydrated assists the athlete's body to maintain its water balance and proper blood flow to the extremities and core.

| Figure 5-20 | Frostbite commonly affects the fingers and toes. Blisters will form on the skin. |

Courtesy of Neil Malcom Winkelmann

Figure 5-21	Wind chill chart.

Wind Chill (°F) = 35.73 + 0.6215T - 35.75 (V$^{0.16}$) + 0.4275T (V$^{0.16}$)
Where, T = Air Temperature (°F)   V = Wind Speed (mph)

Courtesy of the National Weather Service/NOAA.

▌ Lightning Injuries

Lightning is a potentially fatal environmental hazard for athletes who exercise outside. The Federal Emergency Management Agency (FEMA) (2013) states on its website that lightning is one of the top three most common storm-related killers in the United States. Therefore, our athletes must avoid exercising outside when a thunderstorm is approaching. Educate your athletes to utilize weather reports or phone apps to determine if lightning or a thunderstorm is probable prior to exercising outdoors. If your athlete is caught outside and an unexpected thunderstorm is approaching, have him or her move quickly indoors into an enclosed building. If a building is not nearby, then the athlete should get into a car. If the athlete is outside without any shelter, he or she should squat down low, in a position similar to that of a baseball catcher. This position makes the athlete less likely to be struck by lightning. Also, because the athlete does not have significant body surface area on the ground, he or she will be less likely to be injured from a nearby strike as compared to if he or she was lying or sitting on the ground.

You can determine approximately how far away the thunderstorm is from your location by utilizing the flash-to-bang and 30/30 methods, or a commercial lightning detector. Begin the flash-to-bang method when you first see lightning. Begin counting until you hear the thunderclap. Then, divide the number of seconds by five. The result is how many miles the lightning is from your location. Utilize the 30/30 rule with the flash-to-bang method. If you hear thunder after 30 seconds of seeing a lightning flash, lightning is only 6 miles away and a strike is imminent. Therefore, leave the location

and take cover immediately. Do not go back outside until 30 minutes after the last sound of thunder. The flash-to-bang and 30/30 methods are very basic methods of determining when a lightning strike is imminent in your location. If you will be working with your athletes outside on a regular basis, consider purchasing a lightning detector. This electronic equipment detects lightning up to 40 miles away, which gives you ample preparation time to get inside. Effective, accurate lightning detectors can be costly, but are well worth the expense because they can save lives.

SUMMARY

Numerous injuries and illnesses affect your athletes. Some of these injuries and illnesses comprise an emergency because they place your athletes in life-threatening situations. Your role as a professional is to recognize the signs and symptoms of these emergency situations without delay. Your role in emergency care is to treat the athlete appropriately and summon EMS in order to give the athlete the best chance of survival.

DISCUSSION QUESTIONS

1. What is the purpose of a primary survey? What must you determine when performing a primary survey on an athlete?
2. Describe four different types of injuries or illnesses that would cause an athlete to become unconscious.
3. Describe how you would use an AED on an athlete that is in cardiac arrest.
4. What is a stroke? Describe the signs and symptoms of a stroke.
5. When faced with an athlete who is having a grand mal seizure, how should you care for the athlete to minimize the potential for injury?
6. Describe in detail how you would care for a conscious, choking adult athlete.
7. Name the different types of shock that commonly occur to athletes. How must you care for an athlete in shock? When must you summon EMS when a person is in shock?
8. What are the different types of diabetic emergencies?
9. Describe the various types of heat illness that an athlete can succumb to when exercising. What are the signs and symptoms for the different types of heat illnesses? How would you treat each of the heat illnesses? What measures can be taken by the athlete to prevent heat illness?

CASE STUDY 1: CLASSROOM SEIZURE

Derek is a healthy 16-year-old at Anywhere High School. He is a star member of the varsity soccer team who trains year-round. Derek has no health issues and no history of any ailments in his family. During health class, Derek is watching a video with his classmates when suddenly he slumps to the side of his desk and begins to have a tonic-clonic, grand mal seizure. His head and upper and lower body begin to shake uncontrollably. The students that are sitting near Derek panic, rush out of their seats, and run to the front of the room near the teacher. Ralph, Derek's best friend, runs over to him and grabs Derek from the back, holding Derek's arms tightly to prevent him from falling to the floor. After approximately 30 seconds, saliva and blood begin to ooze out of Derek's mouth. While restraining Derek, Ralph gets hit in the nose by the back of Derek's head, giving Ralph a nose bleed. Ralph lets go of Derek, who immediately falls out of the chair, hitting his head on one of the desks as he falls to the floor. After about 1 minute, the seizure subsides and Derek's body relaxes.

Upon coming out of the seizure, Derek finds himself lying on the classroom floor. He is groggy and anxious. Derek sees his classmates and teacher hovering over him. He looks around in confusion, and he does not know what happened to him and why he is lying on the floor. Derek complains that he feels tired, his head and body are sore, and he does not remember what just happened. The teacher helps Derek up and has him sit in a chair. She calls the nurse, who then calls 911. Derek is quickly transported to the hospital for further evaluation.

1. What should the teacher have done to ensure that all of the students, including Derek, were safe from harm during the seizure?
2. Was it appropriate for Ralph to restrain Derek? Why or why not?
3. Why do you think Derek was bleeding from the mouth?
4. Why was Derek sore and tired after the seizure?
5. What were the proper steps to take to give Derek appropriate care during and after the seizure?

CASE STUDY 2: SHOCK IN THE GYM

On an early Saturday morning in We R Fit Gym, a 30-year-old client, Tom, was partaking in his usual workout. He was performing three sets of 10 repetitions of bilateral bicep curls using 65-pound dumbbells. When Tom completed his exercise sets, he went to put the dumbbell weights back on the rack. However, due to the sweat dripping down his arms and on his hands, his right hand lost grasp of the dumbbell. Tom dropped the dumbbell onto the top of his foot, and he screamed out in excruciating pain. The surrounding clients were alerted by Tom's screams and summoned the personal trainer, Dave, who was nearby on the floor. When Dave arrived, Tom was sitting in a chair with his sneaker and sock off of his injured foot, crying and grabbing his foot. Immediately, Dave noticed that Tom had significant deformity and bleeding on his foot. It appeared that two metatarsal bones were protruding from Tom's foot.

Within seconds, Tom began to become agitated. His face turned pale, and his eyes became glassy. When Dave asked him what happened, Tom seemed disoriented and confused. Tom answered Dave and said that his foot was broken, and then said he was cold and thirsty. Upon hearing that Tom was thirsty, another client gave him his water bottle to drink from. After looking at his deformed, bleeding foot, Dave panicked. He then became agitated, irritable, and shaken up, because he did not like the site of blood and did not know what to do to help Tom. Another personal trainer, Mary, went over to Tom to see what the commotion was all about. When Mary arrived, she saw that not only Tom was in distress, but also her coworker Dave. She realized that both victims would be in grave danger if someone did not take immediate action. Consequently, Mary called 911 immediately, and then waited with Tom and Dave for the ambulance.

1. Other than Tom's fractured foot, what condition are Tom and Dave suffering from?
2. How should the two victims be treated prior to the arrival of EMS?
3. Could Dave's condition have been prevented? If so, what could have been done?
4. What actions were taken by all parties involved in this emergency situation that were improper and could have made the situation worse?

REFERENCES

American Academy of Orthopaedic Surgeons (AAOS). (2012). *First aid, CPR, and AED Standard* (6th ed.). Sudbury, MA: Jones and Bartlett.

American Diabetes Association. (2012). Symptoms. Retrieved February 14, 2012, from http://www.diabetes.org/diabetes-basics/symptoms/

American Red Cross. (2012). Hands-only CPR for witnessed sudden collapse. Retrieved January 28, 2012, from http://www.redcross.org/images/MEDIA_CustomProductCatalog/m6440194_HandsOnlyCPRsheet.pdf

American Red Cross. (2013). Learn hands-only CPR. Retrieved March 11, 2013, from http://www.redcross.org/prepare/hands-only-cpr

Binkley, H. M., Beckett, J., Casa, D. J., Kleiner, D. M., & Plummer, P. E. (2002). National Athletic Trainers' Association position statement: Exertional heat illnesses. *Journal of Athletic Training*, 37(3), 329–343.

Blake, W. E., Stillman, B. C., Eizenberg, N., Briggs, C., & McMeeken, J. M. (2002). The position of the spine in the recovery position—An experimental comparison between the lateral recovery position and the modified HAINES position. *Resuscitation*, 53(3), 289–297. Retrieved March 11, 2013, from http://search.ebscohost.com

Centers for Disease Control and Prevention (CDC). (2011, July 19). Heat stress. Retrieved April 24, 2012, from http://www.cdc.gov/niosh/topics/heatstress/

Centers for Disease Control and Prevention (CDC). (2008). *Streptococcus pneumoniae* disease. Retrieved February 12, 2012, from http://www.cdc.gov/ncidod/dbmd/diseaseinfo/streppneum_t.htm

Das, B. K., Karmakar, P. S., Santra, G., Mandal, B., Datta, P. K., Roy, M. K., & Das, T. (2011, June). Awareness of stroke among elderly public in Eastern India. *Neurology Asia*, 16(2), 119–126. Retrieved March 11, 2013, from http://search.ebscohost.com

Federal Emergency Management Agency (FEMA). (2013, March 7). Thunderstorms & lightning. Retrieved March 11, 2013, from http://www.ready.gov/thunderstorms-lightning

Gorse, K., Blanc, R., Feld, F., & Radelet, M. (2010). *Emergency care in athletic training*. Philadelphia: F. A. Davis.

Mangus, B. C., & Miller, M. G. (2005). *Pharmacology application in athletic training*. Philadelphia: F. A. Davis.

Mayo Clinic. (2011). Ventricular fibrillation. Retrieved January 28, 2012, from http://www.mayoclinic.com/health/ventricular-fibrillation/DS01158

MedlinePlus. (2010). Ventricular tachycardia. Retrieved January 28, 2012, from http://www.nlm.nih.gov/medlineplus/ency/article/000187.htm

Miller, M. G., & Berry, D. C. (2011). *Emergency response management for athletic trainers*. Philadelphia: Lippincott, Williams, and Wilkins.

Rho, R. W., & Page, R. L. (2007). The automated external defibrillator. *Journal of Cardiovascular Electrophysiology*, 18(8), 896–899. doi: 10.1111/j.1540-8167.2007.00822.x.

Chapter 6

Basic Injury Examination and Care

CHAPTER OBJECTIVES

After you have read this chapter, you will be able to understand:

- The differences between a primary survey and a secondary survey
- The components of a basic injury examination
- The HOPS process
- When and how to properly move an injured or ill athlete
- How to utilize RICE for athlete injury care
- When to refer an athlete for further medical evaluation or to summon EMS

THE BASIC INJURY EXAMINATION

The primary survey is the first step you take to care for your athletes when they have sustained an injury or illness. If your athlete experiences a life-threatening emergency, you will be able perform a primary survey and obtain advanced emergency medical care. However, your care will go beyond the primary survey. Once you have ascertained that your athlete has no apparent life-threatening conditions, is conscious and breathing, or is not in shock or bleeding severely, you will continue to care for the athlete by performing a basic injury examination, otherwise known as a secondary survey. The basic injury examination is a step-by-step, organized process that helps you determine the non-life-threatening conditions that exist. By performing the secondary survey, you will be able to determine the athlete's specific injury or illness, the

appropriate immediate care, and whether medical referral or emergency care is warranted.

Severity, Irritability, Nature, and Stage of Injury

The secondary survey helps you to pinpoint the severity, irritability, nature, and stage (SINS) of the athlete's injury or illness (Schultz, Houglum, & Perrin, 2010). The *severity* of the injury is the degree or extent of structural damage. For example, ligaments can be sprained and muscles can be strained to various degrees—Grade 1 or first degree is considered a mild injury; Grade 2 or second degree is considered a moderate injury; and Grade 3 or third degree is considered a severe injury. With Grade 3 injuries there is an increased possibility that the athlete will need to be referred to a physician or emergency personnel.

Irritability is determined by what the athlete tells you in regard to his or her symptoms. The extent of pain and the actual injury determine the injury's irritability. Ask the athlete if she or he has pain; if she or he says yes, then ask her or him to describe the pain. She or he may describe the pain as sharp, dull, burning, aching, tingling, or radiating. The description can lead you to determine the type of injury. For example, sharp pain is indicative of a fracture. Dull and aching pain occurs with a muscle strain or ligament sprain. Burning, tingling, and radiating pain are signs of a neurological injury. Utilize a pain scale to quantify how much pain he or she is experiencing. Ask, "On a scale of 1 to 10, with 10 being the most pain that you have ever experienced, rate your pain right now." Be sure to ask what caused the most pain that he or she has ever experienced. By identifying the circumstances in which he or she was in the most pain, you can compare the pain from the past experience to the present injury or illness. This comparison gives you an idea of the athlete's pain tolerance. Keep in mind that each athlete has a different perception of pain. Some athletes have a high pain tolerance whereas others do not. Regardless of the athlete's pain tolerance, the higher the athlete's pain scale rating, the more irritable is the athlete's injury or illness.

In its basic form, the *nature* of the injury or illness is a description of the injury or illness that has afflicted the athlete. This description commonly involves the damaged structure or structures and the injury's classification. Ligaments, muscles, and bones are commonly injured anatomical structures. Sprains, strains, contusions, dislocations, and fractures are some injury classifications, whereas illnesses are classified as bacterial, viral, or fungal infections.

The *stage* of the injury is described by three common injury classifications—acute, subacute, and chronic injuries. Similar to the phases of inflammation, the stages of injury are in a continuum and overlap each other. There is no definitive beginning or end of each stage; however, guidelines for the duration of each injury stage exist.

Acute injuries are caused by a traumatic event, which results in sudden inflammation to the injured area. The athlete exhibits signs and complains of symptoms of injury consistent with inflammation. These signs and symptoms last from a week to a month. An example of an acute injury is when one of your athletes approaches you limping in We R Fit Gym. She says that she was just participating in a kickboxing class and experienced a tearing sensation in her hamstring. Now she is in significant pain. You can see her hamstring is swollen and that she has loss of motion. This hamstring injury was caused by a single, traumatic event that resulted in spontaneous signs and symptoms of inflammation. This hamstring injury is considered an acute injury.

After the acute stage, the injury moves into the subacute stage. When an athlete has a subacute injury, the injury has afflicted the athlete for a month or so. Although signs and symptoms of inflammation significantly decrease in this stage, they often still exist and are bothersome. Think about the following scenario: You are training an athlete to participate in a marathon. She has been running on her own on the streets in her neighborhood. Three weeks ago she sustained a Grade 2 lateral ankle sprain when she slipped on some gravel and inverted her ankle. Once her injury was no longer acute, she continued to train with you. For the past few training days she has complained of dull pain, minor loss of motion and strength, and slight swelling after her training sessions. Her injury is clearly in the subacute stage.

The last stage of injury is the chronic stage. Chronic injuries typically have a long **onset**. The athlete is not able to participate in activity at his or her desired level for many months due to the signs and symptoms that accompany the injury (Prentice, 2011; Schultz et al., 2010). A chronic injury requires intervention and rehabilitation and takes an atypical amount of time to heal. A common chronic injury is lateral epicondylitis, which is otherwise known as tennis elbow. The injury occurs over a long duration due to repetitive stress to the wrist extensor muscles that originate at the elbow. The athlete has signs and symptoms including intermittent pain, muscle weakness, and loss of function. The injury remains chronic for months and affects athletic participation and activities of daily living (ADLs). Continual treatment and rehabilitation must be applied before the chronic injury starts to heal.

> **Onset** When the injury begins and becomes apparent to the athlete. Injuries may have a short, long, or insidious (gradual and undetected) onset.

History, Observation, Palpation, and Special Tests

When performing a basic examination on your athlete, your goal is to attempt to identify the specific injury or illness in order to provide the athlete with proper care and/or referral to a physician or emergency medical personnel. Regardless of the stage or severity, carefully detect as many details of the athlete's condition as possible. Perform your exam in an organized manner to accurately determine your next course of action on the athlete's behalf. One organized way to perform your basic examination is by using the acronym HOPS, which stands for history, observation, palpation, and special tests.

History

History is the first portion of HOPS. The history helps you to obtain the athlete's perspective on the injury. In this part of the secondary survey you will gain the athlete's subjective point of view and information regarding the injury from her personal experience. The history consists of a variety of questions that you ask the athlete. These questions should be general at first. As you find out more information regarding the athlete's condition, pose more specific questions to uncover the injury details. The questions must be as open-ended as possible, allowing the athlete to fully describe her condition in detail. Consequently, try to avoid questions that only require the athlete to answer "yes" or "no." For example, one question you must ask the athlete is whether she has pain. Avoid asking a yes or no question such as "Do you have pain?" The athlete will most likely respond only with yes or no. You can add to your question to get a detailed response; for example, you could ask, "Do you have any pain? If you do, please describe how the pain feels." The athlete's descriptive answer gives you some details about the extent of injury. Also, try not to lead the athlete with your questions, which will solicit an unnatural response. For example, if you need to ask questions regarding the location of pain, instead of asking an athlete, "Do you have pain here?" while pointing to the area where you believe her pain exists; ask her, "Show me where you have pain." A variety of questions can be posed to the athlete regarding her injury, with the primary questions directed toward the **mechanism of injury** and her symptoms

> **Mechanism of injury** How the injury or illness occurred, which can be determined by asking the athlete, "What happened?"

(**Table 6-1**). After you pose one question, her answer will assist you in formulating the subsequent question. As she answers each question, think about her response. Ask yourself how her response relates to the injury. Use this information, along with her previous responses, to formulate additional questions related to and expanding upon the previous ones. This method of questioning will aid you in gaining detailed information, or assist you in redirecting your questions onto a different topic related to her injury symptoms. Taking a thorough history is similar to trying to figure out a puzzle with clues given to you by the athlete. At all times during the history, try to encourage the athlete to talk freely, share her experience, and express her feelings in regard to the injury in detail.

When you listen to the athlete's responses, carefully listen to her tone of voice, which can indicate pain perception, fear, anger, anxiety, and many other emotional responses to the injury. Your line of questioning may be short or long depending on a variety of factors. Your history will often be short if you are able to quickly determine the SINS of injury. Also, if you quickly determine that the athlete is in serious distress, then your history will be very brief but direct. For example, brevity is necessary in situations where the athlete has sustained a dislocated joint, a fracture, or shock, so you can provide immediate, necessary emergency care. Your history may be much longer if the athlete does not exhibit significant distress or evident signs and symptoms, such as with a chronic injury like shoulder tendinitis. Over time you will learn which pertinent questions to ask an injured athlete dependent on her specific situation. These pertinent questions help you obtain the information you need to make an informed decision regarding her care. Often after taking a detailed history you will have a good, possibly definitive, idea of the injury that the athlete is suffering.

At times the athlete will not be able to give you a thorough history or respond to your questions at all. The athlete may be unconscious, in shock, or severely injured or ill and be unresponsive. In these cases, you must ask bystanders and witnesses various questions relating to the athlete's injury or illness. Witness accounts can be invaluable in helping you determine the SINS of injury and what athlete care must be provided.

Table 6-1	History Questions

Some questions to ask the athlete when completing the history portion of the basic examination include:
- What happened?
- When did the injury occur?
- Did you hear any unusual sounds when the injury occurred? If so, please explain what you heard.
- Did you have any unusual sensation or lack of sensation at the time of injury or currently?
- Describe your symptoms. How do you feel?
- Do you have pain? If so, where is the pain?
- On a scale of 1 to 10, with 10 being the worst pain you have ever experienced, rate your pain. What is the worst pain you have ever experienced?
- Describe your pain. Is the pain burning, tingling, aching, radiating, dull, or sharp?
- Are you able to move the body part without pain?
- Do you feel joint instability, locking, or catching?
- What movements or positions increase and decrease your symptoms?
- Have you ever injured this body part before? If so, what happened? What did you do to treat and rehabilitate the previous injury?
- Are you taking any medication? If yes, what are the medications and what conditions do they treat?

Tips from the Field

Tip 1 Even if you witnessed how the athlete's injury occurred, and you immediately visualize the injured structures, your first question to the athlete should always be, "What happened?" It is important to obtain the athlete's own perspective and description of how the injury occurred. As observers, we may not see the exact mechanism of injury. Likewise, the athlete may have injured more than one structure, which may not be evident immediately. Therefore, we must determine first and foremost what happened to cause the athlete's injury.

Observation

It may seem that the history ends at some point during the examination, but actually it does not. You continue to ask the athlete questions throughout the entire basic examination process as you discover more pertinent information regarding the injury. As you are taking the athlete's history, you also take part in the observation process. The observation is also referred to as the inspection. Whereas the history is subjective because the athlete tells you how the injury occurred and the symptoms she is experiencing, the observation is objective and identifies the irrefutable signs of injury. Any observer can find the signs of injury. Various signs of injury that you would observe the athlete for include, but are not limited to, bleeding; ecchymosis; red, pale, blue, and other skin color variations and discolorations; bulges, divots, or other lack of **continuity** in muscles; deformity; malalignment; asymmetry; body and limb posture; swelling; athlete grasping the injury; inability to move the body part; breathing rate and quality; lack of coordination and balance; and **gait** (**Table 6-2**). By also observing her body language and facial expressions, you can determine various emotions, such as anxiety, fear, and apprehension, and her extent of pain, visualized by the athlete wincing.

> **Continuity** In muscles, this is when the tissue feels the same to the touch throughout the tissue's entire length and width.

> **Gait** The manner in which the athlete is walking.

You always want to observe and examine the athlete bilaterally, meaning that you observe both the injured and uninjured extremities. For example, if the athlete's right knee is injured, you also examine the athlete's left knee. For other body parts, such as the face or abdomen, visualize the athlete cut in half into two equal right and left sides from the head, down the bridge of the nose, through the sternum and the umbilicus. This division creates two symmetrical left and right halves of the body, and is called the sagittal plane. By looking at the athlete in this manner, you can compare the right and left sides of the entire body for signs of injury. Typically you examine the uninjured area first to get a baseline, or what is normal, for the athlete. In the unusual occurrence that the athlete has the same or a similar injury to both sides (e.g., bilateral lateral ankle sprains), then compare injury to injury while questioning the athlete as to what is a "normal" appearance for the body part.

Although most often you start the examination by taking the athlete's history, sometimes you begin the observation step in HOPS prior to the history, such as when the injured athlete is walking toward you, or you are approaching the athlete. For example, you are working in We R Fit Gym, and suddenly you hear a large crash. Immediately, you start to run toward the sound. On the other side of the room, you see an injured athlete lying on the mat. As you approach the athlete, you see him writhing in pain on the floor by the weight rack. He is grasping his right knee. He is screaming loudly and clenching his teeth. His knee is deformed. In this case, your observation begins before the history. You observe the athlete before you are able to ask your history questions. Once you finally reach the athlete, you say, "What happened?" In this instance, the observation in the basic injury examination began before the history portion. As your line of questioning continues, the observation continues also. The history and observation portions are perpetuated throughout the entire secondary survey.

Palpation

When you have completed the majority of your observation, you move on to palpation, or touching, the injured area. Before you touch your athlete, ask her if she will allow you to touch the injured area, the surrounding tissues, and the **contralateral** side as part of your basic examination. You must be discrete and professional at all times. Do not stray from palpating the injured area and surrounding areas. If at all possible, palpate the athlete's injury with another person present. Palpate the uninjured side first. This contralateral palpation is important for a variety of reasons. When you palpate the contralateral, uninjured side first, your athlete knows what to expect and how you will palpate the injured area. Also, by palpating the uninjured side first, you attempt to earn your athlete's trust, if you have not earned it already. Palpating the uninjured side first also helps you to determine what is normal or a baseline for your athlete's injured side. Along with your observation, contralateral side palpation helps you determine the injured structures by comparing the injured side after the uninjured side via the use of touch.

> **Contralateral** The corresponding structure on the opposite side of the body.

Table 6-2	Observable Signs of Injury

Signs of injury that may be present when an athlete is injured include:
- Redness, ecchymosis, or discoloration of the skin
- Warm skin
- Swelling
- Deformity
- Postural malalignment
- Unusual body position
- Asymmetry
- Abnormal gait
- Facial apprehension
- Abnormal sounds
- Athlete inability to move the area
- Abnormal movements
- Muscular incontinuity

Crepitus A crackling sound.

Muscle guarding An involuntary muscular response that occurs when the muscles around an injured area become tight and rigid in order to protect an injured area from further injury. Muscle guarding typically is not painful to the athlete.

Muscle spasm An involuntary muscular response that occurs when the muscles suddenly contract and shorten. Muscle spasm typically is painful for the athlete, and the athlete cannot relieve the spasm voluntarily.

Point tenderness A sign of injury. When you palpate the athlete's injury, and the athlete claims the area you touched was painful, then that area is considered point tender.

Edema Fluid that accumulates in bodily spaces due to injury or illness. Edema creates the appearance of swelling, especially at the joints and around soft tissue structures.

When you palpate, be cognizant as to what structures you are palpating. Picture the structures in your mind when you are touching the athlete's skin. If you are palpating the quadriceps, visualize the tendons' origins and insertions under your fingers. Imagine each muscle as you palpate the muscle bellies. Recognize all anatomical structures and their location, including the bony and soft tissues, as you palpate. Also distinguish what is abnormal for the athlete. If you find an abnormal bony or soft tissue structure as compared to the contralateral side, this may indicate structural injury. Likewise, various signs of injury can be determined when palpating the anatomical structures. You will feel for signs of injury including, but not limited to, tissue continuity (including divots, bumps, and bulges), **crepitus**, skin temperature differences (including warm skin indicating inflammation or cold skin indicating lack of blood flow to the area), **muscle guarding**, **muscle spasm**, **point tenderness**, and **edema**.

Tips from the Field

Tip 2 During your palpation, you may have some difficulty trying to determine if the athlete has any signs of injury. In this case, while you are palpating a structure, briefly close your eyes. By removing one of your senses, your sense of touch becomes more acute. This method can assist you in feeling for signs of injury. Obviously, if the athlete is in significant distress, you must not break eye contact with her. You need to visualize the athlete and her condition at all times. However, the skill of closing your eyes briefly during palpation, to use your fingers as your eyes, is acceptable when the athlete requires a basic examination for a seemingly chronic condition or when she is not in distress.

Touch and feel both bony and soft tissues in an organized manner. Start furthest away from and gradually work toward the injured area, palpating the injured area last. The manner in which you palpate the uninjured side is exactly how you should palpate the injured side. It is recommended that you palpate the structures in the same order on the injured side as you do on the uninjured side, so you can work in an organized fashion and not mistakenly forget to palpate a structure. You must palpate all bones and soft tissue. When you palpate, begin with a light touch, using your finger pads and not the tips of your fingers, especially if you have long fingernails. Hard and pointy fingernail touch may be very uncomfortable to the athlete, potentially causing the athlete to lose trust in you for causing discomfort or even pain. If the athlete is able to tolerate light touch, then you can gradually increase your pressure as she can tolerate.

Some circumstances would prevent you from palpating the injury. If the athlete has an open wound, a rash, hives, or an unidentified skin lesion, then by no means palpate the area, even if you are wearing gloves. It is contraindicated to palpate over open wounds due to the potential of increasing bleeding or trauma, or introducing infectious substances into the wound. If you palpate a skin condition, you may spread the infection on the athlete or perhaps have it transmitted to you. Other times when you would not palpate the injury would be if the injury occurred in an area such as the breasts on a female, the groin or buttocks on both males and females, and any other area for which you or the athlete may feel uncomfortable. Do not forget to always be discrete and to have the athlete give you consent to palpate before you do so. If at all possible, you need the athlete to discreetly expose the injured area and the contralateral side not only to observe and compare the areas, but also to palpate both areas for differences in bone and soft tissue. Athletes commonly wear clothing such as bathing suits, sports bras, t-shirts, and shorts during activity. Consequently, it is often easy to visualize both the uninjured and injured body parts.

Remember to always obtain permission to touch the athlete before you do so. Also, at all times, palpate the athlete in a public area, while being discreet and exemplifying professionalism. Give an explanation of what you are going to do even before palpating the uninjured side. If at any time the athlete does not want you to palpate the area or no longer wants you to touch them, stop immediately and refer the athlete to a physician or emergency personnel if his or her injury or illness warrants advanced medical referral. The principles of palpation are discussed in **Table 6-3**.

Table 6-3	Principles of Palpation

The following principles of palpation will assist you during the basic examination:

- Obtain permission from the athlete to touch the injury and surrounding area. Do not touch the athlete if she or he does not give you permission.
- Explain to the athlete the purpose of palpation.
- Explain to the athlete what structures you will palpate.
- Ask the athlete to bare the area as necessary to allow you to palpate and visualize the skin surface.
- Demonstrate to the athlete how you will palpate the injured body part by palpating the contralateral side first.
- Utilize your finger pads and the palms of your hands to palpate.
- Begin with light pressure, and then gradually increase pressure as the athlete tolerates.
- Tell the athlete that if he or she has any pain or other symptoms during palpation, to inform you immediately.
- Palpate the uninjured side in an organized manner, and visualize the structures that you are palpating as you touch them.
- Palpate the injured side in the same manner as the uninjured side.
- Always palpate the athlete with another person present.
- Be discreet and do not have the athlete remove any clothing that would put you or the athlete in an awkward or unprofessional situation.
- Do not palpate the area if a rash, lesions, hives, open wounds, or the like exist, even if you are wearing gloves.
- If at any time the athlete asks you to stop palpation, immediately stop your exam and refer the athlete to a physician or EMS.

Special Tests

Special tests refer to various testing procedures used to examine, rule out, and confirm the extent of the athlete's joint and muscular function; strength; vital signs, including circulation, respiration rate, and blood pressure; and peripheral nerve function. During your basic examination, after you have palpated the injured and surrounding areas bilaterally, you begin to determine the athlete's active and passive range of motion (ROM). Active ROM (AROM) is the amount of joint motion that the athlete creates by contracting her muscles voluntarily. Passive ROM (PROM) is the available amount of motion around a joint without muscular contraction. PROM is involuntary motion that is created when you move the athlete's joint while the muscles are relaxed. Regardless of whether you are checking AROM or PROM, you always check the athlete's ROM first on the contralateral side to determine the athlete's normal motion. By checking the uninjured side first, you also familiarize the athlete with what active and passive testing you will perform on her injured extremity.

To begin determining the athlete's ROM, you first determine the extent of the athlete's AROM. During AROM, the athlete controls the motion by voluntarily contracting his muscles. If the athlete experiences any pain during the AROM, he is able to stop the motion and avoid further pain. Before the athlete performs the AROM, explain what you want him to do and then demonstrate the motion. If you want the athlete to perform active hip flexion, lie down on your back on a table or mat. Show him how to flex the hips, one at a time, with his uninjured side first (**Figure 6-1**). Move through the entire available ROM, and then have the athlete do the same. Tell him in advance that if any motion is painful, or if he has difficulty completing the motion for any reason, he should stop the motion. Immediately ask him where the pain is or what is the difficulty in moving the joint through an AROM. After he performs AROM on both sides you can then determine if he has any deficits.

You can also use a **goniometer** to determine the actual, numerical degrees of motion as compared to researched norms and the

> **Goniometer** A protractor-type device used to measure angles and joint range of motion.

athlete's contralateral side (**Figure 6-2**). Using a goniometer takes significant instruction and practice to yield accurate results. Consequently, further discussion of goniometry is not purposeful for this text.

As the athlete performs AROM, observe various characteristics regarding the athlete's motion. Look at the fluidity of the motion and determine if it is smooth throughout the entire ROM. If the athlete is having a hard time actively moving the joint due to pain or other issues, the athlete's motion may be choppy or stop at different points throughout the range. Also, by observing the athlete's facial expressions you can tell if the athlete is experiencing pain or difficulty moving the

Figure 6-1	AROM of hip flexion.

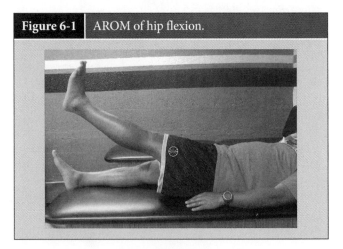

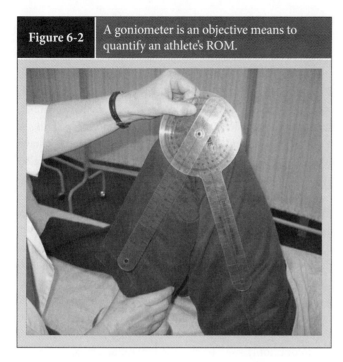

Figure 6-2 | A goniometer is an objective means to quantify an athlete's ROM.

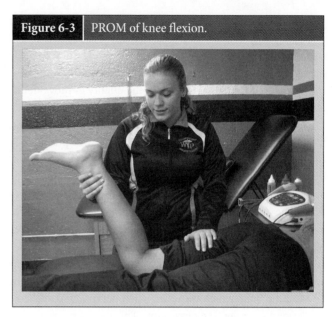

Figure 6-3 | PROM of knee flexion.

body part. If the athlete has no pain or difficulty with active ROM throughout the entire range, you can conclude that the muscles and tendons acting on the joint are intact and most likely not injured.

Once you have determined if the athlete can actively move the affected joint and contract the surrounding muscles, then test the athlete's PROM. First have the athlete relax in a comfortable position. Place the athlete in a chair or have her lie on a table or a mat on the floor. The other joints and limbs must be as stable as possible. Moving the limb when the athlete is lying on a treatment table or the floor, or sitting in a chair is easier than if she is standing or unsupported. The position that you place your athlete in depends on the body part being moved. For example, if you are going to passively move the athlete's knee into flexion and extension, have her sit on the edge of a table or in a chair, her feet dangling off the edge, and her knee bent at a 90-degree angle. This position can also be used to test knee joint AROM.

In order to test the athlete's PROM, attempt to move the distal limb. In the case of extension, stabilize her thigh by having her seated on a table with her legs hanging off the edge. For knee flexion, have the athlete on her stomach. Your hand stabilizes her thigh while you grasp the distal tibia. Tell the athlete to relax and not contract her muscles while you move her tibia. Then move the knee joint throughout a full ROM by moving the tibia (**Figure 6-3**). As you are moving the joint through a PROM, note the smoothness of the motion;

the athlete's facial expressions, which can indicate apprehension or pain; joint instability; and any abnormal qualities of motion such as catching, grating, clicking, or popping. Move the athlete's joint as far as the joint can go without the athlete experiencing pain. If at any time the athlete complains of pain, instability, or an abnormal or lack of sensation, immediately stop performing the passive motion. If the athlete complains of pain around the joint surface when PROM is being performed, then the ligaments or other noncontractile soft tissues around the joint may be injured. If the athlete complains of muscular pain when PROM is being performed, then the muscles may be inflexible, stiff, or strained. At this point, because pain or other signs and symptoms of injury exist, refer the athlete to a physician for further evaluation.

In order to further test muscular integrity and strength, you would perform manual muscle testing (MMT). MMT entails the athlete performing AROM while you are applying resistance to the distal, moving limb, and tests muscles that act on the joint. Using the knee joint as an example, the quadriceps muscle group as a whole is strength tested when performing knee extension and the hamstring muscle group is strength tested with knee flexion. Of course, you can isolate an individual muscle at any joint by knowing the muscle's action and the appropriate position in which to isolate the muscle. In order to perform MMT, begin with the contralateral side and place the joint and body segments in the same position as you have the athlete placed in during an AROM test. Then have the athlete move through an AROM. Afterwards, place your hand at the same location on the moving limb as during PROM.

Instruct the athlete to perform AROM while you apply moderate resistance to the distal segment. Allow the athlete to go through the entire ROM. Do not apply too much resistance to prevent the athlete from moving the joint. While the athlete is moving the contralateral side, note the quality of movement, and the muscles' ability to create force against your resistance.

After performing the MMT on the uninjured side, perform MMT on the injured side, exactly as it was performed on the uninjured side. Compare the two sides to determine if the injured side is weaker than the uninjured. When you apply resistance, you can tell if any bilateral muscular force production variations exist. If the uninjured side moves more smoothly through a full ROM and with greater force output against the same resistance as compared to the injured side, then the injured side most likely has a muscular injury such as a strain, or a neurological injury. A neurological injury such as a neuropraxia, which is caused when nerves are stretched, causes nerve conduction disruption. This disruption prevents the muscle from creating force and contracting, preventing the muscle from moving the joint through a full ROM, or any ROM in some cases. If you find a discrepancy in movement quality or muscular strength, accompanied by pain or other significant signs and symptoms of injury, then refer the athlete to a physician.

AROM and PROM are means to determine the quantity and quality of active and passive joint motion, while MMT will help you determine muscular strength. These special tests also assist you in determining the athlete's pain. The tests identify injury signs and symptoms in regard to the inert or noncontractile structures around the joint, as well as the muscles during motion, muscular contraction, and force production. Always keep in mind when performing special tests that you need to explain to the athlete what you are going to do, demonstrate the tests on another athlete or colleague, and then perform these motions on the athlete's contralateral side first. Before beginning, tell her that if any motion is painful she must inform you immediately. If she has difficulty in completing the AROM or MMT for any reason, tell her to stop the motion and describe the symptoms. Continue with your HOPS sequence as appropriate.

In the basic examination, the special tests also include checking the athlete's vital signs, including circulation, respiration rate, and blood pressure. For musculoskeletal injuries, checking the athlete's circulation by evaluating her pulse distal to the injured area is important. By checking the circulation distal to the injury, you determine if adequate blood flow is being supplied to the injured area and the rest of the extremity that is lower, or distal to, the injury. Compare pulses bilaterally. While comparing both sides, determine the pulse rate and quality to see if they are equal. The pulse rate, or

heart rate, is the number of pulses per minute. For an adult, the average pulse rate at rest, taken in the morning before rising, is 60 to 100 beats per minute (bpm). For an elite or well-trained athlete, the average heart rate may be as low as 40 bpm (Laskowski, 2010). The quality of pulse is a description of the pulse strength during palpation. The pulse may be weak, strong, or nonexistent as compared to the uninjured side. A weak or nonexistent pulse means the athlete does not have adequate blood flow to the distal extremity. A weak pulse also can indicate various illnesses such as shock or heat exhaustion. A nonexistent pulse could also indicate that the person has succumbed to cardiac arrest. A strong pulse can indicate an illness such as heat stroke.

Taking a pulse is not difficult. Find the artery distal to the injury and palpate it with your second and third fingers. Do not use your thumb because it has a pulse of its own and you may mistake your pulse for the athlete's. Most often you can palpate pulses bilaterally at the same time. For example, if the athlete has an upper extremity injury, the radial pulse is most commonly used to check circulation. The radial pulse is located over the radial bone on the lateral side of the wrist, approximately an inch from the wrist joint (**Figure 6-4**). You can easily palpate and evaluate both pulses simultaneously. You can also take a pulse at the brachial artery if the injury is at the shoulder. The brachial artery is located at the inside of the upper arm between the biceps brachii and triceps brachii muscles. This artery is not often utilized for taking a pulse as compared to the radial pulse, since the radial pulse is more easily accessible and at the most distal portion of the upper extremity; however, the brachial pulse is easily identifiable. If the lower extremity is injured, check the athlete's circulation at the popliteal, posterior tibial, or dorsal pedal (also called

| **Figure 6-4** | Location of the radial pulse. |

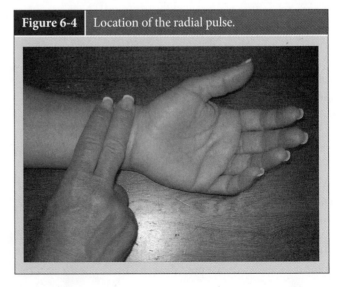

the dorsalis pedis) arteries. Choose the artery that is distal to the injury. The posterior tibial artery and dorsal pedal arteries are most commonly used to examine lower extremity pulses. The posterior tibial artery is found on the medial side of the ankle between the medial malleolus and the Achilles tendon. This artery is easily found due to its location; however, the dorsal pedal artery is not as easily palpated (Mowalvi, Whiteman, Wilhelmi, Neumeister, & McLafferty, 2002). The dorsal pedal artery is located between the first and second metatarsals on the top of the foot by the carpal bones.

After finding the artery upon palpation, take the pulse rate by counting the beats per minute while watching the second hand on a clock or wristwatch for 10 seconds. Then multiply the number of beats by six. The resulting number is the athlete's heart rate in beats per minute (Laskowski, 2010). You can take the pulse rate for a longer duration (i.e., 30 seconds, and then multiply by 2, or for 60 seconds) to obtain a more accurate reading. The pulse quality is subjective. Attempt to determine whether the pulse quality is the same or differs as compared to the uninjured side. The pulse may be slow, normal, fast, weak, or bounding as compared to the uninjured side. If pulses are not equal in rate or quality between the injured and uninjured sides, then refer the athlete for further medical evaluation. In cases of common illnesses, the pulse quality and rate should be identical and normal on both sides. In the case of shock or heat stroke, the quality and rate are not normal. With shock, the pulse is rapid and weak; in contrast, during heat stroke the pulse is rapid and strong. For musculoskeletal injuries, if the distal pulses are equal in rate and quality, then adequate blood flow and oxygen are being supplied to the injured area. Having some knowledge regarding normal pulse quality is important to determine whether the athlete needs immediate emergency care when she has sustained an injury or illness.

You can also check circulation to the distal extremities by checking capillary refill. The athlete's nail beds are normally a pink color. To check capillary refill, gently squeeze the nail bed of the fingers or toes, depending on the extremity that is injured, one at a time for a few seconds. The nail bed turns white, indicating lack of blood flow to the area. Let go of the pressure, and the nail bed's pink color should return immediately. The pink color indicates adequate blood flow to the extremity. Check capillary refill for each finger and toe on the affected limb. If the pink color does not return quickly, or at the same rate as compared to the contralateral side, then the athlete may have inadequate blood flow to the extremity.

Respiration rate is easily determined by counting the number of breaths per minute. An adult who is at rest has an approximate respiratory rate of 15 to 20 breaths per minute.

An exercising athlete may reach 25 breaths per minute. An ill athlete at rest, including an athlete in shock or respiratory distress, may reach 20 respirations per minute.

Blood pressure (BP) is the force blood creates on artery walls as it moves through the circulatory system. BP is measured in millimeters of mercury (mmHg) and is recorded as systolic pressure over diastolic pressure. Systolic pressure is the force of blood on artery walls as the heart beats; diastolic pressure is the force of blood on artery walls as the heart is at rest between beats. The average, normal adult athlete has a BP of 120/80 mmHg, which is verbalized as "120 over 80." This BP means the athlete has 120-mmHg systolic pressure and 80 mmHg diastolic pressure.

Taking an accurate BP requires a lot of practice. In order to take a BP, you need a stethoscope and a sphygmomanometer, also called a BP cuff, or an automatic BP monitor. You can purchase this equipment at various commercial drugstores or through health-related supply companies on the Internet. Exercise scientists most often utilize a BP cuff, which is inflated and deflated manually, along with a stethoscope to take an athlete's BP (**Figure 6-5**). Athletes who monitor their own BP typically utilize automatic BP monitors because these machines are simple to use (**Figure 6-6**). To begin using either device, have the athlete's biceps brachii and elbow exposed. Place the BP cuff snugly around the athlete's biceps brachii muscle approximately 1 inch from the anterior elbow. When utilizing an automatic monitor, follow the directions that accompany the device, which may include a setting for appropriate inflation. In most cases, the athlete

| Figure 6-5 | Most exercise scientists take an athlete's blood pressure by utilizing a blood pressure cuff and stethoscope. |

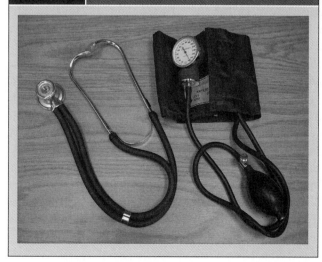

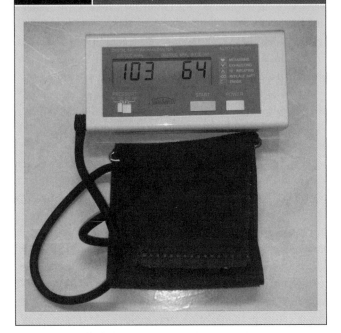

Figure 6-6 Athletes who self-monitor their blood pressure typically utilize automatic blood pressure monitors, such as this one manufactured by Sunbeam®.

Evaluating an athlete's neurological function is extremely important to determine the appropriate course of athlete care. Detailed tests exist to evaluate an athlete's neurological function for all parts of the body, including the brain and spinal cord, which make up the central nervous system (CNS), and the peripheral nerves. These detailed tests are beyond the scope of this text; however, you can perform generalized tests to evaluate the athlete's neurologic function, which can be compromised due to injury. The peripheral, or spinal, nerves arise out of the spinal cord at the cervical, thoracic, lumbar, and sacral vertebrae (**Figure 6-7**). Each nerve has a motor and a sensory branch. Therefore, an individual spinal motor nerve innervates a specific muscle or group of muscles, while an individual spinal sensory nerve innervates an area of the skin. Normally when an athlete sustains a common injury such as a sprain or a strain, evaluating the athlete's neurological function is not necessary. However, you would evaluate the

presses the Start button, which causes the monitor to automatically inflate and then deflate the BP cuff. The monitor then displays the athlete's BP.

When utilizing a BP cuff and stethoscope, place the BP cuff around the biceps brachii so the gauge and bulb tubes are anterior to the elbow. Place the bell of the stethoscope on the brachial artery, slightly superior to the antecubital fossa. Once you hear the "whooshing" sound of the blood flowing through the artery, make sure the bulb valve is shut and inflate the BP cuff by repeatedly squeezing the bulb. Inflate the BP cuff so the pin on the gauge reaches approximately 30 mmHg higher than the athlete's normal systolic BP. At that point, the whooshing sound made by the blood flow ceases. Slowly open the valve so the gauge pin drops approximately 2 mmHg per second. Watch the gauge carefully. When you hear the first "thump" record the number displayed on the gauge at that moment as the systolic BP. Continue to slowly open the valve and watch the gauge. The number on the gauge when the last thump occurs is the diastolic BP. Record the systolic BP over the diastolic BP. To determine the accuracy of the reading, take the athlete's BP three times, with 1 minute of rest between readings. Once you become proficient in taking a BP, you can obtain an accurate reading with one attempt.

Figure 6-7 The peripheral nerves arise from the CNS and function to provide sensation and motor function to the body.

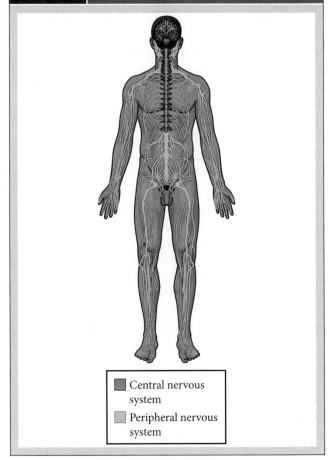

■ Central nervous system
■ Peripheral nervous system

athlete's peripheral nerves if she complains of symptoms such as tingling, numbness, or strange sensations at or around the injured area; muscular weakness; or loss of muscular function (Starkey, Brown, & Ryan, 2010).

A quick and easy means to determine if the athlete's spinal motor nerves are functioning appropriately is to have the athlete perform AROM and MMT testing. You test the injured area as well as the nerves around the injured area. For example, if the athlete complains of "pins and needles" or tingling from her elbow down to her fingers, test the athlete's peripheral motor nerves from the shoulder to the fingers. Have the athlete shrug and abduct her shoulders, flex and extend her elbows and wrists, and flex, adduct, and abduct her fingers. Then have the athlete perform these motions while you apply resistance. Determine if the athlete can perform the movement normally, has difficulty doing so, or has muscular weakness. If the athlete has any deficits, then it is possible that a peripheral motor nerve injury exists. In order to test the peripheral sensory nerves, ask the athlete to close her eyes. Touch her on both sides of her body with a soft touch and then a hard touch. You can perform this touch either on one side and then the other or simultaneously. Ask her if she can feel your touch on both sides equally, and if the sensation is soft or hard. Also ask her to distinguish between two points on her skin. In order to complete this task, have the athlete close her eyes. Put two fingers, spread at least an inch apart, on the same area of the skin. Ask the athlete if she can distinguish between the two points. If the athlete complains of paresthesia or numbness, or is unable to distinguish between the two points, then a sensory spinal nerve may be compromised. After this finding, refer her to a physician for further evaluation. Again, to determine if an injury exists, always compare both the uninjured and injured sides.

Safely Moving an Injured Athlete

For acute injuries, if possible, attempt to keep the athlete at the location where the injury occurred and perform the basic examination. After performing the basic examination, you will determine if the athlete should be moved from the area. If you must move the acutely injured athlete before performing the basic examination, determine how to do so safely without causing further injury or exacerbating symptoms. In certain instances it is evident that you must move the athlete. For example, if an athlete injures himself in the gym and is in the middle of client foot traffic, then you may need to move him, provided it is safe to do so. If an athlete is injured on a playing field in the middle of competition, you may want to move him as long as it is safe to do so. In any situation, you do not move the athlete if moving the athlete may complicate the injury. In some situations you do not move the athlete at all.

For example, if the athlete is in a life-threatening situation and he is not breathing, then leave the athlete where he is and perform CPR. Also, if he has a fractured bone, do not move the athlete.

When you suspect an athlete has a spinal injury, such as when a blow to the head, neck, or spine occurred and the athlete complains of numbness or an inability to move a portion of the body, or any time an athlete is unconscious, the athlete must not be moved and should be transported via spine board to the hospital. Placing an athlete on a spine board appropriately is a difficult task. Staff at your facility must practice this skill on a regular basis to ensure the spine boarding is performed properly and safely for the injured athlete. For some exercise scientists, spine board practice is not practical. Likewise, many organizations, such as gyms or Little League, for example, do not have a spine board on site. Therefore, if you suspect your athlete has a spinal injury, stabilize the head and neck and have someone phone 911. Continue to stabilize the head and neck until the EMTs arrive and physically take over for you. The EMTs are highly trained in moving people onto a spine board for transport. The EMTs may ask you to assist in this task, because at a minimum five people are necessary to appropriately and safely place someone on a spine board (Anderson & Parr, 2011). Do not remove your hands from the athlete's head until directed by an EMT.

In many situations when the athlete is injured, you can move the athlete. An athlete with minor to moderate injuries can be moved. If an athlete sustains a Grade 1 ankle sprain during an aerobics class, you can move her out of the aerobics studio and into an employee office for evaluation. If an athlete has a Grade 2 strain of her quadriceps muscles while performing squats, you can move her away from the flow of client traffic into a safe and noncongested area. If the athlete can walk without pain or exacerbating symptoms, have her walk to a comfortable area for evaluation. If the athlete is in pain, unable to walk, or in a location where she or bystanders would be unsafe if she remained, then you must decide how to properly and safely move her.

If the athlete cannot ambulate on her own, or has pain or exacerbated symptoms of injury, then help the athlete to move from the area. Some means to move an injured athlete include ambulatory assistance, manual conveyance, and spine board transport (Anderson & Parr, 2011). Provide ambulatory assistance to an athlete who can fully or partially weight bear and walk on his own. Typically you provide ambulatory assistance if the athlete has some pain or discomfort in the lower extremity, as with a Grade 1 or Grade 2 ankle sprain, or is unsteady or dizzy, perhaps due to an illness or concussion. You can assist an athlete to ambulate by yourself, but if you have another person help you the move will be easier. In order to provide ambulatory assistance, you need to be approximately the athlete's height. If you are working with another person, position yourselves on either side of the athlete. Put your arm closest to the athlete around the athlete's waist. The athlete's arm closest to you should be placed around your shoulders (**Figure 6-8**). It may be beneficial to hold his arm around your shoulders to make sure it does not slip off while ambulating. Then instruct the athlete to take slow steps to your destination. If you are much shorter or taller than the athlete, you may have a difficult time providing ambulatory assistance. Consequently, have other teammates, clients, colleagues, or others who are the approximate height of the athlete assist him. In this case, before the caregivers move the athlete, demonstrate and describe to the caregivers how to position themselves and support the athlete during ambulation. If you are the only person available to provide ambulatory assistance, position yourself on the athlete's injured side. Instruct the athlete to slightly lean in your direction, and use your body and legs almost as a crutch for his injured lower extremity. Before moving the athlete, always make sure you instruct him that if he experiences any pain or an increase in symptoms while moving to immediately stop and tell you what he is experiencing.

Another means to move the athlete is by manual conveyance, which can be used for an athlete who cannot bear weight on his lower extremity or cannot walk on his own. Also, if the athlete begins to walk with ambulatory assistance and finds that he is in great pain or his symptoms increase, then manual conveyance is warranted. Two caregivers are always needed to move an athlete by manual conveyance. Position the athlete between you and the other caregiver. Place your arms closest to the athlete around his waist as with ambulatory assistance. Then with your other arm, put your forearm under the athlete's thighs. Your assistant takes the same position on the other side of the athlete. Both of you should grasp hands underneath the athlete's thighs. Tell the athlete to slowly lean back to take a seated position in your and your assistant's arms (**Figure 6-9**). Slowly carry the athlete and move him to a safe area. If possible, demonstrate this technique to the athlete first by utilizing another, uninjured athlete who has previously been moved by manual conveyance. If the demonstration is not possible, then carefully describe what you intend to do. Manual conveyance is an appropriate means to move an athlete, but often can be difficult to perform. If the distance to move the athlete is very long, the caregivers can become tired

| **Figure 6-8** | If the athlete can partially weight bear, then ambulatory assistance can be utilized to move the athlete. |

© Debby Wong/ShutterStock, Inc.

| **Figure 6-9** | The proper position to provide manual conveyance. |

© Jones & Bartlett Learning. Courtesy of MIEMSS.

and lose grasp on the athlete. Likewise, if the caregivers are significantly smaller than the athlete, or not strong enough to carry the athlete the distance, then manual conveyance may not be feasible. When manual conveyance is not possible but you must move the athlete, you will have to summon EMS.

Providing Care

Now that you have completed your basic examination and moved the athlete safely, you can assist in providing necessary care. Athlete care involves basic first aid skills, as allowed by your state's statutes. Depending on the credentials, licenses, and the like that you hold and the state in which you work, the care you are able to provide varies. In most circumstances, you can do no wrong if you provide basic first aid and CPR as instructed in formal classes by nationally recognized organizations such as the American Heart Association, the American Red Cross (ARC), the Emergency Care and Safety Institute (ECSI), and the National Safety Council. These organizations offer first aid and CPR courses to become certified in these skills. Even if you are not certified in first aid when you provide proper first aid to an injured athlete, your state's Good Samaritan laws should protect you.

When you care for an injured athlete, start by utilizing the RICE principle. RICE stands for rest, ice, compression, and elevation. When an athlete is injured, he must rest the injured body part and the adjacent tissues to avoid further injury and promote healing. In order to properly rest the body part, the athlete should not move it. To rest the upper extremity from the shoulder down to the fingers, apply a triangular bandage or splint. To rest the lower extremity from the hip down to the toes, apply a splint or commercial brace.

You can also fit the athlete for and teach him how to use crutches or a cane if he needs to rest the lower extremity and cannot fully weight bear. Crutches can also be used while the athlete is partial weight bearing, but he must bear most of his weight on the uninjured lower extremity. You can easily learn how to fit crutches for an athlete. Aluminum crutches typically have different heights marked on the crutch post for easy adjustment. Wood crutches do not have this height designation on the crutch post. Regardless of whether the athlete uses aluminum or wood crutches, position the crutches with the athlete standing so the crutch tips are approximately 2 inches in front of the athlete's toes and 6 inches laterally to the athlete's feet. The axillary crutch pads must be approximately 2–3 inches below the axilla. The athlete's body weight is borne by his hands, not by the axilla. The elbow should be at approximately 30 degrees of flexion (Starkey, 2013). In order to ambulate, the athlete moves the crutches forward approximately 6–12 inches. He steps forward to the crutches

with his uninvolved extremity, then moves the crutches forward once again.

If an athlete can bear a significant amount of weight on the injured lower extremity without pain or other symptoms, the athlete can use a cane instead of crutches. To teach an athlete to use a cane, have him place the cane handle in the hand opposite the injured lower extremity. The elbow is bent and the cane tip rests by the foot in a similar manner as with crutches. Instruct the athlete to move the cane tip forward with the injured lower extremity (Starkey, 2013). The cane acts as a support for the injured lower extremity as it moves forward and bears weight while walking.

Resting the injured body part will give it the chance to heal properly. Rest is particularly important for an acute injury in the inflammatory phase. However, too much rest for long periods of time can be detrimental. Consider an athlete with a relatively minor biceps strain. For the first day postinjury, the athlete complains of pain and weakness while raising his arm. Consequently, you place a triangular bandage on the athlete's upper extremity in order to rest the biceps muscle for the day. The next day the athlete says he still has pain, so you leave the triangular bandage on with his elbow in 90 degrees flexion for another day. After the second day you remove the triangular bandage. The athlete has significant difficulty and pain when attempting to extend his elbow and move his shoulder due to the muscles becoming shortened, contracted, and stiff. In this scenario, too much rest was detrimental. As a rule of thumb, if the athlete needs a triangular bandage, splint, brace, crutches, or a cane as part of injury care, apply such items to make the athlete comfortable and refer the athlete to a physician for medical evaluation.

Ice is the I in RICE. When the athlete is injured, ice facilitates the healing process by decreasing nerve conduction, which decreases pain signals to the brain, acting as an anesthetic and decreasing capillary permeability and vasodilation, which in turn may decrease swelling (Pfeiffer & Mangus, 2012). Ice, in the form of ice cubes or crushed ice, is one type of cold therapy. Other forms of cold therapy used for athletic injuries include ice cups, ice baths, and cold whirlpools. Ice cubes placed in a bag are a very common and typically safe cold therapy utilized for injuries such as sprains, strains, and contusions. Care must be taken when applying ice on an injured medial elbow or lateral knee, because superficial nerves are located at these areas. If ice is left on these structures for too long, the nerve can become damaged. To prepare an ice bag, put as much ice in the bag as is appropriate to cover the injured area. Do not make the bag too heavy or excessive weight will be applied to the injury and the athlete may be very uncomfortable. The ice bag can be applied directly to the skin, unless during questioning you find the athlete has

> **Raynaud's syndrome** A condition in which the athlete has significant lack of blood circulation to the fingers and toes. It is brought on by exposure to cold.

loss of sensation, **Raynaud's syndrome**, or any allergy to cold. In these cases, do not apply the ice and refer the athlete for medical evaluation. Secure the ice bag with an elastic wrap or any commercial ice wrap.

The old saying to apply ice 20 minutes on and 20 minutes off is sometimes not appropriate for some injured areas. For example, this process could actually cause more harm than good in small areas such as the fingers or hand, or over a superficial nerve such as the ulnar nerve. Ice is generally applied for between 5 and 20 minutes, until that area on the athlete is numb. The duration of application depends on factors such as the treatment area size and the tissue depth. For example, the wrist does not have a large quantity of muscle, fat, or other soft tissue and is a smaller area as compared to the gastrocnemius muscle. Consequently, you apply ice for a shorter amount of time, perhaps 5 minutes, as compared to the gastrocnemius, for which ice can be applied for perhaps 15 minutes. At first the ice makes the athlete's soft tissues feel cold. Afterwards the athlete feels burning, then aching, and finally numbness. Once the area is numb, you must remove the ice bag. The ice can be reapplied when the athlete has full feeling, the skin has returned to normal color at the injured site, and the tissues are rewarmed.

During the course of the ice application, frequently ask the athlete how he is feeling. If an athlete has never had ice applied to his body before, check the skin occasionally by briefly removing the ice bag. As the ice is applied and the skin turns cold, the skin changes from pink to red. However, if the skin becomes red, raised, and warm, the athlete most likely has an allergy to the ice, cold, and/or bag. In this case, remove the ice immediately, and monitor the athlete to make sure he does not have any other signs or symptoms of an allergic reaction, such as anaphylactic shock. Also, refer the athlete to a physician for evaluation to be certain the athlete does not have any underlying issues causing the unusual reaction. If at any time the athlete has unusual sensations, begins to feel ill, or has any other abnormal reaction to the ice application, remove the ice bag and begin to take a basic examination.

For injury care, it is important that you have access to ice or cold therapy agents. Most athletic facilities have access to ice. Clinics, hospitals, and similar facilities typically have access to ice via an ice machine. Ice can be made, and reusable, commercial, cold therapy packs can be stored in a freezer. If you do not have a freezer or ice machine available, then cold chemical packs are useful. By squeezing the chemical pack and shaking the contents, the chemical pack turns cold and provides similar effects as ice. When using these chemical cold packs, be careful when applying them to the athlete. They should not be placed directly on the athlete's skin. The chemical cold packs can get tissues extremely cold and freeze the skin, especially upon direct application. If the pack is punctured and the chemicals leak out, the athlete may sustain a chemical burn. Also at times, the chemicals do not mix properly and the bag does not get cold. Squeeze the chemical cold pack and shake it as per the directions on the pack. Then place the chemical cold pack into a sealed plastic bag to prevent chemicals from spilling through the bag and onto the skin. Place one layer or so of toweling on the injured area before placing the pack on the athlete. For those facilities that have access to fallen snow, use snow instead of ice. Snow is an excellent cold therapy agent because you can easily mold and conform it to the injured body part. Place the snow in a sealed plastic bag and use it as you would ice.

Utilizing ice cups can also be beneficial due to the cold and massaging effects. To create an ice cup, place cold water in a small paper cup, approximately three-quarters full. Put the cup in the freezer. Make sure the ice is completely frozen before use. When the water is frozen, carefully rip the top of the cup to expose approximately 1/2 inch of ice. Using a towel to soak up any dripping water, have the athlete rub the exposed ice on and around the injured area. Instruct him to move the cup in small circles or straight lines, for approximately 5–10 minutes, or until the area is numb (**Figure 6-10**). To obtain a massaging effect, the athlete can press deeper into the tissues as tolerated. Ice cup massage, as with any other

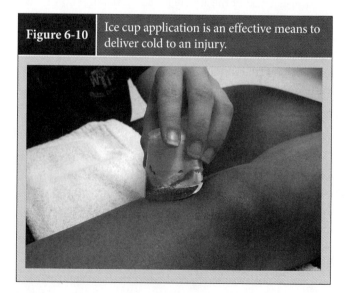

Figure 6-10 Ice cup application is an effective means to deliver cold to an injury.

ice application, should not be done directly over superficial nerves such as the ulnar nerve or the lateral peroneal nerve.

A question that many people ask is, "When can heat be applied to an injured area instead of ice?" The answer is that when an injury is in the first phase of healing, the inflammatory phase, ice must always be applied. Consequently, ice should be applied for the first 48 to 72 hours after injury. If heat is applied, in the form of either a dry or moist heating pad or any other heating element, then blood vessel vasodilation at the injury site will occur. The heat creates increased vascular permeability and edema, and results in increased swelling. These heat effects will cause the healing process to slow down and possibly exacerbate the injury. In most circumstances it is appropriate to apply heat to the injured structures after the inflammatory phase is over. When the athlete states his symptoms are subsiding and you observe decreasing signs of injury, then most likely heat can be applied safely. If at any time you are unsure whether it is appropriate to apply heat, simply continue with ice application. Ice application is appropriate and beneficial throughout all phases of healing.

The purpose of compression, the C in RICE, is to mechanically put pressure on and compress the injured area to assist in supporting the injured and surrounding structures. Compression can also aid in moving edema out of the injured area, which additionally promotes an optimal healing environment for the injured tissue. Compression is most often applied to an acute injured area with an elastic bandage. An athlete with a Grade 2 ankle sprain, for example, commonly has significant ankle swelling. Applying a compression wrap to the ankle, starting from the metatarsal heads and ending at the Achilles tendon origin, can provide support to the injured and surrounding structures, whether or not the athlete is full weight bearing. The compression also forces the edema out of the interstitial areas, which promotes healing. Compression is also applied with commercial neoprene sleeves. These sleeves are made for various body parts including the thigh, knee, and elbow. To assist in preventing swelling due to increased edema, compression is critical in the RICE process.

Tips from the Field

Tip 3 In order to deliver the cold from an ice bag fast to the athlete's tissues, and to provide compression at the same time, take an elastic bandage and wet it with cold water. Wring the elastic bandage and roll it back up. Apply the damp elastic bandage to the athlete's injured area as you would apply any other elastic bandage. Afterwards, place the ice bag on top of the damp elastic bandage and over the injured area. Secure the ice bag with another dry elastic bandage or a commercial ice bag wrap.

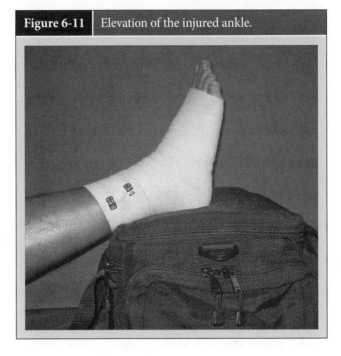

Figure 6-11 Elevation of the injured ankle.

Elevation is the E in the RICE principle. Elevation is used to assist in decreasing edema at the injured site, which as a result decreases swelling. By placing the injured area higher than the heart, gravity helps the circulatory system to transport waste products and fluid out of the injured area. If waste products and fluid are eliminated from the area, healing can be facilitated. If the athlete's ankle is injured, for example, apply an ice bag securely to the athlete's ankle. Have the athlete lie on a treatment table or floor with the affected ankle raised up with his heel on the wall, if feasible. You can also have the athlete lie down and raise the lower extremity up 12 inches on pillows, a gym bag, or the like to have the extremity above the level of the heart (**Figure 6-11**). Utilizing RICE can certainly help the athlete's injury to heal properly and return him to full, pre-injury activity.

SUMMARY

Once the primary survey has been completed, the basic examination is a means to determine what non-life-threatening injuries or illnesses an athlete has sustained. The basic examination's history, observation, palpation, and special tests are integral to determining not only what is wrong with the athlete, but also how to provide proper first aid treatment. What you find in your basic examination will also help you to determine whether the athlete should be moved and referred to a physician or EMS. Although you may not be formally trained in first aid or injury evaluation, by performing a basic examination you can afford your athletes immediate assistance with their injuries.

DISCUSSION QUESTIONS

1. Explain what SINS stands for and how you incorporate this principle into a basic injury examination.
2. Why is taking the athlete's history so important during the basic examination? What history questions are imperative to ask first during the questioning process?
3. When does the basic examination observation begin? What are some observable signs of injury?
4. What signs of injury can you identify during palpation? Why do you palpate the contralateral side prior to the injured side? How can you build a foundation of trust with your athlete prior to and during palpation?
5. What are the similarities and differences of performing active, passive, and resistive ROM (MMT) with your athlete? What do you look for when evaluating the athlete's joint motion and muscular strength?
6. Describe how you properly move an injured or ill athlete.
7. What does RICE stand for, and what are some principles of each RICE component?

CASE STUDY

A Thorough Basic Exam . . . Or Not?

Karen is a healthy 16-year-old softball pitcher with no prior medical history of injury or illness. Today, Karen joins her 12 teammates for a softball game against their league rivals. During the fourth inning, Karen pitches a fastball to the batter, who swings and hits a line drive right back at her. She makes an attempt to catch the ball but misses it, and gets hit in the abdomen with the ball. Karen immediately falls to the ground in pain. The coach runs out to check on Karen and finds her rolling from side to side on her back. Karen holds her arms in a crossed position over her abdomen to try and ease the pain. After about 1 minute, the coach gets her to calm down enough so that she can take a basic examination and try and figure out the SINS of the injury.

The coach begins her basic examination with her history. She asks Karen the following questions: "What happened? Where are you hurt? What does the pain feel like?" Barely able to speak due to the pain and anxiety she is experiencing, Karen answers, "I was hit with the ball in the stomach," as she clutches the left side of her upper abdomen. Karen describes the pain as sharp, and says through the tears, "It really hurts!" While observing Karen, the coach sees that she is doubled over in pain. She asks her to point to exactly where the pain is located. Karen, unable to stand up, slightly pulls up her shirt and clutches the upper left portion of her abdomen. The coach looks at her abdomen and notices that the injured area is slightly swollen and red. Suddenly, Karen says, "Coach, I feel sick to my stomach." The coach notices that Karen is beginning to turn pale. She puts the back of her hand to Karen's forehead, which feels cold and clammy. Karen tells her coach that the pain is spreading up into her shoulder, and she feels faint. The coach asks Karen, "Can I touch your abdomen and feel the area where you were hit?" Karen gives her coach permission to gently feel her stomach, and she notices that the area feels very rigid and warm. As the coach palpates her abdomen, Karen yells out in pain. The coach palpates Karen's right wrist and finds that Karen has a rapid and weak radial pulse. At this point, Karen seems to be calming down, but is still holding her abdomen in pain while sitting on the ground. The coach is not sure what to do next. The coach does not want to further delay the game, so she helps Karen stand up and walk to the dugout to relax. As the game continues, the coach keeps a watchful eye on Karen.

1. What should the coach's next course of action be to assist Karen?
2. Did the coach complete a thorough secondary survey? If not, then what else should the coach have done to complete a thorough basic examination?
3. What injuries may Karen have sustained?
4. At any time during this scenario was Karen in a life-threatening situation, warranting the coach to take a primary survey?
5. What could Karen's coach have done to help improve Karen's condition?
6. Should the coach activate the EMS system? Why or why not?

REFERENCES

Anderson, M. K., & Parr, G. P. (2011). *Fundamentals of sports injury management* (3rd ed.). Philadelphia: Lippincott Williams & Wilkins.

Laskowski, E. R. (2010). Heart rate: What is normal? Retrieved April 1, 2012, from http://www.mayoclinic.com/health/heart-rate/AN01906

Mowalvi, A., Whiteman, J., Wilhelmi, B. J., Neumeister, M. W., & McLafferty, R. (2002). Dorsalis pedis arterial pulse: Palpation using a bony landmark. *Postgraduate Medical Journal, 78,* 746–747. doi:10.1136/pmj.78.926.746.

Pfeiffer, R. P., & Mangus, B. C. (2012). *Concepts of athletic training* (6th ed.). Sudbury, MA: Jones and Bartlett Learning.

Prentice, W. E. (2011). *Principles of athletic training: A competency-based approach* (14th ed.). Champaign, IL: McGraw-Hill.

Schultz, S. J., Houglum, P. A., & Perrin, D. H. (2010). *Examination of musculoskeletal injuries* (3rd ed.). Champaign, IL: McGraw-Hill.

Starkey, C. (Ed.). (2013). *Athletic training and sports medicine: An integrated approach* (5th ed.). Burlington, MA: Jones and Bartlett Learning & American Academy of Orthopedic Surgeons.

Starkey, C., Brown, S. D., & Ryan, J. (2010). *Examination of orthopedic and athletic injuries* (3rd ed.). Philadelphia: FA Davis.

Chapter 7

Wellness, Exercise, and Fitness

CHAPTER OBJECTIVES

After you have read this chapter, you will be able to understand:

- The definitions and benefits of wellness, physical activity, exercise activity, and fitness
- How to prepare your athletes to incorporate cardiorespiratory and strength training exercise activity into their daily schedule
- The importance of conditioning principles in exercise programs
- The FITT principle and how it relates to cardiorespiratory, flexibility, muscular strength, and muscular endurance exercise activity
- The differences between, and advantages and disadvantages of, isotonic and isokinetic exercise
- Various methods for helping your athlete maintain positive mental health

Injuries and illnesses cannot always be prevented; however, we can take action to attempt to avoid them. Many factors play a significant role in injury and illness prevention, but some of the most important are wellness, participation in exercise activity, and fitness. We must educate athletes of all ages about the importance of wellness, exercise, and fitness. As an exercise scientist, your role is to instruct athletes on how to participate in lifelong, beneficial wellness and exercise activities. Because we are the athletes' instructors and mentors, we must participate in these activities as well, and be models for our athletes. This chapter focuses on how you and your athletes can properly incorporate wellness, exercise, and fitness

into an everyday regimen, in order to promote and maintain a healthy lifestyle.

WELLNESS, EXERCISE, AND FITNESS

As exercise science professionals, we instill knowledge in our athletes. We explain and demonstrate the importance of both physical and mental wellness. Wellness is the body's reaction to lifestyle choices. The National Wellness Institute defines wellness as "an active process through which people become aware of, and make choices toward, a more successful existence" (National Wellness Institute, n.d.). If an athlete chooses to smoke, drink alcohol, maintain a stressful lifestyle, and eat nutrient-poor foods, then the athlete will not promote his or her own wellness. With poor wellness, an athlete predisposes him- or herself to illness or disease.

Physical activity is somewhat different than exercise activity. Physical activity is any activity utilizing body movements, such as gardening, cooking, walking, or yoga, that raises the heart rate above normal levels (U.S. Department of Health and Human Services, National Heart, Lung, and Blood Institute [NHLBI], 2012). Along with the heart, the muscles work above resting level. Physical activity is not a regularly scheduled, planned, structured activity; rather, an athlete participates in physical activity on a casual basis. Everyone should participate in some form of daily physical activity to promote a healthy, good quality of life.

Exercise activity is planned exercise activity in which an athlete participates on a regular basis (NHLBI, 2012). Examples of exercise activity include strength training exercise in the gym, running on a treadmill, participating in aerobics classes, walking around town, and bicycling. As long as the activity raises the athlete's heart rate and he or she participates in a regular, planned exercise schedule, then the activity is considered exercise. Daily exercise activity will promote wellness, which in turn will help avoid injury and illness.

Depending on the athlete's level of activity and competition, the athlete may not be as fit as he or she should be. Fitness is the body's response to daily exercise. If an athlete is fit, then he or she can participate in many activities with energy. The athlete can perform strenuous daily activities with ease. Due to his or her fitness, he or she can participate in these activities without excessive fatigue. The term *fitness program* is often used to describe the type of exercise program that an athlete undertakes in order to improve his or her health. Fitness programs include exercises specifically focused on various components of fitness the athlete wants to improve to promote a healthy lifestyle.

Various components of fitness exist. The components are divided into two categories—health-related fitness and skill-related fitness (**Table 7-1**). Health-related fitness includes muscular strength, endurance, and flexibility; cardiorespiratory (also sometimes referred to as cardiovascular) endurance; and body composition (Hoeger & Hoeger, 2013). Each of these health-related fitness components are important in promoting overall physical health. Muscular strength is the muscles' ability to produce force. Muscular endurance is the muscles' ability to produce force over a period of time without undue fatigue. Flexibility is the muscles' ability to lengthen and stretch in order to allow the joints to move through a full range of motion (ROM). Cardiorespiratory endurance is the ability of the heart and lungs to work hard enough for the athlete to meet exercise training demands. Body composition is the amount of lean soft tissue, including muscle and fat, in the body.

Although these health-related fitness components are seemingly different, they are closely related. Exercises incorporated into common fitness programs should touch on each health-related component of fitness to make the athlete healthy and fit.

Unlike health-related components of fitness that focus on the athlete's general physical health, the skill-related components of fitness focus on athletes' specific skills during sport activities. These skill-related components of fitness include agility, balance, coordination, power, reaction time, and speed (Hoeger & Hoeger, 2013). Agility is the athlete's ability to change direction very quickly with coordinated body motion. Balance is the ability to hold the body in a stable position. Coordination is the ability of all body parts to function together and create smooth motion. Power is the muscles' ability to produce a large amount of force in a short amount of time. Reaction time is how quickly the body responds and the motions that result. Speed is how fast motion occurs over a distance. Skill-related fitness is crucial for a competitive athlete because he or she needs to enhance his or her motor skill function for competition. However, an average athlete who wants to maintain, or obtain, health and does not need to enhance skill should concentrate on the health-related fitness components.

If an athlete exercises for a minimum of 30 minutes a day, 5 days per week, then his or her fitness level will improve (MedlinePlus, 2012). However, daily physical activity and exercise are not the only factors that promote fitness. Wellness, accomplished by making healthy lifestyle choices, is highly linked to promoting a good quality of life. An athlete may be physically fit, but he or she may make detrimental lifestyle choices (**Table 7-2**). These choices ultimately result in poor

Table 7-1	Health- and Skill-Related Fitness Components
Health-Related Fitness Components	**Skill-Related Fitness Components**
Muscular strength	Agility
Muscular endurance	Balance
Muscular flexibility	Coordination
Cardiorespiratory endurance	Power
Body composition	Reaction time
	Speed

Table 7-2	Detrimental Lifestyle Choices

The following lifestyle choices are detrimental to an athlete's health:
- Smoking
- Chewing tobacco
- Drug abuse
- Leading a sedentary lifestyle
- Excessive or improper (i.e., not nutritious) food consumption
- Unwillingness to wear seatbelts
- Excessive alcohol consumption
- Participating in high risk behaviors (e.g., unprotected sexual activity, careless driving, etc.)
- Participating in violent behaviors (e.g., fighting, gang-related activities, etc.)
- Inadequate hygiene
- Unprotected environmental exposure (e.g., sun, chemicals, pollutants, etc.)
- Unwillingness to manage psychological stress

wellness. An athlete may believe that if he has a bad habit, or makes a poor lifestyle choice, such as smoking, he can negate these detrimental effects by taking part in beneficial lifestyle choices. An athlete may believe that even though he smokes, with daily exercises and proper nutrition he will be well, fit, and lead a healthy life. Unfortunately this is not the case. Explain to the athlete that participating in exercise or another beneficial lifestyle choice does not negate one poor lifestyle choice. Although exercise is beneficial, smoking will decrease his wellness, promote illness, and potentially cause disease. Ultimately, an athlete should adopt positive lifestyle choices and participate in exercise activity. Hopefully, by choosing to partake in activities that promote physical and mental wellness, performing daily exercise, and maintaining a satisfactory level of fitness, our athletes can live a healthy, long, good quality life.

LIFE EXPECTANCY

In today's society, people do not often consider how their current lifestyle will affect their quality and length of life. People tend to live for the moment. Many people, including athletes, take on destructive habits and lifestyle choices that are detrimental to their health. Some destructive habits include

> **Sedentary lifestyle** A lifestyle without regular physical activity or exercise.

smoking, excessive alcohol consumption, overeating, and lack of exercise. A **sedentary lifestyle** can also lead to injury, illness, and disease early in life. These lifestyle practices have been linked to illness and diseases, including cancer and heart disease (Centers for Disease Control and Prevention [CDC], 2009). The lack of physical and mental wellness commonly results in a poor quality of life and a shorter life expectancy.

The average life expectancy in the United States in 2015 has been projected to be 78.9 years—76.4 years for men, and 81.4 years for women (U.S. Census Bureau, 2011). The aver-

> **Chronological age** The actual number of years that an athlete has been living.
>
> **Biological age** The age an athlete is classified when factoring in her or his overall health as compared to other athletes who are her or his chronological age.

age life expectancy has risen and continues to rise annually; however, what truly matters is not the athlete's **chronological age**, but rather his or her **biological age**. Biological age is the age of the cells and organs in the body. It is determined by various factors includ-

ing an athlete's fitness level, including cardiovascular fitness, muscular strength, and flexibility, along with blood pressure, cholesterol values, skin elasticity, and cognitive ability. An athlete who is 50 years old and in exceptional health more than likely has a biological age less than her chronological age. As an example, her biological age could be 5 years less than her chronological age. On the other hand, an athlete who is 50 and in extremely poor health, smokes, and is obese may have a biological age that is 20 years more than his chronological age. As professionals, we should educate our athletes to be more concerned with their biological age rather than their chronological age. The athletes must consider their behaviors while they are young, and recognize that negative behaviors will definitely be a detriment to their future health.

HEALTHY PEOPLE 2020

In 2010, the U.S. Department of Health and Human Services put forth the Healthy People 2020 initiative (http://www.healthypeople.gov/2020/about/default.aspx) with the goal of promoting healthy, long lives for everyone in the United States. Healthy People 2020's "overarching goals" include the ability for all people throughout the nation to

> *attain, high-quality, longer lives free of preventable disease, disability, injury, and premature death; achieve health equity, eliminate disparities, and improve the health of all groups; create social and physical environments that promote good health for all; promote quality of life, healthy development, and healthy behaviors across all life stages.* (U.S. Department of Health and Human Services, 2012)

Unlike previous health goals, which focused on treatment of illness and disease, Healthy People 2020 goals focus on community education, measures to prevent illness, and disease prevention. The overarching goals are measured and assessed in regard to the progress made. Ultimately, Healthy People 2020's vision is "a society in which all people live long, healthy lives" (U.S. Department of Health and Human Services, 2012).

Many benefits of wellness, exercise, and fitness programs exist that collectively help a person to live a long, good quality life. The benefits are not only physical, but also mental, including emotional and social benefits. Physical benefits gained from participating in wellness, exercise, and fitness programs include, but are not limited to, the following:

- Increased vigor and ability to perform tasks
- Increased muscle tone and decreased fat tissue
- Increased bone strength, which can decrease the possibility of an athlete having osteoporosis
- Increased heart and lung function, which will increase the efficiency and effectiveness of the cardiorespiratory system

- Increased ability for the body to regulate blood sugar and insulin levels, which is crucial for athletes with type 2 diabetes
- Decreased weight, consequently decreasing body mass index (BMI)
- Decreased cardiovascular/heart disease risk factors
- Decreased cancer risk factors
- Decreased fatigue in performing exercise and activities of daily living (ADLs)
- Decreased mental stress, which will decrease anxiety and physical muscle tension
- Decreased blood pressure, which will decrease stress on the heart and cardiorespiratory system
- Decreased total cholesterol, decreased low-density lipoprotein (LDL), and increased high-density lipoprotein (HDL), which will help decrease the chance of cardiovascular disease and heart attack

When an athlete begins to participate in wellness, exercise, and fitness programs, he or she will see and feel the benefits immediately. These benefits may progress slowly or quickly depending on the individual athlete. However, the athlete should be assured that he or she will become healthier with a renewed opportunity to obtain a longer, good quality of life.

READINESS TO PARTICIPATE IN A WELLNESS, EXERCISE, AND FITNESS PROGRAM

In order to begin a wellness, exercise, and fitness program, you and your athlete must evaluate his or her current status of wellness and fitness. Various resources exist to accomplish this self-evaluation. The Internet offers reliable sources that can help an athlete to determine his or her current state of health. A government publication, "Be Active Your Way: A Guide for Adults," can be downloaded at www.health.gov/paguidelines/pdf/adultguide.pdf. This publication gives an inactive athlete who wishes to begin an exercise program many recommendations on how to do so properly.

Physical Activity Readiness Questionnaire (PAR-Q)

Standardized, common tools exist to evaluate an athlete's current state of wellness, readiness to participate in exercise, and fitness. The PAR-Q is a questionnaire that adults ages 15–69 can use to determine their readiness for exercise participation. The questionnaire was devised in Canada and promoted by the Canadian Society for Exercise Physiology. The PAR-Q is commonly used in the United States as an exercise readiness questionnaire. The athlete completes the questionnaire, and if he or she answers yes to any question, then a physician examination is necessary before beginning an exercise

program. The PAR-Q can be found at www.csep.ca/cmfiles/publications/parq/par-q.pdf.

Healthstyle: A Self-Test

Another means to determine the athlete's current health status is by using Healthstyle: A Self-Test, which was devised by the U.S. Department of Health and Human Services. The self-test is used as a reliable means to determine if the athlete's lifestyle choices put him or her at risk for illness or disease (**Activity 7-1**). This test requires the athlete to answer a variety of questions that pertain to the following lifestyle choice categories: use of tobacco, alcohol, and other drugs; eating habits; exercise/fitness; stress management; and safety. For each question within the categories, the athlete will respond almost always, sometimes, or almost never in regard to his or her participation in the activity. Each response is worth a certain number of points. At the end of the self-test, the athlete sums up the total number of points in each category. A high score represents the athlete's good health in regard to the category. For example, if the athlete scores high in the stress management category, you can conclude that the athlete is able to handle his or her stress well. However, if the athlete scores low in the eating habits category, then the athlete has significantly poor eating habits. This self-test identifies which health-related behaviors and lifestyle choices the athlete has under control. The self-test also identifies the behaviors and lifestyle choices the athlete must change to obtain overall wellness and a healthier lifestyle. With the self-test results and your expertise and assistance, your athlete can create wellness goals to incorporate into his or her wellness, exercise, and fitness program.

Tips from the Field

Tip 1 When meeting with an athlete for the first time to help them develop an appropriate personal wellness, exercise, and fitness program, give him or her an assumption of risk form, waivers, medical history, and preparticipation questionnaires. Also give him or her a Healthstyle, PAR-Q, and any other wellness and exercise readiness questionnaires or self-tests that are applicable. Have on hand a list of credible, reliable websites for your athlete's daily reference. For example, many websites offer downloadable programs that your athlete can download to his or her cell phone or computer. These programs assist your athlete in tracking his or her daily nutrition intake, exercise activity, emotional status, and so on. Some programs are free whereas others are accessible once the athlete pays a fee. One free site named Fatsecret (www.fatsecret.com) allows the athlete to actually chat with other people regarding his or her diet and exercise. Weight Watchers Online is a popular paid weight and exercise tracking program (www.weightwatchers.com) that offers a variety of interactive tools to assist your athlete in meeting his or her goals. In this era of increasing technology use, athletes may be more inclined to stay focused on a wellness, exercise, and fitness program if they utilize innovative technology tools to record their progress.

Body Composition Evaluation

Body composition evaluation determines the amount of lean soft tissue, including muscle and fat, in the body. This evaluation is important for people who begin a wellness, exercise, and fitness program because it gives them a baseline to assess their progression. Various tools to evaluate body composition exist, and more than one tool should be utilized to obtain an accurate evaluation for your athlete.

Skinfold Thickness Measurement

One means for an athlete to assess his or her body composition before beginning a wellness, exercise, and fitness program is by utilizing skinfold thickness measurements. These measurements give an approximation of the athlete's body fat content. Skinfold thickness measurements taken throughout the course

of the program assist the athlete in continually tracking his or her progress. The measurement is called a skinfold thickness measurement because the assumption is that most body fat lies directly below the skin. To measure skinfold thickness, calipers are necessary. A caliper is a handheld, pressure-sensitive measurement tool used to measure body fat (**Figure 7-1**). You can purchase calipers from various stores or websites. Exercise scientists should regularly practice taking skinfold measurements to become proficient.

Skin thickness measurements are taken at different sites on the body depending on whether your athlete is a woman or a man. Women are measured at the middle of the triceps, the superilium (right above the anterior iliac crest by the hip), and the anterior, middle thigh. Men are measured at the chest between the shoulder and nipple, the abdomen about 1 inch to the right of the umbilicus, and the anterior, middle thigh. Gently but firmly grasp the athlete's skin and slightly pull it away from the muscle. Then take the calipers and place them perpendicular to the fold. Take the measurement approximately 1/2 inch below where you are holding the skin. Take the measurements in each location three times in millimeters, releasing and grasping the skin each time, while recording each measurement. Average the measurements for

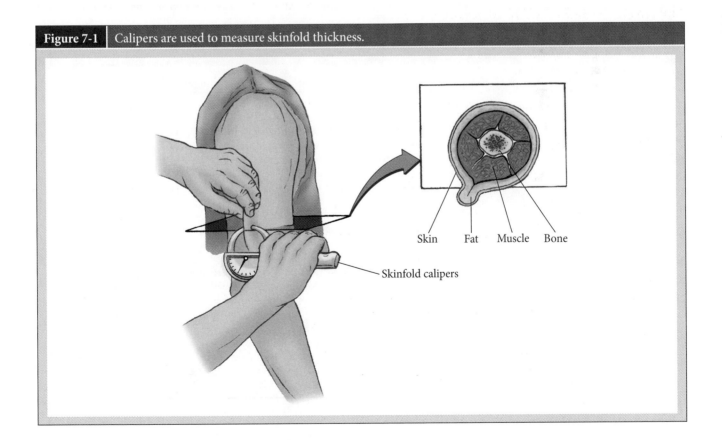

Figure 7-1 | Calipers are used to measure skinfold thickness.

Skin   Fat   Muscle   Bone

Skinfold calipers

each location, and then add together each location's averages. Then take the final calculation and find that number on a skinfold chart, which uses the gender, age, and sum of the three skinfolds to designate the athlete's body fat percentage (**Activity 7-2**). On the average, women should have a body fat percentage between 25-31% and men between 18-24%. Female athletes should have between 14-20% body fat and male athletes between 6-13%. Women who have over

32% body fat and men who have over 25% are considered obese (Muth, 2009).

Body Mass Index

Another tool that tracks the athlete's progress is body mass index (BMI), which evaluates an athlete's weight relative to his or her height. BMI indicates whether the athlete is underweight, normal, overweight, mildly obese, moderately obese, or severely obese (**Figure 7-2**). For both men and women, a BMI of 18.5–24.9 is considered normal. A BMI chart helps the athlete to determine a normal weight for his or her height. The athlete identifies his or her height and weight on the chart, and then determines if he or she has a normal BMI (**Figure 7-3**). The U.S. Department of Health and Human Services, National Heart, Lung, and Blood Institute has various resources for calculating BMI on the Internet, including BMI calculators, charts, and cell phone applications (www.nhlbisupport.com/bmi/bmicalc.htm). By determining his or her BMI, the athlete can set appropriate weight loss goals, aiming for a BMI within a normal range. A normal BMI has been shown to decrease an athlete's risk of illness, disease, and death; however, BMI should not be the only tool an athlete uses to determine risk of illness, disease, mortality, or overall health because it has a notable limitation—BMI does not take into account the body's quantity of muscle. Muscle has a greater density and weighs more than

Figure 7-2	Classification of BMI values.

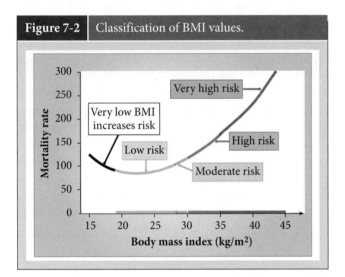

Figure 7-3	BMI chart.

BMI	19	20	21	22	23	24	25	26	27	28	29	30	31	32	33	34	35	36	37	38	39	40	41	42	43	44	45	46	47	48	49	50	51	52	53	54
Height (inches)												Body Weight (pounds)																									
58	91	96	100	105	110	115	119	124	129	134	138	143	148	153	158	162	167	172	177	181	186	191	196	201	205	210	215	220	224	229	234	239	244	248	253	258
59	94	99	104	109	114	119	124	128	133	138	143	148	153	158	163	168	173	178	183	188	193	198	203	208	212	217	222	227	232	237	242	247	252	257	262	267
60	97	102	107	112	118	123	128	133	138	143	148	153	158	163	168	174	179	184	189	194	199	204	209	215	220	225	230	235	240	245	250	255	261	266	271	276
61	100	106	111	116	122	127	132	137	143	148	153	158	164	169	174	180	185	190	195	201	206	211	217	222	227	232	238	243	248	254	259	264	269	275	280	285
62	104	109	115	120	126	131	136	142	147	153	158	164	169	175	180	186	191	196	202	207	213	218	224	229	235	240	246	251	256	262	267	273	278	284	289	295
63	107	113	118	124	130	135	141	146	152	158	163	169	175	180	186	191	197	203	208	214	220	225	231	237	242	248	254	259	265	270	278	282	287	293	299	304
64	110	116	122	128	134	140	145	151	157	163	169	174	180	186	192	197	204	209	215	221	227	232	238	244	250	256	262	267	273	279	285	291	296	302	308	314
65	114	120	126	132	138	144	150	156	162	168	174	180	186	192	198	204	210	216	222	228	234	240	246	252	258	264	270	276	282	288	294	300	306	312	318	324
66	118	124	130	136	142	148	155	161	167	173	179	186	192	198	204	210	216	223	229	235	241	247	253	260	266	272	278	284	291	297	303	309	315	322	328	334
67	121	127	134	140	146	153	159	166	172	178	185	191	198	204	211	217	223	230	236	242	249	255	261	268	274	280	287	293	299	306	312	319	325	331	338	344
68	125	131	138	144	151	158	164	171	177	184	190	197	203	210	216	223	230	236	243	249	256	262	269	276	282	289	295	302	308	315	322	328	335	341	348	354
69	128	135	142	149	155	162	169	176	182	189	196	203	209	216	223	230	236	243	250	257	263	270	277	284	291	297	304	311	318	324	331	338	345	351	358	365
70	132	139	146	153	160	167	174	181	188	195	202	209	216	222	229	236	243	250	257	264	271	278	285	292	299	306	313	320	327	334	341	348	355	362	369	376
71	136	143	150	157	165	172	179	186	193	200	208	215	222	229	236	243	250	257	265	272	279	286	293	301	308	315	322	329	338	343	351	358	365	372	379	386
72	140	147	154	162	169	177	184	191	199	206	213	221	228	235	242	250	258	265	272	279	287	294	302	309	316	324	331	338	346	353	361	368	375	383	390	397
73	144	151	159	166	174	182	189	197	204	212	219	227	235	242	250	257	265	272	280	288	295	302	310	318	325	333	340	348	355	363	371	378	386	393	401	408
74	148	155	163	171	179	186	194	202	210	218	225	233	241	249	256	264	272	280	287	295	303	311	319	326	334	342	350	358	365	373	381	389	396	404	412	420
75	152	160	168	176	184	192	200	208	216	224	232	240	248	256	264	272	279	287	295	303	311	319	327	335	343	351	359	367	375	383	391	399	407	415	423	431
76	156	164	172	180	189	197	205	213	221	230	238	246	254	263	271	279	287	295	304	312	320	328	336	344	353	361	369	377	385	394	402	410	418	426	435	443

Courtesy of the National Heart, Lung, and Blood Institute.

fat. An athlete's body may be composed of a large quantity of muscle and very little fat. Consequently, an athlete who has a large quantity of muscle may have a high BMI that categorizes him or her as overweight or even obese. Therefore, BMI should not be the sole predictor of an athlete's future health.

▌ Other Tools

This chapter describes only two of the many tools utilized to prepare an athlete for wellness, exercise, and fitness programs. Other, more highly accurate tests to determine body composition exist. For example, some testing procedures performed by specialists in an office setting utilize medical equipment. More commonly, the methods mentioned in this chapter are utilized as a quick and easy means to give an approximation of the athlete's current health status. When you assist your athlete in evaluating his or her current health status, utilize and recommend to your athlete valid resources such as governmental resources, validated by research, and commonly accepted and effective health and wellness methods.

GOAL SETTING

When an athlete wishes to begin a wellness, exercise, and fitness program, ask her to explain why she desires to participate and what she wants to accomplish. Speak with her and gain a history of why and how she arrived at this decision. Listen to the athlete, educate her, and offer suggestions for a healthier lifestyle. At this point, evaluate her current state of wellness and fitness using the aforementioned self-tests. Assist her in examining the results. The results, along with her history, will assist you in helping her set long- and short-term program goals.

Long- and short-term goals help guide a wellness, exercise, and fitness program. These goals are set when an athlete begins a program and are modified as necessary. Goal setting gives an athlete motivation and challenges during her journey to achieve better health. Work with the athlete to help her set reachable goals. Make sure the athlete does not set unreachable, unhealthy, or inappropriate goals. Long-term goals are general and focus on the program's end result. Two common long-term goals are to lose weight and stop smoking. On the other hand, short-term goals are set with the intent that the athlete can reach them within a week or two. These goals are objective and measurable; challenging, yet obtainable. These goals help the athlete to reach her long-term goals. Examples of short-term goals are to lose 1–2 pounds per week and to smoke only 15 cigarettes per day instead of 20. These short-term goals act as motivators for the athlete to continue on her quest for a healthier lifestyle.

Always explain to your athlete that short-term goals are motivators. Encourage her to give her best effort to reach these goals. Let the athlete know that during almost every program, setbacks occur. For example, the athlete may only lose 1/2 pound by the week's end. At this point, discuss the short-term goal, the program, and the athlete's effort in reaching the goal. Identify why the athlete did not reach the goal. The short-term goal may have been too difficult for the athlete, and consequently needs to be modified. The athlete may not have made an adequate effort to reach the goal. Keep in mind that short-term goals should challenge the athlete, but if you find she is not reaching the goals on a consistent basis, then the goals may be too difficult. As a result, the athlete can become discouraged and want to give up on her long-term goal. Also, if the short-term goals are too easy, the athlete can get a sense of being infallible. Then the athlete acquires a sense of being able to conquer all tasks and reaching all short-term goals. Consequently, when the athlete faces a challenging short-term goal and does not reach it, she will feel defeated. To avoid short-term goal setbacks, keep your athlete motivated. By creating measurable, challenging, and reachable long- and short-term goals with your athlete, you can prepare your athlete to obtain a healthier lifestyle.

PRINCIPLES OF CONDITIONING

After assisting your athlete in setting long- and short-term goals, you can begin to assist him/her in devising an exercise program. When assisting an athlete in devising an exercise program, educate him/her about the importance of the principles of conditioning. These principles include the following: warm-up, cool-down, progression, intensity, overload, adaptation, individuality, specificity, and safety (Prentice & Arnheim, 2010). The warm-up prepares the body, in particular the muscles, for exercise. The warm-up should be approximately 15–20 minutes long and consist of continuous **aerobic** activity that incorporates the entire body. Examples of aerobic activities include fast walking, jogging, jumping rope, bicycling, and calisthenics. One means to determine that the body is warmed up enough and the athlete is ready to exercise is if he has broken a sweat. Sweating means the body, including the muscles, has reached a state of readiness to participate in exercise activities. The warm-up includes stretching exercises that promote muscle lengthening and flexibility. Stretching principles and exercises are discussed in detail in the flexibility section of this chapter.

After exercise, a cool-down is necessary in order to return the body to a normal state. The cool-down takes place immediately after the exercise activity for approximately 10 minutes. The cool-down activities include similar aerobic activities as in

> **Aerobic** When the body, in particular the cardiorespiratory system, utilizes oxygen during activity.

the warm-up, but at a significantly lower intensity. Stretching of the muscles during both the warm-up and cool-down promotes flexibility, which increases ROM and function.

Progression describes how the exercise activities are sequenced throughout the exercise program duration. By utilizing the principle of progression, the preliminary exercise activities are simple, and then continue to become progressively more difficult. The activities begin at a low intensity and increasingly become more intense. An adequate progression is necessary in order to advance the athlete's exercise program, meet the athlete's fitness goals, and avoid injury.

The intensity of exercise is the extent that exercises challenge the athlete. When an athlete begins an exercise program, the intensity should be low and then progress to be higher. The intensity increases as the athlete's body becomes accustomed to the intensity. Likewise, as you incorporate new exercises into the athlete's program, the new exercises are at a low intensity and are increased as tolerated.

When the muscles are subjected to progressively increasing intensity, over time the muscles become accustomed to the intensity. For example, if you progressively increase the resistance that the athlete is utilizing during exercise, the muscles become accustomed to the resistance. As a result, the muscles become larger and stronger. This principle of conditioning is called overload.

Adaptation is a principle of conditioning that is similar to overload; however, adaptation deals with various components of fitness and not solely the muscles. The principle of adaptation is otherwise known as the specific adaptations to imposed demands (SAID) principle. The SAID principle means that when the body is presented with a challenge or a stressor, it becomes accustomed to the challenge or stressor and reacts in either a positive or negative manner. For example, if an athlete wishes to increase muscular flexibility, he must increasingly provide a stretch to the muscles during each exercise session. The stretch is a type of stress. The muscles respond to the stress by lengthening and providing the athlete with increased flexibility.

Individuality is the principle of conditioning that takes into consideration each athlete's activity level, personal characteristics, goals, and body type. Each wellness, exercise, and fitness program must address each athlete's needs in a specific manner due to the differences in athletes' attributes. Although you utilize some exercise skills and other programmatic methods from one athlete to another, consider that all athletes are not the same, and personalize each athlete's program. Athletes have different needs and goals. Therefore, modify each athlete's program as appropriate.

Specificity is a principle of conditioning that goes hand-in-hand with individuality. Specificity means that programs must be tailored to the athlete's specific needs and goals. The exercise program includes general exercises that benefit the athlete and also exercises that mimic skills utilized in the athlete's regular exercise activity. For example, if the athlete wants to play tennis, then her exercise program should focus on lower body muscular endurance, upper body power in her dominant arm, cardiorespiratory endurance exercises, and agility.

As for the safety principle of conditioning, always make sure the exercise programs do not put the athlete in harm's way. The athlete must be able to complete the exercise activities with the least possibility of injury. The exercises should be challenging; however, intense, difficult exercises predispose the athlete to harm. Likewise, the environment in which the athlete exercises should be safe at all times. The principles of conditioning must always be taken into consideration when you devise an exercise program for your athlete. By utilizing these principles as a framework, you can plan, evaluate, and adjust the athlete's exercise program effectively.

THE FITT PRINCIPLE

Assisting your athlete with his goals and educating him on the principles of conditioning are important tasks to complete before your athlete begins an exercise program. Along with these tasks, you and your athlete collaboratively decide what type of exercise program will be most effective in order to meet his long-term goals. An athlete who wishes to lose weight, increase muscular tone and strength, and increase heart and lung efficiency requires a combination of cardiorespiratory and strength training exercise. When planning the athlete's cardiorespiratory endurance exercise program, incorporate the FITT principle. FITT stands for frequency, intensity, time, and type of exercise.

Frequency of exercise is the number of days per week that an athlete exercises. In order to increase cardiorespiratory endurance, an athlete should exercise a minimum of 3 days a week and progress to 5 days per week. Some highly competitive athletes exercise more than 5 days per week due to their sport activity demands. However, for the average athlete to gain cardiorespiratory benefits, 5 days of cardiorespiratory exercise is optimal.

The *I* in FITT is intensity. Intensity is a principal of conditioning, but is also applied to cardiorespiratory exercise programming. During cardiorespiratory exercise, an athlete works continuously at a percentage of his **heart rate reserve** (HRR). HRR takes into account the athlete's resting heart rate (RHR) and his maximum heart rate (MHR). The HRR percentage is referred to as the

> **Heart rate reserve (HRR)**
> The difference between an athlete's RHR and MHR. The heart rate reserve is used to calculate the THR for the athlete during cardiorespiratory exercise.

target or training heart rate (THR). The higher THR indicates a higher intensity. Most athletes work at an intensity that is 60–80% of HRR. Some sedentary or unfit athletes may need to begin cardiorespiratory exercise at 40–60% of HRR.

In order to determine his MHR, determine the athlete's RHR. The RHR is the number of heartbeats per minute when an athlete is at rest. Typically, the best time for the athlete to calculate the RHR is in the morning, while he is still lying in bed. He can also take his RHR after sitting or lying still for at least 15 minutes. To find RHR, the athlete must find his radial pulse first. The radial artery is located by the wrist and pulsates with each heartbeat. Finding the radial pulse is not difficult. Place your palm up and place your opposing index and middle fingers approximately 1 inch below the wrist joint on the thumb side of the hand. The beating sensation is the radial pulse. The athlete can also take his pulse by utilizing the carotid artery. To find the carotid artery, place the index and middle fingers below the chin on the middle of the throat. Then slide the fingers about an inch to the side of the neck (**Figure 7-4**). The carotid artery pulse will be evident due to its strength. Either the radial or carotid pulse is entirely appropriate to utilize when determining RHR and THR. Once your athlete has found the pulse, have him count how many pulses occur within 10 seconds, and then multiply the number of pulses by six. The final number of pulses is the RHR in beats per minute (bpm). The average person has an RHR of approximately 60–100 bpm (Mayo Clinic, 2010). Your athlete should take his RHR in the same manner (e.g., in bed before waking,

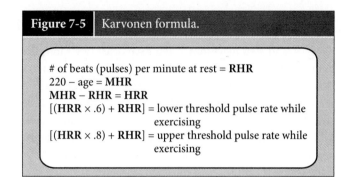

| **Figure 7-5** | Karvonen formula. |

# of beats (pulses) per minute at rest = **RHR**
220 − age = **MHR**
MHR − RHR = HRR
[(**HRR** × .6) + **RHR**] = lower threshold pulse rate while exercising
[(**HRR** × .8) + **RHR**] = upper threshold pulse rate while exercising

sitting at rest for 15 minutes) for 3 days, and average the three RHR values to determine the true RHR.

In order to get an athlete's lower and upper heart rate training thresholds, take the athlete's RHR and utilize the Karvonen formula (**Figure 7-5**). Maximum heart rate (MHR) is calculated first. Maximum heart rate in bpm is determined by calculating 220 minus the athlete's age. Therefore, a 40-year-old's MHR is 220 − 40 = 180 bpm. Then an athlete's HRR must be calculated. To calculate the HRR, an athlete takes the MHR − RHR. If the 40-year-old athlete has an RHR of 70 bpm, then his HRR is 180 − 70 = 110 bpm. Finally, to calculate the athlete's THR, the athlete calculates (HRR × 0.60) + RHR = the lower value of the THR, approximating 60% MHR, and (HRR × 0.80) + RHR = the higher value of the THR, approximating 80% MHR. Therefore, a 40-year-old athlete with an RHR of 70 bpm, a MHR of 180 bpm, and an HRR of 110 bpm has a lower threshold THR of (110 × 0.60) + 70 = 136 bpm, and a higher threshold THR of (110 × 0.80) + 70 = 158 bpm. When performing cardiorespiratory exercise, the athlete's pulse must range between 136 bpm and 158 bpm to get the beneficial cardiorespiratory effects. Have the athlete determine his lower and upper THR before exercise.

Once the athlete has completed his warm-up and begins his exercise program, have the athlete complete approximately 20 minutes of cardiorespiratory exercise before taking his pulse. Inform him to take his pulse while continuing to exercise at a lower intensity, without stopping entirely. If the athlete stops suddenly during exercise, his blood may pool to the extremities and he may faint. After taking a pulse, if the athlete's heart rate is not within training levels, he can modify the exercise accordingly to meet his desired intensity.

An athlete can choose from many commercial heart rate monitor devices to utilize during exercise to determine if he is meeting his THR. Heart rate monitors are devised as wrist-watches with or without touch screens, which can quickly determine an athlete's current heart rate. Some monitors are worn during exercise and monitor heart rate for the duration

| **Figure 7-4** | Location of the carotid pulse. |

of exercise, whereas others only take single readings when prompted. Exercise equipment, such as treadmills, stationary bicycles, and step machines, often have heart rate monitors built into the equipment. An athlete places his hands on the heart rate monitor, and the machine determines his heart rate while exercising. It is beneficial to use these commercial heart rate monitors because the athlete does not need to slow down his exercise, which quickly reduces heart rate, to calculate his heart rate. Continuous reading heart rate monitors are beneficial because the athlete can constantly visualize the increases in his heart rate while exercising, and consequently modify his workout immediately.

The third component of the FITT principle is time, which is the duration of the exercise session. To obtain positive cardiorespiratory effects, an athlete must exercise continuously at heart rate training levels for at least 20 minutes when beginning an exercise program, and gradually progress to 60 minutes. Positive cardiorespiratory effects are evident in athletes participating in only 20 minutes of continuous exercise per day for 3–5 days per week; however, a 60-minute exercise session is optimal.

The last component of the FITT principle is type. Aerobic activities are a type of exercise activity. The athlete must take part in aerobic activities in order to obtain positive cardiorespiratory effects. Aerobic activities that include whole body movements, utilizing both the arms and legs, are most beneficial. Swimming and jogging are two whole body movement, aerobic activities. Riding a stationary bicycle or utilizing a step machine is aerobic and beneficial, but these activities only utilize lower body movements. An upper body ergometer is also an aerobic exercise machine, but the athlete utilizes only the upper body (**Figure 7-6**). Regardless of which machine an athlete utilizes, he will gain beneficial cardiorespiratory effects.

CARDIORESPIRATORY EXERCISE PROGRAM READINESS

As the athlete's exercise scientist, evaluate her current level of cardiorespiratory fitness before she begins a cardiorespiratory program. The best and most accurate way to measure cardiorespiratory fitness is to measure your athlete's maximal oxygen uptake or VO_{2max}. This measure shows how efficiently the cardiorespiratory system utilizes oxygen. Unfortunately, the most conclusive VO_{2max} tests are performed under laboratory conditions with expensive equipment by highly trained exercise science professionals. However, you can utilize a few simple tests to estimate your athlete's VO_{2max}. These tests include the Rockport Fitness Walking Test, the YMCA Step Test, and Cooper's 1.5-mile run/walk test (Thygerson & Thygerson, 2013). For both the Rockport Fitness Walking Test and the YMCA Step Test, the athlete performs cardiorespiratory exercise, takes her pulse, and refers to the respective charts to determine her fitness level. The Rockport Fitness Walking Test requires the athlete to walk 1 mile before taking her heart rate, whereas the YMCA Step Test requires the athlete to step onto a 12-inch-high stable step or bench (**Activities 7-3 and 7-4**). For the Cooper's 1.5-mile run/walk test, the athlete times how long it takes her to complete a 1.5-mile run/walk. Afterward, the athlete refers to the Cooper's 1.5-mile run/walk test chart to determine her fitness level (**Activity 7-5**). Although these tests are not exact determinants of cardiorespiratory fitness, they are inexpensive, easy, common tests utilized to give an approximate baseline cardiorespiratory fitness level.

FLEXIBILITY

Flexibility is important for an athlete who participates in either a cardiorespiratory or strength training program. Good muscular flexibility assists the athlete in gaining a full, unrestricted ROM for her activity. Flexibility also helps the athlete maintain good blood flow to the working muscles, improves posture, and reduces muscular tension. Consequently, she will obtain optimal performance with her exercise activity and ADLs. A flexibility program for both cardiorespiratory and strength

| **Figure 7-6** | Upper body ergometer. |

training programs is necessary, because flexible muscles allow for more joint ROM.

It is important to determine your athlete's current state of flexibility before beginning a cardiorespiratory or strength training program. You can use a variety of methods to test your athlete's current state of flexibility. The basic and commonly used method is called the sit-and-reach test. This test evaluates general flexibility of the back musculature and hamstrings (**Activity 7-6**). A shoulder flexibility test (**Activity 7-7**) and additional flexibility tests for various areas of the lower body (**Activity 7-8**) can also assist you and your athlete in determining your athlete's current state of flexibility.

In order to obtain positive effects from a flexibility program, the athlete first performs a proper warm-up, which prepares the muscles and tendons for stretching activities. The flexibility program incorporates the FITT principle. The athlete's frequency starts at 3 days per week and progresses to daily stretching activities. The intensity of the stretch must be sufficient to create muscular tension. The athlete lengthens the muscles to the point of tightness and discomfort, but not pain. By stretching the muscles to the point of discomfort, the athlete deforms the muscle fibers, and makes them longer. Explain to the athlete that performing a stretch to the point of pain is very detrimental. If your athlete stretches and feels pain, she is actually tearing the fibers, creating injury and causing inflammation as a result. The duration of the stretch is important to cause the muscle fibers to deform and lengthen. The athlete holds the stretch for approximately 10–30 seconds at least three times. Each time the muscles are stretched, the muscle fibers become accustomed to the stretch, as per adaptation and the SAID principle, and remain at the lengthened state. The athlete performs additional **repetitions** if she needs to obtain further immediate muscular lengthening prior to or after exercise activity. Remind the athlete to stretch the contralateral muscle or muscle group so they are equally flexible.

> **Repetitions** How many times the exercise, stretch, or the like is performed.

Static, dynamic, or proprioceptive neuromuscular facilitation (PNF) stretching activities are used to promote muscular flexibility. However, the stretching activity utilized depends on the athlete's current flexibility and specific goals. A static stretch is a passive motion. The athlete places the muscle on tension and lengthens it to the point of discomfort. An example of static stretching is when the athlete sits on the floor in a hurdler's stretch and leans forward in an attempt to put her chest to her thigh. This static stretch results in elongation of the hamstring muscle group. Static stretching is a very common and safe stretching method. Therefore, an athlete who

is inflexible should begin a stretching program using static stretching.

To perform a dynamic stretch, the athlete performs active range of motion (AROM), which requires active muscle contractions. Simultaneously, the athlete lengthens the muscles and creates muscular tension. Once the athlete has an adequate amount of flexibility resulting from performing static stretching exercises, she can begin dynamic stretching exercises. An example of a dynamic stretch is a walking lunge. The athlete stands with her feet together. She places one foot forward so her knee is at approximately a 90-degree angle, allowing her to assume a lunge position. She will feel muscular tension and stretch at the quadriceps and hip flexor muscle groups. Afterwards, she alternates the lower extremities, brings the back extremity forward, and assumes the lunge position again. She continues the dynamic stretching exercises by alternating right and left lower extremities to perform walking lunges. The athlete must not bounce when performing dynamic stretching exercises, because the bouncing (ballistic) movements can cause muscle strains.

To properly perform PNF stretching, the athlete requires your assistance. PNF stretching involves **isometric** and **isotonic contractions** with periods of relaxation and stretching. PNF stretching utilizes the principles of autogenic and reciprocal inhibition. During autogenic inhibition, the **antagonist** is isometrically or isotonically contracted. Then the antagonist's contraction is released and the athlete allows the muscle to relax. Following the muscle relaxation, the muscle is stretched. Reciprocal inhibition differs from autogenic inhibition because the antagonist is stretched simultaneously as the **agonist** is isometrically or isotonically contracted. In order for the agonist to contract, the antagonist must relax. The most opportune time to stretch the antagonist is when it is in this relaxed state.

> **Isometric contraction** When the muscle contracts and creates tension. The muscle does not cause movement, shorten, or lengthen.
>
> **Isotonic contraction** When the muscle contracts and creates tension while moving through a partial or full ROM.
>
> **Antagonist** The muscle to be stretched.
>
> **Agonist** The muscle that is contracted and opposes the antagonist.

Three PNF stretching techniques commonly used are hold–relax, contract–relax, and slow-reversal–hold–relax. Hold–relax utilizes autogenic inhibition. The antagonist is first placed in a stretch. Then the athlete isometrically contracts the muscle against your manual resistance as forcefully as she can. The contraction is held for 10 seconds. Then on your command, the athlete releases the contraction and allows the muscle to relax. The relaxation phase lasts 10 seconds. After this time, move the muscle into a new, elongated position, and hold the stretch for 10 seconds. The entire process is repeated a few times as necessary for the athlete, and then performed on the contralateral side. Contract–relax also utilizes the principle of autogenic inhibition. The antagonist is first placed in a stretch. Then the athlete isotonically contracts the muscle against your manual resistance as forcefully as she can. The contraction is held for 10 seconds. On your command, the athlete releases the contraction, allowing the muscle to relax. The relaxation phase lasts 10 seconds. After 10 seconds, she minimally contracts the agonist to perform AROM, while you move the muscle into a new, elongated position. The stretch is held for 10 seconds. As with hold–relax, the entire process is repeated a few times as necessary for the athlete, and then performed on the contralateral side. Slow-reversal–hold–relax utilizes both autogenic and reciprocal inhibition. The antagonist is first placed in a stretch. Then the athlete isometrically contracts the muscle against your manual resistance as forcefully as she can. The contraction is held for 10 seconds. On your command, the athlete releases the contraction, allowing the muscle to relax. The relaxation phase lasts 10 seconds. After 10 seconds, and on your command, she maximally contracts the agonist to perform AROM against your resistance for 10 seconds. Afterwards, she relaxes the agonist while you move the antagonist into a new, elongated position. The stretch is held for 10 seconds. As with hold–relax and contract–relax, the entire process is repeated a few times as necessary for the athlete, and then performed on the contralateral side.

PNF stretching is effective, but requires good communication between you and your athlete. This stretching technique has the potential to cause injury if not performed properly. Consequently, demonstrate the techniques and practice them carefully with your athlete. Static, dynamic, and PNF stretching methods are effective, valuable means to increase an athlete's flexibility. Therefore, choose the methods that best meet the athlete's abilities and goals.

STRENGTH TRAINING PROGRAMS

Most athletes incorporate strength training activities into their exercise programs. Strength training activities build muscular strength, endurance, and power. Many principles of conditioning, especially overload, adaptation, intensity, and progression, come into play when an athlete incorporates strength training into his exercise protocol. Strength training exercises involve resistance, or weight, applied to a muscle or group of muscles. The muscles move the resistance through a ROM. The muscles are overloaded and adapt to the resistance by becoming larger

and stronger. To continue gaining positive strength training benefits, the athlete increases the resistance and exercise intensity in a progressive manner.

Strength training programs consist of isotonic and isokinetic exercises. Both exercises involve muscular **concentric contractions** and **eccentric contractions**.

Isotonic Exercise

Isotonic exercise is performed with a fixed resistance through a full or partial ROM; however, the speed of the exercise is variable. For example, if you hold a 20-pound dumbbell, the weight of the dumbbell does not change during the exercise. The speed of the exercise is variable, however, because the athlete will not move this 20-pound dumbbell at the exact same speed throughout the entire ROM (even though he may try to do so).

Isotonic exercises include the use of equipment such as resistance machines, free weights, barbells, dumbbells, sandbag weights, bands, and tubing. Resistance machines, commonly found in gyms and fitness centers, are simple and generally safe to utilize with prior, proper instruction. Bands and tubing are commonly utilized as isotonic exercise equipment. A leading company in the production of resistance tubing or bands is Thera-Band (www.thera-band.com/store/index.php). Thera-Band has created various colored resistance exercise tubing and bands, with each color signifying the resistance. The tan band is very thin and offers the absolute minimal resistance, the thick gold band offers maximal resistance, and a variety of colored bands offer resistances in between. These bands and tubes are very helpful in creating muscular strength. They are portable and inexpensive for our athletes. Although bands and tubing are utilized for isotonic exercise, unlike with dumbbells, sandbags, and the like, the athlete cannot quantify exactly how much resistance she is moving. She only is able to record her progression in regard to band or tubing color. Also, when using bands or tubing the resistance is greater at one point and less at another due to the band's or tubing's position relative to the body. Inexpensive free weights

---

Concentric contraction
When the muscle contracts and shortens. An example would be when the biceps brachii in the upper body are lifting an object while the athlete is flexing his or her elbow, and the gastrocnemius in the lower body when the athlete is pushing off his or her toes during jumping.

Eccentric contraction
When the muscle contracts and lengthens. An example would be when the biceps brachii in the upper body assist in lowering an object while the athlete is extending his or her elbow, and the hamstrings in the lower body when the athlete is slowing down during running.

can be purchased to utilize at home, or commercial resistance elastic tubing or bands can be packed in a suitcase to utilize when traveling.

Tips from the Field

Tip 2 If your athlete does not have access to weights or resistance tubing at home, have him or her use items around the house that can be weighed to continue his or her isotonic workouts at home. For example, an athlete can take an empty plastic milk gallon jug that has a handle, clean it out, let it dry, and put in sand, rocks, or even water to create the resistance. He or she can do the same with a tennis ball can. Have the athlete weigh the jug or can to prior to exercise. Depending on how much resistance your athlete uses, he or she can also utilize other household objects, such as unopened food cans or bungee cords, to complete his or her workouts.

Isotonic exercise produces many positive effects for the athlete. It builds strength throughout the entire ROM. The athlete performs the activities at various speeds, which makes the exercises functional and applicable to their activities. The athlete moves the resistance in functional patterns, as she would when performing activities such as throwing or kicking. Consequently, isotonic exercise is very appropriate for athletes to gain strength specific to their chosen exercise activities.

> **Stick points** Specific locations within the ROM when the athlete is unable to move the resistance because the resistance is too great, the muscle is too weak, or both.

Isotonic exercise does have some disadvantages. One disadvantage is in regard to **stick points**. Commonly, while an athlete moves a resistance through a ROM, she comes across a particular point within the ROM where she is unable to move the resistance. At this point in the ROM, the athlete is forced to stop her motion and switch to a lighter weight to complete the ROM. If she tries to move the resistance and it is too heavy for her, she will probably injure herself. Another disadvantage of isotonic exercise is that resistance machines, found in gyms and fitness centers, typically focus on one muscle or muscle group. Consequently, the athlete must use numerous machines in order to build strength throughout the body. These machines take up a large amount of space and are costly. Therefore, athletes typically do not have each, individual machine within their homes. Barbells are simple to utilize; however, an athlete requires assistance from another athlete (called a *spotter*), who helps if the athlete loses her grip on the bar and drops it while performing a lift. The spotter also helps the athlete to lower

and place the barbell correctly back on the rack. This assistance can be viewed as a disadvantage because the athlete does not always have a spotter when performing barbell activities at home or in other venues. Also, as previously mentioned, quantifying resistance with bands and tubing is not readily possible. Resistance applied to the body segment changes as the tube's or band's position changes. For purposes of recording resistance measures and building strength through a full ROM, bands and tubing may not be the isotonic equipment of choice. Despite these disadvantages, in general isotonic exercise is a very beneficial, common means for an athlete to gain muscular strength.

Isokinetic Exercise

Isokinetic exercise is different than isotonic exercise because the resistance is accommodating and the speed is fixed. Special machines, such as those manufactured by companies such as Cybex and Biodex, are utilized for isokinetic training. Accommodating resistance means that the resistance is placed on the athlete throughout the ROM in response to how hard the athlete pushes against the machine. The athlete does not know the amount of resistance applied during the motions. The accommodating resistance challenges the athlete's muscles throughout the entire ROM. The isokinetic exercise speed is fixed. As an exercise scientist, you set the machine for a specific speed at which the exercise is performed. If you want the athlete to move slowly to build muscular strength and power, then set the machine to move at a low speed such as at 60 degrees per second. If you want the athlete to move quickly, to build muscular strength and endurance, then set the machine to move at a high speed such as 360 degrees per second.

Isokinetic exercise has many benefits. The athlete is able to gain muscular strength through a full ROM, without any stick points because the machine accommodates the resistance output. The machine can be set to allow the athlete to move at a variety of speeds, in order to focus on muscular strength along with muscular endurance and power. The computer software allows the athlete to immediately view her effort on the monitor and print out her progress.

Of course, disadvantages also exist. The exercises are performed in straight planes and do not simulate functional movements. Therefore, isokinetics are not functional for sport-specific activities. The machines are large and not portable, so an athlete cannot perform isokinetic exercise at home. Isokinetic machines are also expensive. Some machines, including the accessory equipment needed for the machine, cost tens of thousands of dollars. When utilizing the machine, the athlete has to overcome a large learning curve. You need to instruct the athlete on its use as well as have training or practice sessions so she can familiarize herself with the machine, utilize it safely, and learn its limitations before utilizing it for training. Although isokinetic exercise has its disadvantages, it is valuable and does have a place in an athlete's strength training program.

Beginning a Muscular Strength and Endurance Program

Before an athlete begins a strength training program, you should test his current state of muscular strength and endurance. As with cardiorespiratory and flexibility exercises, have your athlete perform a variety of tests to determine his current state of muscular strength and endurance. The most common way to determine your athlete's current state of muscular strength is by using the One-Repetition Maximum Test (1 RM) (**Activity 7-9**). The findings from this test give a baseline from which you can determine the starting resistance for your athlete's strength training program. The Hand Grip Strength Test utilizes a handheld device called a dynamometer. The athlete grips the dynamometer, applies a full force contraction, and the dynamometer reads the force produced (**Activity 7-10**). An easy test for muscular endurance is having the athlete perform as many push-ups as he can (**Activity 7-11**). The YMCA Bench-Press Test is another means to measure muscular endurance, especially for larger athletes (**Activity 7-12**). The YMCA Half Sit-up Test (Partial Curl-up Test) is also valuable to determine the athlete's current state of muscular endurance (**Activity 7-13**). These muscular strength and endurance assessment tests are critical to utilize in determining your athlete's baseline capabilities, and to create an effective, safe strength training program.

When devising an athlete's strength training program, also referred to as a strength training protocol or strength training prescription, keep in mind the principles of conditioning. Also remember that one athlete has different goals than another. Although you can use the same exercise skills from one athlete's program to another, each athlete must be treated as an individual (the individuality principle of conditioning). Plan the program according to his specific activity needs and goals (the specificity principle of conditioning). As always, the program must be safe for the athlete (the safety principle of conditioning), and include a warm-up and cool-down (the warm-up and cool-down principles of conditioning). An appropriate progression of overload and intensity (the overload and intensity principles of conditioning) is necessary so the athlete's muscles can adapt to the stresses placed on them and benefit from the training (the adaptation and SAID principles of conditioning).

Along with the principles of conditioning, utilize the FITT principle when creating your athlete's exercise prescription. Devise the athlete's program based on the athlete's goals. Typically when an athlete begins strength training, the athlete participates three times per week. Upper, lower, and core body activities comprise the program. Typically, an athlete trains one body group each of the 3 days. Perhaps on Mondays the athlete performs upper body exercises, on Wednesday he performs core body exercises, and on Friday he performs lower body exercises. During the additional 2–3 days per week, the athlete performs cardiorespiratory activities. The athlete completes flexibility exercises each day.

The exercise intensity must be great enough to progressively overload the muscles. If the specific muscles performing the exercise are not entirely fatigued by the last repetition, then the muscles were not overloaded enough due to the intensity being too low. If the intensity is too low, then your athlete will not see the benefits from exercise.

In regard to exercise program time, each exercise session begins with the standard 15- to 20-minute warm-up, and ends with the 5- to 10-minute cool-down. However, the duration for the other exercises varies according to the type and number of exercises incorporated into the program each day. Typically, an athlete should complete approximately 10 different exercises per strength training session. The athlete can complete more or less than 10 exercises depending on the athlete's goals and the number of weeks the athlete has been participating in the strength training program. The longer the athlete has been participating in the program, the longer the strength training session may take due to an increase in types of exercises, repetition, and **sets**.

The types of exercises include isometric, isotonic,

> **Sets** A series of repetitions. An athlete may perform 10 repetitions in one set. In this case, three sets make up 30 repetitions.

and/or isokinetic exercises, utilizing the equipment previously discussed. The athlete can also utilize his own body weight to provide resistance, which is done when performing lunges, push-ups, pull-ups, and sit-ups. The exercises should include open kinetic chain (OKC) and closed kinetic chain (CKC) exercises. OKC exercises include isotonic activities, such as utilizing dumbbells, with the distal extremity (the hand or foot) moving through space. The hand or foot is not fixed in OKC activities. With CKC activities, such as lunges or push-ups, the distal extremity is fixed on a stable object such as the floor, table, or wall. OKC activities strengthen muscles around a particular joint, whereas CKC exercises strengthen muscles throughout the entire extremity that is fixed. OKC activities are important to incorporate into an athlete's strength training program if the athlete cannot weight bear on either the upper or lower extremity. However, OKC activities are not as safe as CKC activities, because with CKC activities the athlete has entire limb control and can stop the motion immediately if necessary. Both OKC and CKC exercises incorporate isometric, isotonic, and isokinetic exercises effectively into your athlete's strength training program.

In order to devise specific resistance exercises to incorporate into your athlete's strength training program, first determine why he wants to strength train. His goals direct you to devise a specific, individual program for the athlete. Ask him if he wants to gain muscular strength to perform everyday activities and obtain optimal health, muscular endurance to perform activities for a long period of time, or muscular power to perform forceful activities for a short period of time. All athletes must have some muscular strength to perform ADLs and other physical activities. Some athletes are content with only obtaining this goal; however, many athletes want to continue with strength training and obtain muscular endurance or power capabilities.

Guidelines for a Strength Training Program

The amount of resistance utilized, along with the number of repetitions and sets in a strength training program, varies depending on your athlete's goals. Experts differ on how many repetitions and sets are needed, as well as the amount of resistance necessary to obtain desired results. Therefore, after reviewing the literature, including resistance recommendations from the National Academy of Sports Medicine (n.d.), the following guidelines can be utilized.

To obtain optimal muscular strength in order to perform ADLs and promote a healthier lifestyle, include approximately 8–12 repetitions and 3 sets of activity into your athlete's strength training program. A low resistance of approximately 70–85% of the athlete's 1 RM is used. The rest time between sets is approximately 1 minute.

For an athlete who wishes to gain muscular endurance, approximately 12–16 repetitions and 3 sets of each activity are incorporated into his strength-training program. The resistance is approximately 50–70% of the athlete's 1 RM, which is a greater resistance than utilized for general muscular strength gains. Rest time is the same as for muscular strength exercises.

Approximately 2–4 repetitions with 1–3 sets is appropriate for gaining muscular power. The athlete uses approximately 30–45% of 1 RM of resistance, with a longer rest period of approximately 2–5 minutes between sets.

Regardless of whether the athlete wants to gain muscular endurance or power, when he is beginning a strength training program, have him perform general muscular strength exercises first. Later, after the muscles **hypertrophy**, you can modify your athlete's program to focus on muscular endurance or power.

> **Hypertrophy** When a muscle increases in size due to progressive overload of the muscle by increasing the resistance.

MENTAL READINESS

Although determining your athlete's physical readiness for cardiorespiratory, flexibility, and strength training exercise programs is important, do not forget to make sure your athlete is mentally ready for exercise. If the athlete is not mentally ready, injury can result. When taking your athlete's history, you can tell if he is mentally ready for exercise by how he behaves and what he says. Watch his body language, including his facial expressions. You know he is mentally ready if he expresses confidence and a positive attitude. An athlete beginning a new program most often expresses his excitement and readiness to make a lifestyle change. He relays to you his motivation along with any anxieties. It is normal for an athlete to state he is anxious. If he shows signs of anxiety or fear, offer suggestions on how to manage stress by performing relaxation techniques. Although for some athletes exercise itself helps relieve mental stress, additional stress reduction techniques can be incorporated into an athlete's daily schedule.

Athletes typically know what works best to manage their stress. Some examples of stress management and relaxation activities include listening to music, reading, or playing video games. Some athletes receive full body massages to relieve physical tension along with mental stress. Athletes also participate in other exercise activities that focus on body and mind relaxation, such as yoga and tai chi. Even though the athlete participates in these activities, he may need additional stress reduction and relaxation methods. Three stress management methods athletes can utilize are imagery, meditation, and Jacobson's muscular relaxation technique.

Imagery

Imagery is a method of visualizing something pleasant that creates positive thoughts. An athlete may start an exercise program to help her to lose body fat. The athlete imagines her body as it will appear when she has reached her goal. Another athlete may choose to picture a place, such as a beautiful, serene island, that creates a calming effect for her. The athlete performs the imagery anywhere at any time. To get the most beneficial effects, instruct her to perform the imagery alone in a quiet, low-lighted room. Tell her to lay down on a couch or bed, or find another comfortable position, with her eyes closed. The athlete must not be disturbed while performing the imagery activity. The imagery session takes as long as the athlete needs. When the athlete feels a decrease in mental stress that is sufficient, then the imagery was successful and the session can end.

Meditation

Meditation is similar to imagery in a variety of ways including body positioning and environment; however, meditation requires slow and controlled breathing. The athlete breathes in through the nose and out through the mouth. He focuses on a word or phrase to repeat in his mind, with the intent to block all negative or unnecessary thoughts. Have the athlete incorporate meditation into his daily activities. The meditation session should begin at approximately the same time each day and must be uninterrupted for approximately 10–20 minutes.

Jacobson's Muscular Relaxation Technique

In the early 1900s, Edmund Jacobson, MD, PhD, created a muscular relaxation technique that helps to decrease muscular tension, which results in a decrease of mental stress (Gessel, 1989). The progressive relaxation techniques consist of voluntary, forceful muscle group contractions. Jacobson wanted his patients to focus on the awareness of muscular tension and then relaxation. He concluded that this awareness decreases physical tension as well as mental tension.

The athlete sits or lays in a low-lighted, quiet room in a comfortable position. During the first session, the athlete creates a fist, noting the muscular tension produced. Then the athlete voluntarily relaxes the muscles. The athlete performs subsequent sessions of upper extremity, trunk and core, and lower extremity voluntary muscular contractions. Voluntary relaxation follows each contraction. The athlete progresses to eventually complete the muscular contractions and relaxations in a systematic fashion throughout the entire body in one session.

These relaxation techniques do not always result in benefits immediately. As the athlete continues to perform these techniques and learns how to listen to his body, the techniques will become very beneficial in managing his mental stress.

SUMMARY

As professionals in the field of exercise science, we have many roles in regard to our athletes. We guide our athletes to lead a healthy lifestyle. We educate them to understand how wellness, exercise, and fitness are beneficial to decrease the chance of injury, illness, disease, and death. We recommend many helpful, and potentially lifesaving, tools to begin a wellness, exercise, and fitness program. The roles we assume are imperative to create a better quality of life for our athletes.

DISCUSSION QUESTIONS

1. Name the health-related components of fitness. Name the skill-related components of fitness. What do each of these components measure? Why are the health-related components of fitness important for all athletes?
2. What tools can an athlete utilize to determine his or her current health status and to predetermine his or her readiness for exercise?
3. What are the principles of conditioning? Describe how each principle of conditioning is incorporated into an athlete's exercise program.
4. What assessment tests are utilized to determine your athlete's current state of cardiorespiratory, flexibility, and muscular strength and endurance? Why is it important to assess your athlete's current state of cardiorespiratory, flexibility, and muscular strength and endurance prior to devising her or his exercise program?
5. What does FITT stand for, and how is this principle utilized for cardiorespiratory, flexibility, and muscular strength and endurance exercise programs?
6. Name different methods of promoting your athlete's mental health.

CASE STUDY: FITNESS WISHES, BUT DANGEROUS HEAT!

It is a warm, sunny Saturday afternoon in July. The ambient environmental temperature is 85 degrees, and the relative humidity is 80%. Dan, a 35-year-old man, wants to become more fit in order to feel better both physically and mentally. To become more fit, Dan knows that he needs to lose some weight. Dan is 5'9" tall and weighs 205 pounds. Therefore, his BMI is 30.3, which means Dan is considered obese. Although Dan is taking an active role in becoming healthier, he smokes approximately one pack of cigarettes per day. Dan admits that he is not ready to quit smoking. He figures the exercise will combat the detrimental effects of smoking and make him healthier.

Dan wants to take advantage of the beautiful weather. He decides to begin his fitness program by exercising outside today. Dan has not participated in any exercise for approximately 1 year. He takes part in casual physical activity, but realizes he needs to have structure with his exercise program. Dan sets a goal to progress and increase the exercise activity intensity as his body allows, and as a result, he will lose fat tissue. He also wishes to overload his muscles to make him stronger. To get back into shape, he wants to incorporate jogging into his exercise protocol. Dan figures that he can exercise approximately 30 minutes or so a day to start, and then increase the duration of the exercise over time.

After taking care of a few chores around the house, and having another cigarette, Dan gets dressed in sweatpants and a t-shirt, laces up his sneakers, and heads outside. Dan will jog slowly, because he has not jogged in a long time. Consequently, he believes a warm-up or stretching is not necessary. Dan heads out to jog to the park. The park is about 2 miles from Dan's house. Dan plans on running from his house to the park and back for a total of 4 miles. He figures it will take him approximately 40 minutes or so to jog this distance. After all, over a year ago when he was more physically fit he remembered that he could run a 6-minute mile; however, Dan knows he must take the jog slow. He also believes that because he is relatively healthy, he will attempt to jog the 4 miles without stopping.

A half mile into his jog, Dan begins to become thirsty. He realizes that he has not eaten or drank anything since breakfast, and does not have any water or electrolyte drinks with him. The park does not have any water fountains available. Dan figures that he will be fine, so instead of turning around and going back to his house he decides to continue on to the park. Dan reaches the mile mark in 15 minutes. It is taking him longer to run than he thought it would. At this point Dan is extremely thirsty, is sweating profusely, has labored breathing, and is becoming extremely tired. However, Dan continues on, figuring that the thirst, sweat, breathing, and fatigue are side effects from lack of conditioning. Shortly into his second mile, Dan begins to get a headache. He becomes increasingly nauseous and dizzy, and his breathing is becoming more difficult. Again, Dan continues to jog. Now Dan is into his third mile. He begins to become uncoordinated, weak, and disoriented.

At this point, the discomfort is too much for Dan. He sees a park bench up ahead, so he jogs to the bench, immediately stops jogging, and sits on the bench to rest. While he is sitting down his calf and hamstring muscles begin to cramp in his right leg. He begins to feel very ill. His breathing is extremely fast and shallow. Dan feels like he cannot catch his breath. A woman walking her dog by Dan notices that he does not look okay. She walks over and asks him what is wrong. She notices that he is profusely sweating and his face is very pale. Barely able to speak due to his breathing difficulty, he tells her how he feels. She asks him for permission to assist him with his condition and he welcomes the help.

1. How much weight would Dan have to lose to maintain a BMI that is considered normal?
2. Should Dan have warmed up and stretched prior to exercise? If so, what exercises should Dan have incorporated into his warm-up?
3. What should Dan have considered in regard to the FITT principle, considering this is the first time he has exercised in approximately 1 year?
4. Should Dan have gone jogging at this time of day, with the outside temperature and humidity as it was? Why or why not?
5. How do you think the detrimental lifestyle choice of smoking has affected Dan's ability to jog the 4 miles?
6. What should Dan have done to better prepare for his jog?
7. What should the bystander do to assist Dan? Should she activate the EMS system? Why or why not?

REFERENCES

Centers for Disease Control and Prevention (CDC). (2009, November 16). Heart disease behavior. Retrieved April 6, 2012, from http://www.cdc.gov/heartdisease/behavior.htm

Gessel, A. H. (1989). Edmund Jacobson, M.D., Ph.D.: The founder of scientific relaxation. Retrieved April 23, 2012, from http://www.progressiverelaxation.org

Hoeger, W. W. K., & Hoeger, S. A. (2013). *Fitness and wellness* (10th ed). Independence, KY: Cengage Learning.

Mayo Clinic. (2010). Heart rate: What's normal? Retrieved April 16, 2012, from http://www.mayoclinic.com/health/heart-rate/AN01906

MedlinePlus. (2012, April 6). Exercise and physical fitness. Retrieved April 10, 2012, from http://www.nlm.nih.gov/medlineplus/exerciseandphysicalfitness.html

Muth, N.D. (2009). What are the guidelines for percentage of body fat loss? Retrieved March 18, 2013, from http://www.acefitness.org/acefit/expert-insight-article/3/112/what-are-the-guidelines-for-percentage-of/

National Academy of Sports Medicine. (n.d.). How much weight do I use for muscle endurance? Retrieved March 3, 2013, from http://www.sharecare.com/question/weight-use-for-muscle-endurance

National Wellness Institute. (n.d.). Defining wellness. Retrieved March 18, 2013, from http://www.nationalwellness.org/?page=Six_Dimensions&hhSearchTerms=definition

Prentice, W. E., & Arnheim, D. D. (2010). *Essentials of athletic injury management* (8th ed.). New York: McGraw-Hill.

Thygerson, A. L., & Thygerson, S. M. (2013). *Fit to be well*. Sudbury, MA: Jones and Bartlett.

U.S. Census Bureau. (2011). Births, deaths, marriages, & divorces: Life expectancy. Retrieved March 18, 2013, from http://www.census.gov/compendia /statab/2012/tables/12s0104.pdf

U.S. Department of Health and Human Services. (2012). About Healthy People. Retrieved March 1, 2013, from http://www.healthypeople.gov/2020 /about/default.aspx

U.S. Department of Health and Human Services, National Heart, Lung, and Blood Institute. (2012). What is physical activity? Retrieved April 10, 2012, from http://www.nhlbi.nih.gov/health/health-topics/topics/phys/

Chapter 7 Activities

ACTIVITY 7-1: HEALTHSTYLE: A SELF-TEST

This self-test, which is a modified version of the one developed by the U.S. Public Health Service, assesses several health-related behaviors. Although these behaviors apply to most individuals, pregnant women and people with chronic health concerns should follow the advice of their physicians. Answer each of the following questions by circling the number of the response that applies best to you. Add the number of points under each health-related behavior category to obtain a score for that category. Use the scoring guide at the end of the test to determine the level of risk you are incurring by your health-related behavior.

Tobacco, Alcohol, and Other Drugs

If you have never used tobacco products, enter a score of 10 for this section, and skip questions 1 and 2.

	Almost always	Sometimes	Almost never
1. I avoid using tobacco products.	2	1	0
2. I smoke only low-tar cigarettes.	2	1	0

Smoking Score:

	Almost always	Sometimes	Almost never
3. I avoid drinking alcoholic beverages, or I drink no more than one or two drinks per day.	2	1	0
4. I avoid using alcohol or other drugs (especially illegal drugs) as a way of handling stressful situations or problems in my life.	2	1	0
5. I avoid driving while under the influence of alcohol and other drugs.	2	1	0
6. I am careful not to drink alcohol when taking certain pain medications or when pregnant.	2	1	0
7. I read and follow the label directions when using prescribed and over-the-counter drugs.	2	1	0

Alcohol and Other Drugs Score:

Eating Habits

	Almost always	Sometimes	Almost never
8. I eat a variety of foods each day, including fruits and vegetables, whole-grain products, lean meats, low-fat dairy products, seeds, nuts, and dry beans.	3	1	0
9. I limit the amount of fat that I eat, especially animal fats such as cream, butter, cheese, and fatty meats.	3	1	0

(continues)

Eating Habits (Continued)

	Almost always	Sometimes	Almost never
10. I limit the amount of salt that I eat, by avoiding salty foods and not using salt at the table.	2	1	0
11. I avoid eating too much sugar, by eating few sweet snacks and limiting sugary soft drinks.	2	1	0

Eating Habits Score:

Exercise/Fitness

	Almost always	Sometimes	Almost never
12. I maintain a body weight that is reasonable for my height.	3	1	0
13. I do vigorous exercise (for example, running, swimming, or brisk walking) for at least 30 minutes at least three times per week.	3	1	0
14. I do exercises to enhance my muscle tone and flexibility (for example, yoga or calisthenics) for 15 to 30 minutes at least three times per week.	2	1	0
15. I use part of my leisure time participating in individual, family, or team activities that increase my level of physical fitness (for example, gardening, bowling, or golf).	2	1	0

Exercise/Fitness Score:

Stress Management

	Almost always	Sometimes	Almost never
16. I take time every day to relax.	2	1	0
17. I find it easy to express my feelings.	2	1	0
18. I recognize and prepare for events or situations that are likely to be stressful.	2	1	0
19. I have close friends, relatives, or others I can talk to about personal matters and contact for help when needed.	2	1	0
20. I participate in hobbies that I enjoy or group activities such as religious or community organizations.	2	1	0

Stress Management Score:

Safety	Almost always	Sometimes	Almost never
21. I wear a seat belt while riding in a motor vehicle.	2	1	0
22. I obey traffic rules and speed limits while driving.	2	1	0
23. I have a working smoke detector in my home.	2	1	0
24. I am careful when using potentially harmful products or substances, such as household cleaners, poisons, and electrical devices.	2	1	0
25. I avoid smoking in bed.	2	1	0
Safety Score:			

WHAT YOUR SCORES MEAN

Scores of 9 or 10 for each section: Excellent! Your responses show that you are aware of the importance of this area to your health, and that you are practicing good health-related habits. As long as you continue to do so, this area of health should not pose a risk.

Scores of 6 to 8 for each section: Your health practices in this area are good, but there is room for improvement. Look at the items that you answered with "Sometimes" or "Almost Never." What lifestyle changes can you make to improve your score and reduce your risk?

Scores of 3 to 5 for each section: Your health-related behaviors are risky. What lifestyle changes can you make to improve your score in this area of health and reduce your risk?

Scores of 0 to 2 for each section: You may be taking serious and unnecessary risks with your health and, possibly, the health of others. What lifestyle changes can you make to improve your score and reduce your risk?

Source: Healthstyle: A self-test. Hyattsville, MD: U.S. Public Health Service, 1981.

ACTIVITY 7-2: CALCULATE YOUR SKINFOLD MEASUREMENTS

There are three sites where skinfolds are most commonly measured:

Men	
Chest	Measure halfway between the right shoulder crease and the nipple.
Abdomen	Measure about 1 inch to the right of the navel.
Thigh	Measure on the front of the right thigh, midway between the hip and the knee joint.

Women	
Triceps	Measure on the back of the right arm, half the distance between the tip of the shoulder and the tip of the elbow.
Suprailium	Measure at the top of the right iliac crest.
Thigh	Measure on the front of the right thigh, midway between the hip and the knee joint.

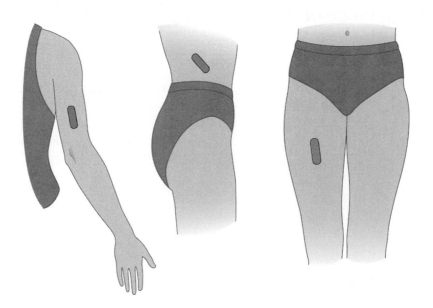

TECHNIQUES FOR TAKING SKINFOLDS

1. Before measuring, if you prefer, mark the anatomical site with a water-soluble felt-tip pen.
2. Take all measurements on the right side.
3. Grasp the skinfold firmly by the thumb and finger of your left hand and pull away from the body. This is usually easier on thin people. Do not pinch the skinfold too hard. The skinfolds are normally pinched in a vertical rather than a horizontal line.
4. With your right hand, hold the caliper perpendicular with the skinfold, keeping the skinfold dial up so that it can be read. The caliper should be a quarter- to a half-inch away from the thumb and the forefinger so that the pressure of the caliper will not be affected.
5. Do not place the skinfold caliper too far into the skinfold or too far away on the tip of the skinfold.
6. Read the dial 1 to 2 seconds after releasing your grip. Take a minimum of two measurements at each site. Allow at least 15 seconds between measurements to permit the skinfold site to return to normal. If the repeated measurement varies by more than 1 millimeter, take another measurement until there is consistency.
7. Do not take measurements when the skin is moist, because dampness makes it easier to grasp the extra skin and thus obtain larger values. Do not take measurements immediately after exercise because exercise makes the skin moist.
8. Be sure to grasp the same size of skinfold consistently at the same location every time. This requires practice.

Results	
Men	
Chest	mm
Abdomen	mm
Thigh	mm
Total of measurements	mm
Women	
Triceps	mm
Suprailium	mm
Thigh	mm
Total of measurements	mm

DETERMINING BODY FAT PERCENT

Add the measurements of your three skinfolds, and then find the body fat percent corresponding to your total in Table 9.A5 for men or Table 9.A6 for women.

Your body fat percent = _____%

Use the following tables to analyze your results.

Percent Fat Estimates for Men: Sum of Chest, Abdominal, and Thigh Skinfolds

Sum of skinfolds (mm)	Age to the last year								
	Under 22	23–27	28–32	33–37	38–42	43–47	48–52	53–57	Over 58
8–10	1.3	1.8	2.3	2.9	3.4	3.9	4.5	5.0	5.5
11–13	2.2	2.8	3.3	3.9	4.4	4.9	5.5	6.0	6.5
14–16	3.2	3.8	4.3	4.8	5.4	5.9	6.4	7.0	7.5
17–19	4.2	4.7	5.3	5.8	6.3	6.9	7.4	8.0	8.5
20–22	5.1	5.7	6.2	6.8	7.3	7.9	8.4	8.9	9.5
23–25	6.1	6.6	7.2	7.7	8.3	8.8	9.4	9.9	10.5
26–28	7.0	7.6	8.1	8.7	9.2	9.8	10.3	10.9	11.4
29–31	8.0	8.5	9.1	9.6	10.2	10.7	11.3	11.8	12.4
32–34	8.9	9.4	10.0	10.5	11.1	11.6	12.2	12.8	13.3
35–37	9.8	10.4	10.9	11.5	12.0	12.6	13.1	13.7	14.3
38–40	10.7	11.3	11.8	12.4	12.9	13.5	14.1	14.6	15.2
41–43	11.6	12.2	12.7	13.3	13.8	14.4	15.0	15.5	16.1
44–46	12.5	13.1	13.6	14.2	14.7	15.3	15.9	16.4	17.0
47–49	13.4	13.9	14.5	15.1	15.6	16.2	16.8	17.3	17.9
50–52	14.3	14.8	15.4	15.9	16.5	17.1	17.6	18.2	18.8
53–55	15.1	15.7	16.2	16.8	17.4	17.9	18.5	18.1	19.7
56–58	16.0	16.5	17.1	17.7	18.2	18.8	19.4	20.0	20.5
59–61	16.9	17.4	17.9	18.5	19.1	19.7	20.2	20.8	21.4
62–64	17.6	18.2	18.8	19.4	19.9	20.5	21.1	21.7	22.2
65–67	18.5	19.0	19.6	20.2	20.8	21.3	21.9	22.5	23.1
68–70	19.3	19.9	20.4	21.0	21.6	22.2	22.7	23.3	23.9
71–73	20.1	20.7	21.2	21.8	22.4	23.0	23.6	24.1	24.7
74–76	20.9	21.5	22.0	22.6	23.2	23.8	24.4	25.0	25.5
77–79	21.7	22.2	22.8	23.4	24.0	24.6	25.2	25.8	26.3
80–82	22.4	23.0	23.6	24.2	24.8	25.4	25.9	26.5	27.1
83–85	23.2	23.8	24.4	25.0	25.5	26.1	26.7	27.3	27.9
86–88	24.0	24.5	25.1	25.7	26.3	26.9	27.5	28.1	28.7
89–91	24.7	25.3	25.9	25.5	27.1	27.6	28.2	28.8	29.4
92–94	25.4	26.0	26.6	27.2	27.8	28.4	29.0	29.6	30.2
95–97	26.1	16.7	27.3	27.9	28.5	29.1	29.7	30.3	30.9
98–100	26.9	27.4	28.0	28.6	29.2	29.8	30.4	31.0	31.6
101–103	27.5	28.1	28.7	29.3	29.9	30.5	31.1	31.7	32.3
104–106	28.2	28.8	29.4	30.0	30.6	31.2	31.8	32.4	33.0
107–109	28.9	29.5	30.1	30.7	31.3	31.9	32.5	33.1	33.7
110–112	29.6	30.2	30.8	31.4	32.0	32.6	33.2	33.8	34.4
113–115	30.2	30.8	31.4	32.0	32.6	33.2	33.8	34.5	35.1
116–118	30.9	31.5	32.1	32.7	33.3	33.9	34.5	35.1	35.7
119–121	31.5	32.1	32.7	33.3	33.9	34.5	35.1	35.7	36.4
122–124	32.1	32.7	33.3	33.9	34.5	35.1	35.8	36.4	37.0
125–127	32.7	33.3	33.9	34.5	35.1	35.8	36.4	37.0	37.6

Percent fat calculated by the formula by Siri: Percent fat = $[(4.95/BD) - 4.5] \times 100$, where BD = body density.

Modified from Pollock M. L., Schmidt D.H., and Jackson A. S. Measurement of cardiorespiratory fitness and body composition in the clinical setting. *Comprehensive Therapy* 1980; 6(9):12–27. Reprinted with kind permission of Springer Science and Business Media.

Percent Fat Estimates for Women: Sum of Triceps, Suprailium, and Thigh Skinfolds

Sum of skinfolds (mm)	Age to the last year								
	Under 22	23–27	28–32	33–37	38–42	43–47	48–52	53–57	Over 58
23–25	9.7	9.9	10.2	10.4	10.7	10.9	11.2	11.4	11.7
26–28	11.0	11.2	11.5	11.7	12.0	12.3	12.5	12.7	13.0
29–31	12.3	12.5	12.8	13.0	13.3	13.5	13.8	14.0	14.3
32–34	13.6	13.8	14.0	14.3	14.5	14.8	15.0	15.3	15.5
35–37	14.8	15.0	15.3	15.5	15.8	16.0	16.3	16.5	16.8
38–40	16.0	16.3	16.5	16.7	17.0	17.2	17.5	17.7	18.0
41–43	17.2	17.4	17.7	17.9	18.2	18.4	18.7	18.9	19.2
44–46	18.3	18.6	18.8	19.1	19.3	19.6	19.8	20.1	20.3
47–49	19.5	19.7	20.0	20.2	20.5	20.7	21.0	21.2	21.5
50–52	20.6	20.8	21.1	21.3	21.6	21.8	22.1	22.3	22.6
53–55	21.7	21.9	22.1	22.4	22.6	22.9	23.1	23.4	23.6
56–58	22.7	23.0	23.2	23.4	23.7	23.9	24.2	24.4	24.7
59–61	23.7	24.0	24.2	24.5	24.7	25.0	25.2	25.5	25.7
62–64	24.7	25.0	25.2	25.5	35.7	26.0	26.7	26.4	26.7
65–67	25.7	25.9	26.2	26.4	26.7	26.9	27.2	27.4	27.7
68–70	26.6	26.9	27.1	27.4	27.6	27.9	28.1	28.4	28.6
71–73	27.5	27.8	28.0	28.3	28.5	28.8	28.0	29.3	29.5
74–76	28.4	28.7	28.9	29.2	29.4	29.7	29.9	30.2	30.4
77–79	29.3	29.5	39.8	30.0	30.3	30.5	30.8	31.0	31.3
80–82	30.1	30.4	30.6	30.9	31.1	31.4	31.6	31.9	32.1
83–85	30.9	31.2	31.4	31.7	31.9	32.2	32.4	32.7	32.9
86–88	31.7	32.0	32.2	32.5	32.7	32.9	33.2	33.4	33.7
89–91	32.5	32.7	33.0	33.2	33.5	33.7	33.9	34.2	34.4
92–94	33.2	33.4	33.7	33.9	34.2	34.4	34.7	34.9	35.2
95–97	33.9	34.1	34.4	34.6	34.9	35.1	35.4	35.6	35.9
98–100	34.6	34.8	35.1	35.3	35.5	35.8	36.0	36.3	36.5
101–103	35.3	35.4	35.7	35.9	36.2	36.4	36.7	36.9	37.2
104–106	35.8	36.1	36.3	36.6	36.8	37.1	37.3	37.5	37.8
107–109	36.4	36.7	36.9	37.1	37.4	37.6	37.9	38.1	38.4
110–112	37.0	37.2	37.5	37.7	38.0	38.2	38.5	38.7	38.9
113–115	37.5	37.8	38.0	38.2	38.5	38.7	39.0	39.2	39.5
116–118	38.0	38.3	38.5	38.8	39.0	39.3	39.5	39.7	40.0
119–121	38.5	38.7	39.0	39.2	39.5	39.7	40.0	40.2	40.5
122–124	39.0	39.2	39.4	39.7	39.9	40.2	40.4	40.7	40.9
125–127	39.4	39.6	39.9	40.1	40.4	40.6	40.9	41.1	41.4
128–130	39.8	40.0	40.3	40.5	40.8	41.0	41.3	41.5	41.8

Percent fat calculated by the formula by Siri. Percent fat = $[(4.95/BD) - 4.5] \times 100$, where BD = body density.

Modified from Pollock M. L., Schmidt D. H., and Jackson A. S. Measurement of cardiorespiratory fitness and body composition in the clinical setting. *Comprehensive Therapy* 1980; 6(9):12–27. Reprinted with kind permission of Springer Science and Business Media.

ACTIVITY 7-3: ROCKPORT FITNESS WALKING TEST™

This activity assesses cardiorespiratory (aerobic) fitness. To perform the test, you need a watch with a second hand to record your time, and you need to wear good walking shoes and loose clothes. You should have your physician's consent before undertaking this exercise test.

INSTRUCTIONS

1. Find a measured track or measure 1 mile using your car's odometer on a level, uninterrupted road.
2. Warm up by walking slowly for 5 minutes.
3. Walk 1 mile as fast as you can, maintaining a steady pace. Note the time that you began walking.
4. When you complete the mile walk, record your time to the nearest second and keep walking at a slower pace. Count your pulse for 15 seconds and multiply by 4, then record this number. This gives your heart rate per minute after your test walk.

   Heart rate at the end of 1-mile walk: _____ beats per minute

   Time to walk the mile: _____ minutes
5. Remember to stretch once you have cooled down.
6. To find your cardiorespiratory fitness level, refer to the appropriate Rockport Fitness Walking Test™ charts based on your age and sex. These show established fitness norms from the American Heart Association.

   Using your fitness level chart, find your time in minutes and your heart rate per minute. Follow these lines until they meet, and mark this point on your chart. This tells you how fit you are compared to other individuals of your sex and age category.

   These charts are based on weights of 170 lb for men and 125 lb for women. If you weigh substantially less, your cardiovascular fitness will be slightly underestimated. Conversely, if you weigh substantially more, your cardiovascular fitness will be slightly overestimated.

How fit you are compared to others of the same age and gender:

Level 5 = high
Level 4 = above average
Level 3 = average
Level 2 = below average
Level 1 = low

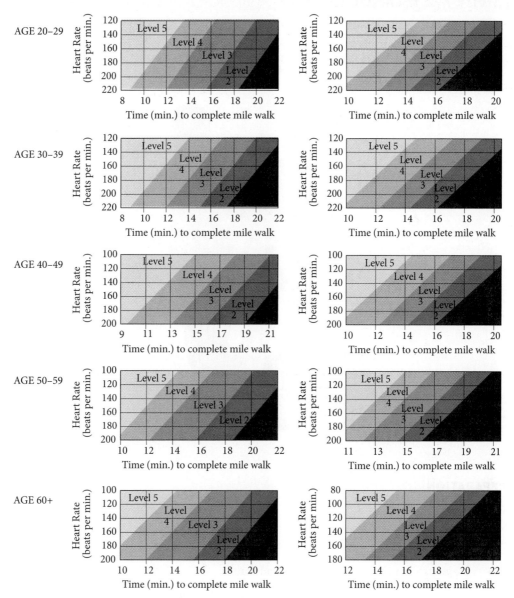

MEN'S FITNESS LEVEL CHART

WOMEN'S FITNESS LEVEL CHART

AGE 20–29

AGE 30–39

AGE 40–49

AGE 50–59

AGE 60+

Rockport Fitness Walking Test™

Courtesy of the Rockport Company, Inc.

ACTIVITY 7-4: YMCA STEP TEST

Complete the PAR-Q questionnaire. Do not take the test if you suffer joint problems in your ankles, knees, or hips, or if you are obese.

PREPARATION

You will need the following:

- 12-inch-high sturdy bench
- Metronome
- Stopwatch, watch, or clock with a second hand

Warm up for 5 minutes before taking the test. Practice before, but you should be well rested with no prior exercise of any kind for several hours before the test.

PROCEDURE

1. Set the metronome at 96 beats per minute (four clicks of the metronome equals one step-cycle: up—1, 2; down—3, 4).
2. Step up and down on the 12-inch bench for 3 minutes.
3. After the 3 minutes of stepping, sit down and within 5 seconds count your radial pulse for 1 full minute.
4. See the following table for your fitness rating.

3-Minute Step Test to Estimate the Quality of VO_2max by Utilizing Age, Gender, and Heart Rate (bpm)				
	Quality of VO_{2max}			
Men Aged	**Excellent to Good**	**Above Average to Average**	**Below Average to Poor**	**Very Poor**
18–25 years	<84	85–100	101–119	>119
26–35 years	<85	86–102	103–121	>121
36–45 years	<88	89–105	106–124	>124
46–55 years	<93	94–111	112–126	>126
56–65 years	<94	95–109	110–128	>128
65+ years	<92	93–110	111–126	>126

	Quality of VO_{2max}			
Women Aged	**Excellent to Good**	**Above Average to Average**	**Below Average to Poor**	**Very Poor**
18–25 years	<93	94–110	111–131	>131
26–35 years	<92	93–110	111–129	>129
36–45 years	<96	97–112	113–132	>132
46–55 years	<101	102–118	119–132	>132
56–65 years	<103	104–118	119–135	>135
65+ years	<101	102–121	122–133	>133

ACTIVITY 7-5: COOPER'S 1.5-MILE RUN/WALK TEST

The 1.5-mile run/walk test is recommended for those who are motivated, experienced in running, and in good condition before taking the test. Do not take the test unless you can already jog non-stop for 15 minutes. It is not recommended for the following people:

- Those failing the PAR-Q questionnaire
- Sedentary people older than 30 years of age
- Severely deconditioned people
- Those with joint problems
- Obese individuals

Sedentary individuals (especially those older than 30 years of age) should participate in a walking/running program for 1 to 2 months before taking the test. For those in hot or cold environments, do not take this test unless you have been exercising in these conditions.

PREPARATION

You will need the following:

- Stopwatch, watch, or clock with a second hand
- Oval running track
- Appropriate running shoes and clothing

Warm up for 5 to 10 minutes before the test.

PROCEDURE

1. Complete a 1.5-mile distance in the shortest possible time. If outdoors, the test should be conducted in favorable weather conditions. Physically fit individuals can cover the distance either by running or jogging. Less fit individuals can run and jog, but may need to walk some of the time.

2. Attempt to keep a steady pace throughout the test.

3. When completed, record the time (minutes and seconds) it took to complete the 1.5-mile distance.

   Time to finish the 1.5-mile distance: _____

4. See the following table to find your fitness rating.

   Fitness rating: _____

Fitness Categories for Cooper's 1.5-Mile Run Test to Determine Cardiorespiratory Fitness						
Fitness category	**Age (years)**					
	20–29	**30–39**	**40–49**	**50–59**	**60–69**	**70–79**
Men						
Very poor	>14:34	>15:13	>15:58	>17:38	>20:19	>22:52
Poor	12:53–14:00	13:24–14:34	14:11–15:24	15:26–16:58	17:11–19:10	19:24–21:47
Fair	11:41–12:38	11:58–12:58	12:53–13:50	15:26–16:58	15:23–16:46	17:12–18:38
Good	10:43–11:29	11:06–11:54	11:40–12:24	12:36–13:35	13:52–15:04	15:14–16:43
Excellent	9:34–10:09	10:01–10:46	10:28–11:15	11:10–12:08	12:20–13:23	13:24–14:34
Superior	<9:17	<9:33	<9:51	<10:37	<10:09	<11:58

Fitness category	**Age (years)**					
	20–29	**30–39**	**40–49**	**50–59**	**60–69**	**70–79**
Women						
Very poor	>17:38	>18:37	>19:35	>21:38	>23:37	>25:49
Poor	15:14–16:46	15:58–17:38	16:46–18:37	18:37–20:44	20:52–22:52	22:07–24:06
Fair	13:48–14:50	14:28–15:43	15:13–16:31	16:46–18:18	18:37–20:16	19:43–21:31
Good	12:24–13:24	12:53–14:08	13:45–14:53	15:13–16:35	16:46–18:27	18:21–19:36
Excellent	11:10–11:58	11:33–12:24	12:11–13:23	13:40–14:34	14:53–16:33	16:40–17:51
Superior	<10:28	<11:00	<11:33	<12:53	<4:05	<14:21

Times are given in minutes and seconds (> = greater than, < = less than)

Reprinted with permission from The Cooper Institute, Dallas, Texas. Available online at www.CooperInstitute.org.

ACTIVITY 7-6: SIT-AND-REACH TEST

PRECAUTIONS

1. Warm up.
2. Stop the test if pain occurs.
3. Do not be competitive. This is a test to help assess your spine/back flexibility, not a game. Do not perform fast, jerky movements.
4. If any of the following apply, seek medical advice before performing tests:
   A. You are presently suffering from acute back pain
   B. You are currently receiving treatment for back pain
   C. You have had a surgical operation on your back
   D. A health-care professional told you to never exercise your back

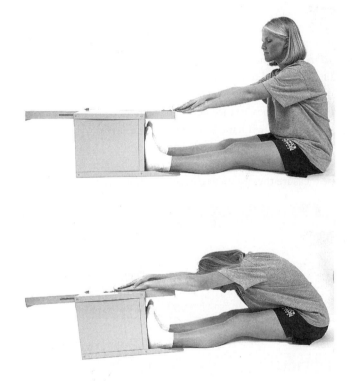

PROCEDURE

Step 1: Sit on the floor with your legs straight, knees together, and toes pointing upward toward the ceiling.

Step 2: Place one hand over the other. The tips of your two middle fingers should be on top of each other.

Step 3: Slowly stretch forward without bouncing or jerking. Stop when tightness or discomfort occurs in the back or legs.

Step 4: Repeat this test two more times and record scores as follows:

- First attempt: _____ points
- Second attempt: _____ points
- Third attempt: _____ points
- Total points = _____ divided by 3 = _____ points, which is rated as _____.

How to Score (average of 3 attempts)	
Reached well past toes	1 point; excellent
Reached just to toes	2 points; good
Up to 4 inches from toes	3 points; fair
More than 4 inches from toes	4 points; poor

Data from Imrie D. *The Backpower Program*, 1st ed. Wiley Publishing, Inc., 1990.

ACTIVITY 7-7: SHOULDER FLEXIBILITY TEST

PRECAUTIONS

- Briefly warm up with a few minutes of stretching.
- Avoid rapid or jerky movements during the test.

PROCEDURE

Step 1: Bring the right hand around to the back of the neck.
Step 2: Bring the left hand around to the small of the back.
Step 3: Try to touch the fingertips of both hands behind the back.
Step 4: Have someone measure the distance between the fingertips.
Step 5: Do the test the other way, left hand to the back of the neck, right hand to the small of the back.
Step 6: Try to touch the fingertips of both hands behind the back.
Step 7: Have someone measure the distance between the fingertips.

How to Score	
Can clasp hands together	Very good flexibility
Fingertips almost touch	Good, but needs work
Not within an inch of touching fingertips together	Poor, needs a lot of work

Adapted from Schlosberg S. *Fitness for Dummies*, 3rd ed. Wiley Publishing, Inc., 2005.

ACTIVITY 7-8: ADDITIONAL LOWER BODY FLEXIBILITY TESTS

These additional flexibility tests can be used to evaluate an athlete's general lower body flexibility. While performing the flexibility tests, the athlete may feel some discomfort due to the muscular stretch. This sensation is entirely normal, and the athlete's flexibility may be evaluated at the point of discomfort. However, keep in mind that while performing these flexibility tests, under no circumstances should the athlete experience any pain or abnormal sensations. If the athlete experiences pain or abnormal sensations, the flexibility test must stop immediately. After performing the flexibility tests, the athlete's muscles are considered "flexible" or "inflexible." For purposes of this activity, the term *inflexible* means that the athlete has room to increase the muscles' flexibility.

ILIOPSOAS AND RECTUS FEMORIS (HIP FLEXOR MUSCLES)

Directions:

- Have the athlete lie on her back on a table with her knees bent at a 90-degree angle over the edge.

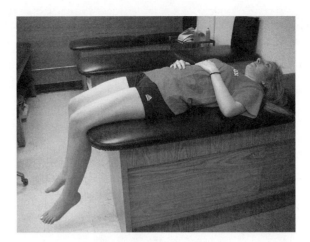

- Instruct the athlete to flex her hip and raise one leg up to her chest with her knee flexed.
- Tell the athlete to grasp her thigh and hold her leg with both hands in this position.
- Evaluate her flexibility.
- Repeat with the other leg.

Results:

While grasping her thigh:

- The athlete has flexible hip flexors if her opposite thigh remains flat on the table and her knee remains flexed.
- The athlete has an inflexible iliopsoas if her opposing hip flexes.
- The athlete has an inflexible rectus femoris if her opposing knee extends.
- The athlete has both an inflexible iliopsoas and an inflexible rectus femoris if both the opposing hip flexes and the knee extends simultaneously.

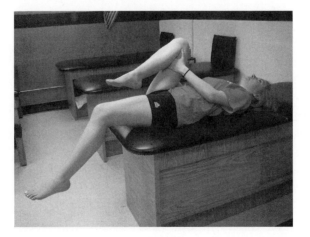

VASTUS MEDIALIS, VASTUS INTERMEDIUS, VASTUS LATERALIS, AND RECTUS FEMORIS (QUADRICEPS MUSCLE GROUP)

Directions:

- Have the athlete lie on her stomach and relax her legs.

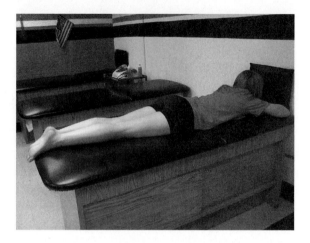

- Firmly grasp one ankle and passively flex her knee to the point where you feel resistance and the athlete feels a stretch.
- Evaluate her flexibility.
- Repeat with the other leg.

Results:

- The athlete has a flexible quadriceps muscle group if her heel touches her buttocks.

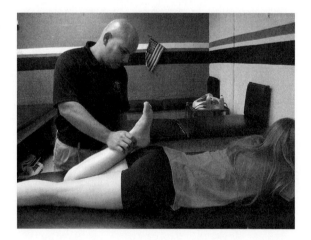

- The athlete has an inflexible quadriceps muscle group if her heel cannot touch her buttocks.

SEMITENDINOSUS, SEMIMEMBRANOSUS, AND BICEPS FEMORIS (HAMSTRING MUSCLE GROUP)

Directions:

- Have the athlete sit in a "modified hurdler's position," with one leg extended and the other with the sole of the foot touching the opposite knee's medial side. The athlete's legs will appear like a forward or backward number 4.

- Have the athlete reach forward toward the extended leg, in an attempt to rest her chest on her thigh and touch her toes.

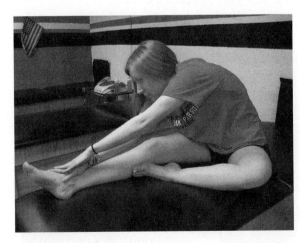

- Evaluate her flexibility.
- Repeat with the other leg.

Results:

- The athlete has a flexible hamstring muscle group if she is able to place her chest to her thigh and/or touch her toes.

- The athlete has an inflexible hamstring muscle group if she is not able to place her chest to her thigh and/or touch her toes.*

*An athlete's upper or lower extremity length, not hamstring muscle group flexibility, may prevent her from touching her toes. If this is the case, then evaluate her hamstring muscle group flexibility by determining if she can bring her chest to rest upon her thigh.

ILIOTIBIAL BAND

Directions:

- Have the athlete lie on her side on a table, with her hips and knees flexed to 90 degrees and relaxed.

- Stand by the table, facing the athlete's back.
- Grasp the athlete's upper ankle with one hand and stabilize her hip with your other hand.

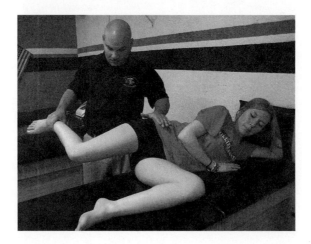

- Utilizing passive motion, slightly extend the athlete's hip, while the knee remains flexed and the hip stabilized.
- Carefully allow her leg to drop.
- Evaluate her flexibility.
- Repeat with the other leg.

Results:

- The athlete has a flexible iliotibial band if, when the upper leg is dropped, it falls to the table.

- The athlete has an inflexible iliotibial band if, when the upper leg is dropped, the leg does not fall to the table and remains suspended in air (abducted).

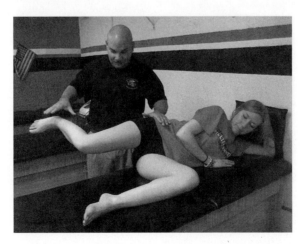

GRACILIS AND ADDUCTOR MUSCLE GROUP (GROIN MUSCLES)

Directions:

- Have the athlete sit on the floor with the soles of her feet together and her knees bent in a "butterfly position."

- Passively abduct her hips by slowly pushing her knees toward the floor until you feel resistance and the athlete feels a stretch.

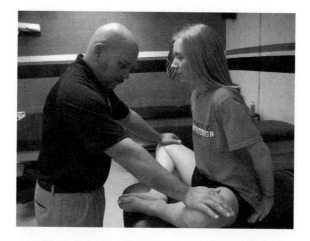

- Evaluate the flexibility of both legs.

Results:

- The athlete has flexible groin muscles if her knees can be moved to become parallel to the floor.
- The athlete has inflexible groin muscles if her knees cannot be moved to become parallel to floor.

GASTROCNEMIUS AND SOLEUS (CALF MUSCLES)

Directions:

- Have the athlete sit on a table with her legs straight and knees extended.

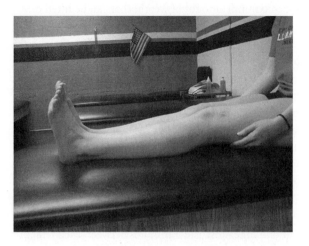

- Her ankles and feet should be in neutral positions, so it appears as if her ankles are at 90-degree angles.
- Stabilize her distal lower leg with one hand while grasping her foot with the other.
- Passively move her ankle so her toes are pointed toward her (dorsiflexion).

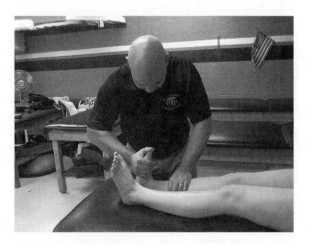

- Evaluate her flexibility.
- Repeat with the other ankle.

Results:

- The athlete has flexible calf muscles if her ankle can be passively moved into dorsiflexion approximately 15 degrees past the starting, neutral position.
- The athlete has inflexible calf muscles if her ankle cannot be passively moved into dorsiflexion approximately 15 degrees past the starting, neutral position, and/or if the athlete's knee flexes when the ankle is passively moved.

ACTIVITY 7-9: ONE-REPETITION MAXIMUM TEST (1 RM)

The one-repetition maximum (1 RM) test for muscular strength is not recommended for older individuals and unconditioned individuals because of possible injury. The 1 RM test should be used only after several weeks of strength training. Muscular strength can be measured by the 1 RM test, which measures the maximum amount of weight that can be lifted one time.

PREPARATION

You will need the following:
- Barbell and various weights with collars
- One or two spotters for safety
- The bench press, shoulder press (military press), and arm curl are the most common methods for assessing muscular strength. Warm up by performing the selected lift to be used several times.

PROCEDURE

- For the selected muscle group to be tested, choose a starting weight that you can lift without a great deal of stress. Then, gradually add weight until you reach the maximum weight that you can lift one time. Rest 2 to 3 minutes between each trial or new attempt to lift the new weight.
- If you can lift the weight more than once, add more weight until you reach a level of resistance that can be performed only once.
- Compute your strength score by dividing your 1 RM weight (in pounds) by your body weight (in pounds) and then multiply by 100.

$$\frac{1 \text{ RM weight (lb)}}{\text{body weight (lb)}} \times 100 = \text{muscle strength score}$$

Strength Ratings for the Maximum Bench-Press Test

	Pounds lifted/body weight (lb)					
Men	**Very poor**	**Poor**	**Fair**	**Good**	**Excellent**	**Superior**
Age: Under 20	Below 0.86	0.89–1.01	1.06–1.16	1.19–1.29	1.34–1.46	Above 1.76
20–29	Below 0.84	0.89–1.01	0.99–1.10	1.14–1.26	1.32–1.48	Above 1.63
30–39	Below 0.75	0.78–0.86	0.88–0.96	0.98–1.08	1.12–1.24	Above 1.35
40–49	Below 0.69	0.72–0.78	0.80–0.86	0.88–0.96	1.00–1.10	Above 1.20
50–59	Below 0.60	0.63–0.70	0.71–0.77	0.79–0.87	0.90–0.97	Above 1.05
60 and over	Below 0.56	0.57–0.65	0.66–0.70	0.72–0.79	0.82–0.89	Above 0.94
Women	**Very poor**	**Poor**	**Fair**	**Good**	**Excellent**	**Superior**
Age: Under 20	Below 0.52	0.53–0.57	0.58–0.64	0.65–0.76	0.77–0.83	Above 0.88
20–29	Below 0.50	0.51–0.58	0.59–0.68	0.70–0.77	0.80–0.90	Above 1.01
30–39	Below 0.45	0.47–0.52	0.53–0.58	0.60–0.65	0.70–0.76	Above 0.82
40–49	Below 0.42	0.43–0.48	0.50–0.53	0.54–0.60	0.62–0.71	Above 0.77
50–59	Below 0.38	0.39–0.43	0.44–0.47	0.48–0.53	0.55–0.61	Above 0.68
60 and over	Below 0.36	0.38–0.41	0.43–0.46	0.47–0.53	0.54–0.64	Above 0.71

Reprinted with permission from The Cooper Institute, Dallas, Texas from a book called "*Physical Fitness Assessments and Norms for Adults and Law Enforcement*". Available online at www.CooperInstitute.org.

ACTIVITY 7-10: HAND GRIP STRENGTH TEST

PREPARATION

You will need the following:

- Dynamometer
- Dry hands

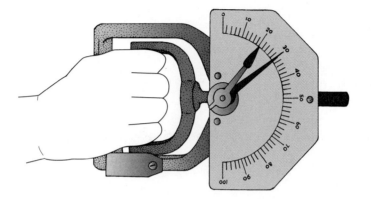

Dynamometer.

PROCEDURE

- Adjust and comfortably place the dynamometer in the hand to be tested. The second joint of the hand should fit snugly under the handle, which is gripped between the fingers and the palm at the base of the thumb.
- Bend forward slightly, with the hand to be tested out in front of your body. Neither the hand nor the arm should be touching the body or any other object. The arm can be slightly bent.
- During the test, an all-out effort should be given for between 2 and 3 seconds. No swinging or pumping of the arm is allowed. The dial can face you.
- The score comes from the sum of both hands, based on the best of two to four trials each.
- See the following table for your fitness level.

Grip Strength for Males and Females of All Ages

Norms and percentiles by age groups and sex for combined right- and left-hand grip strength (kg)

Age	15–19		20–29		30–39		40–49		50–59		60–69	
Sex	M	F	M	F	M	F	M	F	M	F	M	F
Excellent	≥113	≥71	≥124	≥71	≥123	≥73	≥119	≥73	≥110	≥65	≥102	≥60
Above avg.	103–112	64–70	113–123	65–70	113–122	66–72	110–118	65–72	102–109	59–64	93–101	54–59
Average	95–102	59–63	106–112	61–64	105–112	61–65	102–109	59–64	96–101	55–58	86–92	51–53
Below avg.	84–94	54–58	97–105	55–60	97–104	56–60	94–101	55–58	87–95	51–54	79–85	48–50
Weak	≤83	≤53	≤96	≤54	≤96	≤55	≤93	≤54	≤86	≤50	≤78	≤47

Age	15–19		20–29		30–39		40–49		50–59		60–69	
Sex	M	F	M	F	M	F	M	F	M	F	M	F
Percentiles												
95	125	78	136	78	135	80	128	80	119	72	111	67
90	119	74	127	74	127	76	123	76	114	69	106	62
85	113	71	124	71	123	73	119	73	110	65	102	60
80	110	69	120	70	120	71	117	71	108	63	99	58
75	108	67	118	68	117	69	115	69	105	62	96	56
70	105	65	115	67	115	68	112	67	103	60	94	55
65	103	64	113	65	113	66	110	65	102	59	93	54
60	101	63	111	64	111	65	108	64	100	58	91	53
55	99	61	109	63	109	63	106	62	99	57	89	52
50	97	60	107	62	107	62	104	61	97	56	88	52
45	95	59	106	61	105	61	102	59	96	55	86	51
40	93	58	104	59	104	60	100	58	94	54	84	50
35	90	57	102	58	101	59	98	57	92	53	82	49
30	87	56	100	56	99	58	96	56	90	53	81	49
25	84	54	97	55	97	56	94	55	87	51	79	48
20	81	53	95	53	94	55	91	53	85	50	76	47
15	77	51	91	52	91	53	89	51	83	48	73	45
10	73	49	87	50	87	51	84	49	80	46	69	43
5	67	45	81	47	81	48	76	46	74	42	62	39

ACTIVITY 7-11: PUSH-UP TEST FOR MUSCULAR ENDURANCE

PREPARATION

- Use a large space on the floor, clear of obstructions.
- Warm up for 3 to 5 minutes before starting. Give yourself a couple of minutes to recover after warm-up before beginning the test.

PROCEDURE

- Assume the standard position for a push-up, with the body rigid and straight, toes tucked under, and hands about shoulder-width apart and straight under the shoulders.
- Lower the body until the elbows reach 90°. Some prefer to place an object such as a paper cup beneath to touch.
- Return to the starting position with the arms fully extended.
- The most common error is not keeping the back straight and rigid throughout the entire push-up.
- Perform as many push-ups as you can without stopping.
- See the following table for your fitness level.

Ratings for the Push-up and Modified Push-up Tests						
	Number of push-ups					
Men	**Very poor**	**Poor**	**Fair**	**Good**	**Excellent**	**Superior**
Age: 20–29	Below 19	22–27	29–35	37–44	47–57	Above 62
30–39	Below 15	17–21	24–29	30–36	39–46	Above 52
40–49	Below 10	11–16	18–22	24–29	30–36	Above 40
50–59	Below 7	9–11	13–17	19–24	25–30	Above 39
60+	Below 5	6–9	10–16	18–22	23–26	Above 28

(continues)

Ratings for the Push-up and Modified Push-up Tests (Continued)						
	Number of modified push-ups					
Women	Very poor	Poor	Fair	Good	Excellent	Superior
Age: 20–29	Below 15	17–22	23–29	30–34	36–42	Above 45
30–39	Below 9	11–17	19–23	24–29	31–36	Above 39
40–49	Below 4	6–11	13–17	18–21	24–28	Above 33
50–59	Below 4	6–10	12–15	17–20	21–25	Above 28
60+	Below 1	2–4	5–12	12–15	15–17	Above 20

Reprinted with permission from The Cooper Institute, Dallas, Texas from a book called *"Physical Fitness Assessments and Norms for Adults and Law Enforcement"*. Available online at www.CooperInstitute.org.

Women tend to have less upper body strength and therefore should use the modified push-up position to assess their upper body endurance. The test is performed as follows:

- Directions are the same for women as for men, except that women should perform the test with the knees remaining on the floor. Make sure that your hands are slightly ahead of your shoulders in the up position so that when you are in the down position, your hands are directly under the shoulders.
- Keep the back straight and rigid throughout the entire push-up.
- Perform as many push-ups as you can without stopping.

ACTIVITY 7-12: YMCA BENCH-PRESS TEST

The YMCA developed a bench-press test for muscular endurance, using a standardized weight. This test offers several advantages, but it discriminates against lighter individuals.

PREPARATION

You will need the following:

- Barbell with weights and collars to hold them in place
- For the test, men use an 80-pound barbell and women use a 35-pound barbell

- Another person to "spot" for you
- Flat bench
- Metronome, set for 60 bpm

Warm-up should include doing a few bench presses with a small amount of weight to practice bench pressing. Give yourself a couple of minutes to recover after warm-up before beginning the test.

PROCEDURE

- Lie on the flat bench with your feet on the floor.
- Your spotter hands the barbell to you. The down position is the starting position (elbows flexed, hands shoulder-width apart, palms facing up).
- Press the barbell upward to fully extend (straighten) the elbows. After each extension, the barbell is returned to the original down position with the bar touching the chest. Do not bounce the bar on your chest. Do not arch your back.
- Keep up with the rhythm of the metronome—lift the barbell on one beat and lower it on the next. Your spotter counts the number of bench presses you perform (each time the barbell is in the down position); each click represents a movement up or down for 30 lifts per minute.
- Perform as many reps as you can without stopping, and keep with the rhythm. Stop the test when any of these occur: (1) you are unable to reach full extension of the elbows, (2) you are unable to keep up with the rhythm of the metronome, or (3) you are unable to do any more bench presses.
- See the following table for your fitness level.

YMCA Bench-Press Test Scoring							
Your score is the number of completed bench presses. Refer to the appropriate portion of the table below for a rating of your upper body endurance. Record your rating below.							
Rating: _____							
			Number of bench presses				
Men	**Very poor**	**Poor**	**Below average**	**Average**	**Above average**	**Good**	**Excellent**
Age: 18–25	Below 13	13–19	20–23	24–28	29–33	34–43	Above 43
26–35	Below 12	12–16	17–20	21–25	26–29	30–40	Above 40
36–45	Below 9	9–13	14–17	18–21	22–25	26–35	Above 35
46–55	Below 5	5–8	9–11	12–15	16–20	21–27	Above 27
56–65	Below 2	2–4	5–8	9–11	12–16	17–23	Above 23
Over 65	Below 2	2–3	4–6	7–9	10–11	12–19	Above 19
Women	**Very poor**	**Poor**	**Below average**	**Average**	**Above average**	**Good**	**Excellent**
Age: 18–25	Below 9	9–15	16–19	20–24	25–29	30–41	Above 41
26–35	Below 9	9–13	14–17	18–23	24–28	29–39	Above 39
36–45	Below 6	6–11	12–15	16–20	21–25	26–32	Above 32
46–55	Below 2	2–6	7–9	10–13	14–19	20–28	Above 28
56–65	Below 2	2–4	5–7	8–11	12–16	17–23	Above 23
Over 65	Below 1	1–2	3–4	5–7	8–11	12–17	Above 17

ACTIVITY 7-13: YMCA HALF SIT-UP TEST (PARTIAL CURL-UP TEST)

PREPARATION

You will need the following:

- Ruler for measuring 3 inches
- Stopwatch, watch, or clock with a second hand
- Adhesive tape
- Metronome

Sit on a mat or carpet with your legs bent 90° (your feet must remain flat on the floor). Extend your arms so that both hands' longest fingertips touch a strip of tape placed on the floor perpendicular to the body. A second strip of tape is placed on the floor 3 inches toward the feet and parallel to the first. Alternatives to the two tape marks are a 3-inch-width piece of cardboard or two pieces of athletic tape (each is 1.5 inches and can be applied next to each other or a yardstick or similar piece of wood used for the mark nearest the feet).

- Warm-up should include a few sit-ups. Give yourself a couple of minutes to recover after warm-up before beginning the test.
- Set the metronome for 50 bpm.

PROCEDURE

- While lying on the mat or carpet, the curl-up is done by raising your trunk (e.g., curling upward) with arms straight. Fingers slide along the floor until your longest fingertip of each hand touches the second strip of tape or object and then returns to the starting position. You then curl down so that your upper back touches the floor. Keep the 90° bend in your legs. Your feet should not be held down.
- Perform curl-ups to the rhythm of the metronome—curl up on one beat and down on the second beat.
- Perform as many curl-ups as you can without stopping and keep with the rhythm. Stop the test when either of these occurs: (1) You are unable to keep up with the rhythm of the metronome or (2) you are unable to do any more curl-ups. At the end of the test, check your fingertip position. If the fingertips do not touch the near side of the line, your score is not accurate.
- See the following table for your fitness level.

Ratings for the Partial Curl-up Test

Men		Number of curl-ups			
	Needs improvement	Fair	Good	Very good	Excellent
Age: 15–19	Below 16	16–20	21–22	23–24	25
20–29	Below 13	13–20	21–22	23–24	25
30–39	Below 13	13–20	21–22	23–24	25
40–49	Below 11	11–15	16–21	22–24	25
50–59	Below 9	9–13	14–19	20–24	25
60–69	Below 4	4–9	10–15	16–24	25
Women					
Age: 15–19	Below 16	16–20	21–22	23–24	25
20–29	Below 13	13–18	19–22	23–24	25
30–39	Below 11	11–15	16–21	22–24	25
40–49	Below 6	6–12	13–20	21–24	25
50–59	Below 4	4–8	9–15	16–24	25
60–69	Below 2	2–5	6–10	11–17	18–25

Chapter 8
Nutrition and Supplementation

CHAPTER OBJECTIVES

After you have read this chapter, you will be able to understand:

- The roles of macronutrients and micronutrients in the body
- The illnesses and diseases that can overcome an athlete who does not consume the proper macronutrients
- The most commonly deficient minerals in the body
- The various considerations when beginning a weight management program
- Eating disorders, including the signs, symptoms, and effects
- What constitutes the female athlete triad
- The purpose of supplements and nutritional ergogenic aids

The old saying, "You are what you eat," is very true. The variety and quantity of food we eat not only physically shapes our bodies, but also affects the possibility of acquiring a serious illness or disease. An athlete who wishes to become healthy, increase performance, and reduce the possibility of illness and disease has to participate in a wellness, exercise, and fitness program in order to achieve his or her goal. However, an integral component of this program involves the athlete undertaking a proper nutritional program. When an athlete takes proper **nutrients** into his or her body, it produces energy that can be used during exercise, which

> **Nutrients** Substances in food that nourish the body, provide it with energy, and promote its proper function and growth.

benefits his or her health. Nutrients also assist in preventing disease, which helps keep the athlete's wellness in a good state. Proper nutrients incorporated into an athlete's daily dietary plan are beneficial to promoting a long, healthy, and high-quality life.

NUTRIENTS

Our bodies require a variety of nutrients to function optimally. These nutrients include macronutrients and micronutrients. Macronutrients include the basic food components in our everyday **diet** that our bodies require. These macronutrients are carbohydrates, fats, proteins, and water. Micronutrients are

> **Diet** The food and drink we consume each day. *Diet* also refers to a program or plan that an athlete follows when he or she is attempting to modify his or her weight.

substances found in the macronutrients, including vitamins and minerals. Our bodies do not require micronutrients in large quantities as compared to macronutrients. Micronutrients are called *essential* nutrients because our bodies cannot produce them (Fink, Burgoon, & Mikesky, 2009). Consequently, eating a variety of foods that contain micronutrients is imperative. Both macro- and micronutrients are key nutritional components and essential to keep our bodies healthy.

Macronutrients

The four macronutrients are carbohydrates, fats, proteins, and water. Each macronutrient contributes to facilitate optimal bodily function.

Carbohydrates

Carbohydrates (CHO) are the body's main energy source. Athletes need CHO for their bodies to produce enough energy to participate in activities of daily living (ADLs) and athletic activities such as running, bicycling, and other endurance-type exercises. Consuming enough quality CHO promotes adequate energy, which can maximize an athlete's performance.

CHO are made of carbon, hydrogen, and oxygen, along with water. The body breaks down two forms of CHO, complex and simple, to form glucose, also known as blood sugar. Glucose is the body's primary energy source. The liver stores glucose for future energy needs in the form of glycogen. Complex and simple CHO are either natural or refined. Natural CHO are in their original state and high in vitamins, minerals, and fiber. Refined CHO have been placed through manufacturing processes and do not contain essential nutrients. Often refined CHO have added sugar and chemicals which can be detrimental to the body. Complex CHO are starches such as pasta, brown rice, grains, whole grain bread, **legumes**, vegetables, and fruits. Simple CHO include milk, processed foods, sugar, desserts, and candy. Complex CHO are better for an athlete to eat than simple CHO because they are healthier. Some simple CHO do not have any nutritional value. Many simple CHO do not contain vitamins or minerals, and are considered "empty calories." Likewise, simple CHO that are processed, such as food made with white flour, white rice, and snack foods, have a drastic effect on blood sugar levels.

The glycemic index is used to determine the best CHO choices for an athlete, so blood sugar levels are not drastically and suddenly increased. Each CHO has its own glycemic index (**Table 8-1**). A food with a glycemic index of 85 or

> **Legumes** Pod-type foods including, but not limited to, beans, lentils, peas, soy, and peanuts.

Table 8-1	Glycemic Index and Glycemic Load of Common Foods					
Food Glycemic Index (Glucose = 100)		**Glycemic Index (White Bread = 100)**	**Glycemic Index Category***	**Serving Size (g)**	**g CHO/ Serving**	**Glycemic Load**
White bread, Wonder	73±2	105±3	High	30	14	10
White rice, boiled	64±7	91±9	High	150	36	23
Couscous	65± 4	93±6	High	150	35	23
Gatorade	78±13	111	High	250 mL	15	12
Ice cream	61±7	87±10	High	50	13	8
Sweet potato	61±7	87±10	High	150	28	17
Baked potato, russet	85±12	121±16	High	150	30	26
Cranberry juice cocktail	68±3	97	High	250 mL	36	24
Grapenuts	71±4	102±6	High	30	21	15
Cornflakes	81±3	116±5	High	30	26	21
Blueberry muffin	59	84±8	High	57	29	17
Power bar	56±3	79±4	Med	65	42	24
Honey	55±5	78±7	Med	25	18	10
White rice, long grain	56±2	80±3	Med	150	41	23
Coca-Cola	58±5	83±7	Med	250 mL	26	16
Sweet corn	54±4	78±6	Med	80	17	9
Carrot	47±16	68±23	Med	80	6	3
New potato	57±7	81±10	Med	150	21	12
Banana	52±4	74±5	Med	120	24	12
Orange juice	50±4	71±5	Med	250 mL	26	13
Chickpeas	28±6	39±8	Low	150	30	8
Kidney beans	28±4	39±6	Low	150	25	7
Xylitol	8±1	11±1	Low	10	10	1
Lentils	29±1	41±1	Low	150	18	5
Chocolate cake, frosted	38±3	54	Low	111	52	20

(continues)

Table 8-1	Glycemic Index and Glycemic Load of Common Foods (Continued)					
Food Glycemic Index (Glucose = 100)		**Glycemic Index (White Bread = 100)**	**Glycemic Index Category***	**Serving Size (g)**	**g CHO/ Serving**	**Glycemic Load**
Fructose	19±2	27±4	Low	10	10	2
Tomato juice	38±4	54	Low	250 mL	9	4
Skim milk	32±5	46	Low	250 mL	13	4
Smoothie, raspberry	33±9	48±13	Low	250 mL	41	14
Apple	38±2	52±3	Low	120	15	6

*Category = High (>85); Medium (60–85); Low (<60) using GI white bread = 100.

Adapted from: Foster-Powell K, Holt SHA, Brand-Miller JC. International table of glycemic index and glycemic load values. Am J Clin Nutr. 2002;76:5-56. Reprinted with permission from the American Society for Nutrition.

higher is considered a high glycemic index food, 60 to 85 is considered a medium glycemic index food, and 60 or below is a low glycemic index food. Athletes should attempt to ensure their daily CHO intake consists mainly of low glycemic index foods, because they are better for the athlete's body and overall health. Typically, complex CHO, especially those made of whole grains, have a low glycemic index. Low glycemic index foods have proved to decrease the potential of heart disease.

Cholesterol is a fat-like substance that is made by the body, found in the body's cell walls, and carried through the blood. Cholesterol assists the body in digestion, as well as in hormone and vitamin D production (U.S. Department of Health and Human Services, 2011). Although the body produces adequate amounts of cholesterol, many foods we eat, such as egg yolks, meat, seafood, and whole milk products, also contain cholesterol. Too much cholesterol will build up in arteries. This buildup of cholesterol, along with calcium, fat, and other substances, inside the arterial walls is called plaque (**Figure 8-1**). Eventually the inside of the artery becomes increasingly small due to the increasing amount of plaque, and blood flow is blocked. This condition is called atherosclerosis. When atherosclerosis occurs in the **coronary arteries**, the heart does not get the oxygen it needs. As a result, the athlete can have a heart attack.

> **Coronary arteries** Supply the heart with oxygenated blood.

Lipoproteins carry cholesterol through the blood. Two predominant lipoproteins exist—low-density lipoprotein (LDL) and high-density lipoprotein (HDL). The LDL are the "bad" cholesterol that build up in the bloodstream and stick to the arterial walls, causing heart disease. HDL are the "good" cholesterol that help decrease the LDL in the blood.

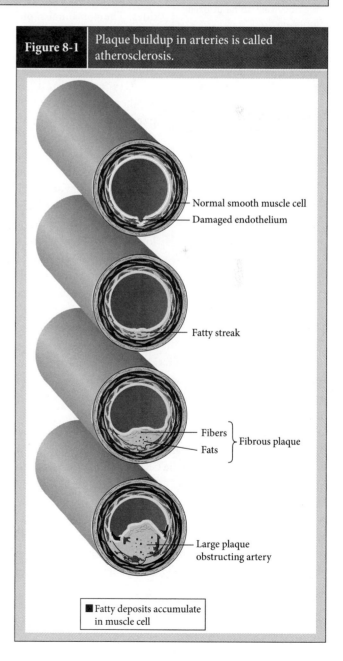

Figure 8-1 Plaque buildup in arteries is called atherosclerosis.

- Normal smooth muscle cell
- Damaged endothelium
- Fatty streak
- Fibers
- Fats
- Fibrous plaque
- Large plaque obstructing artery
- ■ Fatty deposits accumulate in muscle cell

> **Triglycerides** Also called *blood fat*. They are fats that very low-density lipoproteins (VLDL) carry in the blood. Excess sugar in the blood or unnecessary calories consumed that are not burned off with physical activity are converted into triglycerides.
>
> **Insulin** A hormone that is released when blood glucose levels increase. The hormone transports blood glucose into the body cells to be utilized for energy.
>
> **Type 2 diabetes** The inability of the body to utilize or make insulin properly. Consequently, sugar remains in the blood. If the sugar level is not regulated, over time the athlete can succumb to eye conditions including blindness, foot conditions including ulcers, kidney damage, heart attack, and stroke. Athletes who are overweight and obese are predisposed to acquire Type 2 diabetes.

High glycemic index foods increase **triglycerides** while decreasing the body's HDL (Frost et al., 1999). High triglycerides and low HDL cholesterol put an athlete at risk for heart disease.

Complex CHO take longer for the body to break down than simple CHO, and do not cause as much of a rapid increase in **insulin** as simple CHO does. The continual rapid increase in blood sugar can predispose an athlete to acquire **Type 2 diabetes**.

Glycemic load is another measurement utilized when referring to CHO and its effect on blood sugar levels. The higher the glycemic load, the greater, more detrimental effect the food has on blood sugar and insulin levels. A glycemic load of 20 or higher should be avoided. Foods with a glycemic load of 10 or less are beneficial to consume. To calculate the glycemic load, multiply the glycemic index by the grams of CHO in the food, and then divide this number by 100. Examples of foods and beverages with a glycemic load of 10 or under (per serving) include the following: an apple, one slice of whole wheat bread, skim milk, and tomato juice. Examples of foods and beverages with a glycemic load of 20 or over (per serving) include the following: raisins, a frozen white bagel, instant oatmeal, white rice, and apple juice.

Regardless of whether an athlete eats complex or simple CHO, if excessive CHO are ingested and not utilized for energy during exercise, then the CHO eventually is converted into fat. Therefore, an athlete cannot just eat CHO without exercising daily. CHO have only 4 calories per gram. The recommended daily allowance (RDA) for CHO for adult athletes is approximately 40–60% of total caloric intake. This CHO intake should mostly be composed of complex CHO starches and any simple CHO that are natural sugars, such as milk, fruits, and vegetables.

Fiber is another CHO, which differs significantly as compared to complex or simple CHO. Dietary fiber is necessary for the athlete's diet, but it is not broken down and utilized as an energy source. Dietary fiber is important to assist digestion, to prevent constipation, to help make an athlete feel full when eating, and to help her or him maintain optimal weight. Adequate dietary fiber has also been linked to a decrease in the potential of acquiring Type 2 diabetes, heart disease, constipation, and diverticulitis, or large intestine inflammation.

Fiber is classified as soluble or insoluble. Soluble fiber helps slow down digestion, and has been proven to assist in lowering cholesterol (MedlinePlus, 2010). Foods containing a decent amount of soluble fiber include legumes, lima beans, peas, lentils, beans, broccoli, nuts, almonds, sunflower seeds, whole-grain cereal, oatmeal, rye and pumpernickel breads, prunes, oranges, apples, and pears (**Table 8-2**). Insoluble fiber is not broken down as soluble fiber is. Consequently, insoluble fiber assists in moving food through the digestive system. Many foods that contain soluble fiber also contain insoluble fiber. Carrots, celery, corn, asparagus, whole grain pasta and bread, apples, grapes, and pears are all good sources of insoluble fiber. Athletes can also take in fiber via fiber supplements, which come in forms such as powders mixed with liquid, gummy chews, or tablets. Some fiber supplements have additional vitamins and minerals included in them, such as vitamin D and calcium. For an adult athlete, the average fiber RDA is approximately 20–35 grams. Men tend to need more fiber than women, and athletes over 50 years old require less fiber than athletes under 50 years old.

Fats

Fat in the body serves a variety of purposes. Fat helps insulate and cushion the body's organs, is utilized as an energy source when glycogen is not available, is necessary for fat-soluble vitamins to dissolve in the body, and assists in hormone production. Although fat has benefits, fat intake should only comprise approximately 25–35% of nutrient intake per day. For the average adult athlete on a 2,000-calorie diet, the fat grams in his or her diet per day would be approximately 56–77 grams. At 9 calories per gram, fat is the densest nutrient in terms of calories per gram. Too much fat in the diet can prove to be harmful to athletes. Excess intake has been shown to increase the chance of acquiring Type 2 diabetes, heart disease, and cancer (Mayo Clinic, 2011). Athletes who continuously consume an inordinate amount of fat are predisposed to becoming obese. Also, these athletes most often have high LDL cholesterol levels.

Certain types of fat cause these adverse conditions, illnesses, and diseases. Two detrimental fats are classified as saturated and trans fat. Most foods high in saturated fat are solid at room temperature. Examples of saturated fat foods

Table 8-2	Dietary Fiber Recommendations and Sources

The National Academy of Sciences' Institute of Medicine gives the following daily total fiber recommendations for adults:

	Age 50 and younger	Age 51 and older
Men	38 grams	30 grams
Women	25 grams	21 grams

Foods with Soluble and Insoluble Fiber

Soluble Fiber	Insoluble Fiber
• Apples • Oranges • Pears • Peaches • Grapes • Prunes • Blueberries • Strawberries • Seeds and nuts • Oat bran • Dried beans • Oatmeal • Barley • Rye • Vegetables	• Whole grain • Whole wheat breads • Barley • Brown rice • Bulgur • Whole-grain breakfast cereals • Wheat bran • Seeds • Vegetables: ▪ Carrots ▪ Cucumbers ▪ Zucchini ▪ Celery ▪ Tomatoes

Foods with High Fiber

Vegetables Serving Size Total fiber (grams)	Fruits Serving Size Total fiber (grams)	Legumes, Nuts & Seeds Serving Size Total Fiber (grams)	Grains, Cereal & Pasta Serving Size Total Fiber (grams)
Peas 1 cup 8.8	Apple, with skin 1 medium 4.4	Cashews 18 nuts 0.9	Bread, mixed grain 1 slice 1.7
Potato, baked with skin 1 medium 4.4	Apricots, dried 10 halves 2.6	Peanuts 28 nuts 2.3	Bread, whole-wheat 1 slice 1.9
Corn 1 cup 4.2	Raisins 1.5 ounce box 1.6	Pistachio nuts 47 nuts 2.9	Bread, rye 1 slice 1.9
Popcorn, air-popped 3 cups 3.6	Orange 1 medium 3.1	Almonds 24 nuts 3.3	Oatmeal 1 cup 4.0
Tomato paste 1/4 cup 3.0	Peaches, dried 3 halves 3.2	Baked beans, canned 1 cup 10.4	Bran flakes 3/4 cup 5.1
Carrot 1 medium 2.0	Blueberries 1 cup 3.5	Lima beans 1 cup 13.2	Spaghetti, whole-wheat 1 cup 6.3
Pear 1 medium 5.1	Pear 1 medium 5.1	Black beans 1 cup 15.0	
		Lentils 1 cup 15.6	

Data from Institute of Medicine, Food and Nutrition Board. Dietary Reference Intakes for Energy, Carbohydrate, Fiber, Fat, Fatty Acids, Cholesterol, Protein, and Amino Acids. © 2005 by the National Academy of Sciences, National Academies Press, Washington, DC.; U.S. Department of Agriculture, Agricultural Research Service. USDA National Nutrient Database for Standard Reference, Release 25. 2012.

include animal fats, beef, lard, butter, and coconut oil. In excess, these fats specifically increase LDL cholesterol, consequently increasing the athlete's chances of acquiring heart disease. Some foods containing saturated fats, such as whole milk products and avocados, are beneficial in moderation. Trans fat sources are found in saturated foods, but can also be created during the processing of foods. Trans fats are found in cooking oil, butter, margarine, animal meats such as beef and pork, fast food such as french fries, frozen food such as pizzas, cereals, potato chips, cookies, cakes, and candy. Trans fats can cause similar adverse conditions as saturated fats, including a decrease in HDL cholesterol and an increase in LDL cholesterol (Mayo Clinic, 2011). These effects can precipitate heart disease. Therefore, both saturated and trans fats should be limited, or avoided if possible, in your athlete's diet.

Not all fat is bad. Some fats are healthier than others and can promote a healthier diet. The healthier fats are classified as monounsaturated and polyunsaturated fats. These fats are liquid at room temperature and include oils such as olive, vegetable, canola, and sunflower oil, as well as nuts. Monounsaturated fats can improve cholesterol levels, which helps decrease the chance of an athlete acquiring heart disease. Monounsaturated fats also assist in regulating blood sugar levels, especially for an athlete with Type 2 diabetes. Polyunsaturated fats are classified as either omega-6 or omega-3 polyunsaturated fats. Omega-6 polyunsaturated fats include oils such as soybean, corn, and safflower oil. Omega-3 polyunsaturated fats include fish such as salmon and trout, walnuts, flaxseed, and oils such as soybean and canola oil. Both omega-6 and omega-3 polyunsaturated fats provide the essential fatty acids the body needs to function. Polyunsaturated fats can decrease the possibility of succumbing to Type 2 diabetes and high blood pressure. Omega-3 polyunsaturated fats can possibly decrease the risk of coronary artery disease (Centers for Disease Control and Prevention [CDC], 2011). Educate your athletes to consume monounsaturated and polyunsaturated fats instead of saturated and trans fats whenever possible. **Table 8-3** shows the fat content of a variety of foods.

Proteins

Proteins are called the building blocks of the body, and are a component of almost every part of the body including the

Table 8-3   Fat Content of Various Foods

Food Item	Serving Size	Total Fat (grams)	Saturated Fat (grams)	Monounsaturated Fat (grams)	Polyunsaturated Fat (grams)
Grains					
Oatmeal, dry	1/2 cup	2.5	0.5	1.0	1.0
English muffin	1 muffin	1	0.1	0.2	0.5
Pasta, cooked	1 cup	0.9	0.1	0.1	0.4
Brown rice	1 cup	1.8	0.4	0.6	0.6
Whole wheat bread	1 slice	1.2	0.3	0.5	0.3
Whole wheat pita	1 pita (6 1/2")	1.7	0.3	0.2	0.7
Blueberry muffin, made from a mix	1 muffin	6.2	1.2	1.5	3.1
Biscuit	1.2 oz	4.6	0.9	2.8	0.2
Fruits/Vegetables					
Pear	1 medium	1	< 0.1	0.1	0.2
Orange	1 medium	0	0	0	0
Watermelon	1 cup	0.7	0.1	0.2	0.2
Banana	1 medium	0.5	0.2	< 0.1	0.1
Spinach, raw	1/2 cup	0	0	0	0
Broccoli, cooked	1/2 cup	0.1	< 0.1	< 0.1	< 0.1
Carrots, cooked	1/2 cup	0.1	< 0.1	< 0.1	< 0.1
Avocado	1 medium	27	5.3	14.8	4.5
Milk/Alternative					
Skim milk	8 oz	0.5	0.4	0.2	< 0.1
1% milk	8 oz	2.6	1.6	0.7	0.1
2% milk	8 oz	4.7	2.9	1.4	0.2
Whole milk	8 oz	8	5.1	2.4	0.3
Cottage cheese, 2%	1/4 cup	4.4	2.8	1.2	0.1
Swiss cheese	1 oz	8	5.0	2.1	0.3
Soy milk	8 oz	5	0.5	1.0	3.0

(continues)

Table 8-3   Fat Content of Various Foods (Continued)

Food Item	Serving Size	Total Fat (grams)	Saturated Fat (grams)	Monounsaturated Fat (grams)	Polyunsaturated Fat (grams)
Meat and Beans/Alternative					
Ground beef, lean	3 oz	13.2	5.2	5.8	0.4
Chicken with skin	3 oz	9	2.4	3.4	1.9
Chicken without skin	3 oz	3.1	0.9	1.1	0.7
Turkey, white meat, without skin	3 oz	3	1.0	0.6	0.9
Turkey, dark meat, without skin	3 oz	6	2.2	1.5	2.0
Pork chop	3 oz	6.9	2.5	3.1	0.5
Salmon, pink	3 oz	4	1.0	0.8	0.6
Orange roughy	3 oz	1	< 0.1	0.5	< 0.1
Veggie burger	1 patty	0.5	0.1	0.3	0.2
Almonds	1 oz	15	1.1	9.5	3.6
Oils					
Margarine, stick	1 T	11	2.1	5.2	3.2
Butter	1 T	12	7.2	3.3	0.4
Olive oil	1 T	14	1.8	9.9	1.1
Salad dressing, ranch	2 T	18	2.5	NA	NA
Salad dressing, reduced calorie ranch	2 T	5	0.4	NA	NA

organs, tissues, and cells. They help repair cells and tissues, and assist in growth and development. After proteins are ingested, they are digested and broken down into amino acids. Later on, amino acids bind together to make up the proteins. Twenty amino acids exist; they are classified as either essential, nonessential, or conditional amino acids (MedlinePlus, 2012b). Nine essential amino acids are necessary for proper body function. These amino acids are not made by the body, and must be supplied by daily food intake. Nonessential amino acids are created in the body by protein breakdown as well as by the essential amino acids. Consequently, nonessential amino acids are plentiful in the body, unlike essential amino acids. Conditional amino acids are not necessary for the body unless the athlete is ill or experiencing stress.

An adult athlete needs approximately 10–35% of his or her daily diet to consist of protein. Endurance athletes or body builders may need a greater amount of daily protein due to the utilization, breakdown, and repair of muscle tissue (**Table 8-4**). Most often these athletes consume enough protein in their diet, so protein supplements are not necessary. Proteins offer the body 4 calories per gram, which is the same as CHO. Good sources of proteins and amino acids include meat, especially lean cuts of meat; fish and shellfish; milk products; eggs; kidney, black, garbanzo, and pinto beans;

Table 8-4   Daily Protein Recommendations for Athletes

Type of Athlete	Daily Grams of Protein/Kilogram Body Weight	Percentage of Total Calories Contributed by Protein
Sedentary individual	0.8 g/kg	12–15%
Strength athlete	1.4–2.0 g/kg	15–20%
Endurance athlete	1.2–2.0 g/kg	12–18%
Team sport athlete	1.2–1.6 g/kg	12–16%
Weight gain/loss	1.6–2.0 g/kg	16–20%

legumes; peanuts; walnuts; almonds; and soy (**Table 8-5**). An athlete should be careful not to eat too much meat or eggs, because meat has a large quantity of fat and egg yolks are high in cholesterol. Athletes should choose leaner cuts of red meat, pork, or chicken, and trim off excess fat, to obtain an appropriate amount of protein while limiting the amount of fat from these sources. Eating egg whites instead of the entire egg affords the athlete protein but no cholesterol.

Vegetarians may not get enough essential proteins because they do not eat meat. They may need to take protein supplements in liquid, gel, powder, or bar form. Encourage your vegetarian athlete to consume a variety of plant-type proteins to supply the body with enough essential amino acids.

Table 8-5	Protein Content of Various Foods	
Food Item	**Serving Size**	**Protein Content (grams)**
Grains		
Whole wheat bread	1 slice	3
Brown rice	½ cup	3
Pasta	½ cup	3.5
Fruits/Vegetables		
Apple	1 medium	0.3
Banana	1 medium	1.2
Carrots	½ cup	1
Broccoli	½ cup	1.3
Milk/Alternative		
Skim milk	8 fl oz	8
Low-fat yogurt	6 oz	6
Cheddar cheese	1 oz	7
Soy milk	8 fl oz	5
Soy yogurt	6 oz	7
Meat and Beans/Alternative		
Beef	3 oz	25
Chicken	3 oz	27
Turkey	3 oz	26
Pork	3 oz	24
Tuna	3 oz	22
Black beans	1½ cup	23
Lentils	1½ cup	27
Tofu	½ cup	20
Tempeh	½ cup	16
Mixed nuts	1 oz	5

Data from Pennington JA, Douglas JS. Bowes & Church's Food Values of Portions Commonly Used, 18th ed. Philadelphia, PA: Lippincott Williams and Wilkins; 2005.

Obviously, protein is very beneficial for an athlete's health. In addition to assisting in tissue and cell repair, and growth and development of the body, protein offers other benefits for the body. Protein helps to maintain a properly working immune system. This macronutrient also is beneficial for athletes who wish to lose weight. Over the years, athletes who consume a greater percentage of protein with reduced CHO have lost weight more rapidly than athletes eating primarily CHO. Larger quantities of protein in the diet as compared to CHO helps curb appetite, and with exercise improves triglyceride levels. High protein, high fat, and low CHO diets have been shown not to significantly increase triglycerides, HDL, or blood pressure, and insulin levels can be positively affected (Gardner et al., 2007).

At times, athletes can become protein deficient or have excess intake. Both extremes can cause difficulty for the athlete and his or her body. Because athletes typically consume enough daily protein, a protein deficiency, called kwashiorkor, is rare. Most cases of kwashiorkor occur with people in poor countries who do not have access to adequate protein, or to the elderly or others who are unaware of how much protein to include in their diet (PubMed Health, 2012). If an athlete has a protein deficiency, the signs and symptoms of illness include, but are not limited to, fatigue, changes in skin pigmentation, a decrease in muscle mass, diarrhea, swelling, rash, and irritability. If you suspect your athlete has a protein deficiency, refer her or him to a physician for a full physical exam and blood tests.

More often, athletes consume excess daily protein. Many athletes believe that because protein helps repair muscles and assists in growth and development, consuming more protein will create more muscle. This theory is not factual. In reality, excessively high protein diets cause the kidneys to work harder than they should to excrete waste, which could result in kidney damage. Likewise, high protein diets may also contain high amounts of fat, which can cause illnesses or diseases previously mentioned. Although protein is an important nutrient to incorporate in your athlete's daily nutrient intake, always consider the consequences of excess protein intake.

Water

The last macronutrient is water. The body is composed of approximately 60–75% water. Water is crucial for body organ and cellular functions. It dissolves minerals and other nutrients in the body so they can be utilized. Water prevents constipation, alleviates heat from the body via perspiration, flushes out waste products from the kidneys and liver, lubricates joints, and moistens tissues. Water is so essential for body functioning that without water, the body can only sustain itself for a few days.

Obviously, an athlete should drink plenty of water each day in order to provide the body with a sufficient amount. According to the National Council of Strength and

Fitness (n.d.), when someone is thirsty, they have already lost approximately 0.8–2% of their body weight due to water loss. This water weight loss can detrimentally affect an athlete's performance. The amount of water an athlete should drink per day varies, depending on the athlete's age, health, and activity level. According to the Institute of Medicine of the National Academies (2004), approximately 80% of water supplied to the body comes from beverages and 20% is supplied by food. On the average, women require a total of 2.7 liters of water from beverages and food per day, while men require 3.7 liters. Therefore, women need approximately 2.16 liters (9 cups) and men need 2.96 liters (12.5 cups) of water per day. Very active athletes and those who sweat profusely need increased water consumption. Water is also found in various foods. Foods and drinks with high water content include milk, soup, leafy green lettuce, watermelon, cantaloupe, grapefruit, strawberries, tomatoes, cucumbers, carrots, celery, and broccoli. Many of these foods have other nutritional benefits, including preventing illnesses and diseases. Keep in mind that fluids containing caffeine are not as beneficial compared to decaffeinated drinks because caffeine is a **diuretic**, and the athlete may end up dehydrated.

> **Diuretic** Something that causes the kidneys to produce urine, which consequently increases the rate of urination. Other than prescription and over-the-counter diuretic drugs and caffeine, pineapple juice, leafy green vegetables, garlic, and onions are some examples of natural diuretics.

Many athletes choose to drink electrolyte drinks instead of water. Electrolyte drinks are composed of water; electrolytes such as sodium, chloride, and potassium; CHO; sweetener; and flavoring. Some electrolyte drinks include caffeine, which should be avoided before, during, and after exercise. Others contain a large quantity of CHO and simple sugars, which do provide energy. When a large quantity of CHO is in an electrolyte drink, the body focuses on breaking down the CHO prior to delivering the water to the body. This process results in delayed hydration. Some companies make lower CHO and simple sugar sports drinks. Approximately 6% CHO in electrolyte drinks is claimed to be optimal. Some drinks are sweetened with aspartame instead of sugar. These sports drinks may be a better choice for some athletes for hydration; for example, diabetic and overweight athletes can gain the benefits of electrolyte drinks without ingesting excess sugar and calories. The water and electrolyte content in these drinks is certainly beneficial for athletes. Research studies have concluded that athletes tend to hydrate better due to the electrolyte sports drinks' taste. Also, electrolyte drinks have been shown to minimize the body's water loss and increases in core body temperature when exercising in the heat (Bergeron, Waller, & Marinik, 2006).

An athlete knows if she or he is properly hydrated if she or he is urinating frequently and the urine is a light yellow to clear color. If the urine is dark yellow and has a foul odor, then the athlete is dehydrated. Some vitamins and supplements also turn an athlete's urine a dark yellow, however. Therefore, the existence of additional signs and symptoms of dehydration are warranted before making a determination that the athlete is dehydrated. Other signs and symptoms of dehydration include dry mouth, thirst, fatigue, headache, lack of or no sweating, constipation, rapid breathing and heart rate, and low blood pressure. If the athlete experiences sign and symptoms of dehydration, he or she needs to hydrate immediately. If it appears that his or her body is not readily responding to hydration attempts or is experiencing shock, call 911 because the athlete is in a life-threatening situation.

When exercising, athletes must always have water, decaffeinated drinks containing water, or electrolyte drinks on hand to replenish the water loss from perspiration. Typically, exercising athletes should drink 4–8 ounces of water every 15–20 minutes of exercise. This consumption varies depending on the intensity of exercise, the ambient temperature and relative humidity, and the athlete's age, health, and fitness level. Water is essential to the body, and athletes must always have adequate water content in the body to continue to perform activities of daily living and exercise.

Micronutrients

◼ Vitamins

Vitamins are organic compounds that do not supply energy and are not made by the body. Two categories of vitamins exist: fat-soluble vitamins and water-soluble vitamins. Fat-soluble vitamins are vitamins A, D, E, and K. These vitamins require fat in the body to assist in breaking down and dissolving the vitamins. The body does not readily eliminate fat-soluble vitamins. The fat-soluble vitamins not utilized by the body are not eliminated in urine. Consequently, if fat-soluble vitamins are regularly consumed in excess, toxicity results. Water-soluble vitamins break down and dissolve in water. The water-soluble vitamins include vitamin C and the B-complex vitamins, which include the eight B vitamins: thiamine (B_1), riboflavin (B_2), niacin (B_3), pyridoxine (B_6), cobalamin (B_{12}), folic acid (B_9), panthothenic acid (B_5), and biotin (B_7) (Thygerson & Thygerson, 2013). The major vitamins are listed in **Table 8-6**.

Vitamins are imperative for a variety of bodily functions. They enter into the body when an athlete eats a variety of plant and animal foods. An athlete must be cognizant of the vitamins in her or his food. She or he must consume a variety of foods that have many different vitamins; if not, she or he may become vitamin deficient. If an athlete has a

Table 8-6 | Major Vitamins Necessary for Bodily Functions

Vitamin	Major Functions	Rich Food Sources	Deficiency Signs/Symptoms	Toxicity Signs/Symptoms
A and provitamin A (beta-carotene)	Vision in dim light, growth, reproduction, maintains immune system and skin, antioxidant	Liver, milk, dark green and leafy vegetables, carrots, sweet potatoes, mangos, oatmeal, broccoli, apricots, peaches, romaine lettuce	Poor vision in dim light, dry skin, blindness, poor growth, respiratory infections	Intestinal upset, liver damage, hair loss, headache, birth defects, death (betacarotene is less toxic than vitamin A)
D	Bone and tooth development and growth	Few good food sources other than fortified milk and eggs	Weak, deformed bones (rickets)	Growth failure, loss of appetite, weight loss, death
E	Antioxidant: protects cell membranes	Vegetable oils, whole grains, wheat germ, sunflower seeds, almonds	Anemia (rarely occurs)	Intestinal upset, bleeding problems
C	Scar formation and maintenance, immune system functioning, antioxidant	Citrus fruits, berries, potatoes, broccoli, peppers, cabbage, tomatoes, fortified fruit drinks	Frequent infections, bleeding gums, bruises, poor wound healing, depression (scurvy)	Diarrhea, nosebleeds, headache, weakness, kidney stones, excess iron absorption and storage
Thiamine	Energy metabolism	Pork, liver, nuts, dried beans and peas, whole-grain and enriched breads and cereals	Heart failure, mental confusion, depression, paralysis (beriberi)	No toxicity has been reported
Riboflavin	Energy metabolism	Milk and yogurt, eggs and poultry, meat, liver, whole-grain and enriched breads and cereals	Enlarged, purple tongue; fatigue; oily skin; cracks in the corners of the mouth	No toxicity has been reported
Niacin	Energy metabolism	Protein-rich foods, peanut butter, whole-grain and enriched breads and cereals	Skin rash, diarrhea, weakness, dementia, death (pellagra)	Painful skin flushing, intestinal upset, liver damage
Vitamin B6	Protein and fat metabolism	Liver, oatmeal, bananas, meat, fish, poultry, whole grains, fortified cereals	Anemia, skin rash, irritability, elevated homocysteine levels	Weakness, depression, permanent nerve damage
Folate (folic acid)	DNA production	Leafy vegetables, oranges, nuts, liver, enriched breads and cereals	Anemia, depression, spina bifida in developing embryo, elevated homocysteine levels	Hides signs of vitamin B12 deficiency; may cause allergic response
B12	DNA production	Animal products	Pernicious anemia, fatigue, paralysis, elevated homocysteine levels	No toxicity has been reported

deficiency, she or he may have to take vitamin supplements specifically to address the deficiency. An athlete who eats a well-rounded diet most likely does not need vitamin supplementation; however, it is a very common practice for both men and women to take a daily multivitamin that gives them the proper vitamin RDA.

Pediatricians recommend that children take a daily children's multivitamin because their bodies are growing. Many children also have erratic and unhealthy eating habits, so they may not consume all vitamins in the quantity necessary per day. Consequently, daily vitamin supplementation for children is necessary. Some athletes also must take vitamin supplementation upon their physician's recommendation due to conditions or deficiencies they may have. Pregnant women are directed by their physicians to take a daily multivitamin, along with extra supplementation of folic acid. The B complex vitamins can potentially help fight heart disease. Therefore, physicians often recommend to athletes who have atherosclerosis to supplement their diets with extra B vitamins. Although

vitamin supplementation seems to be an easy means to obtain the RDA of necessary vitamins, remind your athletes that vitamin supplementation should not replace healthy eating.

Minerals

Micronutrients include not only vitamins, but also minerals. Minerals are inorganic substances that are required daily for adequate body function. Similar to vitamins, minerals do not supply energy, but are important in many body functions. Minerals assist with the functioning and production of enzymes, hormones, body fluids, the heart, hair, teeth, and bones. Macrominerals are essential micronutrients that are needed by our bodies in large amounts. These macrominerals include calcium, magnesium, potassium, sodium, phosphorous, sulfur, and chloride (MedlinePlus, 2012a). Trace minerals are required by our bodies in small quantities. Trace minerals include iron, selenium, copper, zinc, iodine, cobalt, manganese, and fluoride. **Table 8-7** lists some of the essential minerals our bodies require.

Table 8-7	Essential Minerals Necessary for Bodily Functions			
Mineral	**Roles**	**Rich Food Sources**	**Deficiency Signs/ Symptoms**	**Toxicity Signs/ Symptoms**
Calcium	Builds and maintains bones and teeth, regulates muscle and nerve function, regulates blood pressure and blood clotting	Milk products; fortified orange juice, tofu, and soy milk; fish with edible small bones such as sardines and salmon; broccoli; hard water	Poor bone growth, weak bones, muscle spasms, convulsions	Kidney stones, calcium deposits in organs, mineral imbalances
Potassium	Maintains fluid balance, necessary for nerve function	Whole grains, fruits and vegetables, yogurt, milk	Muscular weakness, confusion, death	Heart failure
Sodium	Maintains fluid balance, necessary for nerve function	Salt, soy sauce, luncheon meats, processed cheeses, pickled foods, snack foods, canned and dried soups	Muscle cramping, headache, confusion, coma	Hypertension
Magnesium	Regulation of enzyme activity, necessary for nerve function	Green, leafy vegetables, nuts, whole grains, peanut butter	Loss of appetite, muscular weakness, convulsions, confusion, death	Rare
Zinc	Component of many enzymes and the hormone insulin, maintains immune function, necessary for sexual maturation and reproduction	Meats, fish, poultry, whole grains, vegetables	Poor growth, failure to mature sexually, improper healing of wounds	Mineral imbalances, gastrointestinal upsets, anemia, heart disease
Selenium	Component of a group of antioxidant enzymes, immune system function	Seafood, liver, and vegetables and grains grown in selenium-rich soil	May increase risk of heart disease and certain cancers	Hair and nail loss
Iron	Oxygen transport involved in the release of energy	Clams, oysters, liver, red meats, and enriched breads and cereals	Fatigue, weakness, iron-deficiency anemia	Iron poisoning, nausea, vomiting, diarrhea, death

No food contains all the important minerals the body requires. Therefore, the athlete's diet must include various foods in order to obtain all necessary minerals. Minerals are found in foods such as bananas, leafy green vegetables, spinach, legumes, milk and dairy products, salt, whole grains, and red meat. Similar to vitamins, if minerals are deficient in the body, illness can result.

Sodium is an important mineral that assists in nerve function; however, according to the 2010 *Report of the Dietary Guidelines Advisory Committee on the Dietary Guidelines for Americans* (U.S. Department of Agriculture, 2010), sodium is overconsumed by the public. Athletes typically overindulge in salty foods such as fast food; potato chips; frozen, breaded foods; lunch meats; and condiments. Many athletes add sodium in the form of table salt to their food, which also creates excess in their diet. Excess sodium can cause hypertension, which can lead to heart problems and stroke. Excess sodium has also been shown to lead to osteoporosis, fluid retention, and kidney stones. An athlete's typical diet contains a sufficient amount of sodium, so additional sodium is not recommended.

The Dietary Guidelines for Americans report also shows that calcium and potassium are two underconsumed minerals. Calcium helps with bone strengthening, muscle contractions, and nerve conduction. Although calcium is important for all adults and children, it is of particular importance to female athletes. As female athletes age, their bones tend to become weakened. Weakened bones are predisposed to fracture. The bones also lose their density. Calcium sources include milk and dairy products, soy, broccoli, spinach, and calcium-fortified foods such as orange juice. If female athletes consume the RDA of calcium throughout their lives, then the risk of bone weakening and loss will be minimized. Potassium is important for adequate nerve conduction, muscle contraction, blood pressure and heart rate regulation, and cellular fluid maintenance. Athletes deficient in potassium can become weak and hypertensive. They can experience muscular cramping and irregular heartbeats. Potassium deficiency can even cause death. Sources of potassium include vegetables, such as raw spinach, sun-dried tomatoes, green beans, and mushrooms, and fruits, such as bananas, oranges, peaches, and apricots.

Iron is an important trace mineral. Iron's primary function is to make hemoglobin, which carries oxygen in red blood cells. Iron is a common mineral often deficient in babies under 2 years of age; teenage girls; women, including pregnant women; and the elderly. If an athlete has an iron deficiency, her red blood cells cannot carry as much oxygen as they should. The athlete experiences a variety of iron deficiency symptoms including fatigue, mental problems, sleep difficulties, pale skin, and **anemia**. Good iron sources include meats, fish, eggs, dried beans, and fruit. The body readily absorbs iron from these sources. Other foods include iron, such as some vegetables, legumes, and whole grains, but the body does not absorb it as well. Iron-deficient athletes, as well as vegetarians, may need to take iron supplements. If an athlete experiences any iron deficiency symptoms, refer him or her to a physician for evaluation.

> **Anemia** When an athlete has a decreased amount of hemoglobin and/or red blood cells in the body. Consequently, because hemoglobin carries oxygen in the red blood cells, if an athlete has anemia, she or he will have decreased oxygen in the body.

MYPLATE.GOV

The U.S. Department of Agriculture has created a tool called MyPlate (http://www.ChooseMyPlate.gov) in response to the 2010 Dietary Guidelines for Americans (**Figure 8-2**). MyPlate recommends healthy nutrients for daily consumption, and the necessary proportions. Fruits and vegetables should be plentiful and varied in the diet, whole grains should be at least 50% of total grains, proteins should be low fat, and dairy products should be consumed with each meal in order to ingest the proper amount of calcium. If an athlete incorporates MyPlate into his or her daily food regime, he or she will ingest all required macro- and micronutrients.

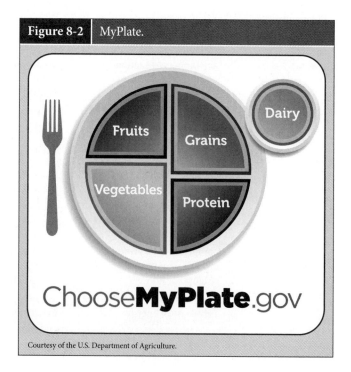

Figure 8-2 | MyPlate.

Courtesy of the U.S. Department of Agriculture.

RECOMMENDED DIETARY ALLOWANCE VERSUS DIETARY REFERENCE INTAKE

Throughout this chapter, the abbreviation RDA has been used. RDA, or recommended dietary allowance, is the average amount of a nutrient that a person's body requires per day in order to function properly. RDA is utilized to determine the recommended daily value (RDV), which is used as the basis for the percent daily value (%DV) that is printed on the Nutrition Facts labels on food and supplement packaging (**Figure 8**-3). This %DV indicates the nutrient values and percentage of total RDV for each nutrient for a 2,000 calorie per day diet. The %DV on these Nutrition Facts labels is a tool for athletes to determine if they are consuming an adequate amount of required nutrients per day.

In 1997, the term *dietary reference intake (DRI)* was devised as another means to describe dietary intake. According to the National Institutes of Health, Office of Dietary Supplements (n.d.), DRI includes various reference measurements used to determine whether the general population is meeting intake requirements. DRI measures include RDA, estimated average requirements (EAR), adequate intake (AI), and tolerable upper intake level (UL). EAR is the standard amount of a nutrient required for the average person. AI is the amount of a nutrient that a person must consume to be healthy. UL is the highest amount of a nutrient that a person can consume without any detrimental effects. DRI is used by U.S. governmental agencies as a scientific means to research and determine these values for specific foods, and then to report the findings to the public. Although DRI is more comprehensive, an athlete can easily and successfully use the nutrients' RDA and the %DV on Nutrient Facts labels to determine how well she or he is meeting the governmental recommendations.

Tips from the Field

Tip 1 Your athlete may not be aware of the best food choices to include in his diet. Likewise, he may not know how to utilize the valuable information listed on the nutrient labels. Once you have assisted him in setting his goals and devised his daily nutrient requirements, take your athlete to the grocery store to have an educational session. First, show the athlete the various foods that would qualify under each section of MyPlate. Then show him how to utilize the nutrient information and %DV on Nutrient Facts labels. Once you educate the athlete to incorporate this information into his dietary plan, over time he will be able to make healthy food choices on a regular basis without assistance.

WEIGHT LOSS AND WEIGHT GAIN

As part of being healthy, an athlete must manage his or her weight. Due to the current prevalence of obesity, and the resulting illnesses and diseases, the athlete must pay particular attention to keeping his or her body weight at normal values. Some athletes do need or want to gain weight, and should set goals to gain lean muscle mass versus fat.

To begin a weight maintenance program, your athlete must understand that for each pound of fat he or she wants to lose, his or her weekly caloric intake must decrease by 3,500. He or she can also expend calories to assist in meeting this goal. To gain lean muscle mass, the athlete must increase his or her caloric intake by adding protein to his or her diet along with exercise, in particular strength training exercise. A safe weight loss or gain goal would be to lose or gain 1 to 2 pounds per week. In order to make this weight management program work, the athlete must incorporate good nutrition and eating habits along with daily exercise. For weight loss, restricting calorie intake alone is not successful long term; the athlete loses weight at first, but then plateaus. Without incorporating exercise, the athlete most likely will gain the weight back. Likewise, exercise alone does not help an athlete lose weight, especially if the athlete does not change his or her eating habits.

When an athlete wants to begin a weight management program, he or she must set long- and short-term goals. Help him or her be realistic with weight management goals, as with exercise goals. Determine how much weight he or she wants

---

Figure 8-3 | An example of a Nutrition Facts label as it would appear on a food package.

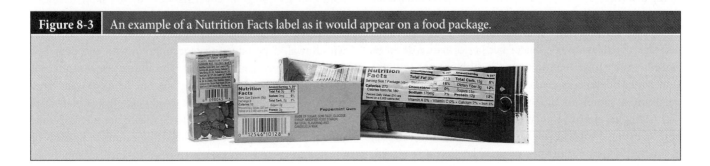

to lose or gain. Have him or her complete a daily food diary of current nutrient consumption, including a calculation of calories ingested and expended. This food diary is very important for creating short-term goals, and determining what dietary changes must be made. Advise your athlete to continue keeping the food diary when beginning the weight management program, and to continue even after reaching the goal weight. After reaching the weight goal, this food diary will assist him or her in continuing a nutritionally balanced diet.

Tips from the Field

Tip 2 When an athlete is beginning a nutritional program, ask her how she would feel most comfortable keeping track of her nutrient intake. Have a variety of paper tracking documents as well as website and cell phone application programs available for the athlete to try. Review the website and application sites first and determine their ease of use. Also determine the athlete's cost for these tools. Some are free, whereas others require a monthly, yearly, or one-time fee. Whichever your athlete chooses, make sure she has some means to track her progress on a daily basis.

Much research is available to review in regard to the best dietary plan for your athlete. As previously mentioned, low CHO, high protein, and high fat dietary plans may work for some athletes. Endurance athletes most likely need a high CHO and low protein and fat dietary plan, which is recommended by governmental agencies. Your athlete may inquire about a certain dietary plan that he or she has read or heard about. Help him or her to determine the dietary plan's safety and effectiveness by looking up information about it utilizing reputable, research-based sources. If you cannot provide the athlete with this information, or need additional assistance, contact a registered dietician (RD) who is an expert in the field.

EATING DISORDERS

When the term *eating disorder* is mentioned, anorexia nervosa and bulimia often come to mind. Although these illnesses are eating disorders, binge-eating disorder and obesity are also eating disorders that affect both male and female athletes. All four eating disorders can be caused by psychological and emotional issues manifested within the athlete. When an eating disorder affects an athlete, his or her performance declines, and his or her physical and mental health are not optimal. Unless the athlete seeks medical assistance to combat the eating disorder, significant illness, disease, and death may result.

Although anorexia nervosa and bulimia are the most notable eating disorders, obesity truly falls into this category of illnesses. Obesity is defined as an athlete having a significant amount of body fat and weight for his or her height, as compared to a healthy, normal weight athlete. Obese athletes have a body mass index (BMI) of over 30. Obesity does not have a single cause; rather, it results from a myriad of factors. If an athlete has poor nutritional habits and consumes more calories than he or she expends during exercise, then over time he or she will gain weight and could become obese. An athlete who has low self-esteem, emotional issues, and trauma in his or her life may rely on food as a comfort and become obese. Also, a medical condition called hypothyroidism and certain prescription medications such as corticosteroids may cause an athlete to gain significant weight. If an athlete becomes obese and remains in that state, he or she can acquire a variety of illnesses. Obese athletes are prone to the following conditions and illnesses, including, but not limited to, heart disease, stroke, cancer, high cholesterol, high blood pressure, Type 2 diabetes, **gout**, sleep apnea, and other respiratory problems. In order to help an athlete lose weight, refer him or her to a physician for evaluation, a registered dietician for consultation,

> **Gout** Caused by uric acid in the blood that crystallizes. The crystals move into the joints and body tissues, especially in the foot. This condition creates painful arthritis and is often recurrent.

and a psychologist or counselor for therapeutic sessions.

Whereas an obese athlete has a high amount of body weight due to body fat, an athlete with anorexia nervosa is extremely thin. Anorexia nervosa begins when the athlete's mental and emotional issues result in self-starvation. Most anorexic athletes are women in their teens and 20s. Males, especially wrestlers and those who need to continually manage their weight, also can become anorexic. Typically an athlete feels out of control with some issue or event in her life; however, she feels she can control the amount of food she consumes. The athlete may also feel peer, coach, or public pressure to be thin. Consequently, she severely limits the amount of nutrients that she consumes. As a result she becomes significantly underweight. Signs and symptoms of anorexia nervosa include, but are not limited to, significant underweight appearance, fatigue, constipation, amenorrhea, thinning and falling out hair, soft hair covering the body, dry skin, dizziness, fainting, low blood pressure, and arrhythmias. The athlete also may exhibit behavioral signs of anorexia such as social withdrawal, depression, a preoccupation with and denial of food, and fear of gaining weight. The athlete visualizes herself as being fat, even though she is not. She tends to wear large bulky clothes to hide her drastic weight loss. If an athlete does not get professional assistance to deal with her mental, emotional, and physical condition, she will succumb to a variety of illnesses such as anemia, electrolyte imbalance, osteoporosis, kidney failure, heart attack, and even death.

Bulimia is an eating disorder in which an athlete binges and purges, typically in secret. The athlete binges by eating thousands of calories of food and then purges or eliminates the food by induced vomiting, or by utilizing laxatives or enemas. The athlete may also attempt to rid her body of calories by excessively exercising. Bulimia has many of the same characteristics as anorexia nervosa. Bulimic athletes typically are females of the same age as anorexic females. Similar to anorexia nervosa, bulimia is a mental and emotional illness as well as a physical illness. A bulimic athlete tends to binge and purge food in secret, is preoccupied with food, and is overly concerned with her weight. Unlike anorexic athletes, bulimic athletes are approximately the same weight as if they were not bulimic. Signs and symptoms of bulimia include tooth and fingernail decay, gum disease, depression, anxiety, obsessive-compulsive disorder, and fainting. If a bulimic athlete does not seek professional help, she may succumb to an electrolyte imbalance, osteoporosis, arrhythmias, esophageal ulcers, kidney damage, and even death.

Binge-eating disorder is similar to bulimia because the athlete consumes large quantities of food in one sitting on a regular basis, but she does not purge after eating. Athletes who tend to binge-eat typically are depressed, anxious, and have other mental and emotional issues. The food acts as a comfort for the athlete. The athlete eats when she does not feel hungry. She consumes food until her stomach is painfully full to the point of illness. The binging takes place in secret. The athlete wants to stop binging, but feels like she is incapable of stopping. She becomes upset and unhappy with herself after binging. The athlete remains at her normal weight for a period of time, but with continued binging she gains weight and most likely becomes obese.

Although obesity and anorexia are evident from the physical appearance of the athlete (if the anorexic is not wearing large, bulky clothing), bulimia and binge-eating are typically not as evident. If you suspect your athlete has an eating disorder, obtain guidance from professionals on how to handle the situation and approach the athlete. You must have a relationship built on mutual trust to discuss her illness with her and offer assistance. Because we often have close relationship with our athletes, they may open up, admit they have an illness, and communicate their feelings to you before discussing the issue with anyone else. When approaching the athlete to assist her, expect her to be defensive. Do not attack the athlete and bluntly accuse her of having an eating disorder. You may need to discuss other topics with the athlete and transition into a conversation regarding her weight and eating habits. You could discuss reevaluating her exercise and nutritional goals. Show her care and compassion during your communication. Listen to everything she has to say, and do not pass judgment. Hopefully the athlete verbally communicates her feelings in regard to her illness and wants assistance. Offer her support and encouragement. Assure her that she can confide in you and trust you to help her. An athlete who does not realize she has an eating disorder cannot admit her problem. If she does not admit her problem, consult an eating disorder expert to get advice on how to handle the situation and get the athlete professional treatment.

FEMALE ATHLETE TRIAD

The female athlete triad occurs when a female athlete is suffering from a disordered eating habit, amenorrhea, and osteoporosis (**Figure 8-4**). These three conditions combined are severely detrimental to the athlete's body. As a part of the

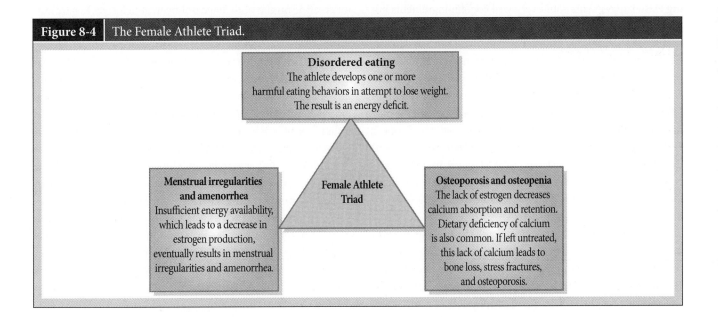

Figure 8-4 | The Female Athlete Triad.

Disordered eating
The athlete develops one or more harmful eating behaviors in attempt to lose weight. The result is an energy deficit.

Female Athlete Triad

Menstrual irregularities and amenorrhea
Insufficient energy availability, which leads to a decrease in estrogen production, eventually results in menstrual irregularities and amenorrhea.

Osteoporosis and osteopenia
The lack of estrogen decreases calcium absorption and retention. Dietary deficiency of calcium is also common. If left untreated, this lack of calcium leads to bone loss, stress fractures, and osteoporosis.

female athlete triad, an athlete is affected by either anorexia nervosa or bulimia. Due to an athlete's exercise regimen, hormonal imbalance, and changes in body weight due to the eating disorder, amenorrhea occurs. Osteoporosis, or bone weakening and loss, occurs due to hormonal imbalances, as does prolonged amenorrhea (Hobart & Smucker, 2000). The female athlete triad is a detrimental cycle of these three conditions, which continues until the athlete receives treatment. If you suspect that your athlete is affected by the female athlete triad, refer the athlete to her physician, a psychologist, and a registered dietician for evaluation and treatment.

SUPPLEMENTS AND NUTRITIONAL ERGOGENIC AIDS

Supplements, also called dietary supplements, are nonfood substances that athletes add to their diet. These supplements include not only vitamins and minerals, as previously discussed, but also herbs, botanicals, amino acids, and metabolites. Supplement manufacturers claim that their products have nutrient value and health benefits, and cause structural and functional improvements (Fink et al., 2009). Because supplements are not drugs, the manufacturers cannot claim supplements have a pharmacological use or that they can cure illness or disease. Over-the-counter (OTC) and prescription drugs are put through mandatory, rigorous testing for safety or effectiveness by the Food and Drug Administration (FDA). Supplements are not tested or regulated by the FDA. The FDA does not approve the supplement's ingredients, dosage, or anything else before the supplement is put on the market. The supplements have labels on them that list the ingredients; however, these labels are also not regulated or approved by the FDA. Therefore, because no FDA testing and no approval requirements for product labeling exist, supplements could very well contain ingredients not listed on the label. This fact could pose significant problems and health risks for athletes. Additional ingredients not listed on the label could interfere with other supplements, OTC drugs, or prescription drugs the athlete is taking. Supplements may also create an adverse situation if the athlete has a medical condition with which the supplement interferes. Some supplements may have ingredients that are banned by the National Anti-Doping Organization of the United States (USADA), the National Collegiate Athletic Association (NCAA), governmental agencies, and other organizations. In this case, an athlete may be found positive for banned substances during an employment or athletic activity drug test.

Athletes must take precautions when utilizing supplements. Recommend to your athlete to consult a physician regarding the supplements that he or she wishes to take. The physician can determine if the supplements are beneficial and safe for the athlete. Also, the physician knows if any supplements are contraindicated due to the athlete's conditions and medications. The athlete should get the supplement tested by a laboratory if possible before using it. If this testing is not feasible, then the athlete should do as much research as possible to determine if the supplement is safe to consume.

Athletes take supplements for a variety of reasons. They are competitive and want any advantage they can get over their competitors. Many athletes believe that by taking supplements they can obtain this advantage. Many male athletes consume protein and whey supplements, or any supplement that assists them in gaining muscle mass. Many female athletes consume weight loss, vitamin, mineral, and energy enhancement supplements (Fink et al., 2009). Most supplements do not give athletes an advantage in competition. Likewise, some supplements do not create the effects that the manufacturers claim. However, many supplements do exist that can enhance an athlete's performance. These supplements are considered nutritional ergogenic aids. Nutritional ergogenic aids are made from nutrients produced by the body or found in food. Two examples of commonly used nutritional ergogenic aids are creatine and caffeine.

Creatine is made by the body from amino acids. In addition, it is typically taken into the body by consuming high protein foods including meat and fish or by supplementation in pill and powder forms. This substance is a natural ergogenic aid because it decreases fatigue and recovery time, while increasing energy and the ability to exercise longer during a session. Creatine has been shown to benefit and increase performance, particularly for short-term, high-intensity exercise (Andres, Sacheck, & Tapia, 1999). Some side effects of utilizing supplemental creatine are water retention in the muscles, resultant weight gain, muscle cramping, and diarrhea. Unfortunately, to date, long-term studies regarding the effects of creatine on the body have not been conclusive. Regardless, creatine has been widely researched and consistently proven to work as a nutritional ergogenic aid.

Caffeine in moderate quantities also acts as a natural ergogenic aid. Caffeine is different than creatine because it is not produced by the body. This substance must be taken into the body from substances such as coffee, tea, soda, chocolate, and other commercialized drinks and food. Caffeine is a central nervous system stimulant and can assist an endurance athlete to continue with her activity for a longer duration. The athlete also has more energy at the end of her exercise activity than if she did not consume caffeine. Caffeine increases the athlete's metabolism, which assists her in expending more calories. Also, caffeine releases stored fat into the blood, which is utilized as an energy source during exercise. When ingested in moderation, these characteristics of caffeine make it a valuable aid to many athletes. Because caffeine does work as an ergogenic aid, its use is limited by organizations, such as the NCAA.

Consequently, athletes who may be drug tested must be mindful of the quantity of caffeine ingested prior to competition.

Many other nutritional ergogenic aids are used by both endurance athletes (**Table 8-8**) and strength and power athletes (**Table 8-9**). These ergogenic aids have a range of effectiveness from low to high. Some supplements have no side effects, whereas some have significant side effects that can be severely detrimental to the athlete's body. Some supplements are

Table 8-8	Common Nutritional Ergogenics Used by Endurance Athletes				
Supplements (other names)	**Claimed Action**	**Human Research**	**Potential**	**Banned**	**Comments/Concerns**
Branched chain amino acids (BCAA)	Essential amino acids that are touted to enhance endurance performance	Yes	Low	No	BCAAs are supplied by whole foods, which also provide other nutrients.
Caffeine (kola nut, guarana)	Enhances performance by increasing serum FFA/use of muscle triglycerides, sparing muscle glycogen	Yes	Moderate	No	Elevates heart rate and blood pressure; can cause irritability, nervousness, and gastrointestinal distress.
Coenzyme Q$_{10}$ (ubiquinone or CoQ$_{10}$)	Enhances function of electron transport chain; increases endurance performance	Yes	Low for athletes	No	Potential for cell damage when consumed in large amounts and exercising intensely.
Energy bars	Provides energy for prolonged endurance performance	Yes	High	No	Should not be used as a meal replacement.
Energy gels	Quick supply of carbohydrates during endurance exercise	Yes	High	No	Consume with 8–12 oz of fluid; may be better tolerated taken in small amounts.
Ginseng	Increases stamina; ability to adapt to training stressors; enhances immune function	Yes	Low	No	Ginseng content in supplements can vary greatly; may increase blood pressure.
Glycerol	Energy source during exercise; promotes hyperhydration status before endurance exercise	Yes	Low-moderate	Yes	USOC/IOC bans use. May cause gastrointestinal upset and cramping.
L-carnitine	Fat transporter within cells; increases endurance performance	Yes	Low	No	Avoid D-carnitine supplements, as they may be toxic and can deplete L-carnitine.
Medium-chain triglycerides (MCT)	Quickly metabolize fatty acids that spare glycogen and thus delay fatigue	Yes	Low	No	May cause gastrointestinal upset and cramping.
Multivitamin/mineral	Supply essential vitamins and minerals to endurance athletes for optimal health and performance	Yes	Moderate	No	Look for supplements containing no more than 100–200% of the Daily Value.
Pyruvate	Accelerates Krebs cycle; enhances use of glucose; greater fat loss; increases glycogen storage	Yes	Low-moderate	No	Limited research available on ergogenic effects and side effects of long-term use.
Sodium bicarbonate	Buffers lactic acid, thereby delaying the onset of fatigue	Yes	Low	No	May cause nausea, diarrhea, irritability, and/or muscle spasms.
Sodium/electrolyte tablets	Prevents hyponatremia by supplying sodium during exercise and other electrolytes as buffers	Yes	High	No	Avoid supplements using mainly sodium bicarbonate; can cause diarrhea/cramping.
Sports beverages	Enhances endurance performance and delays fatigue by supplying fluid, carbohydrates, and electrolytes	Yes	High	No	Practice during training to avoid gastrointestinal distress during competitions.

Table 8-9	Common Nutritional Ergogenics Used by Strength and Power Athletes				
Supplements (other names)	**Claimed Action**	**Human Research**	**Potential**	**Banned**	**Comments/Concerns**
Chromium	Increases muscle mass, decreases fat mass, improves blood glucose and lipid levels	Yes	Low	No	Sufficient amounts can be consumed in the daily diet.
Creatine	Increases anaerobic output (strength/power) in events lasting 6 seconds to 4 minutes	Yes	Mod-High	No	Long-term effects (> 5 years) are still unknown.
Conjugated linoleic acid (CLA)	Increases production of growth hormone, weight loss, fat loss, increased muscle mass	Some	Low	No	Most research showing benefits was conducted on animals. Watch for gastric/ intestinal distress.
Human growth hormone	Increases muscle mass, strength, and power; decreases fat mass	Yes	High	Yes	Causes pathological enlargement of organs and increases risk of chronic disease.
Beta-hydroxy-beta-methylbutyrate (HMB)	Prevents protein breakdown and enhances synthesis; increases strength; improves body composition	Yes	Mod-High	No	Long-term effects unknown. Benefits appear to decline with continued use.
Protein powder/bars	Increase strength; aid in muscle growth and development	Yes	Low-Mod	No	Effective only for athletes who are protein deficient. Watch for other added ingredients.
Steroids	Increase muscle mass and strength	Yes	High	Yes	Harmful side effects: abnormal growth, liver and heart disease, stroke, and aggression.
Medium-chain triglycerides (MCTs)	Increase energy and muscle mass; decrease fat mass	Yes	Low	No	Side effects often experienced are intestinal cramping and diarrhea.
Multivitamin/mineral	Supplies essential vitamins and minerals to athletes for optimal health and performance	Yes	Moderate	No	Look for supplements containing no more than 100–200% of the Daily Value.

banned by the U.S. Olympic Committee and the International Olympic Committee. If an athlete wishes to utilize a nutritional ergogenic aid supplement, help him in researching the supplements. First and foremost, assist the athlete in determining if the supplement is safe for consumption. After taking the athlete's history, conclude whether the supplement will interfere with any of the athlete's current supplements or drugs, or cause any complications with the athlete's current conditions or illnesses. For those athletes who work or compete for an organization that mandates drug testing, identify whether the supplement is banned. If all of these considerations prove to be acceptable, then discuss with the athlete whether the particular supplement would assist him in meeting his goals.

SUMMARY

In order for athletes to truly be healthy and live a good quality of life, they have to not only participate in a wellness, exercise, and fitness program, but also take an active role in their dietary plan. Exercise will not be the only factor in creating a better, healthier life for your athletes. We must assist our athletes in devising the best, most effective, practical nutritional plan that they can utilize for the rest of their lives.

DISCUSSION QUESTIONS

1. What are the differences among CHO, fats, and proteins? What is the role of each macronutrient?

2. Why is water important for an athlete to drink during exercise and on a regular, daily basis?

3. Why are vitamins and minerals important for an athlete to consume? If an athlete is deficient in ingesting vitamins and minerals, what can occur to his or her body?

4. What are some considerations before beginning a weight management program?

5. What are the prevalent eating disorders, their causes, and signs and symptoms? What illnesses or diseases can an athlete acquire if she or he has an eating disorder?

6. What are natural ergogenic aids, and how can they assist an athlete in increasing his or her performance?

CASE STUDY

A New Beginning

Rebecca is a 45-year-old English teacher at Old State High School. She is well respected by her peers, administrators, and students alike. Rebecca has been married for 10 years, and has two children. She is financially secure, has many friends, and is an active participant in her community's activities. Rebecca's family, friends, and coworkers believe that she is happy, due to her outgoing personality. Rebecca could not ask for her life to be any better except for one aspect, which is that she is suffering from obesity.

Rebecca played basketball in college and was in the best physical shape of her life. However, once she graduated from college and stopped playing basketball, she no longer exercised on a regular basis. Her weight began to increase slowly and steadily. Now, after 24 years, she fights a battle with her weight every day. Rebecca's obesity makes her extremely unhappy inside.

Recently, Rebecca went to her physician for her annual physical. She was diagnosed with Type 2 diabetes, high LDL cholesterol, and high triglycerides. Her blood pressure was elevated. Rebecca never had these conditions before. She realized that her health was failing. Her physician told Rebecca that she had to make a conscious decision to help herself and improve her health. She recognized that she had a significant problem.

The day after her physical, Rebecca woke up feeling sullen and depressed. She stepped on the scale, and saw that she weighed 230 pounds. Rebecca looked at herself in the mirror. She finally decided to dedicate herself to leading a healthy lifestyle and losing weight. At 5 feet 10 inches tall with a BMI of 33, she figures she has to lose 60 pounds to get down to a normal, healthy weight. In order to lose weight, Rebecca knows that she must not only exercise, but also consume nutritious foods.

Because Rebecca played college basketball, she has a basic idea of how to create and participate in her own exercise program; however, she admits that she knows little about healthy eating. Having two young children and working full time leaves her very little time to cook. Therefore, her diet consists of quite a bit of fast and processed foods, as well as large quantities of empty calorie foods such as cakes, cookies, and potato chips. Rebecca tends to drink a few cans of sugared soda along with caffeinated coffee daily. Because Rebecca is not knowledgeable about how to create a healthy, nutritious diet plan, she makes an appointment with a registered dietitian, Ms. Tully. Rebecca is certain that Ms. Tully will help her reach her goals, and is excited to begin a new, healthy lifestyle.

1. What information should Ms. Tully provide to Rebecca as far as caloric requirements are concerned?

2. How much weight should Rebecca plan on losing per week?

3. How should Ms. Tully formulate Rebecca's daily diet in regard to quantity of CHO, protein, and fat?

4. What suggestions can Ms. Tully give Rebecca regarding the types of foods she should eat in each category of macronutrients? What foods should Rebecca avoid?

5. What information should Ms. Tully give Rebecca in regard to the importance of dietary fiber? What foods should Rebecca eat that are high in fiber?

6. What foods can Ms. Tully suggest for Rebecca to eat that would help fight against Type 2 diabetes, high LDL cholesterol, and high triglycerides?

7. Should Ms. Tully suggest that Rebecca take vitamin and mineral supplements? Why or why not?

8. Why would Ms. Tully tell Rebecca to avoid drinking sugared soda and caffeinated coffee? What should Rebecca drink instead?

REFERENCES

Andres, L. P. A., Sacheck, J., & Tapia, S. (1999). A review of creatine supplementation: Side effects and improvements in athletic performance. *Nutrition in Clinical Care, 2*(2), 73–81. doi: 10.1046/j.1523-5408.1999.00087.x.

Bergeron, M. F, Waller, J. L., & Marinik, E. L. (2006). Voluntary fluid intake core temperature responses in adolescent tennis players: Sport beverage versus water. *British Journal of Sports Medicine, 40*(5), 406–410. doi: 10.1136/bjsm.2005.023333.

Centers for Disease Control and Prevention (CDC). (2011). Polyunsaturated fats and monounsaturated fats. Retrieved April 30, 2012, from http://www.cdc.gov/nutrition/everyone/basics/fat/unsaturatedfat.html

Fink, H. H., Burgoon, L. A., & Mikesky, A. E. (2009). *Practical applications in sports nutrition* (2nd ed.). Sudbury, MA: Jones and Bartlett.

Frost, G., Leed, A. A., Dore, C. J., Madeiros, S., Brading, S., & Dornhorst, A. (1999). Glycaemic index as a determinant of serum HDL-cholesterol concentration. *Lancet*, 353(9158), 1045–1048, Retrieved April 30, 2012, from http://search.ebscohost.com

Gardner, C. D., Kiazand, A., Alhassan, S., Kim, S., Stafford, R. S., Balise, R. R., et al. (2007). Comparison of the Atkins, Zone, Ornish, and LEARN diets for change in weight and related risk factors among overweight premenopausal women. *Journal of the American Medical Association*, 297(9), 969–977. doi:10.1001/jama.297.9.969.

Hobart, J. A., & Smucker, D. R. (2000). The female athlete triad. *American Family Physician*, 61(11), 3357–3364.

Institute of Medicine of the National Academies (2004). Dietary reference intakes: Water, potassium, sodium, chloride, and sulfate. Retrieved March 16, 2013, from http://www.iom.edu/reports/2004/dietary-reference-intakes-water-potassium-sodium-chloride-and-sulfate.aspx

Mayo Clinic. (2011). Dietary fats: Know which types to choose. Retrieved April 30, 2012, from http://www.mayoclinic.com/health/fat/NU00262

MedlinePlus. (2010). Fiber. Retrieved April 30, 2012, from http://www.nlm.nih.gov/medlineplus/ency/article/002470.htm

MedlinePlus. (2012a). Minerals. Retrieved May 7, 2012, from http://www.nlm.nih.gov/medlineplus/minerals.html

MedlinePlus. (2012b). Protein in diet. Retrieved May 1, 2012, from http://www.nlm.nih.gov/medlineplus/ency/article/002467.htm

National Council on Strength and Fitness. (n.d.). Maintaining proper hydration. Retrieved February 13, 2013, from http://www.ncsf.org/enew/articles/articles-properhydration.aspx

National Institutes of Health, Office of Dietary Supplements. (n.d.). Nutrient recommendations: Dietary reference intakes (DRI). Retrieved February 13, 2013, from http://ods.od.nih.gov/health_information/dietary_reference_intakes.aspx

PubMed Health. (2012). Kwashiorkor. Retrieved May 1, 2012, from http://www.ncbi.nlm.nih.gov/pubmedhealth/PMH0002571/

Thygerson, A. L., & Thygerson, S. M. (2013). *Fit to be well.* Sudbury, MA: Jones and Bartlett.

U.S. Department of Agriculture. (2010). Report of the Dietary Guidelines Advisory Committee on the dietary guidelines for Americans, 2010. Retrieved February 13, 2013, from http://www.cnpp.usda.gov/DGAs2010-DGACReport.htm

U.S. Department of Health and Human Services. (2011). What is cholesterol? Retrieved April 30, 2012, from http://www.nhlbi.nih.gov/health/health-topics/topics/hbc/

Part II

Chapter 9
The Head and Face

CHAPTER OBJECTIVES

After you have read this chapter, you will be able to understand:

- The mechanisms of injury and signs and symptoms of a mild traumatic brain injury
- The differences among intracerebral, epidural, and subdural bleeding
- The emergent care for traumatic brain injuries
- The various facial fractures and specific signs and symptoms for each
- Which eye, nose, and ear injuries require immediate emergency medical care
- The various sideline and computer program tests that help you to determine if an athlete has a concussion
- How to determine whether an athlete has uncomplicated epistaxis versus a brain injury

Injuries to the head and face occur frequently, especially in activities where contact occurs among participating athletes. Many of these injuries are severe and life-threatening; therefore, treat the athlete as if he or she has a cervical spine injury and maintain in-line stabilization until you determine that he or she has not sustained such an injury. Also, it is common practice to wear gloves when caring for an athlete with a head or face injury, regardless of whether blood is present. Any possible contamination (e.g., dirt in the athlete's eyes or mouth) must be avoided. As an exercise scientist, your role is to know the mechanism, or cause, of injury; recognize the signs and symptoms; provide immediate care to the athlete; and identify whether the injury warrants immediate medical referral. The care you give could save the athlete's life.

INJURIES TO THE HEAD

Mild Traumatic Brain Injury (Cerebral Concussion)

Mild traumatic brain injury (MTBI) is also known as a cerebral concussion. The brain is jarred in the skull, which results in altered consciousness and neurological deficits. The injury is typically not life-threatening. For this reason, the injury is classified as a mild traumatic brain injury; however, the injury can be very serious and result in long-lasting signs and symptoms.

Mechanism or Cause of Injury

MTBI can be caused by a direct blow to the head, such as when an athlete hits his or her head against the wall when playing racquetball, or by a fall or force to the **core body**, which causes jolting or jarring of the brain. As a result, the brain is damaged when it hits the skull. The impact force does not need to be significant for MTBI to occur.

> **Core body** The area of the body not including the upper and lower extremities. The core body includes the spine, chest, and abdominal and pelvic cavities.

The forces are either linear or rotational. A linear force involves a direct blow to the head. Typically a blow to the forehead causes the brain to accelerate and then decelerate. Coup and contrecoup injuries result. A coup injury occurs when the brain injury is located at the impact site; a contrecoup injury occurs on the opposite side of the impact. A contrecoup injury occurs because the brain is basically "floating" inside the skull (**Figure 9-1**). A rotational force typically occurs with a blow to the side of the head. The cervical spine and head suddenly and violently rotate, causing a shearing brain injury. When the impact is on one side of the head, the brain then moves to the opposite side of the skull and forcefully hits the bones, which results in the brain injury.

Signs and Symptoms

Signs and symptoms of MTBI can occur immediately or be delayed. The signs and symptoms can also last a very short amount of time (hours to days) or be prolonged (weeks or months). MTBI signs and symptoms include headache, tinnitus, nausea, vomiting, and sleepiness. The athlete may have impaired cognitive or mental function, **retrograde amnesia**, **post-traumatic amnesia**, and inability to concentrate. Balance and coordination problems, along with changes in emotions including sadness and irritability, may exist. He or she may complain of visual disturbances including blurred vision, **diplopia**, and sensitivity to light. The athlete may also have unequal pupil size. The eyes may be unable to move at the same rate and in a specific direction (up, down, or side to side). The athlete may or may not have experienced loss of consciousness. He or she

> **Retrograde amnesia** The inability to remember events that occurred before the MTBI occurred.
>
> **Post-traumatic amnesia** The inability to remember events that occurred after the MTBI injury occurred.
>
> **Diplopia** Double vision.

may say that he or she "blacked out" or "saw stars," which is indicative of a brief, temporary loss of consciousness.

Immediate Care

If you suspect that an athlete has an MTBI, remove the athlete immediately from activity and have him or her rest. If you are unsure whether the athlete has sustained an MTBI, perform some of the sideline tests noted in Tips from the Field Tip 1. For MTBI and all injuries and illnesses where the athlete is a minor, contact the parents or guardians immediately to inform them of their child's injury. Tell them what care you are presently giving the athlete, and if he or she needs advanced medical care. If the athlete is an adult, ask them whether they wish you to inform anyone of their situation. If the athlete has any MTBI signs and symptoms, refer them to a physician immediately for evaluation. Do not have the athlete drive to the physician's office or ER. Instead, have another valid driver (i.e., parent, sibling, family member, or close friend) transport the athlete. Call 911 if the athlete has no means to get to the physician or ER, if the athlete has suffered any loss of consciousness, or if the athlete's signs and symptoms rapidly worsen.

> ### Tips from the Field
>
> **Tip 1** When you suspect an MTBI, test your athlete's cognitive function to determine the extent of injury. Some quick sideline cognitive function tests include asking the athlete to state the alphabet or the months of the year backwards. The "serial 7s" test has the athlete add 7 and 7, then continue adding 7s (7 + 7 = 14 + 7 = 21, and so on) to test cognition. You can tell the athlete three words to remember, then after 5 minutes ask the athlete to repeat the words. Ask them questions regarding orientation such as "Where are you?" and "Who is your competitor?". If the athlete is not able to perform these tasks at a normal rate of speed or cannot perform them correctly, then suspect that the athlete has an MTBI. You can also administer the King-Devick test (http://www.uphs.upenn.edu/news/News_Releases/2011/02/sideline-test-detects-concussions/). The athlete reads a list of single-digit numbers that you write down on an index card. As the athlete reads the digits, note how long it takes him or her to read one digit to the next. If the time progressively increases between numbers, then the athlete has positively tested for a concussion.
>
> Other concussion tests have athletes use various computer programs. One such test is the popular Immediate Post-concussion Assessment and Cognitive Testing (ImPACT) program (http://www.impacttest.com), which is utilized to test athletes who are at risk for concussions. The test is given to athletes as a baseline prior to injury,

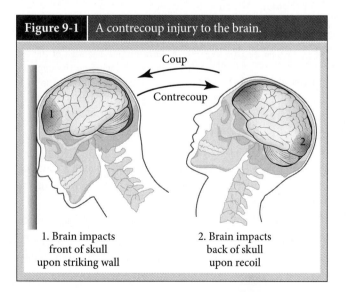

Figure 9-1 | A contrecoup injury to the brain.

Coup

Contrecoup

1. Brain impacts front of skull upon striking wall

2. Brain impacts back of skull upon recoil

immediately after injury, and throughout the healing process as one measure for return-to-play guidelines. This test is highly effective in determining and monitoring an athlete's MTBI, and has been at the forefront of concussion testing in recent years at all levels of competition. Although the simple sideline tests for MTBI are effective in determining if an athlete has sustained an MTBI, computerized testing is something you and your organization should consider if you work with athletes of all ages who are at a high risk of MTBI.

When the athlete returns to your facility, you cannot let them participate, even if they claim their signs and symptoms of MTBI have resolved. You must not only abide by your employer's, local, state, federal, and governing body protocols, but also require written return to activity verification from the athlete's physician for continued participation at your facility. Under no circumstances should you allow the athlete to participate in activity without this written clearance. As part of the athlete's MTBI evaluation, the physician and other experts in the field of concussion management complete a variety of mental and physical tests. With this information, the athlete's physician gives the athlete a proper return to play timeline with guidelines. If the physician does not give you written return to play guidelines, ask your athlete for permission to contact the physician in order to obtain the athlete's limitations for participation. Your athlete will have to sign a Health Insurance Portability and Accountability Act (HIPAA) form in the physician's office for you to obtain his or her medical information. Likewise, ask the physician for information as to the appropriate intensity, frequency, and type of activities for the athlete; which activities should be avoided; and the duration of this protocol. Be certain to utilize your expertise and judgment, along with research, to determine the athlete's return to play activities. The National Athletic Trainers' Association Position Statement: Management of Sport-Related Concussion thoroughly describes MTBI with proper concussion management and detailed return to play guidelines (Guskiewicz et al., 2004).

Prevention

Prevention of MTBI includes having the athlete wear appropriately fitted and safe equipment, such as headgear and helmets, during activities as required. Mouth guards can assist in minimizing MTBI injury by distributing forces away from the head when the jaw has succumbed to a direct blow. Mouth guards can be purchased over the counter or custom made. The athlete needs a mouth guard with a secure fit to protect against injury. Some over-the-counter mouth guards are moldable (utilizing hot water) to fit the athlete's teeth. Custom-made mouth guards can be made by a dentist. These mouth guards provide the best fit, allow for the most nondisruptive breathing, and are generally the most comfortable for the athlete. Athletes must be taught how to properly perform their skills and adhere to their instructors' directions while participating in activities so they do not get hurt. Activity areas must be kept safe and free from potential hazards (Centers for Disease Control and Prevention [CDC], 2012).

Second Impact Syndrome

Second impact syndrome occurs when an athlete's brain rapidly swells, bleeds significantly, and herniates due to a second cerebral concussion, typically while the athlete was still experiencing signs and symptoms of the previous cerebral concussion. Brain herniation occurs when the brain tissue is forced out of normal position due to brain swelling and increased skull pressure. In severe cases, death can occur within 2–5 minutes, with no time for advanced medical personnel to assist the injured athlete (Bey & Ostick, 2009).

Mechanism or Cause of Injury

Second impact syndrome can occur from a blow or jarring force to the head. When the second impact occurs, the athlete is still experiencing signs and symptoms from a previous concussion. The second blow or jarring force does not need to be as forceful as the first concussive blow to the head to cause injury. The impact may be extremely mild, which may not raise a concern at the time.

Signs and Symptoms

Athletes experiencing second impact syndrome produce signs and symptoms of injury that include those of an MTBI, such as headache, nausea or vomiting, fatigue, disorientation, memory problems, and loss of consciousness.

Immediate Care

Because second impact syndrome is life-threatening, call 911 immediately. Monitor the athlete and make sure his or her airway is open and he or she is breathing. If he or she is not breathing, administer cardiopulmonary resuscitation (CPR). Maintain in-line stabilization until emergency medical services (EMS) arrives, and do not move the athlete unless absolutely necessary (i.e., your lives are in danger). If the athlete vomits while you are maintaining in-line stabilization, roll the athlete to his or her side as a unit with the assistance of bystanders and clear his or her airway. Make sure the athlete is breathing on his or her own. Again, if he or she is not breathing, administer CPR. For these severe injuries, always treat the athlete for shock.

Prevention

The first course of action to prevent second impact syndrome is to not allow a concussed athlete to return to play who has not been cleared by his or her physician (as discussed in the MTBI section). An athlete may feel that his or her concussion has resolved because he or she no longer has signs and symptoms of MTBI at rest. However, if when exercising, the concussion signs and symptoms reappear, then the athlete should not participate in athletic activities. If you suspect the athlete is experiencing MTBI signs and symptoms even though he or she has been formally cleared by his or her physician, remove the athlete from activity immediately. Refer the athlete back to his or her physician right away, and do not allow him or her to participate until cleared again by the physician.

Cerebral Contusion (Intracerebral Bleeding)

A cerebral contusion is a brain injury in which the brain is bruised, intracerebral bleeding occurs, and blood leaks into the brain tissue. More than one area of bleeding can occur in the brain, depending on where the contusion occurs. The bleeding may be superficial or deep.

Mechanism or Cause of Injury

A blow to the head from an object, a motor vehicle crash, or a fall with the head striking the floor or a stationary object can cause a cerebral contusion. The cerebral contusion may be a coup or contrecoup injury.

Signs and Symptoms

Blood vessels are torn and swelling occurs with a cerebral contusion, so many of the neurological deficits seen in MTBI and second impact syndrome occur. The athlete may have emotional changes including irritability, agitation, or restlessness. He or she may complain of headache, dizziness, or nausea. The athlete may vomit, have memory difficulty, amnesia, loss of motor function and coordination, and sensory deficits. The signs and symptoms may last for hours, or in more severe cases they may last for weeks. Severe contusions may cause brain herniation and death.

Immediate Care

If you suspect that your athlete has a mild cerebral contusion, refer him or her to a physician immediately for evaluation. If the athlete shows significant signs and symptoms of a cerebral contusion, or his or her status is progressively decreasing, call 911 immediately. Maintain in-line stabilization if the athlete shows neurological or functional impairment. The athlete must be transported immediately to the emergency room. Monitor the athlete's airway and breathing and be prepared to give CPR if necessary. If the athlete vomits, clear his or her airway as previously discussed. Make sure that the athlete's parents or guardians are notified if the athlete is a minor.

Prevention

In an attempt to prevent cerebral contusion, the athlete must wear protective headgear as appropriate for the athlete's activity. Make sure your athlete follows safety rules when participating in activities where the potential for a blow to the head exists (e.g., no diving into the shallow end of a pool). Likewise, make sure your athlete is aware of his or her surroundings at all times when participating in these activities.

Epidural Hematoma

An epidural hematoma is a traumatic brain injury that occurs when an artery or vein is damaged and blood accumulates between the skull and the dura mater (the outermost membrane of the brain) (**Figure 9-2**). The blood accumulates rapidly, within a few minutes to hours postinjury. Most injuries occur to younger people versus adults because the dura mater

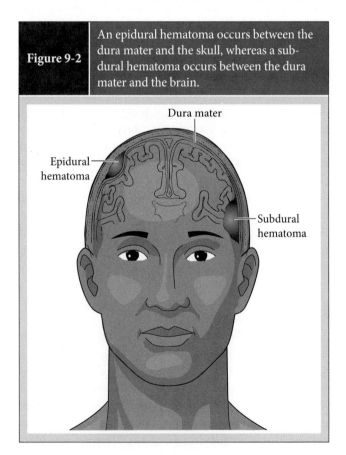

Figure 9-2 An epidural hematoma occurs between the dura mater and the skull, whereas a subdural hematoma occurs between the dura mater and the brain.

is not attached as well to the skull bones in children and teenagers as it is in adults.

Mechanism or Cause of Injury

A direct blow that causes a skull fracture can also cause an epidural hematoma. Often the injury occurs in car and motorcycle accidents. Epidural hematomas are not as common in sport activities.

Signs and Symptoms

The signs and symptoms of an epidural hematoma are similar to those of an MTBI and other head injuries. The athlete may complain of a severe headache, dizziness, confusion, and nausea. The athlete may have one pupil larger than the other, along with muscular weakness on the side of the body opposite from the enlarged pupil (PubMed Health, 2010). It is common for the athlete to have loss of consciousness, then become alert, then become unconscious again.

Immediate Care

This injury is a medical emergency. Rapid hemorrhage and swelling of the brain cause drowsiness that can progress to coma and death. Consequently, care must be immediate. Your role is to summon EMS and care for any life-threatening conditions. Maintain in-line stabilization of the head and neck. The athlete may vomit; if so, while maintaining in-line stabilization, log roll the athlete on his or her side and clear his or her airway. Make sure he or she is breathing, and administer CPR if necessary. Once the athlete is transported to the ER, he or she will most likely have emergency surgery to drill a hole in the skull, which relieves pressure in the brain (PubMed Health, 2010). Even though the athlete receives immediate care, it is common for future complications from the injury to arise, such as loss of function and seizures.

Prevention

Prevention of epidural hematomas includes the same course of action as for MTBIs and cerebral contusions. The athlete must wear appropriate head protection, wear seat and other belts that secure the athlete during activity, perform skills properly, follow safety rules, and pay attention to his or her surroundings including any potential dangers to the athlete's head.

Subdural Hematoma

A subdural hematoma is a rapid accumulation of blood on the brain. The blood fills in the brain tissue quickly and compresses the brain (see Figure 9-2). Subdural hematomas are either acute or chronic. An acute subdural hematoma is life-threatening, whereas a chronic subdural hematoma may not be life-threatening. This injury is one of the most serious brain injuries. The mortality rate for subdural hematoma victims is approximately 60% (Meagher & Young, 2011). Even if treated, a subdural hematoma can cause future neurological complications.

Mechanism or Cause of Injury

An acute subdural hematoma is caused by a serious head injury. Chronic subdural hematomas most often occur with a very mild head injury to an elderly person or someone who is taking **anticoagulant drugs**.

> **Anticoagulant drugs**
> Blood-thinning drugs that an athlete is prescribed to prevent blood clotting. An athlete on these drugs who sustains an injury to the blood vessels will bleed more than if he or she were not taking anticoagulants.

Signs and Symptoms

With an acute subdural hematoma, the blood fills the brain rapidly, which causes immediate signs and symptoms of injury. With a chronic subdural hematoma, the blood fills the brain much slower than with an acute subdural hematoma. Consequently, the signs and symptoms of a chronic subdural hematoma may not occur for days. Many of the same signs and symptoms of injury occur with both acute and chronic subdural hematomas as with the other brain injuries. The athlete may have the following signs and symptoms of injury: a headache, confusion, slurred speech, loss of balance, loss of consciousness, disorientation and confusion, memory loss, visual problems, weakness, fatigue, nausea, and vomiting. Elderly athletes with a chronic subdural hematoma show significant mental decline, including loss of memory, over a few days.

Immediate Care

If you suspect a subdural hematoma, summon EMS immediately. With a head injury of this severity, assume the athlete may also have a spinal injury. Therefore, keep his or her head and neck still and maintain in-line stabilization until EMS arrives. Always monitor the athlete's airway, breathing, and circulation (ABCs), and be prepared to administer CPR if necessary. The athlete may vomit; if he or she does, maintain in-line stabilization, log roll the athlete as a unit, clear his or her airway, and determine if he or she is breathing. If he or she is not breathing, administer CPR.

Prevention

As with other head injuries, instruct your athlete to take precautions to avoid sustaining a subdural hematoma. Your athlete must abide by safety measures at all facilities and venues, wear appropriately fitted headgear and safety belts for activities as required, and pay attention to his or her body while participating in activities, to avoid falls.

Skull Fractures

Although the skull bones are particularly strong in adults, skull fractures can occur in conjunction with other traumatic head injuries. These fractures are particularly serious if the skull bones enter the brain tissue. Various types of skull fractures exist, including a simple, linear, depressed, and compound fracture (MedlinePlus, 2012). A simple fracture is a break in the skull without any further damage to the skin or underlying structures (i.e., brain, meninges). A linear fracture is classified as a break in a line-type fashion without any other damage to the underlying structures. The bone does not splinter and is not otherwise deformed. A depressed fracture is classified by a crushing of the skull bones, which become impacted down into the brain tissue. A compound fracture is when the skull bones break through the skin and cause external bleeding.

▌ Mechanism or Cause of Injury

Skull fractures can occur with any head injury as a result of a significant blow to the head. Although this severe head impact does not happen commonly in general exercise and sport activities, the mechanism of injury likely occurs more frequently in contact sports such as boxing, ice hockey, and football, even though in some of these sports athletes wear headgear. Skull fractures occur more often as a result of car and motorcycle accidents, falling from a height, and being part of a physical attack (i.e., fist fighting).

▌ Signs and Symptoms

Athletes with skull fractures may experience any signs and symptoms of head injuries previously discussed. Additional signs and symptoms that may exist with a skull fracture include deformity, external head bleeding, bruising behind the ears (Battle's sign) or under the eyes ("raccoon eyes"), and a clear fluid mixed with blood coming out of the ears or nose (**Figures 9-3** and **9-4**). The clear fluid is cerebrospinal fluid (CSF). CSF bathes the brain and spinal cord. If CSF is coming from the ears or nose, then the skull injury is significant and most likely a depressed fracture.

Tips from the Field

Tip 2 To determine whether fluid coming from the nose is only blood from a minor nosebleed, or if it is CSF mixed with blood, which indicates a head or brain tissue injury, examine the fluid on a piece of gauze. Put on gloves and take a piece of gauze that has blood from the nose on it

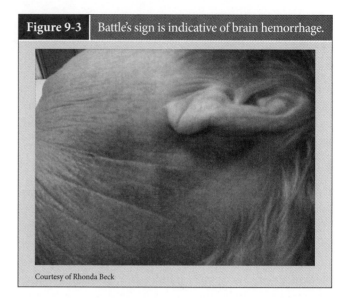

| **Figure 9-3** | Battle's sign is indicative of brain hemorrhage. |

Courtesy of Rhonda Beck

and put it aside. CSF and blood are similar to oil and water, because CSF separates from blood. The CSF is apparent as a straw-colored "halo" or ring surrounding the blood spot on the gauze. If CSF is present, then the injury is a medical emergency and you need to call 911 immediately.

▌ Immediate Care

Skull fractures are serious, potentially life-threatening injuries, Therefore, call 911 immediately. If the person is unconscious, maintain in-line stabilization and check his or her airway and breathing. Administer CPR if he or she is not breathing. If the

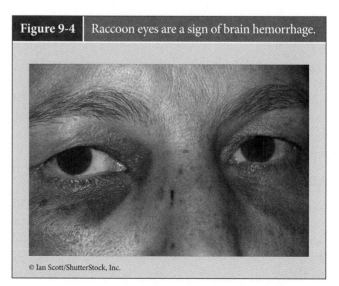

| **Figure 9-4** | Raccoon eyes are a sign of brain hemorrhage. |

© Ian Scott/ShutterStock, Inc.

injury is a compound fracture, apply gloves if you do not have them on already, and then place bulky sterile gauze dressings, a clean cloth, or any clean, absorbent items on the wound site. Be very careful not to apply pressure to the injured area. Pressure on the injured area may force the fractured bones into the brain tissue. If the dressings become saturated, do not remove them. Instead, place more clean dressings on top of the saturated dressings. If you remove the saturated dressings, the bleeding may resume if you have previously stopped it, or continue to flow externally leading to greater blood loss. If an object is protruding from the skull, do not remove it. Attempt to stabilize the object by placing clean bulky dressings around the object, and keep it still until EMS arrives. Do not move the athlete unless a dire emergency presents itself in which your life or the athlete's is in grave danger. If the victim vomits, log roll him or her while maintaining in-line stabilization and clear the airway. After the athlete's airway is clear, log roll them onto their back and check to see if they are breathing. If they are not breathing, administer CPR. Monitor the athlete closely until EMS arrives.

Prevention

As with other head injury prevention tactics, athletes must be aware of their surroundings when participating in activities, abide by activity and facility rules and policies, and wear appropriate headgear, equipment, and seat and safety belts.

Lacerations and Incisions

Scalp lacerations and incisions as well as lacerations to the brain tissue can occur with athletic activity. The scalp has many blood vessels. Consequently, a very minor scalp laceration or incision may bleed significantly. This bleeding creates the appearance of a major wound. Whenever the scalp is bleeding, suspect an additional head injury involving the brain. Lacerations to the brain (cerebral lacerations) can occur if a skull bone is fractured and splinters or is depressed.

Mechanism or Cause of Injury

Scalp wounds and cerebral lacerations typically occur due to a direct blow by an object to the head.

Signs and Symptoms

Other than bleeding, a protruding object and other signs and symptoms of head injuries may exist. The predominance of signs and symptoms will help you determine if the injury is a scalp wound versus a cerebral laceration. If the signs and symptoms are similar to those of head injuries, then the wound may be a cerebral laceration. If the athlete is only bleeding, no other signs or symptoms exist, and the mechanism of injury was a mild force, then the wound is most likely a surface laceration or incision.

Immediate Care

Whether the wound is a surface laceration or an incision, immediately control bleeding. Utilize your personal protective equipment (PPE) and apply gentle pressure on the wound to stop the bleeding, without pressing down into the skull. Utilize clean, bulky dressings (sterile dressings if available), and hold them on the wound. As previously mentioned, apply additional dressings if the blood soaks through the first dressings. Do not remove the saturated dressings. If you suspect a cerebral laceration, provide immediate care as per the other severe head injuries. Call 911 immediately, maintain in-line stabilization, be ready to give CPR if necessary, and monitor the athlete for consciousness, airway, and breathing until EMS arrives. If the athlete's only sign of injury is bleeding, indicating a superficial laceration or incision, after about 15 minutes of applying gentle pressure on the wound, remove the dressing and see if the bleeding has stopped. If the bleeding has not stopped, then continue applying gentle pressure for another 15 minutes. Repeat the application of pressure dressings until the bleeding has stopped. If the bleeding does not stop, or if other signs and symptoms of injury arise, then call 911 immediately. However, once the bleeding has stopped, bandage the wound.

Many scalp lacerations and incisions may need stitches if the wound is deep or the skin edges do not come together. Stitches also are useful to secure the wound because Steri strips, butterfly, or other bandages are difficult to use on the scalp due to the athlete's hair. A liquid bandage can work on the scalp. Liquid bandages are clear, adherent gels or sprays that are applied directly to the wound. These liquid bandages are sold over-the-counter and are commonly utilized by physicians in place of stitches. The benefits of liquid bandages are that they adequately seal the wound shut, prevent pathogens from entering the wound, and maintain an environment conducive to healing. Most often the athlete needs to see a physician immediately to have a liquid bandage or stitches applied.

Prevention

Athletes can prevent scalp lacerations and incisions and cerebral lacerations by wearing appropriate protective head equipment, performing proper activity skills, and being aware of their surroundings.

Migraines

Migraines are severely painful headaches. Athletes experience intense throbbing in the head. According to the Mayo Clinic (2011), these headaches typically occur with nausea, vomiting, sensitivity to light and sound, and visual disturbances. The migraine can last for hours to days. The extent and frequency of the migraine varies from athlete to athlete.

Mechanism or Cause of Injury

Migraines in women can be caused by hormone imbalance, especially estrogen. Some people may also be genetically predisposed to migraines (Russell, 2008). In both men and women, various triggers bring on migraines, including stress; sleep deprivation; intense physical activity to which the athlete is not accustomed; foods and substances including chocolate, caffeine, and alcohol; and environmental changes such as going to a higher or lower altitude where pressure changes, or changes in weather. Smoking also triggers migraines (Rozen, 2011).

Signs and Symptoms

Migraines can arise suddenly and affect an athlete in an instant. The athlete may have indications a couple days before the migraine attacks that warn the athlete the migraine is coming. Indications that the athlete is going to be inflicted by a migraine include hyperactivity, irritability, depression, food cravings, and either constipation or diarrhea. Athletes may also experience an aura before the migraine. An aura may include spots or flashes of light in his or her vision, vision loss, speech difficulty, and tingling in the hands or feet. Each of these symptoms may last up to half an hour. The typical migraine signs and symptoms include throbbing pain in the head, which occurs on one or both sides; sensitivity to light and sound; lightheadedness; disturbed vision; and nausea and vomiting.

Immediate Care

When your athlete complains of a migraine, have him or her stop activity and rest. If he or she has experienced migraines before and has already been evaluated by a physician for migraines, the athlete will know what to do to alleviate the migraine and/or administer medication. If the athlete has never experienced a migraine, then assist him or her in alleviating the symptoms. A migraine can be eliminated if he or she lies down in a quiet room with his or her eyes closed. If the athlete knows what triggered the migraine, make sure the trigger is removed or stopped (e.g., if the athlete is intensely exercising or drinking caffeinated coffee, have the athlete stop exercising and drink noncaffeinated beverages immediately). Refer the athlete to his or her primary care physician or neurologist for evaluation. The physician can give the athlete medication to reduce the incidence of or prevent migraines. The athlete also should participate in stress reduction activities if stress is a trigger for the athlete's migraines.

Do not let the athlete drive if he or she is experiencing a severe migraine that does not allow normal function or is disturbing his or her vision. Instead have a valid driver take the athlete to his or her physician or the ER if necessary. If the athlete experiences the migraine with neck stiffness, severe vomiting or diarrhea, a fever, neurological deficits, or any other significant worrisome signs and symptoms, summon EMS. In these cases, the migraine may be indicative of a more severe illness or condition.

Prevention

In order to prevent migraines, the athlete must be aware of the triggers that cause his or her migraines and eliminate them if possible. If stress is a trigger, the athlete should participate in mental stress reduction exercises and physical stress reduction techniques such as body massages, physical activity, and exercise. The athlete should get plenty of sleep, and avoid caffeine, alcohol, and smoking. Medications can be prescribed by a physician that are either pain-eliminating medications, which are utilized if an athlete sustains a migraine, or preventative medications, which are used by an athlete to deter migraines. If the athlete has been prescribed migraine medication by his or her physician, the athlete must take the prescription as directed.

INJURIES TO THE FACE

Facial injuries occur to the face, eyes, nose, and ears. These injuries happen most frequently during activities in which the face is unprotected. These injuries can be minor, such as an insignificant nosebleed, or severe, such as an orbital fracture. In some instances, depending on the severity, irritability, nature, and stage (SINS) of the injury, the injury may be treated with first aid; however, in other instances EMS must be summoned for advanced medical care.

Facial Injuries

Facial Fractures Including Zygomatic, Maxilla, and Mandible Fractures

Fractures to the bones of the face typically occur to the zygomatic bone (cheekbone), maxilla (the mid-portion of the face above and surrounding the top lip), and mandible (jaw bone). Although the mechanism of injury may be the same for these facial bone fractures, some signs and symptoms of injury vary.

Mechanism or Cause of Injury. Most facial fractures occur in motor vehicle crashes, sport activities, falls, and physical assaults. The specific mechanism of injury is a direct, traumatic impact to the face.

Signs and Symptoms. Some signs and symptoms are similar for all facial areas whereas others are specific to the fractured bone. Common signs and symptoms of facial fractures include pain, deformity, ecchymosis, swelling, inward depression of the bone, and lacerations. Specific signs and symptoms of a zygomatic fracture include visual disturbances, cheek flatness, abnormal sensations, and blood in the eye on the injured side (**Figure 9-5**). An athlete with a maxillary fracture has **malocclusion**, visual disturbances, clear fluid coming from the nose, and difficulty breathing. Mandible fractures cause jaw pain and bruising under the tongue. Malocclusion may be a sign of injury for a mandible fracture as well as a maxillary fracture.

> **Malocclusion** The inability to bring the teeth together in a normal, aligned fashion.

Immediate Care. Any suspected fracture to the face warrants immediate medical care. Summon EMS immediately because facial fractures can disrupt breathing or vision. Likewise, the athlete may go into shock. Keep the athlete as still as possible and treat him or her for shock. You can gently apply a small ice bag to the area, while being careful not to cause further harm by moving or applying pressure to the fractured bones. If the athlete has sustained a laceration that is bleeding, use your PPE and gently place clean dressings, preferably sterile gauze, on the open wound to control the bleeding. If the athlete has **epistaxis**, control the bleeding by placing gauze or an absorbent dressing up the athlete's bleeding nostrils and gently pinch the area just below the

> **Epistaxis** A nosebleed.

bridge of the nose. Have the athlete keep his or her head forward. If the athlete leans his or her head backward, he or she may swallow blood. (See the section "Epistaxis (Nosebleed)" for further information on treating nosebleeds.) Remain with the athlete and monitor him or her until EMS arrives.

Prevention. Preventing facial fractures includes wearing appropriate face masks, as worn during ice hockey and football activities, as well as avoiding any direct trauma to the face, such as a hit by a fist. Make sure your athlete is aware of safety measures and policies when participating in physical activity to avoid injury.

Lacerations and Incisions

Facial lacerations and incisions occur to an unprotected face. Lacerations and incisions may be superficial or deep. Deep lacerations and incisions may involve the underlying structures such as muscles, tendons, nerves, and blood vessels. As with other open wounds, significant bleeding and infection are two primary concerns when an athlete has sustained a laceration or incision.

Mechanism or Cause of Injury. Trauma from impact or a direct blow to the face can cause a laceration or incision. Another mechanism of injury is from an object rubbing and compressing against the skin, such as another athlete's fingernail, jewelry, or exercise equipment. Often the skin is lacerated in conjunction with another injury, such as a facial fracture.

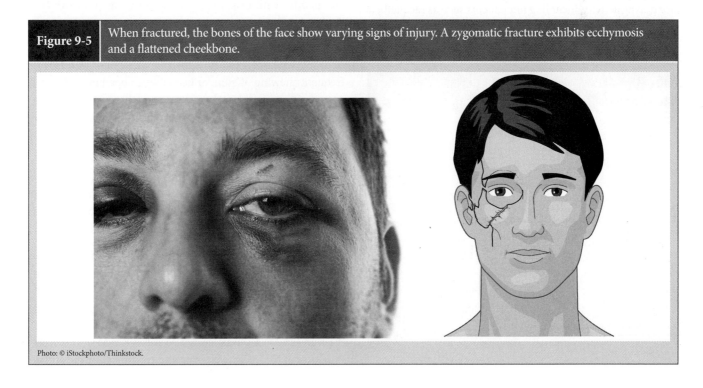

| Figure 9-5 | When fractured, the bones of the face show varying signs of injury. A zygomatic fracture exhibits ecchymosis and a flattened cheekbone. |

Photo: © iStockphoto/Thinkstock.

Signs and Symptoms. The typical signs and symptoms of open wounds are present for facial lacerations and incisions. Bleeding, pain, swelling, point tenderness, ecchymosis, and redness are some signs and symptoms of injury. If the wound becomes infected, then additional signs of fever, increasing redness at the wound site, and pus discharge are evident.

Immediate Care. Sometimes wounds heal with excess scaring or keloids, whether or not appropriate care was rendered. This scarring would potentially alter the athlete's facial appearance. Therefore, proper treatment for facial wounds is critical. To begin caring for the facial wound, put on gloves and stop the bleeding utilizing sterile gauze and direct pressure on the wound site. Once the bleeding has stopped, clean the wound with soap and water. Bandage the wound and refer the athlete to a physician or the ER for stitches. You can apply ice to the area to decrease pain and swelling. Keep in mind that facial lacerations and incisions must be stitched to encourage proper healing, avoid infection, and avoid undue scar tissue. Refer the athlete to his or her physician or the ER to have the wound sutured immediately. Depending on the extent of the wound, the physician may prescribe antibiotics, pain medication, and/or a tetanus vaccination (**Figure 9-6**).

Prevention. In order to prevent lacerations and incisions to the face, your athlete must protect his or her face by wearing facial equipment such as face masks (**Figure 9-7**), goggles, and the like that are required for the particular activity. The athlete should pay particular attention to objects that can strike the face during activity, including implements such as racquetball rackets, hockey sticks, balls, weights, and so on. The athlete needs to be cognizant and aware of his or her surroundings.

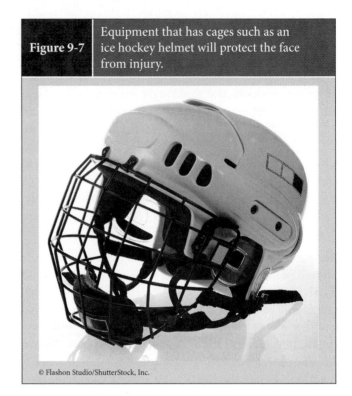

| Figure 9-7 | Equipment that has cages such as an ice hockey helmet will protect the face from injury. |

© Flashon Studio/ShutterStock, Inc.

Temporomandibular Joint (TMJ) dysfunction

The temporomandibular joint (TMJ) is located in front of the ears, and can be palpated when opening and closing the jaw. Similarly to any other joint, the TMJ can become inflamed and painful with overuse. Although rare, the joint can also be dislocated.

Mechanism or Cause of Injury. TMJ dysfunction is common in people who open and close their mouths often, such as with frequent chewing of gum, or keep it in an open position for a period of time, such as when mouth breathing while sleeping. A direct blow to the jaw or TMJ can also create joint inflammation or dislocation.

Signs and Symptoms. TMJ dysfunction signs and symptoms include pain at the joint, decreased jaw motion, inability to close the mouth (predominantly with a dislocation), joint clicking and popping, and jaw and face musculature stiffness. The jaw may also appear to be positioned off-center to the face.

Immediate Care. If the TMJ dysfunction is acute, have the athlete rest the jaw by not chewing gum, talking, or opening the mouth. Apply ice to the TMJ. The athlete can take over-the-counter nonsteroidal anti-inflammatory drugs (NSAIDs), such as ibuprofen or naproxen, for pain and inflammation. If the signs and symptoms do not readily subside with discontinuation of the causative factor and treatment, or the athlete

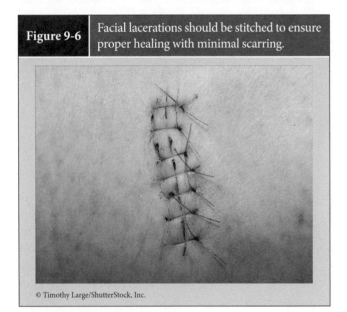

| Figure 9-6 | Facial lacerations should be stitched to ensure proper healing with minimal scarring. |

© Timothy Large/ShutterStock, Inc.

has frequent bouts of TMJ joint pain, clicking, popping, and stiffness, then refer him or her to a physician for evaluation. The physician may give the athlete prescription anti-inflammatory drugs for TMJ dysfunction flare-ups, as well as have the athlete obtain a custom-made mouthpiece to wear while sleeping. This mouthpiece places the jaw in a normal position while sleeping, while also deterring teeth clenching and grinding, which can precipitate TMJ dysfunction. Facial muscle massage also decreases facial muscular tension, which affects the TMJ. If the TMJ is dislocated, care for the athlete by calling 911, checking breathing, treating for shock, splinting the area around the head and jaw, and applying ice.

Prevention. TMJ dysfunction can be prevented if an athlete pays particular attention to his or her jaw motions. The athlete should avoid chewing gum and hard foods that cause continual and forceful mouth opening and closing. If the athlete yawns frequently due to fatigue, he or she should make a conscious effort to get more sleep. The athlete should avoid clenching his or her teeth, and should alleviate any stress by utilizing stress reduction techniques and massage.

Eye Injuries and Conditions

Orbital Fracture

Six bones around the eye make up the orbit—the frontal, lacrimal, ethmoid, sphenoid, maxilla, and zygomatic bones. An orbital fracture is a break in any of these bones. Blowout fractures are fractures to the thin, bony orbital floor.

Mechanism or Cause of Injury. Orbital fractures are caused by a direct blow to the bones surrounding the eye. A significant amount of force is required to break the bones around the orbit. Consequently, if the orbit is fractured, suspect the athlete has sustained a head injury also. The bones can be broken via impact from a baseball, a fist, a crash, a dumbbell, or any hard object that strikes the orbit with force. A mechanism of injury for a blowout fracture is considered indirect because the object causing the trauma does not directly strike the orbital floor. A common mechanism of injury for a blowout fracture is when the orbit is struck by an object that is larger than the eye itself, such as a baseball. As a result of the impact force, the orbital floor breaks.

Signs and Symptoms. Signs and symptoms of orbital fractures vary depending on which of the six orbital bones is fractured. If the zygomatic bone is fractured, then the athlete will have a flat cheek on the injured side. If the frontal bone is fractured, the bone will be flat, or may have a lump at the injured area due to swelling. Athletes with orbital blowout fractures also experience diplopia, sensation problems below the affected eye, and an inability to look upward. For all orbital fractures, the athlete can experience signs and symptoms such as a sunken or bulging eye, an inability to look in various directions, blurred vision, swelling, deformity, raccoon eyes, and bleeding from lacerations.

Immediate Care. Fractures of the orbit are medical emergencies. Call 911 immediately to summon EMS. While you are waiting for EMS to arrive, treat the athlete for shock and control any bleeding. Carefully and gently put a small ice pack on the area, but not directly on the eye. If you utilize a small ice bag to alleviate pain and swelling, do not press hard on the area because you do not want to move the fractured bones and cause further harm. Also, remember that the eyes move simultaneously, so if one eye is injured and the other eye moves, the athlete's injured eye can be further harmed. Therefore, if the athlete is having pain when moving the eyes, bandage both eyes to prevent the eyes from moving.

Prevention. Educate your athlete on the importance of wearing protective eyewear while participating in activities. Athletes are often not required to wear goggles when playing racquetball, but goggles can prevent the ball from striking the orbital area and causing a fracture. Face shields can also assist in the prevention of work-related orbital fractures from flying objects. Recommend to your athlete to always wear seat and safety belts, even in the back seat of motor vehicles, to avoid or diminish the severity of facial injuries during accidents.

Hyphema

A hyphema is blood that accumulates in the anterior chamber of the eye. The anterior chamber is the area between the cornea and the iris.

Mechanism or Cause of Injury. The typical mechanism of injury is a direct blow to the eye. An object, such as a finger, fist, stick, or athletic implement, strikes the eye causing trauma. A hyphema can also be caused by an athlete striking his or her head or eye on an object, such as the ground, due to a fall.

Signs and Symptoms. The primary sign of injury is blood accumulating in the eye's anterior chamber. The blood may not accumulate immediately, but can develop over a couple of days as inflammation progresses. If the injury is significant, the blood accumulates in the anterior chamber, and fills from the bottom up due to gravity. Consequently, the blood may rise to the pupil. The blood can block some or all vision, depending on how much blood accumulates in the anterior chamber. The athlete would see the red color from the blood in front of the pupil. The athlete will have pain, light sensitivity, and blurred vision.

Immediate Care. A hyphema necessitates urgent medical care. Refer the athlete to his or her ophthalmologist immediately. If the athlete is unable to be evaluated by his or her physician, have him or her transported to the ER by calling 911, and treat the athlete for shock.

Prevention. Appropriate safety eyewear can prevent hyphemas. Also, athletes must be aware of their surroundings so they do not have unfortunate falls or accidents.

Retinal Detachment

The retina is tissue in the back of the eye that helps us to see images that pass through the eye's cornea and lens. The retina passes the image to your optic nerve. The image is then transmitted to the brain, which allows us to visualize the image. The retina can become separated from its attachment on the back of the eye and cause significant vision problems.

Mechanism or Cause of Injury. Retinal detachment can be caused by a variety of mechanisms of injury; in addition, certain athletes are at risk for retinal detachment. Retinal detachment appears to be hereditary. Therefore, an athlete is at risk for retinal detachment if he or she has an immediate family member who has had a detached retina. Athletes who are older; have very bad nearsightedness, uncontrolled diabetes, or chronic retinal inflammation; or have had previous retinal surgery are also more at risk for retinal detachment (PubMed Health, 2011). Athletes can experience retinal detachment if they have a hole in their retina. Fluid leaks out of the hole and causes a bubble to form under the retina. Consequently, the retina is pulled off its underlying structural attachment. The retina can also be detached by direct trauma to the orbit or a blow to the head, which can cause a concurrent MTBI.

Signs and Symptoms. An athlete experiencing retinal detachment complains of bright flashes of light, floating spots in his or her field of vision, blurred or partially lost vision, and visualization that a black curtain is coming down in front of his or her eye.

Immediate Care. If an athlete complains of these symptoms, refer the athlete to an ophthalmologist for further evaluation. The athlete must see his or her physician within 24 hours after symptoms appear. The athlete cannot drive while experiencing these symptoms, so another valid driver must take the athlete to the physician. The physician will perform various eye tests including those to check retina function, visual acuity, the ability to detect various colors, and pressure within the eye. Surgery to repair the retina will often be necessary. However, depending on the area and extent of injury, surgery may not be a viable option.

Prevention. If an athlete is at risk for retinal detachment, he or she should make every effort to minimize the potential for acquiring this condition. Obviously, an athlete cannot affect heredity, but he or she can be proactive in decreasing other risk factors. For example, if an athlete is diabetic he or she should carefully control his or her disease with diet, exercise, and prescribed insulin. Age is a risk factor for retinal detachment, but if the athlete takes good care of his or her body, including yearly eye exams, and has a good quality of wellness and fitness, age-related risk factors can be minimized. Also, make sure the athlete wears protective eyewear as appropriate for his or her activity.

Corneal Abrasion

The cornea is the clear, glass-like portion of the anterior eye. With the lens, the cornea helps focus images onto the retina.

Mechanism or Cause of Injury. Corneal abrasions can occur by various mechanisms of injury. Commonly, corneal abrasions occur due to something scraping the cornea. An object enters the eye and then the athlete rubs the eye, which causes the scratch or abrasion. Even an object as small as a grain of sand or dust can cause corneal damage. Contact lenses can scrape the cornea during application and removal. Chemicals, eye drops, and contact solutions can cause a corneal abrasion, especially if these liquids cause an allergic reaction in the eye.

Signs and Symptoms. Athletes with corneal abrasions complain of pain and the sensation of an object in the eye. The athlete's eyes will be teary, red, and bloodshot, especially from rubbing the eye. He or she will complain of blurred and decreased vision and sensitivity to light.

Immediate Care. Immediately discourage the athlete from rubbing his or her eye, because this action can cause further harm. Attempt to determine if an object is in the eye, and if so carefully remove it (see the following section, "Foreign Object in the Eye"). Even if you remove the object, the athlete may continue to complain that something is still in his or her eye. Whether or not a minute object rests in the eye, refer the athlete to an ophthalmologist or ER for treatment. The physician will determine if the cornea has an abrasion by using **fluorescein** strips on the eye. The physician most likely will give the athlete eye drops or ointments and pain medication to heal the abrasion and decrease pain. If the athlete wears

> **Fluorescein** An orange dye that is on a medical test strip of paper. A physician places it onto the cornea to detect injury. The dye covers the cornea, and then the physician looks at the cornea under a blue light. Any areas of the cornea that are green indicate that an abrasion exists.

corrective lenses, he or she will be directed to wear glasses instead of contacts until the abrasion has healed.

Prevention. In order to prevent corneal abrasions, an athlete must wear appropriate protective eyewear when performing daily activities. Contact lenses must be fitted properly for each athlete. When working with any chemicals, the athlete should wear protective eyewear if possible, and make a conscious effort to keep the chemicals away from his or her eyes.

Foreign Object in the Eye

Foreign bodies in the eye range greatly in size. Consequently, the foreign body creates a significant range of injury severity. Obviously a larger foreign body in the eye, such as a nail protruding from the eye, causes significantly more damage than a grain of sand. If the object is small and in the eyelid, such as an eyelash or a small flying insect, then attempt to remove the object; however, if the object is larger and/or protruding from the eyeball, do not remove the object. Removing the object most likely will cause further harm.

Mechanism or Cause of Injury. Foreign bodies can enter the eye when an object flies into the eye, such as a flying insect, or is thrown into the eye, such as sand. An object can touch the eye, such as a finger that has dirt or dust on it, and then transfer the object to the eye. If an object, such as a nail, is shot at the eye, then the object can protrude from the eyeball, causing extensive injury.

Signs and Symptoms. The athlete will complain of many of the same signs and symptoms as exist with a corneal abrasion. If the object is large it will protrude from the eyeball or the eyelid will involuntary remain open.

Immediate Care. Care is very different if the foreign object is small, and can be removed without creating further harm to the athlete, as compared to a large object in the eye that may be protruding from the eyeball. In order to remove a small object from the athlete's eye, first wash your hands and put on non-powdered gloves. In a well-lighted area, have your athlete sit in a chair so you can look down into his or her eyes. Check the eye by gently pulling his or her upper eyelid up, trying to invert it if possible, while the athlete looks down. Then pull the lower eyelid down, inverting it again, while the athlete looks up. If you see the object, have the athlete tilt his or her head to the same side as the injured eye, and irrigate the eye with saline or clean, tepid water. If you irrigate the eye with the head tilted in the direction of the uninjured eye, then the irrigation fluid and the object may be flushed into the other eye. You can use an eyedropper or the tip of the saline bottle to irrigate the eye. Do not touch the tip of the eyedropper or bottle to the eye, because

this action can injure the eye and contaminate the eyedropper and bottle. Once the object is out of the eye, you should have the athlete irrigate his or her eye again to make sure all debris is out of the eye, and to cleanse the area.

Most foreign objects in the eye will be small and can be carefully removed. Rarely will large objects protrude from the eyeball or be stuck in the eye. If you cannot remove the object due to its size or potential for further injury, the athlete's eye is still painful after removing the object, his or her vision is significantly disturbed, or the object is protruding from the eyeball, then call 911 for the athlete to be transported to the ER via ambulance. While waiting for the ambulance, keep the athlete still. Do not remove the protruding object. Instead, apply bulky dressings and bandages around the protruding object to keep it still. Because the eyes move (or track) simultaneously in regard to speed and direction, bandage both eyes to prevent the injured eye from moving. Monitor the athlete for signs and symptoms of shock.

Prevention. To avoid getting a foreign body in the eye, the athlete must wear protective eyewear during activities. The athlete can also protect his or her eyes by wearing sunglasses when outside. A simple way to prevent small foreign objects in the eye is to avoid touching the eyes with unclean hands.

Conjunctivitis (Pink Eye)

Conjunctivitis, or pink eye, is an inflammation of the lining of the eye, which is called the conjunctiva. Pink eye occurs often in children, and is a highly contagious condition. Usually pink eye occurs in one eye, but because it is highly contagious, it can easily spread to the other eye.

Mechanism or Cause of Injury. Various causes of conjunctivitis exist, but the condition typically stems from a viral infection. Conjunctivitis is also caused by bacteria, fungi, allergies, chemicals, and contact lenses.

Signs and Symptoms. An athlete experiencing conjunctivitis has a significant amount of redness or a pink color in the sclera (or white portion) of his or her eye. He or she will complain of an itching eye, pain, blurred vision, and sensitivity to light. The athlete may have significant eye discharge that dries and becomes crusty overnight and keeps the eyelid from opening properly (**Figure 9-8**).

Immediate Care. The athlete must not be allowed to participate in activity at your organization while he or she is contagious. Refer him or her immediately to a physician. In the meantime, the athlete can apply warm compresses to the infected eye to alleviate some discomfort. The treatment varies depending on the type of conjunctivitis. Viral conjunctivitis

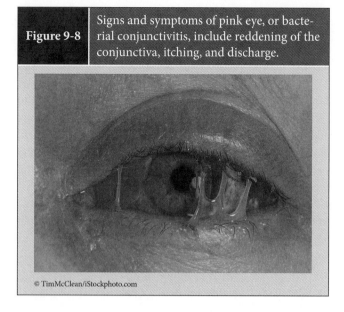

| **Figure 9-8** | Signs and symptoms of pink eye, or bacterial conjunctivitis, include reddening of the conjunctiva, itching, and discharge. |

© TimMcClean/iStockphoto.com

heals on its own. Most physicians prescribe eye drops for both viral and bacterial conjunctivitis, because the viral infection could create a bacterial infection. Allergic conjunctivitis is typically treated with allergy medication. Do not allow the athlete to return to activity until he or she is under a physician's care, no longer contagious, and presents you with a physician's clearance note for return to participation.

Prevention. Prevention of conjunctivitis typically starts with good hygiene. Frequent hand washing, and laundering clothes, towels, and bed linens will help prevent conjunctivitis. Athletes should not share towels, cosmetics, contact lenses, or any object that comes in contact with the eye. Make sure your athletes dispose of previously used eye cosmetics and contact lenses and use new, uncontaminated items.

Stye

A stye is an inflamed sebaceous, or oil, gland in the eyelid, located where the eyelash protrudes.

Mechanism or Cause of Injury. Bacteria enters into the gland and causes inflammation. Typically the stye forms in a few days.

Signs and Symptoms. A stye appears as a red bump that resembles a pimple, which will be point tender and swollen. The athlete may feel like something is in his or her eye. The eye may tear and be sensitive to light.

Immediate Care. Typically styes spontaneously drain without treatment and the eyelid returns to a normal state. The athlete can apply warm compresses to the eye to alleviate any discomfort. He or she must not squeeze the stye because it may cause further harm. Advise your athlete that if the stye does not resolve itself in a week's time, proceeds to worsen, or

exhibits other signs and symptoms such as bleeding, blurred or blocked vision, or extreme sensitivity to light, then he or she should see their physician for treatment. Often, antibiotic ointment is prescribed to treat the inflammation.

Prevention. The best prevention to avoid acquiring a stye is similar to preventing a foreign body in the eye. Make sure your athlete practices frequent, proper hand and face washing, and avoids putting any unclean objects near the eyes.

Ear Injuries and Conditions

Tympanic Membrane (Eardrum) Rupture

The purpose of the tympanic membrane, or eardrum, is to vibrate when sound strikes it. The vibrations travel to the bones behind the eardrum in the middle ear. The vibrations continue on to the inner ear, in order for the nerves to stimulate the brain and process the sound. A ruptured eardrum means there is a perforation in the tissue that forms a hole. Because the ruptured eardrum is unable to vibrate properly, the transmission of vibrations is affected, which subsequently is detrimental to a person's ability to hear.

Mechanism or Cause of Injury. A tympanic membrane rupture is caused by a direct blow to the ear, an ear infection, a foreign object in the ear, a change in pressure, or an extremely loud noise.

Signs and Symptoms. The athlete with a ruptured tympanic membrane has a visible hole in the tissue (**Figure 9-9**), hearing

| **Figure 9-9** | A tympanic membrane (eardrum) rupture. |

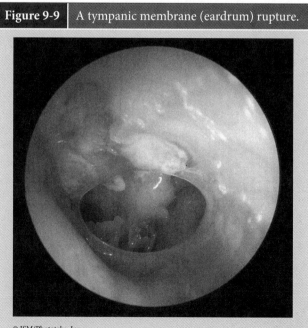

© ISM/Phototake, Inc.

difficulties or loss, discomfort or pain, and possible leakage of fluid or pus (in the case of an ear infection) or blood (in the case of an object forced into the ear).

Immediate Care. Make sure the athlete does not get water in the ear, if possible. He or she can apply warm compresses on the ear to alleviate pain. Refer the athlete to a physician for evaluation. The physician may give the athlete antibiotics to prevent infection (or to treat an ear infection), and pain medication. Most eardrums will heal without treatment within a couple months, and hearing will be restored to normal.

Prevention. Prevention of a tympanic membrane rupture takes a common sense approach. Tell your athletes not to put any foreign objects in the ear. The athlete should not put cotton swabs utilized for cleaning the ear into the external acoustic canal by the eardrum. Explain to the athlete to avoid changes in pressure if the pressure will not be equalized (for example, ascending from deep water quickly, or in an airplane without equalized cabin pressure). Earplugs and noise reduction protective ear wear are necessary if the athlete is in an area with extremely loud noise. Educate your athletes not to slap or hit someone's ear. Finally, recommend to dry the inside of the ear after bathing or swimming. Residual water in the ear can make a great breeding area for bacteria. The bacteria can cause an ear infection, which may lead to a tympanic membrane rupture. To dry the external acoustic canal, utilize a gentle cool hair dryer on low speed held far enough away from the ear so he or she does not blow the air too forcefully into the ear.

Auricular Hematoma (Cauliflower Ear)

Auricular hematoma, or cauliflower ear, is a deformity of the outer ear cartilage that occurs over a period of time. A hematoma in the outer ear is formed, followed by scar tissue. The outer ear tissue is deprived of oxygenated blood due to the injury. The tissue begins to shrink, becomes bumpy, and takes on the appearance of a cauliflower.

Mechanism or Cause of Injury. The mechanism of injury for cauliflower ear is constant friction of the outer ear, on a surface such as a wrestling mat, while the athlete is not wearing protective ear wear. Direct, blunt trauma can also cause cauliflower ear, if the trauma is great enough to cause a hematoma that is not treated or does not heal properly. Some athletes have their outer ear cartilage pierced. If the piercing causes a hematoma to form, the athletes may acquire cauliflower ear.

Signs and Symptoms. An athlete with cauliflower ear may complain of pain, tinnitus, hearing loss, visual disturbances, and headache. The signs of cauliflower ear include the cauliflower deformation appearance; warmth at the area due to inflammation, swelling; and facial swelling.

Immediate Care. In order to care for cauliflower ear, have the athlete apply ice and manual compression to the area. The athlete should be examined by his or her physician. Depending on the severity and how long the athlete has had the condition, the physician may drain the fluid from the ear. After the hematoma has been drained, the physician applies a compression bandage on the area to keep fluid from reentering the site. The physician often prescribes antibiotics to prevent possible infection, as well as pain medication. The sooner cauliflower ear is treated, the greater possibility that the outer ear will not be permanently deformed.

Prevention. To prevent cauliflower ear, the athlete must wear appropriate protective ear wear, headgear, and helmets while participating in activities that can affect the outer ear (**Figure 9-10**). If the athlete's ear is inflamed, the athlete should immediately put ice and compression on the area to prevent cauliflower ear.

Otitis Externa (Swimmer's Ear)

Otitis externa or swimmer's ear is an infection of the outer ear canal.

Mechanism or Cause of Injury. If water remains in the outer ear canal after bathing or swimming and is not removed or dried, it sits in the canal. Eventually bacteria grow in the moist

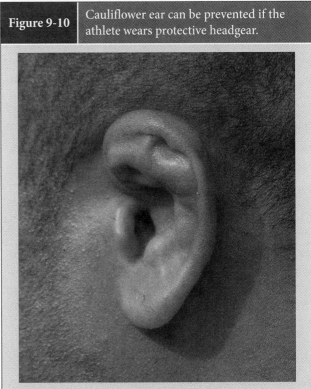

| Figure 9-10 | Cauliflower ear can be prevented if the athlete wears protective headgear. |

© Richard Wareham Fotografie/Alamy Images.

skin environment. Also, if an athlete puts an object in his or her ear and scratches the skin, then bacteria can grow in the skin openings, causing infection.

Signs and Symptoms. An athlete with swimmer's ear may not experience significant signs and symptoms at first. However, the signs and symptoms develop over time if the infection is not treated. The athlete first experiences itching and mild discomfort. The outer ear canal may be red from inflammation, and possibly a slight discharge may exude from the canal. These signs and symptoms progressively increase if the infection is not treated. Pus may drain from and block the canal, which would prevent proper hearing. More significant signs and symptoms exist if the infection is allowed to continue without treatment—the athlete may experience severe pain, redness and swelling, fever, swollen neck lymph nodes, and complete blockage of the outer ear canal, which prevents hearing.

Immediate Care. If the signs and symptoms of swimmer's ear are mild, refer the athlete to a physician. If the athlete is experiencing severe signs and symptoms, then call EMS immediately. The infection is treated with antibiotics for a bacterial infection, or an antifungal drug for a fungal infection. The physician may also prescribe steroids for the inflammation and ear drops to assist in healing the outer ear canal.

Prevention. Advise your athletes to keep their outer ear canals dry after swimming or bathing. To dry the external acoustic canal, utilize a gentle cool hair dryer on low speed held far enough away from their ear so they do not blow the air too forcefully into the ear. Special over-the-counter eardrops or a combination of white vinegar and rubbing alcohol can help dry out the ear. However, if the athlete has scrapes in the canal, white vinegar and rubbing alcohol will burn the skin and cause pain and should not be utilized. Your athlete can utilize earplugs specifically made for swimmers to prevent water from entering the outer ear canal. Tell your athletes not to put anything into their outer ear canal, including cotton-tipped swabs.

Otitis Media (Middle Ear Infection)

The middle ear is the portion of the ear from the tympanic membrane to the inner ear. The middle ear contains the three smallest bones in the body, the malleus, incus, and stapes. Sound vibrations from the tympanic membrane are transferred to these bones and then are transferred to the inner ear. Otitis media is a middle ear infection that occurs most often in babies and children.

Mechanism or Cause of Injury. Bacteria or viruses trapped in the middle ear cause the infection. An athlete who has a cold with nasal passageway and Eustachian tube inflammation

is predisposed to a middle ear infection because the inflammation does not allow the fluid to drain well. Consequently, the fluid backs up into the Eustachian tube and resides in the middle ear. The bacteria then grows in this stagnant fluid and causes the infection.

Signs and Symptoms. Due to the inflammation, the athlete has significant pain, a sore throat, and fluid drainage from the ear. The athlete may complain of muffled hearing due to inflammation and fluid in the middle ear. Children may also complain of difficulty sleeping, and exhibit a low grade fever of approximately 100°F.

Immediate Care. Usually middle ear infections heal without treatment after a few days. The athlete can typically wait to see a physician for 48 to 72 hours after he or she becomes symptomatic in order to see if the infection resolves on its own. In the meantime, the athlete can place warm compresses on the ear. If the athlete has drainage from the ear, refer him or her to a physician immediately. Even though the middle ear infection may heal on its own, the athlete often needs evaluation and treatment from a physician. The physician may prescribe antibiotics and pain medication to treat the infection.

Prevention. To prevent otitis media, recommend to your athlete to get his or her flu vaccination annually. Encourage your athlete to quit smoking and avoid secondhand smoke, which can irritate the passageways. Also, your athlete should attempt to avoid colds by washing his or her hands regularly.

Nasal Injuries and Conditions

Fractures

In athletic activity, a nasal fracture is a common facial injury. Other facial bones are often fractured along with the nasal bones. Likewise, due to the mechanism of injury, a separated septum can also occur with a nasal fracture. Whenever a nasal fracture exists, always consider that the athlete may also have a head and neck injury due to the forceful mechanism of injury.

Mechanism or Cause of Injury. Nasal fractures occur from blunt force trauma to the nasal bones. An object, such as a thrown ball or an opponent's elbow or fist, can strike the nose with enough force to break the bones (**Figure 9-11**).

Signs and Symptoms. The athlete complains of pain and difficulty breathing from the nose. Epistaxis, deformity, point tenderness, and swelling are present.

Immediate Care. Have the athlete sit comfortably with his or her head leaning forward slightly. Tell the athlete to breathe out of his or her mouth. Keep the athlete calm and treat him

Figure 9-11 | A fractured nose can be caused by a straight on or lateral direct blow.

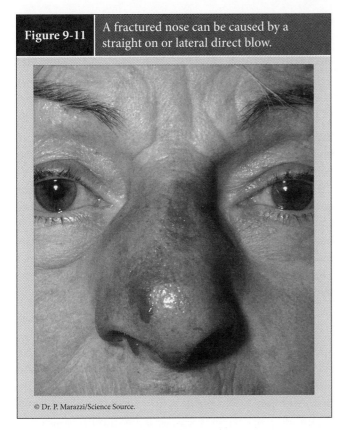

© Dr. P. Marazzi/Science Source.

or her for shock if necessary. Provide the athlete with a small bag of ice to place gently on the injured area. He or she must not apply too much pressure with the ice bag; otherwise, he or she may move the broken bones and cause further harm. If the athlete has epistaxis, then treat him or her accordingly (see the following section, "Epistaxis"). Never attempt to straighten the nose and do not move the athlete if he or she shows signs of a head or neck injury. In the case of a head or neck injury, maintain in-line stabilization on the athlete, and call 911.

Prevention. Nasal fractures can be avoided by wearing protective face guards as appropriate for the activity. Recommend to your athlete to wear seat and safety belts.

▌ Epistaxis (Nosebleed)

Epistaxis typically is not a serious injury unless it is due to a nasal fracture or a head injury. An uncomplicated nosebleed is one that was not caused by any physical trauma to the nose, head, or face. This type of nosebleed can be controlled quickly and the athlete can return to activity. Usually bleeding comes from one nostril unless the bleeding is severe, then the blood can flow into the other nostril.

Mechanism or Cause of Injury. Many causes for a nosebleed exist. Direct trauma, allergies, dry nasal passages, continual inflammation from colds, picking the nose, and drug use (from drugs snorted up the nose) can cause epistaxis.

Signs and Symptoms. Signs and symptoms of a nosebleed are external bleeding from and difficulty breathing through the nose. The athlete may have pain and swelling if a direct blow caused the nosebleed.

Immediate Care. For an uncomplicated nosebleed, have the athlete sit up and pinch his or her nose just below where the bone meets the cartilage. Put on your protective gloves and obtain an absorbent material such as gauze, nose plugs, or commercial nosebleed clotting materials. Carefully insert the absorbent material into the athlete's bleeding nostril. Make sure that the end of the absorbent material is partially protruding from the nostril so it can be removed easily. Have the athlete hold a small bag of ice on the nose to decrease any pain, and to control swelling and bleeding. The athlete should continue to pinch his or her nose with the absorbent plug inserted for about 5–10 minutes.

After 5–10 minutes, remove the plug with a gloved hand and see whether the nostril has stopped bleeding. If the bleeding has stopped, have your athlete clean up his or her face, hands, and any other areas that have blood on them. Remove your gloves, dispose of all bloody materials properly, and wash your hands thoroughly. Make sure that you inform your athlete not to blow or breathe in deeply through the nose for a few hours after the nosebleed. These actions may disrupt the blood clot in the nasal passageway and restart bleeding. If the bleeding has not stopped after the 5–10 minutes of care, apply another absorbent nose plug and have the athlete pinch and apply ice to the nose again for another 5–10 minutes. If after this time the nose still continues to bleed, then summon EMS. If at any time you believe the nosebleed was due to a head injury or some other condition that is potentially life-threatening, or the athlete has a potential neck injury, treat these injuries appropriately and summon EMS immediately. For recurrent nosebleeds, refer your athlete to his or her physician. The physician may **cauterize** the blood vessels that cause the recurrent bleeds.

> **Cauterize** To burn tissue with electricity or a laser in order to assist in the healing process. In the case of epistaxis, blood vessels that bleed regularly are cauterized in the nose.

Prevention. As with nasal fractures, wearing protective face guards can prevent nosebleeds caused by direct trauma. Your athlete should take allergy medicine, irrigate the nose with saline regularly, and utilize humidifiers in the home if his or her nasal passages are dry and susceptible to bleeding. Athletes should not pick their nose or put any foreign objects, including drugs, up their noses.

Deviated Septum

The septum is the portion of the nose that separates the two nostrils inside the nasal cavity. A deviated septum can be a significant injury. When the septum blocks one side of the nasal cavity, breathing difficulties can exist.

Mechanism or Cause of Injury. A deviated septum is caused by a direct blow to the nose due to participating in contact sports, falls, and accidents. An athlete can also be born with a deviated septum.

Signs and Symptoms. An athlete with a deviated septum may have frequent nosebleeds, breathing difficulty due to the septum occluding one side of the nasal cavity, nasal and facial pain, sinus infections due to poor drainage of nasal fluid, and snoring or loud breathing through the nose while sleeping.

Immediate Care. If the athlete's nose is bleeding, treat the nosebleed as previously discussed. Whether or not the athlete's nose is bleeding, refer him or her to a physician for evaluation. The physician may prescribe nasal sprays such as steroids, antihistamines, and nasal decongestants to alleviate signs and symptoms of inflammation and promote nasal fluid drainage. If the athlete continues to have difficulty breathing, the physician may surgically repair the deviated septum by placing it in the middle of the nose. The physician may also choose to reshape the nasal bones along with centering the septum to make a sufficient passageway for air in both nostrils.

Prevention. It is impossible to prevent a deviated septum that occurs to athletes at birth. In order to prevent a deviated septum from direct impact, the athlete should wear protective face gear, and seat and safety belts as necessary.

Tooth Injuries

As with other bony injuries, fractures, subluxations, luxations, and avulsions can occur to the teeth. Some of these injuries require immediate medical attention, whereas others are not as urgent.

Fractures

Tooth fractures can be minor when the break runs through the enamel, which is the outermost layer of the tooth. More significant breaks run through the enamel and dentin (the layer of the tooth inside the enamel). An even more significant fracture is when the break is through the enamel, dentin, and interior pulp (which is inside the dentin) of the tooth. A severe fracture occurs when the break crosses through the root, which is the portion of the tooth in the gum. Fractures, or chips, mostly occur to the enamel and dentin.

Mechanism or Cause of Injury. Tooth fractures are caused by a direct blow or falling on the face or mouth. Fractures can also occur from biting down on or chewing hard food, candy, or the like.

Signs and Symptoms. The athlete will have pain if a direct blow hits his or her face or mouth, but he or she may not have pain if he or she bites down on a hard object and only fractures the enamel and/or dentin. He or she may become sensitive to cold or pressure while chewing food. If the pulp or root is fractured, the athlete will definitely feel pain. The tooth will be jagged and sharp to the athlete's tongue or finger when touched. The athlete will be bleeding if he or she has lacerations to the face, mouth, or gums. Some tooth displacement may be visible.

Immediate Care. A fracture of the enamel, dentin, and pulp is not a medical emergency. The athlete can put some sugarless gum on the jagged edges until he or she is able to be evaluated by a dentist. If he or she is bleeding or has any other facial, head, or neck injuries, appropriately treat those injuries first. For minor fractures, the dentist will re-create the tooth. Significant pulp fractures may need a root canal to save the tooth. For fractures to the root, the dentist may need to pull the tooth and replace it with a prosthetic tooth.

Prevention. Athletes should wear mouth guards whenever possible during activity where the potential for tooth injury exists. Athletes should also wear properly fitted face masks in sporting activities that require the equipment to help reduce the incidence of tooth injury.

Subluxation

A tooth subluxation occurs when it is knocked loose in the socket, but does not fall out. The front teeth are the most commonly affected.

Mechanism or Cause of Injury. A tooth can be subluxed by a traumatic direct blow to or fall on the tooth.

Signs and Symptoms. Usually bleeding occurs to some extent with a subluxation. The athlete most likely experiences some pain and tenderness around the gum line, especially when he or she touches it with his or her finger. The gum line will also appear swollen.

Immediate Care. The athlete must first rinse the mouth out with clean, cool water. Whether the tooth is a baby (primary) or adult (secondary) tooth, instruct the athlete to hold the tooth in place and in proper alignment with a clean finger. Apply ice over the mouth. The athlete should carefully bite down on some rolled up sterile gauze to help keep the tooth in place. Also have him or her place sterile gauze at the injured site to stop bleeding. The socket will eventually close up around the tooth, which makes the tooth stable. If the tooth is very mobile, or you cannot stop the bleeding, refer the athlete to the dentist or ER immediately.

Prevention. Prevention for subluxations of the tooth is the same as for fractures of the tooth.

Luxation

A tooth displacement is a luxation. The displacement can be in any direction. A tooth fracture may occur with a luxation. The front teeth are the most commonly affected.

Mechanism or Cause of Injury. The mechanism of injury is the same for a luxation as for a subluxation, which is usually a direct blow to or fall on the face, mouth, or teeth.

Signs and Symptoms. Luxation signs and symptoms are similar to subluxations of teeth, except displacement will be visible. The tooth can be displaced either outward toward the lips, inward toward the tongue, or to either side. The gums at the site of the luxated tooth will be swollen.

Immediate Care. The athlete must first rinse the mouth out with clean, cool water. With clean fingers, the athlete should attempt to carefully and slowly move the tooth back into its normal position and alignment with the neighboring teeth. Afterwards, have the athlete apply an ice pack to the mouth to decrease pain and bleeding. The athlete needs to see a dentist immediately. Primary teeth will either be removed or repositioned and splinted as per the dentist's recommendations. Secondary teeth will be repositioned and splinted. Antibiotics are necessary to avoid infection, and pain medication can also be utilized.

Prevention. Prevention of tooth luxations is the same as for fractures of the tooth.

Avulsion

A tooth avulsion occurs when the tooth is knocked out of the socket (**Figure 9-12**). This injury typically occurs to young children.

Mechanism or Cause of Injury. The cause of a tooth avulsion is the same as for a subluxation or luxation. Significant trauma is necessary to cause the avulsion. Therefore, determine that

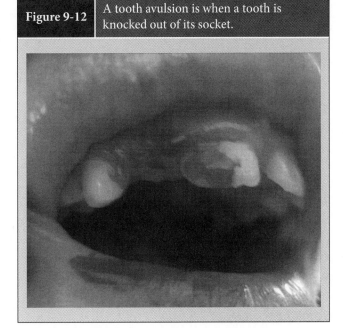

Figure 9-12 A tooth avulsion is when a tooth is knocked out of its socket.

the athlete does not also have a face, head, or neck injury, which must be treated as the priority for care.

Signs and Symptoms. Tooth avulsions exhibit an empty socket where the tooth was knocked out. The socket will bleed and be swollen. The athlete will have a significant amount of pain, even if he or she does not experience another injury to the face, head, or neck.

Immediate Care. If an athlete has knocked out a primary or secondary tooth, he or she should make every attempt to replace the tooth. Without touching any exposed root or pulp, the athlete must clean the tooth first by rinsing it under water. The athlete should not scrub the tooth while rinsing it. Then he or she replaces it in the socket while looking in a mirror in order to visualize proper positioning and alignment. The athlete must see his or her dentist or go to the ER immediately for evaluation, even if he or she has properly replaced the tooth. If the athlete cannot put the tooth in the socket, have him or her put the tooth in saline, milk, or another tooth-saving solution that is sold over-the-counter by commercial vendors. The athlete must see his or her dentist or the ER immediately in an attempt to save the tooth's life. If the tooth is dry for 15 minutes, then the root covering dies and tooth replantation is not possible. The dentist will most likely apply a splint to the tooth once it is replaced. For avulsed secondary teeth, the dentist will perform a root canal at a later date in an attempt to save the tooth. With severe tooth injuries, the athlete may go into shock. Consequently, be prepared to treat shock if you see the signs and symptoms arise.

Prevention.   Prevention for tooth subluxations is the same as for tooth subluxations and luxations.

Tips from the Field

Tip 3 If an athlete's tooth is avulsed and you do not have any milk, saline, or a commercial tooth-saving liquid available, have the athlete place the tooth under his or her tongue en route to the dentist or ER. The athlete must be fully conscious and he or she must not speak in order to keep the tooth under the tongue. If you need to ask him or her questions, then ask "yes" or "no" questions. He or she can then answer you with a head nod or shake, respectively.

SUMMARY

Injuries and illnesses to the head and face may be minor, such as TMJ dysfunction or an uncomplicated nosebleed, requiring nonurgent treatment, or significant, such as with MTBI and most head injuries, which require immediate advanced medical treatment. With any traumatic head or face injuries, you must consider the possibility of a neck injury, neurologic disruption, skull and/or brain bleeding, shock, or unconsciousness. Consequently, with head and face injuries, always be prepared for and know how to provide immediate care for any life-threatening situations that arise.

DISCUSSION QUESTIONS

1. What are some cognitive and neurological signs and symptoms that occur in an athlete who has sustained an MTBI?
2. Which type of bleeding within the skull creates a rapid deterioration of cognitive and neurological function in the athlete?
3. Other than typical signs and symptoms of fractures, what are some signs and symptoms specific for each fractured facial bone?
4. In regard to a migraine, what is an aura?
5. What treatment is appropriate for TMJ dysfunction?
6. What are the differences between otitis externa and otitis media?
7. What should you do to treat epistaxis? When should you call 911 for an athlete who has epistaxis?
8. What are the differences among a tooth fracture, subluxation, luxation, and avulsion? How should you treat each injury?

CASE STUDY

Rock Wall Stumble

Dennis, a 35-year-old, healthy, and fit man, wakes up one Saturday morning excited to go rock climbing with his friends at Northern State Park. When he looks out the window it is pouring rain. He turns on the TV and the weather forecast calls for intermittent heavy rain all day. Dennis calls his friends and they decide it would be safer to climb indoors at the local Northern State Rock Walls gym. Dennis packs his climbing gear. He has climbed the Northern State Rock Walls gym before. For this climb, Dennis and his friends will attempt the 55-foot wall, which is reserved for elite climbers. Although Dennis has never attempted this height before and knows it is challenging, he believes this wall will be nowhere near as dangerous as climbing at Northern State Park. He is anxious and excited to climb today.

The friends arrive at the gym and climb for an hour. Dennis has successfully climbed once already. It is now Dennis' turn to climb again. He chooses a route with a small buttress on it, figuring it would be a good challenge. Dennis has no problem clearing the buttress, but just as he is about to continue ascending he loses his grip and falls just below the buttress. Dennis' momentum makes him swing under the buttress. As he swings, he loses control and hits his head extremely hard against the wall and protruding rocks. Rick, Dennis' friend who is belaying Dennis, lowers Dennis to the ground and asks him if he is okay. Dennis was wearing his helmet as required by the gym; however, he tells Rick that he saw stars and his head is throbbing and hurts. Dennis continues to say that he feels "foggy" and is nauseous. His friends tell him to shake it off, and get up and climb the wall again. At first Dennis does not want to go back up the wall because he starts to feel dizzy, but he succumbs to the peer pressure and begins to climb again.

As he ascends the wall and reaches the top, the dizziness gets worse, and he begins to have significantly blurred vision. Suddenly, Dennis begins to vomit. Rick belays Dennis down and his friends suggest he no longer climbs and rests for the remainder of the 3-hour session. Dennis has never suffered a rock climbing injury like this before, and he has no idea what is happening to him.

1. What injury or injuries may Dennis have?
2. What are some other signs and symptoms of injury that might arise?
3. What course of action should Dennis' friends take to care for Dennis?

4. What type of cognitive evaluation testing can Dennis' friends perform to determine the extent of Dennis' injury?

5. Should Dennis go to the hospital? Why or why not?

REFERENCES

Bey, T., & Ostick, B. (2009). Second impact syndrome. *Western Journal of Emergency Medicine*, 10(1), 6–10. Retrieved May 19, 2012, from http://www.ncbi.nlm.nih.gov/pmc/articles/PMC2672291/

Centers for Disease Control and Prevention (CDC). (2012). Concussion in sports. Retrieved May 18, 2012, from http://www.cdc.gov/concussion/sports/response.html

Guskiewicz, K. M., Bruce, S. L., Cantu, R. C., Ferrara, M. S., Kelly, J. P., McCrea, M., et al. (2004). National Athletic Trainers' Association position statement: Management of sport-related concussion. *Journal of Athletic Training*, 39(3), 280–297.

Mayo Clinic. (2011). Migraine: Definition. Retrieved February 13, 2013, from http://www.mayoclinic.com/health/migraine-headache/DS00120

Meagher, R. J., & Young, W. F. (2011). Subdural hematoma. Retrieved May 19, 2012, from http://emedicine.medscape.com/article/1137207-overview

MedlinePlus. (2012). Skull fracture. Retrieved May 20, 2012, from http://www.nlm.nih.gov/medlineplus/ency/article/000060.htm

PubMed Health. (2010). Extradural hemorrhage. Retrieved May 19, 2012, from http://www.ncbi.nlm.nih.gov/pubmedhealth/PMH0002385/

PubMed Health. (2011). Retinal detachment. Retrieved May 21, 2012, from http://www.ncbi.nlm.nih.gov/pubmedhealth/PMH0002022/

Rozen, T. D. (2011). A history of cigarette smoking is associated with the development of cranial autonomic symptoms with migraine headaches. *Headache: The Journal of Head and Face Pain*, 51(1), 85–91. doi: 10.1111/j.1526-4610.2010.01707.x.

Russell, M. B. (2008). Is migraine a genetic illness? The various forms of migraine share a common genetic cause. *Neurolological Sciences*, 29, S52–S54. doi: 10.1007/s10072-008-0887-4.

Chapter 10

The Upper Extremity

CHAPTER OBJECTIVES

After you have read this chapter, you will be able to understand:

- The various injuries and conditions that an athlete can sustain to the shoulder, elbow, forearm, wrist, hand, and fingers
- Which upper extremity injuries necessitate calling 911 and which injuries only require referral to the athlete's physician
- That the athlete may go into shock after he or she has sustained a significant injury to the upper extremity
- Which upper extremity injuries and conditions require surgery and subsequent rehabilitation in order to restore extremity function

The upper extremity includes the shoulder, upper arm, forearm, wrist, hand, and fingers. This chapter discusses the common upper extremity injuries that may occur to your athletes. Many mechanisms of injury are similar regardless of which area of the upper extremity is injured. However, the severity, irritability, nature, and stage (SINS) of injury vary depending on the injury, and whether the injury is acute or chronic. Some injuries require immediate referral to emergency medical services (EMS) whereas others do not necessitate urgent care. Fortunately, injuries to the upper extremity are not often life-threatening.

INJURIES TO THE SHOULDER AND UPPER ARM

Some athletes think the shoulder is only composed of the ball-and-socket glenohumeral (GH) joint. They are correct that the GH joint is part of the shoulder; however, the shoulder is also composed of the humerus, clavicle, and scapula bones, as well as the scapulothoracic (ST), sternoclavicular (SC), and acromioclavicular (AC) joints. These bones and joints work together for proper shoulder function. When one structure is injured, shoulder function will be hindered.

Fractures

Fractures to the shoulder typically occur to the clavicle and humerus, with the most common fractures occurring to the clavicle. Bones tend to fracture where they change shape and are weakest. Therefore, the clavicle fractures most often at the middle one-third of the bone. The humerus usually fractures below the head of the humerus at the proximal end of the bone. Both fractures can be displaced.

▌ Mechanism or Cause of Injury

A common mechanism of injury for a clavicle or humerus fracture is falling on an outstretched arm. Picture an athlete who falls and tries to catch herself. Her elbow is straight and her wrist is extended as her palm strikes the ground. The forces from the fall, her body weight, and the ground's reaction can cause injury from the fingers, up the extremity, to the sternoclavicular joint. Another mechanism of injury for a clavicle and humerus fracture is a direct blow to the bone or to the tip of the shoulder. The direct blow creates vibrations that travel through the upper extremity, reaching the humerus and clavicle, and cause the bone to break.

Any type of fracture can occur to the humerus. Transverse fractures are common (**Figure 10-1**). The humerus can sustain a spiral fracture when the hand is firmly fixed on a stable surface, such as the floor, but the athlete's body moves. This motion

Figure 10-1	A displaced, transverse fracture of the humerus.

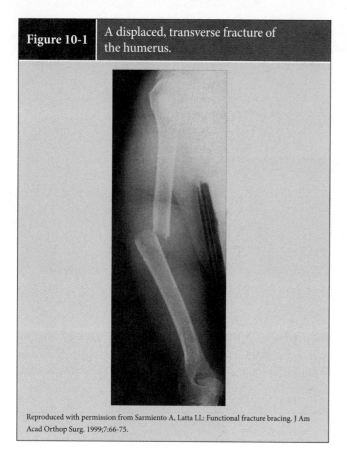

Reproduced with permission from Sarmiento A, Latta LL: Functional fracture bracing. J Am Acad Orthop Surg. 1999;7:66-75.

Figure 10-2	A sling can easily be applied to support many upper extremity injuries.

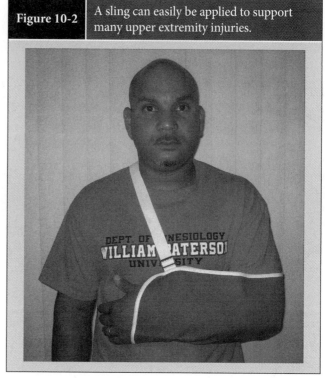

causes a twisting of the humerus, which causes the spiral fracture. A humerus compression fracture can occur when the athlete's palm lands on the ground with the elbow extended. This mechanism of injury is called a fall on an outstretched arm.

Signs and Symptoms

Signs and symptoms of a clavicle or humerus fracture are pain, deformity (such as a prominent bump with clavicle fractures), loss of function or complete inability to move the GH joint, point tenderness, ecchymosis, and swelling. Often, humerus fractures are not displaced and no visible deformity is present.

Immediate Care

If you suspect a clavicle or humerus fracture, tell the athlete to remain still and not to move her arm. Have her sit in a comfortable position supporting the arm. Call 911, or have someone else call for you, so the athlete can be transported to the emergency room (ER). Splint the arm by putting it in a sling, while keeping it as still as possible (**Figure 10-2**). You can also apply an elastic bandage around the arm and splint it to the athlete's body to make the arm immovable. If these splinting materials are not available, you are not trained to properly apply

splints, or you are uncomfortable with splint application, then instruct the athlete to remain completely still and assist her while you wait for EMS to arrive. EMS will appropriately splint the injured area. You can apply a small bag of ice on the injured area. The bag of ice must not move the bones or cause undue weight on the injured area, or it will result in pain or harm. If you see the athlete is going into shock, which is common with shoulder fractures, then treat the athlete immediately.

After sustaining a clavicle fracture, the athlete will wear a "figure 8" brace (shown in **Figure 10-3**) for 3–8 weeks (American Society for Surgery of the Hand [ASSH], 2007). The brace puts a slight traction on the bones. The two broken clavicle pieces straighten out so the ends are in line with each other, which promotes healing. The physician rarely needs to perform surgery to secure the broken bones.

For a humeral fracture that is nondisplaced and remains in normal alignment, the physician will have the athlete wear a sling for approximately 4 weeks before range of motion (ROM) rehabilitation can begin. If the humerus fracture is displaced and the ends of the broken bones are not aligned, then surgery may be the only viable option for proper healing (ASSH, 2007).

Prevention

In an attempt to prevent clavicle or humerus fractures, the athlete must wear properly fitted shoulder padding, especially

Figure 10-3 | An athlete will wear a figure 8 brace to assist clavicle fracture healing.

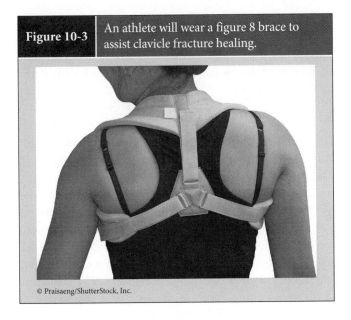

© Praisaeng/ShutterStock, Inc.

Figure 10-4 | An anterior dislocation of the GH joint.

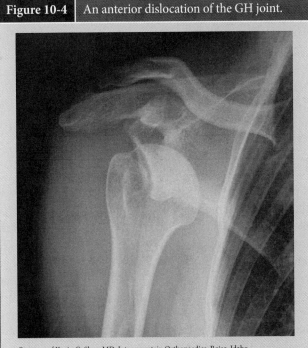

Courtesy of Kevin G. Shea, MD, Intermountain Orthopaedics, Boise, Idaho.

in contact activities such as when playing ice hockey, football, or lacrosse. The athlete should learn how to fall properly, by rolling, instead of falling on an outstretched arm. This skill is commonly executed by volleyball players. Emphasize to the athlete to utilize correct form and skills when performing her activities. She must always be aware of her surroundings, as well as her body positioning during activity, in order to prevent falls. To keep bones strong, the athlete must have a good supply of calcium and vitamin D in her diet, in conjunction with performing weight-bearing activities. Strong bones can minimize the potential of fracture.

Dislocations and Subluxations

A dislocation, or a luxation, and a subluxation of the GH joint are similar because these injuries both involve displacement of the humeral head from its normal position in the joint relative to the glenoid fossa. With a dislocated GH joint, the humeral head moves out of normal alignment and remains in that position. With a GH subluxation, the humeral head moves out of normal alignment and then spontaneously reduces back into normal alignment. Dislocations to the GH joint occur in an anterior, inferior, and posterior manner, with an anterior dislocation being the most common (**Figure 10-4**). Anterior and posterior dislocations are characterized by the head of the humerus protruding from the joint anteriorly and posteriorly, respectively. Posterior dislocations occur when the head of the humerus is displaced back toward the scapula. An inferior dislocation occurs when the head of the humerus protrudes inferiorly into the axilla. Once the athlete has sustained a GH dislocation or subluxation, chances are that the athlete

will sustain another dislocation or subluxation in the future. After a dislocation or subluxation, the athlete's ligaments and joint capsule are permanently stretched, allowing for joint laxity. Therefore, the athlete needs to undergo rehabilitation to strengthen the surrounding muscles to keep the head of the humerus in place during GH motion.

Although the injury is rare, the SC joint can also be dislocated or subluxed. Typically the sternum moves posteriorly with an SC joint dislocation or subluxation. With these injuries, keep in mind that the heart is behind the sternum and may also have been injured. Also, a posterior SC joint dislocation can cause damage to the blood vessels, respiratory difficulty, and other serious complications including death (Hoekzema, Torchia, Adkins, & Cassivi, 2008). Therefore, this injury can be life-threatening.

Both GH and SC dislocations and subluxations are serious injuries. Not only do the bones move out of normal alignment, but the ligaments, tendons, and muscles surrounding the bones are stretched and damaged.

▌ Mechanism or Cause of Injury

A common mechanism of injury for a GH or SC joint dislocation or subluxation is a fall on an outstretched arm. A GH anterior dislocation can also occur when a direct blow occurs to the arm when the upper arm is abducted from the body and the elbow is in a 90-degree angle. An inferior dislocation can be caused by a direct blow down onto the tip of the shoulder while the arm is at the athlete's side. A posterior dislocation can occur when the arm is outstretched and the athlete falls forward, which forces the head of the humerus backwards. The GH joint can become dislocated when the hand is firmly fixed on a surface, such as the floor, and the athlete's body moves and twists the GH joint. The SC joint can receive a direct blow and be dislocated or subluxed.

Signs and Symptoms

A dislocation appears physically deformed. You can see the humeral head or sternum out of normal position. The athlete's complaints include severe pain, inability to move the arm, point tenderness, and loss of feeling into the hand due to trauma to the brachial plexus. Signs of injury include deformity, malalignment, swelling, and ecchymosis. The athlete may be in shock. Signs and symptoms for a subluxation include pain, a feeling of significant movement of the bones during injury, swelling, point tenderness, tingling or numbness in the fingers, and loss of motion. Typically, the signs and symptoms of a GH or SC subluxation are not as significant as with a dislocation.

Immediate Care

If the athlete has dislocated her GH or SC joint, have the athlete stop activity and rest in a comfortable position while you call 911. Splint the arm in the position that you find it (even for a SC dislocation), and apply ice to the injured area. Treat the athlete for shock if signs and symptoms are apparent. While waiting for EMS to arrive, take her bilateral pulse at the radial artery. Compare the pulse rate and quality and determine if her arm has adequate blood flow. Give this information to the EMTs when they arrive. In the ER, the physician will **reduce** the dislocation. Because reduction of the dislocation is painful and the muscles surrounding the joint are tense, the athlete is typically given a sedative or muscle relaxant before the reduction occurs. In some instances, the physician may put the athlete under general anesthesia for reduction. Once in proper position, the athlete's arm is immobilized for up to 3 weeks before rehabilitation begins. The athlete is prescribed nonsteroidal anti-inflammatory drugs (NSAIDs) to assist in decreasing pain and inflammation.

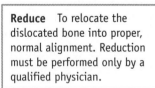

Reduce To relocate the dislocated bone into proper, normal alignment. Reduction must be performed only by a qualified physician.

If an athlete subluxes a GH or SC joint for the first time, splint the arm and ice the area. Depending on the severity of signs and symptoms, you may need to call 911 or refer the athlete to a physician for evaluation. Any time the athlete is in shock, even if the injury is minor, treat the athlete for shock and call 911. For recurrent subluxations without any secondary injuries or complications, refer the athlete to her physician for further evaluation.

Prevention

The athlete must have adequate muscular mass and strength in order to prevent the bones from moving out of alignment when force is applied. Likewise, the athlete must have enough muscular flexibility, active range of motion (AROM), and passive range of motion (PROM) in order to prevent dislocations and subluxations. After the first dislocation or subluxation, surgery may be warranted to prevent additional dislocations and subluxations if rehabilitation alone is not effective. The athlete must wear proper protective gear, and be cognizant of her surroundings, body movements, and positioning to prevent falls, as noted with shoulder fractures.

Separation

A shoulder separation is the term utilized for disruption of the AC joint. The ligaments around the joint are stretched, creating a joint sprain. The injury can be minor, which is referred to as a Grade 1 separation. A Grade 1 separation is a mild AC ligament sprain. A moderate separation, or a Grade 2 separation, is a tear of the AC ligament and a sprain of the coracoclavicular ligament (Starkey, 2013). A severe AC separation is a Grade 3 separation, which is a complete tear, or rupture, of both ligaments. The higher grade of separation requires greater rehabilitation time to restore the athlete's shoulder function.

Mechanism or Cause of Injury

The mechanisms of injury for a separated shoulder are a fall on an outstretched arm or a direct blow to the tip of the shoulder, AC joint, or clavicle.

Signs and Symptoms

An athlete with an AC separation has varying degrees of signs and symptoms, depending on the grade of the injury. The athlete feels discomfort to significant pain. He is unable to move the arm without pain, especially in horizontal adduction (across the front of the body). With higher grades, the AC joint appears deformed, as a large bump, due to the clavicle rising up above the acromion (**Figure 10-5**). The shoulder muscles surrounding the AC joint feel weak.

Immediate Care

Rarely will you need to call 911 for an athlete with an AC separation of any grade. If the athlete goes into shock, which

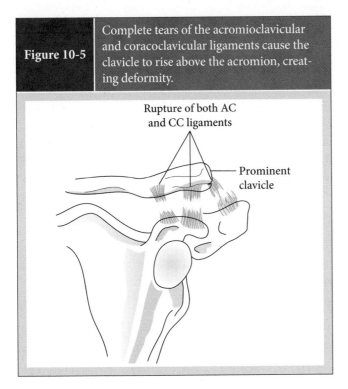

Figure 10-5 Complete tears of the acromioclavicular and coracoclavicular ligaments cause the clavicle to rise above the acromion, creating deformity.

Rupture of both AC and CC ligaments

Prominent clavicle

can occur with many injuries, then call 911 immediately. The athlete may go into shock due to the pain or after visualizing the deformity resulting from a Grade 3 separation. When an athlete sustains a separated shoulder, first perform a secondary survey to evaluate the athlete in an attempt to determine the SINS of the injury. If the athlete has mild signs and symptoms, you most likely do not need to utilize a sling. An ice bag assists in decreasing discomfort. Even with a mild, Grade 1 AC separation, the athlete should not be allowed to return to activity at your facility until he is evaluated and cleared by his physician. If the athlete has moderate to severe signs and symptoms of injury, then utilize a sling to rest the area, and apply ice. You should refer your athlete to his physician for further evaluation.

Typically surgery is not necessary for a Grade 3 AC separation. Proper healing can occur by treating the AC separation with rest, ice, compression, and elevation (RICE). The athlete will most likely wear a specialized immobilization brace to support and rest the arm. The athlete can also take NSAIDs to decrease pain and inflammation. A few weeks of rehabilitation of the shoulder joint and surrounding musculature is necessary in order to regain full ROM and strength.

Prevention

An athlete must pay particular attention to his body position and proximity to other athletes, equipment, and the like to avoid an AC separation. The athlete should also wear protective shoulder padding, depending on what is appropriate for the activity. The athlete must have significant upper extremity ROM and muscular strength in order to prevent an AC separation.

Sprains

Sprains to the shoulder can occur to the AC joint (which was discussed in the shoulder separation section), SC joint, and GH joint. Sprains to the SC joint are not common.

Mechanism or Cause of Injury

A sprain to the SC joint is often caused by a direct blow to the sternum or end of the clavicle. Sprains to both the SC and GH joints can occur due to a fall on an outstretched arm or a blow to the tip of the shoulder. A GH sprain can also be caused by a sudden movement that stretches the joint ligaments. For example, a quarterback who is ready to throw a pass has his shoulder in abduction, away from the body, with his elbow in flexion. If an opposing lineman blocks the pass and strikes the quarterback's arm, forcing it into extension, the anterior GH joint ligaments can be sprained.

Signs and Symptoms

The athlete complains of pain and point tenderness. She cannot move the shoulder through a full ROM without pain. Swelling is present, as well as deformity with Grade 3 SC joint sprains.

Immediate Care

After you have performed a secondary survey, treat the affected joint with RICE. If you suspect the injury is a Grade 2 or 3 sprain, splint the arm to prevent movement, apply ice, and refer the athlete to her physician. Usually Grade 3 sprains are not a medical emergency and do not warrant calling 911. The athlete's physician will prescribe shoulder rehabilitation. Typically the athlete will have to perform GH shoulder ROM as well as shoulder muscle strengthening and flexibility exercises. As with all sprains, the higher the grade of injury, the longer the athlete will be in an immobilized position before rehabilitation begins. Likewise, the duration of Grade 3 SC and GH sprain rehabilitation will be longer. Therefore, the athlete will return to full activity with full shoulder function at a later date as compared to with a Grade 1 or 2 sprain.

Prevention

Entirely preventing shoulder sprains is difficult because direct blows often occur to the area and the shoulder motion is extensive. An athlete must always perform proper body mechanics and skills for her activity. Upper body conditioning in order to

> **Internal forces** Forces that the body creates due to motion and muscle contraction. These forces can cause injury by moving the bones, joints, and soft tissue into a position to which they are not accustomed.

maintain full ROM, flexibility, and strength is important. By having full ROM, flexibility, and strength, her shoulder will be healthy enough to combat any direct blows as well as **internal forces** that can cause a shoulder sprain.

Glenohumeral Joint Instability

GH joint instability is excessive movement of the humeral head out of its normal position as it sits in the glenoid fossa. The instability is classified as anterior, posterior, or inferior, which means the athlete has excessive humeral head motion in these respective directions. Most often, athletes have multidirectional instability, which means the athlete has instability in more than one direction. Typically an athlete has inferior instability concurrently with either anterior or posterior instability. However, an athlete can have instability in all three directions.

Mechanism or Cause of Injury

GH joint instabilities can occur to an athlete who has had a traumatic event such as a GH dislocation or subluxation. The instability can also result over time if the athlete has had severe joint ligament and capsular sprains. Some athletes, such as swimmers and gymnasts, require significant ROM at the GH joint. Over time they have stretched the ligaments and/or capsule surrounding the GH joint. The result is significant laxity or looseness of these soft tissue structures around the joint. This laxity causes instability.

Signs and Symptoms

The athlete complains of "looseness" and joint laxity. He may complain that during motion he feels the humeral head sliding or moving out of joint, along with clicking, popping, or crepitus. The athlete may have pain, especially in the area corresponding to the instability during motion (i.e., if he has posterior instability, he will have posterior pain). He will most likely have a decreased AROM due to joint pain, and muscular impingement, especially with an anterior GH joint instability (Prentice, 2011).

Immediate Care

The athlete should stop activity if he feels GH joint instability, so he does not injure himself further. If he is experiencing pain, provide him with an ice pack to apply to the injured area. Refer him to a physician for further evaluation. He may or may not need surgery, depending on the extent of instability and how much the condition affects his activities, including

ADLs. His physician may prescribe a conservative treatment approach at first, which includes strengthening the musculature surrounding the joint.

Prevention

In order to prevent GH joint instability, the athlete must abide by the prevention strategies for GH dislocations, subluxations, and sprains. The athlete must make sure he has full ROM, flexibility, and most importantly muscular strength around the joint. Muscle strength is important to help the humeral head maintain its position during motion.

Strains

Shoulder muscle strains typically occur to the biceps brachii, triceps brachii, and rotator cuff. Among these three muscle groups, the biceps brachii is most commonly ruptured.

Mechanism or Cause of Injury

As with any other strain, shoulder strains are caused by a forceful concentric or eccentric muscle contraction. A strain can also be caused by a passive muscular stretch. Most often the biceps brachii and rotator cuff muscles are strained during overhead activities, including throwing and swimming. The muscles are typically strained during the eccentric contractions that occur in the follow-through phase of throwing.

Signs and Symptoms

The athlete complains of pain with AROM, especially when mimicking the overhead throwing motion. The pain may not appear immediately; instead, the pain may appear hours after the activity has stopped. She may also complain of a dull ache in the muscles while at rest. Weak and point tender muscles are evident. For Grade 3 strains (ruptures), the athlete cannot contract the injured muscle if the origin or insertion tendon is ruptured. If the tendons are intact but some muscle fibers are ruptured, the athlete may be able to partially contract the muscle. A bulge and/or divot in the muscle indicate the tendon and/or muscle belly fibers are ruptured. The muscle looks deformed (**Figure 10-6**).

Immediate Care

To care for all shoulder muscle strains, apply the RICE principle. Intermittent ice application and rest from the causative activity are effective for treating Grade 1 strains. Referral to a physician for these mild strains may not be necessary; however, the athlete should be referred to a physician for any strain that causes muscular weakness, loss of function, moderate pain, and tingling into the arm and the hand. If you suspect the athlete has sustained a muscle or tendon rupture, has

| Figure 10-6 | A pectoralis major muscle rupture indicating a divot where the tendon has ruptured. |

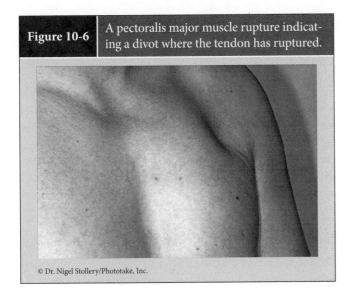

© Dr. Nigel Stollery/Phototake, Inc.

numbness into the arm and hand, or severe pain, then call 911 to summon advanced medical care. The athlete most likely will be in shock when she has sustained a muscle rupture. Treat for shock while you simultaneously splint the injured area and wait for EMS to arrive.

Prevention

In order to prevent shoulder strains, your athlete must have adequate muscle flexibility. The athlete needs adequate muscle strength without one muscle group stronger than another (e.g., biceps brachii significantly stronger than triceps brachii). This muscular strength balance allows for proper co-contractions during movement. The athlete must properly perform the activity skill (e.g., proper overhead throwing) and a proper warm-up and cool-down.

> **Syndrome** A group of signs and symptoms that, when put together, indicate a particular injury, illness, condition, or disease.

Impingement Syndrome

Impingement **syndrome** occurs most often with the supraspinatus tendon, but can also involve the subacromion bursa and long head tendon of the biceps brachii. The extremely small space underneath the acromion process, which is called the subacromial space, is where these soft tissue structures are located. When the humerus is raised away from the body in abduction, the acromion presses upon, or impinges, the supraspinatus tendon. Three stages of rotator cuff impingement syndrome exist (Neer, 1972). The first stage occurs in athletes under the age of 25. The athlete experiences signs and symptoms of an acute inflammatory response at the tendon. Stage 2 impingement affects the 25- to 40-year-old

athlete population. The athlete's tendon is fibrotic, which means excess connective and scar tissue has formed. As well as having a fibrotic tendon, the athlete is classified as having supraspinatus tendinitis. Stage 3 impingement affects athletes over the age of 40. In stage 3, due to the long period of time the syndrome has existed, the acromion has osteophytes, or tiny bone spurs, formed along its arch. At this point, the rotator cuff tendon is significantly weakened and may rupture.

Mechanism or Cause of Injury

The cause of rotator cuff impingement syndrome includes a variety of factors. The athlete may be participating in an activity in which overhead throwing or arm motion occurs in a repetitive manner. Direct trauma to the area can cause impingement. Muscular imbalance, rotator cuff weakness, GH instability, AC joint arthritis, abnormal acromion structure (especially if the acromion is hooked anteriorly), a thickened or calcified coracoacromial ligament, and a thick subacromial bursa are all causes of impingement syndrome (Fongemie, Buss, & Rolnick, 1998).

Signs and Symptoms

Because rotator cuff impingement syndrome is more of a chronic condition than an acute injury, the signs and symptoms appear slowly. As the athlete continues to utilize the GH joint in an overhead position, the supraspinatus tendon continues to be impinged. Over time the tendon develops micro tears and becomes seriously inflamed. The athlete complains of pain, which may even exist at rest and at night while sleeping. She also is unable to raise the arm into a cocked, overhead, abducted, and externally rotated position due to pain and muscle weakness.

Tips from the Field

Tip 1 When performing a secondary survey for an athlete who has a chronic shoulder injury, determine whether the injury is impingement syndrome by asking the athlete to point with one finger where the pain is the worst. If she points at the GH joint from the lateral or anterior sides and states that the pain is coming from deep inside, then suspect the athlete has supraspinatus impingement. If the athlete points anteriorly and is very point tender superficially, then the biceps brachii is most likely impinged.

Immediate Care

If an athlete has impingement syndrome, have the athlete stop all upper extremity activities with the affected arm and refer her to a physician for evaluation. Fortunately, Stage 1

> **Therapeutic modalities**
> Mediums and interventions that can be used to assist in treating an injury or illness. Electrostimulation, ultrasound, and massage are types of therapeutic modalities.

impingement can be treated in most cases with RICE, **therapeutic modalities**, and rehabilitation. Stage 2 and 3 impingement can only be treated with surgery. After surgery is performed, the athlete participates in lengthy rehabilitation. With her physician's consent, the athlete can participate in lower body exercise activities during the course of treatment during any stage of impingement.

Prevention

The athlete must listen to her body in order to prevent impingement syndrome. When performing upper extremity overhead activities, if she begins to feel discomfort, the athlete should immediately apply ice and refrain from activities that cause the discomfort until the discomfort subsides. If she does not take preventative measures, she may develop impingement syndrome in the near future. The athlete needs good flexibility and muscular strength for all muscles that move the shoulder joint.

Tendinitis

The rotator cuff and biceps brachii muscles are commonly inflamed. The tendons can become acutely or chronically inflamed, but most often tendinitis of these muscles is a chronic condition because the injury occurs over a long duration.

Mechanism or Cause of Injury

Shoulder tendinitis can occur due to repetitive, low-intensity contractions; a sudden, violent muscle contraction; acute trauma to the muscle or tendon; and poor upper body posture (MedlinePlus, 2011). If the athlete maintains his arm in a stationary position for a period of time (e.g., when sleeping), the tendons can be stressed. As with impingement syndrome, an athlete who performs repetitive overhead activities, such as a baseball pitcher or swimmer, is more susceptible to tendinitis.

Signs and Symptoms

The athlete feels pain and crepitus. The biceps brachii tendon may subluxate from its position in the bicipital groove. The athlete has point tenderness and loss of function. Over time the tendon thickens and appears larger than on the contralateral side. This thickening causes tendon inflexibility.

Immediate Care

The athlete should utilize RICE in an attempt to make the signs and symptoms of injury subside. If the signs and symptoms do not subside within a few days, then the athlete should be evaluated by a physician. The physician will most likely prescribe NSAIDs, rest, and rehabilitation.

Prevention

The athlete must concentrate on strengthening the affected and opposing muscles (e.g., the triceps brachii muscle opposes the biceps brachii). Avoiding overhead activities and resting the shoulders after strenuous activity can help avoid shoulder tendinitis. The athlete needs to continue to stretch and strengthen the musculature to allow for full ROM and avoid muscular weakness.

Contusion

Because the biceps brachii muscle is an anterior shoulder and upper arm structure, it is very susceptible to contusions.

Mechanism or Cause of Injury

As with any other contusion, the mechanism of injury for a biceps brachii contusion is a direct blow to the muscle. Typically an implement, such as a bat or stick; part of another athlete's body, such as an arm or fist; or an object, such as a ball, strikes the biceps brachii and causes the contusion.

Signs and Symptoms

A biceps brachii contusion results in various signs and symptoms including pain, muscular weakness, loss of function, transitory paralysis, muscle spasm, ecchymosis, swelling, tingling into the hand, and point tenderness.

Immediate Care

When the athlete notifies you of her injury, perform a secondary survey to rule out a humerus fracture. If she does not appear to have sustained a humerus fracture, immediately apply ice and compression to the contused area. If she has significant pain, splint her by utilizing a sling. Instruct the athlete to apply RICE to the area. With a biceps brachii contusion, aggressive stretching should be avoided, and heat should not be applied for the first 72 hours.

A complication that can arise from a deep tissue biceps brachii contusion is myositis ossificans, which is a bony growth that forms in the muscle. Typically, myositis ossificans forms where the hemorrhage exists. Although the exact cause of myositis ossificans has not been determined, aggressive muscle stretching and heat application while the injury is in the inflammatory phase are two predisposing factors for acquiring myositis ossificans.

If after utilizing RICE the signs and symptoms do not subside within a few days, tell the athlete to see a physician for evaluation.

If at any time you are unsure whether the injury is more extensive, treat the injury as if it is a fracture and summon EMS.

▊ Prevention

Athletes should be aware of their surroundings at all times. They can prevent accidental contusions, such as walking into a barbell in the gym, by being cognizant of their actions. Athletes should wear upper extremity protective gear and padding as appropriate for their activities.

Adhesive Capsulitis

Adhesive capsulitis is also referred to as frozen shoulder. The athlete is not able to move the shoulder due to joint capsule inflammation.

▊ Mechanism or Cause of Injury

The actual cause of adhesive capsulitis is unknown; however, it may result from direct or indirect trauma and repetitive motion. The inflammation makes the athlete unable to move the GH joint through a ROM. Other factors that predispose an athlete to having adhesive capsulitis are shoulder surgery, cervical disc disease, open heart surgery, hyperthyroidism, and diabetes (PubMed Health, 2010b).

▊ Signs and Symptoms

Adhesive capsulitis is painful, and due to the significant pain, the athlete is unable to move the shoulder. The shoulder becomes very stiff and, even when pain subsides, the athlete cannot move his GH joint.

▊ Immediate Care

If your athlete has frozen shoulder with a significant amount of pain, have him be evaluated by a physician immediately. Use RICE to make the symptoms subside. Further care for adhesive capsulitis includes NSAIDs, rehabilitation, and possibly steroid injections to alleviate pain and inflammation. The physician may decide that surgery, followed by rehabilitation, is the athlete's only option. Even with treatment, it may take up to a year for an athlete with adhesive capsulitis to have normal shoulder function. Without any treatment, the athlete's shoulder should return to normal function within 2 years (PubMed Health, 2010b).

▊ Prevention

If your athlete has any conditions such as diabetes and hyperthyroidism, these conditions must be under control in order to prevent adhesive capsulitis. Also, if the athlete begins to feel shoulder pain accompanied by stiffness, the athlete must utilize RICE, ROM, and flexibility exercises immediately to avoid the condition progressing to frozen shoulder.

Brachial Plexus Stretch Injury

The brachial plexus is a pathway of nerves located in the neck and shoulder region on both sides of the body. A brachial plexus stretch injury is also called a stinger or a burner. These injuries typically occur in contact sports, most often in football and wrestling.

▊ Mechanism or Cause of Injury

A brachial plexus stretch injury occurs when the shoulder is depressed and the neck is either rotated away or tilted laterally from the depressed shoulder. The shoulder can be depressed by an object or another athlete pressing on the top of the shoulder (e.g., blocking in football), or by another athlete grabbing the athlete's wrist and pulling the injured athlete's arm down (e.g., in wrestling).

▊ Signs and Symptoms

An athlete with a brachial plexus stretch injury feels burning, tingling, or numbness down his arm to the fingers. He will have temporary loss of function for up to a few minutes. In more severe cases, the athlete has abnormal sensations that linger for days after the injury occurred. As time progresses, these sensations subside. When sensation has been restored, function also is restored; however, the athlete may also have residual muscular weakness through the entire arm.

▊ Immediate Care

Immediately after the injury, instruct the athlete to regain sensation in his hand by flexing and extending his fingers by making a fist, then fully opening his hand, as well as moving the wrist in all directions, and flexing and extending his elbow. As he is doing these ROM activities, complete a secondary survey to determine if he has any other injuries that warrant immediate treatment. Within a few minutes he should have full function, including sensation. The athlete cannot return to play if he does not have full sensation, ROM, and strength in the affected upper extremity and neck, as compared to the contralateral side. If the symptoms do not subside quickly, he should go to see his physician as soon as possible. The physician may prescribe pain medication and therapeutic modalities to alleviate pain. Surgery is rarely performed. If the athlete has sustained multiple brachial plexus stretch injuries and nerve damage has occurred, then surgery with rehabilitation following the procedure may be the only option to restore function.

▊ Prevention

Preventing brachial plexus stretch injury is difficult, but the risk of injury can be minimized by performing daily arm and neck ROM, flexibility, and strengthening exercises. Instruct your athlete on how to properly perform all activities, while utilizing proper form and skills at all times.

Thoracic Outlet Syndrome

The thoracic outlet is the area at the neck between the clavicle and the first rib. Nerves and blood vessels run through this area. Thoracic outlet syndrome (TOS) is a condition in which these nerves and/or blood vessels become compressed in this space.

▮ Mechanism or Cause of Injury

Although the specific mechanism of TOS is not often determined, it can be caused by direct trauma or repetitive injuries to the thoracic outlet area. An athlete may have an extra rib, which is an anatomical abnormality. This extra rib can compress on the structures in the thoracic outlet space.

▮ Signs and Symptoms

TOS causes pain in the area, along with tingling or numbness down the arm and into the fingers. The athlete may experience pain in the neck and shoulders, and a dull, weak feeling in the injured arm and hand. The athlete's grip is weakened on the affected side. The pulse on the affected side is slower and weaker, or perhaps nonexistent by palpation, as compared to the uninjured arm.

▮ Immediate Care

Treatment for TOS consists of medication and therapeutic modalities for pain relief and muscle relaxation, along with rehabilitation. In some instances the physician may perform surgery on the athlete to restore function. Rehabilitation will follow surgery. If TOS is not treated, then permanent injury to the nerves and blood vessels can result.

▮ Prevention

TOS can be prevented by not carrying heavy objects, such as boxes, bags, or purses, over the same shoulder repetitively. The athlete should stretch the anterior shoulder and neck muscles, including the pectoralis major. If the athlete is overweight, she must lose weight to prevent or decrease symptoms of TOS. By losing the weight, compression and stress on the nerves and blood vessels in the thoracic outlet space will decrease (Mayo Clinic, 2010).

INJURIES TO THE ELBOW AND FOREARM

The elbow consists of the humerus, radius, and ulna bones. The forearm is considered the area between the elbow and the wrist where the radius and ulna lie. Elbow and forearm injuries can occur alone or in conjunction with other injuries to the upper extremity. As with shoulder injuries, elbow and forearm injuries can be acute or chronic, with some injuries necessitating emergency care.

Fractures

Radius and ulna fractures can occur separately when only one bone is fractured, or both bones can be fractured simultaneously. When a significant forearm injury occurs, such as a fracture, or a dislocation occurs to the elbow, you must determine if the athlete is experiencing Volkmann's contracture. Volkmann's contracture can result from a traumatic injury to the upper extremity, particularly at the elbow, humerus, or forearm, which causes significant swelling. The edema presses on the blood vessels. Consequently, the blood vessels cannot deliver oxygenated blood to the distal upper extremity. If lack of blood flow to the distal extremity continues, then the nerves and soft tissues become damaged. This damage could be permanent. The insufficient blood flow and oxygen cause the hand to take on a claw-like appearance (**Figure 10**-7) due to muscle contracture from lack of oxygen to the tissues. The muscles in the forearm and hand are contracted in a flexed position. The athlete cannot passively extend the fingers. Volkmann's contracture is a medical emergency. As the athlete's caregiver, there is not much first aid that you can perform for Volkmann's contracture, other than to call 911 and treat for shock. Check the athlete's radial pulse and touch her fingers and hand on the affected side and ask her if she can feel your touch. When the EMTs arrive at the scene, inform them of your findings. If the athlete's blood flow to the distal extremity is not restored immediately, via addressing the causative factor such as the fracture or dislocation, then the possibility of losing distal extremity function exists. In cases of Volkmann's contracture, surgery may be necessary.

▮ Mechanism or Cause of Injury

Acute elbow and forearm fractures can occur from a fall on an outstretched arm. Fractures can also be caused by a direct

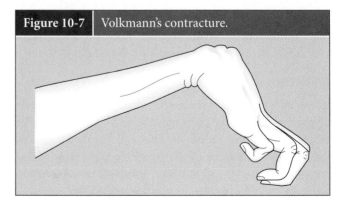

| **Figure 10-7** | Volkmann's contracture. |

blow to the area, which most often occurs in contact sports, especially those utilizing implements, such as lacrosse and field hockey. An athlete can also be in a weight-bearing position where the hand is fixed on an immovable surface, such as the ground or a mat. The athlete twists his body while his hand remains fixed, resulting in a fracture. Due to twisting of the radius and ulna, a spiral fracture would most likely result with this weight-bearing mechanism of injury. This mechanism of injury could occur in gymnastic events such as floor and vault apparatus.

Signs and Symptoms

The athlete experiences severe pain, point tenderness, and loss of function. If the nerves in the elbow and forearm are affected, then he will have loss of sensation. Other signs and symptoms include loss of function, muscle spasm, swelling, and ecchymosis. If he has deformity, then the fractured bones are displaced

Immediate Care

Treat the athlete as you would for any other fracture. Have the athlete keep the arm still, make sure he is comfortable, and call 911. Splint the area using boards, SAM splints (www.sam-medical.com/sam_splint.html), or any other stabilizing materials (**Figure 10-8**). Apply ice on the injured area, while taking care not to apply an ice bag that is too heavy, which would cause an increase in symptoms or complications. Watch for Volkmann's contracture and shock to arise. Once the athlete is at the ER, the physician will evaluate the injury, take x-rays, and cast or splint the area. After the cast or splint is removed the athlete will have to undergo rehabilitation for the entire upper extremity in order to restore full function.

Prevention

Athletes must wear appropriate protective equipment and padding in order to prevent elbow and forearm fractures. Athletes should have adequate ROM, flexibility, and muscular strength at the forearm, as well as muscular coordination and balance, especially if they perform upper extremity weight-bearing activities. Weight-bearing activities help keep bones strong. As noted with shoulder fractures, the athlete must have a good supply of calcium and vitamin D in his diet, to assist in keeping his bones strong. If the athlete has strong bones, the potential for fractures can be minimized.

Dislocations

Dislocations at the elbow occur to the ulna. The ulna is forced out of its alignment with the humerus, most commonly into a posterior position relative to the joint (**Figure 10-9**). As with any other dislocation, an elbow dislocation is a medical emergency, and the possibility of Volkmann's contracture exists. Likewise, dislocations often occur along with elbow and forearm fractures.

Mechanism or Cause of Injury

An elbow dislocation occurs with significant trauma. A direct blow can dislocate the elbow. Also, a fall on an outstretched arm with the elbow in a slight degree of flexion will force the ulna out of alignment and dislocate posteriorly.

Signs and Symptoms

An athlete with a dislocated elbow most likely will be in shock. The elbow appears significantly swollen and deformed. Her forearm on the injured side appears shortened

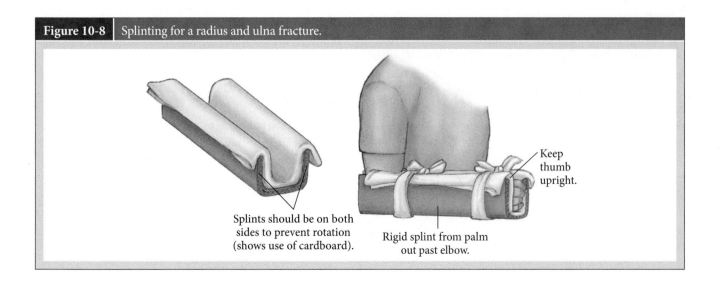

Figure 10-8 | Splinting for a radius and ulna fracture.

Splints should be on both sides to prevent rotation (shows use of cardboard).

Rigid splint from palm out past elbow.

Keep thumb upright.

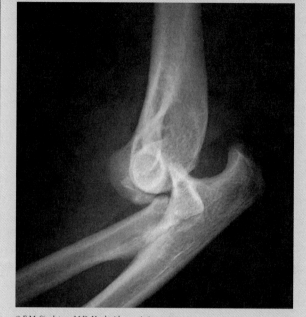

Figure 10-9 An elbow dislocation typically occurs when the ulna is forced posteriorly.

© E.M. Singletary, M.D. Used with permission.

Neurovascular compromise
The body's nerves and blood vessels are detrimentally affected due to trauma. Consequently, the nerves and blood vessels will not be able to perform their actions as they should.

due to its posterior displacement. Severe pain and loss of function may exist, as well as loss of sensation from her forearm to fingers, due to **neurovascular compromise**.

Immediate Care

Treat an athlete with an elbow dislocation as you would for any other medical emergency. Immediately phone 911. Make sure the athlete is in a comfortable position and supporting the injured elbow. Splint the elbow in the position that you find it. Apply ice to the injured area to help decrease pain. Take her radial pulse and determine her hand and fingers sensation as you would for an elbow fracture and Volkmann's contracture. Most importantly, treat her for shock until EMS arrives.

In the ER, the physician will reduce the elbow and put the ulna back into normal alignment. X-rays will determine whether a fracture also exists. The athlete will be splinted with her arm in a sling. The athlete must apply ice frequently to the injured area with the splint removed, as per the physician's orders. Within a few weeks rehabilitation begins. Eventually the splint is removed permanently.

Prevention

Falling on an outstretched arm is a common mechanism of injury, so your athlete should attempt to avoid falling in this manner. If the athlete falls, she should have her body positioned to roll on the ground as she strikes the surface. The athlete must take care when exposing herself to a situation where she could fall. Good muscular strength around the elbow helps to prevent an elbow dislocation.

Sprains

Sprains to the elbow typically occur to the ulnar collateral ligament (UCL) or the radial collateral ligament (RCL). These ligaments support the medial and lateral sides of the elbow, respectively.

Mechanism or Cause of Injury

The UCL and RCL can be injured by a fall on an outstretched arm, a fixed hand with twisting of the arm, or a direct blow to the elbow. The UCL is injured by a force applied to the elbow's lateral side, compressing that area, which results in a traction force on the elbow's medial side where the UCL is located. This force, called a valgus force, stretches and sprains the UCL. Likewise, the RCL is injured by a force applied to the elbow's medial side, compressing that area, which creates a traction force on the elbow's lateral side causing a RCL sprain. This force is called a varus force. UCL injuries often occur when the arm is in a cocked position and the athlete throws a ball with the elbow using an improper side-arm position. Repetitive side-arm throwing motions cause UCL tears, because the athlete's arm is in a valgus position.

Signs and Symptoms

Signs and symptoms of elbow sprains include all inflammation signs and symptoms such as pain, redness, swelling, point tenderness, ecchymosis, increased skin temperature at the injured area, loss of function or function with pain, and joint instability.

Immediate Care

If you suspect the athlete has sustained an elbow sprain, have the athlete discontinue activity and rest. Rule out any other serious injuries such as a fracture or dislocation. Have the athlete apply ice and compression to the elbow. Elevate the elbow by applying a sling. Depending on the severity of the injury, you may need to refer the athlete for a physician's evaluation. The physician will prescribe NSAIDs and possibly have the athlete wear a splint or sling until signs and symptoms of injury decrease. Surgery is not performed for a common, uncomplicated elbow sprain.

Prevention

Athletes must wear protective elbow padding as required by their activity. They must be aware of their surroundings including opponents, implements, immovable structures, and the like when participating in activities in order to prevent sprains to the elbow.

Little League Elbow

Little league elbow is an overuse injury that occurs to the medial elbow of throwing athletes, especially pitchers. This injury is a syndrome that includes growth complications at the medial epicondyle, medial epicondylitis (which will be discussed later in this chapter), and **apophysitis**. The syndrome is considered to be a chronic inflammation of the medial epicondyle.

> **Apophysitis** Inflammation of a bony outgrowth. Common areas of apophysitis include the medial epicondyle (Little League elbow) and tibial tubercle (Osgood Schlatter's disease).

Mechanism or Cause of Injury

Athletes can succumb to little league elbow from repetitive overhead throwing. Usually it occurs to young pitchers who throw too many hard, fast pitches during practices and games. Because the growth plates of children and adolescents are not yet fused, the stress from constant throwing causes weakness at the medial epicondyle, and little league elbow results. The primary force causing this syndrome is a valgus force to the elbow.

Signs and Symptoms

The main symptom of little league elbow is pain at the medial elbow. This pain worsens if the athlete continues to throw, and becomes most painful when the athlete attempts elbow extension. Also, the pain remains for days after the last throwing day. The athlete complains of muscular weakness, loss of coordination, control, and function. The elbow may be swollen and point tender at the medial epicondyle.

Immediate Care

Explain to the athlete the cause of little league elbow, and have him stop the causative factor, which is throwing and/or throwing improperly. If the causative factor is not removed or corrected, then the injury will get worse. Rest is very important for little league elbow. The area needs sufficient time to heal. Have the athlete apply RICE and see how the injury responds to treatment. If the athlete's injury heals well, then he should begin muscle strengthening around the elbow. A slow return to throwing, called a throwing progression, can begin once ROM,

strength, and coordination at the elbow have been regained. If the athlete does not respond to RICE, then he should see his physician for further evaluation. In severe cases where part of the medial epicondyle is avulsed from the humerus, surgery is necessary to secure the fractured bony pieces.

Prevention

The athlete must be aware of how much he throws. Baseball pitch counts are helpful to keep track of how many times the athlete has thrown in one practice or game. The athlete must throw properly, and not subject the elbow to undue valgus forces. Very young athletes should not be throwing breaking balls, such as curve balls and sliders, because these pitches put excessive amounts of stress on the immature medial elbow. Once the athlete is an adolescent, then he can learn the proper way to throw these pitches without predisposing his elbow to little league elbow. A variety of information regarding training and pitch counts for little league players can be found at www.littleleague.org.

Strains

Muscle strains at the elbow most often occur at the biceps brachii, triceps brachii, and anterior forearm muscles. Forearm muscle strains are often referred to as forearm splints; these often occur to athletes who repetitively utilize their wrist in flexion or extension activities. Gymnasts who are pommel horse specialists and keep their wrists in extension for the majority of their routine, and weight lifters who perform wrist curls are two examples of athletes who could sustain forearm splints.

Mechanism or Cause of Injury

The mechanism of injury is a repetitive overuse of the muscles. The muscles can also be stretched for an extended period of time, which can cause the fibers to tear. A one-time forceful muscle contraction or stretch can also cause a muscle strain.

Signs and Symptoms

Elbow and forearm muscle strains are similar in signs and symptoms as shoulder muscle strains, especially because some of the same muscles are involved. The athlete experiences pain, which may appear immediately, hours, or days after injury; loss of function; and point tenderness. The area may be swollen, red, and warm. Ecchymosis may appear. A Grade 3 biceps brachii tendon sprain or rupture at the insertion appears like a large bulge in the middle of the humerus (**Figure 10-10**). A divot or depression would also be present. This divot indicates that the tendon is no longer attached to the bone.

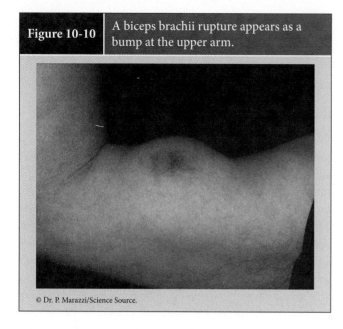

Figure 10-10 | A biceps brachii rupture appears as a bump at the upper arm.

© Dr. P. Marazzi/Science Source.

Immediate Care

Care for an elbow and forearm strain includes RICE. If the athlete is in severe pain, has no muscle function, and/or has any signs or symptoms that indicate a Grade 3 strain, call 911 for advanced medical care.

Prevention

Muscular strength and flexibility are extremely important to prevent and minimize muscular strains. The athlete should strengthen the muscles around the elbow and forearm regularly, which protects them against excessive stress and resultant injury.

Lateral and Medial Epicondylitis

Epicondylitis is chronic overuse injury, which is a type of a muscular strain. It is an inflammation of the tendons that attach to the epicondyles of the humerus at the bony prominence of the elbow. Medial epicondylitis is often referred to as golfer's elbow, whereas lateral epicondylitis is often referred to as tennis elbow.

Mechanism or Cause of Injury

Medial epicondylitis is caused by repetitive, forceful wrist flexion. The injury is called golfer's elbow because during the golf follow-through swing, some golfers incorrectly perform the skill and flex the wrist. Lateral epicondylitis, or tennis elbow, is caused by repetitive forceful wrist extension. A tennis player performs an incorrect backhand and extends the wrist, which is supposed to be straight. Over time, lateral epicondylitis

develops. Both of these injuries most often do not occur from sport activities, but rather from other daily, repetitive, physical activities, such as computer work, gardening, construction, and the like.

Signs and Symptoms

Signs and symptoms for medial and lateral epicondylitis are the same. Pain at the epicondyle, along with muscular weakness, are the prominent signs and symptoms of epicondylitis. Grip strength is weak. Therefore, performing ADLs such as opening a can with a manual can opener, turning a doorknob, and holding a cup is difficult and uncomfortable. The athlete is point tender at the epicondyle, and swelling may be visible. The pain may eventually occur during all activities utilizing the elbow, wrist, and fingers. Without treatment, over time the pain may perpetuate as a dull ache throughout the day at rest.

Immediate Care

In order to stop any further exacerbation of signs and symptoms, have the athlete stop the causing activity and utilize RICE to decrease signs and symptoms. If the signs and symptoms persist throughout the day, then the athlete must see a physician for evaluation. The physician may prescribe NSAIDs to decrease pain and inflammation. The athlete may wear a brace, called a counterforce brace, distal to the epicondyles. This brace decreases stress on the injured tendons as the muscles contract, and also provides compression. In some cases the physician may provide a **corticosteroid** injection to promote healing and decrease pain to the injured tendons and muscles. Rehabilitation must follow the corticosteroid injection. The muscles and tendons around the epicondyle must be strong to prevent recurrence.

> **Corticosteroid** A medication used to minimize inflammation. Corticosteroids prevent detrimental chemical mediators from being produced after injury during the inflammatory phase of healing. They can be given to an athlete by mouth, injection, or intravenously. The medication also comes in eye solutions and topical creams.

Even with treatment, epicondylitis may take many months to subside. If after a year the athlete continues to have significant signs and symptoms of epicondylitis that affect her ADLs and conservative treatment has not proven to be effective, then surgery is performed.

Prevention

The athlete must always use proper form when participating in physical activities to avoid epicondylitis. If the athlete does not know how to perform a skill properly, assist her in learning proper skill execution. Elbow muscles and tendons must be strong enough to minimize the potential for epicondylitis.

Olecranon Bursitis

The olecranon bursa sits on the olecranon between the bone and the skin. Olecranon bursitis is an inflammation of the bursa. Normally you cannot feel the bursa. Fluid collects in the bursa when it is inflamed, however, and you can easily palpate and visualize it in this condition.

Mechanism or Cause of Injury

Olecranon bursitis can be acute or chronic. Acute bursitis is caused by a direct blow to the olecranon when the elbow is flexed. Chronic bursitis is caused by constant rubbing of an object on the olecranon, such as an improperly fitted elbow pad.

Signs and Symptoms

The athlete feels pain and has loss of ROM, especially in elbow flexion. Acute bursitis often makes the elbow appear deformed, because the swelling is very localized. The bursa is swollen and resembles a ping pong ball inside the elbow at the olecranon (**Figure 10-11**). The chronic bursitis swelling is more diffuse

| Figure 10-11 | Acute olecranon bursitis. |

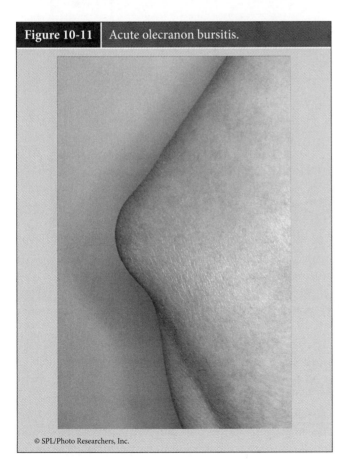

© SPL/Photo Researchers, Inc.

than for acute bursitis. Ecchymosis and point tenderness will most likely be present, as well as red and warm skin.

Immediate Care

The force required to cause acute olecranon bursitis is hard enough to potentially cause an olecranon or proximal ulna fracture. Therefore, apply ice, wrap the arm with an elastic bandage, and put it in a sling. Refer the athlete to a physician to have x-rays taken to rule out a fracture. For chronic bursitis due to friction, advise the athlete to remove the causative factor. Apply ice and a compression wrap. She may be able to continue limited participation if she wears a compression sleeve, applies ice intermittently, and takes over-the-counter NSAIDs. If the athlete's signs and symptoms do not decrease, then refer her to a physician for evaluation. For both acute and chronic olecranon bursitis, the physician will prescribe NSAIDs, therapeutic modalities, compression, and rehabilitation. In some cases, the bursa may need to be drained to relieve the accumulated fluid. Also, corticosteroids may be injected into the bursa.

Prevention

The athlete must wear well-fitted elbow pads whenever participating in activities where the potential for the olecranon to receive a direct blow exists. Likewise, the elbow pads must fit properly in order to prevent rubbing of the pad on the skin.

Ulnar Nerve Injury

The ulnar nerve runs along the elbow's medial side. Because the nerve sits very superficial to the skin and is lodged between the medial epicondyle of the humerus and the ulna, it is often predisposed to injury.

Mechanism or Cause of Injury

The ulnar nerve can be injured by a direct blow to the medial elbow. When this injury occurs, the athlete may say that he "hit his funny bone." Continual pressure on or stretching of the nerve can cause ulnar nerve injury. If an athlete sleeps with his arm flexed, he may awaken to a tingling forearm and fourth and fifth fingers. The nerve may also be compromised if another elbow injury exists, such as medial epicondylitis, little league elbow, a UCL sprain, a fracture, or a dislocation. The edema from the other injury compresses the nerve and create signs and symptoms of an ulnar nerve injury.

Signs and Symptoms

Signs and symptoms of ulnar nerve injury include transient pain at the injury site, and tingling and numbness down the elbow to the fourth and fifth fingers. The hand is also weak, especially when attempting to grip with the fourth and fifth fingers. Over time, if the injury is not treated, the athlete will have visible atrophy of some hand and forearm muscles.

Immediate Care

To care for an ulnar nerve injury that occurs due to a direct blow to the ulnar nerve, have the athlete move his fingers, hand, and wrist as much as possible until feeling is restored. Feeling should be restored within a few seconds to minutes. Typically after a direct blow to the elbow, the athlete does not experience any other complications and can return to activity if he has full elbow, wrist, and hand ROM and strength. Ice should not be applied directly on top of the nerve because the nerve is very superficial. Direct ice on the nerve can damage it if the ice is left on too long.

For other ulnar nerve injuries not caused by a direct blow, or if sensation, ROM, and strength at the elbow do not return to normal, the athlete should be evaluated by a physician. Rehabilitation and perhaps occupational therapy for the elbow and hand will be warranted. Specialized splints can be utilized to wear during the day and while sleeping to assist in keeping the elbow at a comfortable position and avoiding full flexion. The physician may inject corticosteroids into the area to decrease pain and minimize inflammation. Other medications such as over-the-counter or prescription NSAIDs may be prescribed.

Prevention

Preventing ulnar nerve injury includes having the athlete correctly wear properly fitted elbow pads, splints, and other equipment. The athlete should also avoid holding the elbow in a flexed position for long periods of time during the day and while sleeping, if possible.

INJURIES TO THE WRIST, HAND, AND FINGERS

Although the wrists, hands, and fingers are small body areas, they make a significant contribution to body function and activity. The hands and fingers provide grip and dexterity. Full function of each joint is truly important. Many wrist, hand, and finger injuries are not medical emergencies; however, the significance of the injuries and importance of proper treatment cannot be overestimated.

Fractures

Fractures can occur to any of the wrist, hand, and finger bones; however, the most common fractures are to the distal end of the radius (called a Colles' fracture; **Figure 10-12**), the fifth metacarpal (called a boxer's fracture; **Figure 10-13**), the base of the first metacarpal (called a Bennett's fracture), and other

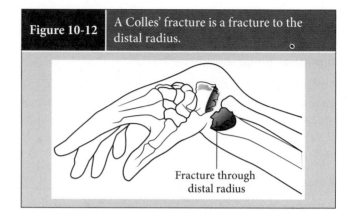

| **Figure 10-12** | A Colles' fracture is a fracture to the distal radius. |

Fracture through distal radius

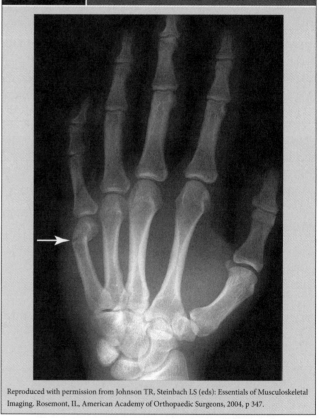

| **Figure 10-13** | A fracture to the distal 5th metacarpal is a "boxer's fracture". |

Reproduced with permission from Johnson TR, Steinbach LS (eds): Essentials of Musculoskeletal Imaging. Rosemont, IL, American Academy of Orthopaedic Surgeons, 2004, p 347.

metacarpals, such as the third metacarpal (**Figure 10-14**), the scaphoid, the hamate, and the phalanges.

Mechanism or Cause of Injury

Fractures to the bones just mentioned are most often injured by a direct traumatic force. A Colles' fracture typically occurs when an athlete falls on an outstretched arm. A boxer's fracture can occur

| Figure 10-14 | A displaced, transverse fracture to the 3rd metacarpal. |

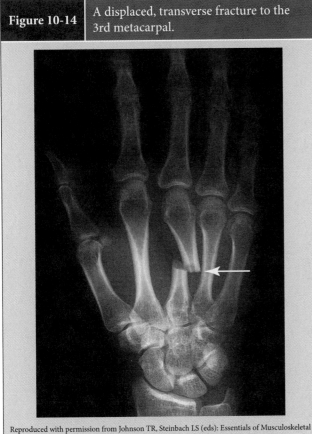

Reproduced with permission from Johnson TR, Steinbach LS (eds): Essentials of Musculoskeletal Imaging. Rosemont, IL, American Academy of Orthopaedic Surgeons, 2004, p 347.

when an athlete strikes a hard, immovable object with a closed fist. A Bennett's fracture occurs when an object strikes or an athlete falls on the tip of the thumb when in slight flexion. A scaphoid fracture can occur by falling on an outstretched arm. Due to the location of the hamate, it is fractured most often when an athlete is holding an implement, such as a field hockey stick or tennis racket, and a traumatic force occurs with the implement in hand. Any metacarpal or phalange can be fractured by getting hit on the tip of the finger, or when the athlete's hand is stepped on. Scaphoid fractures can also occur as stress fractures. Repetitive lower intensity forces over time with the wrist in extension can put undue stress on the scaphoid and eventually lead the bone to break down. This bone does not have a good blood supply. Therefore, without blood to assist in healing, the bone becomes necrotic and dies.

Signs and Symptoms

Fractures of the wrist, hand, and finger cause pain, point tenderness, loss of function, and muscular stiffness. Swelling and ecchymosis may be present. The area may or may not exhibit deformity.

Immediate Care

Treat a suspected fracture of the wrist, hand, or finger as you would any other fracture. Begin with RICE and splint the area. Call 911 if the athlete is experiencing severe signs and symptoms of injury, has an open fracture, has loss of feeling or function, or is in shock. Instances when you may not need to call 911, but should refer the athlete to the ER for x-rays, are for a closed phalangeal fracture, a nondisplaced metacarpal fracture, or any closed wrist, hand, or finger fracture that results in only mild signs and symptoms of injury. The x-rays identify whether a fracture exists. The physician will determine whether a splint or hard cast is necessary, as well as if surgery is required to facilitate proper healing.

Tips from the Field

Tip 2 One simple way to splint a fractured or sprained finger is to "buddy tape" the finger. Have the athlete support the injured finger as you prepare the athletic tape. Take two to three strips of athletic tape that is approximately 1/2 to 1 inch in width and rip or cut them into approximately 3-inch lengths (or longer if the athlete's fingers are large). Place the injured finger in between the other two fingers on either side and have the athlete hold them still. Place the strips of tape around the fingers securely, but not so tight that circulation would be disrupted. The tape should not be directly over the injured area, but should be placed proximally and distally to support the injury. If the injury is to the second or fifth fingers, you can only buddy tape one uninjured finger to the injured finger. If the thumb is the injured finger, then tape the thumb to the hand by placing it next to the second metacarpal and securing it in that position.

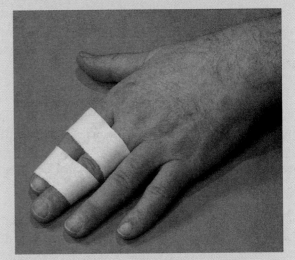

An injured finger is buddy taped to the neighboring finger for support.

© Jones and Bartlett Publishers. Courtesy of MIEMSS.

Prevention

Athletes must learn how to correctly perform activities in order to prevent fractures to the wrist, hand, or finger. The athlete should wear proper protective gear for the area. Vitamin D and calcium ingestion along with weight-bearing activities are important for the athletes to undertake in order to keep bones strong.

Dislocations

Lunate and phalangeal dislocations are very common dislocations that occur at the wrists, hands, and fingers. Lunate dislocations are often assumed to be a wrist sprain until an x-ray confirms the dislocation.

Mechanism or Cause of Injury

When a direct traumatic force strikes the palm of the hand at the lunate, such as when an athlete falls on an outstretched arm, a lunate dislocation can occur. Phalangeal dislocations occur from being stepped on by another athlete, or from a direct blow to the tip of the finger, such as when attempting to catch a basketball.

Signs and Symptoms

The athlete feels the typical signs and symptoms of common dislocations, including pain, and loss of function and sensation at the site of the dislocation. Deformity, especially for phalangeal dislocations, is present along with swelling and ecchymosis (**Figure 10-15**).

Immediate Care

Always treat for shock if necessary when a traumatic injury such as a dislocation occurs. Splint the injury, apply ice, and summon EMS. An athlete may want to reduce his own phalangeal dislocation. Do not allow the athlete or anyone else to reduce the dislocation, because reduction without training can cause further injury or complications.

Prevention

Athletes must be careful not to fall on an outstretched arm. They must be cognizant of their surroundings when participating in activities, especially activities that utilize equipment, implements, and balls that could strike the tip of the finger.

Sprains

Collateral ligaments exist not only at the elbow, but also at the wrist and fingers. The wrist joint and every joint in the finger, including the distal, proximal, and metacarpal phalangeal joints, have a medial collateral ligament (MCL) and a lateral collateral ligament (LCL).

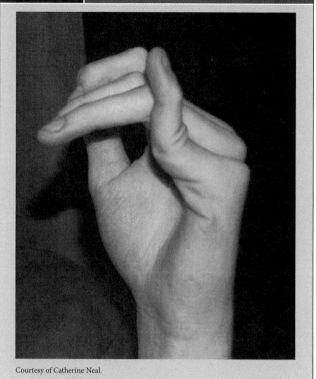

Figure 10-15 A finger dislocation at the PIP joint shows significant deformity.

Courtesy of Catherine Neal.

Mechanism or Cause of Injury

The wrist can be sprained by a fall on an outstretched arm. The phalangeal joints can be sprained by a blow to the tip of the finger. Similarly to the elbow, a valgus force applied to the wrist and phalangeal joints can result in a sprained MCL, whereas the LCL can be sprained by a varus force.

Signs and Symptoms

Sprains to the wrist and fingers result in signs and symptoms of pain, especially during motion; swelling; stiffness; ecchymosis; point tenderness; and increased tissue temperature.

Immediate Care

The first course of action to care for the athlete is to apply RICE. The athlete can also take over-the-counter NSAIDs to decrease pain and inflammation. Once the signs and symptoms of inflammation subside, the athlete can slowly progress to perform AROM and muscle strengthening. With Grade 1 and Grade 2 sprains, physician evaluation may not be necessary. If the signs and symptoms indicate a more significant Grade 2 or a Grade 3 sprain, then refer the athlete to a physician for evaluation. Grade 3 sprains can also occur in conjunction with an avulsion fracture; consequently, when you suspect a Grade 3 sprain, the athlete must be referred to a physician for x-rays. Anti-inflammatory medication, RICE, and a removable splint, followed by rehabilitation, are necessary to return to normal function.

▌ Prevention

An athlete should avoid falling on an outstretched arm with the wrist in extension. Also, the athlete should take precautions to prevent valgus or varus forces to the wrist and fingers in order to minimize trauma to the MCL and LCL.

Carpal Tunnel Syndrome

The carpal tunnel is an area on the anterior wrist that contains the median nerve and nine wrist and finger flexor tendons. Carpal tunnel syndrome is a chronic condition that involves the median nerve. This condition occurs more to women than men, and often occurs to athletes between the ages of 30 and 60 years (PubMed, 2010a).

▌ Mechanism or Cause of Injury

Carpal tunnel syndrome can occur to anyone who utilizes the hand in repetitive motion, especially in conjunction with wrist flexion. Athletes who participate in racquetball, handball, or other activities that require the athlete to grip an implement and perform wrist flexion are most prone to carpal tunnel syndrome. Other people who participate in long periods of computer use, writing, sewing, and driving also can succumb to carpal tunnel syndrome. Rheumatoid arthritis, diabetes, hypothyroidism, obesity, and menopause are conditions that predispose people to carpal tunnel syndrome.

▌ Signs and Symptoms

Signs and symptoms of carpal tunnel syndrome include tingling and numbness in the thumb, index, and third fingers, and the palm of the hand. The athlete has pain with wrist flexion, which can radiate to the elbow and down into the fingers. The athlete's wrist, finger, and grip strength are weak, and function and coordination (including dexterity) are decreased. Over time the athlete's thenar eminence, located at the palm side of the first metacarpal, will slowly atrophy.

▌ Immediate Care

Because this condition is not caused by acute trauma, the athlete would state that the signs and symptoms have worsened over time. Perform a secondary survey that includes a special test, called Tinel's sign, to determine if the athlete has carpal tunnel syndrome. With the athlete's wrist facing up, gently tap over the wrist area where the median nerve is located (**Figure 10-16**). If the athlete feels tingling into the wrist and fingers, then the test is indicative of carpal tunnel syndrome.

The athlete should see a physician, but in the meantime she can utilize RICE or moist heat on the area to eliminate pain and inflammation. Moist heat is acceptable to utilize for carpal tunnel syndrome because the condition is not acute. The athlete should discontinue any activity that causes pain or aggravates symptoms. She can also take over-the-counter anti-inflammatory medication such as ibuprofen or naproxen.

The physician may prescribe NSAIDs and a splint to wear during the day and perhaps at night. The splint assists the athlete in maintaining some wrist extension, which alleviates median nerve pressure. If the carpal tunnel syndrome is caused by improper wrist positioning when utilizing a computer, the athlete can purchase **ergonomic equipment**, such as ergonomic keyboards and mouse pads.

> **Ergonomic equipment**
> Helps place the body in a proper position for optimal performance and to avoid injury.

This equipment assists in placing the wrist in a more comfortable, extended position while typing. Rehabilitation to strengthen the hand and forearm musculature is necessary. If this conservative approach to treatment does not decrease the signs and symptoms, then the physician may choose to give

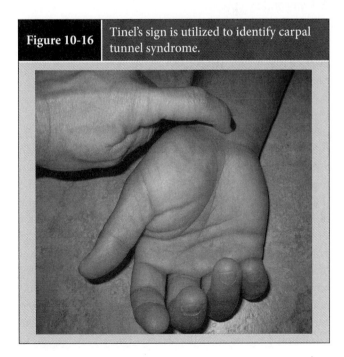

| **Figure 10-16** | Tinel's sign is utilized to identify carpal tunnel syndrome. |

the athlete a corticosteroid injection. Surgery is another option to decrease pressure on the median nerve.

Prevention

In an attempt to prevent carpal tunnel syndrome, the athlete should refrain from keeping the wrist in flexion for long periods of time. Whenever ergonomic equipment is available for the athlete's activities, the athlete should utilize it to keep the wrist in a comfortable, less stressful position of slight extension.

De Quervain's Tenosynovitis

De Quervain's tenosynovitis, which is also referred to as de Quervain's syndrome, is a condition in which the synovial sheath of the tendons that abduct and extend the thumb become inflamed. Consequently, the tendons cannot move properly inside the sheath.

Mechanism or Cause of Injury

Similarly to carpal tunnel syndrome, de Quervain's tenosynovitis is caused by repetitive movements. When the thumb is constantly gripping or in a fist, such as when utilizing an implement like a hammer, racket, or dumbbell, the athlete can irritate the thumb tendons. A repetitive wringing motion, as with wringing out a towel, can also cause inflammation. In particular, people who have rheumatoid arthritis are prone to de Quervain's syndrome.

Signs and Symptoms

The athlete experiences pain at the base of the thumb, especially when gripping objects or making a fist. Swelling, crepitus, and loss of function are also apparent.

Immediate Care

If the athlete complains of chronic pain at the thumb tendons, perform a secondary survey. At the end of the examination perform the following special test called the Finkelstein test: Have the athlete make a fist with the thumb inside, then passively move the wrist medially to apply a stretch to the thumb tendons (**Figure 10-17**). Pain on the wrist area by the thumb indicates de Quervain's tenosynovitis. Treatment for de Quervain's syndrome is similar to that for carpal tunnel syndrome. Have the athlete apply RICE or heat to the area if the tendons are not acutely inflamed. The athlete should see a physician, who probably will prescribe NSAIDs and rehabilitation. The physician may also have the athlete wear a splint to keep the thumb in a rested, straightened position. The athlete should see progress and a decrease in signs and symptoms in

| **Figure 10-17** | Finkelstein test is utilized to identify de Quervain's syndrome. |

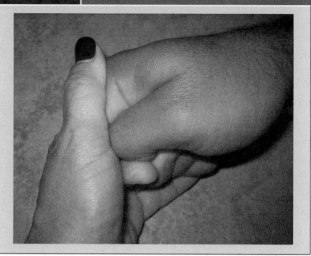

about a month. If this conservative approach to treatment does not work, then the physician may perform surgery.

Prevention

The athlete should attempt to avoid repetitive gripping and wringing activities, and perform AROM of the thumb to avoid de Quervain's syndrome. Ergonomic equipment can assist in preventing this syndrome, as it does with carpal tunnel syndrome. Finger, hand, and wrist muscles should also be strengthened to prevent injury due to repetitive stresses.

Ganglion Cyst

A ganglion cyst is a fluid-filled sac that develops at the wrist and carpal bones. The cyst is benign; however, it may be unsightly and cause functional problems for the athlete.

| **Benign** Noncancerous. |

Mechanism or Cause of Injury

The cause of ganglion cysts is unknown. It is speculated that synovial fluid in the joint spaces among the carpal bones and the wrist joint becomes encapsulated over time and forms the cyst. The athlete would state that the cyst has developed and increased in size over time.

Signs and Symptoms

The cyst is not painful; however, it appears like a large bump (**Figure 10-18**). Upon palpation, the cyst can range from very hard to soft. Palpation of the cyst does not cause point

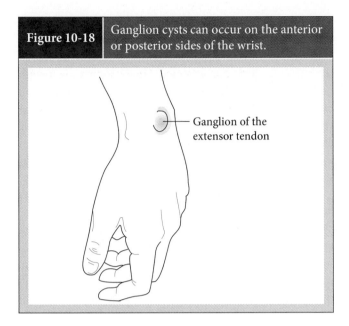

Figure 10-18 | Ganglion cysts can occur on the anterior or posterior sides of the wrist.

Ganglion of the extensor tendon

tenderness. No signs of inflammation exist, and the athlete has full function and sensation.

Immediate Care

Perform a secondary survey to determine that the cyst is not something else. Ganglion cysts typically do not require any treatment. If the athlete is unsure whether the bump is in fact a cyst, pain or loss of function exists, or that athlete believes it is unsightly and wants it removed, then she should see her physician. To remove the cyst, he physician must remove the fluid with a needle and syringe. Then the athlete's wrist will be compressed with a compression wrap or tape. At no time should the athlete try to burst the cyst. If an athlete attempts to burst the cyst, she may cause further injury.

Prevention

Unfortunately, an athlete cannot prevent a cyst from developing. Athletes who have had wrist injuries are predisposed to cysts more than other athletes; consequently, athletes should attempt to avoid wrist injuries.

Gamekeeper's Thumb

Gamekeeper's thumb is a sprain and resultant chronic ulnar collateral ligament (UCL) laxity of the thumb's metacarpophalangeal (MCP) joint. An acute variation of this injury is called skier's thumb.

Mechanism or Cause of Injury

The cause of gamekeeper's thumb is a repetitive valgus force to the thumb when it is in extension and abduction. This repetitive force is placed on the thumb, as it is in a position furthest away from the second finger, creating a forward or backward "L" appearance with the second finger. When a skier falls with the ski pole in hand, a valgus force is placed on the thumb, which causes the injury.

Signs and Symptoms

The athlete has pain and a deficit in grip strength. The pain occurs most often when the athlete makes a pinching motion with the thumb and index finger. Swelling and ecchymosis are present along with joint laxity.

Immediate Care

If the injury is acutely inflamed, the athlete should apply ice to the area and splint the thumb. The athlete should take NSAIDs to decrease pain and inflammation. If the athlete has an increase in symptoms or significant joint laxity, refer her to a physician. If the athlete has significant laxity due to a UCL rupture, she may have to wear a splint for approximately 1 month, or surgery may be warranted. Thumb musculature rehabilitation is necessary regardless of whether surgery has been performed.

Prevention

Athletes should be careful when falling on an outstretched arm or when blocking an opponent with their hands. If the athlete's activity requires utilizing an implement or object in the hand, she should be aware not to fall with the thumb in a hyperextended and abducted position.

Mallet Finger and Boutonnière Deformity

Mallet finger is a rupture of the finger's extensor tendon at the distal interphalangeal (DIP) joint (the joint closest to the tip of the finger). Boutonnière deformity is a rupture of the finger's extensor digitorum tendon at the proximal interphalangeal (PIP) joint (the joint closest to the metacarpal). Avulsion or other fractures can occur with either acute injury.

Mechanism or Cause of Injury

Mallet finger and boutonnière deformity are caused when a force is placed on the tip of the finger and forcefully flexes the finger at the joint. As a result, the extensor tendon ruptures. An athlete can also cut the tendon with an implement, such as a saw or knife, which leads to tendon rupture.

Signs and Symptoms

The athlete has pain and loss of finger extension at the joint by the ruptured tendon. Finger deformity is visible. With mallet

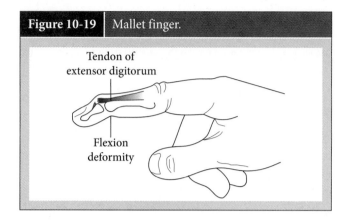

Figure 10-19 | Mallet finger.

Tendon of extensor digitorum

Flexion deformity

finger, the DIP joint appears in slight flexion because the tendon that holds the distal phalange in a normal position is ruptured (**Figure 10-19**). The remainder of the tendon is intact, so the other finger joints remain in a normal position. With boutonnière deformity, the DIP is in slight extension and the PIP is in flexion due to the ruptured tendon (**Figure 10-20**). Swelling, redness, ecchymosis, and point tenderness are present. The athlete may say that he heard or felt a pop or a snap at the time of injury.

Immediate Care

These finger injuries are not medical emergencies unless the athlete goes into shock or is bleeding severely. In these cases, treat him appropriately and call 911. If the athlete is not in shock or severely bleeding then you do not need to summon EMS; however, your athlete does need to see a physician right away. Evaluate the injury by performing a secondary survey. Test to see whether the tendon is intact. Hold the uninjured joints so they are stable. Have the athlete move the affected

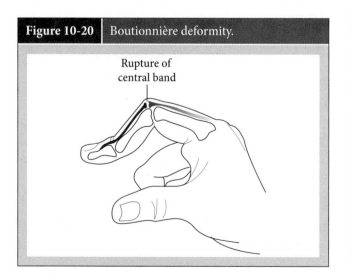

Figure 10-20 | Boutonnière deformity.

Rupture of central band

joint in extension. If the athlete cannot move the phalange, then he may have a ruptured tendon. Before the athlete leaves your facility to see his physician, apply a splint with the injured joint in extension and apply ice. Finger splints made with bendable plastic or thin aluminum pieces covered with foam can assist you in creating a splint appropriate for the injury (**Figure 10-21**). Put the athlete into a sling to keep the area elevated and rested. The physician will take x-rays and splint the finger to promote proper healing. Depending on the athlete's activity, the physician may perform surgery.

Prevention

To prevent mallet finger and boutonnière deformity, the athlete must be careful when catching equipment, such as balls, by utilizing the pads of the fingers and the palm of the hand. Athletes should use proper catching skills to avoid having the ball hit the tip of the finger. Also, athletes must be careful when utilizing sharp objects so they do not cut themselves.

Jersey Finger

Jersey finger is similar to mallet finger because the finger DIP tendon is torn or ruptured. However, the ruptured tendon is the flexor digitorum profundus, which commonly occurs at the fourth finger DIP (**Figure 10-22**). Tears can be partial tears or complete ruptures.

Mechanism or Cause of Injury

Jersey finger was given its name because when an athlete attempts to grab an opponent's jersey, in sports such as rugby and football, the athlete forcefully contracts the finger's flexor

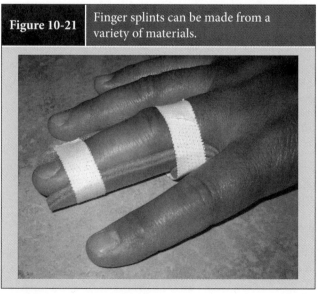

Figure 10-21 | Finger splints can be made from a variety of materials.

Figure 10-22 | Jersey finger.

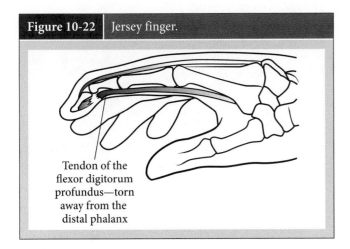

Tendon of the flexor digitorum profundus—torn away from the distal phalanx

tendon, which results in a tendon rupture. The athlete can also cut his flexor tendon with a sharp implement such as a saw or knife.

Signs and Symptoms

The athlete feels pain and has loss of finger flexion. He may say he heard or felt a pop or a snap at the time of injury. Because the flexor tendon is ruptured at the DIP, the athlete cannot flex the finger at this joint. The injury can occur with an avulsion or another phalangeal fracture. The athlete is point tender at the injury site and may complain of numbness at the tip of the finger. Swelling, redness, and ecchymosis are visible.

Immediate Care

Always treat the athlete for shock and call 911 if necessary. Perform a secondary survey if you do not need to summon EMS. As with mallet finger, test to see whether the tendon is intact. Hold the uninjured finger joints so they are stable. Have the athlete move the injured joint into flexion. If the athlete cannot move the phalange, then he may have a ruptured tendon. Refer the athlete to a physician. Apply ice and splint the injured joint in slight flexion. The injured finger joint must be splinted and the arm placed in a sling until he is evaluated by a physician. The physician will take x-rays, prescribe NSAIDs, splint the finger in flexion, and prescribe rehabilitation. Unlike mallet finger, which tends to heal without surgery, surgery is performed for a flexor tendon rupture; otherwise, proper healing cannot occur. Splinting and rehabilitation follow surgery to promote full function.

Prevention

The athlete must use caution when using sharp implements that can cut through soft tissue. Also, the athlete should perform athletic activity skills properly.

Dupuytren's Contracture

Dupuytren's contracture is thickening of tissue underlying the skin in the palm of the hand. Men are more commonly affected than women, and it typically occurs in those 40 years of age or older. The condition can be unilateral or bilateral, with any finger having the contracture. Interestingly, the ring finger is most commonly affected.

Mechanism or Cause of Injury

The cause of this condition is unknown. Dupuytren's contracture is not caused by an athletic activity. It may have some hereditary predispositions. Diabetes, alcoholism, and smoking have been shown to be risk factors for this condition.

Signs and Symptoms

The athlete first feels and then visualizes a bump or nodule on the palm of the hand. This bump is the contracture forming, which eventually forms into a cord-like band. Over time, the athlete's finger becomes contracted into a flexed position, and he cannot straighten it.

Immediate Care

The athlete should see a physician for evaluation. The athlete can utilize heat and ROM exercises in an attempt to loosen the contracture and restore some function. The physician may feel that surgery is warranted to release the contracture, followed by rehabilitation to restore full function. However, the International Dupuytren Society (2013) notes the most recent treatment for the condition is for the athlete to have an enzyme, Clostridial collagenase, injected into the contracture. This enzyme causes the collagen scar tissue bonds to weaken. With ROM exercises, the contracted tissue can be mobilized, which breaks the bonds.

Prevention

The only means to attempt to prevent Dupuytren's contracture would be to avoid the risk factors. Make sure the athlete takes care of himself physically to avoid Type 2 diabetes, does not drink excessive alcohol, and does not smoke.

SUMMARY

Injuries and conditions to the upper extremity vary in regard to severity, but often many mechanisms or causes of injuries are the same. Many upper extremity injuries do not require summoning EMS, but do require the athlete to see a physician for evaluation. Even though most athletes do not weight bear on the upper extremity, upper extremity injuries should be taken seriously. Without shoulder, elbow, forearm, wrist, hand, and finger ROM, flexibility, and strength, the athlete may not be able to perform a variety of activities including ADLs.

DISCUSSION QUESTIONS

1. Which upper extremity injuries warrant you to call 911 immediately?
2. Which upper extremity injuries do necessitate a call to 911, but require referral to a physician?
3. Which upper extremity injuries are considered chronic injuries?
4. What are common mechanisms or causes of upper extremity injuries?
5. Which injuries require surgery followed by rehabilitation in order to restore full function?

CASE STUDY

Kickboxing Shoulder Stress

Lorraine is a married, 45-year-old professional and mother of a 6-year-old boy. Aside from being slightly overweight she is in good health. Lorraine realizes that in order to improve her quality of life she needs to lose weight. She also wants to gain muscle tone, particularly in her arms and legs. She begins to exercise regularly at We R Fit Gym for 2 months by jogging on a treadmill and lifting weights. She has been doing well with her weight loss and muscle tone, but she is becoming bored with performing the same exercises. A trainer at the gym suggests that she try the classes that the gym offers. He suggests that Lorraine try the most popular class, which is impact kickboxing.

Immediately after the first class Lorraine is hooked on kickboxing. The next day she is sore from head to toe, but feels that she is getting a great workout. She is excited to continue the kickboxing classes three times per week. She jogs on a treadmill and performs weightlifting on the alternate 2 days. At the end of the first week, Lorraine notices she has pain at her left anterior shoulder whenever she flexes it. Also, she is unable to raise her arm without discomfort and weakness past 90 degrees of abduction or flexion. In the past she has experienced postexercise soreness for an hour or so after the workouts, so she figures the soreness will decrease in a day or so.

At the beginning of the following week, Lorraine's discomfort in her left arm is gone. She starts the next kickboxing class. During class she decides to increase her intensity when striking the bag with her fists. A few hours after the session, she feels a dull pain and significant weakness not only in her anterior shoulder and down her humerus, but also in her lateral shoulder. As the day progresses, she is not able to perform ADLs that require her arm to be raised into flexion or abduction more than 45 degrees. As night comes and Lorraine goes to bed, she begins to feel tingling "pins and needles" down into her hand and fingers. The dull aching persists throughout the evening.

Lorraine does not continue with kickboxing or upper body weightlifting for the remainder of the week, but continues to jog on the treadmill. The simple motion of her shoulder and arm moving forward and back when jogging is painful. The dull pain in her left shoulder and arm does not subside. The pain continues to affect her daily activities, such as washing her hair, reaching up in her closet to get her clothes, and putting groceries in her cupboard. She is extremely frustrated and does not know what to do. She is ready to quit working out altogether.

1. What structure(s) do you believe is (are) injured?
2. What was the mechanism or cause of the injury?
3. What should Lorraine have done as soon as she felt discomfort at the shoulder and arm to provide immediate care for the injury?
4. What advice would you give Lorraine to care for her shoulder injury? Should she be evaluated by a physician? Why or why not?
5. What should Lorraine have done to prevent this injury?

REFERENCES

American Society for Surgery of the Hand (ASSH) (2007). Shoulder fractures. Retrieved May 30, 2012, from http://www.assh.org/PUBLIC/HANDCONDITIONS/Pages/ShoulderFractures.aspx

Fongemie, A. E., Buss, D. D., & Rolnick, S. J. (1998). Management of shoulder impingement syndrome and rotator cuff tears. *American Family Physician, 57*(4), 667–674.

Hoekzema, N., Torchia, M., Adkins, M., & Cassivi, S. D. (2008). Posterior sternoclavicular joint dislocation. *Canadian Journal of Surgery, 51*(1), E19–E20. Retrieved May 30, 2012, from http://www.ncbi.nlm.nih.gov/pmc/articles/PMC2386312/

International Dupuytren Society. (2013). Enzyme (collagenase) injection to treat Dupuytren's contracture. Retrieved March 3, 2013, from http://www.dupuytren-online.info/dupuytren_collagenase.html

Mayo Clinic. (2010). Thoracic outlet syndrome: Prevention. Retrieved June 1, 2012, from http://www.mayoclinic.com/health/thoracic-outlet-syndrome/DS00800/DSECTION=prevention

MedlinePlus (2011). Rotator cuff problems. Retrieved June 1, 2012, from http://www.nlm.nih.gov/medlineplus/ency/article/000438.htm

Neer, C. S. (1972). Anterior acromioplasty for the chronic impingement syndrome in the shoulder: A preliminary report. *Journal of Bone and Joint Surgery, American Edition, 54*, 41–50.

Prentice, W. E. (2011). *Principles of athletic training: A competency-based approach* (14th ed.). Champaign, IL: McGraw-Hill.

PubMed Health. (2010a). Carpal tunnel syndrome. Retrieved June 4, 2012, from http://www.ncbi.nlm.nih.gov/pubmedhealth/PMH0001469/

PubMed Health. (2010b). Frozen shoulder: Adhesive capsulitis. Retrieved June 1, 2012, from http://www.ncbi.nlm.nih.gov/pubmedhealth/PMH0001490/

Starkey, C. (Ed.). (2013). *Athletic training and sports medicine: An integrated approach* (5th ed.). Burlington, MA: Jones and Bartlett Learning & American Academy of Orthopedic Surgeons.

Chapter 11

The Core Body

CHAPTER OBJECTIVES

After you have read this chapter, you will be able to understand:

- How to evaluate an athlete's posture
- Acute traumatic injuries that occur to the cervical spine
- The similarities and differences between cervical and thoracic spine injuries
- The mechanisms of injury for chronic injuries to the lumbar spine
- The various injuries and illnesses that can occur to the lungs, heart, and other abdominal organs.
- Which core body injuries and illnesses warrant summoning EMS

THE SPINE

The spine consists of the cervical, thoracic, lumbar, sacral, and coccygeal vertebrae. The spinal cord, which is part of the central nervous system (CNS), and the peripheral nerves pass through the vertebrae and provide motor function and sensation to all parts of the body. The vertebral disks located in between each of the cervical, thoracic, and lumbar vertebrae provide cushioning and act as shock absorbers against forces applied to the spine. As a whole, the spine gives the head and body support, maintains the body's shape, provides movement, and protects the spinal cord. Although the spine is well supported by many ligaments and muscles, acute and chronic injuries to the spine frequently occur.

Posture

When evaluating spinal injuries, especially chronic injuries, it is imperative to evaluate the athlete's posture. Posture is the positioning and arrangement of the body parts in relation to each other. If an athlete has correct, normal posture, minimal stresses are placed upon his body. When an athlete has incorrect posture, there is a greater chance that stresses will adversely affect bony and soft tissue structures. The stress on the body due to incorrect posture can cause chronic injury. When an athlete complains of signs and symptoms of chronic injury including pain, loss of function, stiffness, decreased flexibility, muscular weakness, and/or muscular spasm, in conjunction with an **insidious onset**, you should evaluate the athlete's posture. Poor posture can cause chronic

> **Insidious onset** A slow and gradual development of signs and symptoms of injury without any definitive mechanism of injury.

injury not only to the spine, but also to the extremities. Most often the lower extremity is affected by incorrect posture. Because the lower extremity is weight bearing, postural deviations can cause chronic injury down to the feet. Therefore, evaluate the athlete's posture to determine if the faulty posture is the cause of the athlete's lower extremity problem.

If the faulty posture is causing the chronic injury, then the athlete's posture needs to be corrected. Incorrect posture can be genetic and evident at birth. It can also result from incorrect body movements and positioning after injury. The athlete may utilize poor sitting and standing habits, and as he ages, his posture may be affected (Shultz, Houglum, & Perrin, 2010).

To begin evaluating the athlete's posture, you must first recognize what is considered normal posture. By reviewing anatomical pictures of the body, you can visualize what is considered normal posture. In order to evaluate the athlete's posture, examine the athlete from anterior, posterior, and lateral views (**Figure 11-1**). When you examine the athlete in an anterior or posterior view, visualize a line running down the athlete in a sagittal plane, which divides the athlete equally into right and left halves. A plumb line assists you in creating this sagittal plane. A plumb line is string suspended from the ceiling attached to a small weight, similar to a fishing pole weight, which hangs to the floor. Before you examine the athlete, make sure the plumb line is steady. The athlete should stand close to the plumb line during evaluation, but far enough away so he does not touch it.

Tips from the Field

Tip 1 You can make a plumb line to evaluate an athlete's posture even when you do not have a string or weight available. Take the end of some athletic, duct, or masking tape and secure it to the ceiling. Then unroll the tape from the ceiling to the floor. Unroll about 2 feet more than the distance between the ceiling and the floor, and cut the tape.

Figure 11-1	When evaluating an athlete's posture, you must look at anatomical landmarks from the anterior, posterior, and lateral views.

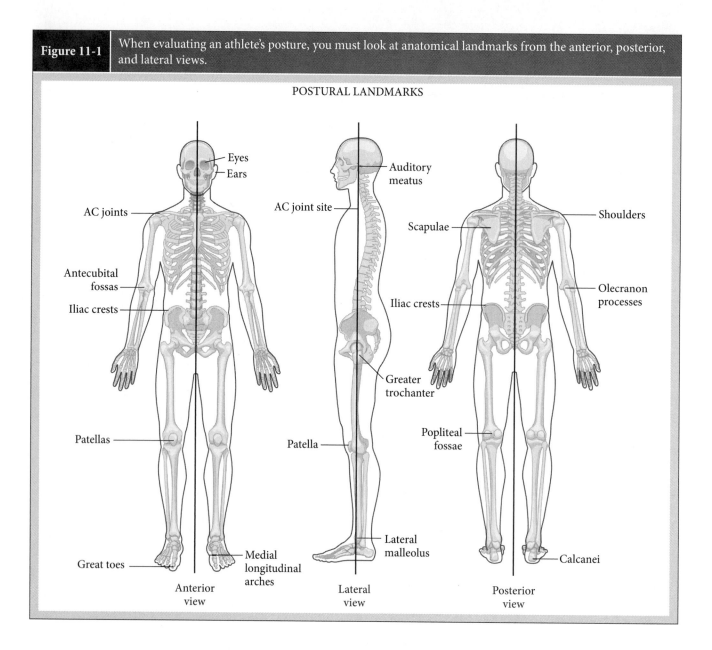

POSTURAL LANDMARKS

Anterior view — Eyes, Ears, AC joints, Antecubital fossas, Iliac crests, Patellas, Great toes, Medial longitudinal arches

Lateral view — Auditory meatus, AC joint site, Greater trochanter, Patella, Lateral malleolus

Posterior view — Shoulders, Scapulae, Olecranon processes, Iliac crests, Popliteal fossae, Calcanei

Then, beginning from the ceiling, roll the tape between the palms of your hands and fingers down to the floor. You should end up with a tight, rolled "string" of tape. Then secure the tape to the floor. Look at the tape string from each view and move it so it is straight from the ceiling and the floor. This task is best accomplished with an athlete standing by the tape. Once the tape plumb line is straight, you can use it to evaluate your athlete's posture.

You can make your own plumb line out of athletic tape.

To examine the athlete's anterior structures, have him stand behind the plumb line facing you. In this position, the athlete's body is divided into two equal halves. The plumb line bisects the athlete's nose, sternum, and umbilicus, and is lined up midway between the feet. With the plumb line in place, observe and compare the athlete's ears, eyes, acromioclavicular (AC) joints, antecubital fossas at the elbows, iliac crests, patellas, medial longitudinal arches of the feet, and great toes. Determine if each of these body parts is in alignment with the matching part on the other side. For example, determine if the AC joint on each upper extremity is aligned at the same height across the body. See if the patellas are at the same height and position. Evaluate the remainder of the body parts to see if postural alignment is correct.

To evaluate his posterior structures, the athlete must stand with his back to the plumb line, bisecting his body into right and left halves as with the anterior view. As you look at the plumb line relative to his spine, the spine should be straight. The spinous processes for each vertebra should be in line with the plumb line. Compare the height and alignment of the following structures bilaterally: the shoulder, olecranon process, scapula, iliac crest, popliteal fossa, and calcaneus. To examine the athlete from the lateral view, have him stand to the side of the plumb line. The plumb line should run through the middle of the ear's auditory meatus, the acromion process, the greater trochanter, slightly posterior to the patella, and in front of the lateral malleolus.

When comparing the contralateral side, if any anatomical landmarks are not aligned or one side of the body does not appear as it should, then the athlete may have a postural deviation. These postural deviations can be the cause of acute and chronic injuries in the body and must be addressed. If you find the athlete has a postural deviation that may be the injury's cause, refer the athlete to his physician for evaluation.

The Cervical Spine

The cervical spine consists of seven vertebrae, with eight pairs of cervical nerves exiting from the intervertebral foramen. The spinal cord starts at the base of the skull, travels through the cervical vertebrae, and continues down to the sacrum. The first two vertebrae, the atlas and the axis, cannot be palpated because they are at the base of the skull. These two vertebrae, along with the articulation of the atlas and the occiput of the skull, provide a lot of movement to the head, including flexion, extension, and rotation. The remaining cervical joints allow for these motions including **lateral flexion**. The cervical spine has a lordotic curve, which is an

> **Lateral flexion** When an athlete bends their neck to the side by moving their head toward their shoulder.

inward curve, or anterior concavity, of the spine when looking at the athlete from a lateral view. Many cervical spine injuries are serious, and potentially limb-threatening; therefore, immediate proper care is crucial.

Fractures and Dislocations

Cervical fractures and dislocations are among the most serious and damaging injuries to the body. The cervical vertebrae can fracture, dislocate, or have a concurrent fracture-dislocation. Vertebral body compression fractures and transverse and oblique fractures to the spinous and transverse processes, laminae, and pedicles are common fractures that occur to the cervical spine. Dislocations can occur between any two vertebrae. Cervical fractures and dislocations that occur at the atlas

(**Figure 11-2**) or axis (**Figure 11-3**) can be life-threatening if the spinal cord is severed in conjunction with the fracture. In this case the nerves affecting heart function and breathing can be affected and the athlete can die immediately. When cervical fractures or dislocations injure the spinal cord, the injury can render the athlete **paraplegic** or **quadriplegic**.

> **Paraplegic**   An athlete who has paralysis of the lower body including the legs. Paralysis usually involves loss of motor function and sensation.
>
> **Quadriplegic**   An athlete who has paralysis of the legs, arms, and torso.

Mechanism or Cause of Injury. A mechanism of injury for cervical fractures and dislocations is a direct impact to the top of the head, when the neck is in approximately 30 degrees of flexion. When the neck is in slight flexion, the cervical spine's lordotic curve is straightened. This straightened spine facilitates force transmission, and compresses and crumples the spine. This injury could occur when a football player has his head down while attempting to tackle an opponent, which is called spearing. Also, an athlete who dives into the shallow end of a pool has her neck in the same position. The cervical spine can also be fractured or dislocated with a forceful flexion-extension that snaps the neck, as occurs with whiplash in a car accident.

Signs and Symptoms. The athlete complains of bony spinal pain, especially with palpation; inability and unwillingness to move the head and neck; and loss of function and/or sensation through the arms and legs. The athlete may say he is unable to move any part of his body, which indicates paralysis. The athlete may show signs of shock.

Immediate Care. The first priority is to see if the athlete is conscious, while checking the athlete's airway, breathing, and

Figure 11-3   A fracture of the axis (C2).

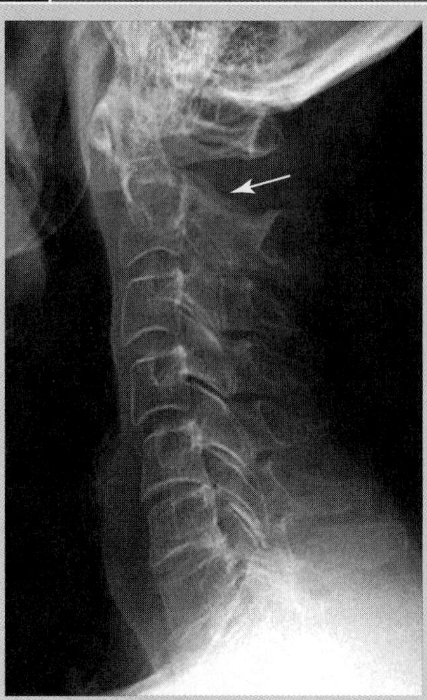

© Living Art Enterprises, LLC/Science Source

circulation. Immediately check to make sure he is breathing, and apply in-line cervical spine stabilization. Tell the athlete not to move, and summon someone to phone 911. If the athlete is in shock, treat him accordingly but do not move him, including his legs. Determine the extent of his consciousness by talking to him. Ask history questions, including those focusing on the extent and location of his pain. Also, without having the athlete move his head and spine, determine if he has feeling in his arms and legs. Ask him if he is able to wiggle his fingers and toes. Touch the extremities while asking him if he can feel your touch. When emergency medical services (EMS) arrives on the scene, the emergency medical technicians (EMTs) may ask you to assist them in spine boarding the athlete (**Figure 11-4**). Listen to the EMTs' directions carefully as they instruct you on how to assist. At the hospital, the physician will give the athlete pain medication and take spine images to visualize the injury. Surgery is immediately necessary for the athlete's recovery.

Prevention. To prevent cervical spine fractures and dislocations, athletes should learn proper athletic activity techniques including diving and tackling. Athletes should always abide by athletic activity rules, such as no diving in shallow ends of pools. Also, athletes must always wear seatbelts when riding in a motor vehicle.

Figure 11-2   Fractures of the atlas (C1) can occur bilaterally.

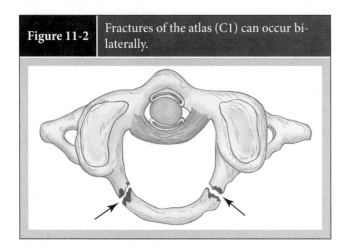

| **Figure 11-4** | If an athlete has a possible cervical spine injury, the athlete must be placed securely on a spine board. |

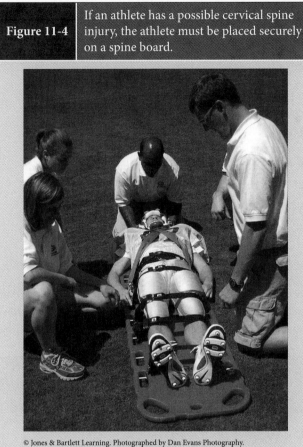

© Jones & Bartlett Learning. Photographed by Dan Evans Photography.

| **Figure 11-5** | A fracture-dislocation of a cervical vertebrae can sever the spinal cord. |

Reproduced with permission from Delamarter RB, Coyle J. Acute management of spinal cord injury. J Am Acad Orthop Surg 1999;7:166-175.

Spinal Cord and Nerve Injuries

Spinal cord and nerve injuries can be traumatic, such as with a severed or contused spinal cord, or chronic, such as a vertebral disk compressing the spinal cord and/or nerve root.

Mechanism or Cause of Injury. Traumatic spinal cord injuries, including a severed and contused spinal cord, typically occur in athletics due to a blow to the top of the head secondary to a cervical spine fracture or dislocation (**Figure 11-5**). These injuries can also occur due to falls onto the head. However, a fracture or dislocation does not need to occur in order to significantly damage the spinal cord. The spinal cord can be contused and swell (which is called *spinal cord shock*). The swollen spinal cord presses on the vertebrae in the spinal canal. Also, the spinal cord can be compressed by blood and fluid from inflammation from a traumatic event. Spinal cord and nerve injuries can also occur from an athlete having a small vertebral foramen (called *spinal stenosis*), which compresses on the spinal cord.

Signs and Symptoms. An injury to the spinal cord can be life-threatening, especially if it occurs at cervical vertebrae 1 or 2 (atlas and axis) level, which affects the breathing centers.

Spinal cord and nerve injuries are more often limb-threatening, which means that an injury to cervical vertebrae 3 through 7 affects motor function and sensation from the arms to the legs. An athlete with a severed spinal cord may be not breathing, in cardiac arrest, or dead if the spinal cord is severed up at the atlas or axis levels. The athlete may be conscious and breathing, but she may have paralysis in the extremities. The athlete may experience pain, incontinence, and muscle spasm. With spinal cord shock, the spinal cord swells and a temporary loss of function and sensation results. Once the spinal cord swelling decreases, then the athlete's function and sensation gradually return. Unlike with acute spinal cord injuries, with chronic spinal cord and nerve injuries, the athlete is conscious. Chronic spinal cord and nerve injuries cause pain, temporary loss of function and sensation, as well as burning, tingling, and numbness throughout all extremities. These signs and symptoms of injury may last for a few minutes or weeks.

Immediate Care. An acute, traumatic spinal cord injury that exhibits loss of motor function and sensation is a medical emergency and must be treated as a spinal fracture or dislocation. Maintain in-line stabilization; monitor airway, breathing, and circulation; and call 911 to summon EMS. Make sure you tell the athlete to lie still. The EMTs will spine board the athlete for transfer to the emergency room (ER). At the ER, the physician will determine the extent of injury. The physician can utilize computed tomography (CT), magnetic resonance imaging (MRI), x-rays, or a **myelogram**. Typically, the athlete is given medication to relieve swelling. The physician may perform surgery to fuse vertebrae or remove fluid that may be causing the signs and symptoms. The athlete will be put on bed rest for a period of time.

> **Myelogram** An imaging test used to determine whether an athlete has a spinal cord injury. The physician injects dye into the spinal column and then takes an x-ray.

For chronic spinal cord and nerve injuries, complete a secondary survey of the athlete's injury, and determine the severity, irritability, nature, and stage (SINS) of his injury. Ultimately, refer the athlete to a physician to determine the underlying cause of the injury. The physician can address this cause of injury by prescribing nonsteroidal anti-inflammatory drugs (NSAIDs), corticosteroid injections, and rehabilitation. Lifestyle modification will most likely be necessary to prevent recurrence.

Prevention. Traumatic spinal cord injuries can be avoided if when the athlete participates in activities he performs the skills properly and abides by activity rules (as with prevention of cervical fractures and dislocations). Sometimes chronic spinal cord injuries cannot be avoided, such as if spinal stenosis exists.

Herniated Disk

A disk is made up of the annulus fibrosus and nucleus pulposus. The annulus fibrosus is the disk's tough, outer portion and the nucleus pulposus is the disk's jelly-like, softer portion. A herniated disk refers to a protrusion of a disk between the vertebrae, which can occur at the cervical, thoracic, or lumbar spine, as pictured in **Figure 11-6**. The disk can actually rupture, and the nucleus pulposus can protrude through the annulus fibrosus (**Figure 11-7**). Most often herniated disks occur to people who have occupations that require heavy lifting, pushing, pulling, or twisting that puts pressure on the disks; people who are middle-aged, due to disk degeneration; or people who are overweight, which places stress on the disks (Mayo Clinic, 2010).

Mechanism or Cause of Injury. Herniated disks typically do not have an acute, traumatic mechanism of injury. As an athlete gets older, disks lose their water content and degenerate. Because the disks are not as strong as when the athlete was young, they are prone to tearing and rupturing with spinal movements. Spinal movements typically are not traumatic

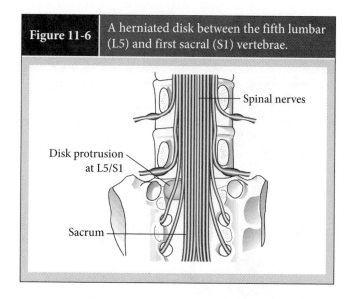

| Figure 11-6 | A herniated disk between the fifth lumbar (L5) and first sacral (S1) vertebrae. |

or exceptionally forceful, but over the years they will further weaken and damage the disks. For example, athletes who continually lift heavy objects improperly, by utilizing their back

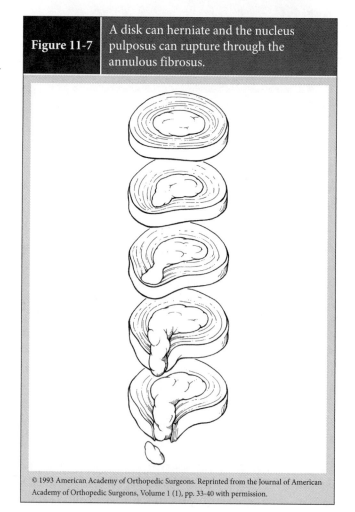

| Figure 11-7 | A disk can herniate and the nucleus pulposus can rupture through the annulous fibrosus. |

muscles, are prone to herniated disks (Mayo Clinic, 2010). As a result, the herniated disks can compress upon the spinal cord and nerves.

Signs and Symptoms. Some athletes do not know that they have a herniated disk because they do not have any signs or symptoms. In many cases, a herniated disk can cause pain, loss of function and sensation, numbness, tingling, or burning down the arms and legs, depending on the site of the herniation.

Immediate Care. If your athlete has any of the signs or symptoms listed, she must see her physician immediately to rule out any other injuries or conditions. The physician will prescribe various medications including over-the-counter or prescription medications including NSAIDs, narcotics, nerve pain medications, muscle relaxants, and cortisone injections. The athlete will participate in rehabilitation, including therapeutic modalities, traction, and exercises, to decrease the pain and increase the strength at the cervical spine. Surgery is rarely needed. If conservative treatment is not improving the athlete's condition, or if a portion of the disk must be removed to allow for the athlete to perform activities of daily living (ADLs) and decrease the signs and symptoms, then surgery is an option.

Prevention. In order to prevent a herniated disk, an athlete must have good posture, including utilizing proper mechanics when lifting, pulling, and pushing heavy objects; have strong core muscles; and maintain a healthy, normal weight.

▌ Sprains and Strains

Cervical sprains and strains tend to occur concurrently. Determining whether the injury is a sprain or a strain is difficult.

Mechanism or Cause of Injury. A sprain or strain to the cervical spine is caused by forceful motions of the neck. Whiplash, which often occurs in motor vehicle accidents, is a common cause of cervical sprains. This mechanism of injury entails a forceful hyperextension of the neck followed immediately by a forceful hyperflexion. These forceful movements along with sudden twisting or rotation motions can also cause cervical strains.

Signs and Symptoms. Cervical sprains and strains have the same signs and symptoms of injury as any other sprain or strain. The athlete complains of neck pain and stiffness, which result in a loss of range of motion (ROM). He is point tender and localized swelling is evident. The athlete may be holding his head and neck very still and have to turn his body to look around him. The athlete does not have nerve dysfunction. This lack of nerve dysfunction rules out more serious injuries.

Immediate Care. If you suspect the athlete has a cervical sprain or strain, have the athlete apply ice to the area. Have him lie on his stomach with his head in a comfortable position to apply the ice pack. The athlete can take over-the-counter NSAIDs to alleviate pain and inflammation. If the athlete cannot move his neck and is in noticeable pain, then the injury is significant enough for him to be evaluated by a physician. The physician will prescribe NSAIDs and perhaps muscle relaxants to alleviate pain, inflammation, and spasm. The athlete rests the area by wearing a Philadelphia collar, which is a soft foam neck brace that assists in stabilizing and resting the neck musculature. The athlete performs rehabilitation including ROM and strengthening exercises, and also has regular application of therapeutic modalities and soft tissue massage. Throughout the rehabilitation process, the athlete should maintain cardiorespiratory fitness levels without putting the neck in further danger of harm.

Tips from the Field

Tip 2 If you need to apply an ice pack to an athlete's cervical spine, do not secure it with a compression wrap or any other securing bandage because you may asphyxiate the athlete. Instead, have the athlete lie on his stomach, prone, on a table or mat. To make the athlete's neck and head comfortable, you can make a temporary face cradle. Take a towel from the longest side and roll it up. Place the ends of the towel together, leaving a hole large enough for the athlete to place his face in. Form the rolled up towel into a circle underneath the athlete's face on the table, with the athlete's forehead and chin on the towel material. Make sure the athlete can breathe normally. If not, then you may need to adjust the towel roll or place the athlete in another position.

A towel roll used as a face cradle can make the athlete more comfortable when he is lying on his stomach during ice application.

Prevention. The athlete must avoid any forceful cervical spine movements in order to prevent sprains and strains. The athlete must have full neck ROM, adequate muscular strength, and flexibility to prevent injuries.

▎Acute Torticollis (Wryneck)

Acute torticollis of the neck is also called *wryneck*. The injury is a sudden, painful neck muscle spasm.

Mechanism or Cause of Injury. Acute torticollis can be caused by acutely bending or twisting the neck, stress, muscular tension, or sleeping in an unusual position for hours in a cold, drafty room.

Signs and Symptoms. The athlete complains of neck pain and stiffness, which occurs typically on one side. She holds her head to the opposite side of the pain. The athlete may state that she went to bed fine and woke up with discomfort and stiffness that became worse throughout the course of the day. The athlete may feel that her neck is "stuck."

Immediate Care. The athlete should see a physician in order to rule out any other significant cervical spine injuries. Therefore, if an athlete approaches you, is in severe pain, and holds her head still and is unable to move it, summon EMS. The physician will evaluate the athlete and take x-rays in order to rule out other cervical injuries. The physician will prescribe medication and therapeutic modalities, including moist heat, to alleviate pain and spasm. The muscles should be massaged and the neck put through gentle ROM and stretching exercises.

Prevention. Prevention of acute torticollis includes maintaining normal posture, even when sleeping. For some athletes, maintaining normal posture may require various ergonomic equipment. For example, pillows are available that can help prevent wryneck that occurs during sleep. The athlete should maintain a low level of stress and participate in stress reduction activities. If the athlete works regularly at a desk or computer, she should take frequent breaks and perform active range of motion (AROM) movements and easy, manual neck muscle stretching exercises.

The Thoracic Spine

The thoracic spine includes the 12 thoracic vertebrae, along with the intervertebral disks, spinal cord, and nerves. Unlike the cervical spine, the thoracic spine has a **kyphotic** curve versus a lordotic curve. The thoracic spine does not have the mobility the cervical spine does due to the shape and configuration of the

> **Kyphotic** An outward, posterior curvature of the spine when viewing the athlete from the side. This curve is found normally at the thoracic and sacral spines.

vertebrae, in particular the spinous processes, as well as the fact that the ribs attach to the thoracic vertebrae.

Thoracic spine injuries have similarities to cervical spine injuries. Thoracic fractures, dislocations, spinal cord injuries, herniated disks, sprains, and strains occur to the thoracic spine as they do to the cervical spine. The same mechanisms of injury and signs and symptoms that occur with cervical spine injuries occur to the thoracic spine with few variations. Instead of reiterating each injury in this section, the differences between these cervical and thoracic injuries are discussed.

Traumatic thoracic injuries, such as fractures and dislocations, do not often occur when an athlete is participating in athletic activities. These injuries typically occur with high impact forces to the spine such as in an automobile accident or a fall from a height onto the head or feet. Thoracic spinal cord injuries are similar to cervical spinal cord injuries, except for the area of the body that is affected. Loss of motor function and/or sensation from a thoracic spinal cord injury occurs into the chest, abdomen, and legs with a severed spinal cord. Herniated disks compressing on the spinal cord and/or nerve root also produce abnormal sensation in the chest and abdomen.

The ligaments that run through the cervical vertebrae also exist at the thoracic vertebrae. Ligamentous sprains produce the same signs and symptoms of inflammation as with cervical sprains, but because the thoracic area cannot create a lot of motion, loss of motion due to spasm is minimal as compared to the loss of motion that occurs with a cervical sprain. Thoracic spine muscle strains occur frequently and exhibit similar signs and symptoms of injury as cervical muscle strains. The muscles attaching to the thoracic spine move the neck, shoulders, and scapula. Therefore, loss of function is noticeable in regard to these structures versus at the actual thoracic spine. Deep muscles that attach to the thoracic spine, such as the erector spinae and rhomboids, can be strained with forceful muscle contraction or sudden stretch. Superficial muscles attaching to the thoracic spine, such as the latissimus dorsi and trapezius, are as susceptible to muscular strains as any other muscle in the thoracic spine area.

Immediate care of these injuries is the same as for cervical injuries. Care for traumatic injuries includes calling 911; maintaining in-line spinal stabilization; monitoring airway, breathing, and circulation; and treating for shock. Care for chronic or nontraumatic injuries is the same as for the respective cervical spine injuries. Prevention of thoracic spine injuries also is similar to prevention of cervical spine injuries.

The Lumbar Spine

The lumbar spine consists of five large vertebrae, intervertebral disks, spinal cord, and nerves. The lumbar spine has a lordotic curve and a notable amount of ROM, similar to the cervical spine. As with thoracic traumatic injuries, such as fractures and dislocations, lumbar fractures and dislocations occur mainly with high impact trauma such as motor vehicle accidents and falls from a significant height, typically when landing on the feet. The lumbar vertebrae are considerably larger and stronger than the other spinal vertebrae; therefore, enormous trauma must occur to fracture or dislocate the bones. Lumbar spinal cord injury can occur, but the spinal cord is not often severed at the lumbar region during athletic activity as compared to the cervical spine. Herniated disks, sprains, and strains occur frequently at the lumbar spine, however.

The human body's center of gravity lies at the lumbar spine, and the upper body weight is borne on the lumbar spine. The lumbar spine performs flexion, extension, rotation, and lateral flexion as the cervical spine does. These motions predispose the lumbar spine to herniated disks, sprains, and strains. These lumbar injuries exhibit similar signs and symptoms as the respective cervical spine injuries. Immediate care and prevention of these injuries are the same as with cervical and thoracic spine injuries.

Spondylolysis and Spondylolisthesis

Spondylolysis and spondylolisthesis are chronic injuries that occur over a period of time. Spondylolysis is a lumbar vertebra stress fracture that occurs most commonly at the fifth lumbar vertebra (L5), and next commonly at the fourth lumbar vertebra (L4) (American Academy of Orthopaedic Surgeons [AAOS], 2007). The stress fracture occurs at the base of the spinous process, which is called the pars interarticularis (**Figure 11-8**). If the stress fracture completely breaks through

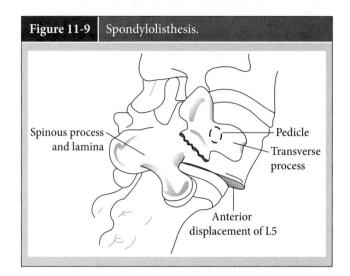

| **Figure 11-9** | Spondylolisthesis. |

Spinous process and lamina — Pedicle — Transverse process — Anterior displacement of L5

the bone, the vertebra becomes unstable. As a result, the vertebral body begins to slide forward on the surrounding vertebrae. This complication of spondylolysis is called spondylolisthesis (**Figure 11-9**). If the L5 vertebra is affected by spondylolysis, then L5 slips forward on the sacrum. If L4 is fractured, then it slips anteriorly on L5. If the vertebra continues to move out of position, it may press on the spinal cord and nerves and cause loss of motor function and sensation into the pelvis and lower extremity.

Mechanism or Cause of Injury. Hyperextension of the lumbar spine predisposes the athlete to spondylolysis and spondylolisthesis. Many of these injuries are found in athletes who participate in sports that require a constant loading of and stress on the low back, such as gymnastics, wrestling, and football (linemen). Genetics can also play a role in creating spondylolysis and spondylolisthesis. Some athletes are born with a thin pars interarticularis, which make the bone susceptible to stress fracture.

Signs and Symptoms. The most common symptom of spondylolysis and spondylolisthesis is diffuse pain across the low back. Due to lack of pain localization, the athlete may think she has a low back strain. Spasm of the low back muscles can occur, which alters posture and gait (AAOS, 2007). Pain may radiate, and the athlete may have burning, tingling, or numbness down the legs if the vertebra has slipped forward enough to affect the spinal cord and nerves.

Immediate Care. Begin caring for the athlete by performing a secondary survey to determine the SINS of injury. If an athlete complains of diffuse pain across her lower back, and has a mechanism of injury that would precipitate spondylolysis and

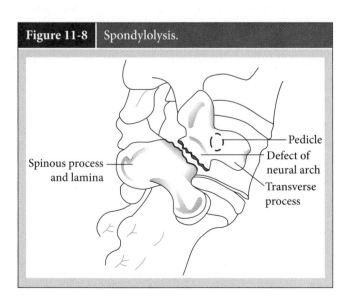

| **Figure 11-8** | Spondylolysis. |

Spinous process and lamina — Pedicle — Defect of neural arch — Transverse process spondylolisthesis, then have the athlete rest from any activity that aggravates the low back, and apply an ice pack and an elastic bandage for support. Refer the athlete to a physician. X-rays will show whether a fracture exists and if the vertebra has slipped anteriorly. If the athlete has either condition, the physician may attempt conservative, nonsurgical treatment first, which includes rest from activities that exacerbate low back pain, NSAIDs, bracing if necessary, and rehabilitation. The core body muscles must be strengthened and stretched in order to attempt to realign the vertebra and decrease symptoms. If rehabilitation does not decrease the pain, and the symptoms begin to affect performing ADLs, then surgery may be the only option to treat the injury. The physician will fuse the lumbar vertebra that has slipped to the vertebra below it to prevent the slippage.

Prevention. Prevention of spondylolysis and spondylolisthesis includes having strong, flexible muscles around the core body. The athlete should avoid continual hyperextension exercises that predispose her to these injuries.

Myofascial Pain Syndrome

Myofascial pain syndrome is a chronic pain syndrome. Although it can occur in the cervical spine area, the lumbar spine is often affected.

Mechanism or Cause of Injury. Myofascial pain syndrome can affect any area of the body that is overused. These muscles are repeatedly contracted during ADLs, hobbies, work duties, and athletic activities. **Trigger points** form in the muscles and refer pain throughout the entire muscle.

> **Trigger points**
> Hypersensitive, hyperirritable nodules in muscle tissue. They are also referred to as *knots* in the muscle.

Signs and Symptoms. The athlete experiences trigger point pain. The pain is a deep, aching pain that is more severe than normal muscular pain. The pain travels throughout the muscle in which the trigger point lies, and worsens over time.

Immediate Care. Usually muscular soreness and even pain resolves quickly when the muscle is treated for inflammation and pain by utilizing rest, ice, and NSAIDs. If your athlete complains of chronic low back pain that does not subside within a few days, especially after rest from activity and utilizing ice packs frequently, then refer the athlete to his physician. A physician can inject corticosteroid medication into the trigger points, and prescribe NSAIDs and muscle relaxants. Rehabilitation, massage, stretching, and relaxation techniques assist in decreasing signs and symptoms.

Prevention. To avoid myofascial pain syndrome, explain to your athletes the importance of exercising and stress management. Exercise, including ROM, flexibility, and strengthening exercises, will help your athletes maintain healthy, strong, pain-free muscles. Your athletes must also find enjoyable ways to relax in order to control stress.

Contusions

Low back musculature contusions are similar to any other muscle contusion.

Mechanism or Cause of Injury. Contusions to the lumbar spine and surrounding musculature occur due to a direct blow to the area.

Signs and Symptoms. Pain with motion, point tenderness, swelling, and ecchymosis are the common signs and symptoms of any contusion. Muscle contusions cause spasm, stiffness, and inability to fully contract the muscle.

Immediate Care. Most often these contusions do not warrant EMS care. Assist the athlete by applying ice and compression with an elastic wrap or low back brace, and telling him to rest from any activity that causes pain. If the signs and symptoms do not subside within a few days, or if they worsen causing persistent pain, then refer the athlete to his physician.

Prevention. Low back contusions can be avoided if the athlete wears appropriate protective equipment. The low back musculature should be strengthened in order to protect against or at least minimize injury due to blunt force trauma.

THE THORAX

The thorax, also referred to as the thoracic cavity, is the area of the body between the neck and the abdomen. The sternum, ribs, thoracic vertebrae, and diaphragm create the thoracic cavity boundaries. Circulatory and respiratory system structures, including the heart, great blood vessels, trachea, bronchi, lungs, and nerves, are located in the thorax, as well as the thymus (an immune system structure) and esophagus (a digestive system structure).

The Ribs

The ribs are located in an area of the body called the thorax. They give the thoracic cavity its shape and protect the heart and lungs. Twelve pairs of ribs, the costal cartilage, sternum, and spine make up the rib cage. The external and internal intercostal muscles are in between each rib and assist respiration.

Fractures

The fifth through ninth ribs are most prone to fractures because they are rigidly secured to the rib cage (Schultz et al., 2010). Also, these lower ribs are not as well protected by the arms, especially if the arms are not down by the athlete's side during activity.

Mechanism or Cause of Injury. Rib fractures occur from a direct blow to the rib cage. The direct blow can occur during contact sport activities, falls, or motor vehicle accidents (**Figure 11-10**). Repetitive twisting of the torso or coughing spells can also fracture a rib.

Signs and Symptoms. With a fractured rib, the athlete has pain on inspiration, especially when taking deep breaths. The rib is point tender and the athlete may experience crepitus upon palpation. Also upon palpation, the athlete may feel a false joint. A false joint is when a crack in the bone is palpable and feels like a joint space. Usually rib fractures are closed fractures.

Immediate Care. Most broken ribs heal on their own within a couple of months. In the meantime, it is important for the athlete to control her pain by utilizing ice packs and NSAIDs. If the athlete's pain causes breathing difficulty or significant pain along the rib, then the athlete should see a physician. The physician will perform an evaluation and take x-rays to determine whether the ribs are fractured. If a fracture exists, the physician will prescribe rest, NSAIDs, and ice packs to decrease pain and inflammation. According to the Mayo Clinic

(2011), compression wraps are no longer used for rib fractures. Compression wraps can hinder deep breathing, which can increase the risk of the athlete acquiring pneumonia.

Remember that various organs lie within the rib cage, and a fractured rib can lacerate one of these organs. Therefore, if you suspect an organ is lacerated, which may be the case if the athlete goes into shock, call 911 immediately.

Prevention. As with any other measures to prevent fractures, athletes need strong bones, which require an adequate intake of calcium and vitamin D. Athletes should wear protective rib equipment as per their activity (**Figure 11-11**), be cognizant of their surroundings, and protect themselves from falls.

Costochondral Separation (Sprain)

A costochondral separation occurs when the costocartilage, which is located between the rib and the attachment to the sternum, is separated from the sternum. The injury is also called a *separated rib*. The separation is considered a severe, Grade 3 sprain.

Mechanism or Cause of Injury. A costochondral separation is caused by a direct blow to the lateral rib cage. The injury can

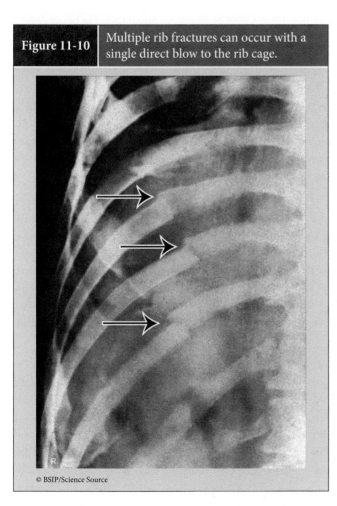

| **Figure 11-10** | Multiple rib fractures can occur with a single direct blow to the rib cage. |

© BSIP/Science Source

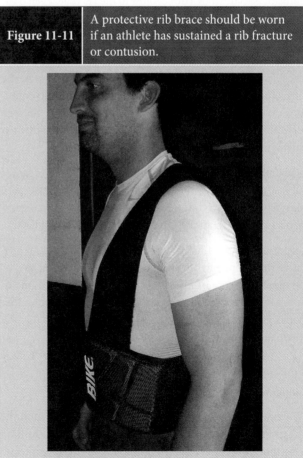

| **Figure 11-11** | A protective rib brace should be worn if an athlete has sustained a rib fracture or contusion. |

Courtesy of Jennifer Eaves and Calvin Bacon.

also be caused by an anterior direct blow to the costochondral area.

Signs and Symptoms. The athlete feels varying degrees of pain, especially upon deep breathing; point tenderness; and crepitus. Ecchymosis and localized swelling may be present.

Immediate Care. Assist the athlete to rest the injured area. Ice packs assist in pain and inflammation control. Treatment should be similar to rib fracture treatment, and 911 should be called in the same circumstances (i.e., breathing difficulty, possible injury to underlying organs, or shock).

Prevention. Costochondral separation prevention is the same as for rib fractures. Athletes need an adequate intake of calcium and vitamin D to strengthen bones. Athletes should wear protective rib equipment as per their activity, be cognizant of their surroundings, and protect themselves from falls.

Contusions

Rib contusions may be mistaken for a rib fracture, due to the similar mechanism and signs and symptoms of injury.

Mechanism or Cause of Injury. Rib and surrounding muscle contusions occur from a direct blow to the rib cage. Even if the athlete is wearing rib protective equipment, a traumatic blow can still contuse the ribs.

Signs and Symptoms. Rib contusions are painful, even when the athlete is not breathing deeply. Swelling, ecchymosis, and point tenderness are present. Unlike rib fractures, rib contusions do not exhibit crepitus or a false joint on the rib. You can utilize the absence of crepitus to differentiate whether the athlete has a rib fracture or a contusion.

Immediate Care. The athlete should immediately apply ice and rest from activity. He can take NSAIDs to decrease pain and inflammation. If the athlete has notable pain when breathing or difficulty breathing, then summon EMS immediately.

Prevention. Prevention of contusions includes wearing protective rib equipment as appropriate for the activity. The athlete must be aware of his surroundings to avoid trauma to the area (e.g., not walking or running into equipment, other people, etc.). The facility should be free from objects that the athlete may walk or run into during activity.

The Lungs

Pneumothorax

A pneumothorax is a collapsed lung. Air collects around the lung in the pleural cavity, which is the space around the lung in the thoracic cavity (**Figure 11-12**). This air causes improper

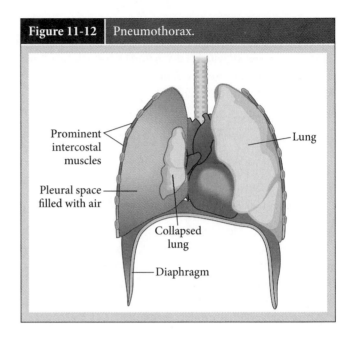

Figure 11-12 | Pneumothorax.

lung functioning, and the lung cannot take in normal amounts of air (PubMed Health, 2012).

Mechanism or Cause of Injury. A pneumothorax occurs when an object punctures a lung. A rib can be fractured, and the fractured bone punctures a lung. A lung can also be punctured by a knife, gunshot, archery arrow, or any penetrating object. Sometimes a collapsed lung occurs spontaneously. Air in the lung escapes and enters into the pleural cavity. This injury is called a *spontaneous pneumothorax*. Athletes who have lung-related illnesses, such as chronic obstructive pulmonary disease (COPD) and asthma, are more prone to having a pneumothorax (PubMed Health, 2012).

Signs and Symptoms. An athlete with a pneumothorax has shortness of breath, pain when breathing (especially when breathing deeply), chest pain, and lightheadedness. The athlete's heart rate is rapid, and blood pressure is low. With prolonged breathing difficulty and without immediate treatment, the athlete can become cyanotic. When listening to the lung with a stethoscope, breath sounds are nonexistent on the injured side. The athlete most likely exhibits signs of shock.

Immediate Care. A pneumothorax is a medical emergency. Call 911 immediately while monitoring the athlete's airway, breathing, and circulation. Treat the athlete for shock if she exhibits signs and symptoms. If the athlete is not treated immediately, then air pressure can build up in the pleural cavity and cause a tension pneumothorax. This air pressure moves toward the heart and healthy lung and compresses

Hypoxia When tissues in the body are deprived of oxygen. If the oxygen deprivation continues for a period of time, the tissues will die.

them. This tension pneumothorax inhibits heart and lung function, and causes significant respiratory distress, **hypoxia**, and death.

A minor pneumothorax, which is a small opening in the lung, often resolves on its own, once the lung is able to inflate with continual breathing. For a minor pneumothorax, the physician may remove some air via a needle inserted into the pleural cavity. The physician can also choose to prescribe rest and supplemental oxygen. A major pneumothorax requires a tube inserted into the chest to pull out air and drain any fluid that has accumulated in the plural space. Surgery may be necessary, especially if this pneumothorax is not the first pneumothorax that the athlete has sustained.

Prevention. A pneumothorax can be prevented by protecting the rib cage as the athlete would for rib fractures and contusions. In order to keep their lungs healthy, athletes should not smoke. An asthmatic athlete must abide by her physician's orders to treat her asthma accordingly.

Hemothorax

A hemothorax is similar to a pneumothorax in regard to mechanism and signs and symptoms of injury. However, a hemothorax is when the pleural space fills with blood instead of air.

Mechanism or Cause of Injury. A hemothorax is caused by the same mechanism of injury as a pneumothorax. Blunt trauma from an object (fractured rib, knife, gunshot, archery arrow, etc.) penetrates the lung and results in hemorrhage. The blood fills the pleural cavity. An athlete can also be predisposed to a hemothorax if he has tuberculosis, lung cancer, or previous lung conditions or surgery.

Signs and Symptoms. Signs and symptoms of a hemothorax include rapid, shallow breathing and shortness of breath; rapid pulse; low blood pressure; and chest pain. The athlete will be anxious and exhibit signs of shock.

Immediate Care. A hemothorax is a medical emergency. Summon EMS immediately. Treat the athlete for shock while monitoring his airway, breathing, and circulation. At the hospital, the physician will perform numerous tests including a chest x-ray, a CT scan, and pleural tests in order to determine if the athlete has a hemothorax. The physician's first objective is to stop the bleeding. If the bleeding does not stop, then the physician will perform surgery. Fortunately, typically the bleeding stops and surgery is unnecessary.

Prevention. Prevention of a hemothorax includes wearing chest protective equipment as required by the activity. In cases where the athlete has a predisposition for hemothorax as mentioned previously, the injury may not be preventable.

Asthma

Asthma is a potentially life-threatening condition in which the respiratory tract airways become inflamed. The airways become swollen and decreased in size. Consequently, not enough air enters the airways and the athlete has serious difficulty breathing.

Mechanism or Cause of Injury. Asthma is caused when an athlete breathes in an allergen or trigger. When a trigger affects an athlete, he has an exacerbation (previously referred to as an *asthma attack*). Triggers can be various substances including smoke, pet dander, pollen, mold, dust, and chemicals in the air. Exacerbations can also be caused by stress; emotions; environmental changes, especially in cold weather; respiratory infections including colds; and exercise. Asthma triggered by exercise is called exercise-induced asthma (EIA). Many athletes who have EIA also have regular asthma. Some athletes have EIA but not regular asthma, which renders the EIA cause as unknown.

Signs and Symptoms. The asthmatic athlete experiences shortness of breath, wheezing, anxiety, coughing, chest tightness, and rapid pulse. The signs and symptoms can last for minutes to days, and tend to worsen in cold weather and with exercise. Severe signs and symptoms also include chest pain, an abnormal breathing pattern, or cessation of breathing for any period of time.

Immediate Care. The first course of action is to remove the athlete from the trigger or vice versa, whichever is safer for the athlete. Assist the athlete in administering his rescue inhaler if he has one available (**Figure 11-13**). Never give the athlete another athlete's inhaler, even if the medication on the label appears to be the same. Try to calm the athlete down. Have him sit in a comfortable position and take slow, controlled breaths. If you do not see that the athlete is beginning to breathe normally within a few minutes, then phone 911 immediately. Monitor the athlete's airway, breathing, and circulation until EMS arrives and treat for shock if necessary. At the ER, the physician will perform many tests to determine what triggers the athlete's asthma, along with the extent of the condition. The physician will take chest x-rays and perform lung function and breathing tests on the athlete. The physician will also give the athlete medication to make the asthma exacerbation subside. The athlete will have to take prescription medication to decrease the potential for exacerbations including long

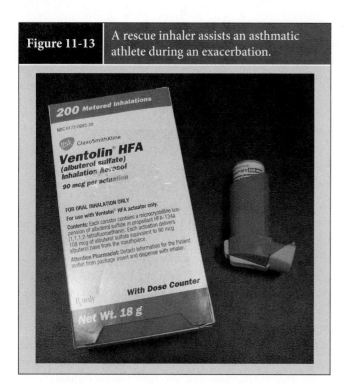

Figure 11-13 A rescue inhaler assists an asthmatic athlete during an exacerbation.

and short duration (or "rescue") inhaled corticosteroids. The long duration corticosteroids assist in preventing exacerbations, and the short duration corticosteroids relieve signs and symptoms if an exacerbation begins.

Prevention. Preventing asthma is not always possible, because an athlete cannot necessarily change how his body responds to allergens. However, to prevent exacerbations, asthmatic athletes should always take their prescription asthma medication as directed by their physician. They should also avoid the asthma triggers. The athlete's home should be clean and free of dust, smoke, and any allergen that triggers the exacerbations. For athletes who have EIA, they should exercise in warm, moist environments, such as in a swimming pool, because this environment tends to decrease the incidence of exacerbations.

Hyperventilation

Hyperventilation is when the blood contains low levels of carbon dioxide.

Mechanism or Cause of Injury. Hyperventilation occurs when an athlete breathes quickly and deeply for a period of time. The quick, deep breathing typically occurs when the athlete is panicking, anxious, angry, or depressed. It can also occur if the athlete has an infection, lung or cardiac disease, stress, or severe bleeding. This type of breathing causes excessive oxygen and low levels of carbon dioxide in the blood.

Signs and Symptoms. The athlete who is rapidly breathing experiences panic, lightheadedness, dizziness, and confusion. She may have chest pain, heart palpitations, and dry mouth.

Immediate Care. In most cases when an athlete is hyperventilating, you can care for the athlete without needing to call 911. Comfort and console the athlete by talking to her in a relaxed tone of voice while reassuring her that she will be okay. Help the athlete gain more carbon dioxide in her blood to normalize the levels. Have the athlete breathe in and out through pursed lips, or have her close her mouth and breathe through only one nostril. Breathing into a paper bag is no longer recommended because the athlete could then become hypoxic. Direct her to breathe slowly and in a regulated manner. The athlete's breathing rate should slowly return to normal within approximately a minute. If the athlete's breathing does not quickly return to a normal rate and depth, or if she has severe chest pain, then call 911 immediately. The physician will evaluate the athlete and perform many tests including a chest x-ray and breathing tests to identify any underlying illnesses that may have triggered the hyperventilation.

Prevention. Preventing hyperventilation begins with stress reduction exercises. These exercises can assist in controlling emotions and panic attacks. The athlete may need to see a professional counselor to assist her in controlling these emotions. The athlete should have annual physicals to make sure she is healthy and free of illness, including lung or cardiac disease.

The Heart

Sudden Cardiac Death Syndrome

Sudden cardiac death (SCD) syndrome is when an athlete dies unexpectedly from cardiac arrest. The athlete may or may not experience any signs or symptoms of illness and may succumb to cardiac arrest with no warning. The athlete who does experience signs and symptoms of cardiac problems and succumbs to SCD dies within an hour after the signs and symptoms first appear.

Mechanism or Cause of Injury. SCD is most often caused by cardiac disease and illnesses such as hypertrophic cardiomyopathy (**Figure 11-14**), atherosclerosis, viral myocarditis, aortic valve stenosis, or drug-induced electrolyte imbalance (Meyer et al., 2003). Less common causes of SCD include conditions such as idiopathic ventricular fibrillation, sick sinus syndrome, atrioventricular node tumor, and Wolff-Parkinson-White syndrome. According to Meyer et al. (2003), approximately 1–5% of athletes who die of SCD do not have any underlying cause. These athletes are classified as having sudden arrhythmia death (SAD) syndrome.

Figure 11-14 | (A) Shows a normal heart. One cause of sudden cardiac death is hypertrophic cardiomyopathy, which is a thickening of the left ventricular wall (B). The ventricle cannot pump sufficient amounts of blood to the body.

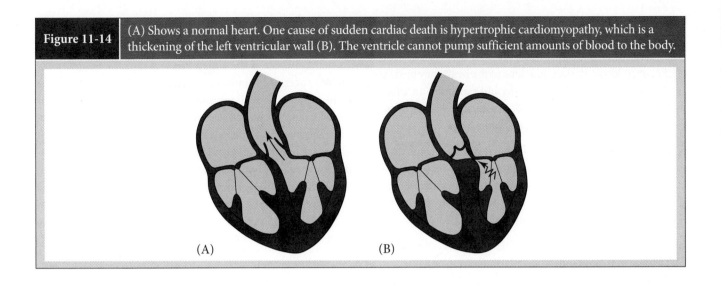

(A)   (B)

Signs and Symptoms. The athlete may experience chest pain, breathing difficulty, confusion, sweaty skin, and unsteadiness immediately prior to cardiac arrest. The athlete loses consciousness, stops breathing, and has no pulse.

Immediate Care. Call 911 immediately and check the athlete's airway, breathing, and circulation. Perform cardiopulmonary resuscitation (CPR) on the athlete and utilize an automated external defibrillator (AED) in an attempt to resume a normal heartbeat. Do not stop CPR until EMS arrives and the EMTs take over for you, another trained person takes over, the environment becomes unsafe, or you are too tired to continue.

Prevention. SCD may not be entirely preventable; however, underlying risk factors can be identified. An athlete should have annual physicals with electrocardiograms taken to determine if he has any heart rhythm abnormalities. The athlete should take care of himself, consume proper nutrients, and maintain normal body weight. He must avoid smoking or drinking excessive alcohol. Participation in physical and wellness activities in order to avoid cardiac disease is imperative. Athletes should gradually progress activity intensity to prevent undue stress to the heart, especially when beginning a new activity or after a long duration of inactivity.

Commotio Cordis

Commotio cordis is a sudden death due to a disruption in the heart's electrical conductivity. The athlete may or may not have an underlying cardiac issue.

Mechanism or Cause of Injury. Commotio cordis occurs when an athlete is struck by an object at the sternum, which overlies the heart. The athlete may be wearing chest protective equipment, but the propelled object's force is so great that the equipment cannot entirely protect the heart.

Signs and Symptoms. Athletes with commotio cordis are unconscious, not breathing, without a pulse, and cyanotic. Ecchymosis appears at the impact point on the chest, which indicates a contusion.

Immediate Care. Call 911 immediately; check for airway, breathing, and circulation; and then immediately start CPR. According to experimental data, AED utilization within 1 minute of loss of pulse gives the athlete a 100% chance of survival (Yabek, 2011). As each minute goes by, the chance of survival decreases significantly. Unfortunately, CPR with AED use is not usually initiated within 1 minute of an athlete with commotio cordis.

Prevention. Athletes must wear properly fitted chest protective equipment for the activity. The protective equipment is not foolproof in preventing commotio cordis, however. The equipment is utilized in an attempt to protect the body and dissipate force from the striking object. When participating in activities where the possibility of receiving a direct blow to the chest exists, the athlete must always be aware of his or her surroundings.

Heart Murmur

Many athletes have heart murmurs. Heart murmurs are extra or unusual sounds that occur when the heart beats. The murmurs can be harmless and not a cause for concern, or may indicate an underlying cardiac problem.

Mechanism or Cause of Injury. The National Heart, Lung, and Blood Institute (2012) notes that "harmless" or "innocent" heart murmurs have an unknown cause. It is speculated that extra blood flow, such as when an athlete is pregnant, may cause a murmur. Abnormal heart murmurs are typically congenital in children. Various portions of the heart may be damaged, which leads to valve problems and murmurs. In adults, murmurs are usually indicative of heart valve disease, which can be caused by infection, disease, and aging.

Signs and Symptoms. Athletes with harmless heart murmurs may experience no signs or symptoms. They may not even know they have a murmur. Some athletes may experience shortness of breath during exertion, excessive sweating without cause, cyanosis, dizziness, fainting, and chest pain.

Immediate Care. If an athlete exhibits signs and symptoms of a heart murmur, have him stop activity and rest, and refer him to a physician for evaluation. If he is in distress, which is not typical, then call 911. First aid is not provided to an athlete if he has an innocent heart murmur. If the athlete has an abnormal heart murmur, his physician will address the cause. If the athlete has another illness or disease that could be causing the murmur, such as hyperthyroidism or anemia, the physician will treat the underlying cause. Once the underlying cause is addressed, the murmur should stop. If the cause is a congenital heart defect, surgery may be warranted.

Prevention. Innocent and abnormal congenital heart murmurs cannot be prevented. However, in an attempt to prevent heart valve disease, the athlete should lead a healthy lifestyle, maintain proper nutrition, and participate in physical activity and exercise on a regular basis.

The Breasts

Breast Cancer

Breast cancer is the most common form of cancer for U.S. women after skin cancer; however, breast cancer can also occur in men. The cancer forms in the ducts of the breast cells.

Mechanism or Cause of Injury. No definitive cause for breast cancer has been identified. The disease occurs when breast cells grow abnormally. Various risk factors predispose an athlete to breast cancer, such as being female, having a familial history of breast cancer, beginning menstruation at a young age, beginning menopause at a young age, taking postmenopausal medications, having the first child at age 35 or older, alcohol consumption, and obesity.

Signs and Symptoms. An athlete with breast cancer experiences a lump in the breast that feels unusual as compared to the other tissue. The lump is not necessarily painful, and remains in the same area. The nipple may be inverted, bleeding, or dimpled. The breast may change shape or size, and the skin may look wrinkled.

Immediate Care. If the athlete has any signs or symptoms of breast cancer, she should see a physician to be evaluated. Even if the athlete has had a recent mammogram, if she develops breast cancer signs and symptoms, she should be evaluated. The physician will order a variety of tests including a mammogram, MRI, ultrasound, and biopsy. A biopsy involves removing some of the abnormal breast tissue mass and testing it to see if it is cancerous. If the athlete has breast cancer, then she can have surgery to remove the mass, the cancerous breast, and/or the lymph nodes. Chemotherapy and/or radiation are prescribed regardless of whether surgery is performed.

Prevention. Mammograms identify abnormal breast tissue. Female athletes should have an annual mammogram beginning at age 40 years. Athletes should exercise, eat nutritious foods, and avoid smoking and alcohol consumption. Female athletes should consider whether postmenopausal hormone therapy is appropriate, because it increases the chance of acquiring breast cancer.

THE ABDOMEN

The abdomen, which is commonly referred to as the *belly*, is the area below the diaphragm and above the pelvis. The abdomen contains the stomach, small and large intestines, liver, gallbladder, pancreas, kidneys, and spleen. The aorta and inferior vena cava also descend from the thorax to the abdomen.

The Kidneys and Urinary System

Kidney Contusions

A kidney contusion is a serious injury. If the kidney does not have adequate time to heal and sustains another injury, complications may occur. Kidney function may deteriorate or the kidney can fail.

Mechanism or Cause of Injury. Blunt force trauma is the cause of kidney contusions. If the force is strong enough, the kidney can actually be lacerated, which is a more significant injury.

Signs and Symptoms. The athlete complains of back pain by the kidney (called the *flank*) and possibly in the abdomen. He also complains of nausea and difficulty breathing. The athlete may vomit and may have some blood in the urine (hematuria), but often this blood is not visible to the naked eye. Ecchymosis and swelling may be visible at the impact site.

Immediate Care. If the athlete has sustained blunt force trauma to the flank area and signs and symptoms indicate that the athlete has sustained a kidney contusion, then refer the athlete to a physician. In the meantime, the athlete must apply ice to the area, rest, and discontinue any contact activities. He can take over-the-counter NSAIDs to reduce pain and inflammation. The physician will perform a urinalysis to check for blood in the urine, and will order a CT scan, an ultrasound, and other tests that evaluate the kidney's function. The athlete should wear padding or a brace over the affected area to protect the area from additional direct trauma until the kidney has healed. Rarely is surgery needed. If the kidney is lacerated or the blood supply to the kidney is damaged, then surgery will be an option to save the kidney.

Prevention. Athletes should wear flank protective gear if they participate in contact activities. The athlete should strengthen the musculature that will help protect the kidney from blunt force trauma.

Kidney Stones

Kidney stones can be found anywhere in the urinary tract, but are formulated in the kidneys. Kidney stones are formed over a period of weeks or months.

Mechanism or Cause of Injury. Kidney stones can form due to the urine containing too much calcium or uric acid. Oxalate, which is found in foods such as spinach, beets, almonds, and sesame seeds, can combine with calcium and form the kidney stones. Kidney stones can be hereditary or caused by medications, such as acyclovir, which treats herpes outbreaks.

Signs and Symptoms. The athlete experiences back pain, nausea, vomiting, chills, fever, and hematuria or abnormal urine color.

Immediate Care: If the athlete believes she has kidney stones, she should be evaluated by her physician. The physician will perform various tests including blood tests, ultrasounds, CT, MRI, and x-rays to determine whether a kidney stone is present and, if so, its location. Treatment for kidney stones is conservative at first because the stones usually pass through the urinary tract on their own. When kidney stones pass through the urinary tract, the athlete may be in a lot of pain and should take NSAIDs. The physician may prescribe narcotics for the pain. If the athlete believes she is passing a stone when urinating, she should strain the urine to collect the stone (**Figure 11-15**). Once the stone is collected, the athlete should give it to her physician for evaluation, in order to determine what caused the stone. If the stone cannot be passed or other complications exist, the physician may need to perform surgery or other procedures to eliminate the stone.

Prevention. The athlete should drink about eight glasses of water per day to make sure adequate urine is being produced and any substances within the urine are diluted.

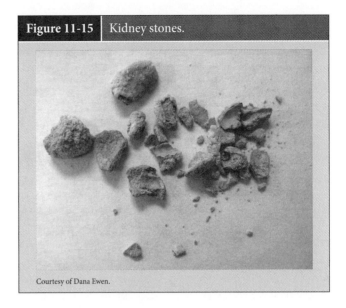

| Figure 11-15 | Kidney stones. |

Courtesy of Dana Ewen.

Urinary Tract Infections

Urinary tract infections (UTIs) occur in both males and females, with the infection occurring more often in females.

Mechanism or Cause of Injury. UTIs occur due to bacteria getting into the bladder and causing cystitis, which is an inflammation of the bladder. A UTI can also occur due to urethritis, which is an inflammation of the urethra. This inflammation can also be caused by bacteria entering the urethra or by sexually transmitted infections (STIs).

Signs and Symptoms. The athlete experiences pelvic pain, as well as severe pain and burning with urination. The athlete constantly feels the need to urinate. The urine is pink or cloudy.

Immediate Care. An athlete with a UTI must see her physician for a urinalysis to confirm the UTI and treatment. Approximately a 7-day course of antibiotics is necessary to eliminate the infection. Rarely does an athlete have a severe UTI that needs to be treated by intravenous antibiotics and hospitalization.

Prevention. UTIs can be prevented by drinking plenty of water each day and emptying the bladder as soon as the urge to urinate exists. Athletes should pay attention to pelvic area hygiene, especially after utilizing the bathroom.

The Digestive System

Peptic Ulcer

Peptic ulcers are sores located in the lining of the esophagus, stomach, and upper small intestines (**Figure 11-16**). Ulcers can become open sores that can hemorrhage.

Mechanism or Cause of Injury. Bacterial infections, especially *H. pylori*, are the most common cause of peptic ulcers. Stomach

Figure 11-16	A peptic ulcer can form in the upper digestive tract.

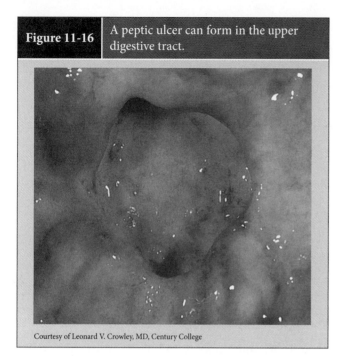

Courtesy of Leonard V. Crowley, MD, Century College

acid and overuse of aspirin and other NSAIDs can wear away the lining of the upper digestive tract. Chemicals from smoking tobacco can also cause the lining to be worn away. When the lining is worn away, an ulcer is formed. Physicians now recognize that stress and food do not cause ulcers.

Signs and Symptoms. Newly formed peptic ulcers exhibit a burning pain at the upper digestive tract, especially when the athlete has an empty stomach or at night. The pain may come and go for weeks at a time. More severe ulcers cause bleeding, and as a result the athlete may vomit blood that is very red in color. The athlete's stools, however, are dark black in color from the blood traveling through the entire digestive tract before being eliminated. The athlete does not have an appetite and most likely loses weight.

Immediate Care. If the signs and symptoms are not significant, the athlete can take over-the-counter antacids. If the athlete has consistent signs and symptoms, then he should see his physician. Through testing, the physician will determine the cause of the ulcer. Antibiotics can treat *H. pylori*. Various medications can be prescribed to prevent or decrease stomach acid production and promote ulcer healing. Antacids can be taken to neutralize stomach acid.

Prevention. Athletes should not overuse NSAIDs. If the athlete is having continual pain requiring NSAIDs, he should consult a physician to determine what can be done to modulate the pain. Athletes should use proper hand washing

practices regularly to prevent the spread of bacteria. Athletes should not smoke.

Gastroenteritis

Gastroenteritis is stomach and small intestine inflammation. When the illness is caused by eating contaminated food, it is referred to as *food poisoning*.

Mechanism or Cause of Injury. Gastroenteritis occurs when bacteria, viruses, or parasites enter the digestive tract. This infection can occur if these contaminants are contained in poorly prepared or uncooked food. The contaminants also can be found in water that the athlete drinks or that is used in food preparation. A person can also pass the contaminants to another person. Noncontagious causes of gastroenteritis are chemicals and other toxins, certain substances found in foods such as seafood and dairy products, and medications.

Signs and Symptoms. The athlete has abdominal pain, nausea, vomiting, and diarrhea. Flu-like symptoms, including fever if the athlete has an infection, and chills are evident.

Immediate Care. Gastroenteritis commonly relieves itself in a short amount of time. Usually the body rids itself of the contaminant within a day to a week. In the meantime, the athlete must treat the signs and symptoms. Ingestion of electrolyte fluids is imperative in order to avoid dehydration. The athlete must ease into eating normal foods after gastroenteritis.

Prevention. An athlete should practice frequent hand washing with soap and water in order to prevent gastroenteritis. She should inform her physician if she has any intolerance or stomach upset with any foods, medications, or toxins.

Vomiting

Vomiting is the body forcing out the stomach contents. Vomiting has many causes. If an athlete vomits, an underlying cause needs to be identified.

Mechanism or Cause of Injury. Many causes for vomiting exist. Vomiting can be caused by illnesses and infections, such as ulcers, gastroenteritis, appendicitis, and the flu. An athlete can vomit when he is in shock, has a migraine, or is in severe pain. Medications, allergens, chemicals, food, and alcohol also can cause an athlete to vomit.

Signs and Symptoms. The athlete feels nauseous, has abdominal pain, and perhaps begins to sweat prior to vomiting. The athlete may become pale, disoriented, and weak.

Immediate Care. First rule out any life-threatening injuries or illnesses by performing your primary survey. Then perform your secondary survey and determine the SINS of illness. If you can readily determine the cause of the vomiting and the athlete is not in a life-threatening situation, then have the athlete vomit into a receptacle, rest, and take slow sips of an electrolyte drink. Remember, if blood is in the vomit, blood-borne pathogens may exist; therefore, wear personal protective equipment (PPE) when assisting the athlete. If vomiting does not stop within 24 hours after it has begun, blood is in the vomit, the underlying cause cannot be identified, or the cause is life-threatening or serious, then immediately call 911. Also, if the athlete is in severe pain or becomes dehydrated, EMS must be summoned. In the ER, intravenous fluids, medication to stop the vomiting, and pain medication will be prescribed. Once the underlying cause is identified, the physician will determine whether it is safe for the athlete to go home or if hospitalization is necessary.

Prevention. The athlete should avoid all substances that may cause him to vomit. The athlete should refrain from being around others who knowingly have a contagious illness such as the flu or gastroenteritis.

Diarrhea

Diarrhea is a loose, watery, frequent bowel movement. If the athlete has three or more of these bowel movements per day, then the illness is classified as diarrhea.

Mechanism or Cause of Injury. Diarrhea can be caused by the same mechanisms of illness as vomiting. Bacteria, viruses, and parasites, as well as illnesses, infection, contaminated food and water, food intolerances, and medications, can cause diarrhea.

Signs and Symptoms. The signs and symptoms include abdominal cramping, bloating, nausea, and the urge to defecate. The stools appear extremely watery and loose. Blood, which appears as very dark red or black, may be in the stool.

Immediate Care. To treat the athlete's diarrhea, remove the causative factor, if you are able to identify it after performing a secondary survey. The athlete should rest in a comfortable place and take slow sips of an electrolyte drink. If the causative factor is not an underlying illness or infection, then the athlete can take over-the-counter antidiarrheal medication. If the causative factor is an underlying illness or infection, the athlete becomes dehydrated, you are not able to identify the cause, or the diarrhea does not stop within 2–3 days, then refer the athlete to a physician.

Prevention. The athlete should practice frequent hand washing. He should refrain from being around others who knowingly have a contagious illness such as the flu or gastroenteritis.

Gastroesophageal Reflux Disease (GERD)

Gastroesophageal reflux disease (GERD) is also called peptic esophagitis and dyspepsia. Some athletes refer to it as indigestion or heartburn. When an athlete eats or drinks, the substances travel through the esophagus, through a sphincter, and into the stomach. The sphincter prevents food and drink from coming back up into the esophagus. If the sphincter is not able to keep the food and drink in the stomach, then reflux, or leaking back into the esophagus, occurs. If the reflux also includes stomach acid, which is created and used for digestive purposes, then the athlete feels a burning sensation or heartburn.

Mechanism or Cause of Injury. GERD can be brought on by drinking alcohol, smoking, obesity, and pregnancy. Various medications, including some high blood pressure, depression, and asthma medications, can cause GERD.

Signs and Symptoms. The athlete with GERD has heartburn, which is a burning sensation into his esophagus. The athlete may have indigestion when he regurgitates his food, or has the sensation that food is stuck in his esophagus by the lower portion of the breastbone. The burning worsens at night and when lying down and sitting.

Immediate Care. An athlete can take a variety of over-the-counter acid reflux medications to prevent, decrease, or neutralize the stomach acid. An athlete should begin to lose weight if he is obese, and quit smoking and drinking excessive alcohol. If the problem persists for weeks to months after self-treatment, then the athlete should be evaluated by a physician. The physician may prescribe medication to assist in decreasing the signs and symptoms of GERD, as well as lifestyle changes to minimize the effects of the illness.

Prevention. Athletes should maintain a healthy weight, not smoke or drink excessive alcohol, and eat slowly at meals in order to prevent GERD. Any foods that aggravate the athlete's digestive system as well as oral anti-inflammatory medications should be avoided.

Irritable Bowel Syndrome (IBS)

Irritable bowel syndrome (IBS) is a common condition of the large intestine. Unlike some other lower intestine illnesses, such as Crohn's disease and colitis, IBS does not produce inflammation. Women are more likely to have IBS than are men.

Mechanism or Cause of Injury. IBS has no known cause. Athletes may have triggers that exacerbate IBS, such as gas, certain foods, stress or other emotions, medications, and hormone changes in women. IBS can also be hereditary.

Signs and Symptoms. IBS causes abdominal pain, cramping, gas, bloating, diarrhea, and constipation. Mucus is visible on the athlete's stools. Most often these signs and symptoms are minor. In rare cases they can be disabling and the athlete must readily see a physician.

Immediate Care. Because IBS has no definitive cause, the athlete must treat her symptoms. The athlete should control her diet by eliminating gas-producing foods, including broccoli and cabbage, as well as foods that can increase signs and symptoms of IBS, such as sugar-free sweeteners, caffeine, carbonated beverages, and dairy products. The athlete should eat fiber-filled foods or take fiber supplements to control constipation. She must manage her stress and exercise frequently. If the athlete has diarrhea, antidiarrheal medications are necessary. If the athlete has stress, anxiety, or depression, she should participate in relaxation techniques, speak with a professional counselor, or see a physician for medication addressing the issue. If the athlete's signs and symptoms are disabling, then refer her to a physician for evaluation. The doctor can prescribe specific medication to treat IBS, along with recommending lifestyle changes to decrease the incidence of signs and symptoms.

Prevention. An athlete can prevent IBS by participating in physical activity. She should regularly participate in relaxation activities. Eating small meals throughout the day, including fiber in the diet, drinking eight glasses of water per day, and avoiding foods that cause IBS signs and symptoms help prevent IBS.

Constipation

Constipation is a common gastrointestinal (GI) problem for athletes. When an athlete is constipated, her stools are hard and difficult to pass.

Mechanism or Cause of Injury. Constipation may occur from a lack of fluid or fiber in the diet. The waste products move too slowly through the GI tract, and lose fluid. This keeps the waste products hard and difficult to pass. Constipation can also occur due to an underlying condition or disease such as diabetes, thyroid conditions, and stroke.

Signs and Symptoms. An athlete with constipation passes less than three stools per week. The stools are hard and difficult and perhaps painful to pass. The athlete feels like the rectum is being blocked, and she strains to produce a bowel movement.

Immediate Care. The athlete can take over-the-counter medications including fiber supplements and laxatives to assist in softening and eliminating the stool. The athlete can also use an enema. Any of these remedies should not be utilized too frequently, because they can irritate the colon and cause

complications. If the athlete continues to pass stools infrequently, then an underlying cause for the constipation may exist and she should see a physician.

Prevention. To avoid constipation, the athlete must increase the amount of fiber in her diet. She can include fiber-filled foods, such as fruits, vegetables, whole grains, and beans, and/or take fiber supplements. The athlete must drink approximately eight glasses of water per day to help move the stool through the colon. Exercise also has been shown to promote colon function.

The Reproductive System

The reproductive system can be affected by systemic disease or by injury.

Testicular Cancer

Testicular cancer is not very common, but is highly treatable.

Mechanism or Cause of Injury: As with breast cancer, no definitive cause of testicular cancer has been determined. Abnormal cells begin to grow in the testes, which create a hard, unusual mass. Risk factors for testicular cancer include undescended or abnormal testicles, and family history. Caucasians are more prone to testicular cancer than other races. Men ages 15–34 years are most commonly affected by testicular cancer.

Signs and Symptoms. A testicular cancer mass feels like a lump in the testicle. The athlete has dull pain in the abdomen and significant pain in the testicle. The scrotum may be swollen due to fluid collecting in the area.

Immediate Care. The athlete should see his physician if he has any signs and symptoms of testicular cancer that persist and do not resolve within a week or two. If the athlete has severe pain, refer him immediately for medical evaluation. Testicular cancer is treated with chemotherapy, radiation, and/or surgery.

Prevention. Testicular cancer is not preventable. However, male athletes should perform testicular self-exams regularly to feel for any abnormalities in the scrotum and testicles.

Scrotal Contusion

A scrotal contusion is similar to any other body contusion in regard to mechanism of injury and signs and symptoms.

Mechanism or Cause of Injury. Scrotal contusions occur due to a direct blow to the scrotum. The athlete could run into an object or be struck by an object in the scrotal area to cause the injury.

Signs and Symptoms. With a scrotal contusion, the athlete has immediate disabling testicular pain. He is typically bent over at the waist due to excruciating pain and feels like he cannot breathe. He also may feel nauseous and vomit. Testicular swelling, ecchymosis, and hematuria may be present.

Immediate Care. Immediate treatment is for the athlete to relax and wait for the pain to subside. An ice pack can be applied to the area and the athlete can take NSAIDs to decrease pain and inflammation. If the athlete has swelling at the scrotum that does not decrease within a few days of rest and ice application, then he must see a physician because he may have another injury such as a hydrocele or spermatic cord torsion (which are discussed in the following sections). The athlete should wear supportive underwear during the healing phases.

Prevention. To avoid scrotal contusions, athletes in sports such as baseball, ice hockey, and football should wear protective equipment for the genitalia.

Hydrocele

A hydrocele is an accumulation of fluid in the scrotal sac around the testicles.

Mechanism or Cause of Injury. Similarly to scrotal contusions, hydroceles are also caused in adults by direct trauma to the scrotum and testicles. Testicle or epididymis infection can also cause a hydrocele.

Signs and symptoms: The athlete rarely feels pain, but sees a significant amount of scrotal sac swelling. He may complain of scrotal sac heaviness.

Immediate Care. Often a hydrocele does not need treatment, but it is prudent for the athlete to be evaluated by his physician to rule out any other conditions such as spermatic cord torsion. A hydrocele typically resolves itself within 6 months or so. If the hydrocele does not resolve, then the physician may aspirate the fluid from the scrotum.

Prevention. Hydroceles are not entirely preventable. Athletes should wear protective equipment for the scrotum to avoid injury due to direct trauma.

Spermatic Cord Torsion

Spermatic cord torsion, also called testicular torsion, can occur to males of all ages. The condition occurs when the spermatic cord and testicle twist around and then are contracted in this position. Because the spermatic cord is twisted, blood supply to the testicle is inhibited or completely cut off. The testicle can become hypoxic and die.

Mechanism or Cause of Injury. Spermatic cord torsion can be caused by a direct blow to the scrotum or can occur during strenuous exercise. The condition can also occur due to an anatomic abnormality where the testes are loose within the

scrotal sac, which causes the scrotum to twist easily, during sleep, or for no apparent reason.

Signs and Symptoms. The athlete complains of a sudden onset of severe scrotal pain on the torsion side and in the abdomen. He feels nauseous, vomits, and has a fever. The scrotum may be red, swollen, and point tender.

Immediate Care. Spermatic cord torsion necessitates immediate care. If the athlete feels like he has a spermatic cord torsion, he should attempt to reverse the torsion manually. Even if he is able to reverse the torsion, the athlete should see a physician immediately. If he is not able to reverse the torsion, call 911 to have him transported to the ER immediately for care. The physician may need to perform immediate surgery in order to return blood supply to the testicle. After surgery, the athlete must rest for proper healing and so the condition does not recur.

Prevention. Spermatic cord torsion is not entirely able to be prevented. Athletes should wear protective equipment for the scrotum to avoid injury due to direct trauma.

Other Abdominal Conditions

Appendicitis

Appendicitis is an inflammation of the appendix that can occur to athletes of all ages. Pus accumulates in the appendix and causes significant signs and symptoms of illness. The appendix can burst, which allows pus to enter into the abdominal cavity. The pus is toxic to the body, and the athlete can die.

Mechanism or Cause of Injury. Appendicitis does not have a definitive cause. The inflammation may be caused by an obstruction of fecal material in the colon by the appendix, or by GI tract infection (**Figure 11-17**).

Signs and Symptoms. From the onset, the athlete complains of an increase in signs and symptoms over the course of the day, which eventually become severe. The athlete feels pain at

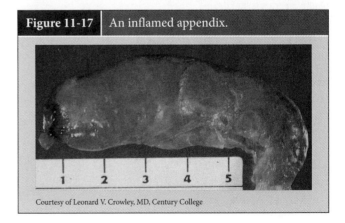

| Figure 11-17 | An inflamed appendix. |

Courtesy of Leonard V. Crowley, MD, Century College

the lower right abdomen at McBurney's point, especially when coughing, walking, or making sudden twisting movements. McBurney's point is a landmark located midway between the umbilicus and the anterior superior iliac spine (**Figure 11-18**). The area is very point tender. The athlete has rebound tenderness, which is absence of pain when pressure is applied to the area, but significant pain when the pressure is released. The athlete may have a low grade (99°F) fever, feel nauseous, and vomit.

Immediate Care. If you suspect your athlete has appendicitis due to the existing signs and symptoms, then refer the athlete to his physician immediately. Call 911 if the athlete has severe abdominal pain that does not subside despite the athlete attempting to get into a comfortable position, and comfort the athlete. The physician will perform an examination and imaging tests to determine whether the illness is appendicitis. If the athlete has appendicitis, the physician will perform surgery to remove the appendix. After the surgery, the athlete must rest and support the area to promote healing.

Prevention. Athletes cannot prevent appendicitis. Signs and symptoms of appendicitis must be recognized in order to seek medical care immediately and avoid a ruptured appendix.

Spleen Injury

Although they do not occur very often, contusions and lacerations of the spleen do occur. The spleen has a vast blood supply. Consequently, if the spleen is injured it can severely hemorrhage. This severe spleen hemorrhage is life-threatening.

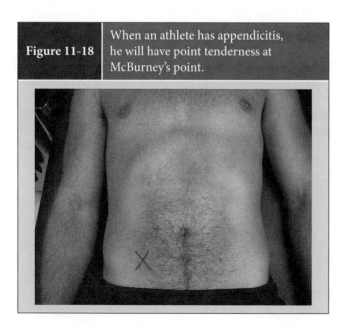

| **Figure 11-18** | When an athlete has appendicitis, he will have point tenderness at McBurney's point. |

Mechanism or Cause of Injury. A spleen injury is caused by blunt force, direct trauma to the upper left quadrant of the abdomen where the spleen is located. This trauma can occur due to a direct blow by another athlete's body, an implement or piece of equipment, falling hard on the ground onto the area, or a motor vehicle accident.

Signs and Symptoms. Typical signs and symptoms of spleen injuries include severe pain at the upper left portion of the abdomen, left shoulder pain (called *Kehr's sign*), nausea, vomiting, shock, abdominal muscle guarding and rigidity, difficulty breathing, and faintness.

Immediate Care. An injury to the spleen is a medical emergency. Call 911 immediately for the athlete to receive immediate medical care. Monitor the athlete's airway, breathing, and circulation while treating him for shock until EMS arrives. For spleen contusions, the physician will have the athlete rest and avoid any contact with others. The athlete cannot come in bodily contact with other people because another less traumatic blow can cause the spleen to rupture. For severe spleen contusions or lacerations, the spleen most likely will need to be repaired or removed surgically.

Prevention. Athletes must wear properly fitted protective equipment to prevent a spleen injury. They should always be cognizant of their surroundings while participating in activities. Athletes should always wear seatbelts in motor vehicles.

Mononucleosis

Mononucleosis, or *mono* as it is often called, is a viral infection.

Mechanism or Cause of Injury. Mononucleosis is caused by the Epstein-Barr virus, which is passed through saliva.

Signs and Symptoms. The athlete with mono exhibits flu-like symptoms including a fever, extreme fatigue and weakness, sore throat, headache, and loss of appetite. She may have night sweats, swollen lymph nodes, and swollen tonsils. Mono can also cause an enlarged, swollen spleen.

Immediate Care. The athlete who has this or any other potentially infectious illness must not be allowed into your facility until her physician verifies that she is not contagious. The athlete must see her physician to be tested. The athlete needs to have significant rest, eat healthy foods, and drink fluids to become well. She should avoid close proximity with other athletes because she can transmit the virus to others. The physician may prescribe antibiotics to treat other bacterial infections, such as tonsillitis, that occur along with mono. Athletes with mono should not come in contact with other athletes or participate in any activity that allows for close physical proximity with athletes, implements, equipment, or the like due to the swelling of the spleen. When the spleen is swollen and engorged with blood, an insignificant direct blow to the spleen can cause it to rupture and create a life-threatening situation for the athlete.

Prevention. Because mono is spread through saliva, your athletes should avoid sharing drinks, utensils, or anything else that has another athlete's saliva on it. Practicing proper hand washing can also prevent virus transmission.

▌ Blow to the Solar Plexus

The solar plexus, or celiac plexus, is located between the sternum and the umbilicus. A blow to this area causes a temporary paralysis of the diaphragm, which is a crucial structure involved in respiration. When this injury occurs, the athlete may say she got the wind knocked out of her.

Mechanism or Cause of Injury. A direct blow to the solar plexus by an object or another athlete, or a fall onto the area causes a temporary paralysis of the diaphragm.

Signs and Symptoms. When the diaphragm is paralyzed, breathing stops for an extremely short amount of time. The athlete feels an inability to breathe, gasps for breath, becomes anxious, and begins to panic.

Immediate Care: Attempt to calm the athlete down. Have the athlete sit comfortably with her knees bent and her body leaning forward slightly (**Figure 11-19**), and loosen any tight clothing, including equipment. Assist her in regulating her breathing by having her perform short inhalations and long exhalations. Within minutes, the athlete's breathing should be restored to a normal rate and depth. If normal breathing does not occur quickly and the athlete is in distress, then call 911.

Prevention. Athletes should wear properly fitted protective equipment that covers the solar plexus area, and should be aware of their surroundings during activities. Athletes should take precautions to avoid falls. All objects and equipment at the facility must be stored away properly so the athlete does not run or walk into the object, causing a blow to the solar plexus.

▌ Stich in the Side

The phrase *a stitch in the side* describes pain and/or cramping on the side of the body, between the flank and abdomen.

Mechanism or Cause of Injury. No definitive cause has been identified as to why a stitch in the side occurs. Various theories include improper conditioning, overeating, intestinal gas, spasm of or lack of oxygen to the diaphragm and intercostal muscles, and constipation.

Figure 11-19 To care for an athlete who has sustained a blow to the solar plexus, have her sit in a comfortable position with her legs bent and regulate her breathing.

Signs and Symptoms. The athlete complains of cramping and pain during activity that occurs below the ribs on the lateral side of the body between the flank and the abdomen. The cramping and pain usually are significant enough for the athlete to stop her activity.

Immediate Care. The athlete should stop activity and rest. She should raise the arm on the affected side and stretch the muscles by leaning away from the injured area (**Figure 11-20**). Usually the stitch in the side subsides with stretching in minutes. If the athlete continues to have a stitch in the side during subsequent activities, then she should be evaluated by a physician, because an underlying condition or lifestyle practice may be the cause.

Prevention. Because the exact cause of a stitch in the side is unknown, prevention is not entirely possible. However, the athlete must stretch her body before exercise, progress the exercises in an appropriate manner, not overeat immediately before exercise, practice proper eating habits and proper nutrition, and go to the bathroom before exercise.

Figure 11-20	The athlete should lean away from the side of pain if she has a "stitch in the side".

Figure 11-21	Abdominal hernias are the most common hernias that affect athletes.

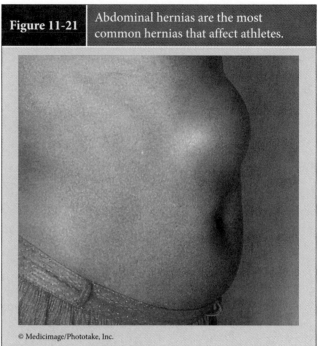

© Medicimage/Phototake, Inc.

Hernia

Hernias are very common and occur to men, women, and children. Various types of hernias exist. An abdominal hernia is a bulging of an internal organ, most often the intestines, through the abdominal wall (**Figure 11-21**). A hiatal hernia is an opening in the diaphragm that allows part of the upper stomach to move into the chest. An inguinal hernia occurs in the groin, a femoral hernia occurs in the upper thigh, and an umbilical hernia occurs around the navel.

Mechanism or Cause of Injury. A hernia may not have a direct cause. Some hernias may be caused by continual heavy, improper lifting. If an action, such as constant coughing, creates significant pressure on the abdominal wall and the abdominal muscles are weak, then these conditions promote an abdominal hernia. Hernias seem to have a familial relation.

Signs and Symptoms. Signs and symptoms of a hernia include a visible bulge at the site. Usually the athlete does not have pain, but some athletes complain of discomfort. The hernia bulge may appear to enlarge when the athlete lifts objects, bends, or strains his abdomen.

Immediate Care. The athlete should see a physician as soon as the hernia is identified. The only course of treatment for a hernia is surgery. The hernia can get bigger over time. If the hernia is not surgically repaired then it can strangulate, which means blood flow is cut off to the area. Hernial strangulation is a medical emergency.

Prevention. Although not all hernias can be prevented, an athlete can strengthen his abdominal muscles and avoid continual lifting of heavy objects, bending, and straining the abdomen.

THE PELVIS

Stress Fractures

Stress fractures of the pelvis typically occur to the femoral neck and to the pubic ramus (**Figure 11-22**). Long distance female runners are most commonly affected by pelvic stress fractures. Also, athletes who are not conditioned and begin an intense running program are more prone to pelvic stress fractures.

Mechanism or Cause of Injury. The repetitive bounding and overload on the pelvic area when running may cause pelvic stress fractures. Athletes who tend to have less muscle tissue to protect the bones, have osteoporosis, utilize an improper running technique, or have a leg length discrepancy are more prone to pelvic stress fractures.

Signs and Symptoms. Pain exists that increases with activity and resolves with rest. If the causative activity continues, then

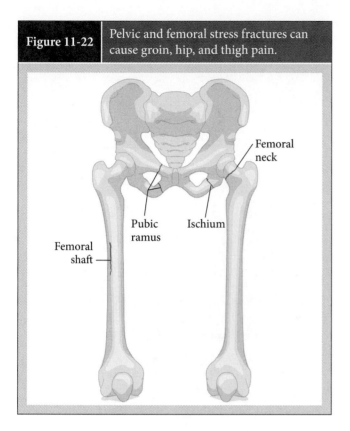

Figure 11-22 Pelvic and femoral stress fractures can cause groin, hip, and thigh pain.

Femoral neck

Pubic ramus

Ischium

Femoral shaft

pain increases and becomes persistent even at rest. The athlete is point tender at the stress fracture site. Eventually the pain causes loss of function. Groin pain is indicative of a pelvic stress fracture, whereas pain down the lateral hip and thigh may indicate a femoral neck stress fracture.

Immediate Care. At the onset of pain, the athlete should rest, apply ice, and compress the area with an elastic wrap. The athlete can take NSAIDs to alleviate pain and inflammation. If the athlete's signs and symptoms do not decrease with rest, ice, compression, and elevation (RICE) and anti-inflammatory medication, then refer her to a physician for further evaluation. If the injury has an insidious onset or the signs and symptoms worsen with treatment, then she must see a physician immediately. The physician will take x-rays, rule out any other injuries, and treat the stress fracture conservatively with rest, minimal weight bearing with the use of crutches or a cane, and NSAIDs. The stress fracture will heal in approximately 1–3 months, and then activity can gradually resume.

Prevention. An athlete can prevent a pelvic stress fracture by progressing the intensity of weight-bearing exercise in an appropriate, safe manner; increasing muscle mass and strength

around the pelvis; ingesting calcium and vitamin D to promote strong bones; and providing the body with sufficient rest periods between lower extremity weight-bearing exercise sessions.

Sacroiliac Joint Dysfunction

The sacroiliac (SI) joints are relatively immovable joints that are created by the articulation between the sacrum and the ilium at the posterior pelvis. SI joint dysfunction is a term used to describe pain around the SI joints that then causes functional deficiencies and other signs and symptoms of injury around the low back, pelvis, and hip.

Mechanism or Cause of Injury. The most common cause of SI joint dysfunction is a wearing away of the cartilage located in the joint between the sacrum and the ilium. Degenerative arthritis results at the SI joint. Other causes for SI joint dysfunction include leg length discrepancy or lower extremity pain that cause improper ambulation and biomechanics; pregnancy, due to pelvic expansion; improper low back posture; and landing on the buttocks or on a single, extended leg. A direct blow to the SI joint can also cause SI joint dysfunction.

Signs and Symptoms. SI joint dysfunction exhibits signs and symptoms of pain and stiffness at the joint, especially when weight bearing on the affected side. Pain can also occur in the lower back, hip, groin, and thigh. The irritation may be severe enough to affect the sciatic nerve, which runs over the SI joint. If the sciatic nerve is affected, the athlete feels a burning and/or aching pain down the back of his thigh. The aching pain in this area may mimic a hamstring strain.

Immediate Care. The athlete must first stop any activity that increases the signs and symptoms of SI joint dysfunction, and rest in the most comfortable position. The athlete should apply ice to the area and take NSAIDs to help decrease pain and inflammation. If the signs and symptoms do not subside, then the athlete should see a physician for evaluation. The physician will take x-rays, an MRI, and/or a CT scan to diagnose the condition. Then the physician will prescribe pain and anti-inflammatory medication, corticosteroid injections, and/or oral steroids such as prednisone. The athlete will have to perform rehabilitation exercises to strengthen and stretch muscles surrounding the SI joints. Manual therapy such as joint mobilization and massage can assist in decreasing signs and symptoms of SI joint dysfunction.

Prevention. SI joint dysfunction can be avoided by maintaining proper low back posture, strengthening and stretching the muscles surrounding the SI joints, and utilizing proper lower extremity biomechanics during activity.

Hip Pointer

A hip pointer is a contused iliac crest. The injury can be disabling for the athlete.

Mechanism or Cause of Injury.   A hip pointer is caused by a direct blow to an unprotected iliac crest. Objects that can bruise the iliac crest include a helmet, another athlete's body, or an implement. The athlete can also fall on the iliac crest, causing the hip pointer.

Signs and Symptoms.   A hip pointer causes pain, ecchymosis, and swelling at the area (**Figure 11-23**). The area is very point tender. Side bending toward the affected side exacerbates pain.

Immediate Care.   The athlete should immediately rest the area, apply an ice pack, and wrap the injury with a compression wrap. The athlete can take anti-inflammatory medication. The signs and symptoms should decrease over a week's time. The athlete can slowly begin to participate in activity. He should wear a hip pointer pad to protect the area (**Figure 11-24**). If the pain persists, then the athlete should see his physician for evaluation. The athlete will have to participate in rehabilitation exercises, which can help regain motion and strength.

Figure 11-24	Hip pointer pads can protect the athlete's iliac crest when it has been contused.

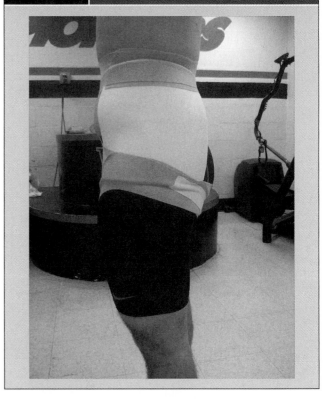

Figure 11-23	A hip pointer can cause significant pain and disability when walking.

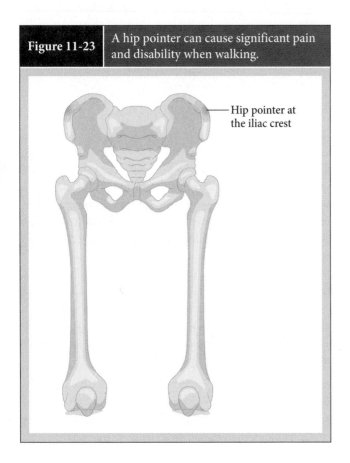

Hip pointer at the iliac crest

Prevention.   Any athlete who participates in contact activities that put the iliac crest at risk for a contusion should wear proper equipment or padding to protect the area. Avoiding falls and being aware of the surroundings can assist the athlete in preventing a hip pointer.

Osteitis Pubis

Osteitis pubis is a chronic inflammation of the pubic symphysis and the surrounding adductor muscles. The inflammation occurs most often to female long distance runners.

Mechanism or Cause of Injury.   The exact cause of osteitis pubis is unknown, but it is apparently caused by overuse and microtrauma to the pubic symphysis. The inflammation can also be caused by muscular imbalance, improper biomechanics, and SI joint dysfunction.

Signs and Symptoms.   The athlete complains of groin pain and point tenderness at the pubic bone. Activity increases the pain, but the pain is relieved with rest. The adductor muscles are inflexible. Contracting or stretching these muscles also elicits pain.

Immediate Care. The athlete must rest the area. She must discontinue participation in aggravating activities that overuse the adductor muscles or bear significant weight on the lower extremity. Ice application and NSAIDs are used to alleviate pain and inflammation. Any biomechanical problem, such as improper ambulation, leg length discrepancy, or SI joint dysfunction, must be addressed and corrected.

Prevention. Osteitis pubis can be prevented by strengthening and stretching the adductor muscles. If the athlete must participate in activities that cause a shearing force across the pubic symphysis, assist her in gradually progressing the activities' intensity and duration to avoid osteitis pubis.

SUMMARY

Athletes commonly sustain injuries and illnesses to the core body. After reading this chapter, you know that many core body injuries and illnesses have similar signs and symptoms. These similarities are often perplexing when you are attempting to determine the injury or illness that the athlete has sustained, and whether it is life-threatening. As with any other injury or illness to the body, when unsure of the care to provide, monitor the athlete's airway, breathing, and circulation; treat for shock; and summon EMS.

DISCUSSION QUESTIONS

1. What are some anatomical landmarks you must observe when evaluating an athlete's posture from the anterior, posterior, and lateral views?
2. What are the various head injuries that can occur to an athlete? Which injuries warrant calling EMS?
3. Name some life-threatening injuries or illnesses that occur to the thorax and abdomen.
4. What injuries to the core body are considered chronic injuries?
5. What core body injuries and illnesses exhibit similar signs and symptoms despite the area affected?

CASE STUDY 1

On a Collision Course

Alyssa is a senior third-baseman for her softball team at Village High School. Today her team is competing in the county championship game against their biggest rival. During the top of the fourth inning, a short fly ball is hit to shallow left field. Alyssa turns and runs full speed to try and catch the ball. Jacqueline, the left fielder, charges in

at full speed, also in an attempt to catch the ball. Neither player realizes that they are approaching each other at full speed. They both call for the ball at the last minute, but it is too late. They collide hard and fall to the ground. Jacqueline gets up rather quickly and goes over to her teammate to see how she is. Alyssa remains on the ground clutching her abdomen in pain. The coach runs out to the field to assess his two players' condition. Jacqueline says that aside from a sore left hip she is fine. Alyssa is still lying on the ground complaining that her abdomen hurts. The coach asks her if she has any other symptoms and Alyssa says no. The coach allows her a minute to gather herself. Alyssa says that the pain is subsiding and she wants to stay in the game. Because Alyssa said that she does not have any other symptoms of injury and is able to move her body normally, the coach allows her to continue playing.

At the end of the inning the players return to the dugout and the coach immediately asks Jacqueline and Alyssa how they feel. Jacqueline says she is fine, but has a bruise on her hip where she hit Alyssa, which is sore and tender to the touch. Alyssa says her abdomen is still painful, but she wants to continue playing. She is still clutching her abdomen with her arm and is leaning over slightly, but the coach allows her to get up to bat. Alyssa is up at bat and gets a hit. She advances each base as her teammates get hits and walks. When she returns to the dugout, Alyssa tells her coach that she feels light-headed. The pain in her abdomen is persistent and increasing. The coach looks at her and notices that she is slightly pale and clammy. He checks her pulse and notices that it is rapid but weak.

1. What possible injury(ies) could Alyssa have?
2. What possible injury(ies) could Jacqueline have?
3. Should the coach activate the EMS system? Why or why not?
4. What immediate treatment should the coach give to both Jacqueline and Alyssa?

CASE STUDY 2

Work Is a Pain

Nathan is a 35-year-old businessman who recently changed jobs. Whereas he used to travel from client to client as a salesperson, he now spends his entire workday behind his desk. All day he is either on the phone or working on his computer.

Nathan is in relative good shape because he regularly goes to We R Fit Gym to perform a variety of cardiovascular exercises. Recently, Nathan has been experiencing some low back discomfort and stiffness on and off throughout the day. He figures that the discomfort and stiffness is a result of his hard work at the gym, and believes the symptoms will eventually go away. As a few weeks pass, the discomfort and stiffness turn into pain. The pain in his low back starts to creep down into his right buttock area. One day Nathan is at his desk for a few hours without rising. He attempts to stand up and immediately feels pain shoot down the back of his right leg, which stops above his knee. The pain feels like a burning sensation, but it disappears after a few minutes. For the remainder of the day Nathan tries sitting in different positions to alleviate the pain. He even gets up every few minutes to walk around, but the pain persists.

The pain continues to affect him the most while seated at his desk. Sitting for short periods of time becomes impossible due to the burning pain down the back of his leg. The pain begins occurring at home and during his daily activities. He cannot sleep without feeling the dull pain in his low back. Driving has become unbearably painful. Working out in the gym on the stationary bike and stair stepper is painful, and this pain prevents him from having full function and strength to complete the exercises.

Nathan finally decides to treat his pain. He decides to take some time off from his cardiovascular exercise and rest his low back and leg. For a week, he rubs Icy Hot on his low back and hamstring to see if it decreases the pain, but the cream brings little, temporary relief. He decides to stretch his hamstring daily to see if that helps decrease his symptoms, but the stretching makes his pain worse. Despite his efforts, the pain persists and nothing he is doing

is making the pain go away. Nathan realizes that he needs advice regarding his pain. Nathan goes to We R Fit Gym and asks one of the personal trainers what he should do.

1. What do you think is the primary cause of Nathan's pain?
2. As Nathan's personal trainer, what would you suggest Nathan do in regard to his condition and pain?
3. Did Nathan take the appropriate course of self-treatment for the pain? Why or why not?
4. Is there anything Nathan can do to change his working conditions at his desk in order to prevent the low back pain in the future?

REFERENCES

American Academy of Orthopaedic Surgeons (AAOS). (2007). Spondylolysis and spondylolisthesis. Retrieved June 11, 2012, from http://orthoinfo.aaos.org/topic.cfm?topic=a00053

Mayo Clinic. (2011). Broken ribs: Treatments and drugs. Retrieved February 25, 2013, from http://www.mayoclinic.com/health/broken-ribs/DS00939/DSECTION=treatments-and-drugs

Mayo Clinic. (2010). Herniated disk: Definition. Retrieved June 10, 2012, from http://www.mayoclinic.com/health/herniated-disk/DS00893/

Meyer, J. S., Mehdirad, A., Salem, B. I., Jamry, W. A., Kulikowska, A., & Kulikowski, P. (2003). Sudden arrhythmia death syndrome: Importance of the long QT syndrome. *American Family Physician*, 68(3), 483–488.

National Heart, Lung, and Blood Institute. (2012). What is a heart murmur? Retrieved February 25, 2013, from http://www.nhlbi.nih.gov/health/health-topics/topics/heartmurmur/

PubMed Health. (2012). Collapsed lung. Retrieved June 11, 2012, from http://www.ncbi.nlm.nih.gov/pubmedhealth/PMH0001151/

Schultz, S. J., Houglum, P. A., & Perrin, D. H. (2010). *Examination of musculoskeletal injuries* (3rd ed.). Champaign, IL: Human Kinetics.

Yabek, S. M. (2011). Commotio cordis treatment and management. Retrieved June 12, 2012, from http://emedicine.medscape.com/article/902504-treatment

Chapter 12

The Lower Extremity

CHAPTER OBJECTIVES

After you have read this chapter, you will be able to understand:

- Lower extremity injuries that occur to the hip, thigh, knee, patella, lower leg, ankle, and foot
- How to identify which lower extremity injuries necessitate calling 911
- Which lower extremity injuries the athlete can treat him- or herself to promote healing
- Which injuries require surgery in order for the athlete to regain full function
- Which lower extremity injuries occur most often to children

The hip, thigh, knee, patella, lower leg, ankle, and foot are the anatomical structures that make up the lower extremity. The mechanisms of injury for lower extremity injuries are often different as compared to upper extremity injuries, due to the fact that the lower extremity is almost always weight bearing during activity. Due to the weight-bearing component, the lower extremity is often injured when the foot is in contact with the ground. When force is applied to the foot, any portion of the lower extremity can be injured due to forces traveling up through the bones and joints. Therefore, when a lower extremity injury occurs while the athlete is weight bearing, always check for injuries that may have occurred from the toes to the hip. As with the upper extremity and core body, the injuries sustained

may be acute or chronic, and mild to severe. Likewise, as with all injuries, the signs and symptoms you find during your secondary survey will assist you in determining the athlete's care.

THE HIP AND THIGH

The hip is a ball and socket joint made up of the head of the femur and the acetabulum of the pelvis. The hip creates a lot of motion because of its configuration as a ball and socket joint. This joint can perform flexion, extension, abduction, adduction, internal rotation, external rotation, and **circumduction**. The thigh consists of the femur and its surrounding musculature. The quadriceps, hamstrings, adductors, and iliotibial band are the thigh muscles commonly injured.

> **Circumduction** The distal end of the extremity (the hand or foot) makes a circular motion moving freely through space while the proximal end (the shoulder or hip) remains stable or fixed.

Femoral Fracture

Even though the femur is the strongest and largest bone in the body, both acute traumatic and stress fractures occur. Most acute fractures occur to the femoral shaft (**Figure 12-1**). Common femoral fracture classifications are oblique, transverse, comminuted, and spiral. Open fractures can also occur. Stress fractures typically occur to the femoral neck. These fractures can take weeks to develop, and are not nearly as severe as acute, traumatic fractures.

Figure 12-1	Acute femoral fractures often occur at the femoral shaft.

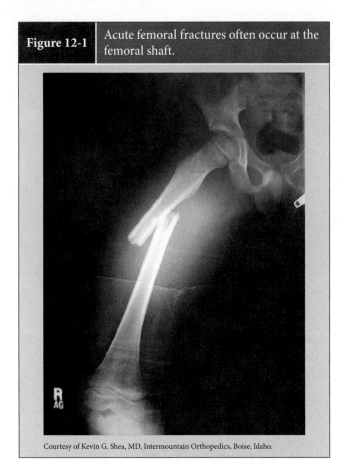

Courtesy of Kevin G. Shea, MD, Intermountain Orthopedics, Boise, Idaho.

Mechanism or Cause of Injury

The amount of force needed to cause a femoral shaft fracture is substantial. The number one cause of acute, traumatic femoral shaft fractures is car accidents (American Academy of Orthopaedic Surgeons [AAOS], 2011). Other causes are motorcycle accidents, pedestrian–car accidents, and falls from a great height. In athletics, the femoral shaft must sustain significant force in order to break. This injury occurs in high velocity collision or contact sports such as football or mixed martial arts.

A femoral neck stress fracture is not a common injury. This stress fracture is caused by repetitive motion and forces applied to the femur during constant weight bearing. These overuse injuries occur most often to females who participate in endurance sports such as long distance running. Long distance runners repetitively weight bear and bound on hard surfaces, which transmits significant forces up the femur to the femoral neck. Athletes who have relatively low body weight and lack muscle mass at the pelvis, hip, and thigh are at risk for femoral stress fractures. Muscles assist in dissipating forces. If an athlete does not have enough muscle to dissipate force away

from the bones, then stress fractures can occur. An endurance athlete who participates in weight-bearing activities; has little muscle mass at the pelvis, hip, and thigh; and is complaining of groin or hip pain that increases with activity may have a femoral stress fracture (Bailie & Lamprecht, 2001).

Signs and Symptoms

An athlete who has sustained an acute, traumatic femoral shaft fracture feels excruciating pain. He most likely is in shock and unable to put pressure or stand on the leg. The femur may be deformed, appear crooked, and look shorter than the uninjured leg. In the case of an open fracture, deformity and visible bleeding exist. An athlete who has a femoral neck stress fracture complains of groin or hip pain that increases with activity. Swelling, point tenderness, inability to fully weight bear on the leg, thigh muscles weakness, loss of hip function, and an abnormal gait may be present.

Immediate Care

When an athlete has sustained an acute, traumatic femoral shaft fracture, he most likely is in shock, so treat him accordingly. Call 911 immediately. Leave the athlete in the position that you find him, provided that his airway is open and he is breathing normally. Without moving the injured limb, splint the limb in the position that you find it and take care of any bleeding (**Figure 12-2**). If you are not trained to properly splint a femoral fracture, feel uncomfortable or not confident enough to splint the injury, or do not have any materials accessible to do so, then keep the athlete still, treat him for shock, and wait until the emergency medical technicians (EMTs) arrive. The EMTs are highly trained to splint femoral and other fractures.

At the hospital, the physician takes x-rays and/or computed tomography (CT) scans to determine the extent of the fracture. When an athlete sustains a femoral shaft fracture, surgery may be warranted to repair the fractured bone. The athlete is splinted and immobilized until he is physically able to have surgery. An athlete who has an open fracture needs surgery immediately. With open femoral shaft fractures, the potential for the athlete to sustain a secondary infection or significant external bleeding exists.

Other complications can arise with femoral shaft fractures. The femoral shaft has a large medullary cavity that contains fatty yellow bone marrow. The fat can escape out of the medullary cavity and cause life-threatening conditions, such as pulmonary embolism. Complications can also arise from the surgery, because metal plates, rods, and other hardware are placed through the bones to promote healing. A non-union of the femoral shaft, blood clots, bone malalignment, and tearing of blood vessels and nerves can also occur (AAOS, 2011).

Figure 12-2 | Splinting a femoral fracture.

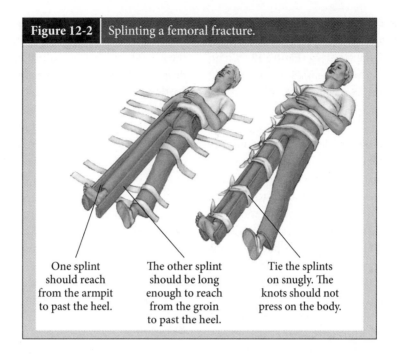

One splint should reach from the armpit to past the heel.

The other splint should be long enough to reach from the groin to past the heel.

Tie the splints on snugly. The knots should not press on the body.

After the athlete's fracture has healed, he will participate in a thorough rehabilitation program in order to regain full extremity function.

If you believe an athlete has sustained a femoral neck stress fracture, have the athlete discontinue any activity that aggravates his signs and symptoms, and apply ice to the area. Apply a compression wrap to his hip and thigh, and fit him for crutches or a cane so he is not fully weight bearing. Anti-inflammatory medication can help decrease his pain. Although the injury is not an emergency, the athlete should see his physician as soon as possible. The physician will take x-rays of the femoral neck to determine if it is fractured. If it is fractured, the physician may need to perform surgery in order to promote bone healing. Whether or not the physician performs surgery, for the stress fracture to heal the athlete must rest from predisposing activities, take anti-inflammatories, weight bear as tolerated, and perform rehabilitative exercises. The stress fracture can take many weeks to heal. Once the physician confirms the stress fracture has healed, then the athlete is able to slowly resume activity.

Prevention

Preventing femoral shaft fractures may not always be possible. Protective sports equipment worn on the thigh is helpful to prevent acute femoral fractures, but the equipment cannot always protect the femur against high impact traumatic forces. Femoral neck stress fractures can be prevented by proper conditioning that includes muscular strengthening. Ultimately, to avoid femoral neck stress fractures, athletes should increase their intensity slowly, participate in muscle strengthening exercises, and progress through activities in a safe manner and as their bodies allow.

Hip Dislocation

A hip dislocation occurs when the femoral head displaces from the acetabulum of the pelvis. The hip joint is severely disrupted and the ligaments surrounding the joint are sprained to varying degrees. Most hip dislocations are posterior dislocations, and the femoral head is forced backwards out of the joint. Hip dislocations can occur with or without concurrent fractures.

Mechanism or Cause of Injury

A substantial traumatic direct blow to the hip, to a flexed knee with force placed upward through the femur, or to the foot can result in a hip dislocation. These traumatic blows occur most commonly in car accidents or by a moving vehicle striking an athlete. Hip dislocations do not commonly occur during athletic activities. High impact events, such as football, rugby, and gymnastics, or events such as downhill skiing and snowboarding when traumatic falls occur can cause a hip dislocation. The hip is flexed, adducted, and internally rotated, or flexed, abducted, and externally rotated when the foot or knee strikes the ground or another object. The hip can also be in this position during a tackle in football or a pile-up in rugby.

Signs and Symptoms

The athlete has extreme pain and is most likely experiencing shock. She cannot sit up or move her hip. A telltale sign of a hip dislocation is the lower extremity's appearance. The hip is in an adducted, internally rotated position, and the injured leg appears shorter than the uninjured leg (**Figure 12-3**). The athlete may have abnormal or loss of sensation down the leg to the foot due to a compromised sciatic nerve.

Immediate Care

Hip dislocations are medical emergencies, so call 911 immediately. Tell the athlete not to move, treat her for shock, and splint the hip and leg in the position you find them. Similar to acute traumatic femoral fractures, if you are not trained to properly splint a hip dislocation, feel uncomfortable or not confident to splint the injury, or do not have any materials accessible to do so, then keep the athlete still, treat her for shock, and wait until the EMTs arrive. Monitor her airway, breathing, and circulation. Perform your quick sensory tests while asking her if she has sensation down her leg and into her foot. Give the EMTs all information regarding the athlete's injury, including signs and symptoms and any other findings, when they arrive on the scene.

At the ER, the physician will order x-rays to determine the extent of injury. Then the physician will give the athlete a

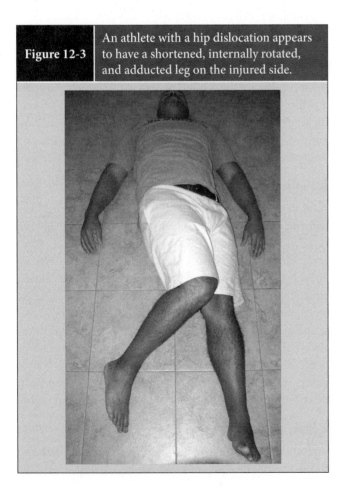

| Figure 12-3 | An athlete with a hip dislocation appears to have a shortened, internally rotated, and adducted leg on the injured side. |

sedative or general anesthesia before reducing the dislocation. Afterwards, the athlete uses crutches for a few weeks to rest the hip. The athlete can take nonsteroidal anti-inflammatory drugs (NSAIDs) or narcotic pain medication and will need to participate in lower body rehabilitation as prescribed by her physician. If the athlete also has a fracture or significant hip joint instability, then she will need to wear a hip stabilizing brace. With proper treatment and rehabilitation, the athlete can return to full activity at approximately 3 months postinjury.

Prevention

Similar to femoral shaft fractures, preventing a hip dislocation is not entirely possible. Athletes must avoid high risk activities in order to avoid hip dislocations. All activity surfaces should be kept clean and safe so the athletes do not slip and fall. As always, athletes need strong hip and thigh musculature to minimize the extent of injuries.

Hip Sprain

Although the hip joint contains the three strongest ligaments in the body, acute sprains to the iliofemoral, ischiofemoral, and pubofemoral ligaments do occur. When a hip is dislocated, the ligaments are sprained to varying degrees.

Mechanism or Cause of Injury

Hip sprains are caused by a forceful stretch of the ligaments due to excessive, involuntary hip joint range of motion (ROM) during activity. The athlete may be standing or running and be hit by an opponent in the thigh. This force pushes the hip joint beyond its normal ROM, which results in sprained ligaments. The hip ligaments can also be sprained by a direct blow to the hip.

Signs and Symptoms

An athlete has hip pain, especially upon hip movement. Consequently, he does not want to move the joint freely. The muscles become inflexible, the joint becomes stiff, and the athlete walks with a limp. The area surrounding the hip may be swollen and point tender.

Immediate Care

To care for the athlete, have him rest the hip by utilizing crutches or a cane, apply ice packs to the area, wear a compression bandage, and elevate the lower extremity whenever possible. Anti-inflammatory medication can modulate pain and inflammation. If signs and symptoms of injury do not decrease over a few days, then the athlete should see his physician. The physician examines the hip to determine the extent of injury and if any secondary injuries exist. Conservative treatment, including rehabilitation exercises, will be prescribed.

Prevention

Athletes can wear hip protective equipment and padding to avoid injury by direct blows. If the muscles surrounding the hip are strong and the athlete has good passive range of motion (PROM) at the hip, then injury to the hip ligaments can be minimized.

Hip Bursitis

The trochanteric, iliopsoas, and ischial bursae are located at the hip. These bursae assist in providing cushion between bone and soft tissue, which allows for unrestricted motion. These bursae, in particular the large trochanteric bursa, can become inflamed. Hip bursitis occurs primarily to middle-aged or older women.

Mechanism or Cause of Injury

Hip bursitis is typically a chronic overuse injury. Athletes who have hip arthritis, previous hip injury or surgery, a leg length discrepancy, or **scoliosis** are prone to hip bursitis. Trochanteric bursitis can also occur if an athlete has a tight iliotibial band that rubs against the bursa. Iliopsoas bursitis occurs from repetitive hip flexion. Ischial bursitis can occur with prolonged sitting or moving the hip from flexion to extension repeatedly, as when riding a bicycle.

> **Scoliosis** A lateral curvature of the spine when observed from a posterior view.

Signs and Symptoms

Hip bursitis produces severe pain at the hip (trochanteric bursitis), the groin (iliopsoas bursitis), or the ischial tuberosity at the buttocks (ischial bursitis). The severe pain becomes a dull, diffuse pain. The pain increases when pressure is applied to the area, such as when sleeping, sitting, or walking. The hip joint may feel stiff, and point tenderness may exist over the bursae. When the athlete moves the hip she may feel a snapping sensation, especially with trochanteric and iliotibial bursitis.

Immediate Care

The athlete should utilize rest, ice, compression, and elevation (RICE) and avoid all activities that aggravate the injury. The athlete must see a physician if she has pain lasting for over a week despite self-treatment; severe hip joint pain that does not decrease each day; ecchymosis, swelling, or redness at the area around the joint; or any intense, shooting pain, which indicates nerve dysfunction. In these cases, the course of treatment includes NSAIDs, rehabilitation, and possibly corticosteroid injections. Surgery may be a possibility if the bursa needs to be drained or removed.

Prevention

Athletes must exercise, maintain a normal healthy weight, and maintain good posture when lifting or sitting in order to prevent hip bursitis.

Legg-Calvé-Perthes Disease

Legg-Calvé-Perthes disease occurs when the femoral head is deprived of blood. The bone becomes necrotic and breaks. This condition is mostly seen in children, especially toddler to pubescent boys, and typically affects one hip.

Mechanism or Cause of Injury

The mechanism of injury for Legg-Calvé-Perthes disease is unknown. For undetermined reasons the head of the femur is deprived of blood and dies. This necrotic area of the femur is weak and becomes unstable. As a result, a piece of the femoral head fractures.

Signs and Symptoms

The child complains of hip pain and/or pain that refers down into the groin and knee. The pain is most noticeable to the child when he is active. At rest the pain decreases or goes away entirely, until he participates in activity again. The child has stiffness, lack of ROM in the hip, and walks with a limp. Upon x-ray examination, the femoral head appears flattened.

Immediate Care

Speak with the child's parents and refer him to his physician for evaluation. X-rays are necessary to determine the extent of the child's condition. If the condition is detected early, the child can return to full function with good outcomes. The physician's treatment protocol may include prescribing anti-inflammatory medication, rehabilitation that focuses on hip ROM, crutches, and bracing to rest the hip. After this nonsurgical approach is attempted, the child's condition is re-evaluated. If the child is not progressing well, then surgery may be required to replace the femoral head in the acetabulum. With treatment, the child should be fully functional without signs and symptoms of the condition, and the femoral head should heal in approximately 2 years.

Prevention

Legg-Calvé-Perthes disease cannot be prevented.

Slipped Capital Femoral Epiphysis

A slipped capital femoral epiphysis (SCFE) is a more common condition of the hip that occurs in children, especially pubescent and adolescent boys who are overweight for their height. The femoral head slips backwards out of the acetabulum.

Mechanism or Cause of Injury

The cause of a slipped capital femoral epiphysis is unknown. The condition can occur slowly during a child's growth. The bone's growth plates are weak during puberty and adolescence, and they grow very fast during this time. As a result, the femoral head moves out of position from the acetabulum. SCFE can also result from acute trauma, such as when a child athlete lands on or receives a direct blow to his hip.

Signs and Symptoms

The child athlete has hip and knee pain. The pain increases when walking, which he does with difficulty and/or a limp. His hip feels stiff and he may not be able to bear weight on the lower extremity. The affected leg appears shorter and turned outward.

Immediate Care

When you believe the child may have SCFE, refer the child immediately to a physician. The condition must be treated within 24 to 48 hours for the best outcome. The physician orders x-rays to confirm the condition. Surgery is necessary to fixate the femoral head to secure it in the acetabulum. After surgery and hospitalization, the child is nonweightbearing on crutches for months. The child begins rehabilitation and weight-bearing activities gradually. It may take up to 2 years for the child to return to normal athletic activities. When SCFE is treated immediately and properly, the child is able to heal and his hip can regain normal function.

Prevention

SCFE is not preventable. Children must maintain a proper weight for their height to decrease the chance of acquiring SCFE.

Piriformis Syndrome

The piriformis is a muscle in the buttocks area that attaches from the sacrum to the greater trochanter of the femur. The piriformis primarily functions to externally rotate the hip. The muscle is important in stabilizing the hip and maintaining balance when weight bearing. When the piriformis is inflamed, the sciatic nerve, which runs under and/or through the piriformis, is compressed by the muscle. Sciatic nerve pain results. This condition is called sciatica.

Mechanism or Cause of Injury

The piriformis becomes inflamed or injured due to overuse. The piriformis is functional during any activity that involves walking, shifting weight from one extremity to another, or externally rotating the thighs. Therefore, these repetitive, continual motions cause piriformis muscle inflammation, trigger points, tightness, and spasm. The sciatic nerve is affected secondarily to the muscular injury.

Signs and Symptoms

The athlete most likely feels signs and symptoms of sciatic nerve pain before she notes the signs and symptoms of piriformis injury. She feels loss of internal hip ROM, burning pain down the posterior thigh to the knee, pain in the buttocks and hamstring area, and tightness, stiffness, and point tenderness at the buttocks over the piriformis. Pain also occurs when the athlete is in a seated position.

Immediate Care

The athlete must treat the primary cause for the sciatic nerve pain, which is the piriformis inflammation. Have the athlete rest from any activity that stresses the piriformis and irritates the sciatic nerve. The athlete can take NSAIDs, and use ice and then heat after approximately 72 hours to relieve the pain and piriformis spasm. Various stretches and exercises to help the piriformis return to its normal state assist in alleviating the sciatica. If the signs and symptoms do not continually decrease after utilizing these treatments, then refer the athlete to her physician. The physician may prescribe anti-inflammatory or muscle relaxant medication, as well as corticosteroid injections to decrease the signs and symptoms. Other beneficial treatment practices include use of therapeutic modalities, such as electrostimulation and ultrasound.

Prevention

Preventing piriformis syndrome and subsequent sciatic nerve pain begins with the athlete gradually progressing the intensity and duration of her exercises. She should always maintain proper posture when sitting, lifting, and running. Flexibility exercises for the piriformis and surrounding muscles as well as hip ROM can help prevent piriformis syndrome.

Groin Strain

The groin muscles run along the medial thigh, and include the adductor longus, magnus, and brevis muscles as well as the gracilis and pectineus. These muscles are commonly injured in athletic activities, especially activities that require running and sudden changes in direction.

Mechanism or Cause of Injury

The groin muscles are injured when one or both of the legs are forced into abduction with or without lower extremity rotation. The foot may or may not be planted on the ground when the injury occurs. The sudden stretch to the groin tears the muscle fibers.

Signs and Symptoms

The signs and symptoms of a groin strain depend on whether the strain is a first-, second-, or third-degree strain. A groin strain causes significant pain and point tenderness on the inside of the thigh up to the pubis. The pain is increased as the athlete contracts the muscles and actively moves the legs together (adduction), or when the legs are passively pulled apart (abduction), which stretches the muscles. The athlete has loss of motion, ecchymosis, swelling, and all other signs and symptoms of injury that exist for any other strain.

Immediate Care

Groin strains typically heal with self-treatment including rest, ice, application of an elastic compression wrap, and anti-inflammatory medication. Fit the athlete for crutches if weight bearing is painful. Once the muscles are in the fibroblastic repair phase of healing and signs and symptoms have decreased, have the athlete begin gentle isometric exercises followed by isotonic strengthening exercises. The athlete should see a physician if he cannot weight bear, he has severe signs and symptoms of injury, or any complications arise.

Prevention

To prevent groin strains, the athlete should have strong, yet flexible groin muscles. He should participate in a daily flexibility program for the muscles. Various agility and cutting exercises must be incorporated into the athlete's regular workout, so the muscles become accustomed to quick, forceful movements.

Quadriceps Strain

Quadriceps muscle strains most often occur to the rectus femoris muscle (Schultz, Houglum, & Perrin, 2010).

Mechanism or Cause of Injury

Quadriceps strains occur when an athlete concentrically or eccentrically contracts the muscles during acceleration or deceleration, respectively. Running, sprinting, and jumping activities often cause quadriceps strains.

Signs and Symptoms

Depending on the degree of severity, the athlete may have pain, muscle spasm, loss of function, and point tenderness. The pain increases when the athlete attempts to contract the quadriceps by moving the knee into extension or the hip into flexion. The pain also increases when the athlete passively moves the knee into flexion and the hip into extension. The quadriceps may be swollen; with a Grade 3 strain, a bulge and/or divot may be present (**Figure 12**-4). The athlete may

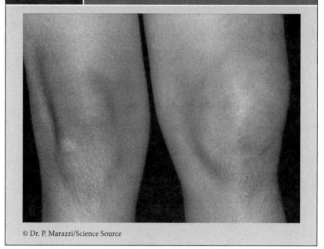

Figure 12-4 The rectus femoris is the most common quadriceps muscle ruptured. The bulge above the patella on the right leg is caused by the ruptured tendon releasing from its bony attachment.

© Dr. P. Marazzi/Science Source

also state that he felt a popping or snapping sensation at the muscle when the injury occurred. The athlete may limp when walking to avoid pain.

Immediate Care

Have the athlete use RICE immediately to decrease the signs and symptoms of injury. If he cannot walk without a limp or pain, fit him for crutches to use until he is able to bear weight on the lower extremity normally. Anti-inflammatory medication assists in decreasing the athlete's pain and inflammation. After the signs and symptoms have subsided, the athlete can begin ROM and strengthening exercises. Return to activity should be slow and as tolerated by the athlete. Signs and symptoms of the muscle strain should not recur when the athlete returns to sport. If they do recur, then the athlete has returned too soon and/or not progressed at an appropriate pace. If an athlete has a ruptured quadriceps muscle, then he should be evaluated by a physician to have diagnostic tests performed and to be certain that no secondary injury exists.

Prevention

To prevent quadriceps muscle strains, the athlete should always complete a proper warm-up and cool-down before participating in any athletic activity. Quadriceps muscle ROM, flexibility, and strengthening programs assist in minimizing potential injury. If the athlete participates in lower body high intensity activities, lower body agility and coordination are important to prevent injury.

Quadriceps Contusion

A quadriceps contusion can disable an athlete and can keep her out of activity for a period of time.

Mechanism or Cause of Injury

As with any other contusion, a quadriceps contusion occurs from a direct blow by an object. This direct blow can occur from an object striking the athlete, such as a batted softball, or the athlete falling on a stationary object, such as a weight bench in the gym. If the muscle is contracted at the time of impact, the injury often is more severe than if the muscle was relaxed during impact.

Signs and Symptoms

Quadriceps contusions may produce signs and symptoms of pain, loss of motion (either when attempting to contract the muscle or when passively stretching the muscle), point tenderness, spasm, increase in temperature, and ecchymosis.

Immediate Care

RICE is used to treat the contusion, along with NSAIDs to decrease pain and inflammation. An ice pack must be applied to the contused muscle with the knee in some degree of flexion as tolerated without pain by the athlete. This position allows the muscles to slowly lengthen. This lengthening assists in increasing ROM and flexibility; however, aggressive ROM and flexibility exercises are not warranted until signs and symptoms of injury notably subside. Also, massage is **contraindicated** for quadriceps contusions in the early stages of healing because massage techniques may promote myositis ossificans (which is discussed in the next section) (Newton & Walker, 2004). While the athlete's muscle is healing, she should wear an elastic compression wrap around the contused muscles. The compression bandage can also hold on padding to cover and further protect the area.

> **Contraindicated** A certain treatment, action, or rehabilitation technique must be avoided due to the particular condition, illness, or injury an athlete has sustained. If the contraindicated treatment, action, or rehabilitation technique is utilized, the athlete's situation most likely will worsen.

Prevention

Athletes must wear appropriate sports protective equipment and padding as required for the activity, especially if they participate in contact or collision sports. The stronger the quadriceps muscle is, the greater possibility that the muscle will not be severely injured by a direct blow. Therefore, participation in a quadriceps conditioning program, as noted for the prevention of quadriceps strains, is crucial in preventing injuries to these muscles.

Myositis Ossificans

Myositis ossificans is an **ectopic** bony growth that occurs in muscle groups, particularly the quadriceps and biceps brachii. Myositis ossificans arises in approximately 20% of quadriceps contusions and strains that have significant hematomas (Torrance & deGraauw, 2011). An athlete who has previously sustained a quadriceps contusion and sustains another contusion at the same muscle is at risk for developing myositis ossificans within that muscle (Newton & Walker, 2004).

> **Ectopic** The formation of soft tissue, a bone, an organ, or the like outside of its normal position or location. Ectopic bone formation is when bone develops outside of the bone in the soft tissue or elsewhere.

Mechanism or Cause of Injury

Myositis ossificans has no definitive cause; rather, the condition is a complication of a muscle contusion or strain. Trauma causes a hematoma within the muscle, which resorbs. As a result, bony deposits form within the muscle. Myositis ossificans has also developed when heat, massage, and aggressive stretching have been utilized too soon after a muscle contusion or strain has occurred.

Signs and Symptoms

If a muscle contusion or strain does not readily heal with conservative treatment, and pain, loss of function, and other signs and symptoms of injury increase, suspect that the athlete has myositis ossificans. Myositis ossificans causes pain upon motion that notably decreases when the knee is flexed. The bony formation may be palpated, depending on its size.

Immediate Care

Whether the athlete has sustained a muscle contusion or a strain that resulted in myositis ossificans, the athlete should continue to treat the primary injury conservatively. These treatment techniques also treat myositis ossificans. By utilizing RICE, and increasing ROM and strength with rehabilitative exercises, the signs and symptoms of myositis ossificans can be controlled. Once the ectopic bone has been formed, it remains in the soft tissue unless it is surgically removed. Surgical removal of the ectopic bone is an option if conservative therapies do not promote healing and decrease signs and symptoms of injury. If conservative treatments do not work, then refer the athlete to his physician.

Prevention

Myositis ossificans cannot be prevented because the mechanism of injury is not definitive; however, muscle strengthening is important to minimize the extent of injury if a contusion or strain occurs. Protective equipment and padding worn during contact sports can dissipate force when a direct blow occurs to the muscle. Heat, aggressive stretching, and massage should be used only in the fibroblastic repair phase of healing, when signs and symptoms of injury have noticeably decreased.

Hamstring Strain

Hamstring strains are more common than quadriceps strains (Schultz et al., 2010), and can occur at any point within the semitendinosus, semimembranosus, or biceps femoris muscles.

Mechanism or Cause of Injury

Hamstring strains occur most often when the muscle is concentrically or eccentrically contracted during activity. For example, the muscle can be strained when a sprinter pushes off the blocks at the start of an event, or as she decelerates at the finish line. The quadriceps muscle group is stronger than the hamstring muscle group; however, if the quadriceps group exceeds the normal strength as compared to hamstrings, then a muscular imbalance occurs between the two groups. Consequently, when the quadriceps muscles contract, they can cause a forceful pull on the hamstrings that results in a strain. Also, high velocity activities, such as running and jumping, and activities that require sudden stops and starts, such as in basketball, can predispose an athlete to hamstring strains. An athlete who has inflexible hamstrings or a prior hamstring strain is also at risk for subsequent strains.

Signs and Symptoms

Signs and symptoms of a hamstring strain are similar to those of a quadriceps strain. The athlete may feel a snap or pop at the time of injury along with immediate severe pain. A defect, a bump, or a divot exists within the muscle at the site of the injury (**Figure 12-5**), as well as swelling, ecchymosis, point tenderness, and loss of ROM and strength. The athlete may not be able to ambulate normally or without pain.

Immediate Care

The athlete can use RICE to treat her injury. The athlete may need to use crutches at first in order to rest the leg. Crutches are also necessary if she cannot bear weight without limping. Anti-inflammatory medication can be helpful to decrease

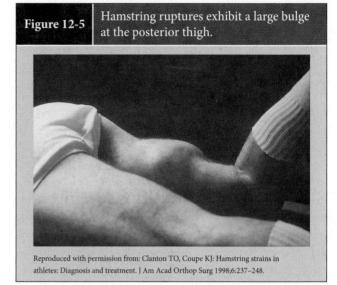

| Figure 12-5 | Hamstring ruptures exhibit a large bulge at the posterior thigh. |

Reproduced with permission from: Clanton TO, Coupe KJ: Hamstring strains in athletes: Diagnosis and treatment. J Am Acad Orthop Surg 1998;6:237–248.

signs and symptoms of inflammation. Surgery typically is not utilized as an option, unless an avulsion exists. The athlete should see her physician if she cannot bear weight, has unusual or loss of sensation down her leg, is in debilitating pain, or is unsure of the extent of the injury.

Prevention

Hamstring strength is important to prevent hamstring strains. The hamstrings should be approximately 40% of the strength of the quadriceps group; otherwise, a muscular imbalance exists. Hamstring strengthening should incorporate eccentric exercises that help the muscles decelerate properly. This type of training can assist in minimizing or avoiding injury. The hamstrings should have adequate flexibility in order to lengthen during activity.

Iliotibial Band Syndrome

Iliotibial band (ITB) syndrome describes an overuse, chronic ITB inflammation.

Mechanism or Cause of Injury

Repetitive, constant friction of the ITB over the lateral femoral condyle causes ITB syndrome. Sometimes the ITB can become inflamed over the greater tuberosity of the femur. This friction occurs with activities that require the athlete's knee to repetitively move from flexion to extension, such as in long distance running and cycling. ITB inflexibility and abnormal gait promote ITB syndrome.

Signs and Symptoms

The athlete may feel pain and a popping sensation or sound that occurs over the lateral femoral condyle or greater trochanter.

This sensation happens during activities that require continual hip and knee flexion and extension. The ITB may feel tight, rigid, and point tender upon palpation. The tighter the ITB, the greater potential for friction and inflammation.

▌ Immediate Care

ITB syndrome treatment includes rest, heat, and stretching prior to exercise, and an ice pack or ice massage after exercise. Heat can be utilized safely and effectively because ITB syndrome is a chronic condition. However, if any acute signs of inflammation arise, have the athlete use ice before and after exercise. The exercises should focus on ITB and surrounding muscle stretching and strengthening. Utilizing massage on the area can help decrease band tightness. NSAIDs can decrease inflammation. If conservative treatment is not effective in restoring the athlete's full, pain-free function, then refer the athlete to his physician. The physician may inject the inflamed site with corticosteroids, and prescribe additional rehabilitation.

▌ Prevention

The athlete should wear properly fitted shoes designed for his sport in order to prevent ITB syndrome. Also, the athlete should participate in a daily ITB flexibility program, as well as ITB stretching before and after exercise.

Tips from the Field

Tip 1 Properly fitting athletic shoes (sneakers, cleats, etc.) help your athlete to avoid many lower extremity injuries. When your athlete is shopping for new athletic shoes, give him advice on how to choose athletic shoes. Tell the athlete that he should expect to pay a moderate amount for quality athletic shoes. Inexpensive athletic shoes may not have the materials and construction necessary to provide proper cushioning and adequate arch support. On the other hand, expensive shoes are often expensive due to brand or athlete endorsement. Expensive shoes may not have better quality construction than moderately priced shoes. The athlete should try on new shoes with the exact socks that he will wear during the intended activity, and should try them on in the afternoon or at the end of the day. At these times, his feet are at their largest size due to weight bearing during the day. A shoe specialist at the store should measure the athlete's foot each time he purchases a new pair of athletic shoes. Athletes who gain or lose weight, younger athletes who are still growing, and aging athletes will have shoe sizes that may vary frequently. The shoe's toe box must be large enough so all toes fit next to each other comfortably and are mobile. The front of the toe box should be about

1/2 inch from the front of the great toe. The heel counter should come high enough above the calcaneus and the Achilles tendon to be supportive, but not cause friction when walking or running. The shoes should be laced up by using equal tension from the toes to the talus. After the shoe is laced, the foot should feel secure in the shoe. When the shoes are properly laced, the athlete can determine right away if the shoe is comfortable while sitting, standing, and walking in the store. If the shoes are comfortable in the store, then they do not need a breaking in period. The athlete can wear them for exercise immediately. Certain athletic shoes have special features such as gel inserts, mesh material to allow for better air circulation, or lightweight construction that may be valuable for your athlete depending on whether he has any foot conditions. Athletic shoes should be replaced whenever the materials become worn, especially on the sole of the foot, or when they no longer feel comfortable or supportive to the athlete.

THE KNEE AND PATELLA

The knee joint is made up of the articulation between the femur and the tibia. The patellofemoral joint is made up of the articulation between the posterior patella and the femur. The patella is the largest **sesamoid bone** in the body. Various disabling injuries occur to both the knee and patella.

> **Sesamoid bone** A bone that is embedded within a tendon, which most often is located over a joint. Other than the patella, which is the largest sesamoid bone, sesamoid bones are located in the hands and feet.

Knee Dislocation

A knee dislocation occurs when the femur or tibia is displaced (**Figure 12-6**). These dislocations are very rare, especially in athletic activities. When knee dislocations occur, other secondary injuries occur to the soft and bony tissues.

▌ Mechanism or Cause of Injury

Direct trauma causes a knee dislocation. An excessive amount of force is needed to separate the femur and tibia from each other. This direct trauma can occur in falls, motor vehicle accidents, and high intensity collision athletic activities.

▌ Signs and Symptoms

The athlete exhibits shock. He may be on the ground, perhaps grabbing his knee in excruciating pain. He may state that he

| **Figure 12-6** | A lateral x-ray of a knee dislocation. |

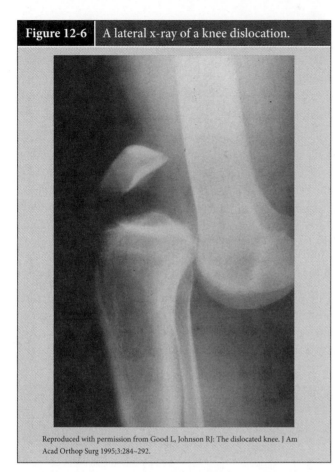

Reproduced with permission from Good L, Johnson RJ: The dislocated knee. J Am Acad Orthop Surg 1995;3:284–292.

cannot feel his lower leg, and circulation may be compromised. The knee appears severely deformed.

Immediate Care

A knee dislocation is a medical emergency. Call 911 immediately and treat the athlete for shock. Stabilize the lower extremity and splint the knee as you find it without moving the lower extremity. Place an ice pack on the knee to assist in decreasing pain. Monitor the athlete until EMS arrives. The physician will take x-rays, determine if any secondary injury exists such as a fracture, and relocate the knee at the hospital. Depending on the findings, the athlete may need surgery to repair the tissues around the knee. The athlete will participate in months of rehabilitation in order to regain full knee function.

Prevention

Knee dislocations are not entirely preventable because the athlete is not able to avoid all high intensity direct trauma. The athlete must participate in strengthening exercises for the

muscles surrounding the knee, while maintaining flexibility and ROM around the joint.

Anterior Cruciate Ligament Sprain

The anterior cruciate ligament (ACL) is within the knee joint. The ACL attaches the tibia to the femur and is tightest in full knee extension. The ligament limits anterior movement of the tibia on the femur, and knee rotation. More females have ACL injuries than males. A Grade 3 ACL sprain is called a *ruptured ACL*. The ACL is one of the most commonly ruptured ligaments in the body. ACL ruptures most commonly occur during competition in noncontact sports. ACL injuries often occur along with medial collateral ligament (MCL) and medial meniscus injuries. These three structures have similar mechanisms of injury; likewise, some fibers of the medial meniscus are attached to the MCL. When all three structures are injured simultaneously, the injury is referred to as an *unhappy triad* injury.

Mechanism or Cause of Injury

An ACL sprain can occur from noncontact or contact activities. A noncontact ACL sprain typically occurs when an athlete is in a weight-bearing position with her foot planted on the ground. The athlete then cuts, twists, or changes direction of her body quickly and suddenly. These motions force the knee into a valgus position in almost full knee extension, and as a result the ligament ruptures. Seven out of ten females with an ACL rupture had them occur in noncontact sports versus contact sports (Kobayashi et al., 2010). The athlete can also fall or land from a height on the foot and sprain the ACL. Contact ACL sprains occur during events in which the athlete's lower leg is hit by another player, such as in football, rugby, and ice hockey.

Female athletes tend to have a higher incidence of ACL ruptures than male athletes due to a variety of factors. Many women have a strength imbalance between the quadriceps and hamstring muscles. Also, hormones, tibial attachment, lower extremity anatomy, and landing biomechanics all predispose females to ACL injuries as compared to males.

Signs and Symptoms

Signs and symptoms vary depending on whether the ACL is stretched (Grade 1 or 2 sprain) or completely ruptured (Grade 3 sprain). At the time of injury, the athlete hears an audible pop, which indicates the ligament rupture. The athlete feels immediate, severe pain and joint instability when attempting to weight bear on the leg. Consequently, she may not be able to weight bear due to pain. Swelling and edema may continue to increase hours after the injury.

Immediate Care

After the athlete has sustained an ACL rupture, her pain will be unbearable and the athlete may be anxious. Calm her down and console her. Immediately utilize RICE to treat the injury. Have the athlete lie down on her back. Wet an elastic wrap with cold water, wring it out, and apply it to the knee to provide compression. Apply ice packs with an elastic wrap on all sides of the knee. While supporting the knee, have the athlete elevate the leg onto pillows, blankets, or other comfortable objects, so the leg is higher than the athlete's heart. Once the athlete is calm and treated, ask the athlete who she would like to transport her home. Fit the athlete for crutches and stabilize the lower extremity with an immobilizing brace. Although an ACL sprain is not a medical emergency, the athlete needs to see a physician for evaluation shortly after the injury is sustained. If the athlete is in extraordinary, severe pain that causes her to go into shock, treat her appropriately and phone 911. Also, if you do not have knee immobilizing materials or crutches readily available, then summon EMS immediately to provide the athlete additional care.

ACL ruptures are most often surgically repaired. If the athlete wishes to be active and/or participates in competitive activities that involve running, cutting, and jumping, then surgery is imperative to repair the ligament and restore joint function. A variety of surgical procedures are utilized. The physician and athlete will discuss the repair options, which include replacing the ruptured ligament with a portion of the athlete's hamstring tendon, patellar tendon, or donor (typically cadaver) tissue. Whether or not the athlete decides to have the ligament surgically repaired, the athlete partakes in a rigorous rehabilitation program to regain ROM, strength (especially hamstring strength), balance, agility, and the like. The physician may prescribe a custom, functional brace to assist in supporting the athlete's knee during activities (**Figure 12-7**). A gradual progression in activities assists the athlete in returning to play safely.

Prevention

Prevention of ACL sprains, especially in female athletes, includes proper nutrition to reduce muscular fatigue, proper calcium intake to keep bones strong, and adequate sleep to promote mental alertness. Athletes should not utilize alcohol, which has a potential neuromuscular contribution to ACL injuries. Controlling stress, overtraining, and burnout are also crucial to prevent ACL sprains (Elliot, Goldberg, & Kuehl, 2010). Other factors to prevent ACL sprains include maintaining a proper quadriceps to hamstring strength ratio (3:2), core body and lower extremity strength and conditioning programs, balance and neuromuscular training, agility exercises, and proper landing techniques and skill performance. The athlete must also wear properly fitted shoes appropriate for the sport and playing surface.

Posterior Cruciate Ligament Sprain

The posterior cruciate ligament (PCL) crosses the ACL in the knee joint, making an *X* appearance with the ACL. The PCL also attaches from the femur to the tibia, but unlike the ACL, the PCL is tight in knee flexion. The PCL functions to control posterior tibial movement on the femur, as well as valgus and varus forces (Rigby & Porter, 2010). Male athletes are more likely to injure their PCL than are female athletes.

Mechanism or Cause of Injury

The PCL is injured by a direct force to the anterior tibia while the knee is in approximately 90-degree knee flexion. PCL sprains most often occur in high-velocity events such as car accidents when the anterior tibia strikes the dashboard.

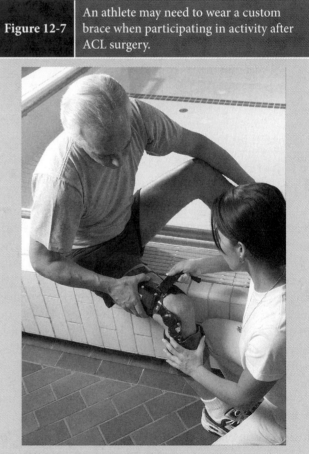

Figure 12-7 An athlete may need to wear a custom brace when participating in activity after ACL surgery.

© AbleStock

The PCL can also be injured in low-velocity events. An athlete can fall or be hit by an object at the anterior tibia while the knee is in flexion, which causes a PCL sprain. As an example, a football player can land on a flexed knee with the ankle in plantarflexion, and a PCL injury can result. The PCL can also be injured by a direct blow to the knee while in hyperextension (Rigby & Porter, 2010).

Signs and Symptoms

Severity of injury dictates the extent of signs and symptoms after a PCL sprain. The athlete may hear a pop at the time of injury and feel severe pain if he has sustained a Grade 3 PCL rupture. Swelling appears and the athlete is point tender in the popliteal area. The athlete has immediate loss of ROM. Knee joint instability may not be present if the athlete has strong quadriceps muscles, which keep the tibia in a normal position while walking.

Immediate Care

Treat the athlete with a PCL sprain as if he has an ACL sprain, and refer the athlete to his physician for further evaluation and imaging. PCL ruptures are not often surgically repaired. Surgery may be an option if an avulsion or other soft tissue structures (i.e., other ligaments, meniscus, and muscle) are severely injured along with the PCL. Conservative therapy is the treatment of choice. Knee immobilization in extension for a few weeks with RICE, anti-inflammatory medication, and rehabilitation that focuses on quadriceps strengthening is prescribed. Quadriceps strengthening keeps the tibia in a normal position relative to the femur. A gradual return to activity can resume after the athlete has rehabilitated the knee and lower extremity enough to have unrestricted ROM, adequate strength, flexibility, coordination, agility, and the like.

Prevention

Attempts to prevent PCL injuries include having adequate quadriceps and hamstring strength and flexibility, avoiding falls on a flexed knee, and wearing protective knee equipment during contact activities.

Collateral Ligament Sprain

The knee has two collateral ligaments on each side of the joint. The MCL attaches from the femur to the tibia on the inside of the knee. The deep fibers of the MCL also attach to the medial meniscus. Consequently, at times due to their anatomical attachment, both the MCL and medial meniscus are simultaneously injured. The lateral collateral ligament (LCL) attaches from the femur to the fibular head on the lateral knee. The MCL and LCL assist in limiting knee rotation and extension. The MCL limits valgus stress on the knee, while the LCL limits varus stress. The MCL is more often injured than the LCL, and the LCL is not as commonly injured as other knee ligaments.

Mechanism or Cause of Injury

The MCL is injured by a valgus force to the knee while the foot is planted, or a direct blow to the lateral side of the knee that forces the joint into a valgus position. The LCL is injured by a varus force to the knee while the foot is planted, or a blow to the medial side of the knee that forces the joint into a varus position.

Signs and Symptoms

With both MCL and LCL injuries, the athlete may feel pain and point tenderness at the site. Swelling and ecchymosis may be present. The athlete may complain that she feels the tibia shifting or sliding when she walks, which indicates joint instability.

Immediate Care

Immediate collateral ligament treatment is the same as for an ACL sprain. Likewise, as with PCL ruptures, MCL and LCL ruptures do not often require surgery. These injuries can be effectively treated with RICE, anti-inflammatories, bracing (**Figure 12-8**), and rehabilitation with a focus on strengthening the musculature on the respective side of the knee where the collateral ligament was injured.

Prevention

MCL and LCL sprains can be prevented by having strong musculature around the entire knee. Proper strengthening and flexibility of the lateral and medial musculature are important to avoid injury due to varus and valgus forces. The athlete should wear protective knee equipment as required by the activity, and perform skills as appropriate.

Meniscal Injury

The medial and lateral menisci are located on the tibial plateaus within the knee joint. They act as shock absorbers for the knee, stabilize and deepen the joint surface, and promote appropriate weight distribution when weight bearing. The menisci are one of the most commonly injured knee structures. Meniscal tears often occur with other knee injuries such as ACL and MCL sprains, due to similarities in the mechanism of injury. The MCL is attached to the medial meniscus; therefore, simultaneous injuries can occur. The meniscus can tear at its periphery or within its body (the horn).

| Figure 12-8 | After a collateral ligament injury, the athlete may need to wear a brace with medial or lateral support. |

Courtesy of DJO Global.

Mechanism or Cause of Injury

The medial and lateral menisci are injured when the knee is in some degree of flexion and then rotates while the lower extremity is weight bearing. As the knee approaches greater degrees of flexion, the femoral condyles sit on the meniscus. With tibial or femoral rotation, the femoral condyles grind on the meniscus and cause a tear. The athlete can also receive a direct blow to the knee, which can cause meniscal injury. As athletes get older, their menisci become weak and thin. Consequently, knee flexion activities that are not seemingly traumatic, such as continual rising from and sitting in a chair, can tear the menisci. In these situations, a mechanism of injury may not be evident.

Signs and Symptoms

Meniscal injuries can produce varying degrees of signs and symptoms. The signs and symptoms may be very mild and the athlete may not even realize he has sustained a meniscal injury. On the other hand, some meniscal injuries are severe and cause significant disability. A meniscal tear produces pain and a feeling of catching or locking within the knee joint. The athlete may say that the knee feels like it is stuck in knee flexion. The knee joint line may be swollen and is often point tender. The athlete may not be able to move the knee through its full ROM.

Immediate Care

An athlete with a meniscal tear who is experiencing minor signs and symptoms of injury requires rest from knee flexion activities, including activities of daily living (ADLs) such as climbing up and down stairs. Have him apply ice packs intermittently as needed, wear an elastic compression bandage, and elevate the leg. The athlete may need crutches if he cannot weight bear or walk without a limp. Although a minor meniscal injury is not a medical emergency, the athlete should go to his physician to be evaluated. If the athlete's tear is a minor peripheral tear and does not prevent knee function, then ROM and strengthening exercises can help to rehabilitate the area. If the athlete's knee is immovable or he is in significant pain, have him rest in a **long sitting position**, splint the knee, apply ice, and call EMS. The physician in the

> **Long sitting position**
> When an athlete is seated on the ground with both legs extended.

emergency room (ER) will evaluate the athlete by performing an examination, or taking x-rays and/or a magnetic resonance imaging (MRI) scan.

Regardless of the type of tear, the athlete may need arthroscopic surgery to repair the meniscus if the tear is creating pain or loss of function. Arthroscopic surgery is used to visualize the inside of a joint, such as the knee, and perform procedures within the joint to repair injured structures. The physician utilizes a camera (arthroscope) placed inside the joint that projects onto a monitor so the physician can see the inside of the joint. Other tools are also inserted into the joint in order for the physician to repair and irrigate the joint during surgery. Quadriceps and surrounding muscles that are damaged and weakened due to the surgical procedure itself must be strengthened during rehabilitation. Return to activity depends on the extent of the meniscal injury, whether or not surgery is performed, and success of rehabilitation.

Prevention

Avoiding deep knee flexion and rotation activities are beneficial in preventing these injuries; however, meniscal injuries due to tissue degeneration are difficult to prevent.

Patellar Fracture

Patellar fractures can create significant disability for the athlete. When the patella is fractured, breaks occur in one or more places. Because correct patellar alignment and movement are imperative for proper ambulation, a fractured patella causes improper ambulation.

Mechanism or Cause of Injury

The patella can be fractured by a direct blow to the bone. An object hits or an athlete falls on the patella and fractures the bone. The quadriceps can also contract forcefully enough to pull on the superior pole of the patella and cause it to fracture.

Signs and Symptoms

The athlete has immediate pain, which increases if she attempts to contract the quadriceps and move the knee into extension. The knee appears in flexion and she cannot extend the knee. Swelling, deformity, ecchymosis, and point tenderness exist.

Immediate Care

If your athlete has a patellar fracture, splint the leg in the position that you find it, apply an ice pack on the area, and treat the athlete for shock. The athlete needs immediate medical evaluation, so call 911. The physician will take x-rays to determine the extent of the fracture, including the type of fracture, and whether it is nondisplaced or displaced. Nondisplaced patellar fractures can be treated by splinting or casting the leg in extension, which allows the bone to heal. The athlete utilizes crutches and is immobilized for a couple of months, at which time she is allowed to bear weight on the leg. Displaced fractures usually require surgery in order to approximate the patella pieces to promote proper healing. Regardless of whether surgery is needed, rehabilitation after the patella has healed includes partial to full weight bearing as tolerated, ROM exercises, and quadriceps muscles strengthening and stretching.

Prevention

Patellar fractures can be prevented by wearing protective knee equipment during contact activities. Stretching and developing good neuromuscular control of quadriceps muscles, along with avoidance of extreme, forceful knee flexion, assist in avoiding patellar fractures.

Patellar Dislocations and Subluxations

The patella is a commonly dislocated or subluxed bone. It commonly dislocates and subluxes laterally from the femoral groove (**Figure 12-9**).

Mechanism or Cause of Injury

Patellar dislocations and subluxations often occur due to an imbalance between the stronger vastus lateralis muscle and

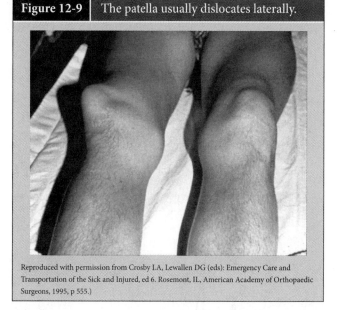

Figure 12-9 | The patella usually dislocates laterally.

Reproduced with permission from Crosby LA, Lewallen DG (eds): Emergency Care and Transportation of the Sick and Injured, ed 6. Rosemont, IL, American Academy of Orthopaedic Surgeons, 1995, p 555.)

the weaker vastus medialis muscle of the quadriceps group. This imbalance causes the vastus lateralis to pull, or track, the patella laterally during motion. Female athletes are more prone to patellar subluxations due to their greater **Q-angle** than are male athletes (**Figure 12-10**). The patella can then sublux when the athlete is running or performing other lower body movement activities, especially when the athlete changes direction suddenly. A direct blow to the medial patella can also cause a dislocation.

> **Q-angle** Stands for the quadriceps angle, which is the relative position of the patella to the tibia, femur, and pelvis.

Signs and Symptoms

An athlete who has sustained a patellar dislocation or subluxation has pain, which is more severe with a dislocation. The dislocation appears deformed because the patella is out of normal alignment with the femur. Swelling and point tenderness exist. With a dislocation, the athlete cannot move the knee joint. With a subluxation, the athlete feels the patella moving out of and then back into place at the time of injury. With a subluxed patella, the athlete can ambulate normally and swelling is minimal to none.

Immediate Care

For a patellar subluxation, apply ice to the area and have the athlete rest. Apply an elastic compression wrap for support. The athlete can take anti-inflammatory medication to relieve

Figure 12-10 | Q-angle measurement.

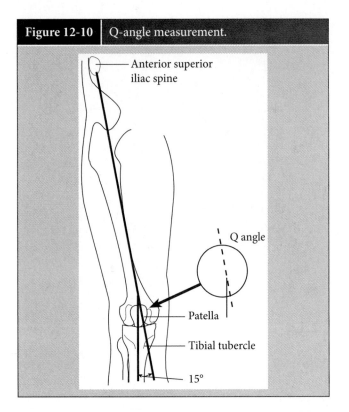

Anterior superior
iliac spine

Q angle

Patella

Tibial tubercle

15°

pain and inflammation. Once inflammation has decreased, the athlete needs to begin a strengthening program for the vastus medialis and medial thigh muscles, and a stretching program for the vastus lateralis and lateral thigh muscles. The athlete can wear a neoprene or other knee brace with a patella cut-out and lateral border to assist in keeping the patella in its correct position. If the athlete has another subluxation or the signs and symptoms get worse with treatment, then she should be evaluated by her physician.

Patellar dislocations are treated like any other dislocation. Have the athlete remain still in whatever position is most comfortable for her, stabilize above and below the knee by splinting the limb, apply ice to the area, treat for shock, and call 911. At the ER, the patella is reduced by a physician. The physician takes x-rays to be certain that the posterior portion of the patella or the femoral condyle did not fracture. The athlete must be nonweightbearing in a knee immobilizer on crutches for a brief time; after that she begins rehabilitative exercises to strengthen medial and stretch lateral knee musculature.

Prevention

Patellar subluxations and dislocations can be avoided if the athlete has a good strength balance between the medial and

lateral knee musculature. The lateral musculature should be flexible enough so the patella is not pulled laterally.

Patellofemoral Pain Syndrome

Patellofemoral pain syndrome (PFPS) is also called patellofemoral stress syndrome. PFPS is a general term used to describe pain at the anterior knee and around the patella.

Mechanism or Cause of Injury

PFPS has an insidious onset and no definitive cause. However, it is speculated that patellar compression against the femur (especially in knee flexion), improper patellar tracking during ambulation, patellar malalignment, biomechanical issues such as flat feet or a high arch, weak quadriceps and hip muscles, tight hamstrings and calf muscles, and muscular imbalance can cause PFPS. Long distance runners and cyclists are susceptible to PFPS, as are athletes who train on inclines and uneven surfaces. Frequent step climbing can predispose a person to PFPS.

Signs and Symptoms

The athlete feels pain between the anterior knee and the posterior surface of the patella, especially when running, climbing stairs, and performing deep knee flexion movements, such as squatting and sitting for long periods of time. Pain at the patella occurring after hours of sitting is called *movie theater sign*. The athlete may also complain of grinding, grating, and point tenderness around and behind the patella. Swelling is not often present with PFPS.

Immediate Care

In order to treat PFPS, the athlete must treat and correct the underlying cause. Therefore, assist the athlete in identifying the underlying cause. Take a secondary survey and perform a postural examination of your athlete in an attempt to identify the mechanism of injury. If you cannot identify the cause, then refer the athlete to a physician for evaluation. To treat the athlete's immediate signs and symptoms, have him discontinue any activities that aggravate the patellofemoral area, especially knee flexion activities. Apply ice on and around the patella intermittently throughout the day and have the athlete take anti-inflammatories to alleviate pain and inflammation. Depending on the underlying cause of PFPS, the physician may prescribe a variety of treatments. A neoprene sleeve with a cut-out for the patella provides some lateral stability (**Figure 12-11**), or taping of the patella with a taping procedure called *McConnell taping* may provide some pain relief for athletes with PFPS. The athlete also may benefit from custom

Figure 12-11	Knee braces with a patellar cutout can help keep the patella in proper position during activity.

Courtesy of Mueller Sports Medicine.

orthotics for his shoes. Custom orthotics are shoe inserts made from a mold of the athlete's foot along with various foot measurements (**Figure 12-12**). These orthotics can assist the athlete in correcting his biomechanical problems. Rehabilitation

Figure 12-12	Custom foot orthotics are created to address each athlete's individual foot condition(s).

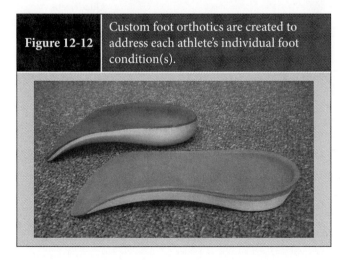

includes stretching and strengthening of knee musculature. Surgery is not typically utilized to correct PFPS.

Prevention

PFPS may not be entirely preventable due to an athlete's structural anatomy. The athlete should perform proper lower extremity conditioning exercises including ROM, flexibility, and strengthening in order to prevent PFPS. Proper footwear that fits appropriately and is purposeful for the sport and playing must be worn.

Chondromalacia Patella

Chondromalacia patella is a type of PFPS that occurs when the cartilage on the lateral posterior portion of the patella softens and degenerates over time. The condition is an overuse injury that may first appear as generalized PFPS, but with repetitive trauma can develop into chondromalacia patella.

Mechanism or Cause of Injury

Chondromalacia patella occurs from the same mechanisms of injury as PFPS. Also, repetitive knee flexion activities, lower extremity malalignments, and previous patella trauma, such as a previous dislocation that has injured the patellar articular cartilage, can cause chondromalacia patella. Athletes who participate in running and jumping activities are most at risk for chondromalacia patella.

Signs and Symptoms

The athlete feels a dull, aching pain, especially when the patella is contacting and being compressed against the femur with knee flexion. The athlete may feel crepitus, grating, or grinding when walking or performing activities requiring knee flexion. Slight puffiness, indicating edema within the area, may be visible around the patella, and the area may be point tender.

Immediate Care

The immediate care is the same as with PFPS. RICE, anti-inflammatories, bracing and taping, rehabilitation, and avoidance of deep knee flexion activities assist the athlete in treating the injury. Refer the athlete to a physician if these treatment methods are not successful. Surgery is not often utilized as a treatment method, but in rare cases a physician will remove damaged cartilage via arthroscopic surgery or realign the patella so it tracks properly in the femoral groove.

Prevention

Athletes should take part in overall conditioning, including lower body strengthening and stretching exercises; wear properly fitted and appropriate shoes for the activity; utilize proper technique; and increase intensity of new knee flexion activities in a progressive manner in order to prevent chondromalacia patella.

Osteochondritis Dissecans

Osteochondritis dissecans (OCD) is another overuse condition. OCD occurs at the patellofemoral joint when the posterior patella and/or the femoral condyles become necrotic due to lack of blood flow to the area. The cartilage degrades and begins to fragment and fracture along with attached bone. This condition occurs most often to adolescent athletes.

▌ Mechanism or Cause of Injury

Although the exact mechanism of injury is unknown, OCD is caused by lack of blood flow to the femur and posterior patella. OCD may also be caused by repetitive microtraumas at the knee and patellofemoral joints that go unnoticed by an athlete.

▌ Signs and Symptoms

Because OCD is an overuse injury, the athlete feels pain that occurs gradually over time. The pain occurs most often after activity has stopped. The athlete may feel grating and catching if a loose bone fragment is within the joints. Some joint line point tenderness and edema may exist. The athlete may have loss of knee ROM. In certain instances, the athlete may not exhibit significant signs and symptoms of injury. If the fragmented cartilage and bone remain near the location from which it broke off, then the fracture may heal on its own. If this is the case, then signs and symptoms typical for OCD are not evident.

▌ Immediate Care

Recommend to the athlete to rest the knee and avoid all painful activities, apply ice, take anti-inflammatory medication, and perform rehabilitative exercises to promote lower extremity ROM, strength, and flexibility. If signs and symptoms of OCD continue, then refer the athlete to a physician. If a loose piece of cartilage or bone is in the joint causing pain or loss of function, then the physician will perform arthroscopic surgery to remove the fragment.

▌ Prevention

OCD prevention includes utilizing proper techniques when participating in athletic activities, as well as participating in lower extremity conditioning and strength training programs on a regular basis.

Patellar Tendon Rupture

The patellar tendon attaches from the inferior portion of the patella to the tibial tuberosity. When the quadriceps muscle contracts, the patellar tendon assists in knee extension. Although a patellar tendon rupture is a rare injury, middle-aged athletes who participate in running or jumping activities are most commonly affected. The tendon can partially or completely tear (rupture) at any point (**Figure 12-13**). When the tendon tears, an avulsion fracture of the patella's inferior pole can also occur.

▌ Mechanism or Cause of Injury

The patellar tendon ruptures from a forceful, sudden quadriceps muscle contraction that forces the knee into extension. The tendon can also rupture from a fall when the athlete lands on the area. If the athlete lands on his feet with his knees in deep flexion after jumping or falling, the patellar tendon can stretch to the point of failure. The patellar tendon can weaken due to illness that disrupts blood supply, such as diabetes, rheumatoid arthritis, infection, and metabolic disease (AAOS, 2009). A weakened patellar tendon along with a forceful stretch or contraction can cause tendon rupture.

▌ Signs and Symptoms

The athlete complains of severe pain immediately after the injury occurs, which may cause him to go into shock. He may say that he felt or heard a pop when the tendon ruptured. The athlete cannot perform active knee extension. A visible defect may be present where the tendon ruptured, along with ecchymosis, swelling, and point tenderness.

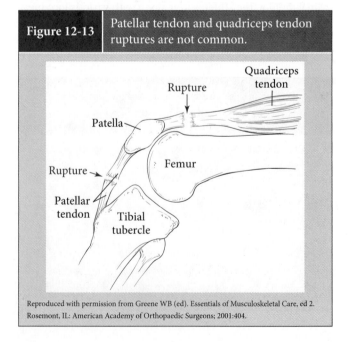

| Figure 12-13 | Patellar tendon and quadriceps tendon ruptures are not common. |

Reproduced with permission from Greene WB (ed). Essentials of Musculoskeletal Care, ed 2. Rosemont, IL: American Academy of Orthopaedic Surgeons; 2001:404.

Immediate Care

If the athlete has ruptured the patellar tendon, he will most likely be in shock, so treat him appropriately. Apply ice, splint the area, and call 911. If the injury is a partial tear with mild to moderate signs and symptoms of injury, then utilize RICE and place the athlete on crutches. He should see a physician for evaluation. For partial or incomplete patellar tendon tears, a nonsurgical approach is taken to treat the injury. The nonsurgical approach includes immobilization for approximately a month and rehabilitative exercises. To treat and promote healing for a completely ruptured patellar tendon, surgery must be performed to repair the tendon. Immobilization and rehabilitation begin after the procedure, with return to activity in approximately 6–12 months (AAOS, 2009).

Prevention

Athletes can attempt to prevent patellar tendon ruptures by performing quadriceps muscle group strengthening and flexibility exercises, and lower extremity conditioning. Avoiding unnecessary high impact, forceful contraction jumping activities is also important. If an athlete's activity includes these jumping activities, as in basketball and volleyball, then a proper warm-up and cool-down are always imperative to avoid muscle and tendon injuries.

Patellar Tendinitis (Jumper's Knee)

Patellar tendinitis is an overuse injury. Repetitive stress that occurs to the tendon causes microtears, which result in tendon inflammation. Over time if the causative stress is not removed, then further damage occurs to the tendon. The tendon becomes very weak and can fail.

Mechanism or Cause of Injury

Patellar tendinitis typically has an insidious onset. The athlete is not able to specify when the tendon first became problematic. The mechanism of injury is repetitive knee flexion concurrent with a quadriceps muscle overload. This mechanism of injury occurs in activities such as weightlifting (i.e., when performing lunges and squats), and basketball and volleyball (i.e., when jumping). Due to the mechanism of injury, the name *jumper's knee* was coined.

Signs and Symptoms

The athlete experiences pain between the inferior pole of the patella and the tibial tubercle. The pain arises at the beginning of exercise activity and again when the athlete has completed the activity. Usually pain subsides during exercise; however, as the tendinitis becomes more severe, the pain occurs at all times during exercise. As the tendinitis continues to worsen, pain is exacerbated during ADLs, including climbing stairs or any motion requiring knee flexion. The area is point tender, but little swelling exists.

Immediate Care

Treat the tendinitis by having the athlete rest and discontinue activities that cause pain. Apply ice and elevate the area. Patellar compression straps, which are similar in function to epicondylitis straps, can be utilized to decrease stress on the tendon. The athlete can take anti-inflammatory medication to reduce inflammation and pain. Once the inflammation and pain are controlled, the athlete should focus on stretching and strengthening the quadriceps muscles. If the tendinitis continues to worsen and interfere with ADLs, such as walking or climbing steps, or if the area becomes red and swollen, then refer the athlete to her physician for evaluation. Along with rehabilitation and NSAIDs, the physician may inject corticosteroids or prescribe topical corticosteroids along with electrostimulation (iontophoresis) or ultrasound (phonophoresis) to decrease inflammation.

Prevention

Stretching and strengthening of the quadriceps group is important to prevent jumper's knee. Eccentric strengthening must be included in the athlete's strengthening protocol, because repetitive eccentric loads of the quadriceps muscles are a cause of patellar tendinitis. Utilizing proper biomechanics, skill, technique, and progression when exercising are also important to avoid patellar tendinitis.

Osgood-Schlatter and Sinding-Larsen-Johansson Diseases

Osgood-Schlatter disease (OSD) is inflammation of the athlete's tibial tubercle apophysis where it attaches to the patellar tendon. Sinding-Larsen-Johansson disease (SLJD), which is not as common as OSD, is an inflammation of the patella's inferior pole at its growth plate, where it attaches to the patellar tendon. These diseases occur most frequently to adolescent boys whose bones are rapidly growing. Athletes who participate in sports that involve jumping, running, and changes in direction are most prone to these conditions. The injuries can occur to one or both extremities.

Mechanism or Cause of Injury

The mechanism of injury for both conditions is the same. The adolescent's body is growing rapidly. The bones grow faster than the muscles and tendons. Consequently, the muscles and tendons are stressed and pulled taut, and pull on the bones.

Over time, this causes an inflammatory response. The injuries occur when the knee is repeatedly flexed during low or high intensity activities. Athletes do not need to participate in athletic activities to sustain either of these injuries. Any activity that requires repetitive knee flexion, such as squatting, lifting heavy boxes, or the like, can cause these injuries. Changes in intensity of activity, improper shoes, poor posture, and faulty biomechanics can also cause OSD or SLJD.

Signs and Symptoms

At first, the child feels pain, especially with knee flexion activities, but it resolves at rest. He may have point tenderness and swelling at the tibial tubercle (with OSD) or the inferior patella (with SLJD). If the stress on the patellar tendon is not eliminated, then eventually the bone stimulation causes new bone to be laid down. The bone formation causes a bump to form on the tibial tubercle. This bump may appear deformed as compared to the contralateral side.

Immediate Care

Instruct the child and his parents to apply ice packs or ice massage throughout the day to alleviate pain. Activities that cause pain and inflammation should be decreased or avoided entirely. Intensity of activities also should be decreased. The child should take anti-inflammatory medication, if possible. Both injuries may last for months, but typically heal on their own when the child stops growing. If the condition worsens or does not get better within a few weeks' time, then refer the child to his physician to determine the extent of injury. The athlete continues with ice application, NSAIDs, and rehabilitation that focuses on quadriceps muscles stretching. The child can also wear a patellar tendon strap to decrease stress on the tendon. The child does not necessarily need to stop all athletic activities during the rehabilitation process. Work with the child to create a safe, progressive, low intensity exercise activity program that allows the child to continue to be active, yet heal appropriately.

Prevention

Activity intensity should be progressed slowly for adolescent athletes who are growing rapidly. Children participating in athletic activities should stretch and strengthen their muscles with advice from and under the supervision of a qualified, trained professional such as an exercise physiologist, credentialed personal trainer, or strength and conditioning coach.

THE LOWER LEG AND ANKLE

The lower leg consists of the area from the knee down to the ankle joint. The ankle joint is composed of the distal tibia and the talus. The fibula borders the lateral side of the ankle. A variety of injuries occur to the lower leg and ankle, ranging from insignificant minor strains to life-threatening compound fractures (**Figure 12-14**).

Lower Leg Fractures

In athletic activities, lower leg fractures occur to the tibia and fibula. The tibia is a weight-bearing bone, whereas the fibula is not. Therefore, stresses from the foot contacting the ground can cause overuse tibial stress fractures. Acute tibial and fibular fractures also occur (**Figure 12-15**). These acute fractures may occur to only one or both bones simultaneously. The fractures can occur anywhere on the bone, but the tibial shaft is most commonly fractured. Fractures can also occur at the epiphyseal plates, tibial tuberosity, and tibial plateaus. A distal fibula fracture is called a *Maisonneuve* fracture (**Figure 12-16**).

Mechanism or Cause of Injury

Acute fractures are caused by a fall, a motor vehicle accident, a direct blow to the bone, or a twist of the lower extremity. In athletics a direct blow by equipment, implements, or another athlete is most common. Stress fractures occur due to constant, repetitive bounding of the foot on the ground. The ground reaction forces are transmitted up to the tibia. Over time, these forces weaken the tibia. The tibia cracks at the weak points and stress fractures form. Stress fractures can occur when an athlete is poorly conditioned, has increased the intensity of or changed her activity too quickly, or wears shoes inappropriate for the activity.

Signs and Symptoms

For acute fractures, the athlete feels pain and is unable to move the body part. She has point tenderness at the fracture site.

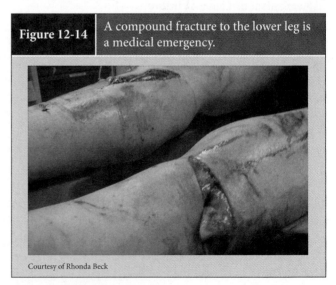

Figure 12-14 A compound fracture to the lower leg is a medical emergency.

Courtesy of Rhonda Beck

Figure 12-15	Lower leg fractures can occur to the tibia, fibula, or both simultaneously as shown in this x-ray.

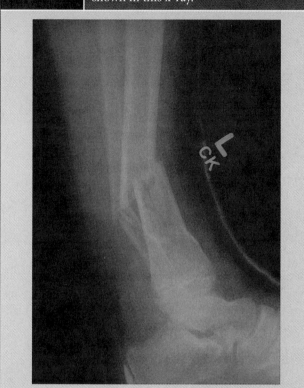

Courtesy of Kevin G. Shea, MD, Intermountain Orthopedics, Boise, Idaho.

The area may exhibit swelling, bruising, and deformity. If only the fibula is fractured, the athlete may be able to walk. Tibial stress fractures may take weeks to develop; consequently, the signs and symptoms take some time to affect the athlete. The athlete begins to experience a gradual onset of localized tibial pain. The pain increases during activity and decreases at rest. As the stress fracture becomes more severe, the pain occurs at rest. The pain may wake the athlete at night. The area where the stress fracture is located is point tender, and the athlete may walk with a limp.

Immediate Care

Care for an acute tibial or fibular fracture as you would for any other acute fracture. Call 911 and treat the athlete for shock. If the athlete has sustained an open fracture, control the bleeding and carefully dress and bandage the wound without moving the leg. Splint the injured extremity in the position that you find it (**Figure 12-17**). Apply ice to the area. Monitor the athlete until EMS arrives. If you suspect that an athlete has a stress fracture, have the athlete stop all weight-bearing activities until she has seen a physician. The athlete can continue to perform upper extremity exercises. The athlete should apply ice intermittently throughout the day and take anti-inflammatories to decrease pain and inflammation.

The athlete's physician will take x-rays or a bone scan to determine whether a stress fracture exists (**Figure 12-18**). The

Figure 12-16	A distal fibular fracture is called a Maisonneuve fracture.

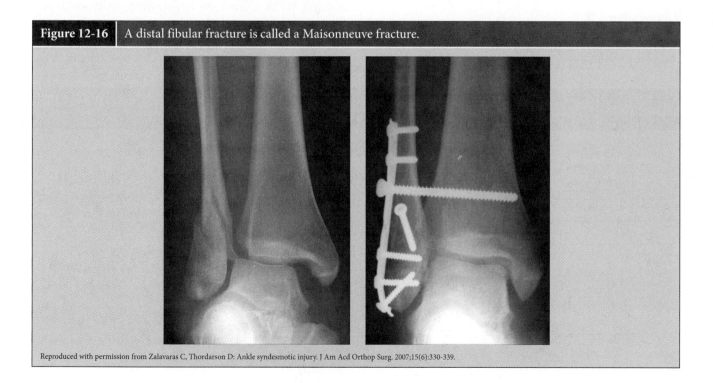

Reproduced with permission from Zalavaras C, Thordarson D: Ankle syndesmotic injury. J Am Acd Orthop Surg. 2007;15(6):330-339.

Figure 12-17 Two methods of splinting tibia and fibular fractures: (A) Anatomic splint using the athlete's body and blankets. (B) Utilizing two boards.

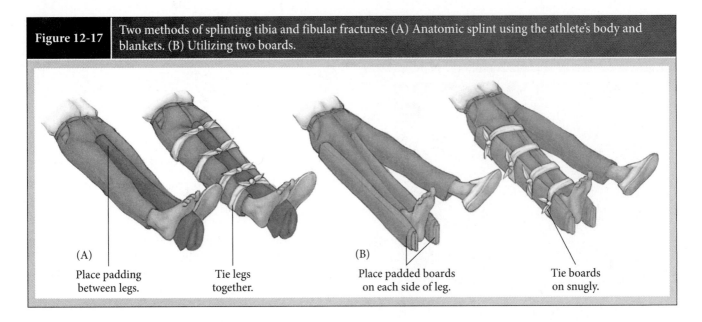

(A) Place padding between legs.   Tie legs together.

(B) Place padded boards on each side of leg.   Tie boards on snugly.

athlete has to rest the area, continue with ice application and anti-inflammatory medication, strengthen the anterior tibial musculature, stretch the gastrocnemius and soleus, correct training errors, properly increase training regimens, and wear proper footwear for her activity. She will gradually return to sport once the inflammation is gone and she has regained some strength in the lower extremity. Depending on the severity of the stress fracture, she can begin to return to activity in about 2 months.

Prevention

To prevent acute fractures, athletes should wear protective equipment such as shin guards when playing soccer. Stress fractures can be prevented by strengthening and stretching lower leg muscles, utilizing proper biomechanics during activity, wearing proper footwear for the activity, and gradually increasing intensity, duration, and type of training.

Medial Tibia Stress Syndrome

Medial tibia stress syndrome (MTSS) is an overuse condition commonly called *shin splints*. MTSS affects the overlying tibial muscles, of which the posterior tibialis is most commonly affected. MTSS occurs most frequently to athletes who perform running activities, especially activities that involve sudden stopping and starting. If the athlete ignores the signs and symptoms of MTSS, does not take steps to treat the condition,

Figure 12-18 Bone scans are used to determine if the athlete has a stress fracture, indicated by black arrow in (A) and white arrows in (B).

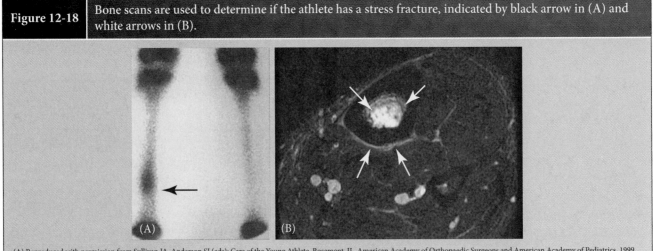

(A)   (B)

(A) Reproduced with permission from Sullivan JA, Anderson SJ (eds): Care of the Young Athlete. Rosemont, IL, American Academy of Orthopaedic Surgeons and American Academy of Pediatrics, 1999, p 408. (B) Reproduced with permission from Johnson TR, Steinbach LS (eds): Essentials of Musculoskeletal Imaging. Rosemont, IL, American Academy of Orthopaedic Surgeons, 2004, p 519.

and continues with the causative activity, then MTSS can progress into a tibial stress fracture.

Mechanism or Cause of Injury

MTSS is caused by an overload of the medial musculature that lies over the tibia. The overload occurs when the athlete increases intensity and duration of activity too quickly; runs on uneven, slanted, or hard surfaces; runs downhill consistently; and performs activities that require sudden stops and starts.

Signs and Symptoms

The athlete has pain and point tenderness on the middle portion of the tibia. The pain decreases or goes away during activity, but then returns at rest. As MTSS continues, the pain persists during rest and activity. Some mild effusion may be present in the area.

Immediate Care

The athlete can treat MTSS herself by applying ice to the area and taking NSAIDs. She does not need to discontinue activity completely, but you should limit her activities that cause pain and inflammation. If signs and symptoms continue even with limited activity, then the activity needs to be limited further or discontinued. The athlete should see a physician if the signs and symptoms of MTSS do not decrease or if they get worse with treatment. If the athlete has sharp tibial pain, call 911.

Prevention

The athlete should strengthen the lower leg anterior musculature and stretch the posterior musculature in order to prevent a muscle imbalance and avoid MTSS. The athlete should wear properly fitted shoes with arch supports. She should seek advice from a professional in order to participate in a safe, progressive exercise activity protocol that poses no harm to the anterior lower leg musculature.

Compartment Syndrome

The lower leg has four compartments that contain muscles, which move the ankle and foot, along with nerves and blood vessels. Compartment syndrome is a condition in which the pressure in the lower leg compartments increases and begins to compromise the nerve and vascular structures. Two types of compartment syndrome exist. Acute compartment syndrome is limb-threatening because pressure on the nerves, blood vessels, and muscles can cause these structures to die. Exertional, or chronic, compartment syndrome occurs during exercise activity and can also be debilitating to an athlete.

Mechanism or Cause of Injury

Acute compartment syndrome is caused by a direct blow or severe trauma to the lower leg, such as a tibial fracture. The muscles in the anterior compartment become inflamed and swollen. The fascia, which contains the muscles in the compartment, does not expand. Consequently, as the swelling and edema increase, the pressure in the compartment increases.

Exertional compartment syndrome is caused by muscular contraction during exercise activity. The muscles fill with blood and expand as they normally should; however, with exertional compartment syndrome, excessive pressure builds up in the compartments. It is not certain why some athletes have exertional compartment syndrome and others do not. Large muscles, thick fascia, high venous pressure, and lower body biomechanics may contribute to exertional compartment syndrome.

Signs and Symptoms

You can differentiate whether the athlete has acute compartment syndrome or a basic contusion. If the pain does not decrease despite treatment efforts, then the athlete most likely has acute compartment syndrome. With acute compartment syndrome, the athlete experiences persistent pain that develops over hours and progressively gets intense. The area may be swollen and red. Athletes with severe compartment syndrome may also have decreased sensation and muscular weakness down the leg and into the foot. An athlete who has exertional compartment syndrome also feels pain come on gradually during exercise that continues to increase until exercise is stopped. The pain lasts until shortly after exercise during rest. The athlete may feel loss of sensation and muscular weakness down the leg during exercise while the compartment pressure exists.

Immediate Care

Acute compartment syndrome is a medical emergency, so call 911. The athlete will have surgery immediately to release the pressure in the compartments. Although exertional compartment syndrome is not a medical emergency, the athlete sometimes requires surgery to release the compartments' pressure. Conservative treatment includes stretching, orthotics, biomechanical changes, massage, and rest from activities. Surgery is more effective than conservative treatment in eliminating exertional compartment syndrome.

Prevention

Acute compartment syndrome can potentially be prevented by wearing protective shin guards for activities in which lower leg injury is possible, such as soccer. Exertional compartment syndrome is not preventable, but the athlete should participate in proper conditioning, such as a warm-up and cool-down, in an attempt to keep the muscles strong and flexible.

Strains

Muscle and tendon strains occur frequently to the lower leg. The gastrocnemius and the Achilles tendon are commonly strained. The Achilles tendon is prone to ruptures (Grade 3 strains), typically to men in their 40s.

Mechanism or Cause of Injury

The causes of a lower leg muscular strain are a forceful muscle contraction or a sudden stretch. Repetitive loading can also cause strains. Most Achilles tendon ruptures occur due to a forceful gastrocnemius and soleus contraction when the athlete pushes off on the ball of his foot.

Signs and Symptoms

Grade 1 and 2 strains exhibit the typical signs and symptoms for strains, as previously discussed. When a muscle or tendon is ruptured, such as the Achilles tendon, the tissue tears away from its bony attachment or at any other portion of the soft tissue. When an athlete's Achilles tendon ruptures, he may describe the incident as feeling like he was struck in the leg with a baseball bat. The athlete feels a snap or pop at the time of injury. The gastrocnemius and soleus muscles roll up and create a bulge in the calf area. This bulge appears deformed as compared to the contralateral side. The athlete experiences severe pain and may exhibit signs and symptoms of shock. He most likely falls to the ground immediately after the injury because he cannot weight bear on the affected leg, and has loss of function.

Immediate Care

Treat Grade 1 and 2 strains with RICE. An athlete with a Grade 2 strain may also need crutches to ambulate. Whenever an athlete needs crutches to ambulate for a Grade 2 strain, the injury is significant enough to warrant seeing a physician. An athlete who has a Grade 3 strain probably is in shock. Consequently, call EMS for assistance. Treat the athlete for shock and use RICE. Keep him comfortable. The physician will evaluate the athlete and determine the extent of injury. An athlete who has sustained a ruptured Achilles tendon typically needs the tendon surgically repaired in order to achieve full function in the future. After the surgery, utilization of therapeutic modalities and rehabilitation begins. The athlete cannot return to full activity for approximately 4–6 months. A nonsurgical, conservative approach includes wearing a cast and boot that elevates the heel and places the athlete's ankle in plantarflexion, in an attempt to properly align the tendon. This conservative approach is not effective if the tendon has snapped up and does not approximate the tendon or the attachment site.

Prevention

Athletes need to undertake a lower leg flexibility program, especially for the gastrocnemius and Achilles tendon. The anterior muscles should also be strengthened so an imbalance between the anterior and posterior muscles is avoided. The athlete's conditioning program must incorporate a variety of exercises other than exercises which require a forceful push-off. Also, the exercise program should follow a safe, progressive increase in intensity and duration in order to avoid lower leg strains.

Tendinitis

Tendinitis can occur in any lower leg, ankle, or foot tendons. The Achilles, peroneal, and posterior and anterior tibialis tendons are commonly affected by inflammation. Tendinitis can be acute or chronic.

Mechanism or Cause of Injury

Tendinitis is caused by a quick stretch or contraction (acute) or repetitive loading to the tendon (chronic). The tendon can also become inflamed due to friction against an object, such as a shoe; improper lower extremity alignment; or faulty biomechanics during activity. Athletic and work-related activities, as well as hobbies and ADLs that require repetitive motions, can cause lower leg tendinitis.

Signs and Symptoms

The athlete experiences pain and possibly crepitus with activity. The tendon may be point tender with mild swelling. As the tendinitis becomes chronic, the tendon noticeably thickens.

Immediate Care

Tendinitis is treated with rest, ice, and anti-inflammatories. The athlete must correct or stop any activity that causes stress on the tendon; otherwise, the tendinitis will persist. If the tendinitis persists and the signs and symptoms interfere with the athlete's ADLs, then refer her to a physician. The physician may recommend treatment including corticosteroid injections, NSAIDs, and rehabilitation, including muscle and tendon stretching and strengthening.

Prevention

Preventing tendinitis includes stretching the muscles and tendons, utilizing proper technique, completing a warm-up and cool-down during an exercise session, and avoiding activities that place undue stress on the tendons.

Ankle Dislocation

Similar to a knee dislocation, an ankle dislocation is rare. The ankle has a decent amount of stability due to the talus and tibia bony configuration. Therefore, a great amount of trauma is necessary to dislocate the ankle. When an ankle dislocates, it commonly has an associated fracture (**Figure 12-19**).

Mechanism or Cause of Injury

In order to dislocate the ankle, a severe force must be placed on the joint. The severe force can be from direct contact, which can occur during a high intensity collision at an athletic event, a fall from a height, or a motor vehicle accident. An athlete also can dislocate an ankle if he twists his ankle beyond the joint's normal ROM.

Signs and Symptoms

The athlete experiences the same signs and symptoms as with a knee dislocation. The athlete has severe pain and is in shock. Deformity, swelling, point tenderness, and abnormal or loss of sensation in the affected limb's toes is present. The athlete cannot move the joint.

Immediate Care

Treat the dislocation as you would any other dislocation by calling 911, treating the athlete for shock, stabilizing and splinting the ankle (**Figure 12-20**), applying ice to the area, and monitoring the athlete until EMS arrives.

Prevention

Ankle dislocations are not entirely preventable. The athlete must keep the muscles around the ankle strong, and make sure the ankle has normal ROM. Unfortunately, unexpected direct trauma forces that cause severe injury cannot always be avoided.

Tips from the Field

Tip 2 If an athlete has a severe ankle or foot injury, do not remove the shoe. The shoe helps to minimize swelling by acting as a compression mechanism. Removing the shoe allows blood and edema to enter the area, and swelling will increase. Also, if the athlete has a dislocation or fracture, removing the shoe may make the injury worse. Splint the injury with the shoe on and apply ice over and around the shoe.

Ankle Sprain

An ankle sprain is one of the most common lower extremity injuries. Ankle sprains occur to the lateral, medial, and anterior tibiofibular ligaments and the syndesmosis.

| Figure 12-19 | When an ankle is dislocated, a fracture often occurs simultaneously. |

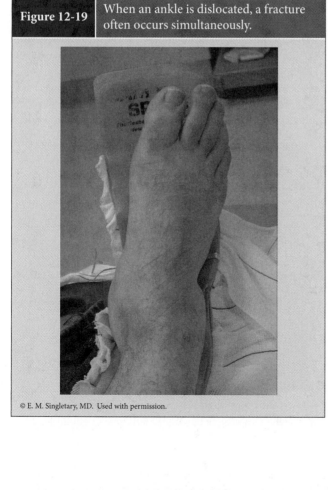

© E. M. Singletary, MD. Used with permission.

| Figure 12-20 | Splint a dislocated, fractured, or severely sprained ankle by utilizing pillows, blankets, clothing, or any other soft bulky materials |

Fold a pillow around ankle and tie it in place.

Mechanism or Cause of Injury

Ankle sprains occur when the joint is forced beyond its normal ROM. A lateral ankle sprain is caused by excessive ankle plantarflexion and inversion, a medial ankle sprain is caused by forceful ankle dorsiflexion and eversion, and a syndesmotic (or high ankle) sprain is caused by forceful dorsiflexion. These excessive forces can occur during athletic activities when running or jumping, or in nonathletic activities such as stepping on an uneven surface, losing balance, or tripping.

Signs and Symptoms

As with other sprains, the severity of the signs and symptoms depends on the grade of sprain. The athlete has pain and point tenderness at the site of injury. Swelling, ecchymosis, redness, joint instability, and loss of function are present. Athletes with Grade 1 sprains may be able to bear weight and ambulate normally, whereas athletes with Grade 2 and 3 sprains walk with a limp or are unable to bear any weight. The athlete may state that she heard a pop at the time of injury.

Immediate Care

Immediately after the injury, apply ice to the area with a compression wrap. Have the athlete lie on her back and elevate the ankle above her heart with her heel against the wall. If the athlete has sustained a Grade 1 sprain, wrap her ankle with an elastic compression wrap after feeling to the ankle has been restored after the ice application. She most likely can ambulate normally without pain or a limp. If the athlete has sustained a Grade 2 or 3 sprain, she may be unable to properly ambulate due to pain and loss of function. Consequently, fit her for crutches and have her ambulate without putting weight on the injured ankle. If an athlete suffers an ankle sprain and cannot walk properly, has severe pain and/or significant loss of function, or has point tenderness on the distal fibula and lateral malleolus, medial malleolus, base of the fifth metatarsal, and/or the navicular bone, then the athlete must see a physician for x-rays to determine whether a fracture has also occurred. A sprained ligament can tear a piece of the bone off with the ligament during injury and cause an avulsion fracture. The excessive force with abnormal movement of the joint can cause bone to strike bone and cause a fracture on the opposite side of the sprain. Regardless of the grade of injury, the athlete requires rehabilitation. She should take NSAIDs, utilize crutches as necessary, wear an ankle brace, and continue RICE for weeks depending on the severity of injury. The athlete can gradually return to full function if she follows this course of treatment.

Prevention

Ankle sprains can be prevented by stretching the gastrocnemius and Achilles tendon; strengthening the muscles that act on the ankle; improving lower body coordination, balance, and agility; and wearing proper shoes for the activity and playing surface.

Tips from the Field

Tip 3 When treating a lateral ankle sprain that has notable swelling around the malleolus, compression of the joint is important to mechanically force the edema out of the joint space. You can promote the movement of the edema by applying a "horseshoe pad" to the ankle under the compression wrap. In order to make a horseshoe pad, you need an approximately 8" × 8" foam or felt sheet that is soft, but not too compressive. You can purchase foam and felt from a medical supply store. Place the felt against the injured ankle. Take a pen and trace a *U* shape on the felt that goes around the tip of the malleolus, so the lateral malleolus and fibula is within the concave portion of the *U*. The lateral malleolus should fit snugly in the bottom portion of the *U* shape. Make the felt horseshoe approximately 1 inch or so wide throughout the *U*. The top of the *U* should come up approximately 4–5 inches above the malleolus. Cut out the horseshoe. Place the horseshoe on the ankle so the lateral malleolus and fibula are within the concave portion of the *U*. Then begin wrapping the elastic compression wrap from the toes over the horseshoe up to approximately where the Achilles tendon meets the gastrocnemius. Along with the compression wrap, the horseshoe forces the edema out of the area underneath the horseshoe. When you remove the compression bandage and horseshoe to apply ice, the edema, including the ecchymosis, should have moved out from underneath the horseshoe. Reapply the horseshoe and compression wrap after the athlete has applied ice and regained full feeling of the ankle.

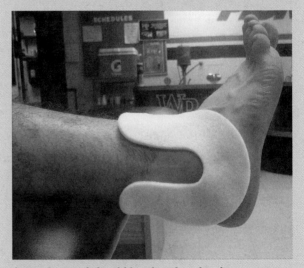

A horseshoe pad should be placed under the compression wrap when an athlete has sustained a sprained ankle.

THE FOOT

Fracture and Dislocation

Foot and toe fractures occur to a variety of bones, including the phalanges, metatarsals, and calcaneus. Some fractures have specific names. For example, a fracture at the base of the fifth metatarsal is called a Jones fracture (**Figure 12-21**); a fracture that results in a proximal metatarsal dislocation is called a Lisfranc fracture. Stress fractures can occur to any of the bones in the foot because they are all weight-bearing bones. Metatarsal stress fractures are commonly called march fractures. Foot dislocations are not common. Other than a Lisfranc fracture, which is a dislocated metatarsal due to a fracture, the phalanges are most likely to dislocate (**Figure 12-22**).

▌ Mechanism or Cause of Injury

The mechanism for an acute foot fracture includes direct trauma to the area. Often an athlete's foot is stepped on by another athlete, which results in a fracture, or the athlete drops a heavy object such as a bowling ball or a dumbbell on his foot. Stress fractures occur from overuse and repetitive weight bearing and bounding on the foot during activities such as continual walking, running, and jumping. March fractures often occur to the second metatarsal when the athlete has a condition called Morton's toe. Usually the first

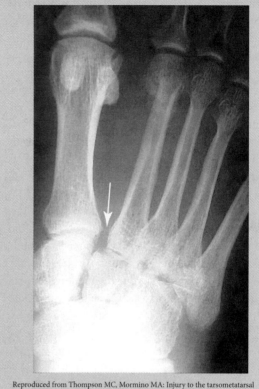

Figure 12-22 | A Lisfranc fracture (noted by the arrow) causes a metatarsal dislocation.

Reproduced from Thompson MC, Mormino MA: Injury to the tarsometatarsal joint complex. J Am Acad Orthop Surg. 2003;11:260-267.

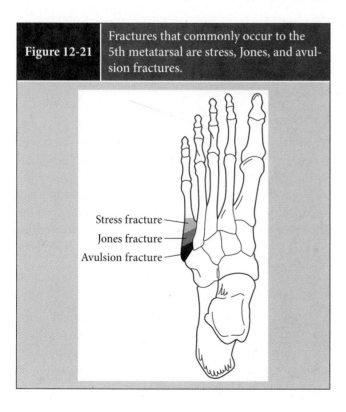

Figure 12-21 | Fractures that commonly occur to the 5th metatarsal are stress, Jones, and avulsion fractures.

Stress fracture
Jones fracture
Avulsion fracture

metatarsal is longer than the second metatarsal; however, with Morton's toe the first metatarsal is shorter than the second metatarsal. Consequently, the majority of pressure is placed on the longer, second metatarsal, which is not typical. Over time this undue stress creates a second metatarsal march fracture. Toe dislocations occur by axial loading, which is a direct blow to the tip of the phalanges. This mechanism of injury transmits force down the adjacent bones. Acute fractures and dislocations can also result from extreme foot torsion while weight bearing.

▌ Signs and Symptoms

Acute foot fractures and dislocations result in the same signs and symptoms as found with any other fracture or dislocation. Pain, point tenderness, swelling, and deformity exist. The athlete may be in shock. Foot stress fractures exhibit the same signs and symptoms as other stress fractures. Pain is dull at first, then becomes sharp and persistent. Point tenderness and mild swelling may exist. The athlete cannot weight bear normally.

Immediate Care

Acute foot fractures and dislocations require immediate advanced medical care and examination. Call 911 immediately. Check the victim for shock and treat him as appropriate. Splint the foot and the ankle in order to rest and stabilize the injury. Apply ice to the area to decrease pain and inflammation. Monitor the athlete until EMS arrives. The athlete may or may not need surgery for the injury, depending on the bony alignment. His foot will be placed in a cast or hard walking boot, and he will utilize crutches until the area heals. Rehabilitation helps the athlete gain full foot ROM and strength. Athletes with suspected foot stress fractures should use RICE. Have him rest the foot by discontinuing weight-bearing activity, and fit him for crutches until he is able to walk without pain or a limp. Apply ice to the injury and an elastic compression wrap to give the foot support and decrease any swelling. The athlete should also elevate the foot above the heart whenever possible. If the athlete continues to have pain, inability to bear weight and walk normally, or any stress fracture signs and symptoms that increase despite treatment, refer him to a physician for evaluation.

Prevention

Athletes cannot always prevent acute fractures and dislocations of the foot. They must be careful not to drop a heavy object on the foot or kick an unyielding object. Athletes who participate in work-related activities with the potential of foot injury, such as construction, should wear appropriate protective footwear. The athlete should perform strengthening exercises for the lower leg and ankle because these muscles and tendons act on and support the foot. The athlete should wear supportive, appropriately fitted shoes for the activity and playing surface to prevent foot stress fractures.

Retrocalcaneal Bursitis

Retrocalcaneal bursitis is an inflammation of the bursa located between the calcaneus and the Achilles tendon. Due to the bursa's location, the athlete may mistake the condition as Achilles tendinitis. The condition is often referred to as *pump bump*.

Mechanism or Cause of Injury

Retrocalcaneal bursitis is caused by friction on the bursa. An athlete who wears tight or poorly fitting shoes combined with repetitive walking, running, and jumping irritates the bursa, which causes inflammation.

Signs and Symptoms

The athlete has heel pain that intensifies when walking, especially up stairs or inclines, and during running and jumping.

Pain continues at rest and even at night while sleeping. Point tenderness and swelling are evident at the injured area.

Immediate Care

The athlete can treat the condition herself. She should avoid any irritating activities; apply ice to the area frequently throughout the day; take anti-inflammatory medication; wear properly fitted work and exercise shoes; stretch the gastrocnemius, soleus, and Achilles tendon; and strengthen the muscles around the ankle. The athlete should place over-the-counter heel wedges in both shoes. These heel wedges raise the heel slightly and decrease some tension on the Achilles tendon. If the signs and symptoms of retrocalcaneal bursitis are not resolved after several weeks of treatment, then refer the athlete to a physician. The physician will recommend the same treatment protocol and perhaps prescribe a corticosteroid injection and/or immobilization to promote healing.

Prevention

Preventing retrocalcaneal bursitis is possible. The athlete should be properly fitted for work and exercise shoes by an expert in the shoe business. These shoes must not cause friction at the calcaneus and Achilles tendon. The athlete should stretch the Achilles tendon frequently, to allow for flexibility in the area. Strengthening the muscles around the ankle is also necessary to prevent retrocalcaneal bursitis.

Plantar Fasciitis

The plantar fascia is a thick band of soft tissue that runs from the calcaneus to the metatarsal heads. It supports the foot's medial longitudinal arch and acts as a shock absorber during weight bearing. Inflammation of the plantar fascia commonly occurs in athletes.

Mechanism or Cause of Injury

When excessive tension is placed on the plantar fascia over a period of time, the tissue begins to fail and inflammation results. Runners are predisposed to acquiring plantar fasciitis due to the stress on the tissue during weight bearing. Also, overweight and pregnant athletes are at risk due to the extra force placed on their feet due to increased body weight. Athletes who wear poorly supportive shoes are commonly afflicted with plantar fasciitis.

Signs and Symptoms

Because plantar fasciitis is an overuse injury, signs and symptoms of injury develop slowly. A signature symptom of plantar fasciitis is sharp pain at the underside of the foot upon waking in the morning and stepping down. During sleep, the foot is in a relaxed, plantarflexed position, which allows the plantar fascia to contract from lack of use. When the athlete steps down for the first time after rising, the plantar fascia is forcefully stretched, which elicits pain. As the athlete walks, the pain decreases due to the plantar fascia becoming stretched and more mobile. Plantar fasciitis usually occurs in one foot, but can be present in both feet (**Figure 12-23**).

Immediate Care

A conservative treatment approach to heal the plantar fascia should begin with the onset of signs and symptoms. The treatment includes NSAIDs, rehabilitation including stretches for the plantar fascia and Achilles tendon, and ankle muscle strengthening. If this treatment does not alleviate signs and symptoms of plantar fasciitis, the athlete should see a physician for additional therapies. A physician can prescribe corticosteroids; therapeutic modalities such as ultrasound; night splints, which are worn to keep the plantar fascia in a stretched position; and orthotics to help decrease stress on the plantar fascia. Usually the athlete's plantar fasciitis signs and symptoms resolve and her foot will be at a pre-injury state within a few months.

Prevention

To prevent plantar fasciitis the athlete needs to wear supportive shoes that are in good condition. Athletes also need to maintain a healthy weight to decrease stress on the plantar fascia.

Figure 12-23	Plantar fasciitis.

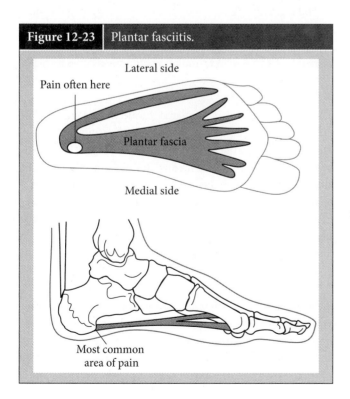

Pes Planus and Pes Cavus

Pes planus and pes cavus are conditions of the foot's medial longitudinal arch. Pes planus is a flat arch called *flat foot*, and pes cavus is a high arch (**Figures 12-24** and **12-25**). Pes planus can be structural or functional. Both conditions can cause various lower extremity conditions and injuries.

Mechanism or Cause of Injury

Structural pes planus occurs in athletes typically from birth. Infants and young children have flat feet, but as they grow older a normal arch forms. For unknown reasons, the arch does not form in some children. Functional pes planus is caused by loose soft tissue structures, including the tendons and plantar fascia, that comprise the plantar portion of the foot. An athlete who has had a foot injury or who is older also may have pes planus.

Figure 12-24	Pes planus is "flat foot" or a flat arch.

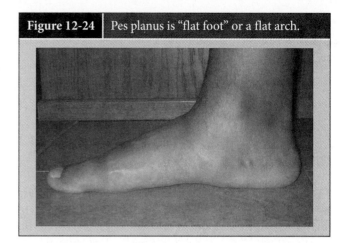

Figure 12-25	Pes cavus is a high arch.

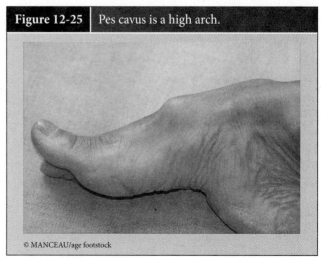

© MANCEAU/age footstock

Pes cavus is not as common as pes planus. It is caused by bone malformations in the foot or nerve problems. Pes cavus can also be caused over time when an athlete continually wears shoes that have a too small toe box. Tight toe boxes force the toes to passively flex and raise the arch. The soft tissue structures shorten and contract in that position, and form pes cavus.

Signs and Symptoms

When observing an athlete with pes planus, the medial longitudinal arch will be flat on one or both feet. An athlete with structural pes planus does not have an apparent medial longitudinal arch when weight bearing and non–weight bearing. The arch is flat in both positions. The athlete who has functional pes planus has a visible medial longitudinal arch while non–weight bearing and a flat arch when weight bearing. Pes planus does not necessarily cause troublesome signs and symptoms, especially if the adult athlete has had flat feet since birth. The athlete may have a tired feeling in her feet after standing, walking, or running for long periods of time due to lack of plantar fascia support.

In contrast to pes planus, pes cavus is painful. If the foot is very rigid, the pain develops when the athlete is on her feet standing, walking, or running. The athlete may complain of secondary problems caused by pes planus or pes cavus, such as MTSS and plantar fasciitis, respectively.

Immediate Care

If the athlete's pes planus or pes cavus does not bother the athlete or cause secondary injuries, then the athlete does not need to treat the condition. If the athlete is experiencing pain or other secondary injury due to pes planus or pes cavus, then he needs to see a physician for evaluation. The athlete may need custom orthotics to assist in decreasing pain and making the foot "normal," as well as correcting any biomechanics that are causing secondary injuries.

Prevention

Flat feet cannot be prevented if the athlete has had structural pes planus since birth. Functional pes planus can be minimized or prevented by strengthening the musculature and wearing shoes that support the medial longitudinal arch. Pes cavus can be prevented by stretching the plantar fascia and musculature that comprise the plantar surface of the foot. Also, athletes should wear shoes that fit their feet well and have adequate toe box size.

Bunion

A bunion is a bony outgrowth that occurs at the base of the medial first metatarsal (**Figure 12-26**).

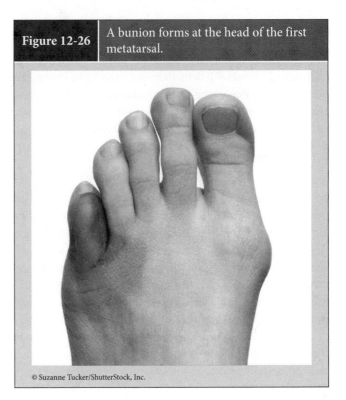

| Figure 12-26 | A bunion forms at the head of the first metatarsal. |

© Suzanne Tucker/ShutterStock, Inc.

Mechanism or Cause of Injury

A bunion forms when an athlete wears shoes that have a tight and pointed toe box. The great toe is forced laterally toward the second toe. This angulation is called hallux valgus. At the same time, the angulation and the shoe cause friction on the medial side of the first metatarsal head. Eventually the bunion forms. Heredity plays a role in formulating bunions, as does arthritis.

Signs and Symptoms

The athlete's great toe is angulated toward the second toe. The great toe may be severely angulated, which results in the great toe lying on top of the second toe. The athlete also has a large bump (the bunion) at the medial first metatarsal head. The athlete's great toe may be red and swollen at the metatarsophalangeal joint due to the inflammation. Likewise, calluses may form at the area. The athlete has soreness or pain at the site of the bunion due to friction when wearing shoes. The first metatarsophalangeal joint function is compromised.

Immediate Care

If the bunion or first digit angulation does not create inflammation, pain, or loss of function for the athlete, then no immediate care or treatment is needed. Those athletes who have problematic, inflamed bunions should wear shoes with a wide toe box. Have the athlete apply ice to the area frequently to reduce pain and inflammation. If the bunion continues to cause pain, the inflammation worsens, or there is loss of function of the first digit, then she should see a physician. A bunionectomy may need to be performed. This procedure involves shaving down the bunion and realigning the angulated toe. The athlete may be able to walk after the surgery, but commonly the athlete wears a walking boot and utilize crutches until the pain and inflammation from the procedure subside. The athlete should be able to return to full activity in approximately 2 months.

Prevention

Athletes should wear comfortable, well-fitted shoes with adequate space in the toe box in order to prevent bunions. Unfortunately, bunions caused by heredity and arthritis are not preventable.

Morton's Neuroma

Morton's neuroma, or metatarsalgia, is a condition that occurs at the ball of the foot. Fibrous tissue thickens around the nerve between the metatarsals and causes various signs and symptoms of nerve injury. The lateral plantar nerve runs between the third and fourth metatarsals. This site is most commonly affected by metatarsalgia.

Mechanism or Cause of Injury

Morton's neuroma is caused by pressure or friction on the ball of the foot, or by previous injury (e.g., metatarsal fracture). Because the ball of the foot between the third and fourth metatarsals is under a lot of pressure and stress when weight bearing, the area becomes irritated. Due to the irritation, fibrous tissue builds up between these metatarsals. Athletes who wear tight shoes, utilize the balls of their feet to participate in sport (e.g., rock wall climbing), or who have pes cavus or hallux valgus are more prone to Morton's neuroma.

Signs and Symptoms

The athlete complains of sharp, burning, shooting pain that is common with nerve injury. The radiating pain may go into the athlete's toes. The athlete may also have tingling or loss of sensation from the ball of the foot to the toes.

Immediate Care

An ice pack or ice massage applied frequently throughout the day will help treat the injury. The athlete can take NSAIDs, must wear footwear that supports the metatarsal arch, and place over-the-counter orthotics in his shoes. The athlete should avoid any aggravating weight-bearing activities on the balls of his feet. If the athlete continues to have pain in his foot that does not decrease a few days after treatment, then the athlete should be evaluated by a physician. His physician may prescribe corticosteroid injections to decrease pain and inflammation. Surgery may be needed to either decrease the tightness of other structures that are compressing the nerve or, in severe cases, remove the nerve.

Prevention

In order to prevent Morton's neuroma, the athlete should wear properly fitting shoes that are not tight. The athlete should also avoid constant weight-bearing activities utilizing the balls of his feet.

Sprain

Toe sprains occur to the medial and lateral collateral ligaments, cartilage, and joint capsule. Sometimes you cannot determine whether the toe is fractured or simply sprained. In fact, a sprain may also accompany a fracture.

Mechanism or Cause of Injury

Toe sprains are caused by hitting the end of the toe on a nonyielding object. An athlete can cause a sprain by kicking a wall, stubbing the toe against the ground, or striking it against another person, such as in martial arts. Stopping short or changing direction while running resulting in the toe hitting the front of the shoe forcefully can cause a sprain. The interphalangeal and metatarsophalangeal joints can also be forced into a valgus or varus position, which sprains the collateral ligaments. The great toe metatarsophalangeal joint is often sprained by forceful hyperextension when kicking. This injury is called *turf toe*.

Signs and Symptoms

The athlete experiences the same signs and symptoms of injury as with any Grade 1, 2, or 3 sprain. She has pain and loss of function at the injured area. The area may be stiff, swollen, and point tender. The toe may appear black and blue from internal bleeding.

Immediate Care

The athlete should use RICE immediately on the toe. Support the injured toe by buddy taping the injured toe to the adjacent toes. The athlete should not weight bear if she cannot do so without pain. If the athlete cannot weight bear, then fit her for crutches. The athlete should also take anti-inflammatory medication. Once the inflammation has subsided, the athlete can perform toe exercises to increase ROM and strengthening exercises for the lower leg muscles that affect the toes. As always, if the athlete's signs and symptoms do not decrease or

Figure 12-27 | Hammer toes.

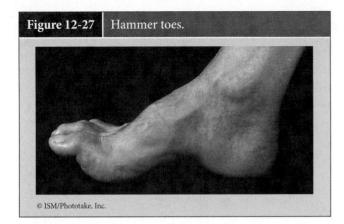

© ISM/Phototake, Inc.

get worse within a few days despite treatment, then the athlete should see her physician to rule out a toe fracture.

Prevention

Prevention of toe sprains includes having good ROM, flexibility, and strength at the toes. The athlete should wear supportive, comfortable shoes with an adequate sized toe box so the toes are not cramped or touching the front of the shoe. The athlete needs to avoid kicking any nonyielding objects.

Hammer Toe, Claw Toe, and Mallet Toe

Hammer, claw, and mallet toe are deformities from tendon contractures. These contractures may take years to develop. Hammer toes are distinguished by metatarsophalangeal joint hyperextension and proximal interphalangeal joint flexion (**Figure 12-27**). Claw toes, which are common with athletes who have pes cavus, are indicated by metatarsophalangeal joint hyperextension, and proximal interphalangeal joint and distal interphalangeal joint flexion (**Figure 12-28**). Mallet toe

Figure 12-28 | Claw toe at the second digit.

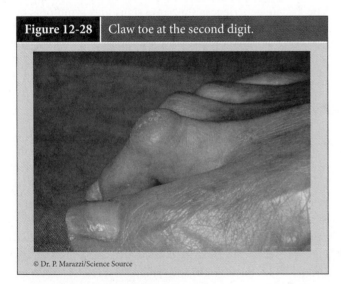

© Dr. P. Marazzi/Science Source

is characterized by flexion of the distal interphalangeal joint (**Figure 12-29**). The deformities can occur to one or multiple toes on one or both feet simultaneously.

Mechanism or Cause of Injury

These toe deformities are caused by wearing shoes that have a tight toe box. Consequently, the shoes do not have enough room at the front of the toe to allow for proper movement when an athlete stops and changes direction. High-heeled shoes also force the toes to become crowded and unnaturally bend into these deformed positions. Nerve damage and previous injury, such as fractures and sprains, can cause hammer, claw, or mallet toe. Also, some athletes inherit the deformities from their parents.

Signs and Symptoms

The athlete's toes are deformed and contracted. The athlete may not be able to move the toes in a normal manner, and feels pain when he tries to do so. Calluses may form where the toes rub against the shoes.

Immediate Care

If the toes are still flexible, then it is possible to correct the deformities. The athlete must wear shoes with a larger toe box so the toes do not hit the front of the shoe when running. He can utilize shoe inserts to help relieve pain and pressure. The athlete needs to perform ROM and flexibility exercises for each affected toe. If the athlete has persistent pain or cannot walk without pain or normal toe function, then he should see a physician. If the toes are tightly contracted and inflexible, the physician may recommend surgery to correct the deformities. The surgical procedure releases the tendons and/or realigns the bones.

Prevention

To prevent hammer, claw, or mallet toes, the athlete must wear properly fitting shoes with low heels and a roomy toe box.

Figure 12-29 | Mallet toes.

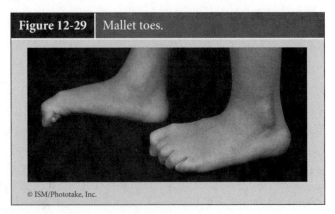

© ISM/Phototake, Inc.

Subungual Hematoma

A subungual hematoma is blood underneath the toenail (**Figure 12-30**).

Mechanism or Cause of Injury

A subungual hematoma is caused by a direct blow to the nail. An athlete who drops a weight on her toe, is stepped on by another athlete, or stubs her toe into a nonyielding object can have a subungual hematoma form.

Signs and Symptoms

The athlete experiences pain as the blood accumulates under the nail due to the pressure created by the blood. The blood under the nail is red at first; as days go by it turns dark purple to black. The nail is point tender. If the nail is significantly damaged, it may fall off during the healing process.

Immediate Care

A minor toe subungual hematoma does not need treatment other than ice application. If the toe is still painful after a few days of ice treatment, then the athlete should see a physician who will drain the blood from the toe. Draining the blood eliminates the pressure from underneath the nail. The athlete instantaneously feels pain relief. The physician releases the blood by utilizing a sterile object such as a pointy scalpel or wire. The hole created to release the blood needs to be treated as an open wound and bandaged to prevent infection and promote healing. In some instances, the nail is significantly damaged and needs to be removed by the physician.

Prevention

Athletes must be careful not to drop heavy items on their toes in order to attempt to prevent subungual hematomas.

SUMMARY

Injuries to the lower extremity vary, but many causes of these injuries are the same. A traumatic, direct blow; torsion of the lower extremity; stress from repetitive, forceful weight bearing; and poorly fitted shoes are common causes of lower extremity injuries. Because the lower extremity is weight bearing during a multitude of activities, forces applied at the foot can be transmitted throughout the extremity and cause injuries at unexpected sites. Consequently, when you examine the athlete's lower extremity, do not assume that an injury is located only where force was applied. Consider the possibility and look for secondary injuries, and treat all injuries appropriately.

DISCUSSION QUESTIONS

1. Which lower extremity injuries have an acute mechanism of injury? Which injuries have a slow or insidious onset?
2. What are common areas of the lower extremity that can sustain a stress fracture?
3. What lower extremity injuries can an athlete treat him- or herself? At what point should the athlete go to see a physician?
4. What lower extremity injuries typically cause an athlete to go into shock? Why does the athlete go into shock when sustaining these injuries?
5. What lower extremity injuries must be surgically repaired, and why?
6. What lower extremity injuries typically occur to men? Women? Children?
7. What role does improper footwear play in causing lower extremity injuries?

| **Figure 12-30** | Subungual hematoma of the great toe. |

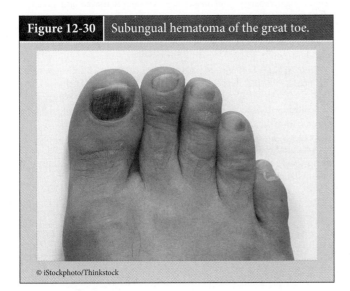

© iStockphoto/Thinkstock

CASE STUDY

Half Marathon Dreams

Taryn is a 22-year-old female who is active but does not exercise on a consistent basis. She decides to do something different to force herself to exercise regularly, so she begins to train for a half marathon. The half marathon will take place in a little over 5 months, so she has to begin to prepare now. Because she did not previously run as part of her exercise routine, she wants to take her training slow and train only 5 days per week. Taryn begins her training and completes 3 miles by the end of her first week. Aside from some delayed onset muscle soreness in her quadriceps and hamstrings, which is alleviated by stretching, she is not experiencing any physical problems. Therefore, after the first week she decides to increased her distance a half mile each week in subsequent weeks.

At the beginning of week four, Taryn adds another half mile to her workout routine, which has her completing 4 1/2 miles. She also begins to run on a new path that includes various surfaces and slight inclines, which mimic the half marathon course. After the second day completing the new mileage and route, Taryn experiences pain at the end of her workouts on the front of both lower legs. She dismisses the pain and speculates that her body is becoming accustomed to the increased mileage and new training route terrain. As she continues her daily workouts and begins her fifth and sixth weeks of training, she feels the pain progressively earlier in her mileage. Taryn's friend suggests that new running shoes will solve her problem.

Early one morning before her run, Taryn goes to her local sporting goods store to purchase a pair of running sneakers. She picks out a stylish pair, figuring that they are probably good for her because they are endorsed by a celebrity and are expensive. She tries the sneakers on and they feel a little tight, but she figures that they will stretch out. She goes home, puts the sneakers on, and goes for her run. In the beginning of her training, Taryn immediately realizes that the sneakers do not help alleviate her pain. The sneakers actually seem to exacerbate her shin pain, because the pain now arises within the first 10 minutes of her run. The pain becomes increasingly stronger as she progresses in mileage. She has to stop running at the 2-mile mark.

Taryn decides to take the next 3 days off from running. On the first day, she notices that her pain is present during the day while she is on her feet at work. Taryn's pain is evident when she perform normal daily weight-bearing activities such as walking up and down stairs. When she touches her medial shins, the area is very tender to the touch. She goes to bed that evening and cannot sleep due to the throbbing pain felt at both medial shins.

Taryn has become extremely frustrated with her condition. She has not been able to complete her training and the pain is not subsiding with rest. Taryn fears that if she goes to see a physician, he will make her stop running for an extended period of time. The rest time will put her behind schedule and ruin her dream of running in the half marathon. Taryn does not know what to do.

1. What injury has Taryn sustained?
2. What is the cause(s) of her injury?
3. What should Taryn have done to treat the injury before it worsened?
4. Should Taryn go to her physician for evaluation? What treatment do you think the physician will recommend?
5. What should Taryn consider when purchasing running shoes?
6. Was the injury preventable? Why or why not?

REFERENCES

American Academy of Orthopaedic Surgeons (AAOS). (2011). Femur shaft fractures (broken thighbone). Retrieved June 16, 2012, from http://orthoinfo.aaos.org/topic.cfm?topic=A00521

American Academy of Orthopaedic Surgeons (AAOS). (2009). Patellar tendon tear. Retrieved June 21, 2012, from http://orthoinfo.aaos.org/topic.cfm?topic=a00512

Bailie, D. S., & Lamprecht, D. E. (2001). Bilateral femoral neck stress fractures in an adolescent male runner: A case report. *American Journal of Sports Medicine*, 29(6), 811–813.

Elliot, D. L., Goldberg, L., & Kuehl, K. S. (2010). Young women's anterior cruciate ligament injuries: An expanded model and prevention paradigm. *Sports Medicine*, 40(5), 367–376. Retrieved June 19, 2012, from http://search.ebscohost.com

Kobayashi, H., Kanamura, T., Koshida, S., Miyashita, K., Okado, T., Shimizu, T., & Yokoe, K. (2010). Mechanisms of the anterior cruciate ligament injury in sports activities: A twenty-year clinical research of 1,700 athletes. *Journal of Sports Science and Medicine*, 9, 669–675. Retrieved June 19, 2012, from http://search.ebscohost.com

Newton, M., & Walker, J. (2004). Acute quadriceps injury: A case study. *Emergency Nurse*, 12(8), 24–29. Retrieved June 19, 2012, from http://search.ebscohost.com

Rigby, J. M., & Porter, K. M. (2010). Posterior cruciate ligament injuries. *Trauma*, 12, 175–181. Retrieved June 19, 2012, from http://search.ebscohost.com

Schultz, S. J., Houglum, P. A., & Perrin, D. H. (2010). *Examination of musculoskeletal injuries* (3rd ed.). Champaign, IL: Human Kinetics.

Torrance, D. A., & deGraauw, C. (2011). Treatment of post-traumatic myositis ossificans of the anterior thigh with extracorporeal shock wave therapy. *Journal of the Canadian Chiropractic Association*, 55(4), 240–246. Retrieved June 19, 2012, from http://search.ebscohost.com

Part III

Chapter 13

Systemic and Local Infections

© Jim Cummins/age fotostock

CHAPTER OBJECTIVES

After you have read this chapter, you will be able to understand:

- The differences between systemic and local infections
- Which infections are highly contagious
- Signs and symptoms of infections
- How to treat systemic and local infections
- When referral to a physician is necessary for an athlete with a systemic or local infection

Systemic and local infections occur frequently to athletes. Athletes who are young or old are more prone to obtaining infections, as are athletes who have immune or other disorders, such as human immunodeficiency virus (HIV) or diabetes. Depending on the athlete's characteristics, the type of pathogen, the body part affected, and the duration the pathogen is on the body or in the bloodstream, both systemic and local infections can be very troublesome.

Bacteria, viruses, and parasites cause systemic and local infections. Local infections can also be caused by fungi. Athletes acquire systemic and local infections in a variety of ways. The pathogens can enter the skin through a cut or mucous membrane. An athlete can consume pathogens that are found in food or water. Some pathogens are transmitted through the air, saliva, blood, skin contact, and animal and insect bites. Pathogens can be found on surfaces such as tables, floors, and mats, and are transmitted to an athlete when touching the contaminated surface.

Systemic infections are caused when a virus or bacterium enters the body. Once in the body, the pathogens spread via the bloodstream. The resulting infection affects a large portion of the body. Signs and symptoms of a systemic infection become apparent throughout the body and not at one particular site. Some classic signs and symptoms of a systemic infection include nausea, vomiting, fever, aches, weakness, and chills. Even though systemic infections are spread through the bloodstream, they are not necessarily more severe than local infections. Some examples of systemic infections include mononucleosis, the common cold, influenza, strep throat, mumps, measles, HIV, hepatitis B virus (HBV), and syphilis. Common minor infections, such as the common cold and influenza, can be treated at home. Other serious infections, such as HIV and measles, require a physician's care. Some systemic infections, such as **septicemia**, are medical emergencies. Septicemia spreads through the body quickly, and can cause septic shock and death. Treatment for systemic infections may include rest, **antipyretics**, fluid intake, and intravenous and other medications.

Unlike systemic infections, local infections do not affect the whole body; instead they are concentrated

> **Septicemia** A life-threatening infection that typically occurs in the body along with another systemic infection. Septicemia spreads through the bloodstream very quickly, and the athlete must be hospitalized and treated immediately. The mortality rate for the infection can be more than 50% (MedlinePlus, 2011).
>
> **Antipyretics** Fever-reducing medications such as acetaminophen, ibuprofen, and aspirin.

in a specific area. These infections do not enter into the bloodstream. Local infections include fungal infections, cellulitis, conjunctivitis, genital chlamydia, and herpes. With the exception of fever, signs and symptoms of local infections are different as compared to systemic infections. Local infections exhibit signs and symptoms of inflammation including redness, warmth and point tenderness at the site, pus, swelling, pain, and a pungent odor with edema drainage. Cleaning the area with soap and water; applying a disinfectant such as povidone-iodine; applying appropriate antifungal or antibacterial ointment, depending on the causative pathogen; and dressing and bandaging the area, can usually treat local infections at home. The athlete should observe the local infection to make sure the signs and symptoms are decreasing and not remaining the same or worsening. In general, if the local infection does not go away within 4 days, or if the signs and symptoms of infection increase, then refer your athlete to a physician. Some local infections, such as cellulitis and sexually transmitted infections, are very serious and the athlete should see a physician immediately. A few local infections, such as gonorrhea, may become systemic if they are not treated. When a local infection has become systemic, the athlete experiences signs and symptoms of a systemic infection. Therefore, if an athlete has obtained a serious local infection or a local infection that has become systemic he or she must be readily evaluated by a physician.

Athletes can avoid infection by practicing cleanliness. Hand, body, and clothes washing with soap and water is crucial to eliminate pathogens from the skin's surface. Athletes should not share toothbrushes, razors, cups, or utensils. Continuously wiping down equipment with an appropriate commercial disinfectant after each athlete's use, and cleaning restroom and shower areas are crucial to prevent infection at your facility.

This chapter divides common infections into five categories. The first category includes common respiratory infections, which is further broken down into upper and lower respiratory system infections. The other four categories are skin, viral, bacterial, and sexually transmitted infections.

RESPIRATORY INFECTIONS

Upper Respiratory System

The upper respiratory system includes the sinuses, nose, mouth, throat, larynx, and trachea. An upper respiratory infection (URI) is a general term for an infection of the upper respiratory system. With these URIs, inflammation exists along with a variety of signs and symptoms.

Acute Rhinitis (Common Cold)

Acute rhinitis is the common cold. Over 100 rhinoviruses exist that can invade the body and cause a cold. A person obtains a cold through various means including contact with nasal secretions from an infected person during hand shaking, water molecules in the air containing the virus transferred by a sneeze, or saliva from sharing a drinking cup. The contagious period is 1–2 days after symptoms arise (Urban, 2009). The person first has a sore throat and a feeling of malaise. Then a runny nose and a cough, accompanied by sneezing, develops. The nasal mucous is clear and thin at first and may turn thick and yellow-green. The cough is dry and hacking, and then may produce mucus. Over-the-counter medications can decrease signs and symptoms of the illness. These medications include decongestants, which thin nasal mucus; antihistamines, which dry out the nasal passages; expectorants, which expel mucus when coughing; and suppressants to quiet the cough. The cold will last about 4–10 days.

Allergic Rhinitis (Hay Fever)

Allergic rhinitis, commonly referred to as hay fever, affects the nose and eyes. Allergic rhinitis is not truly an infection; however, it is included in this section because it is a respiratory condition that exhibits extremely similar signs and symptoms as acute rhinitis. Hay fever is often a hereditary infection that is passed down through the person's parents' genetics, especially the mother (Henochowicz & Zieve, 2011). Exposure to an allergen such as dust, pollen, mold, or pet dander, triggers histamine release. The histamine causes the signs and symptoms of hay fever. Signs and symptoms include sneezing and nasal discharge, which is usually thin. The athlete may have red, watery, and itchy eyes, nose, and throat. As the allergic rhinitis progresses, the athlete may feel fatigued and irritable, along with having a headache, cough, stuffy nose, **postnasal drip**, and puffy eyes.

Postnasal drip The mucus that drains from the nose to the air passages and then to the throat.

In order to treat allergic rhinitis, the athlete must avoid any exposure to the allergens. Over-the-counter and prescription antihistamines can help treat and avoid signs and symptoms of allergic rhinitis. Oral medications include first or second generation antihistamines. First generation antihistamines (e.g., Benadryl Allergy, Chlor-Trimeton) cause drowsiness, whereas second generation antihistamines (e.g., Zyrtec, Allegra, Claritin) maintain athlete wakefulness. Decongestant and corticosteroid nasal sprays, the latter of which must be prescribed by a physician, also help alleviate the signs and symptoms of allergic rhinitis.

Sinusitis

Sinusitis is inflammation of the sinuses, which is caused by a virus, bacteria, or fungus. Sinusitis is classified as acute, subacute, or chronic, depending on the length of the infection. Acute sinusitis is caused by bacteria as a result of a prolonged URI and lasts up to a month. Subacute sinusitis lasts 1–3 months. Chronic sinusitis, which is caused by bacteria or fungus, lasts 3 months or more.

If an athlete has a cold and the nasal passageways are blocked, which prevents the mucus from draining, air cannot flow through the sinuses. As a result, bacteria form in the sinuses and create an infection. People who have a deviated septum or allergic rhinitis, or are smokers are prone to sinusitis. Signs and symptoms of sinusitis include fever, congestion, sinus pain and pressure, sore throat and bad breath from postnasal drip, cough, fatigue, and weakness.

Most acute sinusitis infections can be treated at home and clear up within 2 weeks. Treatment includes nasal sprays, including prescription, over-the-counter, and saline sprays; antipyretics; **analgesics**; and decongestants. A warm or cool mist humidifier utilized while sleeping can assist in moistening air passageways and loosening existing mucus. Flushing the sinuses with a **neti pot** solution helps loosen and remove stagnant mucus in the sinuses. The athlete will require antibiotics to clear up the infection if self-treatment does not alleviate the signs and symptoms within a few days.

> **Analgesics** Pain-reducing medications such as acetaminophen, ibuprofen, and aspirin. These specific medications are also antipyretics. Ibuprofen and aspirin are also anti-inflammatory medications; however, acetaminophen is not.
>
> **Neti pot** A nasal irrigation device that utilizes a saline solution to clear congested nasal passages.

Pharyngitis

The pharynx is the area between the tonsils and the larynx in the back of the throat. Inflammation of the pharynx, or pharyngitis, is also commonly called a sore throat. Pharyngitis can be caused by a viral or bacterial infection, as well as continual postnasal drip or cough, allergies, and smoking. Viral pharyngitis occurs with a common cold or flu. Bacterial pharyngitis infections are caused by Group A *Streptococcus* bacteria. This bacterium is the most common cause for strep throat. Strep throat is a painful inflammation of the throat that most often occurs in children (**Figure 13-1**). Antibiotics are necessary to treat the infection.

Strep throat can cause an athlete to come down with an inflammation of the tonsils, or tonsillitis. Tonsils are lymph nodes located in the throat that normally filter out bacteria; however, with a significant infection such as strep throat, the tonsils become infected and inflamed. Tonsillitis caused by strep throat or other bacteria is treated with antibiotics.

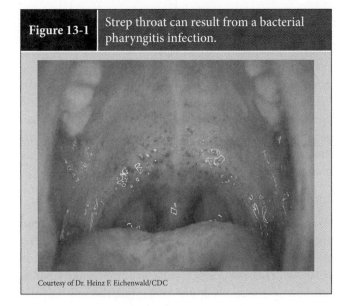

| **Figure 13-1** | Strep throat can result from a bacterial pharyngitis infection. |

Courtesy of Dr. Heinz F. Eichenwald/CDC

Signs and symptoms of pharyngitis include fever, joint pain, muscle aches, headache, swollen lymph nodes in the neck, and nasal congestion. Simple pharyngitis often goes away without antibiotics or other medication. The athlete can lessen the aggravating signs and symptoms by taking oral and topical analgesics (e.g., acetaminophen and sore throat sprays, respectively), utilizing a humidifier and salt water gargles, ingesting fluids, and getting enough rest. If the signs and symptoms do not readily decrease or if they worsen, refer your athlete to a physician. The athlete may need antibiotics to get rid of the infection.

Laryngitis

The larynx, also referred to as the *voice box* or *vocal cords*, is located at the upper portion of the trachea or *windpipe*. The larynx is a passageway to the lungs and functions to produce vocal communication. Laryngitis is classified as acute or chronic. Acute laryngitis is an inflammation of the larynx from a viral infection or by overuse, such as yelling. A bacterial infection rarely can cause laryngitis. Acute laryngitis often occurs with or as a result of a URI. Chronic laryngitis occurs due to work- or habit-related overuse (e.g., singing or continuous talking), smoking, inhaling allergens or pollutants, gastroesophageal reflux disease (GERD), or chronic sinusitis.

Signs and symptoms of acute laryngitis last approximately 1 week, whereas chronic laryngitis signs and symptoms can last a couple of weeks. The signs and symptoms include hoarseness and change in sound of voice; a sore, dry, and painful throat; and coughing. Treatment for laryngitis includes ingesting plenty of fluids to moisten the area, taking analgesics, and resting the throat by decreasing voice communication, singing, and other activities that utilize the vocal cords. If the cause of the laryngitis is a URI, recommend to the athlete to take a decongestant that assists in alleviating symptoms. If the athlete exhibits a fever over 103°F, makes high-pitched sounds, has trouble breathing, drools excessively, or has difficulty swallowing, then refer the athlete to the emergency room (ER) immediately. These signs and symptoms indicate either croup or epiglottitis, which are two severe, potentially life-threatening infections.

Lower Respiratory System

The lower respiratory system includes the trachea, bronchi, and lungs. Infections in this area can be severe because they affect the lungs, which function to receive oxygen and distribute it to the body. When the lower respiratory system is infected, oxygen cannot be delivered appropriately to the body and severe secondary illness or death can occur.

Influenza

Influenza is commonly called the *flu*. Viruses cause this highly contagious and potentially deadly infection. The flu affects the nasal passageways to the lungs. The viruses spread through water molecules when an infected athlete sneezes or coughs. The flu viruses can also thrive on surfaces, such as tables, equipment, and mats. When a person touches the contaminated surface, then puts her hand by her mouth, nose, or eyes, she may become infected. People are contagious a day before flu signs and symptoms are apparent, and approximately 5–7 days afterwards (Centers for Disease Control and Prevention [CDC], 2012b). Signs and symptoms of the flu include fever over 100°F, fatigue, weakness, muscle aches, cough, nasal congestion, and headache.

The CDC notes on its website that "the best way to prevent the flu is by getting a flu vaccine each year" (CDC, 2012b). The flu season predominantly occurs in the winter months. People who are particularly at risk for acquiring the flu—older athletes, young children, and pregnant women—should be **inoculated** each year before the winter season. People who

> **Inoculated** A person has been vaccinated in order to produce immunity against a pathogen.

have diabetes, asthma, or heart disease also should be vaccinated. Because viruses mutate, the flu virus strain changes each year. Consequently, the vaccination required changes each year, and a person must be vaccinated annually to protect against the flu. The flu vaccination is injected into a muscle, typically the triceps. The vaccine causes the body to create antibodies, which protect the person from three flu viruses

that are potentially the most likely to affect people during the upcoming flu season. If a person is not inoculated and is infected with the flu, then she must rest and take in fluids. The flu must run its course, but over-the-counter and prescription (Tamiflu and Relenza) antiviral medications can help to reduce flu signs and symptoms.

Bronchitis

The bronchi are two air passageways, or bronchial tubes, that arise from the trachea. One passageway attaches to the right lung and the other to the left lung. When the bronchi lining are inflamed, the illness is called bronchitis (**Figure 13-2**). Bronchitis is categorized as acute or chronic. Similarly to influenza or a cold, viruses cause acute bronchitis. Acute bronchitis lasts a short duration, 1–3 weeks, as compared to chronic bronchitis, which lasts months or years. Chronic bronchitis is most commonly caused by smoking. Air toxins, including pollutants, chemicals, and gases, can also cause bronchial irritation.

Chronic bronchitis is one of the two illnesses that comprise chronic obstructive pulmonary disease (COPD). Along with chronic bronchitis, COPD also includes emphysema, which is lung tissue degeneration that occurs over a period of years. No treatment exists for COPD. The condition is life-threatening because it causes severe breathing difficulty, lack

| Figure 13-2 | An x-ray of left lung bronchitis. The white area on the x-ray indicates inflammation. |

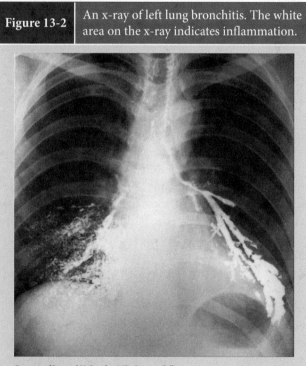

Courtesy of Leonard V. Crowley, MD, Century College

Arrhythmias Abnormal heart rhythms including irregular heart rate; tachycardia, which is a fast heart rate; or bradycardia, which is a slow heart rate.

of oxygen transport, and cardiac **arrhythmias**. Signs and symptoms of bronchitis and COPD include fatigue; chest discomfort, especially when deep breathing and coughing; low grade fever; chills; and mucus production when coughing. COPD signs and symptoms are more severe and prolonged than acute and chronic bronchitis alone.

People who have chronic bronchitis have a productive cough with yellow to green mucus. The cough can continue for years. Self-treatment for acute bronchitis is often effective and includes rest, fluid consumption, cough medicine, and analgesics. Utilizing a warm mist humidifier moistens the air passageways and eases breathing. Chronic bronchitis is a serious illness that commonly requires long-term medication and treatment prescribed by a physician. For chronic bronchitis, the physician may prescribe antibiotics to prevent a secondary bacterial infection.

A person with COPD is continually under a physician's care and needs various medications, including corticosteroid inhalers, to facilitate breathing by reducing inflammation and opening the bronchi. Respiratory therapy is also crucial for a person with COPD. The therapy does not heal the damaged tissue, but instead teaches the person to breathe more effectively in order to perform activities of daily living (ADLs) and other activities. If the cough lasts for more than 3 weeks or produces blood or discolored mucus, refer the athlete to a physician. If the athlete has a 100°F fever or above, along with pain, wheezing, or difficulty breathing, then she must see a physician immediately or call 911 for emergency medical services (EMS).

Pneumonia

Pneumonia is an inflammation of one or both lungs caused by viruses, bacteria, fungi, or parasites. *Streptococcus pneumoniae* is the bacterium that most commonly causes pneumonia. Pneumonia is mild to life-threatening. If left untreated, other illnesses, such as the flu and bronchitis, can progress to pneumonia. Pneumonia can affect people of all ages, but is a significant concern when it affects an athlete age 65 years or older. Athletes who smoke; have COPD, a weak immune system, diabetes, or heart disease; have had a recent cold or flu; or have had recent surgery are at risk for pneumonia.

Pneumonia is classified based on how the person acquired the infection. Community-acquired pneumonia occurs when a person comes in contact with a pathogen during regular contact with an infected person, surface, or object. These pneumonia cases are typically mild. People in hospitals or healthcare centers, in particular kidney dialysis and cancer treatment centers, acquire healthcare-acquired pneumonia. These cases are more serious because the pathogen strains are typically more resistant to treatment than are strains involved with community-acquired pneumonia. Inhalation or aspiration pneumonia occurs when an athlete breathes a pathogen found in his own vomit, food, or fluid from his mouth into his lungs. Opportunistic pneumonia occurs when a person has a weak immune system, as a result of issues such as acquired immune deficiency syndrome (AIDS) or an organ transplant.

Signs and symptoms of pneumonia include fever, chills, fatigue, weakness, headache, breathing difficulty including shortness of breath, chest pain, and cough. The athlete should see a physician if he has a fever 102°F or higher, chills, chest pain, muscular weakness, and continual cough. Athletes who are at risk for pneumonia must see a physician, as should athletes who have a cold or flu that does not resolve in a timely manner or worsens. Because bacterial pneumonia is most common, treatment includes antibiotics, antipyretics, and cough suppressants. If a virus causes the pneumonia, antibiotics are not effective. Antiviral and over-the-counter medications to reduce symptoms may help until the infection runs its course. Depending on the athlete's age and severity of symptoms, the athlete may be admitted to the hospital for treatment.

SKIN INFECTIONS

The skin is made up of three layers—the epidermis (outer layer), dermis (middle layer), and hypodermis (deep subcutaneous layer). The skin protects the body and deters pathogens from entering it. However, at times the skin becomes infected. Skin infections are local infections caused by bacteria, viruses, and fungi. Most skin infections are mild, but some can be severe. If severe skin infections are left untreated, life-threatening sepsis can occur.

Folliculitis

Folliculitis is an inflammation of the skin's hair follicles due to viruses, bacteria, and fungi, with bacteria being the most common pathogen causing the infection (**Figure 13-3**). Cases can be mild to severe. Folliculitis occurs when a pathogen enters a damaged follicle. This infection occurs from shaving, excessive sweating, abrasions and cuts to the skin, and inflammatory skin conditions such as acne and dermatitis. Blocked follicles can also promote bacterial growth. The folliculitis appears as pus-filled or red pimples around a hair that may look like a rash. The folliculitis may be unsightly, especially if many pimples exist in groups on the face or exposed areas of the body. The pimples are itchy, tender to the touch, or painful.

| Figure 13-3 | Folliculitis on the face. |

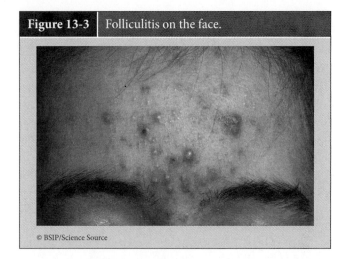

© BSIP/Science Source

They may ooze and crust over. Deep folliculitis exhibits these signs and symptoms, along with a large mass that appears as a lump under the skin. Most often the folliculitis is superficial, and with treatment can be cured in a few days. Have the athlete keep the area clean by washing often with soap and water. Warm, moist compresses promote clearing and draining of the pus in the follicle. Deep folliculitis must be treated by a physician. If the folliculitis spreads or does not resolve within a few days, refer the athlete to a physician. Topical, oral antibiotic, or antifungal medication may be necessary to clear the infection.

Contact Dermatitis

Contact dermatitis is a noncontagious infection that occurs when an object or substance comes in contact with the skin and causes an allergic reaction on the skin's surface. Irritant and allergic contact dermatitis exist. Irritant contact dermatitis affects the epidermis and occurs often to the face and hands. Soaps, cosmetics, and chemicals are common irritants. Allergic contact dermatitis is a hypersensitivity to a substance, and can be caused by poison ivy (**Figure 13-4**), perfume, cosmetics, detergent, latex, and chemicals. These allergens trigger an immune response in the skin. Certain substances, such as cosmetics, can cause both irritant and allergic dermatitis.

The signs and symptoms of dermatitis vary in severity depending on the strength of the irritant or allergen and the length of time the allergen is in contact with the skin. Signs and symptoms of contact dermatitis include red, itchy, blotchy skin that may appear as a rash. Irritant contact dermatitis is most often dry, whereas allergen contact dermatitis creates blisters that ooze fluid. The fluid dries with a crusty appearance. Both types of contact dermatitis may cause tenderness and pain. The irritant or allergen can leave a distinctive red rash, mark, or shape on the skin that identifies the actual object that caused the contact dermatitis. For example, a person can be irritated by costume jewelry that contains nickel. If a person is wearing a ring made with nickel and develops irritant contact dermatitis, the rash appears around her finger in the shape of the ring.

To treat contact dermatitis, assist your athlete in identifying the allergen that caused the contact dermatitis, and promptly remove the allergen. Washing the area with soap and water to eliminate the irritant or allergen is crucial. Athletes can use over-the-counter topical medications (e.g., Caladryl and hydrocortisone creams) to dry the blisters and decrease itching. If the contact dermatitis spreads to other parts of the body (e.g., poison ivy can become systemic for some people and appear at areas other than the contact site) or does not improve after 2 weeks of treatment, then the athlete must see a physician. The physician may prescribe oral corticosteroids to clear up the contact dermatitis.

Cellulitis

Cellulitis is a local bacterial infection that typically occurs at the skin of the lower extremity; however, cellulitis can affect any portion of the body (**Figure 13-5**). If cellulitis is left untreated,

| Figure 13-4 | Poison ivy commonly causes contact dermatitis. |

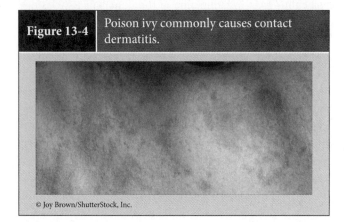

© Joy Brown/ShutterStock, Inc.

| Figure 13-5 | Cellulitis is a serious infection which can occur on any part of the body. |

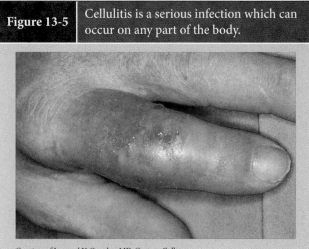

Courtesy of Leonard V. Crowley, MD, Century College

the infection can become systemic and life-threatening. The most common bacteria that cause cellulitis are *Staphylococcus* and *Streptococcus*, which enter through an open wound, break, or crack in the skin surface. Risk factors for cellulitis include people who have athlete's foot, open wounds, a weak immune system, other skin conditions, and swollen extremities. People who are obese or who have had recent surgery are also at risk. Once infected, the skin is very inflamed, red, swollen, hot, and point tender. The person may have a fever and other general infection signs and symptoms, including illness, fatigue, muscular aches and pains, sweating, and chills. The infection can spread rapidly and the skin appears stretched. The athlete must see a physician immediately for treatment to avoid the infection becoming systemic. If the infection is not treated immediately, the bacteria can go deeper into the skin surface and into the bloodstream. An athlete must take oral antibiotics for up to 14 days in order to clear up the infection. If the signs and symptoms do not subside after taking antibiotics for a few days, then the athlete may need hospitalization in order to introduce intravenous antibiotics to the body. If the signs and symptoms of cellulitis exist and the rash is quickly changing shape or expanding in size, then call 911.

Verruca (Common Warts)

Verruca is caused by human papillomavirus (HPV) that enters the body through a crack in the skin. Common warts can be located anywhere on the body, but most commonly appear on the feet and hands (**Figure 13-6**). Warts can spread on the body from one area to another and, less commonly, from one person to another.

The signs and symptoms include raised bumps that may be light gray or brown in color with a scaled surface. Some warts on the bottom of the feet are flat and painful due to

weight bearing. These plantar warts may appear to have black dots within them. These dots are blood vessels that have grown into the wart. Warts are typically unsightly, especially if they are located on the face and hands.

Athletes can treat the warts at home with over-the-counter wart removal preparations (e.g., Compound W or Dr. Scholl's Freeze Away). These preparations should not be used on the face or genitals. If the wart removal preparations do not cure the infection, then the athlete should see a physician, who will treat the wart in a different manner. A physician can utilize electrocautery (burning the wart), cryotherapy (freezing the wart), laser treatment, or stronger prescription topical medication to remove the wart.

Tinea

Tinea is a fungal infection that occurs on the body (tinea corporis or ringworm), the head (tinea capitis), the groin (tinea cruris or jock itch), or the feet (tinea pedis or athlete's foot). Fungi live and flourish in warm, dark, moist areas. Tinea is highly contagious. Therefore, an athlete with tinea must not be allowed to participate in any activity that requires utilization of equipment or contact with other athletes or employees at your facility until cleared by a physician. Athletes are more prone to fungal infections if they sweat frequently, practice poor hygiene, or have minor skin wounds. Athletes who come in contact with contaminated surfaces, such as a shower floor or pool deck; clothing; or other objects that have the pathogen on it can obtain an infection when the fungi enter the skin through a crack or break. The athlete's fungal infection can also spread on the athlete's own body.

The tinea infection appears different depending on the affected area. On the body, ringworm first appears as a red, bumpy, scaly rash that then develops into a red ring with raised edges. On the other hand, with tinea pedis the skin appears scaly and peeling (**Figure 13-7**). The skin may be red

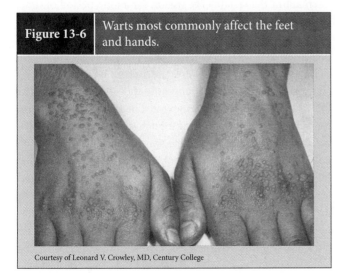

Figure 13-6 Warts most commonly affect the feet and hands.

Courtesy of Leonard V. Crowley, MD, Century College

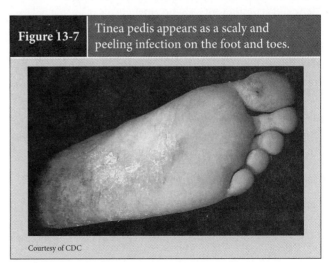

Figure 13-7 Tinea pedis appears as a scaly and peeling infection on the foot and toes.

Courtesy of CDC

and cracked, especially in between the toes. The infection may spread to the toenails, which makes them dry, brittle, cracked, and discolored. Tinea capitis may be itchy, and appear red and scaly with loss of hair and pus-filled sores at the affected area. The athlete may also have a low grade (100°F or so) fever with swollen neck lymph nodes. Tinea cruris appears as red, scaly skin at the groin, which may have blisters that ooze. The area is uncomfortable and itchy.

Treatment of tinea pedis and tinea cruris involves self-treatment with antifungal medications (e.g., Tinactin and Desenex), which are available in sprays, powders, and creams. Tinea corporis and tinea capitis are typically treated under a physician's care with oral or topical prescription antifungal medication (e.g., Diflucan and Nizoral, respectively). A medicated shampoo is also used for tinea capitis. Along with these medications, the athlete must thoroughly wash his or her clothing, practice good hygiene, and keep the skin dry and clean in order to destroy the fungi. The infection should lessen and completely resolve within a few weeks. If self-treatment does not improve the infection soon after treatment begins, or if the athlete has tinea corporis or tinea capitis, then refer the athlete to a physician.

Impetigo

Impetigo is most often caused by the *Staphylococcus aureus* (staph) bacteria, and secondly by *Staphylococcus pyogenes* (strep) bacteria. This infection can occur to people of any age, but most commonly in children and adults who have skin-to-skin contact with other adults. Impetigo is a highly contagious infection. It is spread through physical contact with an infected person. The bacteria do not have to enter through a break or cut in the skin to be transmitted. Therefore, as with tinea infections, athletes with impetigo must not participate at your facility until cleared by a physician. Impetigo has shown to be associated with a URI that occurs 2 to 3 days before the signs and symptoms of infection (Watkins, 2005). Signs and symptoms of impetigo include pustules that enlarge into blisters, which secrete a yellowish liquid. The secretion becomes crusty and honey-colored when dry (**Figure 13-8**). The affected area itches and appears red, but is not painful. The athlete must see a physician for topical, prescription antibacterial medication and oral antibiotics to treat impetigo. Also, the athlete must practice good hygiene, which includes gently washing the area with soap and water. With proper treatment, the impetigo easily heals.

Herpes Simplex (Cold Sores)

Herpes simplex virus (HSV) is classified into two types. Type 1 (HSV-1) is responsible for producing cold sores, also called fever blisters, around the mouth; Type 2 (HSV-2) produces

| Figure 13-8 | Impetigo can be identified by its honey yellow crusted lesions which can occur anywhere on the body. |

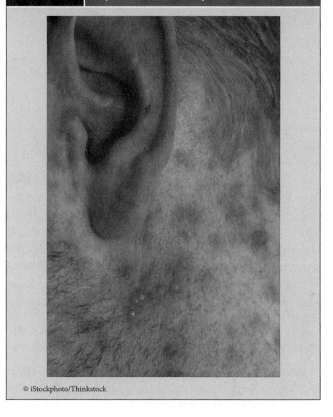

© iStockphoto/Thinkstock

genital sores. HSV-1 and HSV-2 are highly contagious. The virus is transmitted via close contact with an infected person, or touching objects that have the virus (e.g., surfaces, clothing, razors, towels, etc.). Once a person is afflicted with HSV, the virus remains in his or her body for life. HSV can remain dormant in the facial nerve tissues for a long period of time, and outbreaks can occur in which a cold sore erupts on the lip. Usually these outbreaks occur due to ultraviolet light or direct sunlight, fever, trauma, or hormonal changes in women.

Herpes simplex cold sores are painful blisters on the lip (**Figure 13-9**). Signs and symptoms appear a few weeks after infection and can be mild to severe. The first signs and symptoms include tingling, burning, or itching at the area where the outbreak will occur. The athlete may have a fever, sore throat, and swollen glands. The blisters erupt and are visible on the lips, mouth, gums, and/or throat, and they may break and leak a clear, yellowish fluid. These blister outbreaks can occur numerous times throughout the year. When herpes simplex affects the area around the eyes, the infection can cause blindness. Outbreaks over a large portion of the body can be

Figure 13-9	HSV-1 sores commonly erupt on the lips.

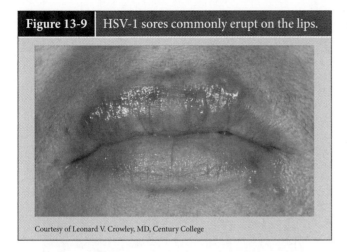

Courtesy of Leonard V. Crowley, MD, Century College

Figure 13-10	MRSA may appear to look like a pimple or spider bite.

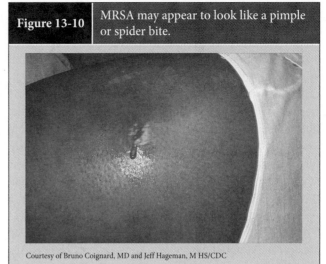

Courtesy of Bruno Coignard, MD and Jeff Hageman, M HS/CDC

life-threatening if the athlete has a weakened immune system as a result of contracting other illnesses such as cancer or HIV.

Because a virus causes herpes simplex, no medication exists to destroy the virus. Treatment is symptomatic, and prescription medications (e.g., Zovirax and Valtrex) can decrease the number and severity of outbreaks. Athletes should frequently wash the area with soap and water, utilize salt-water rinses, take over-the-counter pain-relieving medication, and apply an ice pack to the area if pain exists. If an athlete has blisters form around the eyes, or signs and symptoms that persist for more than 2 weeks, then his physician must examine him.

Methicillin-Resistant Staphylococcus Aureus (MRSA)

Methicillin-resistant *Staphylococcus aureus* (MRSA) was first identified as a significant pathogen in the 1960s. MRSA causes a serious bacterial infection. Staph bacteria are often found on 25–30% of people's bodies, in particular in the nose (Gorwitz et al., 2008); however, these bacteria do not harm or cause signs and symptoms of infection. This type of staph bacterium is considered colonized, which means it is not infectious. Presently, only 1.5% of people have the MRSA bacteria on their bodies. The bacteria are asymptomatic; however, they can enter the body via an open wound or mucosa and cause a life-threatening situation. Risk factors for death due to MRSA infection include age (an older person has an increased chance of death), organ impairment, and residence in a nursing home (Pastagia, Kleinman, Lacerda de la Cruz, & Jenkins, 2012).

MRSA is resistant to the methicillin antibiotic, which is similar to penicillin and amoxicillin. Therefore, MRSA is not easily treated in all cases. When the infection first was viable, patients in hospitals acquired the pathogen due to invasive surgical procedures. This type of MRSA is called healthcare-associated MRSA (HA-MRSA). In 1990, community-associated MRSA (CA-MRSA) developed and was first acquired by athletes. Skin-to-skin contact with an infected athlete, in activities such as wrestling, can cause MRSA transmission. MRSA has also been transmitted in overcrowded or unclean settings, such as child care facilities and military training camps. The bacteria enters the body through open wounds, cracks, or breaks in the skin surface, as well as mucous membranes. Once the bacteria are in the body, they spread throughout the bloodstream, organs, bones, and joints.

Signs and symptoms of MRSA include fever, chills, and other flu-like symptoms; the presence of a wound that does not heal; or a lesion, pimple, boil, or rash that erupts on the skin (**Figure 13-10**). The lesion may look like a spider bite and turn into a painful **abscess**. Regardless of the infection's severity, a physician should treat MRSA.

> **Abscess** A collection of pus within the skin's superficial and deep layers due to a pathogen. The abscess causes swelling and inflammation at the affected area.

Mild cases of MRSA may require only lesion draining. Severe cases require a long course of antibiotics to fight the infection. If an athlete has signs and symptoms resembling MRSA that do not decrease, and the wound or lesion does not readily heal, then refer the athlete to a physician for evaluation. To prevent the possibility of spreading MRSA, all equipment, tables, and the like that are utilized by one athlete must be immediately disinfected prior to use by another athlete.

VIRAL INFECTIONS

Viruses are small microorganisms that cause illness. Once in the body, they take over the body's healthy cells. Viruses live in the cells, replicate, and eventually kill the cells. Some viruses are stronger than others. The viral infections discussed in this chapter are highly contagious. Consequently, if your athlete has one of these infections, he or she must not be allowed to continue participating at your facility until he or she is no longer contagious and has been cleared by a physician. Likewise, the facility must be thoroughly and regularly cleaned with appropriate disinfectant to avoid spreading the infection to other athletes and employees. Viral infections do not respond to medications such as antibiotics; consequently, these infections are difficult to treat. Vaccines exist for some viral infections, which can help protect people from obtaining the infections in the first place.

Measles

Measles is a viral respiratory infection that most often affects children. Signs and symptoms of measles include an itchy, red rash from head to toe; fever; sneezing; coughing; sore throat; runny nose; muscle pain; fatigue; conjunctivitis; white spots in the mouth; and sensitivity to light. According to the CDC (2009), simultaneously with measles, 10% of children also sustain an ear infection, and 5% come down with pneumonia, which most often causes death in children. A vaccine for measles exists, which is given in conjunction with a vaccine for mumps and rubella (referred to as the measles, mumps, rubella or MMR vaccine). Inoculated people are immune to the disease. Some adults do not have their children inoculated due to fear that the MMR vaccine may cause **autism**; however, many research studies have shown that no link between the MMR vaccine and autism exists. Measles is so highly contagious that 90% of people who are not inoculated and come in contact with a contagious person will become infected. A person is contagious 4 days before and 4 days after the rash appears. If an athlete suspects that she has measles, she must see a physician immediately. No medication can cure measles, so the infection must run its course. The athlete can take acetaminophen for aches and pain, utilize a humidifier to moisten the air passageways, and get plenty of bed rest to combat fatigue.

> **Autism** A developmental disorder of the brain that affects children under 3 years old. An autistic child lacks proper communication and social skills.

Mumps

Mumps is an uncommon viral infection that, like measles, most often affects children. The infection thrives in the parotid glands, which are salivary glands below and in front of the ears. The virus is transmitted by saliva when an infected person sneezes or coughs and another person breathes in the

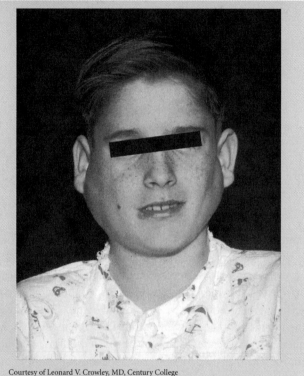

Figure 13-11 The signature sign of mumps is swelling of the parotid glands.

Courtesy of Leonard V. Crowley, MD, Century College

molecules in the air. A person can also be infected if he drinks out of a cup that an infected person has used. The person is contagious for 1 week after signs and symptoms are evident. Signs and symptoms of mumps do not always appear when the athlete first obtains the virus. The signs and symptoms, which can appear 2–3 weeks after infection, include swelling of and painful parotid glands (which appear as if the athlete has apples in his cheeks), fever, fatigue, weakness, and pain with chewing or swallowing (**Figure 13-11**). The only treatment for mumps is acetaminophen, ice or heat packs on the neck, fluids, warm salt-water gargles, and rest. The infection usually clears in 2 weeks. An athlete with suspected mumps must be evaluated by a physician. The MMR vaccination creates immunity for mumps.

Rubella (German Measles)

Rubella, or German measles, is a contagious disease caused by a virus spread through close contact with an infected person or the air. Children are most commonly affected by rubella. As with measles, rubella also causes a rash (**Figure 13-12**). A person is contagious 1 week prior to the rash eruption and 1–2 weeks afterwards. Other signs and symptoms of rubella

| **Figure 13-12** | Rubella produces a similar red rash as measles. |

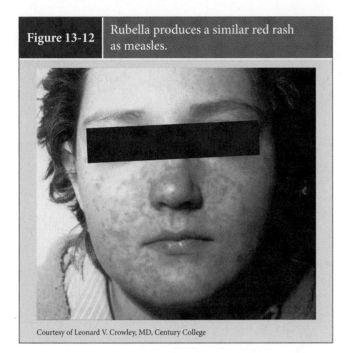

Courtesy of Leonard V. Crowley, MD, Century College

| **Figure 13-13** | Chicken pox. |

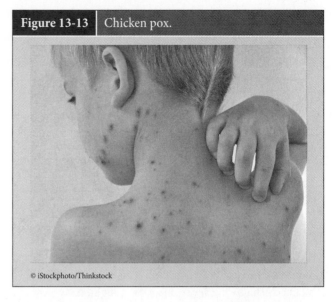

© iStockphoto/Thinkstock

are similar to those for measles. Fatigue, weakness, joint pain, runny nose, and headache may exist, although children have few signs and symptoms. No treatment exists for rubella. Your athlete can take acetaminophen to decrease aches and pains. A person should receive the MMR vaccine as a child to be immune to rubella. MMR booster inoculations may be necessary for older adults and pregnant women, because the vaccine may decrease in effectiveness as the person ages.

Varicella (Chicken Pox)

Varicella, or chicken pox, is caused by the contagious varicella-zoster virus, which affects mostly children. In the past, most children were infected by chicken pox and as a result became immune to the varicella virus as adults. However, now a chicken pox vaccination exists and is given to children. Chicken pox is spread through water molecules in the air from an infected person who sneezes or coughs, or direct contact with the infected person's rash. The infection creates various signs and symptoms resembling the flu, such as fever, aches and pains, fatigue, weakness, headache, dry cough, and loss of appetite. The person has an itchy, red rash that can occur all over the body, including potentially in the eyes, throat, and genitals (**Figure 13-13**). The rash first appears like pink or red bumps, which turn into fluid-filled blisters. These blisters break and crust over. The infected person is contagious for 2 days before the rash appears and until all blisters have crusted over. If you suspect your athlete has chicken pox, refer him or her to a physician. The physician

can prescribe an antihistamine to lessen the itching. For severe infections, the athlete may be prescribed antiviral medications to decrease the duration and signs and symptoms of the infection. These antiviral medications are only effective if taken within 24 hours after the rash appears. After chicken pox infection, the varicella-zoster virus remains dormant in the body's nerve roots. If a person, in particular an older adult, has a weakened immune system, the virus can become active and cause shingles. Shingles appears as a localized, blistering skin rash. A person with shingles may complain of itchiness and pain at the rash site, headache, visual changes including sensitivity to light, and flu-like symptoms (WebMD, 2011). Shingles is treated with antiviral medication, and usually resolves within a few weeks.

BACTERIAL INFECTIONS

Bacteria are single-celled organisms. Some bacteria live on or in our bodies and promote body system function (e.g., bacteria in the intestinal tract help with digestion). Very few bacterial strains cause infection, but the infections that bacteria cause can be fatal. Bacteria reproduce and thrive in the body. They can emit a toxin that in some cases cause an athlete to become extremely ill. Antibiotics are utilized to rid the body of bacteria; however, over years of being exposed to antibiotics, some bacteria have become resistant to the medications.

Lyme Disease

The *Borrelia burgdorferi* bacteria cause lyme disease. This type of bacteria is spread by deer ticks, which ingest the blood of animals and humans (**Figure 13-14**). These small ticks attach to a human's skin and transfer the bacteria. This method of

Figure 13-14 | Deer ticks are very small organisms that are responsible for transmitting Lyme disease to humans.

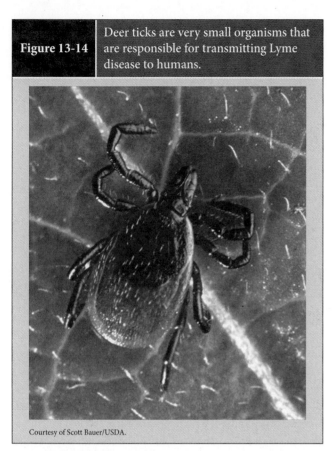

Courtesy of Scott Bauer/USDA.

Figure 13-15 | A bull's-eye formation may appear at the site of the tick bite.

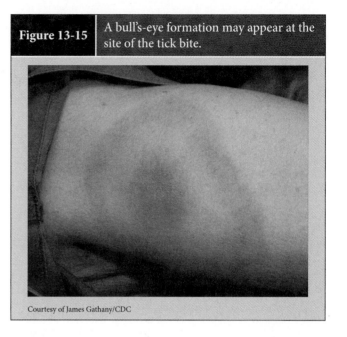

Courtesy of James Gathany/CDC

transmission is the sole means of infection. People cannot spread the infection to others. People who live or participate in activities (e.g., hiking or hunting) in wooded or grassy areas are more prone to acquire Lyme disease.

The signature sign of Lyme disease is a red, bull's-eye pattern rash that develops from a red bump at the tick bite (**Figure 13-15**). Although this sign is indicative of the disease, many infected athletes do not exhibit this bull's-eye rash. The rash may form approximately 1 month prior to other signs and symptoms, which include flu-like symptoms, joint pain that occurs bilaterally and at various body joints, and loss of extremity sensation and function. The athlete's joint pain may appear at first to be a musculoskeletal injury. Consequently, take a thorough secondary survey to rule out any musculoskeletal injury. If your athlete has a deer tick on him, remove it immediately to hopefully avoid bacterial transmission (see Tip from the Field). If your athlete exhibits signs and symptoms of Lyme disease and has been in a wooded or grassy area recently, refer him to a physician. Lyme disease is treated with oral and intravenous antibiotics. How long the athlete has had the disease before treatment affects the treatment duration. Fortunately for most athletes, the treatment destroys the bacteria and rids the athletes of Lyme disease.

Tip from the Field

A tick that is grasping onto a person's skin with its mouth must be removed properly and as soon as possible. Proper tick removal is important so the person does not become injured during the process. Likewise, you want to properly remove the entire tick, including its head, so it can no longer cause harm. It is difficult for a person to remove a tick that is located on his or her back or scalp. Consequently, when the tick is imbedded in these areas you must assist your athlete. Locate the tick and brush aside any hair that is in the way of clearly visualizing the tick. Use fine-tipped, clean tweezers to remove the tick. Grab the tick near its head with the tweezers. Try not to grasp the tick's body because it may release more bacterial toxins into the athlete. Make sure the tweezers are as close as possible to the skin's surface. Grasp the tick firmly with the tweezers and slowly pull upward on the tick without twisting it or pulling its body from its head. The tick should release its grasp from the skin. If a part of the tick's mouth stays on the skin, remove the mouth with the tweezers. Once the tick has been removed, clean the area and your hands with soap and water or an antiseptic. If you cannot remove the mouth, or the tick's head is imbedded in the skin, leave the tick and have the athlete consult his or her physician immediately, because the longer the tick is attached to the skin, the longer it transmits harmful bacteria. Never place petroleum jelly or soap on a tick and wait for it to detach itself from the skin. This method is ineffective. Never burn the tick with a match or other flame because you may burn the athlete's skin. For additional information on how to properly remove a tick, refer to the CDC's website, http://www.cdc.gov/ticks/removing_a_tick.html.

Meningitis

Meningitis is an inflammation of the meninges that surround the brain. Meningitis can be caused by a virus or bacteria. Viral meningitis is typically mild, and the person gets well without treatment. However, bacterial meningitis is a serious, potentially life-threatening infection that must be treated immediately. Bacterial meningitis is transmitted from person to person through saliva (e.g., sharing a cup or kissing an infected person) or from respiratory secretions when the infected athlete coughs or sneezes. *Listeria monocytogenes* is bacteria that cause meningitis that can be transmitted when a person eats contaminated food.

Signs and symptoms of meningitis can develop rapidly and last up to a week. The signs and symptoms include severe headache, a stiff neck, fever, chills, nausea, vomiting, confusion, and sensitivity to light. Bacterial meningitis is a medical emergency, so you must call 911 immediately. Your athlete must be treated in a hospital with intravenous antibiotics. Anyone who has been in close physical contact with the infected athlete must also be treated with oral antibiotics. A meningococcal vaccine to prevent bacterial meningitis is routinely given to children who are 11–12 years old. A booster is given at 16 years old. The CDC (2011) states that the vaccine prevents four types of bacterial infections, including two of the three most common bacterial meningitis infections in the United States.

SEXUALLY TRANSMITTED INFECTIONS

Sexually transmitted infections (STIs) were previously referred to as sexually transmitted diseases (STDs). These infections can be caused by viruses, bacteria, or fungi. Some STIs can be treated and cured, whereas others cannot. The best STI prevention is to refrain from sexual contact with another person. Sexually active people must practice safe sexual intercourse and utilize condoms in an attempt to prevent STIs. The prevalent STIs that people may sustain are discussed in the following sections.

Genital Herpes

Genital herpes is caused by the herpes simplex virus type 2 (HSV-2), which was mentioned earlier in the chapter. The virus is highly contagious and is transmitted by genital-to-genital or mouth-to-genital contact, in which case HSV-1 can cause genital herpes. Women are more often affected by genital herpes than are men. A pregnant woman can pass HSV-2 to her baby during childbirth. The signs and symptoms of genital herpes occur from 2 days to 1 week after infection and are present before an outbreak of genital sores. These signs and symptoms include flu-like symptoms, fever, muscular aches, fatigue, swollen lymph glands, painful urination, and vaginal discharge. Before the sores erupt, the person may feel tingling in the area, which indicates an outbreak will occur. The genital sores are painful, clear or yellow fluid-filled blisters (**Figure 13-16**). These blisters break and crust over. The skin tissue heals in 1–2 weeks. Sometimes the person does not have an outbreak of sores, or the sores are mild and look like pimples or insect bites. In these cases the person may not realize she has been infected with HSV-2. Even if the person does not have sores, she is still contagious. After the first outbreak, the subsequent outbreaks are usually less severe and shorter in duration.

A person with herpes must see a physician for evaluation. Treatment is similar to that for HSV-1 infections, with antiviral medications and good hygiene. Infected people should refrain from unprotected sexual activity. Many people who have genital herpes do not seek treatment due to the mildness and infrequency of outbreaks, and also do not utilize antiviral drugs due to the cost (Emmert, 2000). People with suspected HSV-2 infection should always seek medical evaluation and treatment, because unfortunately the virus can spread to other parts of the body including the brain, lungs, and other organs.

| **Figure 13-16** | HSV-2 causes sores on both male and female genitalia. |

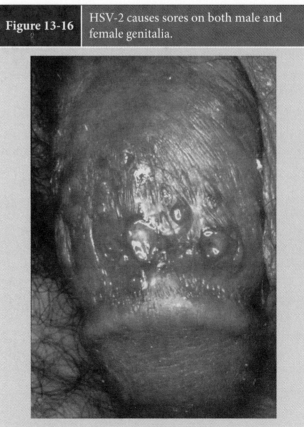

Courtesy of CDC/Dr. N.J. Flumara/Dr. Gavin Hart

Chlamydia

Chlamydia is the most frequently reported bacterial STI in the United States. The infection is most common in sexually active teenagers and young adults who do not utilize condoms. The bacterial infection is passed from one person to another during sexual intercourse, including vaginal, anal, and oral sexual activity, as well as through childbirth. In both males and females, the infection produces mild or nonexistent signs and symptoms, and as a result the person may not know he or she has been infected. Some signs and symptoms of chlamydia are fever, lower abdominal and back pain, and pain during sexual intercourse. Males may have a discharge from the penis, swollen testicles, and burning during urination. Fortunately, chlamydia can be cured with treatment. The person who exhibits signs and symptoms of chlamydia must see a physician immediately to be screened for chlamydia. Chlamydia often occurs with other STIs, including HIV. Oral antibiotics are prescribed to resolve the chlamydia infection. If early treatment is not obtained, then the infection can cause a woman to have serious complications including **pelvic inflammatory disease** and infertility. Untreated chlamydia can cause urethral infection and painful testes in males.

> **Pelvic inflammatory disease (PID)** An inflammation of the pelvis including the uterus, fallopian tubes, and other reproductive organs. PID can cause severe pelvic pain, infertility, ectopic pregnancy, and formation of an abscess.

Trichomoniasis

Trichomoniasis is a very common, curable STI that is caused by a parasite (**Figure 13-17**). The organism is transmitted between sexual partners during intercourse. Men typically have no symptoms, other than possibly painful urination. Women may have painful urination, vaginal itching, and foul-smelling, discolored discharge. Signs and symptoms appear between 5 and 28 days after infection. Athletes with suspected trichomoniasis must see a physician for screening. Both sexual partners need to be examined and treated by a physician, especially because men do not often have any signs or symptoms of infection. The physician will most likely prescribe the oral antibiotic metronidazole (Flagyl), which cures the infection in approximately 1 week.

Human Papillomavirus (HPV)

Human papillomavirus (HPV) is the virus that causes genital warts. Along with causing genital warts, certain types of HPV can cause cervical and other cancers. HPV is the most common STI in the United States. In approximately 90% of HPV cases, the infection is cleared by the body's immune system within 2 years (CDC, 2012a). Both men and women can develop the warts months after infection; however, most women may not know they are infected because most warts develop inside the vagina or on the cervix. The warts can be flat and flesh colored, or raised with a cauliflower-like appearance (**Figure 13-18**). A physician must treat an athlete with HPV. The athlete must not use over-the-counter wart removal

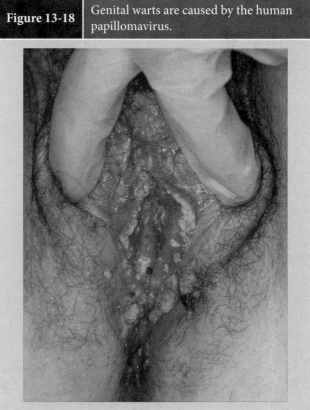

Figure 13-18 Genital warts are caused by the human papillomavirus.

Courtesy of CDC/Joe Miller

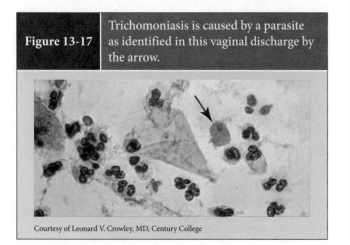

Figure 13-17 Trichomoniasis is caused by a parasite as identified in this vaginal discharge by the arrow.

Courtesy of Leonard V. Crowley, MD, Century College

medications to treat genital warts. A physician prescribes wart removal treatment, which includes topical medications, electrocautery, cryotherapy, or laser therapy. At times, the physician may use surgery to excise the warts. Both males and females ages 9–26 years can become inoculated for HPV with vaccines such as Gardasil and Cervarix.

Gonorrhea

Gonorrhea is a common, highly contagious STI that is caused by bacteria. The infection affects both men's and women's reproductive organs as well as the eyes, mouth, and throat. Transmission occurs through sexual intercourse and childbirth. Signs and symptoms may appear days to months after infection; however, both genders do not always exhibit signs and symptoms of infection. Some signs and symptoms men may experience include discolored discharge from the penis; painful, burning urination; and swollen testicles (**Figure 13-19**). Women may experience very mild symptoms including discolored discharge, painful urination, painful sexual intercourse, and bleeding in between periods. Athletes who suspect that they have gonorrhea must be examined by a physician. Fifty percent of women who have gonorrhea have chlamydia. Both STIs are treated simultaneously. The physician prescribes antibiotics to treat the infection. Untreated gonorrhea can cause pelvic inflammatory disease (PID) and ectopic pregnancy in women, and inflammation of the epididymis in men, which can lead to infertility. Gonorrhea can become systemic and cause arthritic joints and skin lesions on all areas of the body (**Figure 13-20**).

Figure 13-20	If left untreated, gonorrhea can become systemic and affect the entire body, causing pelvic inflammatory disease, infertility, joint arthritis, and skin lesions.

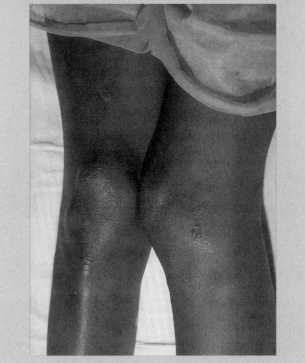

Courtesy of Emory University, Dr. Thomas F. Sellers/CDC

Figure 13-19	Often men and women do not exhibit signs and symptoms of gonorrhea. One sign of infection is genital sores.

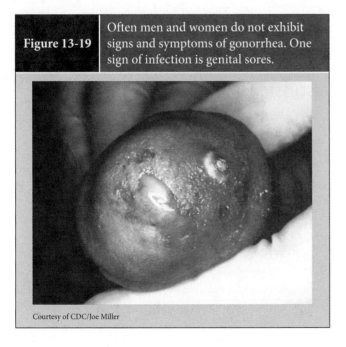

Courtesy of CDC/Joe Miller

Syphilis

Syphilis is an STI that is caused by bacterial infection. Men and women are both affected by this STI. The infection can affect the genital and anal area, as well as the lips and mouth. Syphilis is transmitted when a person comes in contact with an infected person's open sore. As with most other STIs, syphilis can be passed to a fetus while in utero and through childbirth if the pregnant mother is infected.

Signs and symptoms of syphilis may not appear for years, but the average time they appear after infection is approximately 3 weeks. An early sign of syphilis is a painless, open sore, called a chancre, where the person was infected (**Figure 13-21**). The chancre heals, but without treatment the infection produces a rash, which is not itchy, that can be located anywhere on the body (**Figure 13-22**), but most often on the hands and feet. The rash also disappears, and the person may be asymptomatic, yet contagious, for years. The last stage of syphilis may cause chancres on the body, numbness, paralysis, blindness, dementia, and death (**Figure 13-23**). An

Figure 13-21	In the early stages of infection, syphilis produces chancres on the genitals.

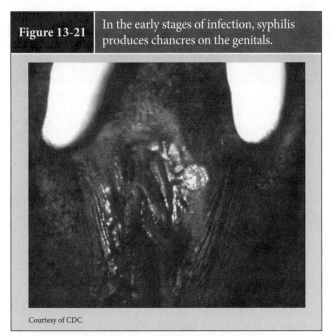

Courtesy of CDC

Figure 13-22	In the second stage of the syphilis infection, a rash erupts somewhere on the body.

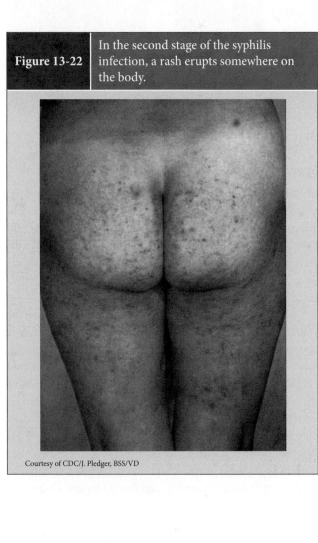

Courtesy of CDC/J. Pledger, BSS/VD

Figure 13-23	in the tertiary stage of syphilis infection, chancers erupt on other parts of the body. A chancre is visible on this man's nose.

Courtesy of J. Pledger/CDC

athlete with syphilis must be under a doctor's care. With early treatment, syphilis can be cured by doses of injectable penicillin, or other antibiotics if the athlete has a penicillin allergy.

SUMMARY

Systemic and local infections are numerous, and undoubtedly at one time or another our athletes will be infected by a pathogen. The severity and duration of the infection varies according to the type and strength of the pathogen, the athlete's characteristics and health, and the treatment available. Educate your athletes about the various infections that exist. They should be aware of the signs, symptoms, and treatment of these infections. The transmission of infections can be prevented at your facility among your athletes and employees. Therefore, require everyone at your facility to take proper steps to prevent the transmission of systemic and local infections.

DISCUSSION QUESTIONS

1. What are systemic and local infections? How can local infections become systemic infections?
2. What are common methods of transmission for URIs? Skin infections? Viral infections? Bacterial infections? STIs?
3. Which infections can an athlete treat at home? Which infections require immediate referral to and treatment by a physician?
4. Which URIs can become severely complicated for the athlete if infection remains untreated?
5. What are some common signs and symptoms of the various skin infections?

6. Which viral or bacterial infections can become life-threatening?
7. Which STIs are caused by bacteria? Viruses? Parasites?
8. Which STIs cannot be cured with treatment?

CASE STUDY 1

Ice Hockey Fever

Ryan is a 16-year-old varsity hockey player at Vegas High School. With Ryan's hockey talent, the season has been very successful. The team is tied for first place in the conference, and Ryan is one of the top scorers. Over the past 3 days, Ryan has been battling an annoying, intermittent dry cough, but otherwise he has felt fine. Today, Ryan woke up with a stuffy nose and a sore throat. He was tired and generally did not feel well. He went to school feeling very weak and fatigued. At after school practice he told his coach how he felt. The coach told Ryan that he probably had a cold. The coach said that the cold would probably go away within a few days. The coach said to Ryan that if he felt up to practicing today, he could. So Ryan decided to practice. He put on his gear and skated onto the ice. During practice Ryan skated slow and was always a step behind his teammates. He had difficulty catching his breath and, on a few occasions, asked a teammate for a substitution due to his fatigue.

At the end of practice the coach pulled Ryan aside and told him to go home, eat a nutritious dinner, drink fluids, and go to bed early to rest his body. Ryan took the coach's advice, but at home he did not eat much due to his lack of appetite. He went to bed early, but had trouble falling asleep because of his frequent cough, which was now producing a light green, thick mucus. At one point during the night Ryan broke out in a sweat, so he got up and took his temperature, which was 100°F. Ryan thought it was strange to have a fever because during the night he was also having frequent chills.

The next morning when he woke up, Ryan was exhausted. He was congested and had a headache. Ryan felt weak despite eating a small, nutritious breakfast. The team's conference game was in 2 days, so Ryan had to attend school in order to be eligible to practice and compete in the game. At practice, Ryan did not perform well. Each time he skated, he felt worse. He continued to cough up the mucus, began to have breathing difficulty due to the congestion, and experienced some chest discomfort when he exerted himself.

When Ryan went home after practice he told his parents how he felt. They took his temperature, which was

101.5°F. Because Ryan had been ill for 5 days and his signs and symptoms were getting worse, his parents decided to take him to his physician. Ryan's parents made an appointment for Ryan to see his physician early in the morning, and Ryan went right to bed to rest.

1. What advice should the coach have given Ryan the first time Ryan came to him complaining of symptoms?
2. What possible respiratory infections could Ryan have?
3. If left untreated, what could happen to Ryan if the illness progresses?
4. What do you think the physician will prescribe to treat the infection?

CASE STUDY 2

Unidentified Lesion

Alexandra has been working out at We R Fit Gym for approximately 6 months. She has been using treadmills and stair machines to increase her cardiorespiratory endurance, and weight machines and yoga to tone her muscles. One day after a workout, she was showering and felt what seemed to be a pimple on the back of her right leg. She was not concerned about the pimple, because she frequently got them from excessive sweating. Alexandra washed the area thoroughly and figured the pimple would go away on its own in a few days, as the other pimples normally did.

Three days later while dressing for work, Alexandra looked in the mirror and noticed that her pimple had increased in size and was swollen. The pimple was red and contained what appeared to be pus under the skin. She touched the pimple. It was very tender to the point of being almost painful. Alexandra attempted to pop the pimple in order to relieve the pressure. A small amount of pus oozed out, but the pimple was now more inflamed. She was going to be late to work, so she put some acne medicine on the area and covered it with a bandage.

When Alexandra returned home from work, the pimple was now the size of a dime. The area around the pimple was very red and now painful to the touch. More pus was evident within the pimple. Some pus had oozed out and left a dried yellowish crust around the area and on the bandage. Alexandra was now concerned because the pimple did not look like a normal pimple anymore. After she bathed, she put antibiotic ointment and a bandage on the pimple. The area was still sore when Alexandra went to bed.

The following morning as Alexandra was getting ready to go to the gym, she removed the bandage and looked at the pimple. The pimple was extremely inflamed and had increased in size. Alexandra was worried and wondered what she should do.

1. What type of skin lesion could Alexandra have? What led you to make this determination?
2. How do you think she acquired the lesion?
3. How must Alexandra treat the area?
4. Should Alexandra seek medical attention? Why or why not?
5. Can Alexandra continue to participate in exercise and fitness activities at We R Fit Gym? Why or why not?

REFERENCES

Centers for Disease Control and Prevention (CDC). (2012a). Genital HPV infection—fact sheet. Retrieved July 3, 2012, from http://www.cdc.gov/std /HPV/STDFact-HPV.htm

Centers for Disease Control and Prevention (CDC). (2012b). Key facts about influenza (flu) and flu vaccine. Retrieved July 2, 2012, from http://www .cdc.gov/flu/keyfacts.htm

Centers for Disease Control and Prevention (CDC). (2011). Meningococcal vaccines: What you need to know. Retrieved February 27, 2013, from http://www.cdc.gov/vaccines/pubs/vis/downloads/vis-mening.pdf

Centers for Disease Control and Prevention (CDC). (2009). Transmission of measles. Retrieved February 27, 2013, from http://www.cdc.gov/measles /about/transmission.html

Emmert, D. H. (2000). Treatment of common cutaneous herpes simplex virus infections. *American Family Physician*, 61(6), 1697–1704.

Gorwitz, R. J., Kruszon-Moran, D., McAllister, S. K., McQuillan, G., McDougal, L. K., Fosheim, G. E., et al. (2008). Changes in the prevalence of nasal colonization with *Staphylococcus aureus* in the United States, 2001–2004. *Journal of Infectious Diseases*, 197, 1226–1234; doi: 10.1086/533494.

Henochowicz, S. I., & Zieve, D. (2011). Allergic rhinitis. Retrieved July 1, 2012, from http://www.ncbi.nlm.nih.gov/pubmedhealth/PMH0001816/

MedlinePlus. (2011). Septicemia. Retrieved June 30, 2012, from http://www .nlm.nih.gov/medlineplus/ency/article/001355.htm

Pastagia, M., Kleinman, L. C., Lacerda de la Cruz, E. G., & Jenkins, S. G. (2012). Predicting risk for death from MRSA bacteremia. *Emerging Infectious Diseases*, 18(7), 1072–1080.

Urban, M. (2009). Common cold. Retrieved July 1, 2012, from http://www .merckmanuals.com/home/infections/viral_infections/common_cold.html

Watkins, P. (2005). Impetigo: Aetiology, complications and treatment options. *Nursing Standard*, 19(36), 51–54.

WebMD. (2011). Shingles—Topic overview. Retrieved March 24, 2013, from http://www.webmd.com/skin-problems-and-treatments/shingles/shingles -topic-overview

Chapter 14

Special Populations

CHAPTER OBJECTIVES

After you have read this chapter, you will be able to understand:

- The exercise and nutritional considerations for youth, masters, and older adult athletes
- What specific needs athletes with cardiovascular, immunological, metabolic, neuromuscular, orthopedic, respiratory, and other conditions have when participating in physical activity and exercise
- Limitations that affect an athlete's participation in physical activity and exercise
- How to modify and vary an athlete's exercise protocol based on his or her specific condition to facilitate safe and purposeful participation

Adults and children alike should participate in wellness, exercise, and fitness programs to promote and maintain a good quality, long life. Many of these individuals are among the special populations afflicted with cardiovascular, immunological, metabolic, neuromuscular, orthopedic, respiratory, and other conditions. These conditions affect the body in various ways, and can influence how the individual performs during physical activity and exercise. In some manner, the condition places limitations on participation in physical activity and exercise. In most cases, individuals with these conditions are not able to participate in activity as individuals unaffected by these conditions would. Exercise program modification is necessary so the individual can participate in an effective, safe manner. As an exercise science professional, you must have in-depth knowledge of each individual's specific condition, physical capabilities, and limitations in order to create an appropriate, safe physical activity and exercise program. Under your direction, and guidance, these individuals can participate in a structured, personalized physical activity and exercise program in order to maintain a better quality of life.

AGE

An athlete who is in the prepubescent through adolescent age group is considered a youth athlete. Masters athletes are over the age of 40 or 50 (Fink, Burgoon, & Mikesky, 2009). Older adult athletes are age 65 years or older (American Psychological Association [APA], 1998). Each age group has special considerations in regard to physical activity, exercise, and nutrition. Most physical activity, exercise, and nutritional programs focus on the average-age, typical athlete who is in a relatively healthy state. Due to their ages, young, masters, and older adult athletes have specific needs that differ from those of the average athlete. These needs must be considered when devising a physical activity, exercise, and nutrition program.

Youth Athletes

Youth athletes are growing physically and emotionally (**Figure 14-1**). Their bodies are constantly changing. Their bones are growing during the pubescent and adolescent years. The epiphyseal plates, or growth plates, at the ends of long bones are delicate during the youth years. Consequently, these areas are susceptible to fractures. A youth athlete's muscles do not grow as quickly or in the same proportion as the bones. When bones grow, they create tension on the muscles and

| Figure 14-1 | Youth athletes have different needs in regard to exercise and nutrition as compared to their adult counterparts. |

tendons, which causes stretching of the soft tissues. When a young athlete creates joint movement, the bones pull the muscles, which can cause microtears, or the tendon can pull off its attachment causing apophysitis (i.e., Osgood-Schlatter disease). Likewise, youth muscles are not as flexible as adult muscles, which predisposes the muscles to strains.

A youth athlete can be injured while participating in activities including sports and conditioning exercise due to a number of factors. Youth athletes do not tolerate the heat as well as average-aged adult athletes. They tend to take in more heat from the environment and sweat less. Consequently, in a hot, humid environment, youth athletes should not participate as long or as intensely. These athletes should acclimatize for a period of 10–14 days (Cuppett & Walsh, 2012). Many youths today are obese and sedentary, with no previous physical activity, which makes them at risk for injury. Unfortunately, many inexperienced coaches fail to teach youth athletes proper skills, as well as proper conditioning. Youth athletes often do not condition their bodies at all or may condition too much. Too much or intense conditioning along with incorporating powerful and ballistic movements, and

forceful, repetitive muscular contractions can cause injuries throughout the youth's body.

Youth athletes must be properly fitted with helmets and other equipment appropriate for the sport. For example, too often pee-wee athletes are poorly fitted with notably loose football helmets and shoulder pads. This poorly fitted equipment can predispose the athlete to severe injury.

Conditioning and strength training youth athletes was considered harmful in the past due to their skeletal immaturity. Research has shown that when properly executed with appropriate progression and intensity, conditioning and strength training exercises can be beneficial for youth athletes. Most weight training injuries and deaths have occurred when the youth was unsupervised. The American Academy of Pediatrics (AAP) suggests that powerful Olympic-type lifts must not be performed until after skeletal maturity has been reached (Stricker, 2012). Young athletes can perform weight training successfully with supervision, using low weights and more repetitions while avoiding high-weight, explosive repetitions. Aerobic capacity in youth athletes is lower than in adult athletes. Also, youth athletes are not as capable of determining proper exercise intensity or calculating heart rate properly, especially those under 8 years of age. Therefore, exercise intensity is more difficult to determine and progressively increase within a youth's conditioning program. The AAP has created guidelines for youth participation in sport (http://www.healthychildren.org/English/healthy-living/sports/pages/Sports-Sense.aspx). These recommendations include activity participation for no more than 5 days per week and in one sport per season, varying training exercises so undue stress is not placed on the same body area, and being mindful of the ambient temperature, humidity, and environment in general in which the youth athlete participates.

Masters and Older Adult Athletes

Many considerations must be taken into account regarding exercise for masters and older adult athletes. As with athletes of all ages, masters and older adult athletes should have a thorough preparticipation examination along with a stress test to be certain they are able to handle the physical activity and exercise demands (Nied & Franklin, 2002). Aerobic exercise for sedentary masters and older adults should start gradually and at a very low intensity (**Figure 14-2**). Progression of activities can be as tolerated. Masters and older adult athletes are not as able to handle hot, humid environments as when they were young adults. They may take prescription medication, have chronic diseases, and have less muscle mass. These factors affect their body's ability to tolerate environmental heat and dissipate body heat through sweat. Consequently, masters and

Figure 14-2 Aerobic exercise for masters' and older adult athletes should begin slowly.

© T-Design/ShutterStock, Inc.

older adult athletes should use caution when exercising in the heat. They should drink plenty of fluids, acclimatize appropriately, shorten the exercise duration, and decrease workout intensity in hot environments.

Older adult athletes commonly have more barriers to exercise that can hinder exercise programming as compared to other adult athletes. Some of these barriers include balance difficulties, cognitive decline, musculoskeletal discomfort, a negative attitude toward exercise, fear of injury, lack of self-confidence in completing activities, and daily habits and routines that they are uncomfortable changing (Nied & Franklin, 2002). In order to make an older adult athlete become comfortable with physical activity and exercise, assist her by thoroughly discussing and setting her goals. Discuss with the athlete how to best fit exercise into her daily routine. Learn the intricacies of her personality and determine her motivation toward exercise. The athlete will be more compliant if she participates in activities she finds most enjoyable. Therefore, develop her exercise program to include her primary interests.

Because muscle mass decreases with age, masters and older adult athletes do not require the same amount of total

calories per day as younger adults. If these athletes consumed the same amount of total calories as when they were in their 20s or 30s, they would undoubtedly gain weight. However, with age, masters and older adult athletes must increase vitamin D, calcium, and magnesium intake to maintain optimal nutrition. Iron requirements decrease as women become postmenopausal, and become equal to men's requirements. To obtain optimal results, consider these nutritional needs when you develop a master's or older adult's physical activity and exercise program.

CARDIOVASCULAR CONDITIONS

Adults who have cardiovascular (CV) conditions such as angina, hypertension, and CV disease can significantly benefit from physical activity and exercise. Exercise benefits include increases in heart and lung efficiency and maximum oxygen consumption, along with decreases in body weight, fat stores, low-density lipoprotein (LDL) cholesterol and triglycerides, heart rate, blood pressure, and symptoms of angina. Consequently, these benefits assist adults with CV conditions in living a good quality of life. Fortunately, these benefits are applicable not only to adults with CV conditions, but all individuals with various conditions who participate in physical activity and exercise. Consider these cardiovascular conditions, the adult's capabilities, and his or her physical limitations when developing a safe exercise program.

All adults with CV conditions must be under the supervision of a physician. Obtain the athlete's consent to communicate with his or her physician in order to devise and execute a safe, effective physical activity and exercise program. Work closely with the physician to determine the athlete's needs. Whenever you are changing the athlete's program (e.g., changing protocol in regard to the frequency, intensity, time, and type [FITT] principle), consult with the athlete's physician. Prior to their exercise participation, all adults with CV conditions should be stress tested by an exercise science specialist who is trained to perform the test. The stress test assists you and your athlete in designing an exercise program within his or her capabilities.

As mentioned previously, angina, hypertension, and CV disease are three very common CV conditions that your athletes may have.

Angina

Angina is chest pain created due to a lack of oxygenated blood flow to the heart. Often this lack of blood flow is due to plaque buildup within the coronary arteries due to high LDL cholesterol and triglyceride levels. Stable angina is diagnosed when the pain occurs in a predictable manner during physical activity and exercise. The pain can also spread to the neck, shoulders, and arms. Exercise can help decrease coronary artery plaque, which decreases the athlete's CV risk. Exercise also helps increase oxygenated blood supply when the athlete is at rest, which can reduce the incidence of angina.

Adults with angina must follow a warm-up and cool-down protocol, as well as all other conditioning principles. When you assist an athlete in beginning a physical activity and exercise program, begin by setting achievable goals. Each exercise science professional may have personal preferences when creating exercise prescriptions, but general exercise programming goals exist. One goal is for the athlete to perform 30 minutes of physical activity, gradually progressing in intensity, for a minimum of 5 days per week. One option is for the athlete to begin with more sessions per week (5–7 days) with short duration sessions (5–10 minutes), and then progress to less sessions per week but longer individual sessions (Durstine, Moore, Painter, & Roberts, 2009). Aerobic physical activity should be performed, which may include walking and household activities including cleaning and gardening. Adults with angina can perform resistance training 2 days a week for 15-minute sessions. The strength training should focus on circuit training with light resistance. Flexibility exercises are beneficial for the athlete's upper and lower body. Stretching muscles 2–3 days per week can help decrease the risk of musculoskeletal injury.

During the athlete's program orientation, educate him on the importance of communication. He must inform you immediately when he is experiencing symptoms of angina during exercise. Be aware of any medication that the athlete takes for angina. His medication must be on hand during his exercise sessions in case he experiences symptoms. For example, if an athlete is prescribed nitroglycerine and he has angina during exercise, he must take the medication immediately. Before and after exercise, evaluate and record the athlete's heart rate (HR) and blood pressure (BP). The athlete must take his HR throughout an aerobic exercise session. During strength training activities, athletes must avoid performing a **Valsalva** maneuver so that BP, blood volume, and HR are not detrimentally altered during exercise. If at any time the athlete's angina symptoms change or increase during or due to the physical activity and exercise sessions, you must immediately stop the program and inform the athlete's physician.

> **Valsalva maneuver** When an athlete holds his or her breath and attempts to forcefully expire through his or her closed mouth and nose.

Hypertension

Hypertension is high blood pressure (HBP). When all athletes exercise, their systolic BP rises. Exercising athletes who have HBP see more dramatic increases of systolic BP than do athletes without HBP. Therefore, the individual needs to make every attempt to lower BP on a daily basis. Many individuals who have HBP are overweight. A primary goal should be for the individual to lose weight and eat nutritious foods such as vegetables, fruits, and low-fat and low-cholesterol foods. Adults with HBP should also make lifestyle changes to assist in decreasing BP, including quitting smoking, limiting alcohol consumption, and reducing salt intake. In regard to exercise, adults with HBP must progress to a goal of completing 30 minutes of aerobic physical activity or exercise for as many days per week as possible. Eventually the athlete should be performing physical activity or exercise 7 days per week. Low intensity exercise is effective in decreasing BP. The hypertensive athlete should work up to 40–60% maximum HR for positive effects. Circuit training has been shown to be more purposeful than strength training in decreasing BP for athletes with HBP. Overall, athletes with HBP should attempt to expend at least 300 kcal/week at first and then increase the intensity, duration, and frequency of exercise to expend 2,000 kcal/week, which includes decreasing caloric intake. Monitoring BP is important before and after exercise (**Figure 14-3**).

An individual who has a systolic pressure greater than 200 mm Hg or a diastolic pressure greater than 115 mm Hg should not exercise until the BP is controlled with medication (Durstine et al., 2009). Some athletes with HBP may be

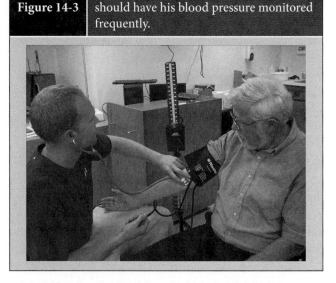

Figure 14-3 An athlete who has hypertension should have his blood pressure monitored frequently.

taking medication comparable to other athletes with CV, such as beta-blockers and diuretics. These medications can lower HR and BP, respectively. Pescatello et al. (2004) created a position stand for the American College of Sports Medicine titled *Exercise and Hypertension* that is beneficial for all exercise scientists who are working with hypertensive athletes and creating exercise programs for them.

Cardiovascular Disease and Heart Attack

Cardiovascular disease, also referred to as heart disease, is a broad term utilized to describe ill conditions of the heart. Cardiovascular disease includes heart rhythm and congenital abnormalities, infections, and coronary artery insufficiencies. These conditions are typically treated with medication and lifestyle changes, including hypertension, diabetes, and cholesterol control; smoking cessation; stress management; proper nutrition; and daily exercise (MayoClinic, 2013). If CV disease is not controlled, then serious secondary conditions, such as angina, and life-threatening emergencies, such as heart attack, can occur.

Cardiovascular disease can cause significant damage to the heart and result in a heart attack. A heart attack, also called a myocardial infarction, occurs when one of the coronary arteries is blocked due to plaque. As a result, not enough oxygenated blood is delivered to a portion of the heart and as a result that portion dies. Individuals who have sustained a heart attack complete four phases of cardiac rehabilitation, which include physical activity and exercise. Phase I exercise includes simple exercises such as moving from a standing to a sitting position and back again. These exercises make the body accustomed to changes in stress on the heart due to various positions and movements. Phases II through IV involve aerobic exercise utilizing both upper and lower body movements. Mild, circuit training resistance exercises performed 2–3 days per week can be introduced during Phases II through IV for athletes who are stable in regard to their symptoms. Flexibility exercises are performed frequently to help decrease the risk of injury.

As with individuals suffering from angina, individuals who have sustained a heart attack must avoid performing a Valsalva maneuver during exercise, which often can occur during isometric exercises or lifting greater resistance than what the athlete is accustomed to. Athletes with any CV condition or who have suffered a heart attack should not participate in physical activity in extreme environments, both hot and cold, due to circulatory changes that can detrimentally affect their condition. Adults who are on medication, such as beta-blockers, can have a decreased HR and exercise capacity while exercising. Any medications that affect the central nervous system (CNS) may cause the athlete to become dizzy or faint. Each of these factors must be seriously considered when the individual is commencing a physical activity and exercise program.

IMMUNOLOGICAL CONDITIONS

When a pathogen has entered and adversely affects the body, sometimes the immune system cannot destroy the pathogen. Also, diseases can cause the athlete's body to attack itself. These diseases are called autoimmune diseases. In either case, individuals with these immunological conditions can participate in physical activity and exercise, which hopefully can make the individual's body stronger in an attempt to fight off pathogens and promote a healthy lifestyle.

Cancer

Cancer is an uncontrolled, abnormal growth of cells in the body. The cancer cells can stay localized in one part of the body or they can spread to distant sites. At this time, cancer cannot be readily prevented because no vaccine or cure exists; however, some cancers are more easily treated than others. For the most part, all athletes with cancer can benefit from exercise. Exercise for cancer patients produces many benefits including maintenance of body weight; increased body image, quality of life, and positive outlook; and decreased depression. Studies have shown that physical activity increases energy balance, decreases fatigue, and increases survival rates for adults with breast cancer (National Cancer Institute, 2009).

When designing an exercise program for an individual with cancer, consider each individual's specific situation. As with CV conditions, communication with the athlete's physician and exercise testing by an exercise science specialist are necessary before the athlete begins a formal physical activity and exercise program. Some history questions to ask the athlete include the following: Where is the cancer in your body, and is it localized or **metastatic**? What treatment are you undergoing, and what are the side effects? Are you in **remission**? Individuals with cancer may have exercise limitations. An individual with lung cancer, for example, has decreased respiratory capability and shortness of breath. He or she will be especially tired and weak after chemotherapy and radiation

> **Metastatic** When cancer cells move from one site in the body to another.
>
> **Remission** When a disease has decreased or become absent in the body. In regard to cancer, if a physician cannot detect cancer cells within an athlete's body via imaging and other diagnostic tests, then the athlete is in remission.

treatments. Individuals with cancer may have loss of range of motion (ROM) and muscular weakness due to inactivity. Often cancer patients have other conditions, such as hypertension, obesity, previous myocardial infarction, and angina, which may affect their exercise capabilities. Consider these and any other limitations when developing an exercise program for these individuals.

Explain to the individual that the physical activity sessions will vary in duration and intensity depending on his or her cancer treatment sessions. Communicate with the athlete and his or her physician and gain a thorough understanding of the treatments' side effects. Some side effects can include diarrhea, vomiting, nausea, severe fatigue, and pain. If at any time the athlete has these side effects, postpone exercise until the athlete feels well.

In general, the athlete should participate in aerobic exercises composed of large muscle activity including walking, cycling, and water aerobics. Incorporating a daily flexibility program is important because cancer patients typically lose ROM and flexibility due to lack of motion and a sedentary lifestyle. Strength training, including free weights and resistance bands, can be utilized to help maintain muscle mass and strength. Circuit training is also beneficial. By incorporating activities of daily living (ADLs) into the program, you assist the athlete in improving his or her daily life and promoting his or her sense of individuality and independence. These ADL activities include walking up and down stairs, reaching for high objects, and moving from a seated to a standing position and vice versa.

Chronic Fatigue Syndrome

Chronic fatigue syndrome (CFS) is a condition that affects mostly middle-aged women. The athlete who has CFS is continually tired, which interferes with ADLs. The athlete may also have headaches, sore throat, low grade fever, difficulty concentrating, confusion, and memory loss. Rest does not relieve the symptoms. The condition is not caused by illness or disease. Although no specific cause of CFS has been determined, CFS is thought to result from an improperly working immune system. No cure exists for CFS, but the symptoms of depression and mental anguish can be treated. One means to treat these psychological symptoms is exercise.

Exercise has been shown to be a valuable treatment for individuals with CFS (Edmonds, McGuire, & Price, 2004). Although exercise does not dramatically improve the athlete's physical capabilities, exercise has shown significant positive changes by increasing her perceived quality of life. Before beginning the exercise, inform the athlete that she may be more tired than usual after the first few exercise sessions,

which is completely normal. Mild, graded physical activity benefits the athlete. Have the athlete begin with low intensity and duration of aerobic, strength training, flexibility, and functional exercises as any able-bodied athlete would. However, the athlete with CFS may not be able to progress as quickly. Completion of moderate intensity exercises is a primary goal. An athlete with CFS may not be able to tolerate high intensity exercises due to the condition. She may become discouraged after exercise, due to fatigue caused by physical exertion. Encourage and support the athlete. Reiterate that the exercise program's purpose is to maintain strength, CV endurance, and flexibility with a goal to promote easier ADLs for the athlete. Explain that the postexercise fatigue will decrease over time as exercise sessions are continued. Discuss with the athlete when she typically feels least fatigued, so you can schedule this time for exercise.

The athlete should exercise 3–5 days per week. The sessions should be of short duration at first with simple activities; for example, the athlete can begin walking at a low intensity for a 5-minute session, 1–2 times per day. The athlete can work up to a 1-hour session per day. Do not be concerned with progressing the athlete's intensity. The athlete's **rate of perceived exertion (RPE)** dictates when to increase the time and frequency of exercise. An RPE of approximately 9 (very light) to 12 (light to somewhat hard) is the goal for each exercise session (**Table 14-1**).

Mild physical activity can also increase the athlete's self-image. As the athlete becomes in control of her exercise program, she will eventually realize that she can be in control of her body and her life. When an athlete has her "good days" and feels that she can perform more exercise during the session, encourage her not to do so. She may have a relapse in CFS symptoms due to the sudden exercise program progression.

> **Rate of perceived exertion (RPE)** The athlete's opinion of how hard he or she is working during exercise. The method was developed by Gunnar Borg, a Swedish psychologist. The RPE is rated by the athlete on a scale of 6–20, with 6 being no exertion at all and 20 being maximal exertion. See the CDC website www.cdc.gov /physicalactivity/everyone /measuring/exertion.html for more information on RPE and the RPE scale athletes can use during exercise.

Fibromyalgia

Fibromyalgia is a chronic condition that most often affects middle-aged women. The condition causes joint pain and stiffness as well as inflexibility and contracture of soft tissues. No specific cause for the condition exists. The condition has

Table 14-1 | Rate of Perceived Exertion

The rate of perceived exertion scale was developed by Gunnar Borg, a Swedish psychologist. An athlete can utilize the Borg scale to determine his or her effort during exercise. While exercising, the athlete rates his or her exertion utilizing the following scale:

6 No exertion at all
7 Extremely light
8
9 Very light
10
11 Light
12
13 Somewhat hard
14
15 Hard (heavy)
16
19 Extremely hard
20 Maximal exertion

According to the American College of Sports Medicine (www .acsm.org/docs/current-comments/perceivedexertion.pdf), the rate of perceived exertion can be effectively utilized to monitor progress, and revise athletes' exercise programs.

been associated with CFS, as well as symptoms of anxiety, depression, and sleep disturbances. Exercise can be beneficial for adults with fibromyalgia because exercise can decrease pain and joint stiffness, while increasing muscle and tendon flexibility. Exercise facilitates the decrease of depression and anxiety symptoms by giving the athlete social interaction and a sense of personal control. Adults with fibromyalgia typically are more hesitant to exercise than are normal adults due to fear of increased pain. These athletes often state that cold or hot environments exacerbate symptoms. Therefore, it is important to begin the exercise and progress the athlete slowly in a neutral environment. Inform the individual that symptoms may possibly increase after the first few exercise sessions, until the athlete's body adapts.

Your encouragement and support, as well as exercising in a group or with a partner, can improve the athlete's compliance to physical activity. Minimize any movements or exercises, including eccentric activity, that can increase symptoms. Consider the time of day that the athlete should exercise in order to minimize symptoms and promote activity; for example, the athlete may have greater loss of ROM due to joint stiffness and muscle inflexibility in the morning. Therefore, the exercise sessions should take place in the early afternoon once the athlete has been moving around and symptoms decrease. In order to promote adherence to exercise,

begin with easy exercises such as walking or utilizing the upper body ergometer (UBE) without resistance. The aerobic exercise program continues to incorporate large muscle aerobic activity, such as biking and aquatic therapy. The athlete should begin with 20 minutes of exercise, 2 days per week. The athlete can work toward completing 40-minute exercise sessions, 3 days per week. The exercise program must move very slowly for these adults in order to address the athlete's physical and psychological considerations. Isotonic, flexibility, and functional exercises also need to be incorporated. The functional activities should mimic the athlete's ADLs. To make these activities useful for your athlete, ask her about her typical day and what ADLs she performs. It also is important to determine what ADLs she cannot perform due to the fibromyalgia, in order to set goals to improve her symptoms. Stress management and relaxation exercises are also beneficial for an athlete with fibromyalgia.

METABOLIC CONDITIONS

Metabolic conditions develop when the body's normal **metabolism** is disrupted by abnormal chemical reactions, including decreased or loss of vital organ function. Diabetes and obesity are two very common and related metabolic conditions that affect children and adults worldwide.

> **Metabolism** How the body ingests food, breaks it down, and creates energy to utilize.

Diabetes

Diabetes is a disease in which high levels of sugar exist in the blood. The three common types of diabetes are type 1, type 2, and gestational diabetes. Type 1 diabetes is also called insulin-dependent diabetes. This form of diabetes often is diagnosed in children. The beta cells in the pancreas produce little or no insulin. Consequently, the glucose remains and builds up in the bloodstream instead of moving into the cells. The athlete may experience signs and symptoms including thirst, hunger, unexplained weight loss, sensation deficiencies, blurred vision, and diabetic ketoacidosis. Type 2 diabetes is also referred to as non-insulin-dependent diabetes. Type 2 diabetes is the most common type of diabetes, and although it can affect children it mostly affects adults. Adults and children with type 2 diabetes cannot utilize insulin properly, so sugar builds up in the bloodstream. Individuals with type 2 diabetes have similar signs and symptoms as individuals with type 1 diabetes. Adults who are predisposed to type 2 diabetes are obese, sedentary, older adults, who have poor diets. Cases of type 2 diabetes in children are increasing due to increases in childhood obesity. Gestational diabetes occurs when hormones produced during pregnancy block the utilization of insulin. Signs and symptoms of gestational diabetes are most often mild, but the woman can have similar signs and symptoms as type 1 diabetes.

All diabetics can benefit from exercise. These benefits include an increased insulin sensitivity (i.e., insulin can be utilized more effectively), a decrease in body fat, and an increase in CV health. A type 2 diabetic can have decreased blood glucose levels with exercise, but this decrease does not readily occur with type 1 diabetics.

When the athlete exercises, he utilizes glucose as an energy source. The athlete must have a simple carbohydrate snack available during exercise, such as orange slices or juice, or the athlete's glucose becomes depleted and he may experience insulin shock. Normal fasting blood glucose levels are under 100 mg/dl. The athlete should measure his blood glucose level before exercise (**Figure 14-4**). He should not exercise if his blood glucose is over 250 mg/dl or below 70 mg/dl (Durstine et al., 2009). In these cases, his blood glucose levels should be reduced with insulin or increased with glucose ingestion (respectively) prior to exercise.

Utilizing the FITT principle, the diabetic athlete can perform aerobic and anaerobic activities at levels that an athlete without diabetes would. Strength training activities focus on muscular endurance training with low resistance and high repetitions. Exercise performed for a long duration, as well as strenuous exercise, creates hormones that combat the effects of insulin.

Diabetic individuals have progressively poor circulation in their extremities. Consequently, the athlete needs to wear properly fitted, cushioning sneakers during exercise to protect the feet when weight bearing.

Obesity

Obesity is an excessive amount of body fat. An adult that has a body mass index (BMI) over 30 is considered obese (**Figure 14-5**). Obesity detrimentally affects the individual's health due to numerous factors. One of these factors is that obese individuals are usually physically inactive. Fortunately, even a small amount of physical activity and exercise can improve the athlete's condition. Along with caloric modification, obese individuals who are physically active and perform exercise can lose body fat, which leads to weight reduction. If an athlete exercises regularly his energy expenditure increases, which promotes weight loss. Weight reduction can also eliminate many of the other conditions (e.g., hypertension, type 2 diabetes, high blood pressure) that an obese individual may have, as well as promote a healthy lifestyle. Before beginning a program, communicate with the athlete and his physician to determine if the athlete has any condition that may affect his ability to exercise.

When initially working with an obese child or adult, consider that he most likely is sedentary relative to other normal weight children or adults. His program must begin with mild

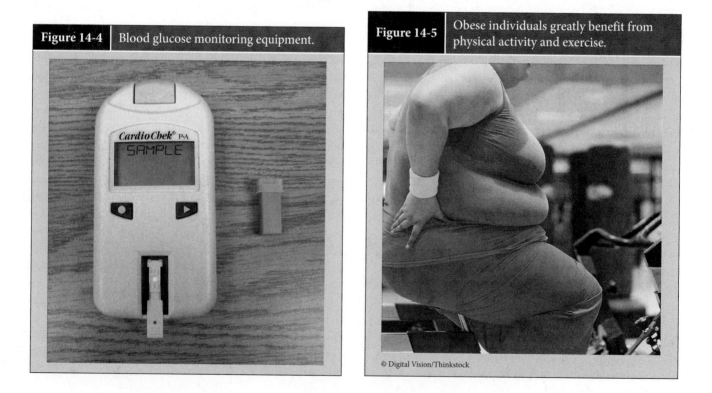

| **Figure 14-4** | Blood glucose monitoring equipment. |

| **Figure 14-5** | Obese individuals greatly benefit from physical activity and exercise. |

© Digital Vision/Thinkstock

intensity activities. Depending on the inactivity and the athlete's weight, lower extremity activities may need to include both weight-bearing and non-weight-bearing exercises. Incorporate simple exercises such as active range of motion (AROM), gentle stretching, and isometric activities into the program and progress the athlete as tolerated. Have the athlete take part in devising his own program. He can describe enjoyable activities to you, which should be integrated into the exercise sessions. Sessions do not have to consist of one long session per day. Rather, obese, sedentary individuals may prefer and better tolerate two shorter sessions per day. The athlete can obtain optimal effects with 5–6 days of exercise per week. Motivation is the key for the exercise program to be successful. The athlete will be more motivated and compliant if he sees progress.

The athlete must continually hydrate before, during, and after exercise because obese athletes lose a lot of water through sweat due to increased body heat production. The athlete should be wearing clothing that allows the sweat to dissipate from his body, and he should exercise in cool temperatures. Eventually, when the athlete begins to see progress, his sense of well-being and appreciation for a healthy lifestyle will develop.

NEUROMUSCULAR DISORDERS

Neuromuscular disorders are conditions in which the nerves in the body improperly function. This improper functioning affects communication between nerves and muscles. Consequently, the muscles do not function as they should.

Cerebral Palsy

Cerebral palsy (CP) is a brain and nervous system condition that develops in utero or within the first 2 years of life. CP occurs during brain development. Suspected causes for CP include in utero brain hypoxia, bleeding, or injury; a genetic condition; or a neurological disorder. Damage and abnormal development occur to the portion of the brain responsible for the spinal nerves and motor control. Consequently, CP causes problems with a person's motion, motor control, reflex capability, balance, muscle tone, and posture. CP can also affect oral motor function, including swallowing and speech. CP affects children and adults in very individualized ways. Consequently, one individual may have different needs than another. Signs and symptoms range from mild to severe and include contracted joints and resultant loss of ROM, shortened musculature and resultant inflexibility, lack of coordination, deficiencies in fine and gross motor skills, and delays in motor and speech function while growing from infant to child.

Individuals with CP can obtain the same benefits from physical activity and exercise as any able-bodied athlete would.

Figure 14-6 Wheelchair bound athletes can participate in many of the same activities as able-bodied athletes.

© Shariff Che' Lah/Dreamstime.com

Most importantly for CP athletes, exercise can decrease the condition's signs and symptoms, which includes reducing muscle spasticity and contractures, and increasing mobility and muscle tone. Physical activity can also promote the athlete's well-being, independence, and social interaction with others. Before your athlete begins the exercise program, determine if he is taking any medications and how the drugs affect his ability to perform exercise. Obtain the athlete's permission to speak with his physician to gain this information prior to developing his exercise protocol.

CP athletes may need to use a wheelchair to mobilize (**Figure 14-6**). These wheelchair-bound individuals may have increased lower extremity symptoms as compared to CP athlete who can ambulate, because the wheelchair-bound athletes are more sedentary due to continual sitting. Include flexibility, aerobic, and strength training exercises in order to facilitate performing ADLs. The exercises should focus on gaining muscular endurance so the athlete can withstand the stresses of ADLs. The specific aerobic exercises depend on whether the athlete is ambulatory or wheelchair bound. If the athlete is ambulatory, then a UBE and a Schwinn Airdyne (**Figure 14-7**) are useful. If an athlete is in a wheelchair, he can utilize a UBE. For endurance activities, the wheelchair-bound athlete can utilize his wheelchair as equipment by pushing it various lengths and speeds to gain muscular endurance. Many athletes with CP are able to perform aquatic exercise including swimming. The specific activities incorporated into the exercise program greatly depend on the severity of the individual's CP.

Figure 14-7 A Shwinn Airdyne is aerobic exercise equipment which can be utilized by many individuals within the exercise protocol.

Tips from the Field

Tip 1 Prior to creating an exercise program for a wheelchair bound athlete, literally put yourself in their position. Sit in a non-motorized wheelchair and mobilize the chair in various directions using only your upper extremities. Then mobilize your upper and lower extremities and trunk by mimicking the exercises you will have your athlete complete. Bind your legs together so you cannot move them and attempt to perform upper extremity and trunk exercises. By partaking in these wheelchair activities yourself, prior to instructing the wheelchair bound individual, you can have an idea of any constraints caused by the wheelchair. You will become familiar with the amount of difficulty and effort required by the wheelchair bound individual during exercise. Also, you will understand the stress that the athlete's body will undertake when performing exercises.

Multiple Sclerosis

Multiple sclerosis (MS) is a disease that affects the CNS. Nerve damage occurs due to inflammation of the myelin sheath that covers the nerves. The nerves themselves can also be damaged. In either case, scar tissue develops around the nerve. The nerve damage and scar tissue cause the nerves to malfunction. Although MS is a neuromuscular disease, it is also considered an autoimmune disease. The cause of MS has not been determined, but autoimmune responses, the environment, genetics, and pathogens are currently being studied in order to determine an exact cause (National Multiple Sclerosis Society, 2012). Signs and symptoms of MS can be mild to severe and include loss of sensation in the extremities, muscle tremors, spasm, weakness, incoordination, paralysis, and fatigue. Athletes with MS may also be sensitive to heat and have loss of bladder control.

Exercise benefits athletes with MS in the same manner as athletes without MS. Exercise can assist an athlete with MS by increasing mobility, flexibility, strength, endurance, and well-being, while decreasing spasm, stiffness, fatigue, and depression. You should be informed of the athlete's medications along with the side effects. Some medications may cause muscle weakness, decreased sweating, fatigue, or shortness of breath. Some athletes with MS are unable to maintain adequate blood flow to the muscles during exercise. This inadequate blood flow can cause difficulty with sustaining exercise and may cause fainting during exercise (Karpatkin, 2005). The MS disease progresses over time. Symptoms may become exacerbated due to the condition's progression, but not due to exercise (Karpatkin, 2005). Therefore, over time your athlete's exercise program may need frequent modification.

Aerobic, strength, and flexibility training should be incorporated into the athlete's exercise programs. Although no specific regimen exists, athletes with MS can perform aerobic and strength training activities utilizing the FITT principle, just as an athlete without MS would. Flexibility exercises are performed each day. Many athletes with MS have decreased or no sweat production. Consequently, the exercise environment needs to be maintained at a normal or slightly cooler temperature. Hydration is important for the athlete to avoid heat illness before, during, and after exercise. The athlete can also cool herself by utilizing cold therapy to decrease core body temperature prior to aerobic exercise, in an attempt to avoid heat illness. As with athletes with CP, some athletes with MS may be wheelchair bound; consequently, modification of their activities is imperative.

Spinal Cord Injury

When a child or adult has a spinal cord injury, she can experience a multitude of signs and symptoms, in particular loss of function and sensation. An individual with a severe spinal cord injury has partial or complete loss of function in the torso and all extremities (quadriplegia or tetraplegia) or the lower extremities (paraplegia). The spinal cord injury causes the person to have reduced or complete inability to perform gross motor function. A quadriplegic athlete has lower cardiac output than does a paraplegic athlete. Exercise assists the athlete in decreasing muscle contracture and spasm, while increasing ROM and flexibility of the movable limbs. The physical activity facilitates a decrease in depression and an increase in self-worth and independence.

Before you devise her exercise program, determine if the athlete has any special considerations due to the spinal cord trauma, including any other noteworthy conditions. Always closely supervise the athlete during exercise. Quadriplegic individuals in particular do not adapt well to extreme heat or cold. Consequently, the athlete needs to exercise in a comfortable, controlled environment. Because the athlete is in a wheelchair for prolonged periods of time, she may develop pressure sores. With your assistance, have her change positions during exercise to relieve the pressure. You must learn the proper way to perform lifts and transfers from equipment to her wheelchair and vice versa from a trained professional. If she has core body deficiency or paralysis, utilize belts and straps to make sure she is safely stabilized while exercising. If the athlete has hyper- or hypotension, monitor her BP before and after exercise. Have the athlete empty her bladder, bowel, and urine or colostomy bag prior to exercise. If the athlete has any signs or symptoms of fainting, change in color, dizziness, nausea, or extreme weakness, then stop the exercises immediately.

The exercise program should include activities within the individual's capabilities. Some activities include utilizing a UBE, mobilizing the wheelchair, utilizing parallel bars to ambulate, manual resistance exercises, neck AROM, and extremity passive range of motion (PROM) performed with your assistance. The aerobic exercises can include swimming with the athlete wearing a flotation device, seated aerobics classes utilizing arm movements only, UBE, and wheelchair cranking (propulsion). The paraplegic athlete can participate in aerobics class instruction with able-bodied athletes, performing upper and core body activities, in order to promote social communication. Strength training exercises include free weights, bands, and tubing. Begin the athlete's aerobic and strength training exercises slowly, using the FITT principle as is done with able-bodied athletes. Flexibility exercises are performed daily and before and after exercise. Always provide encouragement and explain to the athlete that she will notice small but beneficial improvements each week.

ORTHOPEDIC CONDITIONS

Orthopedic conditions can affect any individual at any age. Unfortunately, as we get older, our bodies cannot adapt to stress in the same manner as when we were young. Exercise helps athletes to decrease the effects of two common orthopedic conditions that arise with aging: arthritis and osteoporosis.

Arthritis

Arthritis is a chronic condition that involves inflammation of the joints. Arthritis typically affects middle-aged men and women. The condition is caused by cartilage breakdown within the joints. The decrease of cartilage causes the bones comprising the joint to rub against each other. The rubbing causes inflammation, joint pain, swelling, and stiffness. Arthritis can also be caused by infection, injury, or an autoimmune condition, which occurs when the body breaks down the joints for unknown reasons. If the arthritis is treated with medication, therapeutic modalities, and exercise, then it may heal or become asymptomatic; however, many people have chronic arthritis. Osteoarthritis, otherwise known as degenerative joint disease, is the most common type of chronic arthritis. Osteoarthritis is caused by the wearing down of the joint's bone surface, which occurs with the aging process. Osteoarthritis cannot be healed, but the symptoms can be treated. Rheumatoid arthritis is an autoimmune disease characterized by synovial membrane inflammation around the joints. This inflammation causes eventual cartilage and joint surface breakdown.

Exercise is beneficial for arthritic adults. Typically an arthritic individual is deconditioned due to inactivity and joint pain. Consequently, he may be hesitant to exercise. Educate the individual and explain how moderate exercise can improve his quality of life. Improvements in cardiovascular status, neuromuscular control, flexibility, aerobic capacity, and muscular strength and endurance can be gained with only 30 minutes of daily exercise. AROM and flexibility exercises performed at the arthritic areas help to decrease stiffness and increase ROM during ADLs. The athlete can increase his activity level and energy expenditure on a daily basis. Arthritic athletes can participate in almost any activity that does not put undue stress on the joints. Safe activities include walking, cycling, and swimming. Running, jumping, and any high impact activities are contraindicated.

When developing an athlete's program, begin the exercises at a low intensity and duration. Swimming and water exercise are excellent activities for arthritic athletes due to the buoyancy property of water. Buoyancy helps decrease stress on the upper and lower extremities. Flexibility exercises should be incorporated daily, but the athlete should not overstretch the tendons surrounding the joints because further irritation could occur. Strength training can include any activity that a nonarthritic athlete can perform including circuit training, dumbbells, weight machines, bands, and tubing. Proper footwear that cushion the soles of the feet are extremely important to reduce any unnecessary ground reaction forces and stress on the athlete's lower extremity joints. Inform the athlete that some discomfort may occur at first during the beginning stages of exercise and when new exercises are introduced. Discomfort may also occur at the end of the exercise session or 24–48 hours postexercise until the athlete becomes accustomed to the exercise program. If at any time pain or swelling develops, have the athlete stop the causative exercise and modify his program.

Osteoporosis

Osteoporosis affects both men and women, but is more pronounced in women age 50 years or older. Our bones become thin, brittle, and weak with age. As we get older, the body does not create bone to replace lost bone; consequently, osteoporosis occurs. The body may also resorb too much bone, which causes osteoporosis. Osteoporosis causes the bones to be at risk for fracture. The individual with osteoporosis may not have significant signs and symptoms of the condition in its beginning stages. In later stages she may have pain and point tenderness at and around the area that has the decreased bone density. The pain and point tenderness can also indicate a fracture. Osteoporosis of the spine causes a decrease in the person's height.

Exercise, especially weight-bearing exercise, is crucial for adults with osteoporosis. Weight bearing assists the bones in maintaining their density and strength. Therefore, weight-bearing exercise can help slow down progression of the condition. The athlete can perform exercises as per the FITT principle. The type of exercise depends on the athlete's motor and cognitive function, and previous physical activity. Weight-bearing activities include walking, jogging, aerobics classes, and playing organized sports such as racquetball and tennis. Strength training activities can incorporate any type of resistance equipment. Flexibility and functional activities are also incorporated to improve ROM and the ability to perform ADLs, respectively. An athlete's diet must have increased calcium and vitamin D, which helps the body absorb calcium, in order to keep the bones dense and strong. The athlete's diet needs calcium supplementation as well as high calcium foods such as dairy products, green leafy vegetables, and calcium-fortified foods.

Athletes with osteoporosis may have a fear of falling and breaking a bone. Assist the athlete in controlling her anxiety and fear by having her begin to perform simple exercises that are low to the ground. Have her utilize two feet while weight bearing to create a wide stance, which promotes greater balance when performing exercises. Also teach the athlete stress management exercises, which can alleviate anxiety.

RESPIRATORY CONDITIONS

Respiratory conditions are problematic for individuals who exercise because their lung function is compromised. Consequently, they may not be able to exercise as easily as an athlete without a respiratory condition would due to the decreased oxygen provided to the body. However, with continued exercise the respiratory condition can be improved, as can the athlete's overall health.

Asthma

Asthma is a condition that causes the bronchi to swell and become narrow. Because the passageways are not as large as normal, an inadequate amount of oxygen is transported to the lungs. Asthmatic individuals perform better when exercising in warm, moist environments versus cold environments. Swimming or other aquatic exercises are appropriate activities that decrease asthma symptoms. Shorter duration exercises with intermittent bouts are better tolerated by asthmatic athletes than are long duration strenuous activities. Aerobic activities such as walking, aerobics, and cycling are good activities that bring about the least exacerbations. Over time, aerobic activity produces more efficient lung capability to take in and utilize oxygen, decreases exacerbations, increases general overall fitness and cardiorespiratory endurance, and promotes easier and better ADL performance. Aerobic activity produces breathing efficiency, less breathing complications, and a decrease in wheezing. The type, intensity, and duration of exercise depends on the severity of the athlete's asthma. Strength training includes dumbbells, tubing and band exercises, and isotonic machines. Flexibility exercise is always incorporated into the exercise program.

If prescribed by the athlete's doctor, have the athlete utilize her bronchodilator prior to exercise. Make every attempt to have the athlete exercise in an environment free of any triggers and allergens. However, avoiding potential triggers is not always possible. For example, if the athlete must exercise in a cool environment (e.g., skiing) or an environment with allergens (e.g., running outdoors in the midst of high pollen season), then have her wear a scarf or material that covers the nose and mouth. This will warm the air as it enters the respiratory tract. The facial covering also helps to keep allergens out of the passageways, which decreases the risk of exacerbations. The athlete must have her rescue inhaler medication with her at all times during exercise in case she experiences an exacerbation.

Chronic Obstructive Pulmonary Disease

Chronic obstructive pulmonary disease (COPD) is a common respiratory condition that involves chronic bronchitis and/or emphysema. COPD most often affects men over the age of 60 who smoke or have smoked consistently in the past. A person with COPD cannot be cured; however, signs and symptoms can be treated and decreased through medication and exercise, which includes respiratory therapy. Signs and symptoms of COPD include a persistent cough, wheezing, inability to breathe at a normal rate, decreased lung volume, and shortness of breath, especially with exertion. Along with the typical benefits of exercise, individuals affected by COPD benefit from increased efficiency of the functional lungs and cardiovascular system, decreased wheezing and shortness of breath with everyday activity, and decreased respirations and oxygen necessary to perform ADLs.

When devising a physical activity and exercise program for an individual with COPD, you must take into account how the disease affects the individual. Athletes with COPD have similar bronchodilator medication as asthmatic athletes. Make sure they have immediate access to their medication at all times during exercise. Always consult with the athlete's physician prior to devising an exercise program to determine the effects of the medications on the athlete's ability to exercise. For example, some medications may produce hypotension, muscle weakness, cardiac palpitations, and tachycardia. Athletes with COPD may have difficulty maintaining lean muscle mass. Strength exercises along with proper nutrition including lean meats and fish, fruits, and vegetables, help the athlete's body to build and maintain lean muscle mass. Some athletes may need supplemental oxygen during exercise. Therefore, learn about the equipment, how it is utilized, and any mobility constraints affecting the athlete during exercise. Because COPD is a progressive disease, many adults are also treated for depression. Group exercise, for example a yoga or tai chi class with peers, can promote social activity and assist in relieving depression symptoms.

Skeletal muscle dysfunction is a key indicator of COPD advanced stages, and exercise can assist in reversing this dysfunction. Strength training also has been shown to improve health-related quality of life more than endurance training (Puhan et al., 2005). All exercises incorporated into an asthmatic individual's program can be included in an individual with COPD's program. During aerobic exercise, use a rated perceived exertion (RPE) of approximately 11–13 (light to somewhat hard) to determine the appropriate exercise intensity. Always closely supervise your athlete to make sure he does not experience **dyspnea** during the session. Completion of and progression during the session are more important than exercise intensity for the athlete with COPD.

Dyspnea	Shortness of breath.

Cystic Fibrosis

Cystic fibrosis (CF) is a hereditary, life-threatening disease characterized by an abnormal quantity of thick, salty mucus that exists in and clogs the air passageways and other body organs such as the lungs and pancreas. The mucus can cause lung infections and digestion complications. A child is usually diagnosed before the age of 2 years. The gene that causes CF is inherited from both parents. Signs and symptoms of CF include constipation, nausea, loss of appetite, discolored stools, fatigue, nasal congestion, coughing, recurrent pneumonia, and pancreatitis. Individuals with CF can particularly benefit from exercise by increasing cardiorespiratory efficiency, which assists in clearing mucus from the air passageways, which in turn increases oxygen consumption. Aerobic and strength training exercises have been shown to benefit the individual with CF by increasing lean body mass, maximum oxygen consumption, respiratory muscle endurance, and health-related quality of life. As with other respiratory conditions, athletes with CF are prescribed bronchodilators. Some athletes with CF need to utilize the bronchodilator prior to exercise. The individuals may also be taking additional medications for their condition. These medications, as well as the bronchodilators, may cause side effects such as tachycardia, muscular weakness, and increased BP, which may affect how you devise the athlete's exercise program. The athletes can tolerate exercise in the heat even though they lose excessive salt when sweating, and require adequate fluid replacement during exercise. Some athletes with severe CF may have lower extremity joint pain that hinders their capability to perform lower-body weight-bearing exercise.

Aerobic activities should include large muscle group exercises such as swimming, walking, jogging, and bicycling. Many athletes with CF can tolerate high intensity prolonged exercise, which has been shown to be highly beneficial. However, exercise sessions should be under 20 minutes when the athlete begins an exercise program, and session length should increase very slowly. The athlete eventually can perform 30-minute sessions for 3–4 days per week. Intensity progresses to 80% maximum heart rate (HR). Strength training activities involve large muscle groups, and functional activities focus on ADLs.

OTHER CONDITIONS

Many other conditions that affect athletes can benefit from exercise. These additional conditions include anemia, mental illness, pregnancy, and vision and hearing impairment.

Anemia

Anemia is a condition in which an individual's blood contains insufficient red blood cells, which results in decreased oxygen to the body. Anemia is caused by lack of iron and vitamins in the diet, especially B_{12} and folate; decreased red blood cell (RBC) production; the body's breakdown of RBCs; blood loss due to gastrointestinal (GI) bleeding or injury; and chronic disease. Signs and symptoms of anemia include fatigue, cold extremities, headaches, dyspnea, and dizziness. Various types of anemia exist, and some are more severe than others. Common anemia conditions include iron deficiency and vitamin deficiency anemia. These conditions are easily controlled. Most athletes affected by iron deficiency anemia are women. Sickle cell anemia is a hereditary condition that typically occurs with African American men. With this type of anemia, the individual's RBCs are a sickle or crescent shape instead of a normal circular shape; consequently, oxygen-carrying capacity is diminished. Also, due to the RBCs' sickle shape they can become lodged in a small blood vessel, which blocks blood and oxygen flow to the tissues.

Anemic individuals have decreased oxygen to the muscles at rest because iron, which is the oxygen-binding site in hemoglobin, is not sufficient in the body. When the athlete exercises, oxygen to the muscles is increased and is comparable to nonanemic athletes. Sickle cell anemic individuals can participate in high intensity exercise most often without any issues. However, to decrease any risk of illness, keep the athlete's exercise at a moderate level. Various aerobic activities following the FITT principle and progression are appropriate for the anemic athlete. With regular exercise, anemic athletes can improve their cardiorespiratory endurance significantly.

Athletes who have iron deficiency anemia must supplement their diet with iron-rich foods including red meat, chicken, turkey, fish, spinach, beans, broccoli, and any iron-fortified foods. Iron supplements may be necessary for individuals with severe cases of iron deficiency anemia. To treat vitamin deficiency anemia, the athlete's diet must contain foods rich in vitamin B_{12} and folate. Good sources of B_{12} vitamins include fish and shellfish, cheese, beef, and eggs. An individual may safely ingest B_{12} supplements. The body eliminates excess B_{12} vitamins because they are water-soluble. Good sources of folate include nuts, beans, spinach and leafy green vegetables, eggs, broccoli, and squash. An individual can take a daily prenatal vitamin that combines iron, B_{12}, and folate, even if the individual is not pregnant.

Mental Illness

Mental illness includes a variety of conditions such as depression, stress, panic and anxiety disorders, obsessive compulsive disorder (OCD), and posttraumatic stress disorder. Athletes with these illnesses should be under a physician's and/or mental health specialist's care. If not, refer the individual to the appropriate physician or mental health specialist for evaluation and treatment. Exercise is beneficial for these individuals. They are commonly taking daily prescription medication, which may cause side effects. With the athlete's permission, communicate with his or her physician or mental health specialist to determine any effects of the medication on exercise. Some side effects of mental illness medications include dizziness, weight gain, fatigue, or insomnia. Often athletes with mental illness have a secondary condition or illness that may affect their exercise program. Discuss these secondary conditions and illnesses with the athlete's physician or mental health specialist. This information is imperative to create an appropriate, successful exercise program for the individual.

Exercise has been shown to improve the athlete's mood; balance emotions; decrease depression, stress, and anxiety; and increase social communication and well-being. When devising the individual's exercise program, utilize the same principles as with an athlete without a mental illness. If the athlete has a secondary illness, such as diabetes or asthma, for example, then modify the program to address those conditions. Aerobic activity should begin at a low intensity (40% max HR) and duration (20 minutes) for first-time participants, and progressively increase as with any healthy athlete. These athletes typically respond well to structure, so plan the activities well in advance. Giving the athlete an advance copy of the daily program and recording the activities in a log (see Tips from the Field Tip 3) may make the athlete feel more comfortable. By utilizing these tactics, the athlete knows the daily exercise expectations and sees his or her progress. As a result, the athlete may exhibit decreased mental illness signs and symptoms during exercise. Athletes with social anxiety issues most likely need to begin an exercise program with individual versus group exercises. Hopefully with your encouragement and as time progresses, the athlete develops a social connection to others in the facility and chooses to exercise with a partner or in small groups.

Tips from the Field

Tip 3 Many individuals are not motivated to exercise, and individuals classified into special populations are no different. Some individuals may have no desire to exercise due to their condition. For example, depression may cause an individual to be withdrawn and not willing to venture out of the home to exercise. An obese individual may be embarrassed to exercise in a gym due to his or her appearance. An individual with COPD may be fearful that exercise will exacerbate his or her condition and cause a life-threatening emergency. Consequently, these individuals are often unwilling to participate in exercise. Part of your role as an exercise scientist is to motivate individuals to begin their journey to obtain a healthier lifestyle with exercise as part of their daily regimen. One successful means to motivate an individual is to begin an exercise program by participating in the exercises with the individual. The exercises should take place in a setting that is familiar and comfortable for the individual. Plan a weekly exercise schedule that accommodates both of you. Vary the daily exercise routine to maintain the athlete's interest, which will hopefully promote self-motivation. Once the athlete sees positive results and becomes motivated to exercise, then he or she most likely will be able to exercise regularly on his or her own.

Pregnancy

Although pregnancy is not an illness or disease, it is a condition that affects a woman's ability to exercise. Pregnant women greatly benefit from exercise, provided the exercise is performed within the physician's recommendations (**Figure 14-8**). Benefits of exercise during pregnancy include all cardiorespiratory benefits, maintenance of healthy weight, a decrease in back pain during later pregnancy stages, a decreased risk of gestational diabetes, an increase in energy, and an increase in muscle endurance. The woman's physician must approve exercise throughout the pregnancy. The physician may not clear a pregnant women for exercise if she has been bleeding or spotting, had previous miscarriages or previous premature births, a low placenta, or a weak cervix. With the woman's consent, develop a relationship with her physician

| Figure 14-8 | In consultation with her physician, you can devise a safe and effective exercise program for a pregnant woman. |

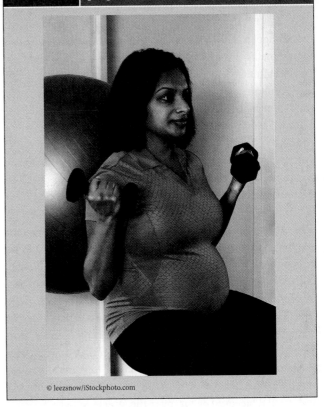

© leezsnow/iStockphoto.com

to regularly discuss her status in regard to exercise. Knowing the woman's, and the baby's, current health status as well as any exercise limitations throughout each of the trimesters is necessary to develop a safe exercise program.

Pregnant women can benefit from at least 30 minutes of moderate exercise as tolerated as many days per week as possible. Exercises focus on aerobic and flexibility exercises versus strength training exercise. If the woman was previously sedentary, she should perform 5 minutes of exercise and increase each session as tolerated, working to complete 30-minute sessions. A woman who was exercising regularly prior to pregnancy can probably continue at her pre-pregnancy level of exercise with her physician's approval, until she is in her second and third trimester. Aerobic activities such as walking, aerobics classes, bicycling, and swimming are best for pregnant woman. Stretching and relaxation activities such as yoga and tai chi are beneficial.

The athlete should exercise on a flat surface, wear comfortable supportive shoes, and eat a nutritious meal or snack at least an hour or two before exercise. As a woman enters her second and third trimester, she gains weight. Consequently, her balance may change while ambulating and moving from various positions. She must be careful when utilizing and getting on and off machines (e.g., treadmill and stationary bike) and up from the floor (e.g., during a yoga session). After pregnancy, the woman can begin low intensity exercises approximately 2 weeks after a vaginal birth, and approximately 4 weeks after a caesarean birth.

Pregnant women are more prone to iron deficiency anemia because the iron must adapt to the increased blood volume, which occurs due to the pregnancy as well as the addition of the fetus's blood volume. Pregnant women need iron, B_{12}, and folate supplementation from sources previously mentioned. They must avoid dehydration and exercising in the heat. The environment must be comfortable and they need to drink plenty of water during exercise. Activities that predispose athletes to falls, high altitudes, or forceful contact with another athlete or implement resulting in trauma need to be avoided. Any activity that requires jumping, hopping, bouncing, twisting, and deep knee or trunk bending should not be incorporated into a pregnant woman's exercise program. If the athlete has any signs or symptoms of dizziness, fatigue, uterine cramping, vaginal bleeding, or dyspnea during exercise, stop the athlete's exercise immediately. Have her cool down briefly to restore CV and respiratory function to normal values, and then have her sit down and hydrate. If uterine cramping and vaginal bleeding occur, refer the athlete to her physician immediately or call 911.

Vision and Hearing Impairments

Athletes who have visual and hearing impairments can exercise similarly to any other sighted or hearing athlete. They can perform and be self-sufficient in carrying out their individualized exercise programs. When dealing with visually impaired athletes, you have to complete many tasks to assure your athlete's safe and effective exercise program. Be certain the exercise area is safe for the athlete. Familiarize the athlete with the facility's layout and physical surroundings. Have the athlete "see" the equipment with his hands. He should use his walking stick if he has one. Make sure as he is seeing the equipment you verbalize what structures he is touching. Describe but avoid any objects that can cause injury to the athlete (e.g., lacerations to the fingers or hands of a Schwinn Airdyne while in motion).

If an athlete is hearing impaired or deaf, she may be able to read lips. Regardless, some words may cause difficulty for the athlete to comprehend due to how they are pronounced by others. Communicate with a hearing-impaired athlete by facing her while talking and speaking slowly. Some deaf athletes may have speech difficulty. If the athlete is unable to read lips, a sign language translator, who can also be a workout companion, may be necessary. The athlete can also communicate via specialized electronic devices for the hearing impaired. If communication is a problem, then the athlete may have less social interaction during exercise. Therefore, take an active role in determining how to involve your athlete to exercise with others. For example, aerobics, kickboxing, and other classes require little to no communication. The athlete is able to see the instructor performing the motions, and the athlete can feel the gym floor vibrate from audio system music. Also, if the athlete is versed in American Sign Language (ASL), you can easily learn and utilize this method of communication. Ultimately, ask the athlete what she prefers in regard to mutual communication. Utilizing facial expressions, eye contact, and visual cues is important for communication.

Aerobic, strength training, and flexibility exercises follow the FITT principle for both visually and hearing impaired individuals. Progress the athlete as he or she can tolerate. All benefits of exercise are applicable to visually and hearing impaired athletes. Demonstrate each exercise activity. Visually impaired athletes can touch your arm, leg, and so on to visualize the activity during your demonstration. They also must have the exercise explained thoroughly and clearly. You can audio record your explanation so the athlete can revisit it on an mp3 player. The athlete may need to use touch during activities for spatial awareness. For example, when a visually impaired person jogs, he can do so on a treadmill holding the handrail, or touching a companion jogger's arm while outside. If the athlete is able to read large lettering or braille, have the instructions also available to him in these forms. Make sure the sound in your facility is not disruptive when you give the athlete verbal instructions, in order for the athlete to hear you clearly. Hearing impaired athletes must remove any hearing devices before swimming or participating in any contact activity. An athlete with hearing loss may have balance issues, so begin her exercise program on a flat surface with her stance in a wide base of support. During the athlete's preparticipation examination, identify any other illnesses or conditions that the athlete has. If he or she does have other conditions, then communicate with the athlete's physician to be sure he or she is cleared for exercise participation.

SUMMARY

Whenever any adult or child with a special condition is participating in physical activity or exercise for the first time, thoroughly test them to determine their capabilities. Along with the preparticipation examination, the exercise testing identifies baseline fitness levels as well as any exercise limitations that must be taken into consideration when devising an exercise program. Athletes with special conditions may experience signs and symptoms that affect exercise, take medications that cause side effects, and have physical and/or mental limitations due to their condition. All of these factors determine physical activity and exercise program modification on an individual, regular basis. Researching these special conditions and discussing the athletes' capabilities and limitations with their physicians is crucial to setting up safe, effective nutritional, physical activity, and exercise programs for these special individuals.

DISCUSSION QUESTIONS

1. Can athletes with special conditions obtain the same exercise benefits as healthy athletes? If yes, what are those benefits? If no, then why not?

2. What special conditions may an athlete have that require daily medication? How can this medication affect exercise performance?

3. When creating an exercise program for an athlete who has any of the three respiratory conditions mentioned, what are your major concerns?

4. What special conditions require you to take the utmost caution with the exercising athlete, and why? What special conditions, if any, do not have exercise limitations?

5. What are some tactics that can be used to assist a visually or hearing impaired athlete to perform safe exercise?

CASE STUDY

A Dire Situation

Gil is a 62-year-old male who has been advised by his physician to improve his lifestyle immediately, or serious illness could result. Gil is sedentary. He sits behind a desk all day at work and leads a very inactive lifestyle. He has poor nutritional habits and consumes too many calories. Consequently, Gil is obese. Gil also suffers from asthma, and is on various medications to prevent exacerbations. His blood pressure is on average 150/95. He takes beta-blocker medication and diuretics in order to keep his hypertension under control. In addition, due to his weight, Gil has acquired type 2 diabetes. However, at this point, he is not insulin dependent. Gil's physician has advised him to control his sugar intake by monitoring his diet, but Gil has not been successful with this task. He smokes about half of a pack of cigarettes daily and occasionally has an alcoholic drink.

After his physician informed Gil about his health, Gil realized his situation is dire. He decides to watch his food intake and eat healthier. He vows to quit smoking someday. In the meantime, he is determined to go to the gym tomorrow and start exercising with the help of a personal trainer. Although self-motivation has not been a strong personal characteristic, Gil realizes he needs to change his lifestyle to live longer and have a good quality of life.

1. What are the various conditions that Gil has acquired?

2. If you were Gil's personal trainer, what special considerations would you need to take into account when devising Gil's physical activity and exercise program?

3. How would you begin Gil's physical activity and exercise program? What parameters would you utilize?

4. What can Gil do to increase his motivation and compliance toward exercise?

REFERENCES

American Psychological Association (APA). (1998). Practitioners working with older adults. Retrieved July 6, 2012, from http://www.apa.org/pi/aging/resources/guides/practitioners-should-know.aspx

Cuppett, M., & Walsh, K. M. (2012). *General medical conditions in the athlete* (2nd ed.). St. Louis: Elsevier.

Durstine, J. L., Moore, G. E., Painter, P. L., & Roberts, S. O. (Eds.). (2009). *ACSM's exercise management for persons with chronic diseases and disabilities* (3rd ed.). Champaign, IL: Human Kinetics.

Edmonds, M., McGuire, H., & Price, J. (2004). Exercise therapy for chronic fatigue syndrome. *The Cochrane Library*, 3, 1–22. Retrieved October 16, 2012, from http://cfids.best.vwh.net/cfs-inform/Exercise/edmonds.etal04.pdf

Fink, H. H., Burgoon, L. A., & Mikesky, A. E. (2009). *Practical applications in sports nutrition* (2nd ed.). Sudbury, MA: Jones and Bartlett.

Karpatkin, H. I. (2005). Multiple sclerosis and exercise: A review of the evidence. *International Journal of MS Care*, 7, 36–41.

MayoClinic (2013). Heart disease: Lifestyle and home remedies. Retrieved March 25, 2013, from http://www.mayoclinic.com/health/heart-disease/DS01120/DSECTION=lifestyle-and-home-remedies

National Cancer Institute. (2009). Physical activity and cancer. Retrieved March 1, 2013, from http://www.cancer.gov/cancertopics/factsheet/prevention/physicalactivity

National Multiple Sclerosis Society. (2012). What causes MS? Retrieved March 1, 2013, from http://www.nationalmssociety.org/about-multiple-sclerosis/what-we-know-about-ms/what-causes-ms/index.aspx

Nied, R. J., & Franklin, B., (2002). Promoting and prescribing exercise for the elderly. *American Family Physician*, 65(3), 419–427.

Pescatello, L. S., Franklin, B. A., Fagard, R., Farquhar, W. B., Kelley, G. A., & Ray, C. A. (2004). Position stand: Exercise and hypertension. *American College of Sports Medicine's Medicine & Science in Sports & Exercise*, 533–553; doi: 10.1249/01.MSS.0000115224.88514.3A.

Puhan, M. A., Schunemann, H. J., Frey, M., Scharplatz, M., & Bachmann, L. M. (2005). How should COPD patients exercise during respiratory rehabilitation? Comparison of exercise modalities and intensities to treat skeletal muscle dysfunction. *Thorax*, 60, 367–375; doi: 10.1136/thx.2004.033274.

Stricker, P. R. (2012). Weight training: Risk of injury. Retrieved July 7, 2012, from http://www.healthychildren.org/English/healthy-living/fitness/Pages/Weight-Training-Risk-of-Injury.aspx

Appendix

INTRODUCTION

An understanding of human anatomy is imperative to the study of Exercise Science. The athletic injuries and illnesses you have learned about in this text have an obvious effect on the body. Without background knowledge focused on the anatomy of the body, it is difficult to appreciate the basic science behind and intricacies associated with the various systems that play a major role in such injuries and illnesses. This appendix has been established to provide a learning base for understanding human anatomy as an interdependent, multi-functional system. Use the following figures as a learning tool to uncover the complexity of the human body and learn the structures essential to injury and illness recovery.

Nine anatomical figures have been included to assist you in recognizing the anatomical structures that are referred to throughout this text. The labels used will help in discerning the role and function of different parts of each system. These figures include: the skeletal system and bones of the skull; anatomy of the spine; the muscular system; anatomy of the ear, eye, and skin; the respiratory, visceral, and digestive systems; female and male reproductive systems; the circulatory system; the heart and blood vessels; and the nervous system and brain. Not all the anatomical figures referenced in the text are represented but these essential systems are often affected by sports injuries and illness. They will prove to be a helpful reference in your continued study of Exercise Science. Be sure to bookmark this page to allow for easy reference as you work your way through the text.

THE SKELETAL SYSTEM AND BONES OF THE SKULL

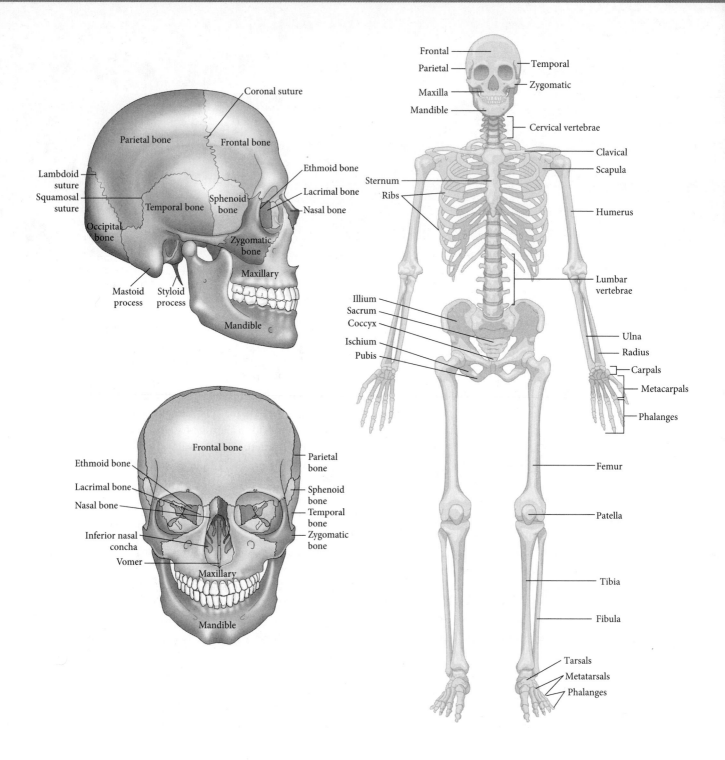

Coronal suture

Parietal bone

Frontal bone

Lambdoid suture

Squamosal suture

Ethmoid bone

Lacrimal bone

Sphenoid bone

Nasal bone

Temporal bone

Occipital bone

Zygomatic bone

Maxillary

Mastoid process

Styloid process

Mandible

Frontal bone

Ethmoid bone

Parietal bone

Lacrimal bone

Sphenoid bone

Nasal bone

Temporal bone

Inferior nasal concha

Zygomatic bone

Vomer

Maxillary

Mandible

Frontal

Temporal

Parietal

Zygomatic

Maxilla

Mandible

Cervical vertebrae

Sternum

Clavical

Ribs

Scapula

Humerus

Lumbar vertebrae

Illium

Sacrum

Coccyx

Ischium

Pubis

Ulna

Radius

Carpals

Metacarpals

Phalanges

Femur

Patella

Tibia

Fibula

Tarsals

Metatarsals

Phalanges

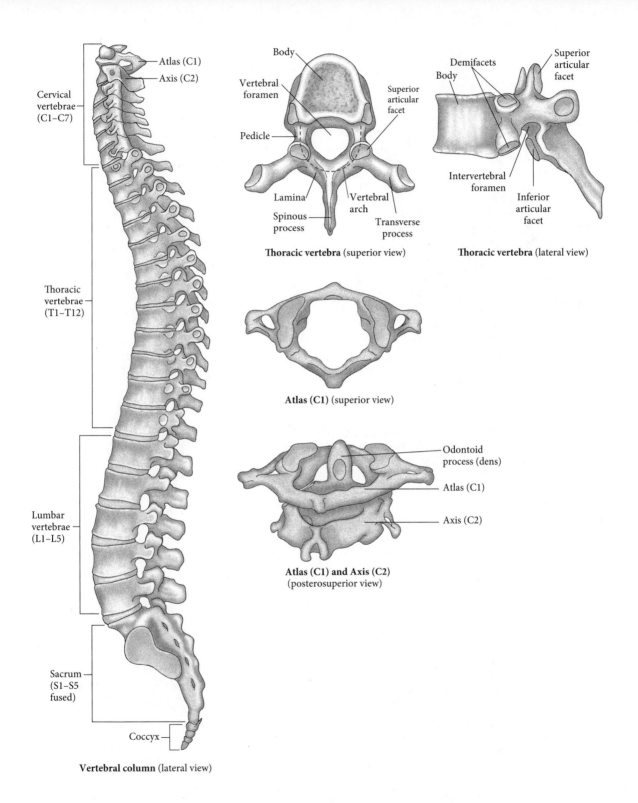

Atlas (C1)

Axis (C2)

Cervical
vertebrae
(C1–C7)

Thoracic
vertebrae
(T1–T12)

Lumbar
vertebrae
(L1–L5)

Sacrum
(S1–S5
fused)

Coccyx

Vertebral column (lateral view)

Body

Vertebral
foramen

Pedicle

Superior
articular
facet

Lamina

Spinous
process

Vertebral
arch

Transverse
process

Thoracic vertebra (superior view)

Demifacets

Body

Superior
articular
facet

Intervertebral
foramen

Inferior
articular
facet

Thoracic vertebra (lateral view)

Atlas (C1) (superior view)

Odontoid
process (dens)

Atlas (C1)

Axis (C2)

Atlas (C1) and Axis (C2)
(posterosuperior view)

THE MUSCULAR SYSTEM

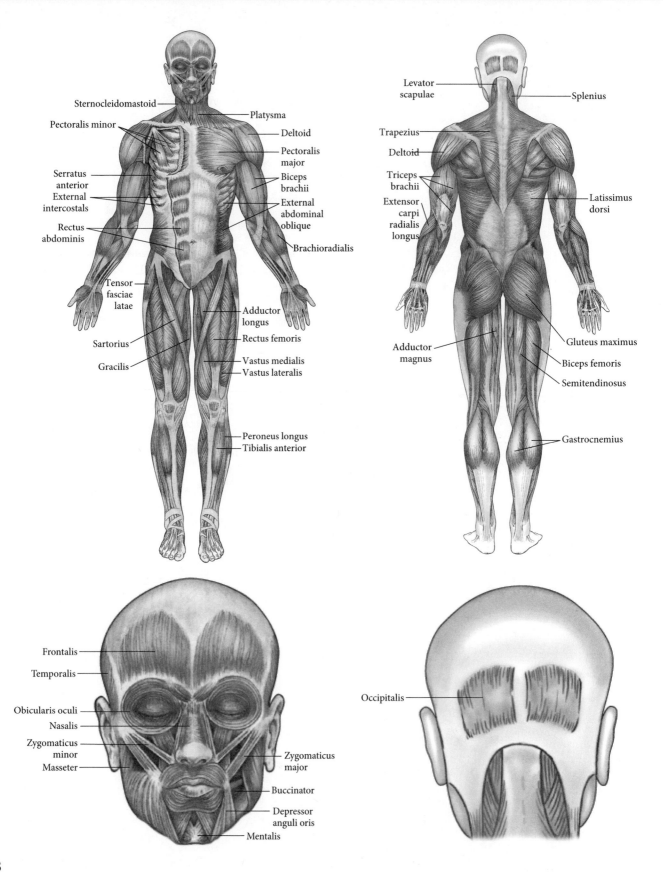

Sternocleidomastoid
Pectoralis minor
Serratus anterior
External intercostals
Rectus abdominis
Tensor fasciae latae
Sartorius
Gracilis

Platysma
Deltoid
Pectoralis major
Biceps brachii
External abdominal oblique
Brachioradialis
Adductor longus
Rectus femoris
Vastus medialis
Vastus lateralis
Peroneus longus
Tibialis anterior

Levator scapulae
Trapezius
Deltoid
Triceps brachii
Extensor carpi radialis longus
Adductor magnus

Splenius
Latissimus dorsi
Gluteus maximus
Biceps femoris
Semitendinosus
Gastrocnemius

Frontalis
Temporalis
Obicularis oculi
Nasalis
Zygomaticus minor
Masseter

Zygomaticus major
Buccinator
Depressor anguli oris
Mentalis

Occipitalis

ANATOMY OF THE EAR, EYE, AND SKIN

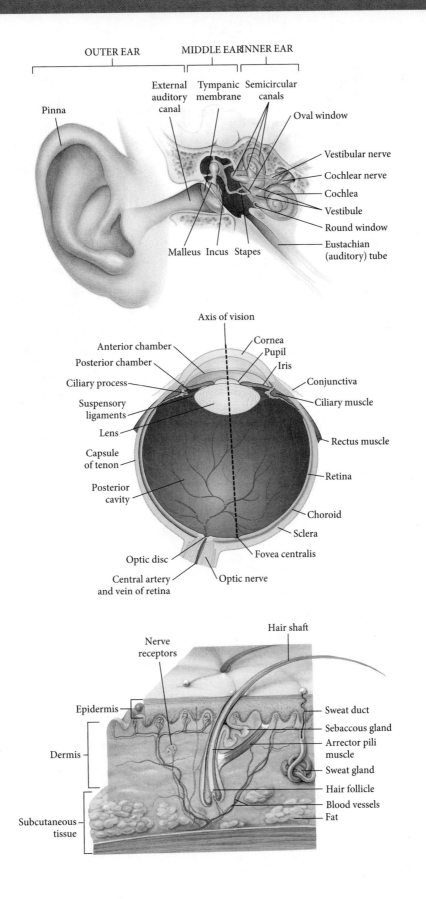

OUTER EAR · MIDDLE EAR · INNER EAR

Pinna

External auditory canal

Tympanic membrane

Semicircular canals

Oval window

Vestibular nerve

Cochlear nerve

Cochlea

Vestibule

Round window

Eustachian (auditory) tube

Malleus · Incus · Stapes

Axis of vision

Anterior chamber

Posterior chamber

Ciliary process

Suspensory ligaments

Lens

Capsule of tenon

Posterior cavity

Optic disc

Central artery and vein of retina

Optic nerve

Cornea

Pupil

Iris

Conjunctiva

Ciliary muscle

Rectus muscle

Retina

Choroid

Sclera

Fovea centralis

Hair shaft

Nerve receptors

Epidermis

Dermis

Subcutaneous tissue

Sweat duct

Sebaccous gland

Arrector pili muscle

Sweat gland

Hair follicle

Blood vessels

Fat

THE RESPIRATORY, VISCERAL, AND DIGESTIVE SYSTEMS

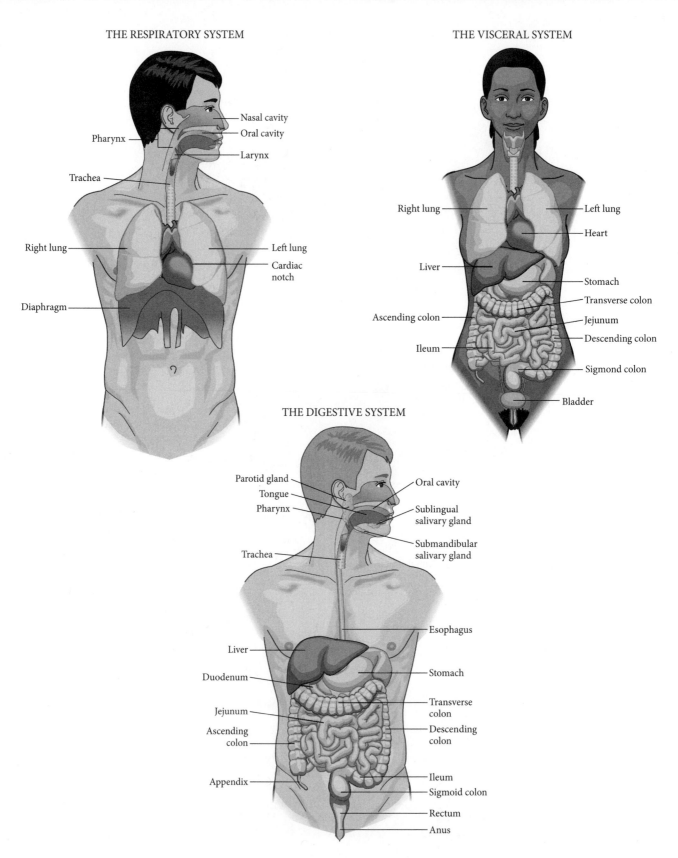

THE RESPIRATORY SYSTEM

Nasal cavity
Oral cavity
Pharynx
Larynx
Trachea
Right lung
Left lung
Cardiac notch
Diaphragm

THE VISCERAL SYSTEM

Right lung
Left lung
Heart
Liver
Stomach
Transverse colon
Ascending colon
Jejunum
Descending colon
Ileum
Sigmond colon
Bladder

THE DIGESTIVE SYSTEM

Parotid gland
Tongue
Pharynx
Oral cavity
Sublingual salivary gland
Submandibular salivary gland
Trachea
Esophagus
Liver
Duodenum
Stomach
Jejunum
Transverse colon
Ascending colon
Descending colon
Appendix
Ileum
Sigmoid colon
Rectum
Anus

FEMALE AND MALE REPRODUCTVE SYSTEMS

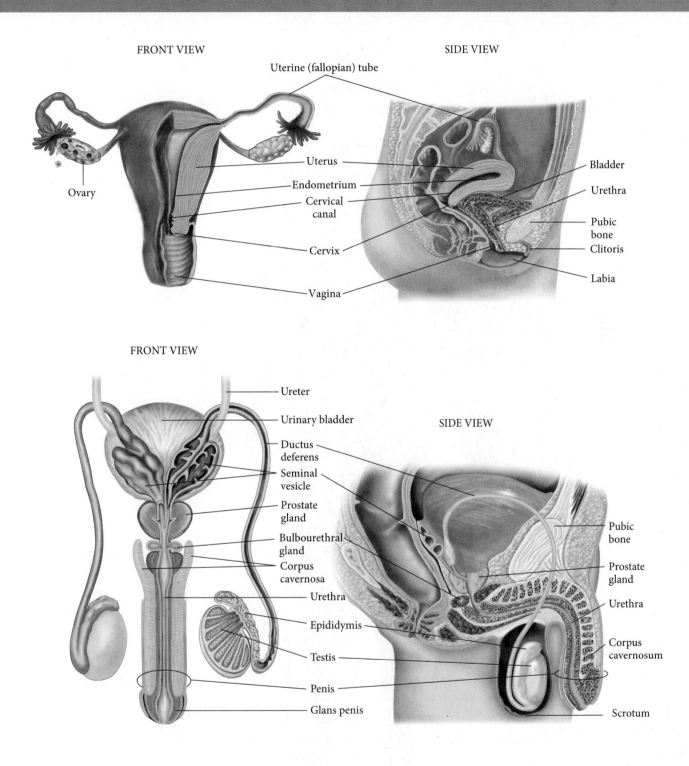

FRONT VIEW

SIDE VIEW

Uterine (fallopian) tube

Ovary

Uterus

Endometrium

Cervical canal

Cervix

Vagina

Bladder

Urethra

Pubic bone

Clitoris

Labia

FRONT VIEW

SIDE VIEW

Ureter

Urinary bladder

Ductus deferens

Seminal vesicle

Prostate gland

Bulbourethral gland

Corpus cavernosa

Urethra

Epididymis

Testis

Penis

Glans penis

Pubic bone

Prostate gland

Urethra

Corpus cavernosum

Scrotum

THE CIRCULATORY SYSTEM

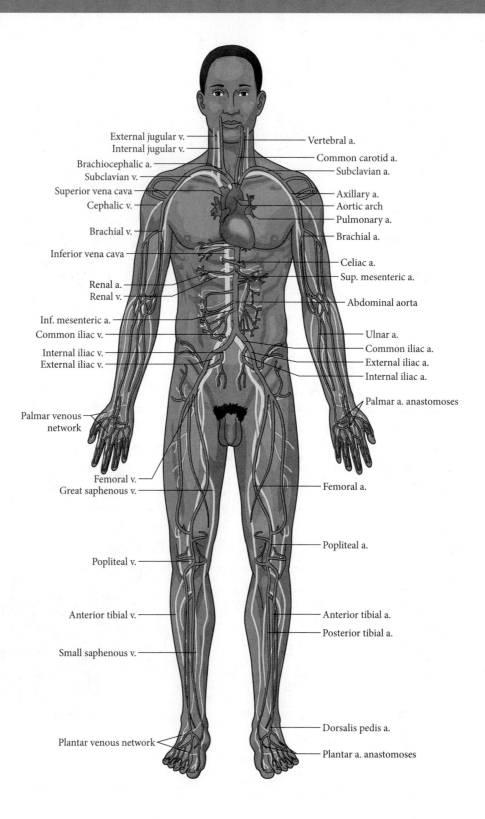

External jugular v.

Internal jugular v.

Brachiocephalic a.

Subclavian v.

Superior vena cava

Cephalic v.

Brachial v.

Inferior vena cava

Renal a.

Renal v.

Inf. mesenteric a.

Common iliac v.

Internal iliac v.

External iliac v.

Palmar venous
network

Femoral v.

Great saphenous v.

Popliteal v.

Anterior tibial v.

Small saphenous v.

Plantar venous network

Vertebral a.

Common carotid a.

Subclavian a.

Axillary a.

Aortic arch

Pulmonary a.

Brachial a.

Celiac a.

Sup. mesenteric a.

Abdominal aorta

Ulnar a.

Common iliac a.

External iliac a.

Internal iliac a.

Palmar a. anastomoses

Femoral a.

Popliteal a.

Anterior tibial a.

Posterior tibial a.

Dorsalis pedis a.

Plantar a. anastomoses

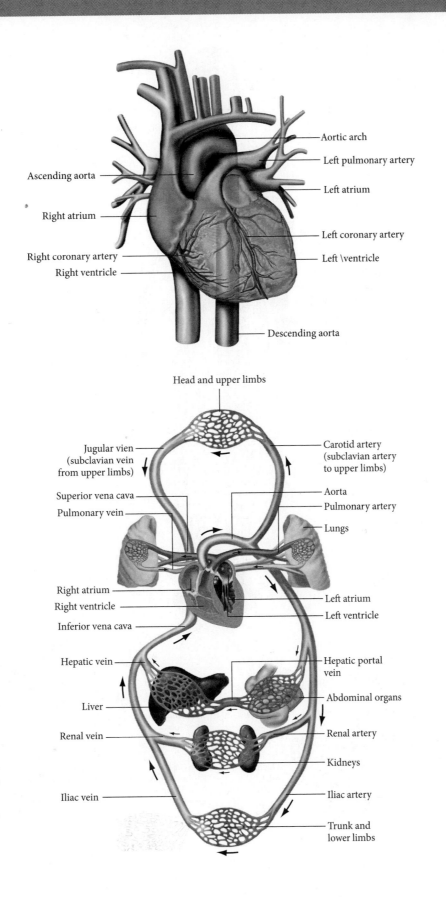

Aortic arch

Left pulmonary artery

Ascending aorta

Left atrium

Right atrium

Left coronary artery

Right coronary artery

Left \ventricle

Right ventricle

Descending aorta

Head and upper limbs

Jugular vien
(subclavian vein
from upper limbs)

Carotid artery
(subclavian artery
to upper limbs)

Superior vena cava

Aorta

Pulmonary vein

Pulmonary artery

Lungs

Right atrium

Right ventricle

Left atrium

Left ventricle

Inferior vena cava

Hepatic vein

Hepatic portal
vein

Liver

Abdominal organs

Renal vein

Renal artery

Kidneys

Iliac vein

Iliac artery

Trunk and
lower limbs

THE NERVOUS SYSTEM AND BRAIN

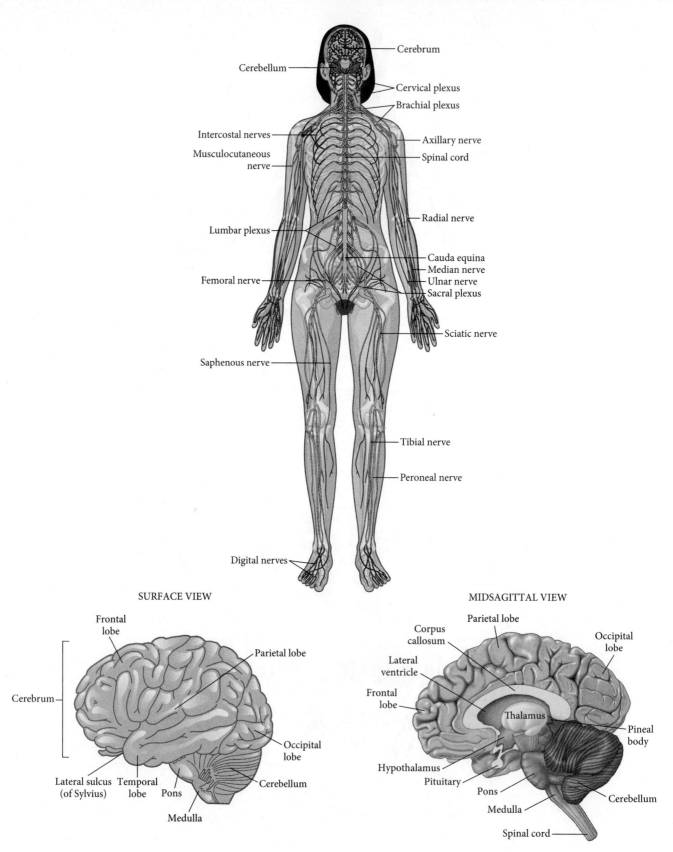

Cerebrum

Cerebellum

Cervical plexus

Brachial plexus

Intercostal nerves

Axillary nerve

Musculocutaneous nerve

Spinal cord

Radial nerve

Lumbar plexus

Cauda equina

Median nerve

Femoral nerve

Ulnar nerve

Sacral plexus

Sciatic nerve

Saphenous nerve

Tibial nerve

Peroneal nerve

Digital nerves

SURFACE VIEW

Frontal lobe

Parietal lobe

Cerebrum

Occipital lobe

Cerebellum

Lateral sulcus (of Sylvius) Temporal lobe Pons

Medulla

MIDSAGITTAL VIEW

Parietal lobe

Corpus callosum

Occipital lobe

Lateral ventricle

Frontal lobe

Thalamus

Pineal body

Hypothalamus

Pituitary

Pons

Cerebellum

Medulla

Spinal cord

Glossary

Abscess A collection of pus within the skin's superficial and deep layers due to a pathogen. The abscess causes swelling and inflammation at the affected area.

Acute injury Occurs when the body is suddenly afflicted by trauma or damage to its tissues, which consequently initiates inflammation.

Aerobic When the body, in particular the cardiorespiratory system, utilizes oxygen during activity.

Agonist The muscle that is contracted and opposes the antagonist.

Allergen A substance or object that causes sensitivity or an allergy.

Analgesics Pain-reducing medications such as acetaminophen, ibuprofen, and aspirin. These specific medications are also antipyretics. Ibuprofen and aspirin are also anti-inflammatory medications; however, acetaminophen is not.

Anemia When an athlete has a decreased amount of hemoglobin and/or red blood cells in the body. Consequently, because hemoglobin carries oxygen in the red blood cells, if an athlete has anemia she or he will have decreased oxygen in the body.

Angina Occurs when a part of the heart does not get enough oxygenated blood. The athlete feels pain similar to an athlete who is experiencing a heart attack, but most often not as severe.

Antagonist The muscle to be stretched.

Anticoagulant drugs Blood-thinning drugs that an athlete is prescribed to prevent blood clotting. An athlete on these drugs who sustains an injury to the blood vessels will bleed more than if he or she was not taking anticoagulants.

Antigen A substance that, when introduced into the body, stimulates the immune system to produce antibodies. Antibodies help the body to destroy foreign substances such as bacteria.

Antimicrobial A substance that attempts to kill pathogens such as bacteria, viruses, and fungi.

Antipyretics Fever-reducing medications such as acetaminophen, ibuprofen, and aspirin.

Antiseptics Substances that assist in cleansing a wound and destroying pathogenic bacteria that may have entered the wound.

Apophysitis Inflammation of a bony outgrowth. Common areas of apophysitis include the medial epicondyle (little league elbow) and tibial tubercle (Osgood Schlatter's disease).

Approximate When the damaged, cut portions of the skin of an open wound fall back in line and are in close proximity.

Arrhythmias Abnormal heart rhythms including irregular heart rate; tachycardia, which is a fast heart rate; or bradycardia, which is a slow heart rate.

Assumption of risk When an athlete knowingly recognizes the inherent risk of injury, and voluntarily participates in the activity.

Aura An abnormal feeling of the mind and body that may come directly before an athlete experiences a seizure.

Autism A developmental disorder of the brain that affects children under 3 years old. An autistic child lacks proper communication and social skills.

Autonomic nervous system Controls automatic bodily functions such as the abdominal organs, pupils, heart rate, breathing, digestion, and other unconscious or involuntary functions of the body.

Benign Noncancerous.

Biological age The age an athlete is classified when factoring in her or his overall health as compared to other athletes who are her or his chronological age.

Booster vaccination A dose of the antigen administered to the body, after the original vaccination was given, in order for the body to create additional antibodies to fight against infection.

Cardiac arrest When an athlete's heart is significantly damaged, it will no longer function properly and stops beating.

Cauterize To burn tissue with electricity or a laser in order to assist in the healing process. In the case of epistaxis, blood vessels that bleed regularly are cauterized in the nose.

325

Chronic injury Occurs when an injury is no longer acute, yet remains in the later inflammatory phase or early fibroblastic repair phase of the healing process.

Chronological age The actual number of years that an athlete has been living.

Circumduction The distal end of the extremity (the hand or foot) makes a circular motion moving freely through space while the proximal end (the shoulder or hip) remains stable or fixed.

Cirrhosis An irreversible liver disease that occurs over time. The liver tissue is replaced with scar tissue, and eventually liver function terminates.

Clonic A state in which the muscles rapidly and forcefully contract and then reflexively relax.

Closed wound An injury to the tissues underlying the skin. Unlike open wounds, bleeding occurs but does not exit the body.

Collagen A strong protein that comprises bone, soft tissue including skin, cartilage, and other connective tissues.

Comparable fault When the court assigns some fault to both the defendant and the plaintiff.

Concentric contraction When the muscle contracts and shortens. An example would be when the biceps brachii in the upper body are lifting an object while the athlete is flexing his or her elbow, and the gastrocnemius in the lower body when the athlete is pushing off his or her toes during jumping.

Continuity In muscles, this is when the tissue feels the same to the touch throughout the tissue's entire length and width.

Contraindicated A certain treatment, action, or rehabilitation technique must be avoided due to the particular condition, illness, or injury an athlete has sustained. If the contraindicated treatment, action, or rehabilitation technique was utilized, the athlete's situation most likely will worsen.

Contralateral The corresponding structure on the opposite side of the body.

Contralateral The opposite side of the body symmetrical to the injured side. If the injury is at the right knee, then the contralateral side is the left knee.

Contributory negligence When a plaintiff is deemed to be responsible to some extent for her or his injury.

Core body The area of the body not including the upper and lower extremities. The core body includes the spine, chest, and abdominal and pelvic cavities.

Coronary arteries Supply the heart with oxygenated blood.

Corticosteroid A medication used to minimize inflammation. Corticosteroids prevent detrimental chemical mediators from being produced after injury during the inflammatory phase of healing. They can be given to an athlete by mouth, injection, or intravenously. The medication also comes in eye solutions and topical creams.

Crepitus A crackling or grating sensation that you and an athlete may feel during movement or palpation when a structure is injured.

Crepitus A crackling sound.

Cyanotic A blue color of the skin that occurs when lack of oxygen and increased carbon dioxide are present in the tissues.

Diet The food and drink we consume each day. *Diet* also refers to a program or plan that an athlete follows when he or she is attempting to modify his or her weight.

Diplopia Double vision.

Direct contact When a person's infected blood has physically touched another person's body.

Diuretic Something that causes the kidneys to produce urine, which consequently increases the rate of urination. Other than prescription and over-the-counter diuretic drugs and caffeine, pineapple juice, leafy green vegetables, garlic, and onions are some examples of natural diuretics.

Doctrine A rule or principle of law.

Duty When a person is liable and responsible for the athlete's well-being, due to the special relationship with the athlete at the time of injury.

Dyspnea Shortness of breath.

Eccentric contraction When the muscle contracts and lengthens. An example would be when the biceps brachii in the upper body assists in lowering an object while the athlete is extending his or her elbow, and the hamstrings in the lower body when the athlete is slowing down during running.

Ecchymosis A black and blue, bruise-like color of the skin that can occur with internal bleeding.

Ectopic The formation of soft tissue, a bone, an organ, or the like outside of its normal position or location. Ectopic bone formation is when bone develops outside of the bone in the soft tissue or elsewhere.

Edema Fluid that accumulates in bodily spaces due to injury or illness. Edema creates the appearance of swelling, especially at the joints and around soft tissue structures.

Epistaxis A nosebleed.

Ergonomic equipment Helps place the body in a proper position for optimal performance and to avoid injury.

Exposure Contact with blood or other potentially infectious bodily fluids via mucous membranes, eyes, nose, mouth, broken skin, or injection into skin or mucous membranes.

Exudate Formed by plasma fluid and cells; it is located in the space outside of the blood vessels.

Fluorescein An orange dye that is on a medical test strip of paper. A physician places it onto the cornea to detect injury. The dye covers the cornea, and then the physician looks at the cornea under a blue light. Any areas of the cornea that are green indicate that an abrasion exists.

Gait The manner in which the athlete is walking.

Goniometer A protractor-type device used to measure angles and joint range of motion.

Good Samaritan laws Statutes that protect people from legal liability when assisting injured or ill people in an emergency situation.

Gout Caused by uric acid in the blood that crystallizes. The crystals move into the joints and body tissues, especially in the foot. This condition creates painful arthritis and is often recurrent.

Guarding Occurs when an abdominal organ is injured. The abdominal muscles spasm and become tense in order to protect the injured abdominal organs from further injury.

Heart rate reserve (HRR) The difference between an athlete's RHR and MHR. The heart rate reserve is used to calculate the THR for the athlete during cardiorespiratory exercise.

Hypertrophy When a muscle increases in size due to progressive overload of the muscle by increasing the resistance.

Hypoxia When tissues in the body are deprived of oxygen. If the oxygen deprivation continues for a period of time, the tissues will die.

Inoculated A person has been vaccinated in order to produce immunity against a pathogen.

Insidious onset A slow and gradual development of signs and symptoms of injury without any definitive mechanism of injury.

Insulin A hormone that is released when blood glucose levels increase. The hormone transports blood glucose into the body cells to be utilized for energy.

Internal forces Forces that the body creates due to motion and muscle contraction. These forces can cause injury by moving the bones, joints, and soft tissue in a position to which they are not accustomed.

Isometric contraction When the muscle contracts and creates tension. The muscle does not cause movement, shorten, or lengthen.

Isotonic contraction When the muscle contracts and creates tension while moving through a partial or full ROM.

Jaundice A yellowing of the skin and whites of the eyes that can occur with liver inflammation, infection, or disease.

Kyphotic An outward, posterior curvature of the spine when viewing the athlete from the side. This curve is found normally at the thoracic and sacral spines.

Lateral A structure's location furthest away from the midline when the body is bisected into right and left halves through the umbilicus.

Lateral flexion When an athlete bends their neck to the side by moving their head toward their shoulder.

Legumes Pod-type foods including, but not limited to, beans, lentils, peas, soy, and peanuts.

Limb-threatening When an athlete sustains a significant injury resulting in loss of motor function and/or sensation of the arm(s) or leg(s).

Long sitting position When an athlete is seated on the ground with both legs extended.

Lymphocytes White blood cells in the body that help the immune system fight illness and disease.

Malocclusion The inability to bring the teeth together in a normal, aligned fashion.

Mechanism of injury How the injury or illness occurred, which can be determined by asking the athlete, "What happened?"

Metabolism How the body ingests food, breaks it down, and creates energy to utilize.

Metastatic When cancer cells move from one site in the body to another.

Muscle guarding An involuntary muscular response that occurs when the muscles around an injured area become tight and rigid in order to protect an injured area from further injury. Muscle guarding typically is not painful to the athlete.

Muscle spasm An involuntary muscular response that occurs when the muscles suddenly contract and shorten. Muscle spasm typically is painful for the athlete, and the athlete cannot relieve the spasm voluntarily.

Myelogram An imaging test used to determine whether an athlete has a spinal cord injury. The physician injects dye into the spinal column and then takes an x-ray.

Negligence When a person did not act as a reasonable, prudent person would, and damages occurred to another person or his or her property.

Neti pot A nasal irrigation device which utilizes a saline solution to clear congested nasal passages.

Neurovascular compromise The body's nerves and blood vessels are detrimentally affected due to trauma. Consequently, the nerves and blood vessels will not be able to perform their actions as they should.

Nutrients Substances in food that nourish the body, provide it with energy, and promote its proper function and growth.

Onset When the injury begins and becomes apparent to the athlete. Injuries may have a short, long, or insidious (gradual and undetected) onset.

Open wound A cut in the skin through which external bleeding occurs.

Opportunistic infections Illnesses or diseases that invade the body of an athlete who has AIDS.

Paralysis The inability to move a body part, with or without an inability to feel sensation.

Paraplegic An athlete who has paralysis of the lower body including the legs. Paralysis usually involves loss of motor function and sensation.

Pelvic inflammatory disease (PID) An inflammation of the pelvis including the uterus, fallopian tubes, and other reproductive organs. PID can cause severe pelvic pain, infertility, ectopic pregnancy, and formation of an abscess.

Point tenderness A sign of injury. When you palpate the athlete's injury, and the athlete claims the area you touched was painful, then that area is considered point tender.

Point tenderness Discomfort or pain when an injured area is touched.

Postnasal drip The mucus that drains from the nose to the air passages and then to the throat.

Post-traumatic amnesia   The inability to remember events that occurred after the MTBI injury occurred.

Prosthesis   A synthetic body part that is custom made to replace an amputated body part.

Q-angle   Stands for the quadriceps angle, which is the relative position of the patella to the tibia, femur, and pelvis.

Quadriplegic   An athlete who has paralysis of the legs, arms, and torso.

Rate of perceived exertion (RPE)   The athlete's opinion of how hard he or she is working during exercise. The method was developed by Gunnar Borg, a Swedish psychologist. The RPE is rated by the athlete on a scale of 6–20, with 6 being no exertion at all and 20 being maximal exertion. See the CDC website www.cdc.gov/physicalactivity/everyone/measuring/exertion.html for more information on RPE and the RPE scale athletes can use during exercise.

Raynaud's syndrome   A condition in which the athlete has significant lack of blood circulation to the fingers and toes. It is brought on by exposure to cold.

Reduce   To relocate the dislocated bone into proper, normal alignment. Reduction must only be performed by a qualified physician.

Relative humidity   The amount of water molecules in the air, which is designated by the percent of air saturation.

Remission   When a disease has decreased or become absent in the body. In regard to cancer, if a physician cannot detect cancer cells within an athlete's body via imaging and other diagnostic tests, then the athlete is in remission.

Repetitions   How many times the exercise, stretch, or the like is performed.

Retrograde amnesia   The inability to remember events that occurred before the MTBI occurred.

Rigidity   Occurs as a result of an abdominal organ injury. The abdominal muscles become stiff upon palpation.

Saturated   When materials, such as gauze, bandages, or a towel, have soaked up the maximum amount of blood or bodily fluid they can hold.

Scoliosis   A lateral curvature of the spine when observed from a posterior view.

Sedentary lifestyle   A lifestyle without regular physical activity or exercise.

Septicemia   A life-threatening infection that typically occurs in the body along with another systemic infection. Septicemia spreads through the bloodstream very quickly, and the athlete must be hospitalized and treated immediately. The mortality rate for the infection can be more than 50% (MedlinePlus, 2011).

Sesamoid bone   A bone that is embedded within a tendon, which most often is located over a joint. Other than the patella, which is the largest sesamoid bone, sesamoid bones are located in the hands and feet.

Sets   A series of repetitions. An athlete may perform 10 repetitions in one set. In this case, three sets make up 30 repetitions.

Shock   A life-threatening condition that occurs when oxygenated blood in the body is not getting to the vital organs, including those in the chest, abdomen, and brain.

Statute of limitations   A finite number of years that a person has to file a negligence claim in court. The statute of limitations is determined by and varies from state to state.

Stick points   Specific locations within the ROM when the athlete is unable to move the resistance because the resistance is too great, the muscle is too weak, or both.

Syndrome   A group of signs and symptoms that when put together indicate a particular injury, illness, condition, or disease.

Systemic   Throughout the entire body.

Tactile   The sense of touch.

Therapeutic modalities   Mediums and interventions that can be used to assist in treating an injury or illness. Electrostimulation, ultrasound, and massage are types of therapeutic modalities.

Tinnitus   Ringing in the ears.

Tonic   A state in which the muscles are in constant contractions.

Tort   A civil wrong that occurs to a person's body or property; not a criminal act.

Trigger points   Hypersensitive, hyperirritable nodules in muscle tissue. They are also referred to as *knots* in the muscle.

Triglycerides   Also called *blood fat*. They are fats that very low-density lipoproteins (VLDL) carry in the blood. Excess sugar in the blood or unnecessary calories consumed that are not burned off with physical activity are converted into triglycerides.

Type 2 diabetes   The inability of the body to utilize or make insulin properly. Consequently, sugar remains in the blood. If the sugar level is not regulated, over time the athlete can succumb to eye conditions including blindness, foot conditions including ulcers, kidney damage, heart attack, and stroke. Athletes who are overweight and obese are predisposed to acquire Type 2 diabetes.

Valsalva maneuver   When an athlete holds his or her breath and attempts to forcefully expire through his or her closed mouth and nose.

Waiver   A type of contract that releases an organization under which the athlete participates from liability.

Work practice controls   Policies and procedures that your employer creates to assist you in reducing the chances of bloodborne pathogen exposure in the workplace.

Index

Note: Page numbers followed by "*f*" and "*t*" indicate figures and tables, respectively.

A

abdomen injuries
    appendicitis, 235–236
    digestive system, 231–234
    hernia, 238
    kidneys and urinary system, 230–231
    mononucleosis, 236–237
    reproductive system, 234–235
    solar plexus/celiac plexus, 237
    spleen injury, 236
    stitch in the side, 237
abrasions, 47
acquired bloodborne pathogens, 33
acquired immune deficiency syndrome (AIDS), 36
act of commission, 5
active range of motion (AROM), 86–88, 91, 110
    of hip flexion, 86*f*
activities of daily living (ADLs), 82, 148
actual harm/damages, 5
acute injuries, 18, 21–22, 82

acute subluxation, 29
acute torticollis (wryneck), 222
Additional Lower Body Flexibility Tests, 133–137
adhesive bandage, 52
adhesive capsulitis, 199
ADLs. *See* activities of daily living
AED. *See* automated external defibrillator
aerobic activity, 105, 108
age group
    masters and older adult athletes, 298–299
    young athletes, 297–298
agility, 100
agonist, 109
allergens, 70
allergic rhinitis (hay fever), 280
aluminum crutches, 93
American Heart Association, 93
American Red Cross (ARC), 93
Americans with Disabilities Act (ADA), 36
amino acids, 153
amputations, 49–50, 49*f*
    objects causing, 49
analgesics, 281
anaphylactic shock, 30, 70